Cloud Computing and MicroServices

Jinmin Yang

Cloud Computing and MicroServices

Springer

Jinmin Yang
Hunan University
Changsha, China

ISBN 978-3-031-93477-3   ISBN 978-3-031-93478-0 (eBook)
https://doi.org/10.1007/978-3-031-93478-0

© The Editor(s) (if applicable) and The Author(s), under exclusive license to Springer Nature Switzerland AG 2025

This work is subject to copyright. All rights are solely and exclusively licensed by the Publisher, whether the whole or part of the material is concerned, specifically the rights of translation, reprinting, reuse of illustrations, recitation, broadcasting, reproduction on microfilms or in any other physical way, and transmission or information storage and retrieval, electronic adaptation, computer software, or by similar or dissimilar methodology now known or hereafter developed.
The use of general descriptive names, registered names, trademarks, service marks, etc. in this publication does not imply, even in the absence of a specific statement, that such names are exempt from the relevant protective laws and regulations and therefore free for general use.
The publisher, the authors and the editors are safe to assume that the advice and information in this book are believed to be true and accurate at the date of publication. Neither the publisher nor the authors or the editors give a warranty, expressed or implied, with respect to the material contained herein or for any errors or omissions that may have been made. The publisher remains neutral with regard to jurisdictional claims in published maps and institutional affiliations.

This Springer imprint is published by the registered company Springer Nature Switzerland AG
The registered company address is: Gewerbestrasse 11, 6330 Cham, Switzerland

If disposing of this product, please recycle the paper.

Preface

Cloud computing is currently the mainstream computing paradigm that has emerged after the highly developed network communications. It makes a fundamental change in the way that small and medium enterprises (SMEs) build and operate their business information systems. Enterprises no longer need to consider such matters as construction of server room and network, purchase of servers and support software, employment of IT operation personnel, and replacement or upgrade of equipment. Enterprises rent computing and storage resources from cloud service providers, migrate their business information systems to run on the cloud, and outsource system operation to cloud service providers. This paradigm enables enterprises to greatly reduce the cost of building and operating their business information systems, thus greatly improving the price-performance ratio. Through the scale effect, the resource utilization rate for cloud service providers is significantly improved. Thus, the service price and quality become attractive. Cloud computing enables service providers and their customers to be in a mutually beneficial and win-win situation. Therefore, the whole society has been embracing cloud computing.

Cloud computing has promoted informationization, bringing about new challenges to servers. Servers are facing the double pressure of increasing data volume and customer requests, with the issue of service quality becoming increasingly critical. In this situation, microservices become the mainstream server architecture, whose aim is to deal with these challenges in an adaptable manner.

As popular technologies, cloud computing and microservices are highly sought after by the society. The industrial sector keeps launching products and services and providing cloud development supports, while the academic sector keeps contributing theoretical research results through papers. There are also many books about cloud computing and microservices. A common feature of these books is that they are centered on products or systems, describing their architecture, functionalities, and methods of use, without the revelation of the ins and outs of the technologies and their causes and consequences. The description of characteristics seems to be somewhat arbitrary and generalized, thereby being difficult for readers to understand. This situation leads to many people's knowledge of cloud computing and microservices staying in the state of knowing what, but not knowing why and how.

To be an innovator, it is not enough to know what the tools and products are and how to use them. It is necessary to know the origins of problems, as well as the characteristics of the evolution of technologies, and to know the strategies and methods for solving problems. This book tries to reveal the essence of cloud computing and microservices from the perspective of technology evolution and to convince people by case study as well as analysis and reasoning.

This book has the following characteristics:

1. It focuses on the core issue in cloud computing and microservices, i.e., how to deepen resource sharing, and associates technologies in cloud computing and microservices with effective management strategies and methods in people's daily work and life, making this book concise, vivid, interesting, and easy to understand.
2. It uses typical cases to demonstrate the evolution process of computing paradigms, involving the problems faced at each stage, as well as the solution ideas, strategies, and methods.
3. It closely follows the basic principles and criteria to demonstrate how to deepen resource sharing by problem presenting, analysis, reasoning, argumentation, and asking questions, so as to enable readers not only to know what, but also to know why and how.

This book aims to enable readers interested in cloud computing and microservices to have a clear perceptual understanding of the basic problems, solution ideas, architecture, characteristics, and key technologies in cloud computing and microservices and then the ability to solve practical engineering problems reasonably and to achieve innovation.

From the perspective of deepening resource sharing, this book summarizes the two leaps of the computing paradigm: from stand-alone computing to cluster computing and then from cluster computing to cloud computing. On the basis of cluster computing, cloud computing has to further solve two key problems: (1) application programs can run everywhere on the cloud and (2) application programs running on the same computer do not interfere with each other. This concise and clear technical vein can enable readers to know the ins and outs of technology evolution and the causes and consequences of cloud computing and microservices.

Each chapter of this book contains the origin of problems, solution ideas, solution schemes, characteristic analysis, problem thinking, and summarization. This layout will guide readers gradually from studying knowledge to understanding the knowledge and then from learning knowledge to applying knowledge.

The book is divided into six chapters. It focuses on analyzing and discussing the resource-sharing issues, revealing the deepening approaches of resource sharing, and demonstrating the grace and artistry of the solutions. The book also explores the motivation behind the evolution of technologies, tracks the latest technologies and their development trends in the industry, and helps readers flexibly cope with the challenges brought about by the development and change of IT technology.

Chapter 1 provides an overview of cloud computing and microservices. Resource sharing is the driving force behind the evolution of computing. The computing approach has experienced an evolution from stand-alone computing to cluster computing and then from cluster computing to cloud computing. In stand-alone computing, sharing means that multiple processes execute concurrently and they share resources on the same computer. Cluster computing extends sharing across computer boundaries. Cloud computing makes further efforts to reduce costs by deepening sharing. Specifically, it utilizes scale effect to achieve a mutually beneficial win-win situation for service providers and their customers. Under the sweeping tide of informationization, servers are facing the double pressure of increasing data volume and customer requests. The strategies and methods to enable server programs' efficient operation, elastic operation, secure operation, rapid development, and rapid revision and upgrading as well as fast startup are collectively known as microservice technologies.

Chapter 2 explains the techniques for realizing resource sharing in a stand-alone computer. The most basic form of resource sharing means that resources on a single computer are shared by multiple applications running on that machine. The central issue is the concurrent execution of multiple tasks and the consequent sharing of resources. For this purpose, the program code is structured into two parts: the operating system and the application, where the operating system plays the role of a resource manager, and the application acts as a client. The interaction between the application and the operating system is realized by means of function calls. Shared resources include hardware resources such as CPU, memory, and network as well as code and data. The operating system manages the various shared resources in separate categories. This chapter explains the implementation of sharing on resources such as CPU, memory, network, code, and data files. It focuses on exploring the problems encountered in code sharing and on their solutions.

Chapter 3 explains the techniques for implementing resource sharing across computer boundaries. Resource sharing across computer boundaries is also known as distributed computing. Distributed computing evolved from stand-alone computing and elevated resource sharing to new levels. With the support of network communication, the boundary concept of resource sharing has been broken and borderless sharing has been realized. Borderless sharing is the dialectical unity of inheritance and magnificence, which can also be described as the dialectical unity of change and invariance. The invariance is manifested in the sharing mode, and the change is manifested in the expansion and extension of the sharing boundary as well as the improvement of service quality. In resource sharing, the access conflict problem is always one of the most fundamental problems. In addition, the data consistency problem becomes exceptionally prominent in distributed computing. This chapter focuses on the strategies and methods to realize borderless sharing.

Chapter 4 explains decentralized computing. Common service systems are centralized systems. They are characterized by the fact that the data correctness of the system, the fairness of the service, and the availability of the service are all controlled by a single service provider. Decentralized computing tries to change this. The idea is that one service is no longer provided by a single service provider, but is instead provided by multiple service providers. In terms of system composition, the system is no longer composed of a single node, but of multiple nodes. Different nodes belong to different service providers. Therefore, everything is no longer decided by a single service provider, but by multiple service providers. Any one service provider is no longer essential to the service, but optional. This chapter focuses on the problems encountered in decentralized computing as well as strategies and methods for solving them.

Chapter 5 explains virtualization and cloud computing. Cloud computing evolved from cluster computing with one goal: to enable enterprise customers to migrate their business information systems to the cloud without modification and to run successfully on the cloud. Compared to cluster computing, cloud computing once again raises resource sharing to a whole new level. Based on cluster computing, cloud computing addresses two key issues. The first one is that enterprise customers' applications can run successfully everywhere on the cloud. The second one is that multiple applications running on the same computer do not interfere with each other. This chapter structures the application into two parts, the application itself and the runtime environment, and then transforms the above two problems into the questions that whether applications can run on a cloud and whether it can run successfully. A solution to these two problems is then derived using virtualization strategies.

Chapter 6 explains microservice technology. Servers running on a cluster or cloud are dynamic in nature. This dynamism is manifested in three ways: (1) the computer on which a server program runs cannot be determined in advance, but in real time at runtime; (2) the number of replicas of a server is dynamically variable for the sake of service availability and throughput; and (3) when the amount of data in a server grows to an upper limit, the server is split in two. In addition, servers face the dual pressures of growing data volumes and increasing loads and face increasing security threats. This chapter explores strategies and methods for making servers run efficiently, securely, and resiliently as well as for enabling rapid development and deployment of server programs, rapid revision and upgrade, and rapid startup. Collectively, these strategies and methods are referred to as microservice technologies.

This book is innovative, illustrated, and easy to understand. It is particularly suitable as a textbook for computer and related majors in higher education institutions or for engineering and technical training. This book is also very suitable for researchers and engineers to read, from which they can realize the connotation of cloud computing and microservices, and appreciate their subtleties.

For beginners to thoroughly understand cloud computing and microservices, it is necessary to read, practice, and think about the connotations and associations between the knowledge. Based on this consideration, each chapter of the book, after the important knowledge points, is provided with reflection questions to guide the reader to think back and around, in order to test the learning effect, deepen the understanding of knowledge points, and train pioneering thinking. The exercises in this book have been carefully selected and organized to cover the important knowledge points.

The book has some complementary materials such as syllabus, teaching PPT, small-group discussion topics, course experiment guidance, and answers to exercises. Readers can download the corresponding resources from the author website (https://csee.hnu.edu.cn/people/yangjinmin). Readers are welcome to criticize and correct the errors in the book.

This book does with the support from the College of Computer Science and Electronic Engineering in Hunan University, China. Its publication cannot be separated from the assistance of editors, Susan Evans Grove, Pradeep Rajasekaran, Mahalakshmi Saravanan, et al, as well as three anonymous review experts.

Changsha, China   Jinmin Yang

Competing Interests The author has no competing interests to declare that are relevant to the content of this manuscript.

Contents

1	**Introduction to Cloud Computing and Microservices**............	1
	1.1 Resource Sharing...	3
	1.2 Resource Management.....................................	5
	1.3 Resource Sharing Characteristics	7
	1.4 Scale Effects..	9
	1.5 Resource Sharing Categories................................	11
	1.6 Distributed Systems.......................................	15
	1.7 Data Consistency...	18
	1.8 Availability of Services	20
	1.9 Efficient Data Processing..................................	22
	1.10 Security of Systems	25
	1.11 System Scalability	28
	1.12 Combined Systems for High-Performance Computing..........	30
	1.13 Big Data Processing......................................	33
	1.14 Cloud Computing...	36
	1.15 Cloud Native Programs	38
	1.16 Virtualization and Virtual Machines	41
	1.17 Abstraction and Dynamic Adaptation	44
	1.18 Microservices...	46
	1.19 History of Technological Evolution..........................	48
	1.20 Summary of the Chapter	55
	References..	56
2	**Sharing of Computer Resources**	59
	2.1 How Computers Work	61
	2.2 Implementation of a Single-Task Operating System	64
	2.3 Multitasking Operating Systems	68
	2.4 Process Scheduling and Management	69
		2.4.1 Process Scheduling	70
		2.4.2 Process Management...............................	76
		2.4.3 Concurrent Multitask Execution	77

xiii

	2.5	Kernel Space and User Space	78
	2.6	Memory Sharing	80
	2.7	Network Sharing	82
	2.8	Code Sharing	88
		2.8.1 Address Relocation	90
		2.8.2 Cross-Module Function Call Based on Indirect Addressing	94
		2.8.3 Static Versus Dynamic Links	97
		2.8.4 Base Address Selection in Relative Addressing	97
		2.8.5 Virtual Memory	99
		2.8.6 Local Variable Storage Allocation and Implementation of Function Calls	104
		2.8.7 Dynamic Storage Allocation for Global Variables	107
		2.8.8 Global and Static Variables and Multithreading	113
		2.8.9 Sharing of Global Variables in Operating Systems	116
	2.9	Sharing of Data Files	117
	2.10	Interaction Between Processes	119
		2.10.1 Signal Handling	120
		2.10.2 Message Queues	125
	2.11	Process-Peripheral Interaction	127
	2.12	Exception Handling	132
		2.12.1 Characterization of Exception Handling	133
		2.12.2 Exception Handling Implementation	137
		2.12.3 Application of Exception Handling	143
	2.13	Summary of the Chapter	146
	References	151
3	**Distributed Computing**	153
	3.1	Function Calls Across Machine Boundaries	155
		3.1.1 Remote Procedure Calls	156
		3.1.2 WEB Interaction	165
		3.1.3 Summary of Function Calls	167
	3.2	Network Transmission	167
		3.2.1 Abstraction of Network Communications	173
		3.2.2 Synchronous I/O and Asynchronous I/O	182
		3.2.3 Gateway Servers	186
		3.2.4 Application Layer Protocols	198
	3.3	Concurrency Control for Transaction Processing	198
		3.3.1 Concurrency Control Based on Access Conflict Identification	201
		3.3.2 Fine-Grained Concurrency Control	207
		3.3.3 Deadlock Avoidance by Enhancing Conflict Identification Conditions	213
	3.4	Transaction Processing and Fault Recovery	215
		3.4.1 Transaction Processing	216

		3.4.2	System Faults and Their Recovery Strategies	218
		3.4.3	Log-Based Fault Recovery	220
		3.4.4	Recovery from Disk Fault	226
		3.4.5	Recovery from Disaster Fault	228
		3.4.6	Implementation of Fault Detection and Recovery	229
		3.4.7	Summary of Transaction Processing and Fault Recovery	231
	3.5	Distributed Transaction Processing		232
		3.5.1	Distributed Servers	232
		3.5.2	Transaction Processing and Fault Recovery in a Distributed Server	236
	3.6	Summary of the Chapter		239
	References			242
4	**Decentralized Computing**			243
	4.1	Paxos Consensus Protocol		245
		4.1.1	Id Application in the Absence of Faults	247
		4.1.2	Impact of Faults on Id Applications	250
		4.1.3	Impact of Faults on System Consistency	251
		4.1.4	Implementation of Replica Consistency in the Presence of Faults	254
		4.1.5	Characterization of the Protocol	257
		4.1.6	Fault Recovery of Replicas	259
	4.2	Specific Implementation of the Paxos Protocol		260
		4.2.1	Handling of Proposal Messages	264
		4.2.2	Handling of Vote Messages	268
		4.2.3	Handling of Decision and Acknowledge and Validation Messages	269
		4.2.4	Handling of Termination and Outcome Messages	272
		4.2.5	Handling of Timeout Messages	274
		4.2.6	Handling of Recovery and Progress Messages	276
		4.2.7	Handling of Fetch and Item Messages	278
		4.2.8	Characterization of Implementations	279
	4.3	Practical Byzantine Fault Tolerance Protocols		280
	4.4	Implementation of the PBFT Protocol		285
	4.5	Summary of the Chapter		287
	References			288
5	**Virtualization and Cloud Computing**			291
	5.1	The Application and Its Runtime Environment		293
	5.2	Compilation Versus Interpretation of Application Programs		295
		5.2.1	Features of the High-Level Programming Language	296
		5.2.2	Compositional Characteristics of the Source Program	297
		5.2.3	Compilation Process and Methods	298
		5.2.4	Intermediate Code Optimization	304
		5.2.5	Interpreted Execution on Applications	307

		5.2.6	Interpreter Implementation	309
		5.2.7	Interpreted Execution on Instructions	314
		5.2.8	Mapping Logical Addresses to Memory Addresses	321
		5.2.9	Characteristics of Interpreted Execution	326
		5.2.10	Intermediate to Machine Code Translation	328
		5.2.11	Code Optimization Based on Instruction Pipelining Processing	329
		5.2.12	Cache-Based Code Optimization	330
		5.2.13	Multicore Processor-Based Code Optimization	332
		5.2.14	Interpretation-Compilation-Based Hybrid Run Mode	333
	5.3	Virtualization of the Runtime Environment		336
	5.4	Virtualization of Files		338
	5.5	Virtualization of Functions		341
		5.5.1	Proxy-Based Decoupling and Encapsulation Scheme	344
		5.5.2	Solutions Based on Function Virtualization	346
		5.5.3	Interface Characterization	351
		5.5.4	Getting Another Interface by One Interface	352
		5.5.5	The Essence of Function Virtualization	354
	5.6	Migration of Applications		356
	5.7	Implementation of Virtual Machine		358
	5.8	The Virtual Machine's Own File System		364
	5.9	Virtual-Real Mapping of Server Port Numbers		366
	5.10	Persistent Storage of Data in VMs		368
	5.11	Volume of Resources Owned by the Virtual Machine		371
	5.12	Virtual LAN Implementation		374
	5.13	Updates to Applications on Virtual Machines		377
	5.14	Containerization of Applications		378
	5.15	Cloud Service Management Systems		380
	5.16	Summary of the Chapter		383
	References			388
6	**Microservices**			391
	6.1	Efficient Data Processing		393
		6.1.1	Tree Indexing	394
		6.1.2	Hash Indexes	398
		6.1.3	Organizing Data Storage Based on Access Characteristics	399
		6.1.4	Thread Pool and Connection Pool	404
		6.1.5	Batch Processing	407
	6.2	Security Technology		408
		6.2.1	Defense Against Injection Attacks	409
		6.2.2	Authentication of Client and Server to Each Other	411
		6.2.3	Defense Against Other Internet Attacks	416
		6.2.4	Management of Client Access Privileges	418
		6.2.5	Audit on Client Access Operations	420

6.3	Server Scalability	421
6.4	Service Cluster	423
6.5	Abstraction and Dynamic Adaptation	425
6.6	Serverless	428
6.7	Summary of the Chapter	430
References		432

About the Author

Jinmin Yang is a professor at the College of Computer Science and Electronic Engineering in Hunan University, China. After graduating with a bachelor's degree from the University of National Defense Technology, he worked as an aircraft repair technician at the aircraft maintenance shops and then served as a senior IT engineer at Changsha Electric Power Company. After obtaining Ph.D. in Computer Applications from Hunan University in 2004, he became a faculty member in the institution. His research interests include distributed computing, database, compiler, and software engineering. He has published three textbooks, respectively, on database, compiler, and cloud computing and microservices. He has won four awards on science and technology progress in Hunan Province.

Chapter 1
Introduction to Cloud Computing and Microservices

This chapter provides an overview of cloud computing and microservices. Resource sharing has been the driving force behind the evolution of computing. The computing paradigm has experienced an evolution from stand-alone computing to cluster computing, and then from cluster computing to cloud computing. In stand-alone computing, sharing means that multiple processes execute concurrently in a computer. Cluster computing extends sharing across computer boundaries. Cloud computing enables server programs to run successfully anywhere on the cloud. Cloud computing has promoted informationization, bringing about new challenges to servers. Servers are facing the double pressure of increasing data volume and customer requests. For servers, the strategies and methods to achieve efficiency, resilience, scalability, availability, security, and consistency, as well as rapid development and deployment, rapid revision and upgrade, and fast startup, are collectively known as microservice technologies.

Distributed system is a familiar and classic concept for IT professionals, but cloud computing [1] is different, often giving people both familiar and unfamiliar feelings. People are familiar with cloud computing, because it is the current hot technology. Industry sector has been developing cloud platforms and tools to support the construction of various cloud systems, while academic sector has been publishing papers on theoretical research results in cloud computing. On the other hand, it is unfamiliar because the difference between cloud computing and distributed computing is not clear, and it is not clear whether it is something completely new or only an evolution of the original technology. Existing literature in the explanation of cloud computing is mostly centered around the products, describing their architecture and their functionalities, without their ins and outs and causes and consequences, often making people know the cloud computing, but do not know the reason.

Some people say that cloud computing is a completely new technology, while others say that it is just an evolution of an existing technology. People who hold these two views often argue about it, each with its own views. These two views seem to be contradictory on the surface, in fact, but also have a unity. Cloud computing is a new technology. This view is true from the point of perspective of its impact on society and the promotion of economic development [2]. If we look at the internal realization of cloud computing [3], it is true that cloud computing is only an evolution of the original technology, and nothing has essentially changed. This unity suggests that it is important to look at cloud computing both in terms of its far-reaching impact on society and as an evolution of the original computing technology. Cloud computing is an advanced stage in the evolution of distributed computing [4].

Cloud computing could not emerge without highly developed network communications. The highly developed network communication is reflected in the four aspects: high availability, high reliability, high coverage, and low cost. Nowadays, mobile communication technology enables business information systems and their users to be no longer limited by time and space, i.e., users can access business information systems anytime and anywhere. It is in this context that the cloud computing paradigm emerges. Cloud computing has led to a fundamental change in the way small and medium enterprises (SMEs) build and operate their business information systems [5]. Enterprises no longer have to consider the construction of server room and network, the purchase of servers and support software, the hire of IT operation personnel, and the replacement of equipment and software. Enterprises rent computing resources and storage resources from cloud service providers, migrate their business information systems to run on the cloud, and move their data to the cloud for storage. The system operation work is also outsourced to the cloud service provider. This scenario greatly reduces the threshold for enterprises to build and operate their business information systems.

Cloud service providers use management software to consolidate a large number of physical servers into one logical server [5]. Logical servers have completely different characteristics than physical servers. A physical server becomes unavailable to its users when it fails, whereas a logical server never appears to fail to users. Physical servers provide limited computing and storage resources, whereas logical servers appear to users to have an infinite number of resources. These two characteristics of logical servers are very popular among users. When users move their business information systems to the cloud, they will no longer encounter the problem of insufficient resources or dropouts due to failures.

For cloud service providers, when the number of users reaches a certain scale, they can play a scale effect to improve their resource utilization and make their services cheaper and better, so as to recruit more users and obtain more profits. When business is profitable, the cloud service provider will also be willing to make additional investments to make the service better, make the scale bigger, and the price lower. This creates a win–win situation for both the cloud service provider and its customers. Because of this, the whole society embraces cloud computing [6].

The essence of cloud computing is to leave professional things to professional companies, and to improve resource utilization through division of labor and specialization, which in turn expands demand, increases scale, and achieves iteration and virtuous cycle. The high degree of development of network communication provides a prerequisite for division of labor and specialization. On top of the communication network, an information service network is constructed [7]. In this information service network, each enterprise is both a provider of a certain service and a consumer of other enterprises' services. The information system takes the service as a unit and evolves and develops continuously through the combination and iteration of services. From the point of view of service combination and iteration, the service program as a basic unit is also called microservice [8].

The goal of cloud computing is to deepen resource sharing and solve the deep-rooted problems faced therein. For example, an organization that migrates its business information systems to run on the cloud does not want its business information systems to be tied to a particular cloud service provider. The advantage of this is that it is easy to migrate the business information system from one cloud platform to another when there is a better cloud service provider to choose from. If their business information systems are tied to a specific cloud service provider, then the migration can be problematic, resulting in a loss of choice.

There are a series of questions to think about when faced with cloud computing. There are 3 most basic questions. The first one is: Why is resource sharing so important? What problems are encountered in resource sharing? How to solve them? The second question is: an enterprise's business information system on the cloud, compared with on the enterprise's own servers, both in the operation costs and quality of service will have a huge advantage, and how to achieve this advantage? The third question is: how can the business information system of an enterprise user, which is to be run on the platform provided by a cloud service provider, be made independent of each other and seamlessly integrated? This chapter will unfold layer by layer around these questions to draw a basic portrait of cloud computing.

1.1 Resource Sharing

Resource sharing is both a goal that people have been pursuing and a driving force for social advance. In the early days of computers, they were so expensive that only research institutes could afford them, making them a precious resource. In order to fully utilize computers, the sharing model is: let a computer with multiple terminals. A terminal consists of a display screen and a keyboard. Thus, one computer can be used by multiple users at the same time. The technical solution to achieve computer sharing is to use a multitasking operating system that runs different users' programs in turn by clock's interrupts. This strategy divides time into time slices by means of a clock's interruption. Within a time slice, the computer runs a program. Once the time slice is over, a clock interruption is triggered to control the computer through software to run another program. Since the time slice is very short, users do not feel the intermittency of the program running. This scheme enables each user to feel as if he or she has a computer all to himself or herself. The implementation of a multitasking operating system will be explained in detail in Chap. 2.

Computers with multiple terminals are often referred to as minicomputers. To use a minicomputer, a user must go to the computer room of a computing center, where the terminals are housed. Thus, the use of computers is limited to scientific calculations and is prevented from office work. In the 1980s, IBM developed the PC and made all of its technology available to the public. IBM's initiative was a crucial catalyst for human society to enter the PC era. As the PC machine is inexpensive, supports office work, and thus is put on the desk, it is also known as a desktop machine. Compared to minicomputers, PCs have a distinguishing feature of low price. For this purpose, PCs used single-tasking operating systems. Single-tasking operating systems are characterized by simplicity, require few computing and storage resources, and are very inexpensive.

The distinguishing feature of PCs is that they are inexpensive. Because of the low price, the number of people who can afford one PC increases. More purchases result in the expansion of scale of production. When the scale of production increases, the cost of production decreases. Lower cost makes the price fall further. Lower prices draw more customers to buy. In addition, when there are many people using the product, product defects and quality problems are fully exposed. The continuous elimination of product defects makes the reliability and quality of the product improve, making the product more popular. This virtuous cycle and iteration are not only driving the technology forward, but also leading to society's advance. The application of PC is rapidly spreading from the office sector to the field of equipment automation.

The digitization of offices and equipment control has resulted in a large amount of business data stored in computers. Thus, data sharing has become an urgent issue. In this context, there appeared network technology. It solved the problem of data transportation, making data transportation fast, low cost, and good quality. Mobile network communication is even better, allowing people to use it anytime and anywhere. PC technology and network communication technology directly bring human society into the information age. Network communication technology will be explained in detail in Chap. 3.

Resource sharing includes hardware sharing, software sharing, and data sharing. From a business perspective, resource sharing is accomplished through the interactions of resource owners and resource users. Resource owners are also called service providers, and resource users are called customers. In terms of how resource sharing is implemented, resources are managed by a server and customers use a client program to access the server. The service provider publishes application programming interface (API) functions for client programs to access the server. Client programs access the server through API function calls. When the client program and the server are not on the same computer, they have to interact over the network. This kind of API function call is also known as remote procedure calling (RPC for short) [9]. The details of function calls are explained in Chaps. 2 and 3.

From an interaction perspective, what a client program transmits to a server is called a service request, and what a server transmits to a client program is called a service response. The server processes each request it receives and then responds with a response result. The client program processes the response result to determine what to do next. Therefore, an API function call means that a client program sends a request to a server, and then gets a response result as the function return value from the server.

Resource sharing is not a modern concept. It was introduced a long time ago. A typical example of resource sharing is the ancient academies. At that time, technology was not well developed and books were very expensive and unaffordable to the vast majority of people. Hence, the academies emerged. Anyone who wanted to read went to the academies to borrow books. Borrowing books was much cheaper than buying them, so everyone was willing to go and borrow books. For an academy, it had many customers and its books could be fully utilized. Even if the individual borrowing fee is very low, its total revenue is still very substantial. This is a typical case of mutual benefit and a win–win situation through resource sharing.

1.2 Resource Management

Resource sharing is closely linked to resource management. Resource is a business term and has a business value. Resources are inseparable from their owners and customers. The value of a resource is realized through its use by customers. Therefore, the owner of a resource will try to recruit customers to make the best use of the resource. A resource cannot usually be used by more than one customer at the same time. Therefore, the resource owner has to effectively manage the use of the resource by customers in order to fully utilize the resource and realize resource sharing. The resource owner should record the current status of each resource. The current state of a resource usually has only two kinds: (1) idle and (2) occupied. Resource state will change in two situations. When an idle resource is assigned to a customer to use by its owner, the state of the resource varies from idle to occupied. When a customer rents a resource back to its owner, the state of the resource changes from occupied to idle. The orderly use of resources is called resource management.

Resource sharing can be mutually beneficial for both the owner of the resource and the customer. There are three roles in the resource sharing model: the resource, the owner, and the customer. The owner of the resource is often referred to as the manager of the resource. Customers make requests to the manager to rent resources, and the manager is responsible for allocating the resources to customers. Take a computer, for example, its hardware resources include memory, disk, CPU, and network. The manager of these resources is the operating system and the client is the application program. The application program requests resources from the operating system by calling API functions, and the operating system allocates the resources to the application program for use.

In resource management, resources usually have category and identification number attributes, and may have other attributes as well. When a client requests a resource from a manager, the category of the resource is usually reflected in the API function name. For example, resources on a computer have categories such as memory, file, and network. An application program calls the API function *alloc* when it requests memory from the operating system, and *fopen* when it requests a file. Resources requested by a client from a manager are identified by IDs. For example, the return value of an application's call to the *alloc* function is the id of the resulting block of memory, and the return value of a call to the *fopen* function is the id of the resulting file. Subsequent accesses by the client to the resource are identified by IDs. For example, when an application wants to write data to a requested file, it does so by calling the *fwrite* API function, whose first argument is the file id.

From a business point of view, resource sharing is also called resource service, and so resource owners are also called resource managers. In an operating system, the manager of file resources is called a file manager, the manager of memory resources is called a memory manager, and the manager of network resources is called a network manager. File sharing is also called file service. Among the file service API functions released by the operating system to customers, the most commonly used ones are *fopen, fread, fwrite, fseek,* and *fclose*. From the customer's point of view, the functionality of *fopen* is to request resources, the functionalities of *fread, fwrite,* and *fseek* are to use resources, and the functionality of *fclose* is to return resources back.

There is a process for a client to access a resource. To access a file, for example, the client first calls the *fopen* function to open the specified file, and then calls the *fwrite* and *fread* functions to write data to the file and read data from the file, respectively. After completing the data reading and writing, then call the *fclose* function to return the file back to the operating system. Specifically, the client calls the *fwrite* function to write the specified length of memory data to the current location of the file, and calls the *fread* function to read the specified length of data from the current location of the file into memory. The client can also call the *fseek* function to move the current location to realize the read and write to any location of the file.

The file manager uses the current access log table to effectively manage the sharing of file resources [10]. An example of the current access log table is shown in Table 1.1. There are three rows of data in this example, indicating that there are currently three clients accessing, where client *A* (whose process id is 18) is accessing two files, and client *B* (whose process id is 19) is accessing one file. The first row of data in this example indicates that the file c:\data\student.dat is currently being used in a read-only manner by the application with process id 18, with the current location pointer value of 64,000, and the file access id of 1. The *memAddr* and *memSize* columns of the table record, respectively, the starting address of the file data in memory and the size of memory occupied by the file.

With the current access log table, the file manager can effectively manage file access. Now, suppose the application program with process id 19 calls the *fopen*

Table 1.1 Table of current access logs

accessId	fileName	clientId	accessModel	memAddr	memSize	curPointer
1	c:\data\student.at	18	R	51200000	10240000	64000
2	c:\data\course.at	18	R	71680000	5120000	0
3	c:\data\enroll.at	19	R|W	92160000	4096000	102400

function for a write operation to the file c:\data\student.dat. When the file manager receives this request, it first consults the current access log table to see if there exists a line with a *fileName* field value of c:\data\sdutent.dat. If it exists, the file is currently being used by another process and there is an access conflict, so the user's request can only be denied. If it does not exist, it indicates that the user's request can be fulfilled, so a row is added to the current access log table to record the access, and the file access id for that row is returned to the client. The client checks the return value of the *fopen* function and if it is −1, it indicates that the request was denied by the service. Otherwise, it indicates that the request was successful and the return value is the file access id.

For the example in Table 1.1, suppose the application with process id 19 calls the *fopen* function for a read operation on the file c:\data\student.dat. Then, the request will succeed for the following reason: a file can be shared by more than one client in a read mode. At this point, the file manager will add a row to the current access log table to note the access. When client *A* (whose process id is 18) calls the *fclose* function to perform a close operation on the file with *accessId* 1, the file manager then performs a delete operation on the first row of data in Table 1.1.

Reflection 1-1: Can you write the implementation code for the *fopen* function based on the current access log table?

Reflection 1-2: For the management of memory shares, what fields should be included in its current access log table?

1.3 Resource Sharing Characteristics

In the resource sharing model, there are three concepts: resource, service provider, and customer. When a customer needs a resource, it sends a resource request to the service provider. Only after the request is approved by the service provider, the customer access the resource. After accessing the resource, the customer notifies the manager so that the service provider can reclaim the resource. This access model is characterized by the fact that the service provider and the client are both independent of each other and can interact with each other. Mutual independence is reflected in the construction of the service program and the client program, without dependency between them. When building a service program, there is no need to consider client programs, only what resources are available to be shared, and the processes and links through which the client accesses the resources. The same is true for the construction of the client programs, which can be programmed and implemented according to the resource access guidelines, without considering the provider of the service program.

There are a number of benefits to service providers and clients being independent of each other. The first benefit is that the service program and the client program are freed from dependencies and constraints on each other. For the provider of a service program, it can focus on the design and development of the service program without having to consider the client program. The same is true for the provider of the client program, which is not constrained by the service provider and can focus on the development of the client program. For example, a communication network provider can focus on the design and development of a communication network without considering communication terminals such as cellular phones. A manufacturer of cellular phones does not need to consider the provider of the communication network either, and can focus only on the design and development of the cellular phones.

A second advantage of the independence of the service provider and the customer is that it allows a service provider to recruit more customers, and it also allows a customer not to be tied to a particular service provider. For example, for communication service providers such as mobile and Unicom, any holder of a communication terminal can be a customer. From another point of view, the holder of a communication terminal, as a customer, is not bound to a particular communication service provider. When there is a better communication service provider to choose from, he can change as he wishes.

Mutual independence is a prerequisite for free competition. The mutual independence of service providers and customers in the resource-sharing model dictates that no one can stop to eat his or her way out. Any person or enterprise is both a money maker and a consumer in society. When making money, it plays the role of a service provider; when consuming, it plays the role of a customer. As a service provider, if you do not improve your service, you will be surpassed by other service providers; thus, your customers will slowly lose, and you will make less and less money. As consumers, they have a choice of service providers. Therefore, the services are obliged to become better and better. It is this mutual independence of service providers and customers that leads to the continuous progress and advance of human society.

In the resource sharing model, the service provider and the customer have to interact. This interaction is characterized by the fact that the client is always the active party and the service provider is the passive party. This type of interaction is also known as Client/Server model or C/S model for short. The client initiates a request to the service provider and the service provider responds to the client's request. From a programming point of view, the request and response are embodied in a function call, where the request is embodied in the real parameters to be passed and the response is embodied in the return value of the function call. From an object-oriented perspective, a request is an instance object of a request class, and a response is an instance object of a response class. For each request class, the service provider has to provide a handler for its instance object, which is naturally a member function of the corresponding request class. Similarly, for each response class, the client provides a handler for its instance object, which is naturally a member function of the corresponding response class.

For a service, there must be a service access protocol, i.e., a consensus and contract for the interaction between the service provider and the customer. The so-called service access protocol is the process by which the customer accesses the service and its links. Each link corresponds to a request from the client and a response from the service provider. From a programming perspective, each link corresponds to a function call. From the object-oriented point of view, each link corresponds to the definition of a request class and a response class. With the service access protocol, the server program and the client application are both independent of each other and can be assembled.

When a service is provided by a company only, the access protocol for that service is defined and published by the provider, e.g., WeChat service is defined and published by Tencent. For general-purpose services, such as file services, database services, email services, DNS services, and web services, the service access protocols are usually defined and published by international standards organizations. For example, WWW is a well-known international standards organization. For WEB services, the service program is called a WEB server, and its most commonly used client program is a browser.

Reflection 1-3: To understand network communication protocols such as HTTP, TCP, and IP from an object-oriented perspective, they actually correspond to a class definition, i.e., the HTTP class, the TCP class, and the IP class. An HTTP packet is an instance object of the HTTP class. Is this the right way to understand network communication protocols? Please give reasons.

Resource sharing also has the property that what time a customer initiates a request to a service provider is entirely up to the customer, independent of the service provider. Furthermore, in the case of a service provider, it has a one-to-many relationship with its customers. That is, a service provider usually has many customers. When there are few customer requests, the service provider is idle; when there are many customer requests, the service provider is busy. In order not to wear itself out when customer requests swarm, a service program should have measures in place to deal with this situation. The simplest way is to reject new customer requests when it is overwhelmed. The fact that a request is rejected by the service provider is not unacceptable to a customer, because the mutual independence of the service provider and the customer is the most basic feature of the service model. How to portray busyness and idleness? What are the responses of the service program to busyness? These questions are addressed in detail in Chaps. 3 and 6.

1.4 Scale Effects

As far as the provision of services is concerned, in terms of service quality, there is a great deal of difference between individuals and organizations. For example, public transportation service, if it is provided by an individual, then the service has no quality assurance for customers. When the driver is sick, or the car breaks down, customers will perceive the service as unavailable. If the bus service is provided by a company, the quality of service will be completely different. In a bus company, a driver getting sick or a bus breaking down is not visible to customers. The reason is that when an on-duty driver is sick, the company can dispatch another driver who is on vacation to fill in, and when a bus breaks down, the company can dispatch another spare bus to fill in. Thus, in the eyes of customers, bus service is never interrupted.

For a company that provides a certain service, the larger it is, the more stable and fault-tolerant its service will be. An example is given to illustrate this property. For a bus company, assume that it operates 10 bus routes and provides uninterrupted service 24 h a day. Also, assume that a driver works 5 days a week, 8 h a day. For this bus service, in a week's time, the company has to employ 40 drivers, with 30 scheduled to work each day and another 10 on vacation. When one of the on-duty drivers falls ill, there is no problem at all in finding one of the 10 vacation drivers to fill in for the sick driver. In contrast, let us say the company is small and only operates 1 bus route. In this case, the company only needs to hire 4 drivers, 3 of whom are scheduled to work each day while the other one is on vacation. When one of the drivers on duty is sick, the one on vacation may not be able to fill in due to an emergency. This does not allow for uninterrupted bus service.

The same is true for a cloud service provider. The more servers it has, the smoother the service it provides and the more assured the quality of service. When a server fails, it can dispatch another backup server to take its place or migrate the work undertaken by the failed server to other similar servers that are functioning normally. For cloud service providers, their servers can be fully utilized when their business volume increases, so they can adjust their service prices even lower. In the view of customers, the service price is low and the quality is guaranteed, so they are willing to consume the service. As customer volume increases, the cloud provider's server size increases further and its services become more popular. This benign iteration drives the rapid development of cloud services.

An organization or company that gathers human and material resources together to form a scale will develop competitiveness. The larger the scale is, the more obvious the scale-sharing effects are, and the stronger the competitiveness brought about. The more inexpensive the service or commodity is, the more popular it will be with customers. In China, lighters are sold at only one RMB a piece, which is a typical example of competitiveness brought about by scale effect. A lighter consists of nine parts, but its sale price is only one RMB, which is totally out of the question. By common sense, it should be sold for 5 to 6 RMB. Lighters can be as cheap as one RMB a piece; it happens only in China. The reason behind it is: China's annual production of lighters has reached a billion. In terms of lighters, China's competitiveness in the world no other country can shake. This is a vivid case of China's supercompetitiveness in the world of small daily commodities.

One more example. Back in 2007, calling from China to Canada costs 18.6 RMB per minute with China Mobile service. Why was it so expensive? Because at that time, China Mobile had invested very heavily in the construction of a cross-border communication network, but the volume of business was small. In order to recover the cost, it had to set the price very high. The high price inhibited the growth of customer volume. Then again, nowadays, you do not even have to pay a separate fee for making international calls through the Internet. On the face of it, China Mobile's turnover should have fallen. On the contrary, compared to 2007, China Mobile's annual turnover has increased 50 times. Why is this happening? Because its customer volume increases exponentially due to price reductions. Compared to 2007, China Mobile's customer base has increased hundreds of times. Everyone has a cell phone now, and communication rates are so low that everyone can afford them. This win–win situation stems from the scale effects.

In the marketing of cloud services, the scale effect is highly valued by major cloud service providers [11]. Tencent Cloud, for example, not only provides free cloud development platforms for WeChat mini-programs, WeChat mini-games, and WeChat official accounts, but also offers preferential conditions for free use of cloud services before customers make profits. Even after customers make a profit, the cloud service charges are also divided into several different grades according to the traffic. Driven by such favorable charging policies, SMEs are naturally willing to migrate their business information systems to run on the cloud. In the next few years, the number of cloud service customers is bound to rise exponentially [12].

In history, there are two events related to scale effects that have had a profound impact on human society. In the 1920s, Ford of the United States built the Ford automobile. At that time, automobiles had just come out. As a rule, new things are rare and fresh, and naturally expensive. Ford had a head start and could have made a lot of money from the high price. But instead of doing so, Ford shouted the slogan of making automobiles affordable for all factory workers. The meaning of this slogan was to make the automobile that just came out cheap and not a luxury item. This philosophy of Ford's accomplished himself and advanced human society. Ford became the king of automobiles, and cars soon entered the homes of ordinary people.

The second event was the development of the PC by IBM in the 1970s. IBM did not make high profits by keeping the technology secret, producing and selling it by itself. Instead, it made all the technology public and allowed any individual or business to produce and sell PCs without paying any royalties to IBM. This move made PCs inexpensive and production climbed rapidly. As PCs were sold in large quantities, had many users, and were widely used, their defects were fully exposed. Therefore, the quality of PCs has become rapidly better, and the performance has been continuously improved. IBM's move appears to be selfless, but in fact it is a long line to catch a big fish. The popularity and popularization of PCs have triggered a huge information industry. IBM quickly became an industrial predator and a giant of the industry in this big wave.

1.5 Resource Sharing Categories

Among resource sharing, code sharing was first proposed. In the early days of computers, they were mainly used for scientific computing. There are a lot of basic and common things in scientific computing, such as trigonometric function solving, matrix operations, Fourier transforms, and so on. The programming implementation of these elements is a very specialized matter. Code sharing not only simplifies the application development cycle and saves development cost, but also improves the software quality. However, code sharing encounters many problems in its implementation. Code sharing is categorized into two ways: sharing at source code level and sharing at binary executable level. The problems faced by source code sharing are: (1) compilation problems due to the different programming languages used by the client program and the service program; (2) leakage of function implementation technology due to the fact that the service provider has to release the source code to its clients. Both of these problems are fatal, so a binary executable sharing scheme is proposed.

In the binary executable sharing scheme, the service provider encapsulates its source code into functional functions and then compiles them into intermediate code or machine code, i.e., converts the source code file into a binary executable file. The readability of binary executable file is very poor and not suitable for human reading, so it is beneficial for the service provider to keep technical secrets. In addition, compilation problems can be solved. Instead of a source code file, the service provider provides the client with a binary executable file (commonly known as a dynamic link library file). Customers do not need to compile the binary executable file, but only link it to their own applications. There are many technical problems encountered in linking. These problems and their solutions will be explained in Chap. 2.

In addition to code sharing, computer sharing is also very important. Computer sharing is the sharing of a computer by multiple applications, i.e., having one computer execute multiple applications. An elementary form of such sharing is to have one computer execute one application before executing another. A single-tasking operating system is a typical solution to realize this elementary way of sharing. The basic principle of a single-tasking operating system is to use one application program (denoted as program A) to execute another application program (denoted as program X). Program A is called the operating system and consists of an infinite loop of code. Thus, program A always runs after it is started up and does not end. The functionality of the code in the loop body is to wait for the user's keyboard to enter the name of the application program to be executed (i.e., Program X), then loads the binary executable file of Program X from disk into memory, and then calls the main function of Program X. When the main function of program X returns, it means that program X has finished executing and program A moves on to the next round of the loop. The specifics of single-tasking operating systems are detailed in Chap. 2.

An advanced form of computer sharing is to allow a single computer to execute multiple applications concurrently. Multitasking operating systems are a typical solution to realize this advanced way of sharing. The principle of a multitasking operating system is that time is divided into time slices, and an application is executed in one time slice. Thus, multiple applications are executed by the CPU in turn, or each application is executed by the CPU intermittently. Since the time slice is very short, the fact that the CPU executes an application intermittently is not perceived by users. It appears to users that each application is running smoothly.

Concurrent execution of multiple tasks means that multiple applications share a computer. The shared resources include the CPU, memory, network, monitor, and other external devices such as keyboards and disks. There are two types of memory: memory and registers. Each type of shared resource has a manager. When an application wants to use a shared resource, it calls an API function to request it from the manager. Thus, a multitasking operating system actually consists mainly of shared resource managers. With multiple applications running at the same time, it is natural to have a manager as well. This manager is called the process manager and manages the startup of applications (i.e., process creation), the switching of processes (i.e., process up and down), and the termination of processes. Thus, it can be said that a multitasking operating system consists of a shared resource manager and a process manager. In addition, the desktop application is essential. It runs all the time and is responsible for human–computer interaction. Its functionalities are: displaying windows and starting applications (i.e., process creation).

In a multitasking operating system, a process is an entity in which a program runs. The operating system creates a process every time an application starts running. Multiple processes can also be created for a single application program. For example, a Word program can be started up multiple times, i.e., multiple processes can be created so that they all run the Word program but handle different Word files separately. The process manager provides API functions for applications to call in order to create a new process to execute an application. In the Linux operating system, the *fork* function functions to create a new process. The new process is cloned from the caller process. The process manager maintains a process table. Each row of data in the process table records one process. A process has only one row in the process table. A process is identified by its id. To create a process, you add a row to the process table; to terminate a process, you delete the corresponding row in the table.

On a computer, clients of a shared resource are processes. In the case of memory, as a shared resource, each process requires it to run. A program consists of code and data. When a program runs, it requires both code and data to be in memory. Code has a read-only property, so code in memory can be shared by multiple processes. For data, each process usually has its own copy, which is not shared. When a process needs memory, it requests it from the memory manager through an API call. The memory manager maintains a memory usage table that keeps track of allocated memory. Every time a block of memory is allocated, a row is added to the memory usage table noting the starting address and size of the block and the id of the client process, and when the client process frees a block of memory, the corresponding row is deleted from the memory usage table.

For a binary executable file, it contains both code and data. Data are divided into variables and constants. Code and constants have read-only properties. Because of this, a binary executable file is usually divided into three segments: the code segment, the constant segment, and the variable segment. Before a process can run, it usually loads the components of its program (one or more binary executable files) from disk into memory. By the time a process wants to load a binary executable file, it may already be loaded into memory. The reason for this is that the binary executable file may also be a component of another process. In this case, only the variable segment must be loaded, while the code and constant segments can be shared. The sharing of code and constants creates a problem: for the later process, its variable and shared parts (code and constants) are not next to each other in memory, which is inconsistent with the compile-time assumptions. The solution to this problem is explained in Chap. 2.

Of the shared resources, the characteristics of the network are completely different from memory and similar to the CPU. CPU sharing, which divides time into time slices and then allows the CPU to take turns executing the current process, gives users the illusion that there are multiple CPUs. The functionality of a network is to transmit data (both receiving and sending). Network sharing divides the data to be transmitted by each process into packets, and then lets the network take turns transmitting the packets, giving users the illusion that there are multiple networks. This strategy is also called multiplexing. Here, multiplexing means that data packets to be transmitted by more than one process are transmitted through a single network. The implementation of network sharing is explained in detail in Chap. 3.

Shared resources include data in addition to hardware and code. Data sharing means that data on a computer are to be read/written by more than one process. For a particular data, when one process is performing a read operation on it, another process is not allowed to perform a write operation on it. Also, when one process is performing a write operation on it, another process is not allowed to perform a read or write operation on it. Thus, data sharing also needs a manager. File managers, database management systems are typical data managers. Application programs access files by calling the API provided by the file manager, access to the database by calling the API provided by the database management system. For data maintained by the operating system, such as process table and memory usage table, the application program accesses them by calling the API provided by the operating system.

There are also data that have no manager, such as static variables defined in a program. Global variables, which are shared by multiple threads in a multithreaded program, also fall into the category of data without a manager. For this type of data, the program can read and write to it directly. The correctness of its sharing is controlled by the program itself. For this purpose, the operating system provides lock service. Programming a multithreaded application, the designer can specify a lock from the operating system and associate it with the shared data. A thread carries out a locking operation before accessing the shared data. After the data have been manipulated, an unlocking operation is performed. The prerequisite for successful locking is that the requested lock has not been occupied by another thread. If the requested lock has been occupied, the requester is stuck in a waiting state until the holder unlocks it.

Resource sharing, as described previously, covers a single computer. It is characterized by the fact that the operating system plays the role of service provider (i.e., resource manager) and applications (i.e., processes) play the role of clients. When the scope of sharing is extended to other computers, e.g., the resources on computer α are to be used by computer β. If so, an application program (denoted as process S) running on computer α needs to play the role of service provider, and another application program (denoted as process C) running on computer β needs to play the role of client. Process C and Process S interact over a network to form a distributed system. This kind of sharing will be explained in detail in Chap. 3.

1.6 Distributed Systems

The most basic distributed system consists of two applications (i.e., processes) running on different computers, with one application acting as a server and the other as a client. The client sends a request to the server, and the server responds to the client. Requests and responses are still expressed as function calls: the name of the function and the real parameters passed express the request, and the function return value expresses the response. The interaction between an application (i.e., a process) and the operating system has both similarities and differences from the interaction between an application and another application. The similarities are in the requests and responses, and in the function calls. The difference is that the interaction between an application (i.e., a process) and the operating system is the matter within a process, while the interaction between an application and another application is between processes.

The operating system is actually a group of dynamically linked library files that provide API functions for applications to call. Data maintained by the operating system, such as the process table and the memory usage table, are not visible to applications. The data that an application can access directly is limited to the data that it defines and maintains. Application's access to OS-maintained data must be accomplished through API calls. Therefore, the complete application code consists of two parts: the application code and the operating system code. Its data also consist of two parts: data maintained by the application program and data maintained by the operating system. The data maintained by the application program are private to the process, while the data maintained by the operating system are shared by all processes.

Reflection 1-4: Many editors provide functionalities for selecting, copying/cutting, and pasting text or images. Is it correct to say that the copying/cutting functionality is to turn process-private data into shared data, and the pasting functionality is to turn shared data into process-private data?

For two processes on the same computer (denoted as Process A and Process B), interaction between them must be accomplished through the operating system. When process A wants to transmit data to process B, it calls an API function from the operating system to make a copy of the data to be transmitted (process A's private data), creating a shared data maintained by the operating system. When process B receives the data, it calls the API function provided by the operating system to convert the shared data maintained by the operating system into process B's private data. This is the implementation scheme for inter-process communication. This scheme is referred to as IPC, where IPC stands for interprocess communication.

If the above process A and process B are located on different computers, then the operating system has to send the transferred data over the network to another computer. In addition to this, it is also important to consider whether the two computers are homogeneous or not. If they are heterogeneous, then the operating system at both ends will have to translate the data received or sent. The reason for this is that heterogeneous computers do not recognize each other's memory data. Different computer models may have different memory representations of data, such as integers and real numbers. For example, with an X86 model, a 32-bit computer uses 4 bytes to store an integer, while a 64-bit machine uses 8 bytes to store an integer, which differs from each other. For characters, different operating systems may use different encoding standards. This leads to translation being an essential task when transferring data between two heterogeneous computers.

The diversity of data expressed by computers is similar to the diversity of human languages in the world. There are many languages in the world, such as Chinese, Russian, German, Japanese, and so on. When people from different countries communicate, they usually use English. English is recognized worldwide as the standard language of communication. This means that everyone has the same job to do, which is to learn English well. If you learn English well, you will be able to communicate with anyone in the world. The same is true for communication between computers, which also defines standard expressions for data. For example, integers and real numbers are expressed in characters, and characters are encoded in UTF-8. Thus, each operating system does the same thing: when it sends data, it translates its own memory data into standardized data; when it receives data, it translates standardized data into its own memory data. Serialization of data objects usually refer to is the translation from memory data to standard data; while deserialization of data objects is the translation from standard data to memory data.

Reflection 1-5: Converting an integer or a real number to a string is done in C using the sprintf function. Which function is used to convert a string to an integer or a real number respectively in C language?

In a distributed system, a client sends a request to a server via a function call whose return value is the response result. Since clients and servers are independent of each other, there is uncertainty as to what time the response result will be available. For API functions about interactions, the timeout setting should be considered when programming. If the timeout occurs and the response result has not been received, the function will also return. However, the function's return value at this point expresses an error rather than a normal response result. The program can further check the error information, know the reason for the error, and make the appropriate processing. For example, if the error is a timeout, you can send another request again. If all three requests time out, it can be concluded that the server has failed. On the server's side, client requests may be duplicated. In server programming, the handling of duplicate requests is essential.

The classic way for an application to access resources managed by the operating system is that the resource class is expressed by a function name. When there are multiple instances of a particular resource class, the instances are then identified by name. For example, there may be multiple serial ports on a computer, each identified by name. One special case, though, is a file. A file is identified by a path in addition to its name. Programming a file identified by a path plus a filename poses a problem. Here is an example. Assuming that the application *studentManage* was developed with the data file identification set to "D:/data/student.dat", the application is now to be installed on a computer that has only a C disk, not a D disk. Since the student.dat file cannot be installed on the D disk specified during development, the application will not run successfully.

In order to solve the above problem, files are programmed to be identified with just the filename, without the path. This has the advantage of simplicity and unification with other types of resource identification. The problem that arises is: which path to go to at runtime to find the file in question? The solution is: first go to the path where the application is located to find the file. If it is not found, then go to the path indicated by the environment variable PATH. In the above example, you would first look for the student.dat file in the path where the *studentManage* application is installed. When you start running *studentManage*, the path will be known. The advantage of this approach is that no matter where the application *studentManage* is installed, the program will run normally and the student.dat file will be found.

For distributed systems, there is an extra thing in resource identification, and that is to identify the server first. The server is identified with four items: IP address, port number, username, and password. The ideal way to handle this is to still identify the server by name only. The advantage of this approach is twofold. The first is that it maintains the uniformity of the programming pattern, which is indistinguishable from classic local access. The second benefit is applicability. The server referred to by name is only a logical concept at the time of programming. The physical server to which the name refers is not determined until the application is installed. That is, the name is not mapped to a server until the application is installed, giving the server's IP address, port number, username, and password. An example of this kind of processing is: the Windows operating system's control panel has a functionality to configure data sources. A data source is identified by its name, and each data source carries configuration parameters for the resource it refers to. When the application is programmed, the data sources are identified by name. In the implementation of the API function for accessing the database, the data source name is used to look up the identification parameters of the server to which it refers in the control panel.

For cloud computing, the requirements are even higher. The physical server to which the name refers is not determined at the time of installation of the application, but only at runtime. It even changes during runtime. In cloud computing, the server program runs on the cloud, and exactly which server it runs on has dynamic changeability. As soon as the change occurs, the new identification parameters have to be updated in the service registry. Once the client discovers that the network communication is disconnected, it has to go to the service registry to reacquire the identification parameters of the server by the service name and re-establish the network connection with the server. The server has a one-to-many relationship with its clients, and when it changes dynamically, it affects multiple clients. Therefore, it is desirable that the dynamic changeability of the server be transparent to its clients. The solution is to add a service agent, also called a service broker, between clients and the server. In the view of clients, the service broker is the server. The feasibility and concrete implementation of this solution will be explained in detail in Chap. 5.

In a distributed system, an application may be both a service provider and a client. This situation is similar to human society. A business is both a provider of some product and a consumer of some other component. This dual role of an application makes the servers throughout the Internet constitute a service network. Servers are identified by name. There are also standards for name identification. For example, the server's name "https://www.hnu.edu.cn: 8080/" expresses not only the network communication protocol, the domain name of the server, but also the listening port number of the server. In actual network communication, it is the server IP address that is needed, not the domain name. The domain name is used to get its IP address. This kind of service is provided by DNS servers. Therefore, in the implementation of the API function for network connection, the DNS server is accessed to get the IP address of the domain name, and then a network connection is established with the server by IP address. The advantage of this scheme is that the domain name visible to clients is a logical address with eternal immutability.

Reflection 1-6: When programming applications, try not to use physical identifiers but logical identifiers, so that the developed applications are well generalized and adaptable. The conversion of logical identifiers to physical ones is encapsulated in the implementation of API functions. For example, in the implementation of a database application, when accessing a database, it is better not to splice SQL statements to directly manipulate the data in the tables of database, but to do it by calling stored procedures, why? Please give reasons.

1.7 Data Consistency

Section 1.6 mentions access control management on reading and writing to shared data. A specialized manager can be set up so that clients cannot read or write to shared data directly. With this approach, clients must call API functions provided by the manager to access the data. If a thread can read and write to the shared data directly, then the access control management is up to application developers. The common approach used to avoid access conflicts is that a lock is associated with the shared data, and each thread accesses the data on condition that it has occupied the lock. After accessing, the lock is released by the occupant thread so that other threads can lock it. When a thread calls API function *lock* to hold the lock occupied by another thread, it will be trapped in a waiting state until the lock is released by the holder thread. This shows that a lock is actually shared data. Locks have a manager, which is the operating system. Access control management on the shared data is necessary to ensure that the data are correct.

There is also a class of applications that involves performing updates on two or more items of data. An example of such an application is a bank transfer. Transferring $100 from account A to account B involves two operations: adding 100 to the balance of account B and subtracting 100 from the balance of account A. Two operations must both be performed successfully for the transfer operation to be considered successful. It is not permissible to perform only one operation in a transfer operation. In practice, however, it is possible to perform only one operation in a transfer.

For example, the system crashes abnormally after the first operation is performed, which leads to the second operation not to be performed. Additionally, it is possible that the second operation fails. The reason is that the balance in account A is not enough for 100 dollars. As you can see, for business operations such as transfers, a manager must be in place to ensure that the business operation is performed correctly. This type of business is called a transaction characterized by involving updates on two or more items of data. Correctness means that all operations contained in a transaction are either all executed successfully or none of them are executed.

The above example is used next to further illustrate other characteristics of transactions. The account data in the bank's database server are naturally shared data. While the server is accepting and processing the above transfer request (set as request 1), it may simultaneously receive another transfer request (set as request 2): a transfer of $200 from account A to account C. This is entirely possible. When account A belongs to a big company, it has several financial cashiers working at the same time, each dealing with their own business. Assume that before these two requests are processed, the balance in Account A is 900. Request 1 contains six data operations: Read (B, B_1); $B_1 = B_1 + 100$; Write (B_1, B); Read (A, A_1); $A_1 = A_1 - 100$; Write (A_1, A). Request 2 also contains six data operations: Read (C, C_2); $C_2 = C_2 + 200$; Write (C_2, C); Read (A, A_2); $A_2 = A_2 - 200$; Write (A_2, A).

The database server processes concurrent requests. For the two concurrent requests mentioned above, the execution scheduling scheme may be as follows: the first four data operations of request 1 are executed first, followed by the six data operations of request 2, and then the last two data operations of request 1. When executed according to this scheme, the result is obviously incorrect. After execution, the balance of account A becomes 800. The correct result should be 600. The reason for the incorrect result is that in the process of reading and writing account A by request 1, the reading and writing operations of account A by request 2 are interspersed, which obviously violates the basic principle of shared access. Incorrect data resulting from a violation of the sharing principle or from a transaction not being executed as a whole is called a consistency error. When a server performs concurrent processing of requests, the scheduling scheme executed must ensure data consistency.

For a transaction, the data it wants to update may be distributed across different servers. For example, if the bank transfer mentioned above is an inter-bank transfer, then account A is on a database server in one bank (noted as server A) and account B is on a database server in another bank (noted as server B). At this point, the transaction manager sends a transfer out request to Server A and a transfer in request to Server B. To ensure that the transaction is holistic, the transaction manager has to make a final decision after receiving the response results from Server A and Server B. As long as one of the two responses is unsuccessful, then the entire transaction should be revoked to ensure the consistency and atomicity of the transaction. For example, if Server A fails to perform the operation, then the transaction manager has to further send an undo request to Server B to undo the just transferred operation. To complete a transaction, there are two round-trip interactions between the transaction manager and member servers. This interaction protocol is called the two-phase commit protocol. This protocol will be explained in detail in Chap. 3.

For transactions such as bank transfers, processing results cannot be lost due to failures. Failures are inevitable. For example, if a database server stores data in memory, memory data will be lost when an abnormal system failure, such as a blue screen, occurs or when a power failure occurs. When a database server stores data on disk, although the above failures do not cause disk data to be lost, disk data will also be lost when a disk failure occurs. In short, failures can lead to data loss. For transaction processing, it is required that the results of processing are not lost. The solution to this paradox is storage redundancy, i.e., multilocation storage. When data stored in one place are lost due to a failure, data stored in another place still exists, thus enabling data not to be lost. Storage redundancy and fault recovery schemes are explained in detail in Chap. 3.

In order to achieve data consistency, the abstract concept of transaction is defined. A transaction is an update operation performed on two or more items of data. For data consistency, transactions are required to have four properties: atomicity, consistency, isolation, and persistence [13]. Atomicity means that the server should treat the transaction submitted by a client as a whole, and the update operations contained in the transaction are not allowed to be executed in one part and not in the other. Isolation means that when the server executes multiple transaction requests concurrently, the results should be the same as if they were executed serially. Persistence means that if a client submits a transaction request and the server responds to the client with a successful execution, the subsequent execution results must be intact and must not be lost due to failures. The four attributes of a transaction require a technical solution to implement them. Specific implementation details will be explained in Chap. 3.

1.8 Availability of Services

For customers, the expectation is that the service will always be available without interruptions. But servers inevitably fail. When a server fails, the service is interrupted and becomes unavailable. Failures include software failures, hardware failures, and environmental disasters. Examples of software failures include resource demands not being met, the system experiencing a blue screen of death exception, and the execution being stuck in a deadlock. Hardware failures include CPUs, memory, motherboards, disks, etc., not working properly. Environmental disasters include power outages, fires, floods, earthquakes, and even terrorist attacks. Failures can be categorized into several levels based on their frequency and impact. Transaction failures affect only the transaction that has failed and are frequent but low impact and easy to deal with. Recovery from software failures usually involves rebooting the system. Recovery from a hardware failure requires replacing the failed component or even replacing the computer. Environmental disasters can

1.8 Availability of Services

destroy an entire machine or even an entire server room, and fault recovery requires a remote backup.

From the service level, an effective way to improve service availability is replication. Replication is the process of cloning a server so that it has multiple copies. As long as one replica is working, the service will not be interrupted. Making a server have multiple replicas improves service availability, but introduces a new set of problems. The first is the problem of replica consistency. Each replica must be synchronized to ensure consistency between replicas when processing client transaction requests. The solution is to set up a replica manager. The replica manager is responsible for accepting requests from clients. When a client's request is a transaction request, the replica manager distributes it to every normal replica for execution. It then collects the results of their processing. Only when the processing results of all replicas are successful, the transaction is recognized as successful; otherwise, the transaction should be withdrawn. When the client's request is a data query request, the replica manager simply forwards it to one replica for execution.

Multiple replicas synchronizing a transaction request can have a short-board effect, where the completion time of a transaction is determined by the slowest replica. The performance of a server is affected by a number of factors, such as the presence of memory leaks, deadlocks, and so on. Therefore, even if each replica has the same hardware and software, there will be a difference between fast and slow in operation. To address this issue, you can choose one of the replicas to act as the Master and the others to act as Standbys. Only the Master is responsible for transaction processing. If the processing is successful, the results will be sent to each Standby, so that the data stored in the Master and Standbys are the same and have consistency. Once the Master fails and becomes unavailable, one of the Standbys is chosen to act as the Master.

For a failed replica, there are two issues: the first is failure discovery and the next is failure recovery. When the replica manager sends a request to a replica, it is recognized that the replica has failed if there is a timeout waiting for a response. The point of failure is naturally after the last normal response. In addition, the replica manager can also send a heartbeat detection request to the computer where each replica resides at regular intervals to determine whether the failure is a software failure or a hardware failure. The natural way to recover from the failure is to restart the server program. If the failure is identified as a software failure, restart may be on the original computer. If the failure is determined to be a hardware failure, restart should be on another standby computer. After restart, the transactions that have been successfully processed by fault-free replicas since the point of failure should be executed once in same sequence by recovery replicas. This execution is called a Redo operation, after which the data owned by recovery replicas is consistent with the data owned by the other normal replicas. Thus, failure recovery is complete. The detailed process of fault recovery will be explained in Chap. 3.

The replica manager may also possibly fail. When it fails, the service becomes unavailable. However, replica managers have completely different characteristics from replicas and are much less likely to fail. First, replica managers have simple things to deal with, so the amount of program code is very small. Simple things are highly reliable, so the probability of a replica manager failing is low. In addition, the replica manager maintains very little state data, and failure recovery is very easy and the recovery time is very short. Therefore, replica manager failures have very little impact on service availability [14]. To improve the availability of the replica manager, multiple replicas can also be set up for it.

When the Master fails, it is necessary to choose one of the Standbys to act as the Master. Since each replica executes the same program and owns the same data, which Standby should be chosen to act as the Master? From the replica management model, it can be seen that the replica manager is the client for both the Master and the Standby. Therefore, when the Master cannot respond to the transaction request of the replica manager, or the Standby cannot respond to the query request of the replica manager, the replica manager determines that the unresponsive one has failed. In addition, for Standby, Master is its client, so Standby failure can also be sensed by Master. From this, it can be seen that which Standby is chosen to act as the Master should be decided by the replica manager; the fault sensing and fault recovery of the replicas (including the Master and Standby) are also the responsibility of the replica manager.

Who is responsible for replica manager's fault sensing and fault recovery? Clients of the service send requests to the replica manager and get response results. Therefore, clients of the service are able to sense replica manager failures, but are not able to make a contribution to fault recovery. The replica manager is up and running by the cluster/cloud manager of the service operator. Therefore, the cluster/cloud manager should be responsible for fault sensing and fault recovery of the replica manager. Fault sensing can be done using heartbeat detection. The cluster/cloud manager is the top manager and must be available at all times. The implementation is still multicopy. The difference is that there is no more manager on top of the cluster/cloud manager, so the replicas of the cluster/cloud manager have to sense each other's failures and collaborate to determine a new master. Details of implementation will be explained in Chap. 4.

1.9 Efficient Data Processing

A server not only stores and manages data, but also processes clients' requests and responds to them. The load on a server is very heavy and the performance problem of data processing is very prominent. The reason is that all the client requests go to the server and hence the server becomes a load center and faces intensive customer access. In addition, all customer data are stored on the server, so the data on the server are usually massive. Querying and locating the massive data are very time-consuming and labor-intensive. Under this double pressure, the load on the server is very heavy. If data processing is not efficient, then customer requests cannot be responded to in a timely manner, and thus customer performance requirements for

1.9 Efficient Data Processing

the system cannot be met. How to achieve efficient data processing is a core issue in data management [15].

To improve data processing performance, it is first necessary to understand the process of data processing. As far as data processing is concerned, a computer can be modeled as consisting of three components: CPU, memory, and disk. The data are stored on disk and its processing is done by the CPU. The process is to transport the data from disk to memory and then from the memory to CPU. If the data are updated, then it is also transported from CPU to memory and then from memory to disk. These three components of a computer vary greatly as far as sensitivity is concerned. CPU is very responsive and fast at processing, while disk is slow, and memory falls somewhere in between. The role of memory is to mitigate the incoherence between CPU and disk. Memory and disk are both storage media for data, but have completely different qualities. The advantage of memory is that it is responsive, but the disadvantage is that it loses data when power is lost, and its capacity is much smaller than that of a disk. Disks have the advantage of high capacity, no loss of data when power is lost, and are far more cost-effective than memory. The disadvantage of disks is that they are slow to respond.

Data are stored on disk with the concept of volume. A large amount of data takes up a large amount of disk platter space. When a piece of data is to be read or written, the magnetic head has to move to where the data is located on the disk. The longer the head travels, the more time it takes and the worse the performance is. Therefore, minimizing the distance the head has to travel is critical to improving performance. One effective way to do this is to place data that are frequently accessed by users in a central location and store closely related data close together. The organization of data storage on disk is closely related to processing performance. How data storage on disk should be organized is described in detail in Chap. 6.

Using memory to cache disk data effectively improves processing performance. If the data to be read are in memory, it need not be read from disk at all. Data to be written can also be cached in memory and not written to disk immediately. It can be deferred until it is free and then written to disk in bulk. As a result, the transportation between disk and memory is greatly reduced, and processing performance is significantly improved. Ideally, all data would be cached in memory. However, the amount of data is usually much larger than the cache capacity, so data are still transported between memory and disk from time to time. When the required data are not in memory, they are transported from disk to memory. When there is not enough free memory space, some memory space must be selected to free up for it before transporting it. For the data in the selected memory, if it is not available on disk, it is exported to disk. Memory selection is critical and has a significant impact on performance. If the data existing in the selected memory will have to be read later, it will have to be transported from disk to memory again at that time. How to select memory is explained in detail in Chap. 6.

The most frequent operation in data processing is to query a row or some rows from a table. The intuitive way to query is to transport all rows of a table from disk to CPU to examine them one by one. For those rows that match the query, they are usually a small portion of all transported rows. Those rows that do not meet the criteria are transported in vain. Reducing the number of futile transports is critical to performance improvement. Creating indexes can significantly reduce the number of futile transports. An index is like a table of contents for a book. If a book does not have a table of contents, when you want to find something in the book, you have to start from the first page and go page by page until you find it. When the book is very thick, it takes a lot of time to find it. With a catalog, the situation is very different. You can find the page number first from the catalog to, and then jump directly to the appropriate page. What is the nature of an index? How to create an index? How do you use an index? These issues will be explained in detail in Chap. 6.

Given that CPU, memory, and disk vary greatly in response speed, concurrent processing of customer requests can significantly improve CPU utilization and thus system processing performance. If the CPU is set to process customer requests in a serial manner, it is idle during the period from issuing commands to obtaining response results when reading and writing data. To improve CPU utilization, the CPU can be allowed to process requests from multiple users simultaneously. Concurrent processing introduces a new problem of access conflicts to shared data. This must be effectively managed and controlled to ensure the correctness of the data. In addition, for multicore processors, concurrency processing can be further utilized in a multithreaded manner. How to realize concurrent processing in a single thread? How does multithreaded concurrent execution differ from single-threaded concurrent processing? These questions will be answered in Chap. 2.

The performance of a server is reflected in its throughput and response time to client requests. Enhancing data processing performance is based on the computer's hardware characteristics, the characteristics of the data itself, as well as the characteristics of access. Effective ways include reasonable organization of data in storage, reducing the distance traveled by the magnetic head in disk space, reducing the number of times the data are transported between memory and disk as well as between memory and CPU, and reducing futile transports of data and vain CPU's processing.

The hardware characteristics of the server, such as the size of the memory, can be determined with a single startup test. However, the characteristics of the data itself, and the access characteristics vary from application to application. For example, the closeness of the relationship between data tables, the closeness of columns and the closeness of rows in a table, all of these are different from case to case. For data access characteristics, some can be predicted in advance, while others need to be detected and captured during operation. For example, a table in a database consists of two parts: schema and data. The access frequency of the schema is significantly higher than that of the data. This characteristic can be predicted in advance. The reason is that the schema holds semantic information, structural information, storage information, and state information of the table. Every time a table's data are accessed, its schema needs to be accessed beforehand. Therefore, it is better to have the schema resident in the cache.

Business characteristics and access characteristics should be explored as much as possible and then utilized. For example, for the university academic affairs management server, for the student data therein, the access frequency of current students is much higher compared with graduated students. This is an obvious business characteristic. In addition, in terms of users, the student class has the most users, the teacher class has the second most users, and the faculty administrators have the least. Therefore, the organization of data storage should give priority to the operations frequently performed by student-type users. For example, students view their course score sheet, which is the most frequent operation, should be prioritized. In addition, operations that students select courses and viewing the records of selected courses are also common and should also be given high priority.

1.10 Security of Systems

In a distributed system, there are three roles: client, client program, and server. All three are independent of each other. This means that anyone can access any server from anywhere, using any client program. This model brings great convenience to clients, but also provides an opportunity for lawbreakers. They often explore system vulnerabilities to invade the system, bringing threats to system security. Speaking of security, from the customer's point of view, the most concerned question is: Is the response result obtained by the client program really from the server? If not, but from a hacker, then there is no way to talk about security. From the server's point of view, the most important question to ask is: did the request actually come from the real client? If not, security loses its foundation. These two questions are fundamental in security. The first is called the client-to-server authentication issue, and the second is the server-to-client authentication. How to authenticate is explained in detail in Chap. 6.

After solving the authentication problem, the next security threats are peeking, tampering, counterfeiting, and repudiation. These four problems stem from network transmission. Clients' requests and servers' responses are transmitted over the public Internet. During the transmission of data over the public internet, it can be peeked and tampered by hackers. When the data are peeked and tampered by hackers, it is not the real data. This situation is obviously unacceptable. These two problems are solved by encrypted transmission technology. Encrypted transmission means that when sending data, the sender first encrypts the data with a cipher for security reasons, obtains a ciphertext, and then passes the ciphertext to the receiver. The receiver receives the ciphertext and decrypts it using a cipher to get the data. After the data are encrypted, hackers cannot know what is being transmitted over the Internet because he does not know the cipher and therefore cannot tamper with it.

However, encryption does not solve the problem of counterfeiting. For example, if a customer uses an online banking system to make outgoing transfers, the customer sends encrypted data to the server once for each transfer operation. A hacker can intercept this encrypted transfer packet from the public Internet, copy it, and send it to the server over and over again. The server will then keep performing this operation of transferring money over and over again, resulting in the customer's money being swindled. In this scenario, the hacker does not need to make any changes to the encrypted packet, but only needs to keep copying and sending it to achieve the fraudulent purpose. For this scenario, the server should have the ability to recognize duplicate requests and discard them. How are duplicate requests recognized? This will be explained in detail in Chap. 6.

The problem of denial can be demonstrated by a case study. Suppose a customer performs a transfer over the public Internet, but refuses to recognize it, suing the bank for stealing his money or saying that the bank leaked its account information to someone else. At this point, the bank also countersues, saying that the user has resisted. Thus, the problem of not being able to determine who is right and who is wrong arises. To solve this problem, the user must sign the transfer request. When the server receives a signed transfer request, it responds by archiving it. In the event of a user denial, the archived signed transfer request is used as evidence that the customer is denying. Asymmetric cryptography is used to digitally sign the data, and the specific implementation scheme will be explained in Chap. 6.

In addition to the above security threats, there is another category of security threats originating from loopholes or flaws in program design. When using the system, hackers distort the program semantics by entering special parameters to achieve the purpose of committing attacks: to illegally steal information for profit or to disrupt the normal operation of the system. The most common such attacks are SQL injection and HTML injection. The following is an example to demonstrate these two types of attack. User login is usually a prerequisite for accessing a system. The user enters an account name and password in the login interface. Many applications handle the user login by first splicing out an SQL statement. The spliced statement is:

```
String sqlState = "SELECT COUNT(*) FROM user WHERE name = '"+
userName +"' AND password = '"+ password +"';"
```

where *userName* and *password* are the account name and password entered by the user in the login interface, respectively. Then, this SQL request is sent to the database server. If the response result value is greater than 0, then it is considered a legitimate user and the login is successful.

When the hacker enters both the username and password as "'oR '1' =' 1", the program splices out the SQL statement as "SELECT COUNT(*) FROM user WHERE name = "'OR '1' = '1' AND password ="' OR '1' = '1' ;". This SQL statement completely breaks the logic of the programmer's preconceived notions. The given selection condition holds true for every row of data in the user table, so the query result value is the number of rows in the user table. Therefore, the response result value is greater than 0, and the user logs in successfully. This is a typical example of SQL injection attack. From this example, it can be seen that SQL injection attack is that the hacker first guesses the processing method of the program, and then takes advantage of the splicing of SQL statements in the program, and makes the SQL statements deviate from the original logic by inputting SQL keywords in the human–computer interface, so as to achieve the purpose of the attack.

HTML injection attacks are similar to SQL injection attacks in that they use keywords in the syntax to distort the semantics of the program. In an HTML

1.10 Security of Systems

injection attack, the hacker utilizes HTML keywords. An example of an HTML injection attack is to attack a web page that contains user comments. Let us say a web page that contains user comments. Under normal circumstances, when user A opens the web page and posts a comment, then when user B opens the same web page, he can see the comment posted by user A. Assuming that User A is a hacker, and that the content entered in the comment box contains HTML keywords and JavaScript script attack code, then when the WEB server generates a web page for User B, it will deviate from the programmer's expected logic. The result is that the JavaScript script attack code injected by the hacker will be executed in User B's browser, attacking User B's computer. For example, a virus or Trojan horse could be placed on User B's computer.

A concrete example of an HTML injection attack is given in Fig. 1.1, where Fig. 1.1a shows the content of the comments entered by the hacker to realize the attack by taking advantage of the generative nature of the web page; Fig. 1.1b shows the processing logic for the display of the comments in the web page; and Fig. 1.1c shows the content of the web page generated for User B. As can be seen from Fig. 1.1b, the logic of the web page designer is that each comment is an item in a list box. In HTML, the tag of the list box is "ol" and the tag of the item is "li". However, when processing the hacker's comment, the list box is distorted into two list boxes by the hacker's input, and JavaScript script code is injected in the middle of the two list boxes, as shown in Fig. 1.1c. Thus, when user B opens the page in the browser, the injected JavaScript script code is executed.

As can be seen from the above examples, security issues such as SQL injection attacks and HTML injection attacks can be put into effect by hackers without the use of any tools. The purpose can be achieved simply by typing special content when using the system. The threshold for this type of attack is low, which only requires an attempt to detect system vulnerabilities and flaws. Once the vulnerability is found, the attack can be easily executed. The attack is very harmful. In the

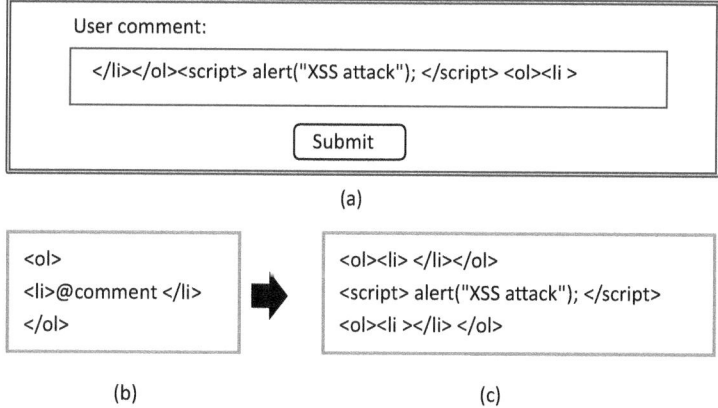

Fig. 1.1 Example of an HTML injection attack. (**a**) Comment input by a hacker; (**b**) Normal HTML for display of comment; (**c**) HTML distorted by the hacker's comment

above HTML injection attack, any user who opens the web page is attacked. How to prevent this type of attack will be explained in detail in Chap. 6.

There is another category of security threats that is different from the above three categories, where the attack uses the strategy of stealing the beam. This type of attack is also demonstrated through an example. In many applications, different categories of users have different access rights. For example, in the case of a teaching management system, there are three categories of users: students, teachers, and faculty administrators. When a user logs in, the server recognizes the user's category. Different categories respond with different functionality pages. If a student user wants to act as a hacker and get the functionality page of the teacher category, he or she only needs to intercept the request made by the teacher category user on the Internet and then use it as his or her own request. An analogy for this problem is as follows. When visiting a palace, the administrator creates different routes for different categories of visitors. These routes are isolated from each other and do not intersect. The checking of the tourists must then be done only at the gate. At the gate, visitors are directed to the corresponding tour route based on their category.

For information systems, checks cannot be placed only at the time of login. Each request from a user should be checked to see if he or she has the authorization for the operation. In the case of the palace tour example above, the category of each tourist is also checked at each attraction to see if he/she has the right to visit the attraction. The management of user rights is a very important matter in information systems, and the problems faced and the solution techniques will be explained in detail in Chap. 6.

1.11 System Scalability

There are many service systems that have more and more customers and manage more and more data. Typical examples are e-commerce service systems such as Taobao and Pinduoduo, and chat service systems such as WeChat and QQ. The number of customers of these services reaches several hundred million, and the volume of business data reaches P-level. With such a large amount of data and business volume, the service provider usually uses tens of thousands of computers, or even hundreds of thousands of computers to store and process. Each of these computers is a server that maintains and manages a portion of the system's data and acts as a member in the system. Another manager manages the members of the system. The manager is the window open to the external and receives client requests. For a client request, the manager first determines which members are involved in the data distribution, and then breaks it down into subrequests, which are submitted to the corresponding members for execution, respectively. For a member, the manager is its client. The manager collects all the responses from the involved members, summarizes them, and returns the summarized results to the client as the response.

The amount of data and customer requests for a system changes over time. In the case of an e-commerce service system, for example, its data volume is increasing,

1.11 System Scalability

and it has ups and downs and fluctuations in the amount of customer requests. For example, the amount of customer requests during promotional periods will be significantly higher than usual, and the system load will be significantly heavier. In this case, it is necessary to scale the system. When the amount of data increases or the amount of customer requests increases, it will be necessary to split a member into two to ensure the quality of service by increasing the resources. When the amount of data decreases or the number of customer requests decreases, it is necessary to merge two members into one to save overhead by reducing resources.

The organization of data storage has a lot to do with the scalability of the system. An example is given below. Assuming that the transaction data in an e-commerce service system is organized in storage based on the time of generation, there is only one transaction data table in a database. At the beginning of the system's launch, only one member is required to store the transaction data due to the small amount of transaction data. When the amount of transaction data stored by this member reaches the upper limit, the manager adds a new member to store the additional transaction records. This storage organization is characterized by distributing transaction records to different members in the order in which they are generated. This seemingly reasonable storage organization is not adapted to the access characteristics of the data, which can lead to very low system performance. The reason is e-commerce systems have an obvious characteristic: customers (i.e., both buyers and sellers) are only concerned with their own transaction records and have to query their transaction records frequently. Such queries are the most frequent operations in the system.

Above storage organization of transaction data based on time faces a low performance problem for e-commerce systems. This pattern results in transaction records of each customer being sparsely distributed across members in the system. Whether a buyer or a seller wants to query his/her own transaction records, the manager has to send subquery requests to all the members that have stored transaction data. Each member performs a query on the transaction data it owns and then returns the query results to the manager. The manager can only respond to the client after it receives the response results from all members and summarizes them. Since each query involves all members, the response time is constrained by the slowest member. Therefore, the performance is obviously not good. Since this kind of query is the most frequent operation in the system, the overall performance of the system will also be very poor.

If the storage of transaction data is organized on a customer-by-customer basis, the situation is completely different. In this pattern of organization, all customers are spread evenly across the members of the system beforehand, and then whenever a transaction record is generated, it is stored under its corresponding customers (i.e., the buyer and the seller). This organization makes each customer's transaction records not only fall on one member, but also be aggregated and stored together. When a customer wants to query his transaction record, the manager then needs to access only one member. The entire query result is provided by one member, instead of calling all members to participate. As a result, performance is significantly improved.

Another benefit that comes from organizing the storage of transaction data based on customers is load balancing. All customers are distributed evenly across the members of the system beforehand. Therefore, the load of both adding and querying transaction records is evenly distributed to each member. There is no intersection between them, so the potential of parallel processing can be fully realized. When the amount of data on a member reaches the upper limit, it can be split into two based on the customer, and one of them can be migrated to a new member. Splitting in this manner still maintains the transaction records of a customer falling on one member. After the split, the mapping of customers to members in the meta information of member maintained by the manager is modified accordingly to reflect the split.

Organizing the storage of transaction data based on a customer basis can improve data availability in addition to achieving efficient querying and load balancing. As an example, suppose member A is split into two, i.e., a new member B is added, and then half of the transaction data in member A is migrated to member B. A customer cannot access his/her own transaction data only during the period that his/her transaction data are being migrated. In contrast, if the storage of transaction data are organized based on time, the entire transaction data are unavailable during the migration. The reason is that the migrated transaction data theoretically covers all customers, and thus any query is involved in the migrated transaction data. If the storage organization is based on a customer-by-customer basis, the situation is completely different. Migration is the process of moving half of the customers from member A to member B. A customer's data contain his/her transaction data. Therefore, only the migrated customers are affected by the migration. In addition, the migration is done one by one with the customers as objects. Therefore, the number of affected customers can be further reduced to one.

The above discusses the benefits that can be brought by organizing the storage of transaction data based on customers, using an e-commerce service system as an example. This way of organizing data storage has its strengths and, naturally, its weaknesses. For example, when the total transaction volume of a certain period is queried, the eligible transaction records are then sparsely distributed on all members, requiring all members to participate in the processing. Therefore, the query overhead is high. However, this kind of query request occurs only occasionally and thus does not have a significant impact on the overall performance of the system. When considering how to organize the data storage, it is important to perform a statistical analysis of customer requests to identify the most frequent operations and give them priority. The organization of data storage will be explained in detail in Chap. 6.

1.12 Combined Systems for High-Performance Computing

Many systems manage very large amounts of data, such as GOOGLE's search engine and Tencent's WeChat. Their data volume reaches P level. In the computer world, the units of data volume have Byte, KB, MB, GB, TB, PB, EB, etc.

1.12 Combined Systems for High-Performance Computing

1 KB = 1024B, 1 MB = 11,024 KB, 1GB = 1024 MB, 1 TB = 1024GB, 1 PB = 1024 TB, 1 EB = 1024 PB, etc. There are else application scenarios where the amount of computation is very large, such as solving partial differential equations in high dimension, multiplying very large matrix, and training neural networks. Ultra-large-scale data processing and ultra-large-scale scientific computing require high-performance computing [16]. Combining multiple computers into a single computer can realize high-performance computing. There are three existing forms of combined systems: supercomputer, cluster system, and distributed system. All three systems use many computing units and storage units for parallel processing to achieve high performance. However, they each have their own favorites and differences.

For supercomputer, the goal pursued is to make the computing and storage units as compact as possible, as close to each other as possible. This makes the connection lines between the units shorter and thinner. The motivation behind this is that data are exchanged very frequently between units in scientific computing. Transferring data from one unit to another is equivalent to transporting an item from one place to another. The transmission delay is proportional to the road length. In scientific computing, transmission delay is a key factor affecting performance.

For the transmission delay, it is also often felt in daily life. For example, when taking a shower at home, hot water flows immediately when you turn on the hot water faucet. When taking a shower in a hotel, it usually takes several minutes to open the hot water faucet before hot water flows out. The prerequisite for hot water to flow out is that the cold water in the pipe from the hot water source to the faucet flows out of the faucet first. The time it takes to run out of cold water is directly proportional to the volume of cold water in the pipe. The volume of cold water is proportional to the length of the pipe and proportional to the diameter of the pipe. Therefore, to get hot water for the shower as quickly as possible, it is best to just put the water heater in the shower room, and also not make the pipes too thick. In the same way, the time delay for an electrical signal to travel from one unit to another is proportional to the capacitance of the line. And capacitance is proportional to length as well as the cross-sectional area of the line. Therefore, it is important to make the line as thin and as short as possible. Because of this, a supercomputer is densely packed with hundreds or thousands of CPU units and memory sticks on a single panel.

When using a supercomputer for scientific computation, data have to be constantly transferred between units. When the transfers become very frequent and the number of transfers is large, the cumulative transfer time will be very long, which becomes a key factor limiting the performance of the system. Therefore, for supercomputers, the pursuit is to do small and fine. Only in this way can the high-performance requirements be met. It can be seen that supercomputers are mainly used to do scientific computing to meet the demand for ultra-large-scale scientific computing. With a lot of computing units and storage units to a panel, high performance is achieved, but the problem of heat dissipation arises. Even with only one CPU unit on the desktop computer, an electric fan is necessary to dissipate heat. For a supercomputing motherboard densely packed with thousands of computing units, heat dissipation is an oversized problem. This is the reason why supercomputers are very expensive.

In contrast to exascale scientific computing, there is usually less frequent data exchange in exascale data processing. The reason for this is that data fusion in data processing is much less deep and the correlation is much less extensive. Therefore, instead of using super computers for exascale data processing, cluster systems are usually used. A cluster system consists of a number of commercial computers that are linked together using a general-purpose local area network (LAN), and then software is used to integrate them into a very large computer system. From the outside, a cluster system is a computer. It differs from an ordinary computer in that it has a large amount of computing power, a large amount of storage space, the ability to provide uninterrupted service to users, the ability to provide fast responses to user requests, and a large amount of throughput. These qualities are exactly what one would expect. These qualities are achieved through the group effect.

Compared to supercomputers, cluster systems are cost-effective, scalable, reliable, and simple and easy to operate and maintain. The members of a cluster are ordinary commercial computers. These computers are very cheap because of their exceptionally large number of users and production. In addition, these computers, because of their widespread use, have had their flaws fully exposed, and thus their reliability is very high after continuous improvement. In contrast, supercomputers, because of their small number of users, are not very reliable, are very expensive, and require specialized personnel for operation and maintenance. Therefore, cluster systems are widely used, and almost all large companies have their own cluster systems deployed in their data centers.

The difference between a cluster and a distributed system is that the member computers in a cluster system are placed in the same building, are all one brand of computer, have the same hardware and operating system, and run the same software. In other words, the members of a cluster are isomorphic to each other. The advantage is that when exchanging data between members, a direct memory copy can be made without the need to do translation. In contrast, the distinguishing feature of a distributed system is that its members are autonomous. Therefore, a distributed system is usually a heterogeneous system. When exchanging data between its members, translation is usually indispensable. Translation involves both sides of the interaction: the sender translates the in-memory data into standard data and the receiver translates the standard data into in-memory data. Therefore, data exchange in a clustered system is very efficient as compared to a distributed system.

A distributed system is usually a confederated system. Its members are not restricted in terms of hardware, software, location, affiliation, etc., but are required to follow standards for accessing external services and providing services to the outside world, and to interact with each other according to defined protocols. The members are usually connected to each other through the public Internet. The frequency of data exchange between members in a distributed system is low compared to a clustered system. Translation is a time-consuming and computationally resource-intensive task. When the frequency of data exchange is low, the translation overhead has little impact on the overall performance.

Another obvious difference in supercomputers compared to cluster systems and distributed systems is the sharing of I/O subsystems, which mainly refers to the sharing of disk storage. In a cluster system or distributed system, its members are independent computers, usually with their own computational units, memory units, and disk storage units. In contrast, a supercomputer is still one computer, and parallelization refers mainly to the computational and memory units, while the I/O subsystems are shared units.

Whether it is a super computer, a cluster system, or a distributed system, it appears to users to be a computer. The things that a user does with a computer are: installing applications, starting applications, closing or suspending applications, and human–computer interaction with applications. Every computer has an operating system. As to the user, the operating system is actually also an application whose name is Program Manager. By starting the computer, the user is actually starting the program manager. The user then engages in human–computer interaction with the program manager. The functionalities provided by the program manager include naturally: (1) installing new applications, (2) displaying installed applications, (3) launching installed applications, (4) displaying launched applications, and (5) closing or suspending launched applications. For launched applications, there is usually a human–computer interface as well. For example, the browser application has a human–computer interface.

A computer system is a dialectical unity of change and invariance. Change refers to the interior of the system and invariance refers to the exterior of the system. In the eyes of users, the system has invariance. The invariance is reflected in the way users use the system unchanged. Since the birth of computers, the way users use computers has been: launching a human–computer interface, then installing applications, launching applications, and closing and suspending applications. There are two types of applications: with and without human–computer interface (HCI). For example, server programs usually do not come with an HCI. Variability is reflected within the system. As systems evolve, there have been supercomputers, distributed systems, cluster systems, big data processing systems, and cloud systems. Supercomputers focus on parallel computing to improve the system arithmetic power. Distributed systems explore standardization for the diversity of members. Cluster systems utilize the group effect to improve service quality and cost-effectiveness, and cloud systems aim to further solve the problem that programs can run everywhere based on the cluster.

1.13 Big Data Processing

Many enterprises, especially Internet companies, store very large amounts of business data in their data centers, up to P-level, often called Big Data [17]. The big data are scattered on each member of the cluster, and unified management is carried out by the cluster manager. These data support the daily business operation of the enterprise on the one hand, and on the other hand, they also support data analysis and mining, such as the portrayal of user profiles, the discovery of abnormal user behavior, etc., and some of them are also applied to machine learning and artificial intelligence. Data analysis and mining can provide support for enterprises to better carry out their business, as well as expand their business.

Big data contain both a large amount of useful data and a huge amount of useless data, or even junk data, and are characterized by a large total amount of value, but a very low density of value. This characteristic means that in data analysis, the ratio of the amount of output data to the amount of input data is very small. Data analysis software is like a factory. In the case of a factory, there is a problem of siting. Does the company build the factory close to the source of raw materials or close to the company's location? The classic approach is to build the factory near the company's location. This model facilitates plant operations and maintenance. However, as the scale of processing increases, the transportation of raw materials becomes a bottleneck in the system. The reason for this is that the throughput of raw materials from the source to the plant is limited by the transportation capacity. In response, the factory model was changed by building factories in close proximity to the raw material sources, or even in each of the raw material sources. The problem was eliminated and production efficiency increased.

The same is true for data analysis. The classic approach is to deploy data analysis software on a separate dedicated computer, and then to fetch data from storage over the network for analysis. In the case of better and better machine performance and larger and larger amounts of data, the throughput of transmitting data is increasingly mismatched with the throughput of machine processing, resulting in a waste of machine performance that cannot be fully utilized. For this reason, it is necessary to change the model to become data centric, in which the program flits close to data. That is, let the program close to the data so that it can be fetched quickly. Another rationale for this change is that the size of programs is much smaller than the amount of data, and the overhead of moving programs is much smaller than the overhead of moving data. When data analysis became data centric, the data analysis model also changed from a centralized model to a distributed model.

Big data distributed processing systems are also commonly referred to as clusters. A cluster consists of a manager and multiple members. Both the manager and the members are obviously servers. The manager is the external service window of the cluster and receives requests from external clients. Inside the cluster, the manager sends requests to the members and thus is the client of the members. The manager provides services externally on the one hand and manages internal members on the other hand. The management of internal members includes adding and releasing members, failure detection, and failure recovery of members. The manager has meta information about the members, knows the distribution of data over the members, and is able to parse requests from external clients into requests to members. It can also summarize the response results of members and finally send the response results to external users.

The cluster described above is dynamic in nature. Dynamism is reflected in the fact that the number of members of a processing task and the computers on which each member is scheduled to run are not configured in advance, but are determined

1.13 Big Data Processing

in real time based on the distribution of the data. For example, the data in the saleRecord.dat file are now to be analyzed using the *saleAnalysis* software. After submitting this task to the big data processing platform, the platform first arranges for a computer to run the *saleAnalysis* Manager. After the *saleAnalysis* Manager runs, it first asks the file manager about the size and storage distribution of the saleRecord.dat file, then decides how many members to use to perform the analysis in parallel and assigns analysis tasks to each member. After this, the manager sends a request to the platform to request that each member be started up. Note: a request to the platform to start a program is accompanied by a number of startup requirements, such as CPU and memory resource requirements, and proximity to a particular computer.

The parallel processing model of big data newly introduces the concept of geographic distribution based on the classical single-computer parallel processing model, which is a distinctive feature of big data processing. In the single-computer parallel processing model, the program (i.e., the master process) is started first, and then the master process creates child processes. Once the master process tells the ids of all the child processes to each of them, the child processes can communicate with each other. Here the master process corresponds to the manager in the cluster and the child processes correspond to the members in the cluster. Therefore, the big data parallel processing model is exactly the same as the classic single-machine parallel processing model, and there is no difference in essence. It can be seen that the original stand-alone parallel processing program can also run on the Big Data platform. There is no change in the logic of the application program. The change is only within the platform, i.e., subprocesses become members, and inter process communication (IPC)-based interprocess communication becomes network-based communication between managers and members and between members and members.

Due to the newly introduced concept of geographic distribution, the manager should add new API functions that can be easily called by clients to get or set geographic distribution information. In the eyes of applications, file services are provided by the file manager of the operating system. A distributed file system is just a server behind the file manager and is not visible to applications. Therefore, the operating system should add a new API function to facilitate applications to obtain the physical storage information of distributed files, such as IP address, file size per location, and even data range per location. The subprocess creation API function provided by the operating system does not consider distributed computing. Therefore, the process manager of the operating system should also add a new API function, so that clients can set the parameters of the subprocess creation instructions, in order to add the ability to create remote subprocesses (i.e., members of the cluster). Of course, only adding a new API function is not enough, it is necessary to modify the internal implementation of the subprocess creation API function to add the function of directional creation of remote subprocesses.

Dynamically creating remote subprocesses (i.e., members of a cluster) faces the new problem of having a program that runs everywhere. Binary executable files are generated for a specific model of computer and operating system by a compiler.

Application code usually contains three layers: the application layer, the support library layer, and the operating system layer. Of these, the support libraries and the operating system are shared at program runtime. Therefore, there is an installation and deployment issue with an application. Installation and deployment are necessary to allow the application to run properly on the specified computer. One of the important tasks is to check whether the support libraries are already installed on the computer and whether there are any sharing conflicts. Now to specify the computer on which the application will run in real time, you may encounter problems with it not running successfully. This may be due to a mismatch between the computer and the operating system model, or a sharing conflict with an already running program (e.g., a service port number conflict). How to make an application run everywhere? The analysis and answer to this question will be given in Chap. 5.

1.14 Cloud Computing

Cloud computing evolved from cluster computing and pursues cost-effectiveness [18]. Traditional cluster computing is characterized by the fact that enterprises build their own cluster systems and run their own server programs. Each computer in the cluster runs typically a server program, and the range of data to be processed is basically determined in advance. In other words, the system layout and load distribution are planned in advance, and the system is of static. Cloud computing is completely different, the programs to be run come from customers, and the data stored is also the customers' data. What the cloud service provider provides to customers is only the infrastructure. Therefore, the number and variety of server programs on the cloud are much more than that on the cluster. It is much less expensive for customers to migrate their business systems to the cloud as compared to building their own infrastructure. In addition, the reliability of the infrastructure on the cloud is much higher than the infrastructure built by themselves. Therefore, customers are willing to use cloud services. For cloud service providers, they can utilize scale effect to achieve the best price and good quality. Thus, cloud computing can bring mutual benefit and win–win pattern.

Every enterprise needs to build its own business information system. According to the traditional practice, the construction of business information systems is involved in the computer room, computer, network, system software, as well as the daily operation and maintenance: fault recovery, system expansion, system upgrades, and other issues. Its cost and overhead are high. Ditching the traditional approach and migrating applications and data to the cloud has the following advantages. First of all, it saves time and effort, as all the specialized things such as server rooms, computers, networks, system software, operation and maintenance personnel, as well as system expansion and upgrades in the construction of business information systems are no longer needed to be considered by enterprises themselves, and are all outsourced to the cloud operators. Cloud operators, as professional service providers, can provide professional and reliable solutions to these problems. This pattern leads to not only quality assurance, but also affordability.

For an enterprise, its business is constantly developing and adjusting, so its business information system has a continuous issue of expansion and upgrading, and requires real-time adjustability. For example, during the period of promotional activities, its business volume increased in vain, which is dozens or even hundreds of times the usual business volume. This requires its business information system to be able to adapt to this load volatility. Hardware platforms with small volumes cannot do this; only platforms with large volumes can. The cloud platform is a large system that provides services with good elasticity and scalability. When the user's data volume and business volume are not large, only a small amount of computing and storage resources can be rented. When the volume of business and data increases, resources can be dynamically increased. Thus, for customers, the original phenomenon of wasteful excess resources, or shortage of resources exists no longer.

A cloud platform is a large pool of shared resources that are organized into a system through software. It utilizes the effects of scale and aggregation to achieve cost-effectiveness and create a virtuous iterative cycle. There is a huge customer base on the cloud platform. For individual customers, their business has ups and downs and volatility. However, for the entire customer base, the total business is smooth. Individual fluctuation and volatility and overall smoothness are the key characteristics of cloud platforms. Therefore, although individual customers have to rent more or less resources, the platform as a whole will not be idle and wasteful or short of resources.

The cloud platform contains an automated monitoring system. It automatically monitors the quality of service of customer information systems running on the platform and automatically makes resource allocation adjustments for them. The platform uses a split or shrink strategy to make the customer information system have good scalability, and uses a replication strategy to enhance the availability and reliability of the customer information system and improve its throughput capacity. Under the premise of meeting the requirements of service quality, optimizing resource allocation and reducing operation and maintenance costs is a basic characteristic of cloud computing. Another characteristic of cloud platforms is that all infrastructures and services are built based on standard technologies. As a result, there is uniformity in the patterns and specifications for accessing services. Various components on the platform can smoothly interface with each other and work in concert with each other. From the customer's point of view, there is no difference between the cloud platform and his own original LAN system in terms of daily operation and maintenance such as installing a server program.

Customers migrate their business information system to run on the cloud, in addition to cost-effective and reliable, another advantage is that the cloud operator can provide statistical analysis report of the characteristics of the system runtime load, such as business volume and user volume with the change of law over time, as well as the user's access characteristics and so on. Thus, customers can timely and accurately understand their business characteristics and features, and can make timely and reasonable business decisions. In short, cloud computing is to outsource professional things to professional companies to achieve mutual benefit and win–win situation.

There are two core problems to be solved in cloud computing: (1) programs should be able to run everywhere; (2) programs should run without interfering with each other. Many of the customer's business programs are historical legacies, with only binary executables and no source code. There are various kinds of programs, for example, some are Windows 32 programs and some are Linux 64 programs. Therefore, it is not possible to modify customer programs to adapt them to the cloud platform. Instead, it is only possible for the cloud platform to adapt to the client programs. In addition, the cloud platform may have to migrate the server program α running on computer A to computer B for resource optimization. For the sake of service availability and throughput, for the server program α running on computer A, it may have to start a new replica for it on computer B. This requires the customer program to be able to run everywhere on the computers in the cloud system.

In cloud computing, in order to fully utilize the resources, multiple server programs from different customers may be running on a single computer. These programs may interfere and disrupt each other when running. For example, when a program has vulnerabilities, such as dead loops and memory leaks, the shared resources such as CPU, memory, service port numbers, etc., are exhausted by it, thus affecting the normal operation of other programs. Client-supplied programs may even intentionally disrupt the system. This interference and disruption are also related to the characteristics of the operating system. The operating system employs a preemptive mechanism for resource allocation. That is, when an application requests a resource, the operating system handles it in such a way that if it can be satisfied, it is satisfied. This model creates a fatal problem of programs interfering and disrupting each other in cloud computing. The problems faced by cloud computing and their solutions will be explained in detail in Chap. 5.

Reflection 1-7: A customer migrates its business information system to run on the cloud, introducing a new data security issue. How can the cloud service provider allay the customer's data security concerns such as data loss, data theft, etc.?

1.15 Cloud Native Programs

Programs running on the cloud are dynamic in nature as compared to running on a particular computer. A cloud system consists of many computers, and exactly which of these computers a program is scheduled to run on is not determined until runtime. In addition, a program running on computer A may have to be migrated to run on computer B for resource optimization. This requires a program to be able to run everywhere on the cloud. When program α acts as a client to access server β at runtime, the physical address of the server β is not known in advance. The reason is that the server β runs on the cloud and its physical address has real-time variability. Therefore, when program α wants to establish a network connection with server β, it has to go and get the physical address of server β in real time. After a network

1.15 Cloud Native Programs

connection is established, it may fail at some subsequent point in time, due to the fact that server β has been migrated to another computer. This requires program α to re-retrieve the physical address of server β and re-establish the network connection as soon as it discovers that the connection has failed.

The meaning of cloud native is: programming and developing programs that run on the cloud for the above-mentioned characteristics of running on the cloud. A program so developed is called a cloud-native program [19]. For a cloud-native server program, it should consist of 2 programs: a manager program and a member program. The manager program is the window to provide services externally, and its functions naturally include: (1) registration of service instances; (2) startup, fault detection, fault recovery, and shutdown of the member program; (3) perception of quality of service; and (4) replica management of members, including creation and release of replicas. The first of these functions is to facilitate client programs to find the physical address of a server instance. When a program acts as a client to access a server, it cannot be programmed to use the physical address directly, but only the name to identify the server. When a client establishes a network connection, the physical address of the service instance should first be found in the registry based on the service name. In addition, during interaction with the server, when an error occurs that the other party closes the connection, the client should re-retrieve server's physical address and then re-establish the network connection.

Cloud-native service programs should be generalized and generic in order to run everywhere. The opposite concept of generalization and universality is diversity. On a computer, the most fundamental software is the operating system. The diversity of operating systems is reflected in the fact that each operating system defines its own APIs for the services it provides, which are different from each other. In order for applications to be adaptable and generic, a standard API has to be defined for the services provided by the operating system, called POSIX [20], which stands for Portable Operating System Interface of Unix. Each operating system manufacturer should provide a library of standard API implementations as a support library for applications. When programming an application, instead of calling the operating system's APIs, you should call the APIs provided by POSIX, so that the application has the characteristics of generalization and universality at the source code level.

Adaptability and generalizability of applications should not stop at the source code level, but should extend to the runtime level. Source code is not directly run by the computer, but is first compiled into binary executable code. Binary executable code is not adaptable and generic because it is associated with a specific model of computer and operating system. In order to make the code independent on the computer and operating system, Java provides a solution: the developer first compiles the source code into intermediate code, and then uses the Java virtual machine [21] to interpret and execute the intermediate code. This solution is characterized by the fact that the intermediate code is independent on the computer and the operating system, and each operating system comes with a Java virtual machine. The essence of this scheme is that the compilation is no longer on the development side, but on the runtime side. In other words, each operating system comes with an intermediate code compiler, which compiles the intermediate code into binary executable code in real time as the program is executed, or interprets and executes the intermediate code.

The operating system acts as a resource manager and manages the resources on a computer, which includes processes in addition to memory, CPU, etc. Resource sharing in the operating system means that the resources on one computer are shared by multiple processes on this machine. For a server program running on the cloud, its manager and members are usually not running on one computer, but are distributed on different computers. Thus, some concepts in the operating system have to be extended from one computer to the cloud system. The registry, for example, was originally a concept in the operating system to store meta information about services and their instances on the local computer. An extension to it is to store meta information about services and their instances on the cloud. Instead of each computer on the cloud having its own registry, there is a common registry. Another example is the concept of subprocesses. An extension to this is to add a new category: the remote subprocess category. The extension is implemented without any modifications to the operating system, just with the addition of a new support library file.

It is not difficult to implement remote manipulation. The operating system provides services to users such as installing and uninstalling applications, starting and stopping applications, and showing the status of applications. In addition, operating systems come with an application program called telnet server. This service program runs with the startup of the operating system. A user can run a telnet client application on a local computer, connect to a telnet server on a remote computer, log in, and interact with it. A telnet client application is like a terminal connected to a remote computer. The user interacts with it to manipulate the remote computer, for example, to start an application program and to view its running status on the remote computer. Telnet service has become a standard service, with corresponding telnet protocol defined for the data structures of the request and the response, as well as the values of some of the member variables and their meanings. Therefore, any program can interact with a telnet server on any computer based on the telnet protocol to manipulate the remote computer.

The concepts of files and functions also need to be extended. In traditional programming concepts, calling a function means calling a local function, and accessing a file means accessing a local file. In cloud native, "local" no longer refers to a computer, but to the cloud. Therefore, function calls encompass calls to functions on the cloud, while file access encompasses access to files on the cloud. Cloud functions and cloud files both appear as services. Therefore, accessing cloud files is actually accessing file services. After being serviced, files have some new characteristics, such as not experiencing data loss due to storage failures. Therefore, there is no need to consider fault tolerance issues when programming. In cloud native, it is ideal to achieve cloud transparency to clients. The specific implementation of transparent calling of cloud functions will be explained in Chap. 3. The transparency of cloud files will be explained in detail in Chap. 5.

Many basic applications are indispensable for every enterprise, such as database server and web server. So many cloud service providers have developed cloud-native database server products and WEB server products. For example, as famous cloud service providers in China, Huawei, Tencent and Ali have developed their own cloud-native database products: GaussDB [13], TDSQL [22] and PolarDB [23], respectively. When customers want to move their business information systems to run on the cloud, they can directly use the products provided by cloud service providers for database servers and WEB servers. Since the database service and WEB service are standard services, customers' business information systems are naturally compatible with any cloud-native database server and WEB server. The more cloud-native server products there are, the fewer obstacles customers will encounter in moving their business information systems to run on the cloud, the lower the costs will be, and the more guaranteed the quality of service will be.

1.16 Virtualization and Virtual Machines

Virtualization and virtual machines are the most central concepts in cloud computing [24]. These two concepts are somewhat general and abstract and thus are not easy to understand. Giving an example is an effective way to turn the esoteric into the popular, and turn the abstract into the concrete. The earliest concept of virtualization is virtual memory. It was proposed to solve the problems encountered in the continuous expansion of computer functionalities. Initially, a computer ran only a single program, i.e., the entire memory was occupied by a single program. In machine language, code and data are identified with memory addresses. Therefore, when compiling source code into machine code, the compiler had to be able to know the memory address of each instruction and each item of data. It is not difficult to do this. The location where the machine code file is loaded into memory at runtime can be set in advance, so the memory address of the first instruction of the code is a known constant. Its address value plus its length is the memory address of the second instruction, and so on. Instructions are generated one by one during compilation, so the compiler can figure out the memory address of each instruction and each item of data.

In a multitasking operating system, a machine has to run multiple programs at the same time. This means that more than one program has to be stored in memory at the same time, so memory is no longer occupied exclusively by one program. This is where the problem arises. For example, program A is started before program B. In this situation, program B cannot be run because the memory space required by program B is already occupied by program A, leading to the loaded location not matching the location set during compilation. For this problem, a virtual memory solution emerged. In this solution, the compilation scheme remains unchanged, and it is still assumed that a computer runs only one program, and the entire memory space is occupied exclusively by one program. However, the addresses in the machine code are no longer treated as physical addresses at runtime, but as virtual addresses. A virtual address is converted to a physical address in real time at runtime. This solution not only adds the new feature of multiple programs being able to run simultaneously on a single computer, but also enables dynamic link libraries to be shared by multiple programs. The efficacy and implementation details of virtual memory will be explained in detail in Chap. 2.

A commonly heard virtual machine is the Java Virtual Machine (Abbreviated as JVM). The emergence of JVM is related to the Internet. After the emergence of the Internet, many popular applications appeared on the Internet, and clients could download them from the Internet and run them on their own computers. The downloaded program has to be a binary executable file in order to run directly on the client's computer. However, binary executables are tightly coupled to the model of the computer and operating system. The developer of an application does not know the model of clients' computer and operating systems. Thus, he/she has to exhaust the mainstream computer and operating system models, respectively, for generation of binary executable files in compilation, and then put them to the Internet for clients to choose and download. Clients need to know the models of their own computer and operating system, and then select and download the corresponding binary executable file. This approach brings great trouble and difficulties to both developers and clients.

The solution to the above problem requires program code that can be executed independently on the model of the computer and the operating system. JVM is one solution. In this solution, program developers first compile the Java source code into Java bytecode (also called intermediate code). Intermediate code is characterized by (1) poor readability, which is similar to machine code in this respect, and (2) independence on the model of the computer and operating system, which is similar to source code in this respect. In addition, every operating system comes with an application program, JVM, which executes Java bytecode. Therefore, for developers, only the intermediate code has to be released when an application is released. For clients, it is just a matter of downloading the program. The problem of choosing a download based on the model of the computer and operating system no longer exists. JVM extends the capabilities of the computer so that the code it can execute is no longer limited to machine code, including Java bytecode. The principles of the implementation of JVM will be explained in detail in Chap. 5.

New computer models are constantly appearing. For example, after the 32-bit X86 model, a 64-bit X86 model was introduced. For 32-bit X86 models, there were Windows 32 operating systems and Linux 32 operating systems. For 64-bit X86 models, there were Windows 64 operating systems and Linux 64 operating systems. The original Windows 32 application can only run under the Windows 32 operating system, and can neither run directly under the Windows 64 operating system nor under the Linux 32 operating system. In order for original Windows 32 applications to run under the Windows 64 operating system, a Windows 64 application must be developed with the name Windows 32 Virtual Machine. Then, use it to run Windows 32 applications. Similarly, if another operating system, such as Linux 32 or Linux64, also provides a Windows 32 virtual machine, you can use it to run Windows 32 applications.

The meaning of virtual machine is very broad. The above two examples, the Java virtual machine and Windows 32 virtual machine, are introduced to demonstrate

1.16 Virtualization and Virtual Machines

how to extend the capabilities of a model to support the execution of more kinds of code. There is another application scenario where you want to run both Windows 32 and Linux 32 operating systems on a 32-bit X86 computer. This function cannot be realized in the following way: installing Windows 32 OS on the computer first, and then Linux 32 OS. This way leads to a result that the installed Windows 32 OS is overwritten by Linux 32 OS. The reason is that the operating system always thinks that it is the sole manager of the computer. The realization of this feature also requires a virtual machine, but here virtual machine has the meaning of a bare metal computer. This virtual machine also needs to be realized by software. VMWare [25] is such a software. The procedure is that VMWare software is installed first on the computer, and then startup VMware, through which you can install Windows 32 and Linux 32 operating systems, respectively.

There is also an application scenario where it is desired to run multiple instances of the Linux 32 operating system simultaneously on a single 32-bit X86 computer. The intent is to divide a computer into multiple computers so that they are isolated from each other and do not interfere with each other. Cloud computing has this application requirement. In cloud computing, a single computer may be running multiple applications, which come from different customers. If they are arranged to run in a single operating system instance, they may interfere with or disrupt each other. This scenario has been exemplified in Sect. 1.14. The solution is to have each customer's applications run on a separate instance of the operating system, as provided by the Docker software. When running an application through Docker [26], it can specify a container for the application. The meaning of container is a virtual machine. The meaning of a virtual machine here is an operating system instance.

There is also a class of virtual machines that function by combining multiple computers to be used as a single computer. Clusters and cloud systems are examples of this type of virtual machine. To users, a cluster or cloud system appears to be exactly the same as a single machine in terms of use and operation. This virtual machine has the qualities of an ideal computer: it never fails, has infinite storage capacity, infinite throughput, and is responsive. The functionality of such a virtual machine is to make transparent to the user the concepts of distribution and composition of the system, the network, as well as the physical location and replication of member, thus simplifying the complexity of using and operating the system, and preserving the coherence and invariance of the original patterns of use and operation. The basic pattern of computer use by users is to view installed applications, install new applications, startup/stop applications, view the status of applications, or interact with an application in a human–computer interface.

When there are multiple instances of an operating system on a computer, applications located on different instances can only communicate with each other over a network. When there is only one network card on a computer, it can naturally be managed and controlled by only one of the operating system instances. Thus, only one instance of the operating system has network communication capabilities, while the other instances do not. In order for all instances to be able to communicate over the network, a virtual network has to be implemented in software, and then all operating system instances have to be connected to the virtual network. The virtual network [27] consists of a virtual switch and virtual network interface cards (NICs). Each operating system (OS) instance has a virtual NIC that is connected to the virtual switch. Thus, the instances can communicate with each other. In addition, the operating system instance that manages and controls the physical network card also acts as a bridge in the virtual network and is responsible for communication with the outside of the computer. Obviously, the implementation of a virtual network requires an operating system to support it. The implementation of virtual networks will be explained in detail in Chap. 5.

1.17 Abstraction and Dynamic Adaptation

Abstraction is an important tool in software engineering to enhance the generality and wide applicability of software. For example, a cell phone can connect to the network either through Wi-Fi, mobile data network, or Bluetooth. The cell phone shows its dynamic adaptivity in network communication: when Wi-Fi is available, it chooses Wi-Fi to communicate; when Wi-Fi is unavailable, it automatically switches to use mobile data network to communicate; when mobile data network is also unavailable, if Bluetooth is available, it automatically switches to use Bluetooth. This dynamic self-adaptation is usually achieved by abstraction. Take network communication as an example, although there are many different communication links, from the customer's point of view, there is no difference between them, and their functionality is to complete the communication. Thus, a network communication interface socket can be abstracted from them. An application as a communication service client only sees the socket interface. As for the bottom of the communication linking in the end with Wi-Fi, or mobile data network, or Bluetooth, the application does not know.

To obtain dynamic adaption, the application sets a socket interface variable. Before calling the interface, the application requests a socket value from the service provider. By request, the application tells the service provider the memory address of the socket variable and asks the service provider to assign a value to the socket variable. Once the service provider gets the address of the socket variable, it can assign a value to the socket variable at any time. For the service provider on the cell phone, when it finds that Wi-Fi is available, it assigns the socket value provided by Wi-Fi to the socket variable. The application then uses Wi-Fi to communicate. When Wi-Fi is found to be unavailable and Bluetooth is available, the service provider assigns the socket value provided by Bluetooth to the socket variable. The application then communicates using Bluetooth. The application only knows to use the socket variable, i.e., the interface call. Whether the value of the socket variable has changed or not, the application neither cares nor knows. This realizes the dialectical unity of abstraction and concreteness.

Another example of dynamic adaption is printing. When printing a document in the document editor, a dialog box pops up asking the user to select a destination printer. Among the available printers are not only just printer, but also fax machine

1.17 Abstraction and Dynamic Adaptation

and even PDF document generator. When the PDF document generator is selected, the print result is to generate a PDF document. Optional printers can be added dynamically. A software can be added to the list of optional printers as long as it implements the print interface. Dynamic adaptive printing is reflected in: the client is only concerned about the abstract concept of printing, that is, calling the print interface. After the user selects a printer and presses the OK button, the program does the following: loads the dynamic link library file that implements the print interface into the process memory space, finds the starting address of the print interface in memory from it, and then calls it. The implementation of function dynamic calls will be explained in detail in Chap. 2.

In cloud computing, the quality of service is checked in real time when a server program is running. The core metrics of quality of service are response time and throughput. When the quality of service is not up to the mark, the reason behind it may be that there are not enough resources or the program is malfunctioning. When there are not enough resources, additional resources are to be added. In case of a failure, fault recovery is started up. The problem encountered in the detection work is that many programs, especially those legacy programs, were not developed with quality-of-service detection in mind. In this case, the detector had to be embedded in the program. A detector in this context is a dynamically linked library file (henceforth referred to as a module) that contains a detection function. The embedding strategy is also commonly used in everyday work and life. For example, a water pipe consists of several sections that are socketed together. When a water meter is to be embedded, one of the joints is unwound and the meter is embedded in it. Embedding is easy to do since the joints at the ends of the meter and the joints at the ends of the water pipe are standardized.

A program is similar to a tap, consisting of multiple modules in series. Module A is connected to module B in the sense that function α implemented in module B is called in module A. Specifically, there is a function variable α in module A, which is used to store the starting address of the function α in memory. A call to function α in module A is implemented by obtaining its starting address from function variable α. Thus, the startup of a program (denoted as program Y) must be done by another program (denoted as program X) that is already running. Program X first loads the main module (i.e., the module containing the main function) of program Y into memory, and then checks which modules the main module is going to daisy-chain, and loads the daisy-chained modules into memory as well. Taking the above example of module A concatenating with module B, after loading module B into memory, we get the value of the memory address of function α and assign it to the function variable α. After all function variables have been assigned with values, we call the main function of program Y. Thus, Program Y is then started up to run. When the main function returns, program Y is finished.

The server program calls the *recv* function in the network communication module to receive the client's request and then the *send* function to send the response result. The QoS module can then be embedded in the middle of the server program module and the communication module. After embedding, both the client's request and the server's response will flow through the QoS module. The QoS detection module senses the response time and throughput by timing and counting the requests and responses. From the above cross-module function call implementations, it can be seen that the QoS module also provides implementations of the *recv* and *send* functions for the server program to call, whose function is to relay requests and responses, as well as timekeeping and counting of requests and responses. In the implementations of *recv* and *send* functions in the QoS detection module, the *recv* and *send* functions in the communication module will be called, respectively. The implementation of module embedding will be explained in detail in Chap. 2.

1.18 Microservices

A server program runs in a cloud environment and is dynamic in nature. The dynamism is manifested in the fact that the computer on which it runs cannot be determined in advance, but in real time at runtime. In addition, the number of replicas of a server is also dynamic for service availability and throughput. When the request volume increases or the availability needs to be improved, the number of replicas will have to be increased in real time. When the business volume decreases, the number of replicas should be reduced in real time to save resources. This feature requires that the service program can be run anywhere, and its startup time is not too long. Startup time is directly related to the amount of code, but also related to the number of modules and their degree of interleaving. If the amount of code is large, the loading time is naturally long. If the number of modules is large and the degree of interleaving is high, then the modules have to be loaded sequentially based on their dependencies, and the function import address list has to be filled in a large amount. This all lengthens the startup time of the program. In addition, shared resources (e.g., port numbers) required by a program may already be occupied by other already running programs on the local machine. In this situation, the program cannot run properly.

Microservices [28] come in response to the three problems mentioned above. A server program that can run everywhere, has a short startup time, and works properly is called a microservice program. The meaning of micro here is not small. For example, Microsoft and WeChat are not small systems. Micro means carefulness. Specifically, if small things are carefully and thoughtfully considered, the whole thing is reliable and trustworthy. Being able to run everywhere does not mean being able to run on any one computer. It means being able to run on many computers in a given system. To reach the goal of a short startup time, it is important to analyze the factors that affect the startup time, and take measures to speed up the startup of the program in several ways. For example, when a binary executable file is generated by using static compilation and linking mode, it can be eliminated to analyze the dependencies between modules and fill in the import address table, and allows the entire program to be loaded at once. One means of making a program work successfully is to have it run in a separate instance of the operating system.

1.18 Microservices

Micro also has the meaning of fast. A distinctive feature of modern server programs is the high frequency of updates. When the program has bugs, or its structure is unreasonable, or new functions need to be added, it has to be updated. When the existing functions need to be improved, it also need to be updated. Program update involves program design and development, testing and validation, as well as on-line deployment. Update to be fast, not only refers to each department to be fast, the transfer from one department to another should also be fast. The source code should be updated quickly, the prerequisite for which is that the program is developed using a popular framework, and following standards in naming and formatting. Only then is it easy for developers to understand the original program, and to quickly find out what to change. In other words, when a standard already exists for a job, it should be followed; when there are automated tools to assist, try to use them. The transfer from one department to another should also be fast, and a proven way to do this is to package the program for transfer along with the support libraries and the required shared resources. The packaged program is called an image. It can then be used out of the box in each subsequent department.

The out-of-the-box implementation [29] can be demonstrated by an example. When using Docker to develop and deploy an application, its developer first downloads a base image from the Docker image repository (denoted as image A) and then starts up the image on his computer, thus creating a container. A container means an operating system instance. Then, you install and configure the application in the container so that it can start up and run properly. The container contains the application and its runtime environment. The container is then packaged into an image (labeled image B). Subsequently, whether in test department or production department, the job of launching the application on a given computer becomes the job of launching image B. This is called out-of-the-box use. Since the image contains the operating system instance information, the application will run in the same runtime environment regardless of the computer on which image B is launched, and will not encounter any obstacle or problem such as sharing conflict.

Reflection 1-8: When you use an integrated development enviroment (IDE) tool to create a project with the category of Server, the tool automatically generates the framework source code for you. You then use the tool to define specific service functions. The tool automatically generates the definition of handler functions on the client requests based on the service definition. The manual coding content is to give a concrete implementation for the handler functions. Other standardization tasks, such as service instance registration, corresponding code is also generated by the tool. What are the characteristics of the source code generated by the tool?

Reflection 1-9: What is the relationship between images and static compilation and linking?

Reflection 1-10: When developing WeChat applets based on the cloud, there is a concept called cloud function, which is characterized by the fact that the function is uploaded to the cloud, runs on the server side, and is called on the front end. What are the similarities and differences between cloud functions and remote procedure calls? Cloud function is an abstraction of remote procedure call, is it right?

On the cloud, online updates to a server program are no longer done using the original replacement method, but instead are done using a switchover method. Replacement is the process of shutting down and uninstalling the old version of a server program, and then installing and launching the new version of the server program. When the replacement method is used, the service is unavailable during the replacement period. The situation where the service is unavailable for a long period of time is not acceptable in many application scenarios, such as the passenger identification service at a train station. The switchover method involves starting up the new version of the server program on another computer, and then the server gateway switches the client requests from the old version to the new version. After the switchover is complete, the old version of the server program is shut down and uninstalled. As you can see, the service is always available without interruption when switching. The switchover is completely feasible on the cloud because there are a large number of computers on the cloud with spare resources. After the switchover, the resources occupied by the old version are released and put into the spare resource pool. The implementation of the switchover is explained in detail in Chap. 5.

For a system, how many server programs should it be divided into, or what functional modules should be classified into a server program? The benchmark should be the frequency of interaction. If two modules are in a single program, their interaction will be in the form of function calls. If they are in different programs, they interact through process-to-process communication. When the two interacting processes are not running on the same computer, they also need to communicate over a network. When the two communicating computers are heterogeneous, translation processing is also required at both ends of the communication. It can be seen that when there is frequent interaction between two functional modules, both of them should be classified into the same server program. This principle of division is also often used in daily life. For example, when arranging dormitories for students, one class should be accommodated in close proximity to each other. For students of a department, the arrangement should be based on the principle of the closest building, because the most common place for students to go is the building.

1.19 History of Technological Evolution

The core problem to be solved by a multitasking operating system is resource sharing, which also establishes the C/S model of resource sharing. The operating system is the resource manager, or resource service provider, on a computer. Applications as clients apply for resources and use them by calling the APIs provided by the operating system. Resource management means recording what and how many resources are available, as well as the current status of resources used by clients, and then responding to new client requests based on the information in the existing records. Client requests may or may not be successful. The running of an application is abstracted as a process in the operating system. The operating system

1.19 History of Technological Evolution

manages processes in addition to resources. As far as processes are concerned, the services provided by the operating system to application programs include creation of processes, shutting down of processes, etc. When the operating system starts up, it creates an *init* process that executes the *init* application. *init* waits for users to log in. After a user does login, the *init* process reads his/her configuration information and creates a new process to run his/her startup script.

To facilitate process control, the process manager records the parent–child relationship between processes. When process A creates a new process B, it is said that process A is the parent of process B. Thus, processes in the operating system have a tree structure, in which the root process is naturally the *init* process. A process can control its children and grandchildren, for example, by shutting them down. In addition, a process can establish contact with another process and communicate with it as long as it has access to the id of that process. When a process calls the operating system API to create a child process, the return value is the id of the child process. Since the parent process knows the ids of all its children, it can communicate with anyone of its children. When the parent process tells all its children the ids of all its children, its children can also communicate with each other.

Two processes residing on different computers can communicate with each other over a network. For multiple processes on a single computer, the network is a shared resource. Therefore, the operating system has a network manager that provides services for processes to send data and receive data. Processes call the APIs provided by the network manager to use the network, including sending data and receiving data. When process α on computer A wants to send data to process β on computer B, it does not know the id of process β because process ids are assigned by the process manager in real time. Therefore, in network communication, the process id cannot be used to identify a process, but only the IP address plus the port number can be used to identify a process, where the IP address identifies the computer and the port number identifies the process. In the operating system, port number is also a shared resource, so a port number can only be occupied by one process. In order to alleviate the port number conflict, common server programs are assigned port numbers in advance. For example, the port number assigned to a web server is 80.

In cloud computing, the exact computer on which a customer's server program is scheduled to run is not determined in advance, but in real time at runtime. This situation makes the problem of server programs not running properly due to port number conflicts exceptionally prominent. For example, the task scheduling manager wants to schedule server program β to run on computer A. If server program α has been already running on computer A and its port number is the same as the port number of β, then server program β cannot run successfully on computer A. To address this problem, customers can be asked to give the port number information when installing and deploying their server programs on the cloud. Once the task scheduling manager knows the port number of every server program, it can do non-conflict scheduling. Taking the above scenario as an example, the task scheduling manager will not schedule service program β to run on computer A if it knows that service program α is already running on computer A and its port number is the same as that of β.

Compared to cluster computing, the most significant feature of cloud computing is the dynamic nature of program running. Dynamism is manifested in: (1) the task scheduling manager determines which computer to run a given program in real time at runtime; (2) a running program may have to be migrated from one computer to another; (3) the number of replicas of a program varies at runtime. These features imply that a program should be able to run everywhere. Java technology provides a strong support for this goal. Java bytecode is independent on the models of computer and operating system. Thus, all computers installed with Java virtual machine can run Java programs. Existing operating systems come with the Java Virtual Machine as an application program. Therefore, it is sensible to use Java to develop a new server program. Java's OS-independence is reflected in the JDK. The JDK is a programming interface for Java, which is a step further than POSIX, and abstracts more functional interfaces. Each Java virtual machine provides its own implementation of the JDK.

The nature of Java technology is to postdate the generation of machine code. In the traditional model, machine code is generated by a developer using a compiler and then distributed to users to run directly on their computers. Users' computers are called the target computers. The advantage of this model is that the developer keeps the source code himself and distributes the machine code. The machine code is extremely poorly readable, which helps the developer protect his intellectual property. In addition to the model of the target computer, there are also versions. For example, for 32-bit X86 computer, there are 386, 486, 586, and so on. The later versions have more registers and other new features than the previous versions. A compiler generates machine code for a particular model and version of the target computer. In a Java program, instead of machine code, the developer distributes bytecode to users. The generation of machine code is transferred from the development side to the runtime side and is carried out in real time by the Java virtual machine on the target computer.

Java solutions not only make programs generic, but also optimize the efficiency of program execution. In the traditional compilation model, the developer does not know the version number of the target computer on which the program is installed, and therefore can only compile conservatively with a low version to ensure that the machine code can be executed on any version of the target computer. If the target computer is a high version, its computational potential is wasted. For example, for a 32-bit X86 computer, machine code compiled based on the 386 version will not utilize the new registers and other new features compared to the 386 version if it is executed on a 586 version. With the Java solution, the machine code is generated by the Java Virtual Machine on the target computer, which naturally knows the model and version number of the computer on which it resides. Therefore, the generated machine code is efficient in execution.

An operating system is designed with the assumption that it is the sole manager of the computer's resources. Therefore, it is not possible to have 2 or more operating systems running simultaneously on a single computer. Many application scenarios require multiple operating systems to be running on a single computer at the same

1.19 History of Technological Evolution

time, hence VMware [25] emerged in 2001, which provides virtual bare metal functionality. After installing VMWare on a computer, you can install multiple operating systems and have them all running at the same time. Since VMWare is installed first and the operating system is installed later, VMWare gains control to the computer, and the operating system becomes an application running on top of it. Even though the operating system considers itself to be the sole manager of resources, when it executes a resource access instruction, it does not have enough privileges and thus triggers an abnormal interrupt, causing the computer to jump to execute the interrupt handling routine, i.e., the code in VMWare. This means that any access to resources by the operating system is done on its behalf by VMWare.

VMWare enables multiple applications running on the same computer to be isolated from each other and not to interfere with each other by allocating resources to the operating systems running on top of it. This gain comes at a performance cost [30]. The reason is that applications are originally called functions in the operating system kernel via soft interrupts. The soft interrupt handling routines can only be coded in VMWare. This is the only way that VMWare can keep the management of resources in its own hands at all times. Thus, application programs cannot directly call the operating system kernel code, and the operating system also cannot access resources directly. Such things have to be completed through the intermediary of VMWare. For example, when an application opens a file, or reads or writes to a file, it does so through the intermediary of VMWare. Since applications cannot interact with operating system kernel directly, performance overhead via VMWare is remarkable. Thus, new application isolation schemes such as Namespace and CGroup [31] emerged in 2013.

Namespace and CGroup are two new functionality modules for the Linux operating system. Namespace is a generic term for operating system configuration parameters, such as computer name and IP address, as well as runtime parameters such as process ids, which are managed by the operating system and shared by all processes. Applications can access and use the parameters in the Namespace by calling the operating system API. For example, a process id can be queried based on the application name, and once the process id is obtained, a signal can be thrown to the process to manipulate it, such as shutting it down. In order to isolate processes from each other and prevent them from conflicting, interfering, or destroying each other, the Linux operating system has added the ability for applications to create Namespace instance objects. When you want to create a child process, you can create a new Namespace instance object and associate the child process with it. Thus, the child process and the parent process will belong to different Namespaces.

Namespace contains only operating system configuration parameters and runtime parameters, and does not contain hardware resources such as CPU, memory, network, etc. Linux's CGroup (abbreviation of Control Group) is a solution specifically for hardware resource isolation. Hardware resources logically belong to CGroup instance objects. Each process belongs to a CGroup instance object and can use the hardware resources in it. A process can create a CGroup instance object for its children, then allocate the resources owned by its own CGroup instance object to the newly created CGroup instance object, and then associate the children with the newly created CGroup instance object. Thus, the parent process and the child process belong to different CGroup instances and are isolated from each other in terms of hardware resources and do not interfere with each other.

The performance overhead of the Namespace and CGroup isolation scheme is much smaller than that of VMWare [25]. The reason is that Namespace and CGroup intermediaries are only needed when applications request resources. When an application interacts with a resource, it no longer needs to go through the Namespace and CGroup intermediaries. For example, when an application opens a file, it has to go through the Namespace and CGroup intermediaries, which has a performance overhead. When applications read or write to a file, which does not need to go through the Namespace and CGroup intermediaries, there is no performance overhead. The usual scenario is that an application first opens a file and then reads and writes to it many times. Therefore, the performance overhead of Namespace and CGroup may be negligible.

Docker is a tool designed to simplify the implementation of applications' isolation. It utilizes Namespace and CGroup technologies to achieve isolation between applications. It let applications run in a container, thereby isolating multiple applications running on the same computer from each other. Container is an abstract concept that graphically describes the scenario where programs are isolated from each other. A container means an operating system instance, and its implementation is not complicated. When the task manager starts up an application, it creates a Namespace instance object and a CGroup instance object for it. Thus, different applications belong to different Namespaces and CGroups and are isolated from each other.

In addition to isolating programs from each other at runtime, Docker enables programs to transfer quickly from development department to test department, and then to production department, with fast startup at runtime. In the traditional model, applications are packaged and distributed by the development department. The test department and the production department install and configure the application on their own computers before launching it, respectively. Since the runtime environments of the three departments are not the same, the application may run successfully in the development department, but not in the test department, or in the production department. Because of this, the latter two departments have to install the program, configure it, and then launch it. Even so, there may be a sharing conflict that prevents the program from running properly. For example, program A wants to use port 80, which has been occupied by program B that has already been started up. Thus, program A cannot run successfully. The reason is that port numbers are shared resources.

To address the above issues, Docker makes all applications run in containers. Containers [32] are virtual machines and have invariance. Thus, the runtime environment in which the application runs also has invariance. This solution overcomes the problem that an application cannot run successfully due to the variability of the runtime environment. At runtime, the mapping of the virtual machine to the physical machine is done automatically by the Docker tool. Applications are then

1.19 History of Technological Evolution 53

packaged and distributed using Docker, eliminating the need for installation and configuration for subsequent users. Instead of calling the packaged program an installer file, Docker renames it an image file. In this scenario, the test department and the production department can take the image file and use it out of the box. Thus, program's transfer from one department to another one can be accelerated, and the startup is also accelerated. In addition, the problem of unsuccessful operation will no longer be encountered. The specific implementation will be explained in Chap. 5.

For a cloud service provider, a software is needed to consolidate all its computers into a single computer. This software is called a cloud service management system. For example, Kubernetes [33] is a well-known cloud service management system. It is naturally a distributed system with two role software: manager and member. The member software runs on each computer and accepts requests from the manager, and is responsible for starting up, monitoring, and shutting down virtual machines on this machine, and also for allocating hardware resources owned by this machine to the virtual machines. The cloud service management system provides cloud services to customers externally on the one hand, and is responsible for member management internally on the other hand. Customers can register an account on the cloud service management system and then migrate their business information system from their own server room to run on the cloud. After the migration, the operation and maintenance of the business information system are all left to the cloud service provider. The specific implementation of migration to the cloud will be explained in detail in Chap. 5.

After a customer migrates his business information system to the cloud, the original system architecture concept remains. However, their original physical LAN now becomes a virtual LAN, and their original physical computers becomes virtual machines. From the operation and maintenance perspective, there is no difference between a virtual machine and a physical computer. Customers can add virtual machines to the virtual LAN and configure them. Customers can also install applications on the virtual machine and then start up the virtual machine or shut it down. The operations and maintenance that the customer performed originally in the physical world now occur in the virtual world. In the customer's view, a virtual machine differs from a physical computer in that it never fails. In addition, the resources owned by the virtual machine, such as CPU, memory, and network bandwidth, are elastic and can be automatically adjusted according to the load. Cloud service providers charge customers based on the volume of resources they consume. Therefore, the amount charged varies from time to time.

Cloud services can be categorized into three levels: (1) IaaS (abbreviation of Infrastructure as a Service); (2) PaaS (abbreviation of Platform as a Service); and (3) SaaS (abbreviation of Software as a Service) [34]. IaaS means that Cloud service providers use software such as VMWare to provide virtual bare-metal services to customers. Then, customers are responsible for installing their own operating systems, support libraries, and applications on the virtual machines. In this way, the customer has the most control over their business information system. PaaS means that the cloud service provider provides the platform and the customer is responsible for installing applications on top of it. For example, Node.js is a kind of service platform, if the customer's application is developed based on Node.js, then this kind of service can be chosen. SaaS refers to that the cloud service provider provides software, and the customer is responsible for applications. For example, cloud database management system is such a class of software, provided by the cloud service provider. The customer is responsible for their own business database definition. When using this approach, the customer is the most trouble-free, does not have to consider software upgrades.

There are private and public clouds [35]. A private cloud is usually owned by an organization, and its customers come from subsidiaries or divisions of the organization. Public clouds are open to the public, and their customers come from all walks of life. Compared with private clouds, public clouds are larger in scale and have more prominent security issues. For private clouds, it is easy to establish a trusting relationship between the cloud service provider and its customers as they belong to the same organization. For public clouds, customers are very concerned about data security and quality of service issues, and cannot accept data loss, errors, and leakage. Because of this, the current public cloud providers are usually well-known Internet giants, such as Amazon, Google, Microsoft, and Ali, Tencent and Huawei in China. For an organization, its business information system is its lifeblood. Migrating it to run on the cloud, reliability and security must be guaranteed. In addition to technical improvements, governance at the legal level [36] is essential to allay customers' concerns.

Decentralization is a solution to the trust problem. Existing service systems are basically centralized systems characterized by a single service provider. Customers use the service system based on their trust in the service provider. In the case of banking services, for example, customers deposit their money into the bank's service system based on their trust in the bank and conduct transactions through the service system. The correctness of the transaction presupposes that the customer trusts the service provider. The service provider has the ability to tamper with the transaction data and transaction rules. Decentralized solutions try to overcome this problem with the strategy that services are no longer provided by a single service provider, but by multiple service providers together. In terms of system composition, the system is no longer composed of a single node, but of multiple nodes. Different nodes are attributed to different service providers. Everything in the system is no longer decided by a single service provider, but by multiple service providers.

Compared with the centralized system, the decentralized system has two obvious new qualities: (1) under the premise of more than half of the normal nodes, any node (or any service provider) is no longer essential to the provision of services, but optional; (2) even if there is a malicious node in the system, which wants to destroy the consistency of the system by messing up, it will not succeed. Therefore, decentralized systems are highly trusted, have good availability, and are very popular among customers. Bitcoin and Ethereum [37] are two transaction service systems built on the concept of decentralization. In a decentralized system, a mutually agreed upon decision is called a consensus. The specific process of reaching consensus is called a consensus protocol, also called a consensus algorithm. Well-known consensus protocols are Paxos [38] and practical byzantine fault tolerance (PBFT) [39]. The problems to be solved in decentralized computing, and the methods to solve them will be explained in detail in Chap. 4.

1.20 Summary of the Chapter

Sharing is the driving force behind the evolution of computing. Computing has gone through 2 times of evolution: (1) from stand-alone computing to cluster computing; (2) from cluster computing to cloud computing. In stand-alone computing, sharing means that multiple processes execute concurrently and they share the resources on the same computer. Cluster computing extends the scope of sharing and realizes sharing across computer boundaries. Cloud computing, on the other hand, reduces costs by deepening sharing and utilizing scale effect to achieve good value for money and mutual benefit. The evolution of computing is a dialectical unity of change and constancy. The constancy is reflected in the way customers use computers. Whether it is a cluster, or the cloud, in the eyes of customers, it is always a computer, with the way of use and operation unchanged. The change is in the characteristics of the computer. Compared to a single computer, a cluster presents the customer with different qualities: it never fails; it is always available; and it has infinite computing power and storage capacity. Compared to clusters, the cloud presents customers with different qualities: excellent quality and reasonable price.

Cloud computing, on the basis of cluster computing, needs to further solve two technical problems: (1) applications can run everywhere; (2) applications running on the same computer can be isolated from each other and do not interfere with each other. The Java virtual machine and the scripting engine enable Java programs and scripting programs, respectively, to run on every computer. It is not enough to make an application run on a given computer; there is also the question of whether it can run successfully. This problem is rooted in the variability of the runtime environment. The way to solve the problem is virtualization. Having a program run on a virtual machine can virtualize the environment in which the application runs. The virtual environment has invariance. The mapping of the virtual environment to the real environment is done by the virtual machine. VMWare is a software that provides virtual bare-metal capabilities. On the virtual bare metal, customers can install their own operating systems, support libraries, and applications. Docker is a software that provides container functionality so that applications running in different containers are isolated from each other and do not interfere with each other.

Under the tide of informationization, service systems are facing the double pressure of increasing data volume and customer requests. The efficiency and security of data processing, the scalability of systems, and the availability of services are becoming more and more important. The number of replicas of a server needs to be adjusted in real time during operation. When the business volume increases or availability needs to be improved, the number of replicas will be increased in real time.

When the business volume decreases, the number of replicas should be reduced in real time to save resources. This feature requires that the startup time of a server program should not be too long. In addition, server programs are constantly being revised and upgraded. Fast revising and upgrading are crucial for the organization and are the basic guarantee to win customers. Revamping and upgrading should be fast, not only meaning that it should be fast in each department, the transfer from one department to another should also be fast. The strategies and methods to achieve program's efficient operation, elastic operation, secure operation, fast update, and fast startup are collectively known as microservice technology.

Exercises
1. Universities use student number to identify a student in their management of students. Is the student number a virtual id, or a real id? Why is the ID number not used to identify the student? Please give detailed reasons. A mobile number used to be a physical id in China because its first 3 digits identified the service provider and next 4 digits identified the city. When a customer wants to change his/her service provider or resident city, he/she had to change his mobile number. What are the disadvantages of changing his/her mobile number for a customer? A customer can now change his/her service provider or resident city without his/her mobile number changed. Does this situation indicate that the mobile number is no longer a physical id, but a virtual id, and who is responsible for the mapping of the virtual id to the physical id?
2. In China, Tencent company has launched WeChat Mini-Program, which provides a platform for customers to build their own business information systems on the Tencent Cloud. Is the platform portable? In other words, can customers migrate their WeChat applets to run on the Ali Cloud or Huawei Cloud? Why does not the cloud service provider want customers to use their own software, but instead use the platform software provided by the cloud service provider? Or why does not Tencent provide the following service for its customers: let them directly migrate their original business information systems to the cloud? This is obviously not a technical issue. Please analyze the reasons.
3. Currently, the customers who are actually migrating their business information systems to the public cloud are mainly micro and small companies. For medium-sized enterprises, what are the doubts and concerns about migrating their business information systems to the public cloud? Why are micro and small companies willing to migrate their business information systems to the cloud?
4. Suppose that after an organization migrates its business information system to the cloud, data loss, or data error, or data leakage occurs. How to determine the responsibility? Is it the customer's own fault? Or should the cloud service provider take the responsibility? How much is the loss? How much is the compensation? Do these questions suggest that governance at the legal level is also crucial in cloud computing?

References

1. Kai, H., Geoffery, C. F., Jack, J.D., *Distributed and Cloud Computing: From Parallel Processing to the Internet of Things*. Morgan Kaufmann Publishers Inc., 2013.
2. Huawei Technologies Co., Ltd. *Cloud Computing Technology*. Springer Nature Singapore Pte Ltd., 2023.
3. Todd, H. *Explain the Cloud Like I'm 10*. New York: Possibility Outpost Inc., 2018.
4. Nayan, B. R., *Cloud Computing*. The MIT Press, 2023.
5. Thomas, E., Zaigham, M., Ricado, P., *Cloud Computing: Concepts, Technology & Architecture*. London: Pearson Education, 2016.
6. Anders, L., *Cloud computing basics*, SpringerLink, 2021.
7. Wilder, B., *Cloud Architecture Patterns*. O'Reilly Media, 2012.
8. Antonio, B., Nicola, D., Schahram, D., et al, Microservices. SpringerLink, 2020.
9. Don, B., *Essential COM*. Addison-Wesley Professional, 1998.
10. David, B., *Using and Administering Linux: Volume 1*. Springer Nature link, 2023.
11. Sean, M., , Zhi, L., Subhajyoti B., et al, *Cloud Computing - The Business Perspective*. Decision Support Systems, 2011, 51(1): p. 176–189.
12. Rai, R., Sahoo, G., Mehfuz, S., *Exploring the factors influencing the cloud computing adoption: a systematic study on cloud migration*. SpringerPlus, 2015, 4(197): p. 1–12.
13. Huawei Technologies Co., Ltd., *Database Principles and Technologies – Based on Huawei GaussDB*. Springerlink, 2023 [access date 05/21/2024]; Available from: https://link.springer.com/book/10.1007/978-981-19-3032-4.
14. Víctor, M., Omer, R., et al, *Adaptive Application Scheduling Under Interference in Kubernetes*. In Proc. of the 9th IEEE/ACM Int. Conf. on Utility and Cloud Computing, 2016, p. 426–427.
15. Arshdeep, B., Vijay, M., *Cloud Computing: A Hands-On Approach*. CreateSpace Independent Publishing Platform. 2013.
16. Weiwei, L., Chennian, X., Wentai, W., et al, *Performance Interference of Virtual Machines: A Survey*. ACM Computing Surveys, 2023, 55(12): p. 1–37.
17. Ali, D., Mengchi, L., *Big Data Systems: A Software Engineering Perspective*. ACM Computing Surveys, 2020, 53(5): p. 1–39.
18. Abdessalam, E., Faiza, S., James, H., et al, *Cloud Brokerage: A Systematic Survey*. ACM Computing Surveys, 2019, 51(6): p. 1–28.
19. Nane, K., Peter-Christian,Q., *Understanding Cloud-Native Applications After 10 Years of Cloud Computing - A Systematic Mapping Study*. Journal of System Software, 2017, 126(4): p. 1–16.
20. Donald A. L., *POSIX Programmer's Guide. Writing portable UNIX programs with the POSIX.1 standard*. 2023 [access date 07/21/2024]; Available from: https://dl.acm.org/doi/book/10.5555/119327.
21. Gough, K.J., Corney, D., *Evaluating the Java Virtual Machine as a Target for Languages Other Than Java*. Proceedings of the Joint Modular Languages Conference on Modular Programming Languages,2000, p. 278–290.
22. Yuxing, C., Anqun, P., Hailin, L., et al, *TDSQL: Tencent Distributed Database System*. Proceedings of the VLDB Endowment, 2024, 17(12): p. 3869–3882.
23. Wei, C., Yang, L., Zhushi, C., et al, *POLARDB Meets Computational Storage: Efficiently Support Aanalytical Workloads in Cloud-Native Relational Database*. Proceedings of the 18th USENIX Conference on File and Storage Technologies, 2020, p. 29–42.
24. Thomas, W., Elhadj, B., *On Resilience in Cloud Computing: A Survey of Techniques across the Cloud Domain*. ACM Computing Surveys, 2020, 53(3): p. 1–36.
25. Orran, K., Phil, M., Arkady, K., *Enabling a Marketplace of Clouds: VMware's VCloud Director*. ACM SIGOPS Operating Systems Review, ,2010,44(4): p. 103–114.

26. Bernstein, D., *Containers and Cloud: From LXC to Docker to Kubernetes.* IEEE Cloud Computing, 2014, 1(3): p. 81–84.
27. Debashis, B., Rohit, T., Serge, M., et al, *Virtualizing Networking and Security in the Cloud.* ACM SIGOPS Operating Systems Review, 2010, 44(4): p. 86–94.
28. Armin, B., Abbas, H., *Microservices Architecture Enables DevOps: Migration to a Cloud-Native Architecture.* IEEE Software Magazine, 2016,33 (03): p. 42–52.
29. Merkel, D., Docker: Lightweight *Linux Containers for Consistent Development and Deployment.* Linux Journal, 2014, 239(3): p. 76–90.
30. Ann, M. J., *Performance comparison between linux containers and virtual machines.* In Proc. of the 2015 Int. Conf. on Advances in Computer Engineering and Applications, IEEE, 2015, p. 342–346.
31. Dan, K., *Virtualization: A Manager's Guide.* O'Reilly, 2011.
32. René, W. S., Steffen, G., *VApp: a Standards-Based Container for Cloud Providers.* ACM SIGOPS Operating Systems Review, 2010, 44(4): p. 115–123.
33. Why you need Kubernetes and what it can do. 2020 [access date 12/11/2023]; Available from: https://kubernetes.io/docs/concepts/overview/#why-you-need-kubernetes-and-what-can-it-do.
34. Funmilade, F., Rami, B., *A Systematic Review of Service Level Management in the Cloud.* ACM Computing Surveys, 2015, 48(3): p. 1–27.
35. Arpan, R., Santonu, S., Rajeshwar, G., et al, *Secure the Cloud: From the Perspective of a Service-Oriented Organization.* ACM Computing Surveys, 2015, 47(3): p. 1–30.
36. Claudio, A. A., Rasool, A., Ernesto, D., et al, F*rom Security to Assurance in the Cloud: A Survey.* ACM Computing Surveys, 2015, 48(1): p. 1–50.
37. Gencer, A. E., Basu, S., Eyal, I., et al, *Decentralization in Bitcoin and Ethereum Networks.* 22nd International Conference on Financial Cryptography and Data Security, 2018, p. 439–460.
38. Leslie, L., *The part-time parliament.* ACM Transactions on Computer Systems, 1998, 16(2): p. 133–169.
39. Miguel, C., Barbara, L., *Practical byzantine fault tolerance and proactive recovery.* ACM Transactions on Computer Systems, 2002, 11(1): p. 62–97.

Chapter 2
Sharing of Computer Resources

There are two levels of resource sharing. The first level refers to the sharing of resources on a single computer by multiple processes running on the machine. This is the most basic form of sharing and the cornerstone of distributed computing. The second level refers to sharing across computer boundaries, i.e., resources on one computer can be shared by processes on other computers. For the sake of distinction and contrast, the first level of sharing is named stand-alone computing, and the second level of sharing is called distributed computing. In stand-alone computing, running instances of an application program are called processes. When multiple processes execute concurrently, the problem of resource sharing is introduced. Shared resources include hardware resources such as CPU, memory, network, and other resources such as code and data files. Computer resources are uniformly managed by the operating system, and processes act as clients to request resources from the operating system. In distributed computing, resource sharing manifests itself as an interaction between two processes running on different computers, with one process acting as a server and the other as a client.

In stand-alone computing, to figure out the implementation of resource sharing, you must first figure out how computers work. The way a computer works is expressed in the execution of a program. A program is a sequence of instructions, also known as code. Normally, the CPU executes the instructions in the code sequentially and one by one. It is only when it executes a branch jump instruction that it breaks the above rule and makes a jump. It is the jumps that allow the CPU to loop through a particular section of code. In addition, computers have interrupt mechanisms [1]. Interrupts can be triggered by components in a computer. Once an interrupt is triggered, the CPU jumps to execute the interrupt handling routine [1] after executing the current instruction. The interrupt handling routine is also a piece of code that ends with the interrupt return instruction *iRet*. When the CPU executes the *iRet* instruction, it jumps again, back to the next instruction that should have been executed before the interrupt. Sect. 2.1 of this chapter explains how computers work, while Sect. 2.2 shows how computers work using the implementation of a single-tasking operating system as an example.

The computer's interrupt mechanism can be used to enable the concurrent execution of multiple tasks. An application program is executed once by the CPU and the corresponding computing task is completed. The computer clock can be set to trigger an interrupt at regular intervals. When the clock interrupt is triggered, the next instruction to be executed is in the instruction register. The interrupt transfers the data in the instruction register to the interrupt register and then places the first instruction of the interrupt handling routine into the instruction register. Thus, the CPU jumps to execute the clock interrupt handling routine. When the CPU executes the interrupt return instruction *iRet*, it restores the value in the interrupt register to the instruction register, so the CPU jumps again and the execution of the application program is resumed.

For every running application, there is the concept of the next instruction to be executed. For applications that are not yet running, the next instruction to be executed is the starting instruction, i.e., the first instruction. Concurrent multitasking is implemented by noting the next instructions to be executed for every running application in the clock interrupt handling routine. They are then rotated into the interrupt register. Thus, the CPU takes turns executing the application programs to be run. The implementation details of concurrent multitasking are explained in Sects. 2.3, 2.4, and 2.5. Sect. 2.3 explains the multitasking operating system [2], Sect. 2.4 explains process scheduling and management [3], and Sect. 2.5 explains kernel space and user space [4].

Concurrent execution of multiple tasks naturally leads to the issue of resource sharing. When computer resources are shared by multiple applications, a manager is needed to manage them. The manager of shared resources is the operating system. The operating system manages various shared resources in different categories. Among them, CPU resources are managed by the process scheduler [5], memory resources are managed by the memory manager [6], network resources are managed by the network manager [2], and file resources are managed by the file manager [1]. Applications, as clients, have to apply to the manager before using the shared resources. The allocated shared resources can be used only after the request is successful. The last four sections of this chapter, starting from Sect. 2.6, explain the implementation schemes for sharing the resources of memory, network, code, and data files. It focuses on analyzing the problems encountered in code sharing and their solutions.

The next Sects. 2.10 and 2.11 explain the implementation of process-to-process interaction [5] and process-to-peripheral interaction [1], respectively. Exception handling [7] is very important for applications, and Sect. 2.12 analyzes the characteristics of exception handling and then discusses its implementation. Section 2.13 concludes the chapter.

2.1 How Computers Work

As soon as a computer is powered up, it executes program code. The computational tasks to be performed by the computer are expressed in the program code. Program code is a sequence of instructions. Each instruction consists of an instruction code and parameters. The instruction code specifies the operation to be performed and the parameters specify the data involved in the operation. In terms of running program code, a computer can be modeled as consisting of two parts: the CPU and the memory. The code and data are stored in the memory. The CPU fetches the instruction from the memory one by one and executes it. Executing an instruction is also known as a one-step computation. One-step computation usually involves reading data from memory, giving it to the CPU to process, getting the result of the computation, and then storing the result in memory. A computational task is usually accomplished by many steps of computation. What each step of computation has to do is identified by an instruction code.

Each model of computer has its own set of instructions. An instruction consists of an instruction code and the parameters it requires. For an instruction, how many parameters it carries, the order of the parameters, and the meaning, width, and value range of each parameter are specified by the computer manufacturer and released to compiler vendors. Compiler vendors develop compilers based on the published machine instructions. Compilers translate source programs into machine codes and generate binary executable files. The binary executable files are loaded into the computer's memory and handed over to the CPU to be executed to get the computation results. Executing an instruction is similar to a function call in a high-level programming language. In a program, the function name serves to identify the functionality. Similarly, an instruction code serves to identify an operation instruction. In terms of a function, how many arguments it takes, the order of the arguments, and the type of each argument, these things are specified at the time of function definition. Similarly, a machine instruction, how many arguments it takes, the order of the arguments, and the type of each argument are defined when the computer hardware is designed.

A program consists of two parts: code and data. To run a program, it is first loaded into memory. Typical memory is RAM. There are two types of memory: RAM and ROM. RAM is characterized by the fact that the contents of the memory are lost when the power is turned off, while ROM is not. Therefore, ROM is often used to store the program code that will be executed first when the computer is turned on. RAM consists of memory units. Each memory unit has 1 byte of storage space and is identified by a memory address. The other type of memory is registers, which can be accessed by the CPU two orders of magnitude faster than memory. However, registers are much more expensive than memory, so the number of registers on a computer is very limited. When a program is loaded into memory, the execution of the program is initiated by loading the memory address of the first instruction in its code section, into the instruction register.

The CPU reads the instruction code from memory based on the value in the instruction register. Once the instruction code is obtained, the CPU parses it and knows how to further read the required parameters from the memory. After reading the parameters, the instruction is executed. Based on the currently executed instruction and the result, the CPU can derive the memory address of the next instruction code and place it in the instruction register. Thus, the next calculation is initiated. An example of this computation mode is shown below. Let a program be loaded into memory with four instructions as shown in Table 2.1. It is assumed that the memory address of line 1 is 4000, and the current value of the instruction register is 4000, i.e., the first instruction is to be executed. Thus, the execution of these 4 instructions is as follows.

1. The CPU reads the instruction code at memory address 4000. Assuming that the width of the instruction code is fixed at 2 bytes, the width of the register identifier is fixed at 1 byte, the width of the memory address is fixed at 4 bytes, and the width of an integer is also fixed at 4 bytes, the CPU will get the instruction code as REG_MEM_INT_ADD. Note that the instruction code has been named here for readability. This instruction code indicates the CPU to do the addition operation on two integers. It also specifies that the first operand is in a register, the second one is in memory, and the result is placed in a register. From this code, it is clear that it is followed by 3 parameters. The first parameter is the register identifier where the first integer is located, with a length of 1 byte. Thus, the CPU reads 1 byte from memory address 4002 to get the register identifier of the first operand. Then, it reads 4 bytes from memory address 4003 to get the memory address where the second operand is located. Last, it reads 1 byte from memory address 4007 to get the register identifier where the result of the calculation is stored.
2. After completing the reading of the instruction code and its parameters, the CPU executes the machine instruction to complete the calculation of the step. From the executed instruction code REG_MEM_INT_ADD, the width of the instruction is 8 bytes. The CPU thus adds 8 to the value of the instruction register to get the memory address where the next instruction is located, i.e., 4008.
3. The CPU reads the instruction code at memory address 4008 and finds that it is INT_LARGER_COMPARE, which means comparing the values of two integers and putting the result of the comparison in the logical flag register. Thus, it is known that it comes with 2 parameters. The first parameter is the memory address of the first integer and the second one is the memory address of the second integer. So the CPU reads 4 bytes from memory address 4010 to get the

Table 2.1 4 lines of instructions in memory

Memory address	Instruction code	Parameters
4000	REG_MEM_INT_ADD	R1, 8000, R2
4008	INT_LARGER_COMPARE	8024, 8028
4018	CONDITION_JUMP	4800
4024	REG_REG_INT_ADD	R2, R3, R2

memory address of the first integer and then reads 4 bytes from memory address 4014 to get the memory address of the second integer.
4. After completing the reading of the second instruction, the CPU executes it to complete the second step of the calculation. From the executed instruction code INT_LAGER_COMPARE, the width of the line of code is 10 bytes. The CPU thus adds 10 to the value of the instruction register to get the memory address where the next instruction is located, i.e., 4018.
5. The CPU reads the instruction code at memory address 4018. It is found to be CONDITION_JUMP, which means if the value in the logic flag register is TRUE, a jump occurs. This operation instruction has only one parameter, i.e., the target memory address to jump. So the CPU reads 4 bytes from memory address 4020 to get the target memory address 4800 to be jumped.
6. The CPU executes the third instruction. At this time, if the value in the logic flag register is TRUE, the CPU sets the value of the instruction register to the parameter value 4800. That is, the memory address where the next instruction to be executed is 4800, i.e., it executes a jump. If the value in the logic flag register is FALSE, then no jump is performed and the execution of the next instruction, i.e., instruction 4, continues. From the executed instruction code CONDITION_ JUMP, it is clear that the width of the code line is 6 bytes. Thus, the CPU does an addition of 6 to the value of the instruction register to get the memory address where the next line of instruction code is located, i.e., 4024.

Programs are executed with an interrupt mechanism. There are various categories of interrupts, such as disk interrupts, keyboard interrupts, etc. The interrupt category is identified by the interrupt number, starting at 0. Interrupts include hard and soft ones. Hard interrupts are triggered by circuitry such as the clock and memory, and peripherals such as the keyboard and disk. Soft interrupts are triggered by instructions executed by the CPU. The instruction code contains the interrupt instruction code. Once the CPU executes an interrupt instruction, a soft interrupt is triggered. Whenever an interrupt is triggered, after the CPU executes the current instruction, the memory address of the next instruction to be executed is in the instruction register. Instead of executing the next instruction, the CPU saves the value in the instruction register to another special register (which is referred to as the interrupt register) in order to free up the instruction register to load the start address of the interrupt handling routine in memory, thus jumping to the execution of the interrupt handling routine.

From the above interrupt handling process, it can be seen that when an interrupt is triggered, the CPU has to know the starting address of the interrupt handling routine in memory, so that it can load it into the instruction register and begin executing the interrupt handling routine. The CPU's design is to put the starting address of each interrupt handling routine into the IDT (abbreviation of Interrupt Description Table). In addition, the starting location of the IDT in memory is specified in the hardware design as a constant. This constant is usually set to 0. For the interrupt number i, the starting address of its interrupt handling routine is put in the ith row of the IDT. In a 32-bit machine, the address width is 4 bytes, so each row in the IDT is 4 bytes wide. Thereby, assume the fifth interrupt is triggered, the CPU knows that the starting address of its interrupt handling routine would be stored in memory at address 20.

The next thing is who sets up the IDT? Setting up the IDT means filling in the IDT with the starting address of every interrupt handling routine in memory. The rule of thumb is that whoever provides the interrupt handling routines is responsible for filling in the IDT. The first program that is executed when the computer is turned on is called the BIOS (abbreviation of Basic Input & Output System in ROM). The starting address of the BIOS in memory is specified in the CPU's design. Therefore, the BIOS is placed in ROM before the computer is shipped from the factory. The functionality of the BIOS is to load the operating system boot code from the disk to a specified location in memory and then jump to execute it. It can be seen that the BIOS has to perform disk I/O which involves disk interrupt. Thus, the BIOS needs to provide the disk interrupt handling routine and set up the IDT.

How does the BIOS know the starting address of the disk interrupt handling routine in memory? The disk interrupt handling routine is a part of the BIOS itself, so the BIOS naturally knows its starting address in memory. Therefore, there is no problem for the BIOS to set up the IDT. After the BIOS reads the operating system boot code from the disk into the memory, it jumps to execute it. The operating system provides its own interrupt handling routines, so it will come and reset the IDT.

As soon as the computer is turned on, the value in the instruction register is set to a constant. This constant is the starting address of the BIOS in memory. Thus, the computer executes the BIOS. The BIOS does three things in sequence: (1) sets up the IDT for disk I/O; (2) reads the operating system boot code from the disk into a specified location in memory; and (3) jumps to execute the operating system boot code. The functionality of the operating system boot code is to read the operating system code from the disk into memory and then jump to execute it. The operating system has its own interrupt handling routines. Thereby, the operating system resets the IDT so that it can manage the entire computer.

2.2 Implementation of a Single-Task Operating System

For the simplest single-tasking operating system, its functionality is to provide human–computer interaction interface, get user's keyboard input, and execute the application program specified by the user. *Cmd* is a command prompt program coming with the Windows operating system. It is in fact derived from the original single-tasking operating system, DOS. *Cmd* consists of a loop of code that waits for a user to input the name of the application file to be executed in each round. When the user hits the key *Enter*, it indicates the end of user input. The next works of *Cmd* are to parse the user's input, load the application program to be executed from disk into memory, determine the starting address of its main function, and then call it. Thus, the application program is executed. When the main function returns, it means that the application program has ended. Thus, the current round of the cycle is over, and

2.2 Implementation of a Single-Task Operating System

the next round of the cycle starts. *Cmd*'s source program implemented in C language is shown in Code 2.1.

Code 2.1 Source Code of Cmd
```
(1)    char input[200];
(2)    int argc;
(3)    char *argv[10];
(4)    int (*appMain)( int, char **);
(5)    while(true) {
(6)       gets(input);
(7)       argc = resolve(input, argv);
(8)       unsigned int loadedAddr = loadLibaray(argv[0]);
(9)       appMain = getProcAddress( loadedAddr, "main" );
(10)      *appMain(argc, argv).
 11    }
```

The meaning of the source program shown in Code 2.1 is as follows. The variable *input* is used to store the command line entered by the user's keyboard. The command line consists of several segments separated by spaces. The first of these segments is the name of the application program file to be executed, and the other segments are the accompanying parameters. Variable *argc* is used to store the number of segments, variable *argv* to store the segments. Line 4 defines a function pointer variable *appMain*, whose definition shows the definition of the function referred to as: the type of the return value is int; there are two formal parameters; the type of the first one is int, and the second one with type of char **. The compiler knows from this definition how to generate the target code that calls the function referred to by the variable. The definition of the function to which the variable refers is identical to the definition of the main function. Therefore, the *appMain* variable can be used to store the starting address of the main function in memory, thus realizing the call to the main function.

As you can see from the while statement on line 5, *Cmd* will keep running and will not end. Line 6 is a call to the C system function *gets* to get the user's keyboard input into the variable *input*. The *gets* function returns only when the user hits the key *Enter*. Line 7 parses the user's keyboard input and slices it into substrings bounded by space characters. The addresses of all substrings are stored in the array variable *argv*, and the number of substrings is stored in the variable *argc*. Line 8 is to call the system function *loadLibaray*, to load the executable file from disk into memory, where the real parameter *argv*[0] points to the filename substring, and the function return value is the memory address of the loaded module. Line 9 is a call to the system function *getProcAddress* to get the starting address of the main function of the loaded module, which is assigned to the variable *appMain*. Line 10 is a call to the main function of the loaded module, which executes the application.

The call to the function *gets* in line 6 of Code 2.1 expresses human-computer interaction. When the program runs to the function *gets*, it will pause, waiting for the user's keyboard input. Until the user hits the key *Enter*, the function *gets* returns. The function *gets* is implemented as shown in Code 2.2. The formal parameter *input* specifies the starting location where the keyboard input character should be stored. The meaning of line 3 is: the value of the formal parameter *input* is assigned to the global variable *charBuffer*, which is intended to tell the keyboard input interrupt handling routine that it now accepts keyboard input and wants to place the character that the user has typed in at the memory location indicated by *charBuffer*. A keyboard input interrupt is triggered when the user hits the keyboard to enter a character. In the keyboard input interrupt handling routine, the value of *charBuffer* is checked and if it is not null, it indicates that a program is waiting for keyboard input. The global variable *charBuffer* is used here as a vehicle for passing information between *Cmd* and the keyboard interrupt handling routine.

Halt in line 4 of Code 2.2 is a computer instruction. Its functionality is to let the CPU pause and not continue executing line 5. Only until the keyboard triggers an input interrupt, the CPU jumps to execute the keyboard input interrupt handling routine. After the interrupt returns, the CPU jumps once again to execute the code in line 5. The meaning of line 5 is that if the user hits the key *Enter*, then the *gets* function will return; otherwise, it will wait for further keystrokes from the user. If the user hits the key *Enter*, the meaning of line 6 is to rewrite the entered character *Enter* to 0, marking the end of the string. The meaning of line 7 is to tell the keyboard input interrupt handling routine to ignore the user's keyboard input afterwards.

The implementation of the keyboard input interrupt handling routine is shown in Code 2.3. Whenever the user hits the keyboard, a keyboard input interrupt is triggered. What the interrupt handler routine does is to fetch the character from the keyboard. First, it checks to see if the value of the global variable *charBuffer* is null. If it is not null, it indicates that a program is waiting for keyboard input, thereby it deposits the entered character into the memory location indicated by *charBuffer*. Note: before the interrupt is triggered, the CPU has finished executing line 4 of the function *gets*. When the keyboard input interrupt handler routine returns, the CPU then executes line 5 of the *gets* function. The question now is: how does the CPU know the memory address of the next instruction to be executed after the interrupt handling routine returns.

When an interrupt is triggered, the instruction register stores the memory address of the next instruction to be executed. In the case of the above *gets* function, for example, the instruction register holds the memory address of line 5. Once the interrupt is triggered, the CPU transfers the value in the instruction register to the interrupt register, so that when the interrupt handling routine returns, it can go back and continue executing the interrupted program. In the case of the above *gets* function, for example, it is to go back and continue to execute line 5. After the CPU has backed up the value in the instruction register, it then reads the starting address of the interrupt routine from the IDT based on the interrupt number and puts it into the instruction register. The CPU then starts executing the interrupt processing routine. The last statement of the interrupt handling routine is *iRet*. *iRet* stands for interruption return, and its functionality is to restore the value in the interrupt register to the instruction register, so the CPU continues to execute the interrupted program.

Code 2.2 Implementation of the Function Gets

```
(1)  void gets(char *input) {
(2)    charBuffer = input;
(3)    while(true) {
(4)      halt;
(5)      if (*charBuffer == carriage return) {
(6)        *charBuffer = '\0';
(7)        charBuffer = null;
(8)        return;
(9)      }
(10)     else
(11)       charBuffer ++;
(12)   }
(13) }
```

Code 2.3 Keyboard Input Interrupt Handling Routine

```
(1)  void keyboardInterruptHandler( ) {
(2)    if (charBuffer ! = null)
(3)      *charbuffer = fetchChar( );
(4)    iRet;
(5)  }
```

From the above interrupt mechanism, it can be seen that when the CPU executes line 4 of the *gets* function, it goes into a suspended state. It is the keyboard input interrupt that wakes up the CPU, and after backing up the value in the instruction register to the interrupt register, it starts executing the keyboard input interrupt handling routine. After the keyboard input interrupt routine returns, line 5 of the function *gets* is executed. The line is an if statement, the meaning of which is: if the user's input is the character *enter*, the input ends, and the *gets* function returns. Otherwise, the *gets* function waits for the next character input.

From the above implementations of the *gets* function and the keyboard input interrupt handling routine, it is clear that their interaction should have a common storage for passing information. In the above example, the global variable *charBuffer* is used as the common storage between them. The *gets* function tells the keyboard input interrupt handling routine whether or not it wants to receive a character from the keyboard by changing the value of *charBuffer*. The keyboard input interrupt handling routine then checks the value of *charBuffer* to determine whether there is a program waiting for keyboard input, and resumes the execution of the interrupted program via *iRet*.

Cmd can be thought of as a single-tasking operating system in its simplest form. Its functionality is to provide human–computer interaction and to run any one application program. Many embedded systems [8] have neither disks nor keyboards, and do not need to have a BIOS or an operating system to run just one application. This means that the application runs on bare metal. At this point, the application replaces the BIOS and is placed in ROM. When the computer is powered on, the first instruction of the application program is executed. Naturally, the first thing the application does is to set up the IDT so that it can communicate with the peripherals for I/O. The embedded application consists of two parts: the function module as well as the interrupt handling routines.

2.3 Multitasking Operating Systems

A multitasking operating system enables a computer to run multiple applications simultaneously. Thus, a computer can act as more than one computer for a user. The benefits are: increased utilization of computer resources, and enabling the computer to do more things. A computer running multiple applications at the same time is in terms of human perception. The essence is to cut the time into time slices, and then let the CPU to the time slice as a unit to sequentially rotate the execution of each application, so that people feel like multiple applications running at the same time.

To make a computer run program *A* and program *B* simultaneously, first load both program *A* and program *B* into memory and then have the CPU execute them alternately. The CPU executes program *A* in the first time slice, then goes to program *B* in the second time slice, and then switches between them repeatedly. If the length of the time slice is small enough, e.g., 0.1 s, program *A* and program *B* are running at the same time from the human perception. This alternate switching is actually the switching of values in the instruction register. Let the next instruction to be executed by program *A* and program *B* have the memory addresses α and β, respectively, then when α is placed in the instruction register, the CPU executes program *A*. When β is placed in the instruction register, the CPU executes program *B*.

Running multiple applications at the same time essentially allows multiple applications to share resources. Shared resources include the CPU, registers, memory, network, and code and data files. Sharing creates access conflict problems. For example, registers are to be used by each application. For program *A*, when the CPU executes it, the memory address of its next instruction to be executed is stored only in the instruction register. If the value in the instruction register is now to be changed so that the CPU goes to program *B*, the current value of the instruction register has to be saved to another place before the value of the instruction register is changed. So that when it comes back to execute program *A* at some later time slice, it will know the memory address of its next instruction to be executed.

In addition, the data required by the CPU to execute an instruction can be either in memory or in a register. Therefore, other registers are shared resources as well as the instruction register. When switching from program *A* to program *B*, the register values of program *A* are first saved and then the register values of program *B* are restored. The reverse is also true. When switching from program *B* to program *A*, the register values of program *B* are first saved and then the register values of program *A* are restored.

Alternate switching of program execution can be achieved by clock interrupts. Set the interval between clock-triggered interrupts to the duration of the time slice, for example, 0.1 s. Thus, every 0.1 s, the execution of the current program will be interrupted, and the CPU goes to execute the clock interrupt handling routine. For example, suppose program *A* is currently executing, and after the clock interrupt is triggered, the value in the interrupt register is the memory address of the next instruction to be executed by program *A*. At this point of time, the values in the registers other than the instruction register are referred to as the context of program *A*. The clock interrupt handling routine first saves the context of program *A* to the memory allocated for use by program *A*, and then restores the context of program *B* to the registers from the memory allocated for use by program *B*. Subsequently, the instruction *iRet* is executed, which conducts the CPU to executes program *B*.

Reflection 2-1: After a clock interrupt is triggered, for program *A*, the memory address of the next instruction to be executed is not in the instruction register, but in the interrupt register. Why? The value in the instruction register is the memory address of the first instruction of the clock interrupt handling routine, why? The value in the instruction register is not the context of program *A* at this time, while the value in the interrupt register is the context of program *A*. Why? To restore the context of program *B* to registers, the memory address of the next instruction to be executed is restored to the interrupt register, why? When the CPU then executes the instruction *iRet* in the clock interrupt handling routine, it jumps to execute program *B*, Why?

2.4 Process Scheduling and Management

Having solved the problem of alternate switching of program execution, the next question is: how does the clock interrupt handling routine know which application is currently executing and which one is next to be executed? This problem is known as the scheduling and management of application execution. For this reason, the concept of process was introduced in operating systems. A process is a running instance of an application program. Multiple applications running at the same time means that there are multiple process objects in the operating system. Processes have the concept of life cycle. To start an application running, a process object is created in the operating system. When the process object is created, you must specify which application should run. To terminate an application is to release a process object from the operating system. Thus, multitasking refers to multiple processes. It is also possible to open the same application several times. For example, in our daily work, we often open several *word* applications and let them edit different word files, respectively. Each open corresponds to creating a process.

2.4.1 Process Scheduling

Processes are recognized from an object-oriented perspective, with the concepts of class and instance object. To create a process is to create an instance object of the class *process*. The end of a process is the release of a process instance object. The process class has the member variable *state*, which records the state of the process. There are only three values for the process state: RUNNING, WAITING, and READY. For scheduling and managing processes, there are further concepts of the current process as well as process table. The current process is the process that is currently being executed by the CPU, and its state attribute value is RUNNING. There is the global variable *currentProcess* in the operating system. Another global variable *processList* stores all the processes in the current operating system. Every time a process is created, a process object is added to *processList*, and every time a process is released, an existing process object in *processList* is deleted.

Only the state attribute of the current process has a value of RUNNING, while the state attribute of other processes has a value of READY or WAITING. The state attribute of the current process changes from RUNNING to WAITING after the process calls one of the operating system-provided wait functions. For example, the value of the state attribute of the current process changes from RUNNING to WAITING when it calls the operating system-provided function *waitForKeyboardInput*. The functionality of this function is to change the value of the state of the current process, and then allow the CPU to execute another process. When a line of characters is entered from the keyboard, the value of the state attribute of the process is changed to READY by the keyboard input interrupt handling routine. On subsequent process switches, the process becomes the new current process again and continues to run.

With the concept of process, alternate switching of program execution naturally means alternate switching of processes. When a process switches, only processes with a state attribute value of READY are eligible to be scheduled for execution. There are only two events that trigger a process switch. The first is the clock interrupt described earlier. The second event is: the current process calls a wait API function, e.g., *waitForKeyboardInput*. The implementation of *waitForKeyboardInput* is used as an example to illustrate the second type of process switch. The function is to wait for Keystrokes to enter a line of characters. That is, the function does not return until the user hits the key *Enter*. Specifically, the first step is to tell the operating system that an application is waiting for keyboard input. This is done by assigning the starting address of the cache where the application receives the character line to the operating system's global variable *charBuffer*. *charBuffer*'s value is checked in the keyboard interrupt handling routine. If it is not null, it indicates that there is a process waiting for keyboard input.

A process calls a function such as *waitForKeyboardInput* to wait for an event to occur. From a process scheduling point of view, this means that the current process changes from running to waiting and voluntarily gives up CPU to another process that is ready. In other words, the value of *currentProcess* must change. There are two scenarios. The first scenario is that all processes are not in the ready state. Thus, the new value of *currentProcess* is set to null, which means that there is no process to run. At this point of time, the CPU has nothing to do but call halt to pause. The second scenario is that the new value of *currentProcess* is not null, which means that there is at least a process in the ready state, and then the CPU is scheduled to run the new current process. The implementation of process switching is shown in Code 2.4.

The function *waitForKeyboardInput* can be implemented as shown in Code 2.5. The meaning of INT 70 in line 2 is to trigger the 70th soft interrupt. Lines 5 through 8 are the implementation of the 70th soft interrupt handling routine. Its functionality is to assign a value to the operating system's global variable *charBuffer*, and then call the function *giveUpCPU* (see Code 2.4) for process switching. The process switching here does two things: (1) saves the context of the current process, as shown in line 4 of Code 2.4; and (2) schedules another ready process to act as the new current process and let the CPU run it, as shown in lines 5 through 9 of Code 2.4.

In process switching, the process that gives up the CPU is called the abdicating process, and the new current process is called the uploaded process. Before switching, the context of the abdicating process is in the registers, where the registers do not refer to a particular register, but to all registers except the instruction register. A process switch is, in fact, a process context switch. Specifically, the context of the abdicating process is copied from the registers to its context member variable, and then the context of the uploaded process is copied from its context member variable to the registers. The process switch is then completed by executing an *iRet* instruction. One of functionalities of *iRet* is to load the value in the interrupt register into the instruction register.

Code 2.4 Implementation of Processes Switching
```
(1)    void giveUpCPU(int eventId ) {
(2)       currentProcess->state =WAITING;
(3)       currentProcess->waitForEvent = eventId;
(4)       currentProcess->SaveContext( );
(5)       currentProcess = processList->getNextProcessToRun( );
(6)       if (currentProcess ! = null) {
(7)          currentProcess->ActivateContext( );
(8)          iRet;
(9)       }
(10)      else
(11)         halt;
(12)   }
```

Code 2.5 Implementation of waitKeyboardInput
```
(1)    void waitForKeyboardInput( char *input) {
(2)      INT 70 (input);
(3)      return;
(4)    }
(5)    void int70Handler(char *input ) {
(6)      charBuffer = input;
(7)      giveUpCPU(KEYBOARDINPUT);
(8)    }
```

When performing a process switch, there may be no uploaded process. That is, current all processes do not have a state attribute value of READY. This is shown by the return value null of the function *getNextProcessToRun* in line 5 of Code 2.4. After the interrupt handling routine has been executed by the CPU, no process needs the CPU to continue its execution, so the CPU executes the instruction *halt* to pause. *getNextProcessToRun* is a process scheduler function. The simplest implementation is to let the CPU take turns executing processes in the ready state.

For the implementation of the function *waitKeyboardInput* shown in Code 2.5, the function *int70Handler* in the operating system kernel cannot be called directly. It must be called through a soft interrupt. When the soft interrupt handling routine *int70Handler* is executed, the value in the interrupt register is the memory address of the next instruction to be executed in the interrupted program. That is, the memory address of the return statement in line 3 of Code 2.5. The interrupt handling routine is being executed at this time, so the value in the instruction register is not part of the context of the abdicating process, whereas the value in the interrupt register is part of the context of the abdicating process. For the abdicating process, after the user hits the key *Enter*, it is dispatched again as the new current process. When it resumes execution, it then executes the return statement in line 3 of Code 2.5.

When process *A* calls the function *waitKeyboardInput*, it changes to the wait state. Process *A* is then changed to the ready state in the keyboard input interrupt handling routine only when the user hits the key *Enter*. The implementation of the keyboard input interrupt handling routine is shown in Code 2.6. Its functionality is to check if there is a process waiting for keyboard entry of a line of characters. If there is, the character is fetched from the keyboard and stored in the cache. If the character typed in by the user is the key *Enter*, then it is necessary to further check which process is waiting for the keyboard entry of the character line and then change the value of its state attribute to READY. Whereupon the waiting process becomes ready to be scheduled for execution during the next round of process switching.

2.4 Process Scheduling and Management

Code 2.6 Implementation of Keyboard Input Interrupt Handling Routine

```
(1)   void keyboardInterruptHandler( ) {
(2)     Process *process = null;
(3)     if (charBuffer ! = null) {
(4)        *charBuffer = fetchChar( );
(5)        if (*charBuffer ! = carriage return)
(6)           charBuffer ++;
(7)        else {
(8)           *charBuffer = '\0';
(9)           process = processList->getFirstItem();
(10)          while (process ! = null) {
(11)             if (process->state == WAITING && process->waitForEvent == KEYBOARDINPUT) {
(12)                process->state = READY;
(13)                break;
(14)             }
(15)             process = processList->getNextItem();
(16)          }
(17)          charBuffer = null;
(18)        }
(19)     }
(20)     checkCurrentProcess( process);
(21)  }
```

Before a hard interrupt is triggered, the CPU may be either in the working state or in the suspended state. Being in the working state means that the CPU is executing a process, i.e., the value of *currentProcess* is not null. In contrast, being in the suspended state means the value of *currentProcess* is null. After a hard interrupt is triggered, the CPU starts executing the hard interrupt handling routine. If the state of a process is changed to ready by the hard interrupt routine, and the CPU was in the suspended state before the interrupt, the process in the ready state should be changed to current process at the end of the hard interrupt routine to allow it to resume running. The implementation of this processing is shown in Code 2.7. In the keyboard input interrupt handling routine, if the character read from the keyboard is the key *enter*, the process waiting for the character line to be entered is changed to the ready state, as shown in lines 9–17 of Code 2.6. Therefore, this code shown in Code 2.7 is to be called at the end of the keyboard input interrupt handling routine, as shown in line 20 of Code 2.6.

Code 2.7 Checking Whether or Not There Is a Process in the Ready State
```
(1)   void checkCurrentProcess(Process *process ) {
(2)      if (currentProcess == null && process == null )
(3)         halt;
(4)      else if (currentProcess == null && process ! = null ) {
(5)         currentProcess = process;
(6)         currentProcess->ActivateContext( );
(7)         iRet;
(8)      }
(9)      else
(10)        iRet;
(11)  }
```

Reflection 2-2: For Code 2.7, *iRet* is executed at both line 7 and line 10. The value in the interrupt register is different when *iRet* is executed at these two places, why? Which process is jumped to execute respectively?

One of functionalities of the clock interrupt handling routine is to perform a process switch, the implementation of which is shown in Code 2.8. At this time, the current process becomes the abdicating process, and the uploaded process is determined from *processList* in accordance with the process scheduling strategy. The variable *abdicatingProcess* is used to record the abdicating process. Its value may be either null or not null. Null means that there is currently no process in the running state. Not null means there is currently at least one ready process. The variable *currentProcess* is used to record the uploaded process (i.e., the new current process). Its value has three possible scenarios: (1) null, showing there is no process is in the ready state among all processes; (2) not null, and not equal to *abdicatingProcess*, implying there is another process in the ready state; (3) not null, and equal to *abdicatingProcess*, indicating that there is no other process currently in a ready state except the abdicating process. In the third situation, the abdicating process had to be allowed to continue running. Combining the abdicating and uploaded processes results in six scenarios.

Reflection 2-3: For Code 2.8, there were six scenarios, but now they have been consolidated into four scenarios. Which two of the six scenarios have been consolidated?

From the above analysis, it can be seen that when process *A* calls the function *waitForKeyboardInput*, it changes to the wait state, and at the same time, the value of *currentProcess* changes. When the user hits the key *Enter*, the state of process *A* is changed to READY by the keyboard interrupt handling routine, and then process *A* may be selected as the new current process again, either by the keyboard interrupt

2.4 Process Scheduling and Management   75

handling routine, or by the clock interrupt handling routine, or by another running process who is calling a wait function such as *waitForKeyboardInput*.

Code 2.8 Implementation of Clock Interrupt Handling Routine
```
(1)   void timerInterruptHandler( ) {
(2)     Process *abdicatingProcess = currentProcess;
(3)     currentProcess = processList->getNextProcessToRun( );
(4)     if (currentProcess ! = null) {
(5)       if ( currentProcess ! = abdicatingProcess) {
(6)         if ( abdicatingProcess ! = null)
(7)           abdicatingProcess->SaveContext( );
(8)         currentProcess->ActivateContext( );
(9)       }
(10)      iRet;
(11)    }
(12)    else
(13)      halt;
(14)  }
```

Reflection 2-4: From the above implementations of interrupt handling routines such as soft interrupt 70, keyboard input interrupt and clock interrupt, it is clear that in the interrupt handling routines, the last instruction to be executed is not necessarily *iRet*, but may also be halt. Under what circumstances is halt executed? and under what circumstances is *iRet* executed?

Reflection 2-5: In the implementation of process switching shown in Code 2.4, the return value of the call to the member function *getNextProcessToRun* at line 5 is definitely not the same as the value of *currentProcess* before the call, why? And in the clock interrupt handling routine shown in Code 2.8, the return value of the call to the member function *getNextProcessToRun* at line 3 could equal to *currentProcess*, why?

Reflection 2-6: In process switching, you have to call the member function *getNextProcessToRun* of *processList* to get the uploaded process. When its return value is null, it means that all processes are in the waiting state, i.e., there is no process to run. At this point, only a hard interrupt can change the state attribute value of a process, why? When no process is running, the CPU has nothing to do but execute the hard interrupt handling routine. Therefore, at the end of the hard interrupt handling routine, *currentProcess* is checked to see if it is null. If it is, the instruction *halt* is executed to pause the CPU. At the end of the hard interrupt handling routine, the last instruction executed is either *iRet* or *halt*. If *halt* is executed, what is the value in the interrupt register when a hard interrupt is triggered again later?

Reflection 2-7: In the implementation of the function *getNextProcessToRun*, the uploaded process is selected from those processes in the ready state. Once the uploaded process is determined, its state should be changed to RUNNING. Suppose the CPU is executing the handling routine of soft interrupt 70, and exactly at this time, the clock interrupt is triggered. Thus, the process switching should be executed in both places, will a sharing conflict problem occur? Is there a sharing conflict problem?

Reflection 2-8: The process object, the current process, and the process table are maintained by the operating system kernel and cannot be accessed directly by the application program. Interrupt handling routines (including soft interrupt handling routines) are part of the operating system kernel and cannot be called directly by the application program. The application program can only call the soft interrupt handling routine through the soft interrupt instruction. What are the similarities and differences between soft interrupts and function calls, and what are the differences and similarities between the instruction *iRet* and *return*?

2.4.2 Process Management

The process manager is an integral part of the operating system. It is responsible for process scheduling, managing processes, and providing service interfaces for clients (i.e., applications) to call and manipulate processes. The service interface includes creating processes, closing processes, suspending processes, and querying processes. A process is a running instance of an application, so it must be associated with an application. To create a process, you load the application's binary executable from disk into memory and then get the memory address of its main function, which is the address of the first instruction the process will execute. Creating a process is actually adding a process instance object to the process table, whose implementation of the interface function *createProcess* is shown in Code 2.9. This implementation omits loading the application executable from disk into memory, obtaining the memory address of the main function, and initializing the process member variables.

Code 2.9 Implementation of the Function createProcess
```
(1)   int createProcess( byte *pMainFunc) {
(2)     return INT 89(pMainFunc);
(3)   }
(4)   int int89Handler( byte *pMainFunc)) { // create a process
(5)     Process *process = new Process(pMainFunc, READY);
(6)     processList->addItem(process);
(7)     iRet process->id.
(8)   }
```

2.4 Process Scheduling and Management

As can be seen from Code 2.9, the application programs interact with the operating system kernel by the soft interrupt 89 to create a process. In the operating system kernel, an instance object of the process class is created and added to the process table. The created process is set to the ready state so that it can subsequently be scheduled for execution by the process manager. The process table variable *processList* is a global variable in the operating system.

In a multitasking operating system, the state of a process can be changed in the following four ways: (1) from RUNNING to WAITING; (2) from WAITING to READY; (3) from READY to RUNNING; and (4) from RUNNING to READY. When a process itself calls a wait function, such as *waitForKeyboardInput* (shown in Code 2.5), its state changes from RUNNING to WAITING. Later, when the event for which a process is waiting occurs, its state changes from WAITING to READY. For example, a process may be waiting for the event of keyboard input by calling *waitForKeyboardInput*. The event occurs when a keyboard input interrupt is triggered. When a process waits for some lock, the event occurs as a result of another process releasing the lock. Locks are shared kernel objects managed by the operating system, and applications naturally release locks they hold by calling the operating system API.

The third and fourth scenarios occur when a process switch is performed. As soon as the current process goes down, a process with state READY is selected to go up and act as the new current process. For the abdicating process, its state changes from RUNNING to READY, and for the uploaded process, its state changes from READY to RUNNING.

Reflection 2-9: Shutting down a process means deleting a process instance object in the process table. Assuming that its API function is defined as: void *killProcess* (int *processId*), can you write its implementation? When the main function of the application returns, the execution is over and the process should be closed. How to realize the process shutdown at this time? Can a process call the function *killProcess* to shut itself down? Please explain why.

Reflection 2-10: Process query is the process of getting the process id of an application by its name. Having obtained the id of a process, one can communicate with it. Can you write the implementation for process query?

Reflection 2-11: *releaseLock* is an operating system (OS) application programming interface (API) function that releases locks, can you write its implementation?

2.4.3 Concurrent Multitask Execution

A computational task is accomplished by the CPU executing a trip of program code. For a computing task, the CPU has the concept of the next instruction to be executed during the execution of the program code. For a computing task that has not yet started, the next instruction to be executed is the starting instruction of the program code, i.e., the first instruction. The process of completing a computing task is abstracted into processes. Thus, concurrent multitask execution refers to the concurrent execution of multiple processes, i.e., the CPU takes turns executing existing processes in time slices, giving the impression that multiple processes are being executed by the computer at the same time. In other words, one computer is turned into multiple computers through software.

The central concept in concurrent multiprocess execution is process switching. A process has a member variable, *nextInstruction*, which is used to record the memory address of the next instruction to be executed. When a clock interrupt is triggered, the CPU jumps from the current process to execute the clock interrupt handling routine. During the jump, the memory address of the next instruction to be executed by the current process, which was originally in the instruction register, is transferred by the CPU to the interrupt register. Thus, in the clock interrupt handling routine, the value in the interrupt register is first read and saved to the member variable *nextInstruction* of the current process, and then the memory address of the next instruction to be executed by the uploaded process is loaded into the interrupt register from its member variable *nextInstruction*. The process switch is realized by executing the interrupt return instruction *iRet*. The reason is that the instruction *iRet* loads the value in the interrupt register into the instruction register.

It can be seen that a process switch is involved in two times of jump of the CPU. The first jump occurs from the current process to the clock interrupt handling routine when a clock interrupt is triggered. The second jump appears from the clock interrupt handling routine to the uploaded process when the instruction *iRet* is executed. The switching is done through a clock interrupt. The switching consists of saving the value in the interrupt register to the member variable *nextInstruction* of the current process and loading the value of the member variable *nextInstruction* of the uploaded process into the interrupt register. The uploaded process becomes the new current process.

A process may want to wait for a certain event to occur by calling a wait API function. Waiting means giving up the CPU, i.e., making a process switch. When there is no the uploaded process, the halt instruction is executed to suspend the CPU. Subsequently, when a hard interrupt is triggered, the CPU is woken up to execute the hard interrupt handling routine.

2.5 Kernel Space and User Space

In a multitasking environment, resource sharing means that resources are shared by multiple processes. For example, the CPU is shared by multiple processes, allowing multiple processes to execute concurrently. In addition to the CPU, memory, and peripherals, such as network cards, are also shared resources. As seen in Sect. 2.4, when a process calls a wait function such as *waitForKeyboardInput*, it performs a process switch, i.e., it accesses *processList* as well as *currentProcess* maintained by the process manager. Process switching is also performed in the clock interrupt handling routine. Therefore, *processList* and *currentProcess* are shared data. In addition, locks maintained by the operating system are also shared data. Both shared

2.5 Kernel Space and User Space

hardware resources and shared data must be accessed in an orderly fashion, or else they will be disorganized and incorrect.

The way to achieve orderly access to a shared resource is to set up a manager for the shared resources. When a process accesses a shared resource, it sends a request to the manager, and the manager returns a response. This process is represented as a function call. The manager opens up its services by providing API functions, and applications as clients access the services by calling API functions. Thus, the operating system is actually a manager of shared resources and the application programs are clients accessing the shared resources. Running instances of an application program are called processes.

There is a boundary between the application program and the operating system. This boundary is represented by soft interrupts. API functions provided by the operating system end up being called with soft interrupts. Soft interrupts and function calls are both different and related. From a functional point of view alone, there is no difference between the two. They both perform jumps. But from a security point of view, they are different. For shared resources, processes cannot access them directly bypassing the operating system; otherwise, the operating system would be useless. This goal is achieved through the interrupt mechanism. There are different levels of machine instructions. High-level machine instructions can only be executed when the CPU privilege level flag is set; otherwise, an exception interrupt will be triggered. High-level machine instructions point to operating peripheral I/O, setting up the IDT, masking interrupt, and so on. Lower-level machine instructions can be executed even when the CPU privilege level flag is reset, such as data arithmetic instructions, branch jump instructions, and so on.

When an interrupt is triggered, the CPU first sets the CPU privilege level flag, and then jumps to execute the interrupt handling routine. Since the CPU privilege level flag is set, high-level machine instructions can appear in the interrupt processing routine. The CPU is said to be in the kernel state when the CPU privilege level flag is in the set state. When the interrupt return instruction *iRet* is executed, it first resets the CPU privilege level flag and then performs a jump to the next instruction to be executed prior to the interrupt. The CPU is said to be in the user state when the CPU privilege level flag is in the reset state. The storage space of a computer is divided into kernel space and user space. When the CPU is in the user state, it is not allowed to access data in the kernel space or jump to execute code in the kernel space. When the CPU is in the kernel state, the situation is completely different. It can both access data in user space and jump to execute code in user space.

Based on the security mechanisms provided by the CPU as described above, kernel space is reserved for the operating system, and user space is reserved for the application programs. So the operating system code is also called kernel space code, and the application program code is also called user space code. Only low-level machine instructions can appear in user-space code, not high-level machine instructions, or else an exception interrupt will be triggered when running. This is the solution that applications cannot bypass the operating system to access shared resources directly. When the CPU is in kernel state, it can jump to execute code in user space. It is better not to have this situation happen. If this happens, then the application code becomes operating system code and can perform any operation. There is no security at all.

Reflection 2-12: OS's global variables stored in kernel space, such as *currentProcess* and *processList*, are known as kernel space data. Each process can access kernel space data through soft interrupts to invoke soft interrupt handling routines. Therefore, kernel space data are shared data. When the CPU is in the user state, there is no need to worry about that hostile applications making a mess with kernel space data, why? On the other hand, when the CPU is in kernel state, if it calls a function in user space, the whole security mechanism will be in vain, why?

2.6 Memory Sharing

The implementation of CPU sharing is given in Sect. 2.4. When the current process is waiting for an event, it gives up its CPU to other ready processes; (2) the ready processes are executed in turn by clock interrupts. CPU sharing is realized through the process manager. Memory is also a shared resource and is shared in the following way. When a process needs a memory resource, it requests it from the memory manager, which allocates a block of free memory to the requestor. When a process no longer needs the acquired memory resource, it should return it to the memory manager so that other processes can use it. This type of sharing is also common in everyday life. For example, this is the case with book sharing. A reader who wants to read a certain book requests it from the library. After reading it, the book is returned to the library, whereupon other readers can borrow it as well. Based on the above memory sharing scheme, the memory manager should provide two API functions for the application to call. One is *allocate*, which is used to request memory, and the other is *release*, which is used to return memory.

To implement memory sharing, the memory manager must know how much memory the system has and the current usage state of memory resource. The memory usage state refers to which memory blocks are currently free and which blocks are occupied by processes. For an occupied memory block, it is important to further record which process is occupying it. Thus, the memory manager has to maintain a memory block table, as shown in Table 2.2. The example data from this table show that the current memory is divided into four blocks. The first block has a memory starting address of 10,000,000 and a space size of 40,000,000 bytes, which is already occupied by the process with id 10. The starting address of each row of data in the

Table 2.2 Memory block table

startAddr	Size	State	processId
10,000,000	40,000,000	Used	10
50,000,000	10,000,000	Free	
60,000,000	20,000,000	Used	2
80,000,000	640,000,000	Free	

2.6 Memory Sharing

table plus the space size is the starting address value of the next row. The reason for keeping track of which process occupies an allocated block of memory is that when the process is terminated, all the memory it occupies is freed.

Allocating memory to a process is a matter of sequentially checking the memory blocks in the memory block table until a block of memory is found that has a status of free and a space size greater than or equal to the client's request. If the found memory block has a space size just equal to the client's request, it is allocated directly to the requestor. If it is larger than the customer's request, it will be split into two pieces, one of which is allocated to the applicant, and the other is kept as free. Based on this principle of memory allocation, the function *allocate* is implemented as shown in Code 2.10. The meaning of line 11 is: to insert a memory block into the memory block table. The insertion location is after the block referred to by the variable *block*.

Code 2.10 Implementation of the Function Allocate
```
(1)   byte * allocate( int neededSize) {
(2)      MemoryBlock *block = memoryBlockList->getFirstItem();
(3)      while (block ! = null) {
(4)         if (block->state == FREE && block->size >=
            neededSize) {
(5)            block->state = USED;
(6)            block->processId = currentProcess->id;
(7)            if (block->size > neededSize) {
(8)               int startAddr2 = block->startAddr + neededSize;
(9)               int size2 = block->size - neededSize;
(10)              MemoryBlock *block2 = new
               MemoryBlock(startAddr2, size2,FREE);
(11)              memoryBlockList->InsertItem(block2, block);
(12)           }
(13)           return (byte *)block->startAddr;
(14)        }
(15)        block = memoryBlockList->->getNextItem();
(16)     }
(17)     return null;
(18)  }
```

Reflection 2-13: When an application calls *release* to return occupied memory, it first finds the corresponding row in the memory block table. Check the row before it, and if it is free, merge both of them. Can you write the code to implement the function *release*?

2.7 Network Sharing

Two processes located on different computers can communicate with each other over a network. For multiple processes on the same computer, they share the network. That is, they all use the network to send data or receive data. Because the network is used by multiple processes, a network manager is necessary to manage it. The model of network sharing is that when a process wants to send data, it makes a request to the network manager and submits the data to the network manager. The network manager slices the data from client into small segments and sends them in turn, i.e., it takes turns to send the small segments of each process one by one by the network card. Since the sending time of each small segment is very short, it appears to a person as if there is a network for each process, and all processes are sending data at the same time. The same is true for receiving data. This shows that network sharing is similar to CPU sharing.

A process may have to communicate with more than one process at the same time, such as server programs. Imagine there is a communication channel between two processes, and both of them use this channel to send and receive data. A communication channel is also called a network connection. When a process communicates with more than one process at the same time, the process has more than one network connection, i.e., the process has a one-to-many relationship with the network connection. In addition, network connections are dynamic. The dynamic nature of network connections means that a process will establish a network connection only when it wants to communicate with another process. Once the communication is complete, the network connection should be released. Network connection is a function implemented through software. A process communicates with another one through a network connection. Therefore, the network manager should provide application programs with API functions (named *createConnection* and *releaseConnection*) to create and release a network connection. For a network connection, the send and receive functions should be provided for applications to call.

For a segment of data received from a network card, the network manager has to be able to recognize which network connection it belongs to. For this purpose, the network manager adds a network connection identifier to a customer's segment when it sends the segment. Thus, the receiver's network manager knows which network connection to deliver the received segment to. A segment with a network connection identifier is called a packet. From this, it can be seen that in order to achieve the function of network connection, a cost has been paid: when transmitting a segment of customer's data, an additional network connection identifier needs to be transmitted. The packet received from the network card thus consists of 2 parts: the customer's data and the network connection identifier.

There is a process of establishing a network connection. The communication between two processes is based on a C/S model: one process acts as a client and the other as a server. First, the server calls the function *createConnection* provided by the network manager to request for the creation of a network connection object

2.7 Network Sharing

dedicated to listening for connection requests from clients. Next, the client calls the function *createConnection* to request for the creation of a network connection object and send a network connection request to the server with the connection identification information of the client end attached. After receiving a client's connection request, the server applies to create a network connection object to interface with the client and informs the network manager to send the client a network connection response with the connection identification information of the server end. Once the client receives the connection response, it knows the server's connection information, and thus a complete network connection is established.

The network manager uses port numbers to identify network connections. Therefore, a network connection has a member variable, *port*, which records its own port number. In addition, there are member variables *oppositeIpAddr* and *oppositePort*, which record the IP address and port number, respectively, of the other party to the communication, thus identifying the other party's network connection. In addition, there are member variables *sendQueue*, *receiveQueue*, and *process*, where *sendQueue* is used to cache data to be sent by the process and *receiveQueue* is used to cache data received. Applications call the member function *receive* of the network connection to receive data. When there are no data in *receiveQueue*, the calling process moves to a wait state. When the network manager receives a packet from the network card, it changes the state of the calling process from WAITING to READY. The network manager uses the port information on the packet to find the corresponding network connection object, and then the process object by the member variable *process* of the network connection object.

A network interrupt is triggered when the NIC finishes sending a packet, or receives a packet. In the network interrupt handling routine, the event category identification data of the NIC are read first. If it is a send completion event, the next packet is sent. If it is a receive event, it will first find the corresponding network connection object based on the connection identification information of the packet, and then the receiving process object based on the member variable *process* of the network connection object. If the receiving process is waiting to receive data from the network, i.e., its *state* and *waitforEvent* attributes are WAITING and NETWORKRECEIVE, respectively, its state attribute is changed from waiting to ready. Otherwise, the data of the packet are placed in *receiveQueue* of the network connection object. The implementation of the network interrupt handling routine is shown in Code 2.11.

In Code 2.11, the meaning of lines 3 and 5 are: read interrupt category identification data and the received packet from the NIC, respectively. *ConnectionList*, *sendingProcess*, and *ipAddr*, appearing in lines 6, 16, and 21, respectively, are global variables in the operating system, storing the network connection objects, the process whose data are currently being sent by the NIC, and the IP address of the computer, respectively. All network connection objects created by the application program are placed in the global variable *connectionList*. The meaning of line 18 is to determine which network connection object to be selected based on the send scheduling scheme. The selected network connection object has data waiting to be sent by the NIC. If there are no data waiting to be sent from any of the network connection objects, the return value of *getNextItemWithDataToSend* is null. Line 22 means to output the packet to the network card, which will send it. Line 28 checks whether a process is currently running. If not, a process switch operation is performed. *checkCurrentProcess* is implemented in Code 2.7.

Code 2.11 Implementation of Network Interrupt Handling Routine

```
(1)   void networkInteruptionHandler() {
(2)      Process *process = null;
(3)      int eventId = fetchEventId();
(4)      if (eventId == RECEIVE) {
(5)         Packet *packet = (Packet * )fetchData( );
(6)         Connection *conn = ConnectionList->getItemById(
            packet->oppositePort);
(7)         process = conn->process;
(8)         if (process->state == WAITING && process-
            >waitForEvent == NETWORKRECEIVE) {
(9)            *conn->receiveBuffer = (byte *) packet->data;
(10)           process->state = READY;
(11)        }
(12)        else
(13)           conn->receiveQueue->addItem( packet->data);
(14)     }
(15)        else if (eventId == SEND_FINISH) { // the NIC has
            finished sending a packet
(16)           process = sendingProcess;
(17)           sendingProcess->state = READY;
(18)           Connection * conn = ConnectionList-
               >getNextItemWithDataToSend( );
(19)           if (conn ! = null ) {
(20)              byte * data = conn->sendQueue-
                  >pickOutSegment( );
(21)              Packet *packet = new Packet(data, ipAddr,
                  conn->port, conn->oppositeIpAddr,
                  conn->oppositePort);
(22)              networkOutput(packet); //submit to network
                  card to send
(23)              sendingProcess = conn->process;
(24)        }
(25)           else
(26)              sendingProcess = null;
(27)     }
(28)     checkCurrentProcess(process ); // see Code 2.7 for
         implementation
(29)  }
```

2.7 Network Sharing

The application calls the function *send* to send data by network. This function is a synchronized function, which means that when sending data, the function will not return until the data have been sent out by the network card. In other words, after the process calls this function, it changes to a wait state. Until a network interrupt is triggered, the network interrupt handling routine changes its state to ready. *send* is implemented as shown in Code 2.12. When a process sends data, the NIC may be busy with data from another process, identified by the global variable *sendingProcess* not being null. In this situation, the data to be sent are placed in the network connection's send queue, *sendQueue*, and scheduled to be sent by the network manager. If the NIC is idle, it is submitted to the NIC for sending. Finally, the sending process is transferred to the wait state, whereupon the function *giveUpCPU* is called to perform the process switch, as shown in line 14. See Code 2.4 for the implementation of the function *giveUpCPU*.

Code 2.12 Implementation of the Function Send
```
(1)   void send( int connectionId, byte * dataToSend) {
(2)     INT 90( connectionId, dataToSend);
(3)     return;
(4)   }
(5)   void int90Handler(int connectionId, byte * dataToSend) {
(6)     Connection * conn =
          ConnectionList->getItemById(connectionId);
(7)     if (sendingProcess == null) {
(8)       sendingProcess = currentProcess;
(9)       Packet *packet = new Packet(dataToSend, ipAddr,
          conn->port, conn->oppositeIpAddr,
          conn->oppositePort);
(10)      networkOutput(packet);
(11)    }
(12)    else
(13)      conn->sendQueue->addItem(dataToSend);
(14)    giveUpCPU( NETWORKSEND );
(15)  }
```

Applications call the function *receive* to receive network data. This function is also a synchronized function, and will not return until network data have been received. Before this function is called, if network data have been received, it is put in the receive queue of network connection. Thus, the calling process can get it directly. However, it is possible that the network data have not been received. In this situation, the calling process has to transfer to the waiting state, and calls the function *giveUpCPU* to perform process switching. Until a network interrupt is triggered, the network interrupt handling routine changes its state to ready. The receive function is implemented as shown in Code 2.13. Note that for synchronization functions [1], the return value is usually undetermined when the soft interrupt handling routine is called, as is the case with the receive function. If the network data have not been received, the location in memory where the subsequently received network data are stored is still undetermined. Only after a network interrupt is triggered is the location determined in the network interrupt handling routine.

For synchronization functions, the data type of the return value can only be void. The reason is that in soft interrupt handling routines, it is not usual to execute the *iRet* instruction, but rather to execute the process switch or the pause instruction *halt*. That is to say, many of the soft interrupt handling routines are not able to determine the result of the return. The return result has to be determined in other interrupt handling routines. For example, the return result of the function *waitForKeyboardInput* is determined in the keyboard input interrupt handling routine. The return result of the receive function is sometimes determined in the network interrupt handling routine. Therefore, for synchronization functions, the return result must be achieved through a formal parameter. When calling a synchronous function, only the address of the variable can be passed as a formal parameter to obtain the return result.

Code 2.13 Implementation of the Receive Function
```
(1)   void receive( int connectionId, byte ** receiveBuffer) {
(2)     INT 91( connectionId, receiveBuffer );
(3)     return;
(4)   }
(5)   void int91Handler(int connectionId, byte **receiveBuffer ) {
(6)     Connection * conn = ConnectionList->getItemById(connectionId);
(7)     *receiveBuffer = conn->receiveQueue->pickOutData( );
(8)     if (*receiveBuffer ! = null)
(9)        iRet;
(10)    else {
(11)      conn->receiveBuffer = receiveBuffer;
(12)      giveUpCPU( NETWORKRECEIVE );
(13)    }
(14)  }
```

An example of calling synchronous functions, *waitForKeyboardInput* and *receive,* is shown in Code 2.14. Here, the address of the variable is passed respectively. In the *waitForKeyboardInput* call, the application program has prepared storage space for the character line to be received. In the receive call, the application has only prepared a pointer variable, data2, to store the starting address of the received network data in memory. In the soft interrupt handling routine of

2.7 Network Sharing

waitForKeyboardInput, the value of the formal parameter is assigned to the global variable *charBuffer*, see line 6 in Code 2.5. In the soft interrupt handling routine of *receive*, the value of the formal parameter is assigned to the member variable of the network connection object, *receiveBuffer*, as shown in line 11 of Code 2.13. The network connection objects are placed in the global variable *connectionList* and are therefore equivalent to global variables. So, in the keyboard interrupt handling routine, you can put the received character into data1; in the network interrupt handling routine, you can assign a value to data2. The result is returned.

Code 2.14 Example of Calling Synchronous Functions
```
(1) byte data1[100];
(2) byte *data2;
(3) waitForKeyboardInput( data1 );
(4) receive( &data2 );
```

Reflection 2-14: For server programs, the network connection object, which is dedicated to listening for connection requests, is used only to receive connection requests, so there is no need to assign values to the member variables *oppositeIpAddr* and *oppositePort*. When creating a network connection object, you can specify a port number or ask the operating system to assign one. Network connection objects in the network connection table *connectionList* are not allowed to have the same port number. How does the operating system manage port numbers? Can you write the implementation code for the function *createConnection*?

Reflection 2-15: In socket programming, the functionality of the connect function is to send a connection request to the server's listening network connection object through a created network connection object, and then wait to receive the connection response. After receiving the connection response, it assigns values to the two member variables of the network connection object, *oppositeIpAddr* and *oppositePort*. Can you write an implementation of the connect function by referring to that of *createConnection*, *send*, and *receive*?

Reflection 2-16: In socket programming, the functionality of the accept function is to receive a connection request of a client from a listening network connection object. Once a connection request is received, a new network connection object is created and a connection response is sent to the requester through this new network connection object. Can you write the implementation code for the accept function by referring to that of *createConnection*, *send*, and *receive*?

Reflection 2-17: What role does the listen function play in socket programming? Are *createConnection* and *listen* synchronous wait functions?

Reflection 2-18: When a process is executing a soft interrupt handling routine, or when the CPU is executing a hard interrupt handling routine, if a hard interrupt is triggered again, then it may cause incorrect data in the operating system. What is the reason? One solution is to mask interrupts when a process is executing a soft interrupt handling routine or the CPU is executing a hard interrupt handling routine, so that the execution of the interrupt handling routine will not be interrupted and will be atomic. What does interrupt mask mean? Is it ignoring the interrupt to be triggered? Why?

2.8 Code Sharing

When a computer runs a program, it loads it from disk into memory, then finds the starting address of its main function in memory, loads it into the instruction register, and starts it running. After the CPU executes an instruction, it can figure out the memory address of the next instruction to be executed, and then puts it into the instruction register, whereupon the CPU executes the next instruction. The process continues iteratively. When the program is running, the data and code in memory are identified by memory addresses. This requires the compiler to know the memory address of each item of data and of each instruction in the code at the time it generates an executable file. Assuming that the starting address of the executable in memory is a known constant at runtime, the compiler will be able to figure out the memory address of each item of data in the executable and each instruction in the code when it generates the code instruction by instruction, and therefore will be able to generate the executable.

When the computer is running only one program, the entire memory space is free and available. There is no problem in loading the executable file into the memory location set for it at compile time. The location conflict problem arises when the computer executes multiple programs at the same time. Assuming that the compiler specifies a memory start location of 1000 for the executable, then at runtime each program asks to be loaded into memory at location 1000, but only one program is actually allowed to be loaded into that location. This is a specific case of a location conflict.

One way to resolve location conflicts is to perform address relocation of the program code after loading the executable into memory if the loaded location is not where it was intended to be. Address relocation [9] means scanning and parsing the entire program code for all address constants and then modifying them. For example, if an executable file is loaded at a predefined location of 1000, but is actually loaded into memory at 3000, then each of the address constants in the code should be processed by adding 2000 to make the code refer to the same address as the actual address. Address relocation brings the problem of long program startup time. Because relocation calculations are large, time-consuming, especially when the program code is large. In many application scenarios, it is unacceptable to have a long program startup time.

The above problem is also known as the misalignment problem. A mismatch is when the memory address value referred to in the program code does not match the actual memory address value at runtime. Another solution to the mismatch problem is to improve the computer itself by adding relative addressing. Relative addressing means that before the CPU executes an instruction, when its parameter is a memory

2.8 Code Sharing

address constant, it treats it as a relative address and adds it to the base address to obtain its absolute address. In other words, in the process of CPU executing an instruction, a link is added to derive the absolute address from the relative address. For example, at compile time, it is set that the executable will be loaded into memory at location 1000 at runtime. At runtime, if the executable is loaded at location 9000, the base address will be 8000. The difference between relative addressing and relocation is that relocation is a one-time event that occurs before the program is run for the actual address calculation, while relative addressing is a real-time event that occurs while the program is running.

Relative addressing makes it possible for an executable file to run correctly regardless of where it is loaded in memory at runtime. However, a program usually does not consist of just one executable file, but of an executable file containing the main function and several library files. Such programs are called multimodule programs. In contrast, a program consisting of a single executable file is called a single-module program. Dividing an application program into multiple modules has two advantages. The first is that it is easy to assemble and maintain. When an upgraded version of a module is available, or when it needs to be replaced by another module with the same interface, it is not necessary to recompile the entire application. It is sufficient to make an overriding substitution for the module being replaced. An additional benefit is the implementation of module sharing in a multitasking environment. For shared modules, only one copy is stored on disk and only one copy is loaded in memory. Thus, storage space is saved.

For two programs, A and B, running simultaneously on a single computer, one or more library files may be part of both. For example, library files provided by the C language are a part of almost every application program. Assuming that program A starts running first and program B starts running later, library α is part of both program A and program B. When loading program B, the ideal situation is that program B does not have to reload its own library α into memory, but instead shares the library α that has been loaded by program A. The library α then has only one copy in memory, saving memory space. This is the specific case of module sharing.

While module sharing saves storage space, it also brings about new problems. The first is the compile-time code generation problem. What to do about cross-module references, such as cross-module function calls? Since the called function is in another module, the memory address of the called function is not known when generating the call instruction. Therefore, for cross-module function calls, a code generation problem is encountered. One of the ways to solve this problem is to set the memory address of each module that makes up the application to be loaded at runtime at compile time. Based on this setting, the memory address of the called function can be calculated. Address relocation is then performed before the program is run. Address relocation will be explained in detail in Sect. 2.8.1. Another way is to add indirect addressing to the computer to solve the problem of cross-module references. Section 2.8.2 will explain the solution based on indirect addressing.

For module sharing in a multitasking environment, the shared content is only the code; the data part is not shared, but each process has its own copy. This creates a new problem. Module sharing is not considered at compilation time, and it is assumed that there is only one copy of the data in the module in memory. How to realize the need to share code but keep data private while keeping the compilation model the same? Section 2.8.3 will explain the solution based on virtual memory. In addition, with code sharing, there is a natural problem of code reentry. That is, the code can be executed by multiple processes, with the effect that the code is the same, but the data handled are not the same. Each process, while executing the same code, handles completely different data, i.e., data are private to a process. The method of achieving this effect is explained in Sect. 2.8.4.

2.8.1 Address Relocation

The compile-time memory layout of multiple modules that make up an application may be inconsistent with the run-time memory layout, causing the application to fail to run. An example is given to illustrate the situation. Suppose program A consists of module *a.exe* and *d.dll* and program B consists of module *b.exe* and *d.dll*. Both of them are compiled with the memory layout of the *d.dll* file immediately after the exe file, as shown in Fig. 2.1a. Program A is started up first to run, and then program B is started up. For program A, the compile-time memory layout is identical to the run-time memory layout. For program B, its own *d.dll* will not be loaded into memory anymore because it may share program A's *d.dll*. The sharing results in the runtime layout of program B being different from the compile-time layout, as shown in Fig. 2.1b. For program B, *d.dll* is not immediately after *b.exe*, resulting in misplaced references to *d.dll* in *b.exe* (such as function calls), i.e., the address in code does not match the real one. Thus, program B cannot run normally.

The above problem is also known as the cross-module reference problem. Cross-module access by direct addressing requires that the memory layout of the modules at runtime follows the compile-time settings, and that the size of each module does not change due to version upgrades. The reason is that the addresses in the code are constants. In other words, the modules that make up an application cannot be changed; otherwise, the addresses in the code will not match its real one at runtime.

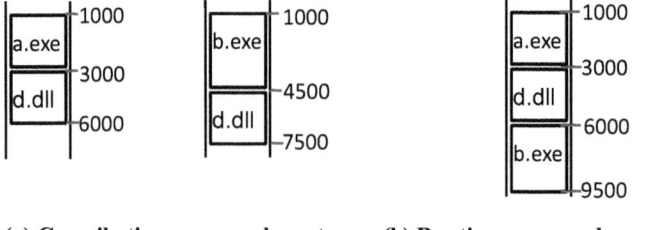

(a) Compile-time memory layout   (b) Runtime memory layout

Fig. 2.1 Differences between the compile-time layout and the actual layout at runtime. (a) Compile-time memory layout. (b) Runtime memory layout

2.8 Code Sharing

It can be seen that when direct addressing is used, an application consisting of multiple independent executable files becomes meaningless, and it is better to combine the modules that make up an application into a single executable file, i.e., a single-module program, at compile time.

The above problem of cross-module references can be solved by performing address relocation before running the program. Address relocation here refers to the relocation of cross-module references. Compared with the relocation of a single module, for an address constant appearing in the code of a module, it can be either an outer address or an inner address. An inner address points to one data or an instruction in the module, while an outer address points to one data or an instruction in an external module. For example, in an instruction in *b.exe* that calls a function in *d.dll*, the address constant pointing to the function is an outer address. Two types of addresses should be relocated by different base address. Taking Fig. 2.1b as an example, *b.exe* is set to locate at address 1000 at compile time, and its size is 3500 bytes, and *d.dll* comes immediately after *b.exe*, and its size is 3000 bytes. Thus, *d.dll* locates at address 4500 at compile time, as shown in Fig. 2.1a.

Now, assume that *b.exe* and *d.dll* are actually loaded in memory at addresses 6000 and 3000, respectively, as shown in Fig. 2.1b. Thereby, the inner address constants that appear in the *b.exe* code should be processed by adding 5000, while the outer address constants (pointing to the contents in *d.dll*) that appear in the *b.exe* code should be processed by subtracting 1500. Furthermore, the compile-time layout shows that if an address constant appearing in the *b.exe* code ranges from 1000 to 4500, it is an inner address. If it ranges from 4500 to 7500, it is an outer address pointing to the contents in *d.dll*. Therefore, if you encounter an address constant in *b.exe* that is 3024, relocate it to 8024; if an address constant is 5264, relocate it to 3764.

Reflection 2-19: How are the above 8024 and 3764 calculated, respectively?

From the above analysis, it can be seen that if direct addressing is used at compile time, the advantage is that the addresses are all actual values, and the runtime code execution is efficient. The problem is that any module that constitutes the application at runtime has to be loaded into the memory location set at compile time. This requirement is usually not satisfied, especially in a multitasking runtime environment. To solve the misplacement problem, address relocation is performed. Address relocation involves scanning and parsing the entire code. Not only is it necessary to identify the address constant in the code, but also to determine to which module it is pointing to data or code. Then, based on the actual loaded address of the target module in memory, its new address is calculated and the old address is replaced.

Reflection 2-20: For a single-tasking environment, the operating system itself can be considered as one program and the application program as another. Therefore, in a single-tasking environment, the application program has to be loaded to the location predetermined at compile time, which is usually still not satisfied at runtime, why?

When starting up a program, to relocate the outer addresses, the executor has to know the memory layout of the program at the time of compilation. For example, in the above example, when encountering an address constant of 5264 in *b.exe*, how do you know that it is an outer address? How do you know that it is an address that points to the contents in *d.dll*? To be able to relocate, it is necessary to note down in the *b.exe* file the memory layout information at compile time as follows: (1) the starting memory address of *b.exe* is 1000, and the size is 3500; (2) the starting memory address of *d.dll* is 4500, and the size is 3000. When relocating, it is also necessary to know the actual starting address of *d.dll* in memory. Only after knowing this information can relocation be realized. The compile-time memory layout information of the modules included in the application program *B* is shown in Table 2.3.

To realize the relocation, there should be a module loading manager, which is responsible for the two tasks of module loading and relocation. The module loading manager provides the API function *loadLibarary* for applications to call in order to load and run a program. The module loading manager keeps track of loaded module so that when the user requests a module to be loaded, it knows whether the module has been loaded into memory. If it has been loaded, it should not be loaded again. The load information includes the filename of the module, and the module's start and end addresses in memory. A record of the memory space occupied by loaded modules at runtime is shown in Table 2.4. When a newly loaded module needs to be relocated, use this table to calculate the new address constants in the code.

The implementation of relocation is shown in Code 2.15. When a user requests a module to be loaded, the manager first looks up in the module record table based on the module filename to see if it has already been loaded into memory or not. If not, it is loaded into memory and then recorded to the module record table. This process is shown in lines 1–4 of Code 2.15. For a newly loaded module in memory, its code is scanned and parsed to find out all address constants to be relocated, as shown in lines 5–19. During the scanning process, for each address encountered, it is necessary to determine its type (outer or inner) according to the compile-time memory layout information contained in the module itself (shown in Table 2.3. If it is an outer address, it is necessary to further find out what module it points to.

Table 2.3 Compile-time memory layout of the modules making up the application

Module name	Starting address	End address
b.exe	1000	4500
d.dll	4500	7500

Table 2.4 Memory space occupied by loaded modules in ModuleList

Module name	Starting address	Final address
a.exe	1000	3000
d.dll	3000	6000
b.exe	6000	9500
……	……	……

2.8 Code Sharing

Code 2.15 Implementation of Address Relocation

```
     Byte * loadLibarary( char * fileName) {
(1)    Module *curModule = moduleList->getItemByName(fileName);
(2)    if(curModule == null) {
(3)       curModule = loadFileFromDisk(fileName);
(4)       moduleList->addItem(curModule);
(5)       Address *addrValue =
          curModule->parseFirstAddrValue();
(6)       while(addrValue) {
(7)          if (*addrValue >= curModule->CompileStartAddr &&
             *addrValue < curModule->CompileEndAddr) {
(8)             if (curModule->CompileStartAddr ! =
                curModule->loadedStartAddr)
(9)                *addrValue = *addrValue +
                   (curModule->loadedStartAddr - curModule-
                   >CompileStartAddr);
(10)         }
(11)         else {
(12)            ReferencedModuleInfo *p;
(13)            p = curModule->getReferencedModuleByAddr(*addrVa
                lue);
(14)            Module *referencedModule =
                moduleList->getItemByName(p->fileName);
(15)            if (referencedModule->loadedStartAddr ! =
                p->compileStartAddr)
(16)               *addrValue = *addrValue +
                   (referencedModule->loadedStartAddr -
                   p->compileStartAddr);
(17)         }
(18)         addrValue = curModule->parseNextAddrValue();
(19)      }
(20)   }
(21)   return curModule->loadedStartAddr;
(22) }
```

Take the *b.exe* module shown in Table 2.3 as an example, when it is loaded into the memory at the actual location of 6000. From the compile-time memory layout table contained in itself (as shown in Table 2.3), it can be seen that it is necessary to implement address relocation for *b.exe*. When scanning and parsing its code, if an address constant is found out with the value of 5264, it can be seen from the compile-time memory layout table contained in *b.exe* itself that it points to *d.dll*. This determination is shown in line 13 of Code 2.15. The next step is to look at the actual location in memory where *d.dll* is loaded. At this point, it is necessary to go to the memory space occupied by the loaded modules recorded in *ModuleList* (such as

Table 2.4) to get the information of *d.dll*. From this, we can see that the actual starting address of *d.dll* in memory is 3000, which is not consistent with the location 4500 set by *b.exe* during compilation. Therefore, to relocate 5264 to 5264 + (3000−45,000) = 3764.

Suppose an address 3024 is encountered, which is known to be inner from the compile-time memory layout table contained in *b.exe* itself. This determination is shown in line 7 of Code 2.15. At this point, it is necessary to see whether the actual address of *b.exe* being loaded in memory is consistent with the address set at compile time. If it does not, address relocation is performed. From the *ModuleList*, a record of the memory space occupied by loaded modules is shown in Table 2.4. It can be seen that relocation is required, with 3024 relocated to 3024 + (6000−1000) = 8024.

As can be seen from Code 2.15, address relocation is a very time-consuming task. Not only does relocation involve parsing the machine code to identify the address constants, but it also involves identifying the module to which the address points and then performing the relocation computation to modify the machine code. All these tasks are very time-consuming, especially when the program is long. Address relocation results in long program startup time, which is unacceptable in many scenarios.

2.8.2 Cross-Module Function Call Based on Indirect Addressing

Indirect addressing is the intermediary to get the memory address of the instruction or data in an external module at runtime. In module *b.exe*, how to call function *f1* in module *d.dll*? The scheme based on address relocation described in the previous section is to scan and parse the whole code of *b.exe*, find out the address constants in it and identify its type (outer or inner), and then modify it to make it consistent with the actual memory location. The concept of indirect addressing is proposed to eliminate the above scanning, parsing, recognizing, calculating, and modifying, so that *b.exe* can start up quickly. The strategy is that a space location is set aside in *b.exe* to store the starting address of the function *f1* at runtime. The space location is named as variable *f1Addr*. When generating code in *b.exe* for calling function *f1*, call instruction is chosen based on indirect addressing, rather than on direct addressing. When indirect addressing is applied, the instruction parameter is not the memory address of the function *f1*, but the memory address of the variable *f1Addr*.

Indirect addressing requires that the memory address of the function *f1* be filled into the variable *f1Addr* before *b.exe* starts running. The solution is to dedicate a space location in *d.dll* to store the relative address value of function *f1*. Name this space location as the variable *f1RelativeAddr*, whose value is the offset of function *f1* in *d.dll*. This offset can be calculated at compile time and is a constant. At runtime, after loading *b.exe* and *d.dll* into memory, the loaded address of *d.dll* is the base address of the function *f1*. The value of this base address plus the value of

2.8 Code Sharing

f1RelativeAddr is the actual memory address of the function *f1*, which is assigned to the variable *f1Addr* in *b.exe* to complete the initialization before startup.

To complete the initialization of *b.exe* before it starts, it is necessary not only to know that it calls a function in the external module *d.dll* in order to load *d.dll* from disk into memory, but also to know the relative address of the variable *f1Addr* in *b.exe* in order to assign a value to it. In addition to this, the relative address of the variable *f1RelativeAddr* in *d.dll* has to be known in order to read its value. To answer the above 3 questions, you need to build the function import table in *b.exe* and the function export table in *d.dll*. In the case of *b.exe*, for any external function it calls, it should be recorded in the function import table of *b.exe*. In the case of *d.dll*, for all the functions that it opens to external calls, they should be recorded in the function export table of *d.dll*. Examples of the function import table in *b.exe* and the function export table in *d.dll* are shown in Tables 2.5 and 2.6, respectively.

Assuming that the program *b.exe* needs to be run, the initialization process before startup is as follows. Load the file *b.exe* into memory, assuming it is loaded to memory location 2000. After loading, check its function import table (shown in Table 2.5), from which it is clear that it has to call the *f1* and *f2* functions in the module *d.dll*, as well as the *sin* function in the module *m.dll*. So the files *d.dll* and *m.dll* are loaded from disk into memory. Suppose they are loaded to memory addresses 5000 and 8000, respectively. From the function import table in *b.exe*, it is clear that functions *f1* and *f2* in file *d.dll* are to be called, so the function export table in file *d.dll* is examined (shown in Table 2.6). The relative addresses of functions *f1* and *f2* are 448 and 892, respectively. The relative address plus the base address is the absolute address, so that the actual memory addresses of functions *f1* and *f2* are 5448 and 5892, respectively, which are filled into the third column of the first and second rows of the function import table in *b.exe*, respectively. Do the same for row 3. After filling in the function import table in *b.exe*, you can execute the program *b.exe*.

From the above scenario, it is clear that function import and export tables play a bridge role in realizing cross-module function calls. When a function is open to the public, the compiler creates the function export table in generating the executable. If the source program calls a function from an external module, the compiler creates

Table 2.5 Function import table example

Module file name	Function name	Memory address
d.dll	f1	
d.dll	f2	
m.dll	sin	

Table 2.6 Function export table example

Function name	Relative address
f1	448
f2	892
f3	2064

a function import table in generating the executable. If an executable has both, then both of function import and function export tables are created. In the source program, you should let the compiler know whether the functions you have implemented are open to the public or not, and you should let the compiler know whether the functions you want to call are from external modules or not. In C/C++ language, for example, when the modifier export is added to a function definition, it indicates that the function is open to the public; when the modifier import is added to a function definition, it indicates that the function comes from an external module. For functions from the outside, the link should also specify the filename of the external module.

In the above scenario of filling in the function import table, how do I know the memory addresses of the function import and function export tables? How do I know the memory address of each row of data in both tables, and the memory address of each column in each row? Only if the above two questions are answered can the contents of the two tables be read and column 3 of the function import table be filled in. The answer to this question relates to the data structure of executables and library files. In any operating system, the data structure of executables and library files is defined and publicized. For example, the data structure is known as the PE format in Windows operating systems and the ELF format in Linux operating systems. Compiler vendors then generate executables and library files based on the data structure published by the operating system vendor. Thus, after an executable file is loaded from disk into memory, it is an instance object of an executable file. The function import table and function export table are both its member variables, and their relative addresses are both known constants.

Both the function import and function export tables also have data structures. In the case of the row in the function import table, for example, the data structure is defined as: class *importRow* {char * *moduleName*; char * *functionName*; unsigned int *functionAdd*r;}. It can be seen that the length of each row of data is a known constant, and the length of each column of data in the row is also a known constant. Therefore, no problems are encountered in figuring out the relative address of each data item in the function import and function export tables. The relative address of the data item plus the base address (i.e., the loaded address of the module in memory) is the absolute address of the data item.

Reflection 2-21: In the definition of the data structure of the executable, the relative address of the main function is its member variable. Imagine what other member variables should be present? What is the data type of each member variable?

Compared with the address relocation method, the advantage of indirect addressing to realize the call of the function in the external module is that there is no need to scan, parse, identify, calculate, and modify the code, but only needs to fill in the function import table. Therefore, it can realize the fast startup of the program. But along with the benefits, there are also costs. Indirect addressing is obviously not as efficient as direct addressing. However, calls to functions in external modules are usually infrequent during program execution, so the overhead is usually small.

2.8.3 Static Versus Dynamic Links

Traditionally, compilation is divided into two sections: compilation and linking. The compilation translates each source program file into a target code file. For example, when running on a Windows operating system, Microsoft Compiler CL compiles a C/C++ source program file with the suffix .c or .cpp into an object code file with the suffix .obj. The linking combines multiple object code files into a single executable file. In the Windows operating system, the executable file has the suffix .exe or .dll. The problem to be solved by linking is mainly the data references and function calls across module boundaries, i.e., the generation of function export and import tables in each executable file.

There are two types of linking patterns: static and dynamic. When a function open to the public in an external library file is called in the project source program, if static linking is selected, then the external library file is also merged into the executable file. Thus, all function calls are within-module calls. In this case, the function import table and the function export table are not required. Advantages of static links are: (1) no need for the target computer to support indirect addressing; (2) highly efficient function calls. The disadvantage is that when the referenced library file has a version update, it is necessary to re-link to generate a new executable file.

If dynamic linking is chosen, the referenced external library file remains independent and is not incorporated into the executable. The advantage of dynamic linking is that when a referenced library file is updated, the old version is replaced with the new version without re-linking. In addition, in a multitasking environment, the referenced library file can be shared by multiple processes, thus saving memory space. The disadvantages of dynamic linking are: (1) it requires the computer running the program to support indirect addressing; (2) function calls are not as efficient as static linking because of indirect addressing.

Reflective 2-22: Embedded applications are characterized by clear and fixed functionality, are not complex, and run in a single-task environment. When linking such applications, should you choose static or dynamic linking? In contrast, complex applications such as browsers run in a multitasking environment, have many referenced libraries, and have frequent version updates. When linking to such applications, should you choose static or dynamic linking?

2.8.4 Base Address Selection in Relative Addressing

Accessing instructions or data within a module by relative addressing does not affect program operation regardless of where in memory the module is loaded. In relative addressing, there is a base address selection problem. If the loaded address of a module is used as the base address, then for a multi-module program, each module has its own base address, which is different from each other. When a cross-module jump occurs due to a function call, the base address must follow. The same is true when the function returns. Here is an example. Assume that the base address is stored in the base address register. When the CPU executes the code in module A, the base address stored in the base address register is that of module A. When jumping from module A to module B, the value in the base address register is first pressed into the base address stack to free up the base address register to store the base address of module B. After the function returns, the top element of the base address stack is popped into the base address register. Thus, the base address of module A is restored to the base address register.

It can be seen that there are differences between cross-module function calls and within-module function calls. A function call within a module is called a local call and does not involve a base address switch. A cross-module function call is called a far call and involves two base address switches. The first switch is executed before the jump and the second switch is executed after the return. For the called function, it does not know whether the caller is from this module or from an external module. Therefore, for cross-module function calls, both base address switches can only be performed by the caller. For the caller, when it calls a function, it knows whether it is a far call or a local call. Therefore, it knows whether to perform a base address switch or not.

For cross-module function calls, a base address switch is performed before the call. This requires the caller to know the base address of the called module. For this reason, a column is added to the function import table to record the base address of the external modules. In the initialization work before startup, when filling in the function import table, the contents include the memory address of the called function, as well as the base address of the called module.

Taking the loaded address of the module in memory as the base address seems very reasonable, but for cross-module memory access, there is not only storage overhead, but also base address switching overhead. The storage overhead is manifested in three places: (1) a register has to be used to store the base address of the current module exclusively; (2) a column has to be added to the function import table to store the base address of the module being called; and (3) the value of the base address register has to be pressed into the base address stack when an external function is called. The switching overhead is manifested in two places: (1) when calling an external function, the current base address has to be saved to the stack, and then the base address of the called module has to be loaded into the base address register; (2) after the function returns, the base address of the caller's module has to be popped from the stack and restored to the base address register.

Both of these overheads can be eliminated entirely if the value in the instruction register is used as the base address. The instruction register stores the absolute address in memory of the next instruction to be executed. Notate the memory address at which the module is loaded as L_a; notate the absolute address in memory of the next instruction to be executed currently in the module as I_a, stored in the instruction register. The relative address of I_a with respect to the starting location of the module is noted as R_0. Then, we have $I_a = L_a + R_0$. The absolute address of an instruction or one data in the module is noted as x. Then we have $x = L_a + R_{x,0}$, where

$R_{x,0}$ is the offset (i.e., the relative address) of the instruction or data with respect to the address of the module being loaded. At compile time, both R_0 and $R_{x,0}$ are constants.

Now let's calculate the relative address value $R_{x,I}$ of the above instruction or data with respect to I_a. From the definition of $R_{x,I}$, it follows that $x = I_a + R_{x,I}$. From the three equations $I_a = L_a + R_0$, $x = L_a + R_{x,0}$, $x = I_a + R_{x,I}$, it follows that $R_{x,I} = R_{x,0} - R_0$, where R_0 and $R_{x,0}$ are constants at compile time, and so $R_{x,I}$ is a constant at compile time as well. Therefore, it is perfectly feasible to use the value in the instruction register as the base address. The instruction register is set up specifically for program execution. The compiler exploits the value in the instruction register by using it as the base address. Therefore, the base address register can then be eliminated. In addition, using the loaded address of the module as the base address has storage and switching overhead for across module accesses. By using the value in the instruction register as the base address, this overhead is eliminated. This solution also makes the far call no different from the local call.

Reflection 2-23: Local function calls apply relative addressing. Suppose a local call instruction in the code is: call $-496(I_a)$, where -496 is the relative address and I_a is the value in the instruction register, i.e., the base address. Suppose the CPU runs to this locally called instruction and the value in the instruction register is 8324, i.e., the absolute address of this locally called instruction in memory is 8324. What is the value of the starting address of the called function in memory?

Reflection 2-24: Indirect addressing is used for cross-module function calls. Let the instruction to call the external function $f1$ somewhere in the executable file A be: *far call ptr* $- 992(I_a)$, where ptr is the abbreviation of pointer, which means indirect addressing, i.e., $-992(I_a)$ is the memory address in the function import table that records the data in the third column of the row of the function $f1$, and its content is the starting address of the called function in memory. Suppose the CPU runs to this remote call instruction with a value of 8884 in the instruction register, i.e., the absolute address of this remote call instruction in memory is 8884. What is the value of the memory address in column 3 of the row recording function $f1$ in the function import table of file A?

2.8.5 Virtual Memory

In multitasking environments, modules cannot be loaded into the location set at compile time, causing misalignment problems and preventing the program from running. For this reason, a relative addressing solution is introduced so that intra-module references occurring in the code are no longer affected by where the module is loaded. For cross-module references, an indirect addressing solution is introduced so that the code is written at compile time and does not need to be relocated at runtime. As a result, code in executables and libraries has read-only properties, enabling fast startup and reliable operation of programs. However, the module sharing problem is not completely solved. The reason is that a module consists of two parts: code and data, and module sharing means code sharing. The data in the module are not shared. Let there are n processes sharing module A, then the data part of module A has n copies in memory, one for each process. But the code will only access one of those copies. Thus, multiprocess sharing of the module runs into a problem.

For the case of data not shared in module sharing, an example is given. Program A consists of $a.exe$ and the library file $d.dll$, implying that the data in $d.dll$ belongs to program A. Program B consists of $b.exe$ and the library file $d.dll$, implying that the data in $d.dll$ belongs to program B. Suppose that program A is started up to run first. When $d.dll$ is loaded, its code and data are loaded into memory. When program B is started up, the module manager sees that $d.dll$ has been loaded into memory and stops loading its code portion, but its data portion still needs to be loaded from disk into memory. The memory layout after loading program B is shown in Fig. 2.2. There are two copies of the data portion of $d.dll$. The first copy starts in memory at 4000 and is attributed to program A. The second copy starts in memory at 9500 and is attributed to program B. However, for the code of $d.dll$, it will only access the data in the first copy and not the data in the second copy because the code is designed to do so without considering sharing.

In order to realize the expectation that code is shared in a module but data are not, a solution based on virtual memory is proposed. With the concept of virtual memory, executables and libraries compiled for a single-task environment can be shared by multiple processes in a multitasking environment. Module sharing means only the code is shared by multiple processes, while each process has its own copy of data in memory. Those copies are separated from each other.

In virtual memory-based solutions, the memory addresses that appear in executables and library files are called virtual memory addresses. When a program is running, before the CPU executes a machine instruction, it performs address mapping to convert a virtual memory address to a physical memory address, and then accesses the memory data based on the physical memory address. The processing is similar to address relocation. In address relocation, the memory space is divided into segments based on the modules that have been loaded in memory, and then a lookup matching strategy is used to determine the module to which an address is attributed, and then the new address value is calculated. In the virtual memory scheme, each segment has the same fixed size of memory space. Thus, a segment of memory is

Fig. 2.2 Example of data not shared in module sharing

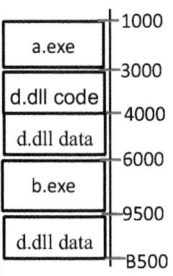

2.8 Code Sharing

called a page of memory. The size of a page of memory is denoted by *pageSize* and is a constant.

Instead of looking up a table to determine the page number in the conversion of a virtual memory address to a physical memory address, the page number is derived directly by dividing the virtual memory address value *virtualAddr* by *pageSize*. In addition, each process maintains a mapping table, which records the starting physical address of each page's virtual address. Thus, the address translation algorithm is: *physicalAddr* = MAP (*virtualAddr* / *pageSize*) + *virtualAddr* % *pageSize*, where *virtualAddr* / *pageSize* is the result of the division, i.e., the page number, and *virtualAddr* % *pageSize* is the remainder of the division, i.e., the offset in the page, and MAP is the mapping of the virtual to the real.

Taking the above program *A* and program *B* as an example, the mapping relationship between virtual memory and physical memory is shown in Fig. 2.3. Here, we assume that *pageSize* is 1024. When the compiler generates an executable file or a library file, it keeps the original assumption that a computer runs only one application program, and the application program uses the entire memory space of the computer. Process 1 and Process 2 are created to run programs *A* and *B*, respectively. *a.exe* and *d.dll* are loaded into process 1's virtual memory space at locations 1024 and 3072, respectively, as shown in the left part of Fig. 2.3. *b.exe* and *d.dll* are loaded into process 2's virtual memory space at locations 1024 and 5120, respectively, as shown in the right part of Fig. 2.3. Note that the virtual memory space performs allocation in pages, so in process 2, the starting address of *d.dll* is not 4524, but 5120. From Fig. 2.3, it can be seen that the code portion of the shared

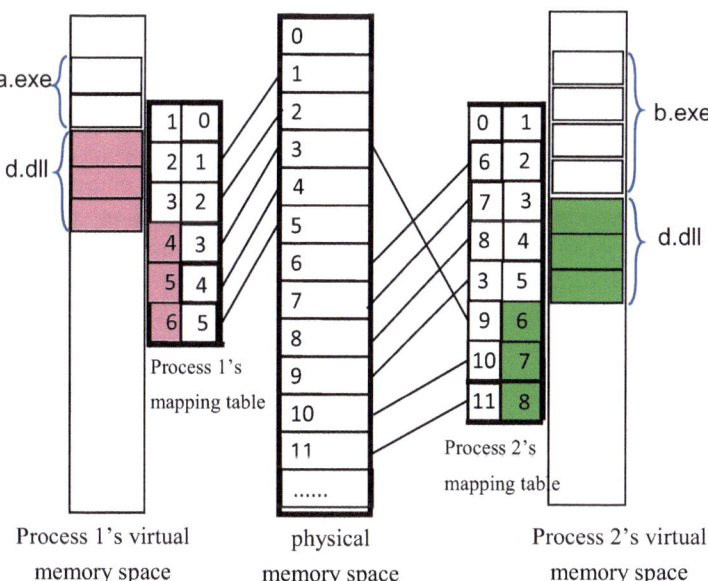

Fig. 2.3 Mapping of virtual memory addresses to physical memory addresses

module *d.dll* has only one copy in memory, which is shared by the 2 processes. Its data portion is not shared and the 2 processes have one copy each.

Although *d.dll* file is loaded in different locations in the virtual address space of the two processes, it does not affect the operation of the code. The reason is that the code in the *d.dll* file uses relative addressing for accessing its data. And the base address is the virtual address of the instruction to be currently executed in the virtual memory space, stored in the instruction register. The relative address value is independent of where *d.dll* is located in the virtual memory space, and is calculated by the compiler when generating the *d.dll* file, and is a constant. For process 1 and process 2, when the CPU executes a certain instruction in the *d.dll* code, the value in the instruction register is not the same, with a difference of 2048. That is to say, the same data in the *d.dll* has the same relative address in the two processes, but the base address is not the same, and therefore the absolute address is not the same either. All the addresses mentioned here are referred to virtual addresses.

Before an instruction in the code is executed, the absolute virtual address is figured out and then converted to a physical address. In process 1, assume that the virtual address of a piece of data in *d.dll* is located on page 5. In process 2, the virtual address is on page 7. This scenario is shown in Fig. 2.3. By checking the mapping table of the two processes, we can see that in process 1, the data are located in page 4 of the physical memory, while in process 2, the data are located in page 10 of the physical memory. In other words, through relative addressing and virtual memory, the code is invariant and shared, but the data are not shared.

Introducing the concept of virtual memory [6] brings the benefit of module sharing, but also the cost of doing so. The cost comes from 2 sources. First, there is storage overhead with the introduction of virtual-real mapping tables for each process. Also, for executable and library file loading, the minimum allocation unit of memory is a page, which is coarse-granular and prone to memory waste. For code segments or data segments of executables, memory waste occurs when their size is not exactly a multiple of the page size. For example, if the size of the file *b.exe* is 3500, 4096 memory space has to be allocated to it, with 596 memory space wasted. Another cost is the overhead of address mapping. Real-time conversions are performed on any address encountered during program execution. The conversion involves 1 division, 1 multiplication, 2 additions, and two memory reads. The first memory read is to read the starting address of the process's virtual-real mapping table, and the second read is to read the mapped value.

As you can see, the overhead of virtual-real address mapping is not small. Because of this, the CPU provides two modes of program operation: real mode and virtual mode. When the virtual mode is turned off, the program runs in the real mode, with no concept of virtual memory, so there is no need for a mapping table, and no overhead for virtual-real conversion.

Note: In the virtual-real conversion, when *pageSize* = 2^m and *virtualAddr* is a binary number, *virtualAddr* divides *pageSize* by shifting *virtualAddr* to the left by *m* bits and filling the right *m* bits with zeros. *virtualAddr* % *pageSize* can be obtained by filling all bits except the right *m bits* of *virtualAddr* with zeros. MAP (virtualAddr / pageSize) reads the value of an array element using *virtualAddr / pageSize*

2.8 Code Sharing

as the index of the array element. The feature of the value is that it is all right m bits are zero, while *virtualAddr % pageSize* has its all bits except the right m bits set by zero. Thus, the virtual-to-real conversion can be realized in hardware.

Reflection 2-25: For the virtual-real mapping table of a process, in order to save storage space, each row of data may not correspond to only one page, you can reduce the consecutive allocated pages into one row, and reduce the consecutive free pages into one row as well, and record only the starting page number. For the free page row, the corresponding physical memory page value is null. For example, the virtual-real mapping table of process 1 and process 2 in Fig. 2.3 can be reduced to 2 rows and 4 rows, respectively, as shown in Tables 2.7 and 2.8, respectively. Based on the reduced virtual-real mapping table, how can address translation be performed? Can you write the virtual-real address conversion algorithm? Is the virtual-real mapping table of a process a very frequently accessed data? Should it be stored in cache? Please justify. The above scheme saves the storage space of the virtual-real mapping table, but it requires checking the virtual-real mapping table, i.e., it imposes a table checking overhead. Should we shrink the storage space of the mapping table or not? Please justify.

Reflection 2-26: The data segment in executables and library files can also be subdivided into a variable segment and a constant segment. The variable segment is used to store global variables defined in the source program. The constant segment is used to store string constants that appear in the source program. For numeric constants and character constants in the source program, the compiler places them directly into the code and does not need to store them separately. Constants have the same read-only property as code. Should the constants be shared with the code, or should each process have its own copy in memory?

Reflection 2-27: If the global variable concept is eliminated, the variable portion of the data is also eliminated from executables and library files. Can a program then be set to run in real mode? What storage overhead and computation overhead can be reduced by running a program in real mode as opposed to running it in virtual mode? Is the elimination of the global variable concept in the Java language relevant?

Table 2.7 Virtual-real mapping table for process 1

Virtual start page number	Real start page number
2	1
7	

Table 2.8 Virtual-real mapping table for process 2

Virtual start page number	Real start page number
2	6
6	3
7	10
8	

2.8.6 Local Variable Storage Allocation and Implementation of Function Calls

For multitasking operating systems, the concept of virtual memory is essential to support forward compatibility. Many of the original source programs have global variables defined in them. When the compiler generates an executable or library file, the global variables are placed in the data segment of the file, andare accessed in the machine code by direct or relative addressing. For such executable programs, virtual memory scheme is an effective way to achieve code sharing without data sharing. When none of the executable modules that make up an application contain global variables, the application can be run in real mode, eliminating address mapping overhead.

In executable modules, global variable is a kind of data, while local variable is another one. A local variable is defined in a function and differs from a global variable in that it has a life cycle concept. When allocating storage space for variables, the compiler can use either a static allocation scheme or a dynamic allocation scheme. Compared with static allocation scheme, dynamic allocation scheme utilizes the life cycle of local variables to save memory overhead, but it requires the CPU to support relative addressing. If the CPU supports only direct addressing, only static allocation scheme can be used.

In a static storage allocation scheme, local variables are treated as global variables and their memory locations are specified at compile time. Thus, the memory address value of each local variable is a constant in the executable file. The formal parameters, return value, and return address of a function call are also treated as local variables, and their memory locations are specified at compile time. Therefore, the memory address values of all variables are constants. When generating function call code, the caller writes the real parameters and the return address value into the memory of the called function's formal parameter and return address, respectively. When generating the function return code, the return value is written into the return value memory. The Fortran compiler uses a static memory allocation scheme to generate executable code, and the C compiler also provides this option.

When a static storage allocation scheme is used to generate an executable, no function recursive calls can appear in the source program. In addition, if direct addressing is used, the program must be loaded at runtime into a memory location set at compile time. The biggest disadvantage of this scheme is the high memory overhead at runtime of the program. The reason is that the program allocates storage space for all data in advance. In other words, formal parameters and local variables do not differ from global variables in terms of memory allocation.

Static storage allocation schemes can be optimized based on function call characteristics. Assuming that function *A* calls function *B* and function *C*, it is impossible for the formal parameters and local variables of function *B* and function *C* to coexist at runtime. Thus, the formal parameters and local variables of function *B* and function *C* can share the same memory space to save the memory space occupied by the formal parameters and local variables of one of the two functions. Based

2.8 Code Sharing

on the above observation, it is necessary to analyze which functions' formal parameters and local variables do not coexist at runtime so that they can share the same memory space. The solution is to build a directed graph of the program's function calls when compiling the source program. The construction method is as follows: when the function β is called in the implementation code of function α, a directed edge is created, pointing from function α to function β. The directed graph of function calls according to the above method can be processed into a directed tree if recursive function calls are not allowed. The tree has the main function as the root node.

From the function call directed tree, we can see that: (1) the functions contained in the path from the root node to the leaf node, their formal parameters and local variables coexist in the program runtime; (2) for those nodes sharing identical parent node, their formal parameters and local variables don't coexist at runtime; (3) in a path from the root node to a leaf node, a function appears at most once. Thus, we can start from the root of the tree and traverse the whole tree with depth-first principle, and sequentially determine storage addresses for formal parameters, local variables, function return address, and return value of each function in turn. This improvement is based on the fact that functions at the same level of a call tree are not active side by side, so their formal parameters and local variables can share the same memory space. When the local variable memory size is reserved at the maximum of their values, the memory requirements of any one of them can be met.

For local variables in a program, a dynamic allocation scheme can also be used to further optimize the amount of memory required at runtime. In this scheme, a function allocates memory space for its formal parameters and local variables only when it is active. A function is active when its code is executed, i.e., when it is called. When the function returns, it frees the memory space occupied by its formal parameters and local variables. Therefore, in this scheme, the functionality of the start instructions of the function is to request memory space for local variables.

In a dymamic allocation scheme, base addresses of both the formal parameters and local variables are not known until the function is called. Therefore, local variables cannot be accessed by direct addressing, but by relative addressing. This requires the computer running the program to support relative addressing. Relative addressing means that the address value given in the code is the relative address, and the base address of the reference is placed in a specific register. For example, the jump instruction *goto 48(B)* uses relative addressing, where 48 is the relative address value and the base address of the reference is stored in register B.

A program calling a function at runtime is called an activity. The activity frame is the content of the data transfer involved in completing a function call. Specifically, the activity frame includes the real parameters to be passed, the return value, and the return address value. The real parameters and return address values are passed from the caller to the callee, while the return value is passed from the callee to the caller. In a directed tree of function calls, an edge expresses a function call relationship, where a parent node function calls a child node function. At runtime, the path from the root node of the tree (the main function) to any other node in the tree expresses a sequence of call progressions, also is called an activity sequence. For example, if you call function A in the main function, and then call function B in function A, then (main, A, B) is a call activity sequence.

A sequence of activities naturally corresponds to a sequence of active frames. Function calls are LIFO, so the stack should be used to store activity frames. The active frame is created in real time by the function caller and its memory allocation is dynamic in real time, so it has a base address. When a dynamic memory allocation scheme is used for local variables, it also has a base address. After the caller has created an active frame, the next thing that happens is that the callee requests memory space for its local variables. If the active frame and the local variables of the callee function are allocated closely together, two base addresses can be reduced to one, thus saving the storage space of one base address. In this case, the active frame is on one side of the base address and the local variables are on the other.

The following example illustrates the implementation scheme of function calls. Let function α call function β. Before the call, the top of the stack is local variables of function α. Suppose that register B is used to store the base address of local variables of function α, as shown in Fig. 2.4a, where the memory address of the stack top is stored in register T. To call the function β, function α allocates memory space on the stack top for the active frame that calls the function β, as shown in Fig. 2.4b. The active frame consists of three parts: the return address value, the return value, and real parameters. It then jumps to the first line of instructions of function β. The first line of instructions of function β is to push the value in register B into the stack. That is, to save the base address value of the caller in the stack, in order to free up register B for storing the base address of its own local variables, as shown in Fig. 2.4c. The instruction in line 2 of the function β is to store the memory address of the stack top (i.e., the value in register T) into register B to get its own base address, as shown in Fig. 2.4d. The third line of instructions of function β is to allocate memory space on the stack top for its local variables, as shown in Fig. 2.4e.

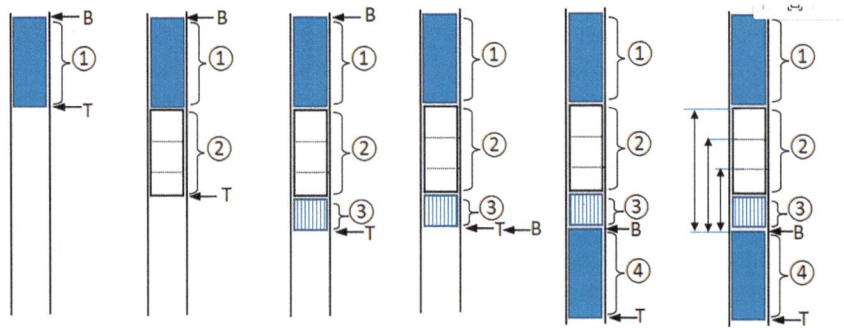

① Local variables of function α; ② Active frame for calling function β; ③ Base address of α; ④ Local variables of function β

(a)　　　　　(b)　　　　　(c)　　　　　(d)　　　　　(e)　　　　　(f)

Fig. 2.4 Implementation of function calls

2.8 Code Sharing

The next problem to be solved is how the function β derives offsets of the return address value, the return value, and each formal parameter at compile time. From Fig. 2.4f, it can be seen that the memory ③ stores the base address of the function α, while the memory ② stores the active frame. The active frame consists of three parts: the return address value, the return value, and the real parameters. The widths of the return value and the real parameter can be derived from the definition of the function β. Therefore, their offsets are constants at compile time. For example, let the definition of the function β be: float f (int i, char* p), assuming that the target computer is a 32-bit machine, then the width of the return value is 8 bytes, the sum of the widths of the two formal parameters is also 8 bytes, and the width of the address is 4 bytes. Thus, the return address value has an offset of -24, the return value has an offset of -20, the second formal parameter p has an offset of -12, and the first formal parameter i has an offset of -8.

When the function β wants to return, it first writes the return value into memory at address $-20(B)$, where register B stores the base address of the function β and -20 is the relative address of the return value. The return address value (whose memory address is $-24(B)$) is then read into the jump register, and then the local variables are popped off the stack, freeing the memory space they occupy. At this point, the stack top is the base address of function α, which is also popped off the stack and stored into register B. The base address of function α is then restored. Next, jump back to function α and execute the instruction after the call, which naturally reads the return value and then pops the active frame off the stack, freeing the memory space it occupied. At this point, the stack is restored to the state it was in before the call to function β.

Reflection 2-28: The print function in C differs from common functions in that the number of formal parameters and the data type of each of them is not explicitly given in the function definition, except for the first formal parameter. When called, the number and data type of all real parameters except the first one are determined by the value of the first real parameter. The data type of the first real parameter is const char *. The number of format output characters (%) in the string corresponds to the number of real parameters closely behind the first one, and their data type should be consistent with its corresponding format output character. When calling a function, the real parameters are stacked upside down, i.e., the last real parameter is stacked first, then the penultimate real parameter is stacked, and finally the first real parameter is stacked. Why are the real parameters stacked backwards? How do you solve for the memory address of each real parameter in the implementation of the print function? Can you write the source code for solving it?

2.8.7 Dynamic Storage Allocation for Global Variables

Early CPUs supported only direct addressing methods. Therefore, the compiler could only use static memory allocation scheme for all variables, including global and local variables, in generating executable programs. Thus, in the program code, the memory addresses of all variables are absolute and constant. Since the CPU does not support dynamic storage allocation, as well as object-oriented programming, i.e., no concept of member variables. For this kind of executable, it must be loaded into the memory location specified at compile time to run. In a single-tasking runtime environment, this requirement is easily satisfied. In a multitasking environment, applications face the problem of load location conflict, i.e., the memory location where they want to be loaded has been occupied by other programs, resulting in the inability to load and run. For the sake of forward compatibility, later CPUs added the ability to run the program in virtual mode, so that multiple programs could be run at the same time. In virtual mode, all addresses appearing in code are treated as virtual addresses.

Later CPUs supported relative addressing. Thus, for local variables, a dynamic storage allocation scheme was used to save memory overhead. For global variables, static storage allocation schemes continued to be used. In object-oriented programming, instance objects of classes also require a dynamic storage allocation scheme, i.e., member variables also use a dynamic storage allocation scheme. The compiler applies relative addressing to generate executable code, which has the added benefit that executables run independently of where they are loaded in memory. Thus, the load location conflict problem is completely solved. Executables generated using the relative addressing scheme can be run in the traditional real mode with high efficiency and good performance.

In a multitasking environment, module sharing is expected as a way to save memory overhead. Module sharing means that the code is shared, while the global variables in the module are one for each process and do not intersect with each other. This feature requires a dynamic storage allocation scheme for global variables. If the compiler uses a static storage allocation scheme, this means the program must run in virtual mode. The dynamic storage allocation of global variables is reflected in the virtual-real separation and virtual-real conversion. The biggest advantage of the virtual mode is that it enables module sharing without any changes to original executables, i.e., it has full forward compatibility. However, the cost paid is too high. Virtual-real mapping has not only computational overhead but also storage overhead. Is it possible to use dynamic storage allocation scheme for global variables at compile time, so as to eliminate the real-virtual mapping and reduce the implementation overhead of module sharing?

Moving to a dynamic storage allocation scheme for global variables means that when a process is created to run a program, memory space should be allocated for global variables for each module that makes up the program. Thus, for a module, there are as many copies of the global variable as there are processes sharing it, one for each process, independent of each other. In this case, the access to global variables in the code can only use relative addressing, using a register to store the base address of the global variable exclusively. The register that stores the base address of the global variable is called the module register. Since each module constituting a program has its own global variables, when the CPU execution jumps from one module to another, the value of the module register should be changed along with it. Thereby, when the CPU executes the code in a module, the global variables accessed are that in this module.

2.8 Code Sharing

CPU execution jumps from one module to another only when executing cross-module function calls. Suppose that a function $f1$ in module B is called from module A. For the called function $f1$, the caller can be in any module, which includes module B. Thus, a change in the value of the module register obviously cannot be the responsibility of the called function $f1$. Looking at the caller again, it calls a function and naturally knows whether it is a local call or a far call. Therefore, the change of the module register value should be put on the side of the caller. Also, the active frame passed by the caller to the called function $f1$ cannot be different for cross-module calls. Thus, for cross-module calls, the caller should save the module register values to the stack before creating the active frame. After a cross-module function call returns, the caller should first restore the value in the module register before reading the function return value. The reason is that it is possible for the caller to assign the function return value to a global variable.

From the above analysis, it can be seen that the cross-module function call contains the following 8-step actions: (1) push the value of the module register into the stack for restoration after the function returns; (2) create the active frame on the stack top and complete the initialization; (3) place the base address of the global variables of the module where the called function is located into the module register; (4) jump to execute the called function; (5) restore the value saved in step 1 to the module register after returning; (6) read the return value from the active frame; (7) free the memory allocated on the stack in step 2; (8) free the memory allocated on the stack in step 1. For function calls within a module, there are no 4-step operations 1, 3, 5, and 8, but only 4-step operations 2, 4, 6, and 7.

Step 4 of the above scenario has to read the base address of the global variables of the module where the called function is located. Now the question is: where is that base address stored? For the above example, the caller is in module A, so it should be in a variable that is accessible in module A. The only variables that can be accessed in module A are the global variables of module A. Therefore, for each module that module A depends on, the compiler should add a global variable in module A for it to store the base address. For example, if Module A depends on Module B and Module C, then the compiler should add two global variables in Module A to store the base addresses of the global variables of Module B and Module C, respectively. Such added variables in each module are henceforth referred to as base address global variables.

The last remaining issue is the initialization of the base address global variables, and the initialization of the module register. The following is an example of how this work is accomplished. Assume that program α consists of four modules: module A, module B, module C, and module D. Module A is the main module and contains the main function. Module A depends on module B and module C. Specifically, module A calls functions $f1$ and $f2$ in module B, and calls function $f3$ in module C. The dependency is expressed in the function import table of module A. Assuming that module B depends on module D and module C depends on module D, a process is created to run the program α. Since the CPU first executes the main function in the main module A, the main module A should be loaded into the memory, and then its global variables are allocated memory, and then the starting addresses of the global variables are assigned to the module register to complete its initialization. Next, each module is initialized according to the module dependency tree.

The initialization of the process is mainly the initialization of the modules, the instruction register and the module register. Its implementation is shown in Code 2.16. Its functionality is to create a process, and then call the function *mouduleInitialize* to complete the initialization of each module, as well as the initialization of the module register, and then the initialization of the instruction register. The value of the variable *argv*[0] in the code points to the filename of the main module. Line 5 is to complete the initialization of the process stack, in which the two real parameters of the call to the main function are to be pushed into the stack as a way to initialize the two formal parameters of the main function call.

Module initialization is to load the module file from disk into memory, fill in the function import table, and allocate memory for global variables and assign initial values. The global variables in a module have the following sequential relationship: the first global variable is of type character pointer, pointing to the module file name, followed by the base address global variables, and finally the global variables defined in the source program. The amount of memory space required for all global variables is calculated by the compiler and written in a specific location in the module file, so it can be read from the module file. Taking the above example of the main module *A*, the value of its first global variable points to the file name of the main module *A*. The second and third global variables are base addresses, which store the base addresses of the global variables of modules *B* and *C*, respectively. The next global variables are that defined in the source program.

Code 2.16 Implementation of Process Initialization
```
(1)  void runProgram(int argc, char **argv) {
(2)    Process *process = CreateProcess();
(3)    process->moduleRegisterValue =
         mouduleInitialize(process, argv[0]);
(4)    process->InstructionRegisterValue =
         getMainFunctionAddress( argv[0] );
(5)    process->stack->initialize(argc, argv);
(6)    return;
(7)  }
```

The module initialization of the process is done by calling the function *mouduleInitialize*, the implementation of which is shown in Code 2.17. Line 2 means loading the module from disk to memory based on the module file name. After loading, it is naturally an instance object of the *ModuleFile* class in memory. Line 3 is to get the size of the storage space occupied by its global variables. Line 4 is to allocate memory for the module's global variables in the heap of the current process. Line 5 is to assign an initial value to the first global variable. Line 6 means moving the pointer so that *dependentObject* points to the second global variable. The next lines, lines 7 through 18, initialize all the base address global variables and also initialize all the other modules. The code implies that the function import table in the module file is scanned to find out which modules it depends on and performs initialization on them in turn.

For a module, there may multiple modules dependent on it. In the above example, both module B and module C are dependent on Module D. In a process, for a module, memory is allocated only once for its global variables, and multiple allocations are not allowed due to dependencies from multiple modules. For this reason, the starting addresses of the module's global variables in memory are recorded in the process's module object table, *moduleObjectList*, see line 12. When memory is to be allocated for a module's global variables, first look it up in *moduleObjectList* to see if it has been allocated or not, shown in lines 9 through 15. If it has not been allocated, perform the allocation and add it to the process's *moduleObjectList*, see lines 10 through 13.

The meaning of line 11 in Code 2.17 is that the initialization of a sub-tree in the module dependency tree is completed by a recursive call. In the above example, the root of the module dependency tree of program α is module A. There are two sub-nodes of module A: module B and module C. Both module B and module C have only one sub-node, namely module D. Therefore, when the function *mouduleInitialize* is called against the main module A, then, in the while loop of line 8, line 11 has a two-level meaning: (1) initialize the second and third base address global variables of the main module A in turn; and (2) initialize the two subtrees, module B and module C, in turn. Line 16 is to move the pointer so that it points to the next global variable in the module. When the CPU executes to line 19, the pointer *dependentObject* is already pointing to the fourth global variable in module A, i.e., the first global variable in the source program. Line 19 initializes the global variables in the source program.

Code 2.17 Implementation of the Function moduleInitialize

```
(1)  byte * mouduleInitialize(Process * process, const char
       *moduleName) {
(2)    ModuleFile *moduleFile = new ModuleFile(moduleName);
(3)    int size = moduleFile->getGlobalVariableSize();
(4)    byte*moduleObject = process->heap->allocate(size);
(5)    (char*)*moduleObject = moduleName;
(6)    dependentObject = moduleObject += sizeof(char *);
(7)    char * dependentModuleName = moduleFile-
       >getFirstDependentModule( );
(8)    while (dependentModuleName! = null) {
(9)      byte *dependentModuleObject = process-
         >moduleObjectList-> getItemByName (
```

```
              dependentModuleName );
(10)      if (dependentModuleObject = null) {
(11)         ( byte *)*dependentObject = mouduleInitialize(pro
             cess,dependentModuleName);
(12)         process->moduleObjectList->addItem
             (*dependentObject);
(13)      }
(14)      else
(15)         ( byte *)*dependentObject =
             dependentModuleObject;
(16)      dependentObject += sizeof(byte *);
(17)      dependentModuleName = moduleFile-
          >getNextDependentModule( );
(18)   }
(19)   initializeProgramGlobalVariable(dependentObject );
(20)   return moduleObject;
(21) }
```

The meaning of line 20 in Code 2.17 is that the return value is passed to the caller as the starting address of the global variables of the main module in memory. The caller places this return value into the module register to complete its initialization.

Reflection 2-29: Does the recursive call at line 11 in Code 2.17 perform a depth-first traversal of the module dependency tree, or a breadth-first traversal? Is the order of module initialization: module *B*, module *C*, module *D*, or module *B*, module *D*, module *C*?

Reflection 2-30: When running a program in a multitasking operating environment, check its type. If it adopts the static storage allocation scheme, then run the program in virtual mode. If it adopts relative addressing, and global variables are allocated using a static allocation scheme, then run the program in virtual mode as well. If it adopts relative addressing, and global variables are allocated under a dynamic storage allocation scheme, then the program can be run in real mode. How does the operating system know the type of the program? Should type information be part of executables and library files? Consult the information on executable file formats and then answer the question.

Reflection 2-31: Can the mode of operation be refined from the process level to the module level? An example is given as follow. Assume that program *A* consists of *a.exe* and the library file *d.dll*, and *a.exe* adopts relative addressing and the dynamic storage allocation scheme for global variables. *d.dll* also adopts relative addressing, but has a static storage allocation scheme for global variables. Therefore, the CPU can execute the code in *a.exe* in real mode, but has to execute the code in *d.dll* in virtual mode. When executing a cross-module function call in *a.exe*, the CPU operation mode is changed to the virtual mode before jumping. After the cross-module function call returns, change the CPU operation mode back to real mode again. Is this processing scheme feasible? Please explain the reason.

Reflection 2-32: The performance overhead of running a program in virtual mode is high, so you should try to run programs in real mode. For this purpose, Java has eliminated global variables. Therefore, it paves the way for running programs in real mode. Microsoft's .NET adopts a dynamic storage allocation scheme for global variables, allowing the program to run in real mode. Java appeared before Microsoft's .NET. Is it time to bring back the concept of global variables to Java? are there other considerations for Java in eliminating global variables? Please review the information about Java and then answer the question.

Reflection 2-33: In a multitasking environment, some processes run in real mode and some in virtual mode. Is the running mode of a process its an attribute? Process switching may be accompanied by a switch in running mode, is it right? Can an instruction that changes the CPU's running mode be executed only in the operating system kernel? Can the instruction be used in an application program? Consult the information on machine instructions and then answer the question.

Reflection 2-34: An application written in the Java language consists, in terms of composition, of java development kit (JDK) library files and application files. There are naturally no global variables in the application, as determined by the Java language. But the JDK implementation is a matter for the java virtual machine (JVM). If there are no global variables defined both in the JDK implementation and in the JVM implementation, then the JVM can run in real mode and it is perfectly feasible. Assuming that the JDK's implementation contains global variables, how do you get a Java program to run in real mode?

From the above analysis, it is clear that the virtual memory scheme is designed to be compatible with historical legacy executables and libraries so that they can still run successfully in multitasking environments and have the qualities of code sharing and data not sharing. The gains come at a cost, including storage overhead and computation overhead. To avoid this overhead, the source program can be recompiled, provided it is available, with a dynamic storage allocation scheme for global variables. The newly generated executable is then able to run in real mode and has the qualities of being code-shared and data-unshared.

2.8.8 *Global and Static Variables and Multithreading*

Running instances of an application program are called processes. A program can have multiple running instances, where each running instance is a process. It is characterized by multiple processes to execute the same program code, but the data handled by each other different. For example, opening the word program several times and letting them edit different word documents is a typical example of concurrent multitasking with the same program code and different data. This efficacy achieved reflects the dialectical unity of change and invariance. Invariance is reflected in the code, while change is reflected in the data. Specifically, the invariance is reflected in the use of base address register to store the base address of the data exclusively, while the change is reflected in the different base address values loaded into the base address register at runtime. Adopting relative addressing to access the data, the program will has only the id of base address register and the relative address of the data (i.e., offset) appear in code, both of which are constants. The dialectical unity of change and invariance requires that the storage allocation of all variables cannot adopt a static scheme, but must adopt a dynamic one.

There are two dimensions for classifying variables in a program. The first-dimension divides variables into three categories: (1) global variables; (2) local variables; and (3) member variables. The second-dimension divides variables into two categories: (1) dynamic variables and (2) static variables. Combined, there are 6 categories. In terms of storage allocation, the six categories can be grouped into four: (1) static variables, including static global variables, static local variables, and static member variables; (2) dynamic global variables (global variables for short); (3) dynamic local variables (local variables for short); and (4) dynamic member variables (member variables for short). For the first three types of variables, the storage allocation code is automatically generated by the compiler based on their semantics. The storage allocation of static and global variables is done at the time of process creation; the storage allocation of local variables is done at the time of function call. For member variables, storage allocation is done when the programmer creates an instance of the class.

It can be seen that for each shared module, when its static and global variables use a dynamic allocation scheme for storage, each process has its own copy and does not get along with each other. For local variables and member variables, their storage is dynamically allocated, which is inherently process-private. In short, processes are data-isolated and do not share a single piece of data with each other in user space. Thus, as long as the execution of the kernel code is atomic, process switching can be performed unconditionally in the clock interrupt handling routine, which guarantees the correctness of concurrent multitasking.

To reduce the implementation cost of concurrent execution, some operating systems have further proposed the concept of thread on the basis of process. Multiple threads can be created within a process and allowed to execute concurrently. There is no difference between a thread and a process in terms of concurrent execution. The central concept in concurrent execution is the next instruction to be executed. Each thread has its own next instruction to be executed. In application scenarios where the code is the same but the data are not the same, multiple threads can be created in a process to execute the same code but handle different data. The concept of threads came later than processes and was intended to be a lightweight implementation of concurrent multitasking. From the perspective of concurrent execution, a process containing *n threads* is equivalent to n processes.

In a process, the program's constituent modules, as well as the heap, are shared by the threads in it. That is, modules, global variables, static variables, and the heap are concepts in a process, and only the stack is a concept in a thread. Threads, as units of operation, of course have their context, i.e., register values. Thus, a process in the traditional sense would contain only one thread. This thread is called the main thread. Applications can also create threads by calling API functions provided by

2.8 Code Sharing

the operating system. To create a thread, you only need to specify the function you want it to execute, i.e., the next instruction to execute. With the concept of threads, the concept of task scheduling is no longer process switching, but thread switching.

The modules that make up an application belong to the concept in process, so the global and static variables in a module are shared by all threads in the process. Thus, modules with global or static variables face access conflict problems in multi-threaded situations. For example, threads $t1$ and $t2$ both write global variables a and b. Assume that $t1$ runs first, and after writing to a, it gives way to $t2$, which writes to a and b, and then gives way to $t1$, which writes to b. At this point, a and b are assigned values by $t2$ and $t1$, respectively. This is clearly incorrect.

From the above analysis, it is clear that for modules with global or static variables that are shared by multiple threads, there is no guarantee that the program will run with correct results. This is another reason why many high-level programming languages eliminate global variables. However, there are many programs left over from history that use global variables, such as the C function library [10]. Because of this, there are several versions of the C library, including those that support multithreading and those that do not. For versions that support multithreading, synchronization control is implemented when accessing global variables. The strategy for synchronization control is to add the concept of locks to the operating system. The principle for an application to access a global variable is to lock it before accessing it and release the lock after accessing it. Locking is a waiting function. If the lock is occupied by another thread, the applicant is put into a waiting state until the lock is released by the occupant.

When a global variable is of type pointer to an instance object of a class, then that instance object also becomes a global variable. This augmentation of global variables is transitive in nature. That is, when an instance object becomes a global variable, if its member variables is also of pointer type, then the instance object being pointed to also becomes a global variable. This spreading nature of global variable augmentation makes it extremely easy to make a program vulnerable (i.e., buggy). This is another reason why many languages like Java want to eliminate global variables and restrict static variables from being pointer variables.

The problems caused by data sharing are mainly manifested in the following three aspects: (1) because of the omission of synchronization control, programs are incorrect sometimes; (2) because of the defective synchronization control, there is a deadlock potential; (3) exceptions cause the operation to release the lock to be skipped, which results in other threads waiting for the lock to freeze. Because of these, some operating systems do not support multithreading. In multi-threaded application design, even if global variables and static variables are not defined in the source code, the program still suffers from hidden problems due to data sharing. The reason is that global variables or static variables are defined in the support library and multi-threading support is not considered.

For the problems caused by multi-threaded sharing of global or static variables, let's give an example. Suppose there is a global variable i. The meaning of $i++$ in the source program is $i = i + 1$, which seems to be an atomic operation no need of synchronization control, but it is not. The reason is that the results of numerical operations can usually only be stored in registers first, and then the register values are stored in memory. Thus, translating i++ into machine code involves at least 2 machine instructions. If a thread switch happens to occur in the middle of these two instructions, it can lead to an access conflict problem. Also, there may be instructions in the middle of these 2 machine instructions. The reason is that by letting the i-value reside in a register, the operation of loading the i-value from memory to the register is eliminated when the i-value is subsequently read. That is, the i-value in memory is not necessarily the latest value. If the thread switch occurs between these two instructions, then the i-value read from memory by the newly uploaded thread is not the latest value and is naturally incorrect.

Reflection 2-35: There is no difference between threads and processes as far as concurrent multi-task execution is concerned. The concept of threads is proposed to realize concurrent execution in a lightweight manner. Lightweight here means storage overhead. What is lightweight specifically? When running an application in virtual mode, the virtual-real mapping table is a concept in process. When running an application in real mode, there is no need to create a virtual-real mapping table for a process. At this point, is the storage overhead significantly less when creating a thread compared to creating a process? Please justify. For global and static variables in each module, is it possible to allocate a copy to each thread as well, so that there is complete data isolation between threads?

2.8.9 Sharing of Global Variables in Operating Systems

For shared data, there are issues of consistency and correctness. An example is given below. A company's bank account is shared by multiple cashiers and accountants, with the cashiers transferring money out of the account and the accountants transferring money in. Now suppose the balance of funds on the account is $1000, and Cashier A wants to transfer $200 out of the funds and Accountant B wants to transfer $300 in. Both the fund transfers out and the fund transfer in have three-step operations: (1) read the value of the fund balance of the account; (2) add or subtract the read balance value to get the new balance value; and (3) assign the new balance value to the fund balance variable of the account. Assume that the CPU executes the operation of Cashier A first, and after executing step 1, it performs a process switch to go to the operation of Accountant B. When the CPU finishes executing the 3 steps of operations of Accountant B, it again performs a process switch and turns back to execute the step 2 and step 3 operations of Cashier A. This is where the problem of inconsistent and incorrect data arises. The fund balance value should be $1100, but is now $800, and the result is clearly incorrect.

For shared data, access to it must be atomic. For the above example, it means that when cashier A is transferring money, no one else can do the transfer. The way to achieve this is to set a lock on the shared data. The locking process is done before accessing the shared data, and the unlocking process is done after accessing it. Take the above transfer as an example, add a lock operation before the first step, and add an unlock operation after the third step. Thus, the whole transfer operation is changed from 3 steps to 5 steps. Lock is a wait function. After cashier *A* succeeds in locking, even though the CPU is given to accountant *B* due to process switching, accountant *B* falls into a waiting state due to unsuccessful locking. At this point, the process switch will be performed again, giving the CPU to Cashier *A*. After Cashier *A* performs the lock release operation in step 5, the state of Accountant *B* will change from WAITING to READY, and the CPU will be given to Accountant *B* only in the next round of process switching.

Lock is also shared data. The difference is that the shared data of the bank account mentioned above belongs to the shared data in the user space, i.e., the shared data in the application program, while the shared data of the lock are in the kernel space, i.e., the shared data in the operating system. Processes atomically access the shared data in the user space by locking the shared data in the kernel space. Now the question is how a process atomically accesses to shared data in kernel space? Answer starts with the scenarios in which the execution of a program is interrupted. There are only two scenarios for process switching: (1) the current process actively gives up the CPU due to a call to a synchronization function, and (2) the current process is forced to give up the CPU due to a clock interrupt. It is the second scenario that destroys the atomicity required for shared data access. For this reason, access to shared data in kernel space is atomic if hard interrupts are masked when the CPU executes kernel code.

The next question is: Why can hard interrupts be masked when the CPU is in kernel state? and why can't hard interrupts be masked when the CPU is in the user state? Hard interrupts should not be masked for a long time, otherwise too many hard interrupts will accumulate in the cache space, leading to cache overflow problems. Also, after masking hard interrupts, you must remember to open hard interrupts. If you miss to open the hard interrupt, then the whole computer is completely out of control. Because of this, masking hard interrupts is only allowed in operating system code, not in application code. When an interrupt handling routine is executed, the last instruction executed is either *iRet* or *halt*, both of which include the functionality of opening hard interrupts. In addition, to ensure that the CPU does not take too long to execute an interrupt handling routine, the operating system imposes row limits on tables such as the number of processes in *processList* to avoid a large amount of data leading to long lookup time in kernel space.

2.9 Sharing of Data Files

System resources in a multitasking environment, including CPU, memory, network, code, and disk files, can be shared by multiple processes. In order to solve the resource access conflict problem, a manager needs to be set up for each type of system resources. When an application program wants to access a resource, it submits a request to the manager of that resource, and the access is accomplished through the resource manager. For example, when program *B* wants to open the disk file "d:\f1.txt" to read and write to it, it should submit a request to the file manager. Here, program *B* acts as a client and the file manager acts as a server. The file manager responds to the client's request based on the current usage of the resource. When the disk file "d:\f1.txt" is not being accessed by any other program, Program B's request is satisfied. If the disk file "d:\f1.txt" is already in use by another program, Program B's request will be denied.

As you can see from the above example, each resource manager acts as a server and provides access interfaces for clients to call, thus enabling client-server interaction. Access interfaces are also called APIs. For example, for disk file access, there are five API functions: fopen, fread, fwrite, fseek, and fclose. Program *B* requests to open the disk file "d:\f1.txt" through the function call fopen("d:\f1.txt", WR), where the real parameter WR indicates that a read or write operation is to be performed. The client's request is reflected in the function name and the real parameter passed. The file manager responds to the received request, and the result is reflected in the function's return value. A return value of −1 indicates that the request was denied. A return value greater than 0 indicates that the request was successful.

For a resource manager to be able to handle a client's request, it must know the state of the resources. For example, for a file manager to be able to handle a client's fopen request, it must know the current state of the requested file. Therefore, the file manager has to record the current state of the managed resources. For a file, the current state information includes: whether it is currently free, or which clients are currently using it; access mode of each client; and the current value of the file pointer for each client. The current state information is usually stored in a table, as shown in Table 2.9. The four columns of the table represent the file identifier, file name, client identifier, access mode, and file pointer value, respectively. In a multitasking environment, the client identifier is usually the process id.

Reflection 2-36: The principle of file sharing is that a file can be opened and used by any client when it is idle. When a client requests to open a file, he or she must specify the access mode. There are three types of access modes: read only (Read), read and write (Read and Write), and append (Add). A file can only be opened by one client in the Read and Write mode, provided that the file is in an idle state. A file can be opened by more than one client in read-only mode, i.e., the file is shared. A file is allowed to be opened by only one client in append mode. Based on the data structure in Table 2.9, can you write the processing flow of the file manager for fopen requests to derive the implementation code for the two functions fopen and fclose?

Note: Table 2.9 only records information about the current state of files, not information about the file itself. The information about the file itself includes how

Table 2.9 Current State Information of files

fileId	fileName	clientId	accessMode	filePointer
1	c:\a.dat	7	R	100
1	c:\a.dat	9	R	20
2	d:\f1.txt	9	WR	0

the file is cached in memory. The cache information includes how many segments of data are cached, the location of each segment in the file, the starting address and length of each segment in memory, and the data change flag. When a client reads a file, if the read data are not in the cache, disk operations are also performed to read the data required by the user from the disk into the cache. When the user closes the file, the data in the cache with a change flag of true are written to disk.

File sharing is a coarse-granular way of data sharing. In contrast, in database management, the sharing granularity is reduced as an approach to increasing the concurrency of multitasking. A database consists of multiple tables. A table consists of multiple rows of data. When a single file is used to store a table, the sharing granularity can be refined to rows. For a row of data, multiple clients can perform read operations on it simultaneously. In this case, the row data have an identification problem. A primary key attribute is defined for the table for this purpose. For the rows in a table, the values of the primary key are unique, i.e., they are not the same as each other. A client can perform four types of operations on the table data: adding rows, deleting rows, modifying rows, and querying rows. When two clients' requests do not conflict with each other, they can be processed concurrently.

From the above analysis, it is clear that an operating system can actually be structured to consist of multiple system resource managers. System resources include CPU, memory, network, and disk files and so on, which can be shared by multiple applications. Thus, there are CPU managers, memory managers, network managers, file managers, module managers, and so on. Application programs access system resources through the resource manager. Thus, the applications become the clients of the system resources and the resource manager acts as the server. The interactions between clients and servers are done through API calls.

2.10 Interaction Between Processes

Interaction between processes refers to the transfer and processing of data between two processes. The interaction between two processes can be modeled as follows: process A passes a data to process B, and process B processes the received data. In the process of processing the data, process B may also pass data to process A. The passed data consist of two parts: (1) the data class id; (2) the specific content of the data. The process receiving the data first read the data class id. With the data class id, the receiving process knows what is the intention of the sending process, i.e., it knows which function should be called to process the received data. The specific content of the data is used as a real parameter in the function call. Inter-process interaction is also called Inter Process Communication (IPC) [1]. Compared with the C/S interaction, it is more relaxed. The data passed can be interpreted as a request, but the receiver may not return a response to the sender.

The operating system provides three ways for processes to interact with each other: shared memory, signals, and message queues. Shared memory is a section of physical memory whose starting address and space size can be obtained by any process by calling an API function provided by the operating system. Thus, processes can both write to and read from the shared memory. Access conflicts to shared memory are considered and resolved by the application programs themselves. In the signal and message approach, a member variable of type table is added to the process class. Since the process table *processList* and the current process *currentProcess* in the operating system kernel are global variables, they are also shared data. Process objects are stored in *processList* and are therefore also shared data. Since the process is shared data, its member variables are also shared data. From this, we can see that the essence of inter-process communication is the same, which is realized through memory sharing. The difference is in access control: the application program's access to signals and messages is done through the operating system.

In inter-process interactions based on either signaling or messaging approach, the receiver of the data should provide an implementation of the handling routines for each type of data. The difference between signaling and messaging is reflected in the way that data handling is initiated. In the signaling approach, the extraction and handling of signals are the responsibility of the operating system. Signal handling has priority over program execution. In the messaging approach, on the other hand, the extraction and handling of messages are the responsibility of the application program itself and are serial in nature. Signal handling is explained next in Sect. 2.10.1. Then, in Sect. 2.10.2, we analyze the characteristics of signal handling and reveal the origin of message queues.

2.10.1 Signal Handling

Signal handling draws on the interrupt mechanism. Interrupts are hardware features. Assuming that the CPU is currently executing instruction I_i and the next instruction to be executed is I_{i+1}, when a hard interrupt is triggered, instead of executing instruction I_{i+1}, the CPU jumps to the interrupt handling routine. When the interrupt handling routine returns, the CPU jumps again and goes on to execute instruction I_{i+1}. From the point of view of jumping, there is no difference between soft interrupt and function call. The difference between the two is that in a soft interrupt, the called function is in kernel space and the caller is in user space. In a function call, both the called function and the caller are either in kernel space or in user space. Thus, soft interrupts isolate user space from kernel space. Isolation is commonly referred to as the operating system running in kernel space and the applications running in user space. The application programs access the services provided by the operating system through soft interrupts. The operating system responds to hard interrupts through interrupt handling routines to achieve interaction with hardware.

For an operating system, it can be understood as a collection of interrupt handling routines, which is naturally a collection of managers of shared resources. Only in a multitasking operating environment is there a sharing problem. Soft interrupts can be understood as services provided by the operating system to the application

2.10 Interaction Between Processes

programs. Some of the services can only be accomplished with the help of hardware, such as network communication. The operating system sends requests to the hardware through I/O instructions and captures the response from the hardware through hard interrupts.

From the above analysis, it is clear that the applications realize interaction with the operating system through soft interrupts. In a multitasking environment, how do applications interact with each other? The operating system provides a signal service for this purpose. Signal is an operating system concept for simulating interrupt triggering and interrupt handling routines to enable interactions between processes. In other words, signal is interrupting simulation implemented in software. Interrupt is a hardware feature, while process is a concept in the operating system. Therefore, triggering a hard interrupt is a hardware behavior and has nothing to do with process. Signal is different, it is a process-specific concept. That is, when a signal is triggered, it must mean that the signal is triggered for a process. Triggering a signal S for process B means that when process B is scheduled for execution, instead of executing its next instruction to be executed, it goes to execute the handling routine of signal S. After the signal handling routine returns, the process B then proceeds to execute its next instruction.

Signal handling routines are not the same as interrupt handling routines, which are associated with processes. When an application calls the API function *setSignalHandler* provided by the operating system to set a signal handling routine, it is referring to setting a message handling routine for the current process. The current process is stored in the operating system with *currentProcess*, so setting a signal handling routine means for the current process. Signals, like interrupts, are identified by serial numbers. Since signals are services provided by the operating system to the application programs, signal handling routines are part of the application programs rather than the operating system. This is another obvious difference between signals and interrupts. When process A triggers a signal to process B, the current process is naturally process A. For process B, it may be in the READY state or in the WAITING state. The signal does not change the original logic of process B. It is only when process B is subsequently scheduled for execution that it executes the signal handling routine.

For process A to trigger a signal S to process B, there is a prerequisite, which is to legally get the id of process B. If process B is created by process A, i.e., process A is the parent process of process B, then process A gets the id of process B when it creates process B, and it can then trigger a signal to process B. In other words, for security reasons, interaction between processes by triggering signals is not unconditional, and is contingent on obtaining each other's process ids.

In the operating system, the IDT is a data structure that supports interrupt processing. To support signal handling, two member variables should be added to the process: (1) a signal vector table, *signalHandlerList*; and (2) a signal-triggered event table, *signalEventList*. The starting memory addresses of the signal handling routines are recorded in *signalHandlerList*, while signal trigger events are stored in *signalEventList*. Setting up a signal handling routine is to add or update a row of data in *signalHandlerList*. Triggering a signal S for process A is to add a row of data to process *A*'s *signalEventList*. When executing a process switch, for the newly uploaded process, first check whether there is a row of data in its *signalEventList*. If not, it is natural to execute the next instruction to be executed by the newly uploaded process. Otherwise, the corresponding signal handling routine has to be called first. One line of data corresponds to one signal handling routine call. After the signal handling routine returns, the next instruction of the newly uploaded process is executed.

The specific implementation of handling signal is shown in Code 2.18. These four lines of code should be embedded in front of the *iRet* in the process switching implementation (there are three scenarios for process switching, see Codes 2.5, 2.7, and 2.8, respectively). The meaning is: before letting the CPU execute a process, check if there are any rows of data in its *signalEventList*. If there is, let the CPU jump to execute the function *callSignalHandler*. After the function returns, let the CPU proceed to execute the next instruction of the process. For this purpose, the next instruction to be executed is pushed into the process stack, and then the starting address of the function *callSignalHandler* in memory is loaded into the interrupt register, as shown in lines 2 and 3 of Code 2.18. Thus, when the CPU executes the *iRet* instruction in the process switch, it next jumps to execute the code in the function *callSignalHandler*. When the function *callSignalHandler* returns, the next instruction of the process is executed.

Code 2.18 Implementation of Calling Signal Handling Routine
```
(1)   if (currentProcess->signalEventList->hasRow( )) {
(2)       currentProcess->stack->push(currentProcess->
          context->nextInstructionAddr);
(3)       setIntruptionRegisterValue(callSignalHandler);
(4)   }
```

In line 2 of Code 2.18, pushing the memory address of the next instruction to be executed into the process stack actually creates the active frame for calling the function *callSignalHandler*. Since the function *callSignalHandler* has no parameters and no return value, the only item in the active frame is the return address. The return address is the memory address of the next instruction to be executed. After the active frame is created, line 3 of Code 2.18, together with the iRet instruction, lets the CPU jump to execute the function *callSignalHandler*. After the function returns, the CPU then proceeds to execute the next instruction of the process. About the implementation of function return, refer to Sect. 2.8.6.

The function *callSignalHandler* is implemented in the support library provided by the operating system. The support library belongs to application programs. This function's functionality is to handle signal-triggered events, i.e., to invoke signal handling routines. Its implementation is shown in lines 1–9 of Code 2.19. It extracts the signal events from the operating system kernel via #96 soft interrupt, and then gets the information about the handling of a signal event: the starting address of the corresponding signal handling routine in memory, and the real parameter to be passed to call it. If a signal event is extracted, the corresponding signal handling routine is called, as shown in line 5. The implementation of the #96 soft interrupt handling routine is shown in lines 10–20 of Code 2.19. Its functionality is to extract the signal event from the *signalEventList* of the process. If there is one, it then reads the starting address of the corresponding signal handling routine in memory from the *signalHandlerList* based on the signal id. In order to get the return value from the #96 soft interrupt handling routine, the address of the data had to be passed, as shown in lines 3 and 6.

Code 2.19 Handling of Signal Events

```
(1)   void callSignalHandler( ) {
(2)     SignalHandling *signalHandling = new
          SignalHandling( );
(3)     INT 96(&signalHandling);
(4)     while (signalHandling->handler ! = null) {
(5)       (FAR CALL)*(signalHandling->handler)
          (signalHandling->parameter,
          signalHandling->moduleBaseAddr);
(6)       INT 96(&signalProcessing);
(7)     }
(8)     return;
(9)   }
(10)  void Interuption96Handler(SignalHandling
        **signalHandling) {
(11)    SignalEvent *signalEvent =
          currentProcess->signalEventList->pickOutItem();
(12)    if ( signalEvent ! = null) {
(13)      (*signalHandling)->parameter =
            signalEvent->parameter;
(14)      SignalHandler *signalHandler = currentProcess-
            >signalHandlerList->getItemById (signalEvent->id);
(15)      (*signalHandling)->handler = signalHandler->handler;
(16)      (*signalHandling)->moduleBaseAddr =
            signalHandler->moduleBaseAddr;
(17)    }
(18)    else
(19)      (*signalHandling)->handler = null;
(20)    iRet;
(21)  }
```

Note: You cannot call signal handling routines directly during process switching. The reason is that the CPU is in kernel state when executing the process switch, while the signal handling routines belong to the code in the user space. When the CPU is in kernel state, it is not allowed to call the function in the user space; otherwise, it will bring security risk. Because of this, it is necessary to wait until the CPU executes the *iRet* instruction and returns to the user state before calling the signal handling routines. For this purpose, the function *callSignalHandler* is introduced and embedded before the next instruction to be executed by the process, thus completing the embedded call to the signal handling routine.

When the CPU jumps to execute the function *callSignalHandler*, the value in the module register is not the base address of the global variable in the module (i.e., the support library) to which the function *callSignalHandler* belongs, but the base address of the global variable in the module where the next instruction to be executed is located. Therefore, global variables cannot be used in the function *callSignalHandler*. As can be seen from Code 2.19, this requirement is met. Apparently, calling a signal handling routine in the function *callSignalHandler* is a cross-module function call, see line 5 in Code 2.19. Because of this, when setting up the signal handling routine, it is necessary to provide not only the memory address of the signal handling routine, but also the base address of the global variable in the module to which the signal handling routine belongs, i.e., the value of the module register. This is what provides the support for far calls.

Calls to signal handling routines have different characteristics than regular function calls. Regular function calls have C/S characteristics: the caller acts as a client and the called function acts as a service. Usually, the service comes first, then the client. Thus, the program has a hierarchical characteristic: functions in lower modules are called in upper modules. Or modules have a dependency relationship. When module A calls a function locating in module B, module A is said to be dependent on module B. A call to a signal handling routine becomes a call in a lower module to a function locating in an upper module. In this situation, Functions like signal handling routines are called callback functions. It is characterized by registration and then calling back. Registration means that the upper module calls the function in the lower module and passes the start address of the callback function in memory to the lower module to save. Calling back means that a lower module calls a function locating in the upper module (i.e., callback function).

The memory address of a runtime callback function is unknown at compile time. How can it be obtained at registration time? The answer to this question starts with the data structure of the executable. From an object-oriented point of view, the data structure of an executable, also called the executable class, is defined by the operating system vendor. The compiler generates the executable based on it. The class has the member variable *loadedAddr*, which is used to store the loaded address of the executable in memory at runtime. When program A loads module α into memory, it gets its loaded address. The module α in memory at this point is an instance object of the executable class. Program A assigns the loaded address of module α to *loadedAddr*, a member variable of module α. The relative address of the function, i.e., the offset in module α, is computed at compile time and is a constant. The relative address of the function plus the value of *loadedAddr* is its absolute memory address.

Reflection 2-37: Is the inability to use global variables in the function *callSignalHandler* another consideration in Java's elimination of global variables?

Reflection 2-38: A process's *signalEventList* and *signalHandlerList* are both data in kernel space, but *signalEventList* is shared data, while *signalHandlerList* is private to the process, why?

Reflection 2-39: Is it necessary for a process to trigger a signal to itself? Please provide a justification.

Reflection 2-40: The signal service API functions provided by the Linux operating system for applications are: (1) the API function to set up a signal handling routine, named *signal* or *sigaction*; (2) the API function to trigger a signal, named *kill* or *sigqueue*. *Sigaction* has two formal parameters, the first one is the signal id and the second one is the signal handling routine (including the memory address of the function and the base address of the global variable of the module to which it belongs). *sigqueue* also has 2 formal parameters, the first one is the signal id, the second one has type void *. Can you give the implementation code for the functions *sigaction* and *sigqueue*?

Many applications do not have signal processing routines set up for themselves, but when a signal is triggered at runtime, it also responds. For example, when running a program using the command prompt program *cmd.exe* in Windows, when the ctrl+C key is pressed, it ends the currently running program and returns to the command prompt state. The implementation of a program usually neither gives the ctrl+C signal handling routine nor sets up the ctrl+C signal handling routine. This means that it is the operating system that sets up the default signal handling routine for all processes. If an application sets up its own signal handling routine, it replaces the default.

2.10.2 Message Queues

In signal-based inter-process interaction, process *A* triggers a signal to another process *B* without any constraints. The current process at the time the signal is triggered must be process *A*. Subsequently, as soon as process *B* becomes the uploaded process, it processes the received signal. This scheme prioritizes starting up signal handling, which may trigger multiple execution flows and thus bring about sharing conflict problems. For example, suppose process *B*, after executing program code, jumps to handle signal 1. There appear two execution streams. One is the program code execution flow, which has the concept of the next instruction to be executed. The other is the signal 1 handling execution flow, which also has the concept of the next instruction to be executed. Suppose that a process switch occurs during the handling of signal 1 due to time slice expiration. When it is process *B*'s turn to become the uploaded process again, it will jump to handle signal 2 because it has received signal 2. At this time, there appear a new execution flow, i.e., the handling execution flow of signal 2.

The sharing conflict problem arises when a process has multiple execution flows. Here is an example. Assume that all three execution flows perform a 1-increment operation on the global variable *count*, which consists of three instructions: (1) read the value of *count* into a register, (2) do a 1-increment operation on the value of the register, and (3) write the new value of the register to *count*. Assume that the three execution flows have the following jump scenarios: flow 1 reads *count* into a register and then jumps, and flow 2 also reads the value of *count* into a register and then jumps. Assuming that the initial value of *count* is 1, the value of *count* is *2* at the end of flow 3, flow 2 and flow 1, respectively. The reason is that 3 flows write the new value of the register to *count*. But the correct value of *count* is 4. It can be seen that when there are multiple flows in a process, there is a sharing conflict problem that possibly makes the data inconsistent or incorrect.

To address the above issue, the first execution flow had better not to access to global variables. The reason is it is of the program code. Another extreme way to handle this is to have the program code consist of only one infinite loop statement. The only line of code in the loop body is a call to the operating system's pause API function, which is a wait function that waits for a signal event in the process's *signalEventList* before returning. Thus, when the process receives a signal, it will be woken up and dispatched to become the uploaded process. Once it becomes the current process, signal handling is performed. After the signal is handled, the program code is executed, i.e., the pause function is called again. In this scenario, all the process has to do is to handle the received signal. Programs like servers, whose business function is to handle signals (i.e., client requests), can be implemented in this way.

Prioritizing signal processing may lead to processes having more than two execution flows, raising data inconsistency and incorrectness issues. This is where the approach of message queuing comes in. In the message queuing scheme, a new member variable *messageList* is added to the process class. Process *A* sends a message to process *B*, similar to triggering a signal, by adding a message to process *B*'s *messageList*. For messages in *messageList*, the operating system does not actively handle it. The application calls the API function *pickOutMessage* provided by the operating system to extract it. *pickOutMessage* is a synchronization function. That is, if there is no message in *messageList*, the process will fall into a waiting state. Until a message is received, the process state will be changed from WAITING to READY. *pickOutMessage*'s return value is a received message.

When processes interact with each other by means of messages, the application program calls the function *pickOutMessage* recursively. Then the extracted message is handled by calling the corresponding message handling routine. Thus, there is only one execution flow, namely the program code execution flow, in the entire process. The problem of inconsistent and incorrect data due to multiple execution flows is solved. A message, like a signal, consists of two parts: message id and message content. The message id represents the message category. The application should provide an implementation of a handling routine for each message category.

Note: Having a message queue does not mean that signal handling can be removed. Signal handling is still indispensable. A signal is triggered for a process when something needs to be prioritized by the process. For example, exceptions should be prioritized. Because of this, the operating system defines a number of signal ids and gives implementations of their handling routines respectively. It is with these signals that the process can be instantly jumped to the execution of a specific code segment (i.e., the signaling routine).

Reflection 2-41: For signal ids, consult the information to see which segment is used by the operating system? Which segment is used by the application program? Which signal ids are specifically defined by the operating system?

Reflection 2-42: Can you give the implementation of the API functions *pause* and *pickOutMessage* with reference to the implementation of the send and receive functions in network communication (see Codes 2.12 and 2.13)?

Reflection 2-43: The API function for sending a message to a process is *postMessage*, whose functionality is to add a message to *messageList* of the receiver process. Can you give an implementation of the *postMessage* function? There is another function *sendMessage* that also sends a message to a process, which differs from *postMessage* in that *sendMessage* does not return until the recipient process calls the *pickOutMessage* function to pick up the message. Can you give an implementation of *sendMessage*? In this case, two identifying attributes are added to the content of each message, one of which is the id of the sender process and the other is the id of the message object. For the receiver of the message, when the *pickOutMessage* function is called to pick up the message, a message (i.e., a response message) is sent to the sender of the message to let it know that the message has been picked up by the receiver.

Reflection 2-44: Should there be an upper limit on the number of message entries in a process's *messageList*, in order to control memory overhead? Under what circumstances would the limit be reached? When the maximum number of messages in *messageList* is reached, no more messages are received. Therefore, the return value of the *postMessage* function indicates whether the message was sent successfully or not. Please modify the implementations of *postMessage* and *sendMessage* to reflect this situation. Note: There can be more than one reason why sending a message is unsuccessful.

2.11 Process-Peripheral Interaction

Many functions provide services for applications to interact with external devices, such as the *send* function that can be used to send data over the network and the *receive* function that can be used to receive data from the network. External devices include disks, keyboards, network cards, USB devices, etc., or peripherals for short.

Machine instructions include Input/Output (I/O) instructions. Input instructions are used to read data from peripherals, and Output instructions are used to output data to peripherals. Peripheral devices then respond to the I/O instructions through hard interrupts. When process A sends a request to a peripheral, it takes time for the peripheral to respond. During the time between sending the request and the response from the peripheral, process A is in the waiting state. The CPU can then be scheduled to execute another process. The peripheral responds with a hard interrupt. When a hard interrupt is triggered, the CPU jumps to execute the interrupt handling routine. Its function is to read the response result from the peripheral and wake up process A. Process A becomes the uploaded process and then goes to handle the response result. From this, it can be seen that the interaction between the process and the peripheral is also in C/S mode.

I/O functions implemented based on the above mode are called synchronization functions [1]. In the implementation of a synchronization function, a process switch is performed to give up the CPU after a request is output to the peripheral. See Codes 2.12 and 2.13 in Sect. 2.7 for implementation details. Many application scenarios involve programs that function to handle the input and output of multiple peripherals at the same time. For example, a router has multiple NICs plugged into it. The function of the routing program is to send a request to each NIC to receive data. When a response is received from one NIC, the received data is forwarded by another NIC. When the synchronous mode is used to implement the routing program, assuming that the number of NICs on the router is n, then $2n$ processes have to be created to implement the routing function. For each NIC, a process should be dedicated to receive data, and another one should be dedicated to send data. The implementations of the receiving process and the sending process are shown in Codes 2.20 and 2.21, respectively.

Code 2.20 The Program Executed by a Receiving Process
```
(1)   while(true) {
(2)     IpPackage *ipPackage = network-> receive();
(3)     int processId =
        getProcessIdToSend(ipPackage->destionationIpAddr);
(4)     postMessage(processId, (void *)ipPackage);
(5)   }
```

Code 2.21 The Program Executed by a Sending Process
```
(1)   while (true) {
(2)     Message *message = messageQueue->pickOutMessage();
(3)     network-> send(message);
(4)   }
```

2.11 Process-Peripheral Interaction

In this implementation, message queues are used for process-to-process communication. When an IP packet is received from a NIC, the destination IP address is used to look up the routing table to determine which NIC to forward it. For example, suppose process 6 is responsible for sending in the third NIC. When process 1 receives an IP packet from the first NIC that should be routed to the third NIC, it forwards the IP packet in a message to process 6. Here *receive*, *pickOutMessage* and *send* are all synchronous functions.

As can be seen from the above routing procedure, the synchronous mode has the advantage of simple and straightforward processing expression. Its disadvantage is that multiple processes have to be created. In addition, the processes interact with each other frequently, and thus process switches have to be performed frequently as well. At the time of process switching, the context of the abdicating process (i.e., the values in all registers) is saved to its member variable *context*, and then the context of the uploaded process is loaded from its member variable *context* into the registers in order to restore the context of the uploaded process to the machine. It can be seen that the process switching overhead is not small and is increasing with the number of registers. Therefore, an important aspect of performance optimization for an application is to reduce the number of processes, which contributes to reducing the process switching overhead. For the above routing program, can $2n$ processes be reduced to one process? This leads to the concept of asynchronous functions [1].

Asynchronous and synchronous are two relative concepts. In the implementation of an asynchronous function, after a request is made to a peripheral using an I/O instruction, the process does not wait for the response result, but continues on to the next level of execution. Therefore, when a process calls an asynchronous function, it returns immediately and does not get stuck in the waiting state. The process can then move on to something else. When the peripheral finishes handling the request, a hard interrupt is triggered. Thus, the CPU jumps to the interrupt handling routine. In the interrupt handling routine, instead of unconditionally changing the state of the requesting process from WAITING to READY, a response message is sent to the message queue of the requesting process. When the process extracts this message from the message queue, it processes it and gets the response result.

When an asynchronous mode is used to implement the routing program, it is possible to reduce the $2n$ processes to a single process, as shown in Code 2.22. In this implementation, the first step is to call the asynchronous function *receive* to each network connection to send a request to receive IP packets, as shown in lines 1–4. Then it enters an infinite loop, where the synchronous function *pickOutMessage* is called in the body of the loop to retrieve a message from the process's message queue. There are two types of messages: (1) the result of the response to a RECEIVE request, with class id NETWORK_RECEIVE, and (2) the result of the response to a SEND request, with class id NETWORK_SEND. When an IP packet is received, based on the destination IP address in it, it goes to the routing table to find out which NIC it should be forwarded out from, as shown in line 8. At this point, if the sending NIC is busy sending, it caches it to the send queue; otherwise, the asynchronous function *send* is called to send it, as shown in lines 9–14.

Code 2.22 Routing Program Implemented in an Asynchronous Manner

```
(1)    for (int networkId = 0; networkId++; networkId <
       networkCardNum) {
(2)      network[networkId]-> receive( );
(3)      isSending[networkId] = FALSE;
(4)    }
(5)    while (true) {
(6)      message *message = pickOutMessage();
(7)      if (messsage->id == NETWORK_RECEIVE) {
(8)        int networkId =
           getNetworkToSendIt(messsage->content->ipPackage-
           >destinationIpAddr);
(9)        if (isSending[networkId] == FALSE) {
(10)         network[networkId]->send(messsage->content->
             ipPackage);
(11)         isSending[networkId] = TRUE;
(12)       }
(13)        else
(14)          sendBufferList[networkId]->addItem(messsage->
              content->ipPackage);
(15)       network[messsage->content->networkId]-> receive( );
(16)   }
(17)   else if (messsage->id == NETWORK_SEND) {
(18)     int networkId = messsage->content->networkId;
(19)     IpPackage *ipPackage =sendBufferList[networkId]
         ->pickOutItem();
(20)     if (ipPackage ! = null)
(21)       network[networkId]->send(ipPackage);
(22)     else
(23)       isSending[networkId] = FALSE;
(24)   }
(25) }
```

When a send response result is received, it means that the requested data have been sent by the NIC, and the next IP packet can then be sent, which is handled as shown in lines 17–24. If there are no IP packets to be sent, set the NIC's transmit state to idle, as shown in line 23. When the NIC's hard interrupt handling routine is executed by the CPU, it means that the NIC has responded to a request from the process, and the state of the process may be WAITING, RUNNING, or READY. If it is WAITING, it is not because of the call to the asynchronous function, but because of the call to the synchronous function *pickOutMessage*, as shown in line 6. In this case, in the NIC hard interrupt handling routine, the process state should be changed

2.11 Process-Peripheral Interaction

to READY after sending the message to the process, so that the process can then resume running.

Comparing the two implementations of the routing program, it is clear whether *receive* and *send* are asynchronous or synchronous functions, it is not a matter of distinguishing them from the function definitions. Whether they are synchronous or asynchronous functions is marked on the network object's member variable *mode*. The network provides API functions for applications to call to set the mode of operation. The default mode is synchronous. Applications can change it to asynchronous mode. The network object also has a member variable *linkedProcess* that records which process is currently a client. In the NIC hard interrupt handling routine, the result of the response from the NIC is processed based on the network object's mode value. If asynchronous, a message is sent to the message queue of the process pointed to by *linkedProcess*. The message id is NETWORK_RECEIVE or NETWORK_SEND, and the message content includes the id of the network object and the response result. The state of the process to which l*inkedProcess* refers is then checked. If it is WAITING and the wait event is MESSAGE, change its state to READY.

Reflection 2-45: When the routing program is implemented in a synchronous manner, $2n$ processes are created in the case of n NICs. Why do you need $2n$ processes? Is it okay to create only n processes? Analyze the features of Codes 2.20 and 2.21 and then answer the question.

Reflection 2-46: In daily life and work, is making a phone call a synchronous mode or an asynchronous mode? What about sending short messages using WeChat or QQ? What about sending emails? What about visiting someone? In today's society, which mode is popular? synchronous or asynchronous. When should you use synchronous mode? When should we use asynchronous mode?

Reflection 2-47: Based on the meaning of asynchronous functions, can the network interrupt handling routine given in Sect. 2.7 (see Code 2.11) be supplemented with the addition of asynchronous mode to handle received IP packets or the response to a sending request?

Reflection 2-48: Based on the meaning of asynchronous functions, can the implementations of the *send* and *receive* functions given in Sect. 2.7 (see Codes 2.12 and 2.13) be supplemented by adding implementations of the asynchronous mode of operation? In the NIC hard interrupt handling routine, the state of the requesting process is checked after sending a message to it. If it is WAITING and the event waited for is MESSAGE, then its state should be changed to READY, why?

Reflection 2-49: The functionality of a routing program is to forward IP packets. The network object in Code 2.22 differs from the connection object described in Sect. 2.7. There is one network object corresponding to each network card. Multiple connection objects can be created for a single network object. Both the network object and the connection object have member functions *receive* and *send*. In socket-based network programming, socket means connection object. Socket objects also have a member variable *mode*. Asynchronous mode is named NOBLOCKING, whose implementation in the socket is not to send a message to the requesting process's message queue. Consult the sources to see which function is called to set the operating mode of the socket? How is the response result handled in NOBLOCKING mode? What is the difference between the processing of a socket and the processing of sending a message to the requesting process? Which way is better? Give reasons.

2.12 Exception Handling

The CPU may encounter exceptions during the execution of an application program. For example, when performing a division operation, if the divisor is zero, the result of the operation will not be obtained. Another example is: the amount of memory in the machine is only 64 K, but when the program reads or writes the memory data, the value of the memory address given is 2 M, so the reading or writing is naturally unsuccessful. Once the CPU encounters an exception during the execution of an instruction, a hard interrupt is triggered, and the CPU jumps to execute the interrupt handling routine. These hard interrupts are called exception hard interrupts. In the exception hard interrupt handling routine, the exception process (i.e., the current process) is first checked to see if it is set up for exception handling [7]. If not, the exception process is considered unnecessary to execute further and is directly terminated. Otherwise, an exception signal is triggered for the exception process. Thus, when the exception hard interrupt handling routine returns and the exception process is scheduled for execution, signal handling is executed first. In the exception signal handling routine, the exception processing is executed according to the settings.

High-level programming languages support the expression of exception handling in source programs [10]. The C++ language, for example, identifies a segment of program code with the curly brace pair '{'and '}'. When a programmer prefaces a segment of code with the keyword *try*, that segment of code is called a try code segment. When an exception occurs while the CPU is executing the try code segment, it skips the rest of its unexecuted portion and moves on to execute the code that follows the try code segment. This is the exact meaning of exception handling. When an exception occurs, the CPU jumps as shown in Fig. 2.5. Here, function *A* has a try code segment. In this try code segment, function *B* is called, and an exception occurs when the CPU executes some instruction in function *B*. The CPU then jumps to execute the interrupt handling routine. When the interrupt handling routine returns and the exception process is scheduled for execution, the CPU jumps to execute the exception signal handling routine, and then jumps again to execute the instruction following the try code segment in function *A*. Obviously, there are instruction segments in both function *A* and function *B* that are skipped and not executed by the CPU, indicated by a single circle in the figure.

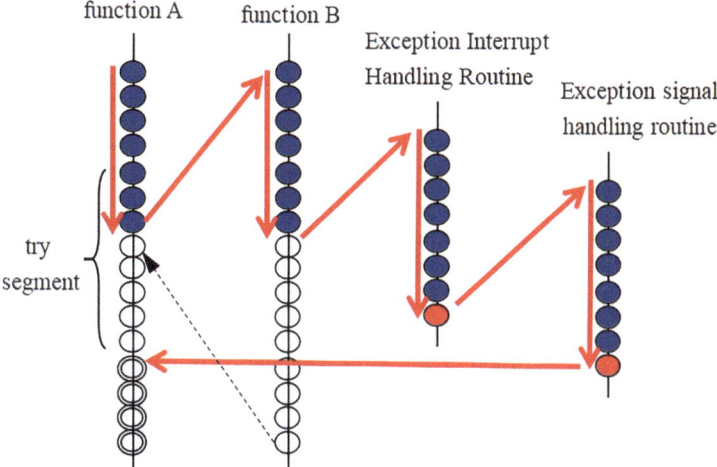

Fig. 2.5 CPU's jumps when an exception occurs

2.12.1 Characterization of Exception Handling

Try code segments may be nested, i.e., there are try code segments nested within another try code segment. This nestedness is similar to the nestedness of function calls, which can be described in terms of an exception tree. If a try code segment *A* has a try code segment *B* embedded in it, then try code segment *B* is a child node of try code segment *A*. It is possible for a try segment to have no parent node, i.e., the parent node is empty. Exception handling has the concept of current try code segment. When the CPU starts executing the main function, the current try code segment is empty. During the subsequent execution, every time a try code segment is encountered, the try code segment becomes the current try code segment, and every time the CPU finishes executing a try code segment, the parent node of the try code segment becomes the new current try code segment again. Once an exception occurs, if the current try code segment is not empty, then the CPU jumps to execute the instruction after it. If it is empty, the process is terminated.

From the above process, it is clear that exception handling requires knowing the memory address of the instruction that follows each try code segment at runtime. The computation of this address is easy. Suppose the try code segment is in module α. After module α is loaded into memory, it is an instance object of the executable class with the member variable *loadedAddr* storing the address at which it was loaded. The relative address of the instruction following each try code segment, i.e., the offset in module α, can be calculated at compile time as a constant. This constant, plus the value of *loadedAddr*, is the memory address of the instruction following the try code segment.

In the implementation of exception handling, the nested relationship of try code segments at runtime should be tracked so as to know the current try code segment.

The information to be tracked is naturally the memory address of the instruction following the try code segment. For this purpose the exception frame class is defined. Whenever the CPU executes a try instruction, it creates an instance object of the exception frame and sets it as the current exception frame. An exception frame has a member variable *jumpAddr*, which records the memory address of the instruction following the try code segment. When the CPU executes the instruction at the end of the try code segment, the current exception frame changes again to the parent of the current exception frame. In order to know the memory address of the parent frame, the exception frame also has the member variable *father*, so the nested nature of the try code segment is manifested as a chain of exception frames in the runtime trace. The current exception frame is the head of the chain, and every time the CPU executes a try instruction, the created exception frame is added to the chain and becomes the head of a new chain. When the CPU executes the end instruction of the try code segment, the head of the chain is deleted and the exception frame it refers to is released.

In order to show the above tracing process clearly, an example is given. Suppose there is a try code segment A in function α, in which there is a try code segment B. In try code segment B, function β is called, and in function β there is a try code segment C. In try code segment C, function θ is called, and when the CPU executes function θ, the contents of the process stack are shown in Fig. 2.6. At this point of time, the top of the stack is local variables for function θ, as shown at the bottom of the figure. There are three exception frames in the stack, from top to bottom corresponding to try code segments A, B, and C. The current exception frame is of try code segment C in function β. There are two chains in the stack: (1) the chain of function call relationships, indicated by dashed arrows in the figure, and (2) the chain of nested relationships of exception frames, indicated by solid arrows in the figure. When function θ returns, the exception frame of try code segment C becomes the top element of the stack. When the CPU finishes executing try code segment C, it pops its exception frame from the top of the stack, and then the current exception frame becomes the exception frame of try code segment B.

With the current exception frame, once an exception occurs, a jump can be implemented in the exception signal handling routine to allow the CPU to go to the

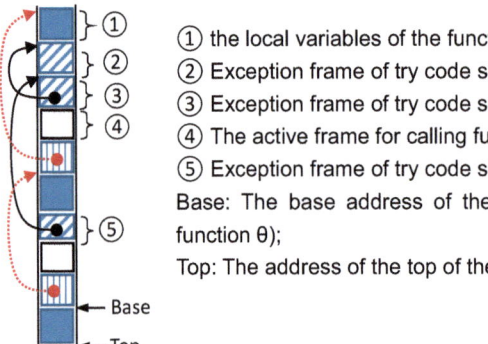

① the local variables of the function α;
② Exception frame of try code segment A in function α;
③ Exception frame of try code segment B in function α;
④ The active frame for calling function β;
⑤ Exception frame of try code segment C in function β;
Base: The base address of the current function (i.e., function θ);
Top: The address of the top of the process stack;

Fig. 2.6 Process stack status when the CPU executes to function θ

2.12 Exception Handling

instruction following the current try code segment. This kind of jump is fundamentally different from the branch jump in the source program. Branch jumps in source programs are intra-function jumps. Since an exception can occur in the called function, the jumps in this case are cross-function or even cross-module in nature. The return operation of the called function is jumped over, causing an imbalance between call and return, and triggering a stack inconsistency error. This is illustrated by the example shown in Fig. 2.6. Suppose an exception occurs when the CPU executes to an instruction in function β, but the instruction is not in try code segment C. The process stack condition at this point is shown in Fig. 2.7a. After the exception jump, the instruction following the try code segment B in function α is executed next. At this point, the current function is not function β, but function α. The expected process stack status is shown in Fig. 2.7b. But the actual process stack situation is as shown in Fig. 2.7a. The two are clearly inconsistent.

The reason for the inconsistency of the process stack is that the jump on an exception may be a cross-function or even cross-module jump, which is also called a long jump. Long jumps leave a lot of code unexecuted, including code that frees the local variable storage of a function before it returns and code that frees the active frame after the function returns. In the example shown in Fig. 2.7, the local variables of function β and the active frame of the call to function β are not released from the process stack, and the value in the base address register of the current function is still that of the local variable of function β. At this point, it is necessary to execute the code in function α. This is clearly wrong. This error is called a stack inconsistency error.

To eliminate stack inconsistency errors, a consistency check should be done on the stack in the exception signal handling routine. If inconsistency is found, the local variables at the top of the stack, the base address of the caller function, and the active frame should be released until the stack is consistent. Therefore, the setup information of the exception handling should also include the local variable base address of the current function, i.e., add a member variable *baseAddr* to the

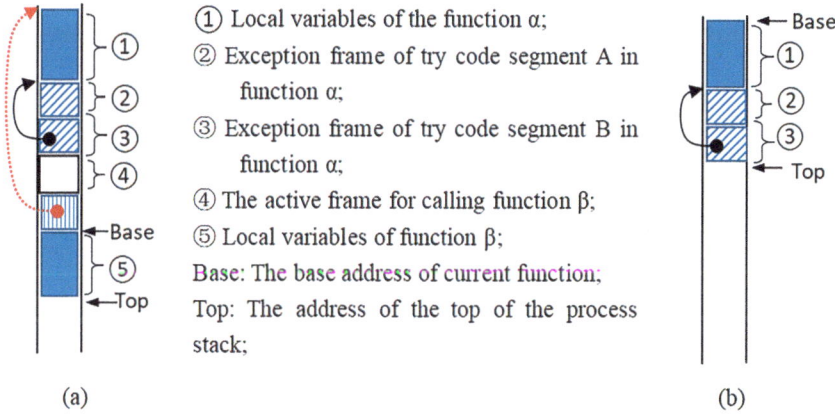

Fig. 2.7 Example of process stack inconsistency due to a long jump. (**a**) status at the moment of the exception. (**b**) Desired status after the exception jump

exception frame class. When doing the stack consistency check, if the value of the local variable base address register is not equal to the member variable *baseAddr* of the current exception frame, then the local variables at the top of the stack, the base address of the caller's function, and the active frame should be popped. This checking and popping continue until it is consistent.

Exception handling has the recovery of register values in addition to the recovery of the process stack. Again, the above example is used to show the origin of the problem. Suppose the CPU executes to an instruction in function β, but the instruction is not in try code segment C, and an exception occurs. At this point, it is necessary for the CPU to jump to execute the instruction after the try code segment B in function α. This long jump has a register value recovery problem. Before calling function β, some data are stored in the registers. When the CPU jumps to execute function β, the code in function β also uses the registers to store data. In order not to destroy the value left in the registers by function α, function β performs a vacating operation on the registers it wants to use, i.e., it stores their values on the process stack. Before the function returns, it restores the value from the process stack to the registers, so the value left in the registers by function α is not affected. A long jump leaves the restoration operation of the register values unperformed, and thus the value left in the register by function α is not restored.

The CPU jumps taken by exception handling, where code segments that should have been executed are not executed, cause many more problems than the above. If the unexecuted code includes an operation that frees a shared resource in the operating system, then the shared resource will never be freed. If the shared resource is a lock, it can cause other processes waiting for the lock to freeze. If an operation to close a file is not executed, then other applications that open and use the file will always fail. If the unexecuted code contains an operation that frees an object, then the object remains in memory, causing a memory leak. As you can see, the use of exception handling in source programs should be done with care and consideration of the potential pitfalls and hazards, especially in collaborative and shared application scenarios.

For the pitfalls caused by exception handling, Java provides garbage identification and recycling mechanisms that help in problem solving, especially memory leaks. Garbage identification is the most critical in garbage collection. Instance objects created by the program and shared objects in the operating system that are requested become garbage if the program is unreachable for them. Thus, at any given moment, instance objects can be divided into two categories: (1) reachable objects and (2) unreachable objects. Unreachable objects are called garbage and the memory they occupy should be freed. Now the question is: how to recognize garbage? The strategy used is: identify the reachable instance objects and the remaining instance objects are naturally garbage.

Program access to instance objects is characterized by chaining. The only possible starting points of the chain are local variables, formal parameters, global variables, and static variables. Local variables and formal parameters at runtime are on the process stack. Global variables and static variables are the contents of the executable file and are always present in memory. Therefore, only the in-memory values of the above four types of variables must be parsed. The portion of them that is of type pointer and has a value other than 0 constitutes the starting set of the chain, also called the root set. The instance objects pointed to by the pointers in the root set is first-level reachable objects. If a member variable of any first-level reachable object is of type pointer and its value is not 0, The instance object pointed to by the pointer is a second-level reachable object. By following this path, all reachable instance objects can be labeled, and the remaining unlabeled instance objects are garbage. For OS shared object identifiers that only appear in garbage, the OS API is called to free them. For the garbage itself, the memory it occupies is reclaimed.

2.12.2 Exception Handling Implementation

The C library functions *setjmp* and *longjmp* can be used to implement exception handling. *setjmp* saves the current context of the process to a specified memory space. *Longjmp* restores the context of the process saved by *setjmp*. The restoration of the instruction register should be placed last, because once the value in the instruction register is restored, the CPU jumps to execute the next instruction indicated by *setjmp*. The meaning of the try keyword is *setjmp*. Once an exception occurs, *longjmp* is called in the exception signal handling routine to make the CPU jump. In C language, for example, exception handling is expressed in the source program as shown in Code 2.23, where try and catch are both keywords. If an exception occurs during the execution of the try code segment, it jumps to the execution of the contents of the catch segment. Otherwise, the contents of the catch segment are not executed. The compiler performs the equivalent transformation in preprocessing, resulting in the source program shown in Code 2.24.

Code 2.23 Exception Handling Representation in Source Programs
```
(1)    try {
(2)       ......
(3)    }
(4)    catch (void *exceptionDescription) {
(5)       ......
(6)    }
```

The meaning of lines 1–4 in Code 2.24 is: create an exception frame and add it to the chain of exception frames as a new chain head. The head of the chain is the current exception frame. Line 5 contains two operations: (1) call the function *setjmp*; (2) read the return value and assign it to the local variable *ret*. The functionality of *setjmp* is to save the current context of the process to the member variable, *context*, of the current exception frame, in order to prepare for the exception handling with the CPU jump. If the value of *ret* is 0, it comes from *setjmp*, otherwise it comes from *longjmp*, which is called in the exception signal handling routine. Therefore, when the return value is 0, the try code segment is executed, otherwise the catch code segment is executed, as shown in lines 6–12. When *ret* is not 0, the return value means a pointer to the exception description. The meaning of lines 13–15 is that the head of the exception chain is extracted from the chain and released, and the current exception frame is changed to a new head of the chain.

The implementation of the exception signal handling routine is shown in Code 2.25. Its functionality is to get the current exception frame and then call the function *longjmp* to restore the process context to the context saved by *setjmp*. The restoration causes the CPU to jump to the instruction that assigns a value to the variable *ret* in line 5 of Code 2.24. The implication of line 6 is to trigger a signal to end the process.

The value assigned to the local variable *ret* in line 5 of Code 2.24 comes from 2 sources: (1) from *setjmp* and (2) from *longjmp*, i.e., the instruction that assigns a value to *ret* will also be executed by the CPU after the call to *longjmp*. Why would two executions of the same instruction result in different values for *ret*? This needs to be answered by delving into the implementation details of *setjmp*. Let Code 2.24 be located in function α. The status of the process stack before calling *setjmp* is shown in Fig. 2.8a. *setjmp*'s code is divided into three segments, which are, in order: (1) the initialization work segment; (2) the business processing segment; and (3) the cleanup and return work segment. The initialization segment does the following: (1) saves the value in the base address register (i.e., the base address of the caller); (2) stores its own base address in the base address register; (3) allocates storage space for local variables; and (4) pushes the value of the registers to be used into the process stack and saves them in order to free up the registers for its own use. The status of the process stack after initialization is complete is shown in Fig. 2.8b. The cleanup before returning is just the reverse of the initialization.

Code 2.24 Exception Handling Implementation

```
(1)   ExceptionFrame *father = getCurrentExceptionFrame( );
(2)   Context *context = new Context( );
(3)   ExceptionFrame *exceptionFrame= new ExceptionFrame(
      context, father );
(4)   setCurrentExceptionFrame ( exceptionFrame );
(5)   int ret = setjmp(exceptionFrame->context);
(6)   if (ret == 0) {
(7)   ....... // The contents in the try block
(8)   }
(9)   else {
(10)    ExceptionDescription *exceptionDescription =
        (ExceptionDescription *) ret;
(11)    ....... // The contents in the catch block
(12)  }
(13)  setCurrentExceptionFrame ( exceptionFrame->father );
(14)  delete exceptionFrame->context;
(15)  delete exceptionFrame;
```

2.12 Exception Handling

Code 2.25 Implementation of Exception Signal Handling Routine
```
(1)  void exceptionSignalHandler(void
     *exceptionDescription) {
(2)  ExceptionFrame *currentExceptionFrame =
     getCurrentExceptionFrame( );
(3)  if (currentExceptionFrame ! = null)
(4)    longjmp(currentExceptionFrame->context, (int)
       exceptionDescription);
(5)  else
(6)    triggerSignal(KILL_PROCESS, (void *) "exception id: 2;
       detail: process exited abnormally");
(7)  return;
(8)  }
```

The business processing segment of *setjmp* does the following: fills the caller's activity frame with the return value and saves the process context. However, the process context that setjmp saves is not that of the current moment, but the moment after the return. The reason is that in *longjmp* it is not for the CPU to jump to re-execute the code in the *setjmp* function, but rather for the CPU to jump to execute the code after *setjmp* returns. As far as the process stack is concerned, the process stack in the current moment is shown in Fig. 2.8b, and the process stack in the post-return moment is shown in Fig. 2.8a. There are obvious differences between the two, such as the base address register value (i.e., Base in the Fig. 2.8) and the top-of-stack address register value (i.e., Top in the Fig. 2.8). For registers to be used in *setjmp*, the values are already stored on the process stack during the initialization phase and are naturally accessible. For specialized registers such as the base address

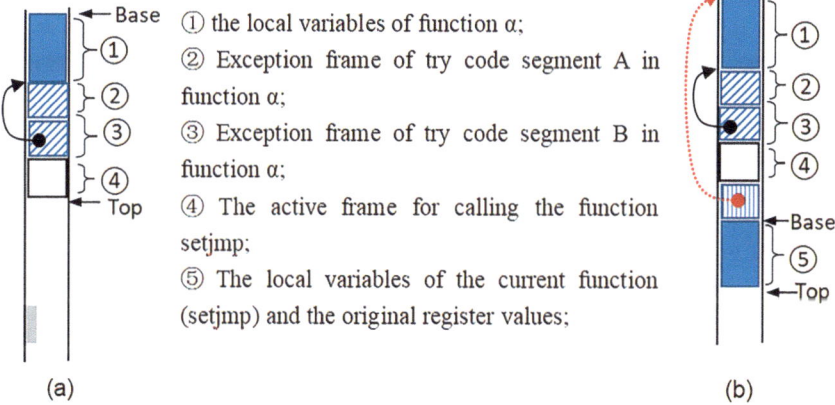

Fig. 2.8 Process stack status change due to a function call. (**a**) status before jumping to setjmp. (**b**) status after setjmp has completed its initialization

register and the top-of-stack address register, can their values in the post-return moment be derived in the current moment? This is the key question to answer.

There are four specialized registers whose values in the post-return moment are significantly different from their values in the current moment. These four registers are: the instruction register, the base address register, the top-of-stack address register, and the module register. In the post-return moment, the instruction register stores the address in memory of the next instruction to be executed after the return (i.e., the instruction that assigns a value to ret). This value is stored in the member variable *returnAddr* in the active frame and is filled in by the caller before the call. The values in the base address register, and the top-of-stack address register are the Base and Top values as in Fig. 2.8a. Comparing Fig. 2.8a, b, the base address register value in the current moment (i.e., the Base value in Fig. 2.8b), minus the width of the pointer variable yields the top-of-stack address value in the post-return moment. This location stores exactly the base address register value in the post-return moment. Therefore, in the current moment, it is not a problem to derive the values of the registers in the post-return moment.

setjmp is a function in the C library module, and its caller is in the application module. Thus, the *setjmp* call in line 5 of Code 2.24 is a cross-module call. The module register value in the post-return moment is the base address of the global variable in the application module. The module register value in the current moment is the base address of the global variable in the C library module. The two are not the same. According to the implementation of the cross-module function call, the caller first presses the module register value into the stack to save it, and then creates the active frame on the top of the stack. Therefore *setjmp*, as a called function, can know where the module register value in the post-return moment is stored on the stack, and getting it is not a problem.

In *longjmp*, the first thing to do is to assign a value to the member variable *returnValue* in the active frame that calls s*etjmp*. This requires knowing the address in memory of the active frame that called *setjmp*. Since the saved process context is the process context just after the return of *setjmp*, it can be seen from Fig. 2.8a that the saved top-of-stack address value (i.e., the Top value) minus the width of the active frame that called *setjmp* (which is a constant) yields the memory address of the active frame. Therefore, filling in the return value in *longjmp* is not a problem. After filling in the return value, the next step is to restore the values of all registers. Of course, the restoration of instruction register values should be placed at the end, because once restored, the CPU will jump to execute the next instruction to be executed just after the return of *setjmp*, i.e., the instruction that assigns a value to *ret* shown in line 5 of Code 2.24. In the process of recovering register values by *longjmp*, some registers, such as instruction register and base address register, are used, so the order and strategy of recovering register values are very critical.

For the registers to be used by *longjmp*, according to the reverse order of recovery, the values to be recovered are read out from the current exception frame and pushed into the process stack, and then finally the values are recovered to each register in turn by popping. For the top-of-stack address register, its value changes with each pop. The value in the instruction register is popped last. The final pop operation not only restores the value in the instruction register, but also restores the value in the top-of-stack address register, killing two birds with one stone.

Note: When the CPU executes the *longjmp* function, the active frame of the call to *setjmp* is actually long gone from the process stack. The call to *setjmp* may have been made a long time ago when the exception occurred. After *setjmp* returns, the caller has to do three things: (1) read the return value, (2) release the active frame of the call to *setjmp*, and (3) restore the values of the module register. Now *longjmp* wants to restore the process status to the status just after *setjmp* returns, so it has to think that the active frame that called *setjmp* still exists and assign a value to its member variable *returnValue*. Considering that the active frame for calling *setjmp* still exists will not be a problem because the data stored in that location have lost its significance and belongs to what was skipped and cleaned up.

Reflection 2-50: Assume that exception handling is set up in the function α shown in Fig. 2.8a. Once the exception occurs, then the CPU moves to execute the function *exceptionSignalHandler* in which *longjmp* is called. At the time the CPU executes the *longjmp* function, the base address register value at this point must be greater than the Top value in Fig. 2.8a plus the width of the pointer type. Why?

Reflection 2-51: The machine code for the *longjmp* function also has three segments, in order: (1) the initialization segment; (2) the business processing segment; and (3) the cleanup and return segment. However, the cleanup and return segment will not be executed by the CPU, why?

The current exception frame pointer value is used in Code 2.24 and also in the exception signal handling routine *exceptionSignalHandler*, see Code 2.25. Code 2.24 belongs to the application module, while the exception signal handling routine *exceptionSignalHandler* belongs to the support library. Where is the appropriate place to store the current exception frame pointer? First of all, it cannot be stored in a global variable in the support library. The reasons are as follows. Suppose the exception occurs when the CPU executes the code in module θ. After the hard interrupt handling routine returns, the CPU jumps to execute the *callSignalHandler* function in the support library. In this function, the function *exceptionSignalhandler* is called. At this time, the value in the module register is the base address of the global variable in module θ, not the base address of the global variable in the support library module. Therefore, global variables cannot be used in the *exceptionSignalhandler* function.

Storing the current exception frame pointer in a global variable in the main module of the application is also problematic. The main module (i.e., the module containing the main function) is the topmost module among the modules that make up the application. Exception handling may also be set up in other lower-level modules, so that the current exception frame pointer value is also read and written. Lower-level modules have to use callback functions to access the upper-level modules. Thus, each module has to set a global variable to store the memory address of the callback function and provide a registration function for the upper-level module to call. But as far as exception handling is concerned, global variables cannot be accessed in the function *exceptionSignalhandler* of the support library. Therefore, it is not feasible to use the global variable in the main module to store the current exception frame pointer. Therefore, it is only possible to store it in the operating system, i.e., to add a member variable to the process to store the current exception frame pointer.

Suppose that the exception occurs when the CPU executes code in module θ and the exception handling is located in module α. When *longjmp* is called, the recovery of the module register value is included in the process context recovery effort. Therefore, after recovery, the value in the module register is no longer the base address of the global variables in module θ, but the base address of the global variables in module α.

When exception handling occurs in a loop statement, each loop performs one exception handling operation: creating an exception frame, initializing it (i.e., saves the context of the process to the exception frame), adding it to the chain of exception frames, and then extracting it from the chain of exception frames and destroying it. Each loop does not change the context of the process. That means loops cause the same thing to be executed over and over again. To optimize performance, loop statements containing exception handling can be equivalently transformed so that the exception handling operation is executed only once. For example, the source program in Code 2.26 can be equivalently transformed into the source program in Code 2.27. Since the exception handling is moved outside the loop, once an exception occurs, it jumps outside the loop and assigns a value to the variable *ret*, see line 5. In line 6, if *ret* is greater than 0, it means that the return value came from *longjmp*, i.e., an exception was thrown. At this point, an unconditional goto statement has to be used to jump from outside the loop to inside the loop, see line 9.

Reflection 2-52: What are the overheads of exception handling, including storage overhead and computation overhead? Is the overhead large? Exception handling is best avoided in code that is frequently executed by the CPU. Is this view correct? Why? Functions in the underlying support libraries are usually frequently called functions, so it is better not to have exception handling in the underlying support libraries. Is this view correct? Give reasons. Is it correct to argue that attention in program design should be focused on avoiding exceptions rather than on exception handling? For the return value of an API function, should the success or failure of execution be considered? Give examples of API functions that take this into account. Is checking whether the value of a variable is within bounds before using it an important means of avoiding exceptions?

Code 2.26 Source Program Example with Exception Handling in a Loop
```
(1)    while(....) {
(2)       ......
(3)       try {
(4)          The contents of the try block;
(5)       }
(6)       catch(ExceptionDescription *e) {
(7)          The contents of the catch block;
(8)       }
(9)       ......
(10) }
```

Code 2.27 Implementation of Moving Exception Handling Outside the Loop

```
(1)   ExceptionFrame *father = getCurrentExceptionFrame( );
(2)   Context *context = new Context( );
(3)   ExceptionFrame *frame= new ExceptionFrame( context,
      father);
(4)   setCurrentExceptionFrame ( frame );
(5)   int ret = setjmp(frame->context);
(6)   if (ret > 0) {
(7)      ExceptionDescription *e =
         (ExceptionDescription *) ret;
(8)      The contents of the catch block;
(9)      goto (14);
(10)  }
(11)  while(....) {
(12)     ......
(13)     The contents of the try block;
(14)     ......
(15)  }
(16)  setCurrentExceptionFrame (frame->father );
(17)  delete frame->context;
(18)  delete frame;
```

2.12.3 Application of Exception Handling

Exception handling can be used to solve many application problems. For example, for the command prompt program *Cmd* in Sect. 2.2 (see Code 2.1 for its implementation), its functionality is to wait for the user's keyboard to enter a command line, i.e., the name of a program file to be executed, and then call the main function in it. Assuming that *Cmd* is now being used to run program *A*, when program *A* contains infinite loop code, the call to the main function of program *A* (see line 10 of Code 2.1) will never return. At this point, the user can no longer interact with *cmd*. Infinite loop code is found in many applications, such as *Cmd* program itself, which contains infinite loop code (see the while statement in lines 5–11 of Code 2.1). To keep *Cmd* program from getting out of control, the user can interrupt the execution of program *A* by hitting ctrl + C, which causes the CPU to jump to the code after line 10 of Code 2.1, i.e., to the next while loop. The user can then interact with *Cmd* program again. This application functionality can be realized through exception handling.

To return *Cmd* program to the state in which it interacts with the user (i.e., the keyboard input state) when the user hits the ctrl+C keys, two things need to be done.

The first thing is to add exception handling to line 10 of Code 2.1. The tenth line of code with exception handling is shown in Code 2.28. The meaning is: in the process of calling the main function, once triggered an exception, jump to the execution of the code in the catch block, that is, the output of the exception description. Exception handling is over to enter the next round of while loop. The second thing is to check if the keyboard input is the ctrl+C key in the keyboard input interrupt handling routine. If it is, it is treated as an exception event and triggers an exception signal to the current process (in this case, the process running C*md* program). The signal id identifies the class of the signal. The operating system defines a number of signal ids and also provides routines for handling these signals in the support library, so that manipulations to a process, such as ending a process, can be performed. The id of the exception signal is included in a list.

Code 2.28 Add Exception Handling to Main Function Calls
```
(1)   try {
(2)      *appMain(argc, argv).
(3)   }
(4)   catch (void *exceptionDescription) {
(5)      print("%s\n", (char *)exceptionDescription);
(6)   }
```

Exception handling is also used in database servers to handle user SQL requests. The database server uses while infinite loop to process user's SQL requests, one SQL request is processed in each round of while loop. Before executing a user's SQL request, a series of legitimacy checks are performed. These checks include: SQL syntax check, object existence check, data integrity check, and security check. Only after all the checks are passed will the SQL be executed. If a check fails, the subsequent checks and SQL execution are skipped and the next while loop is performed. This business characteristic coincides with exception handling. Applying exception handling makes the code very clean and logical. The handling of the SQL request is shown in Code 2.29.

Many of the definitions of legitimacy rules for SQL requests do not have a return value concept. For example, triggers that express data integrity do not have a return value. There are also legitimacy rule definitions placed in stored procedures, which also do not have a return value concept. This situation makes it difficult to programmatically implement the legality checks described above. If the branch statement is used for control, no logical judgment can be made because triggers and stored procedures do not have return values. Even if the branch statement can be used, it will be difficult for the programmer to grasp accurately because of the many branches, deep nesting, complex relationships, and different rules in different modules, which making it very easy to get it wrong. If you use exception handling, the definition of

2.12 Exception Handling

the rule is only one guideline, that is: if SQL request is not legal, then call the API function that throws an exception, do not have to worry about process control issues.

Code 2.29 Example of Exception Handling in Database Servers

```
(1)   try {
(2)     if (SQL statement has syntax error)
(3)       throw(190, "Syntax error code, detail");
(4)     if (the table name and field name in the SQL statement
          do not exist in the database)
(5)       throw(191, "Object does not exist error code,
          detail");
(6)     if (Permission check of SQL statement does not pass)
(7)       throw(192, "No permissions error code, detailed");
(8)     if (SQL statement is an update operation) {
(9)       if (SQL statement is an UPDATE or DELETE operation)
(10)        Execute the corresponding query to get the data
            rows to be updated;
(11)      SELECT * FROM trigger INTO bind_trigger WHERE
          operation = @operation_type AND obj_table = @
          obj_table ORDER BY type;
(12)      if (Existing BEFORE type trigger in bind_trigger)
(13)        Execute the code in each BEFORE type trigger in
            bind_trigger in turn;
(14)      if (bind_trigger has a trigger of type
          INSTEAD OF)
(15)        Execute the code in INSTEAD OF type trigger in
            bind_trigger in turn;
(16)      else
(17)        Executes the SQL statement requested by the client;
(18)      if (Existing AFTER type trigger in bind_trigger)
(19)        Execute the code in each AFTER type trigger in
            bind_trigger in turn;
(20)    }
(21)    else
(22)      Execute the SQL statement requested by the client;
          // a query statement
(23)   }
(24)   catch (exception *e) { ..... }
```

Code 2.30 gives the definition of a trigger. Its meaning is: to add a row to the student table, the value of the student number field cannot be duplicated with the existing records in the table. The meaning of the fifth line of code is: from the student table to find rows of records, the condition is that the student number field value is equal to that of the added row. If the query result is not null, then it means that the newly added row is not legal, so the *throw* function is called to throw an exception. The first real parameter, 200, is the exception number, and the second real parameter is the description of the exception. This trigger is executed on line 13 of Code 2.29. When the exception is thrown, all subsequent code is skipped over to the execution of line 24 of Code 2.29.

Code 2.30 Trigger Definition Example
```
(1)   CREATE TRIGGER insert_row_on_student AS
(2)   BEFORE INSERT ON student
(3)   referencings new row as new
(4)   FOR EACH ROW
(5)     WHEN (EXIST SELECT studentNo FROM student WHERE
          studentNo=@new.studentNo)
(6)       throw(200, @new.studentNo + 'Already exists in
          student table' )
```

As you can see from the above application example, exception handling can also be used to dynamically control the execution flow of a program. Whenever a process triggers an exception signal, it interrupts its current execution flow, allowing the CPU to jump to the code in the catch block. A process can trigger an exception signal for itself as well as for other processes. In the hard interrupt handling routines, a process can also be given an exception signal. Codes 2.29 and 2.30 are examples of a process triggering an exception signal for itself.

Reflection 2-53: The function that throws an exception is *throw*. Can you give its implementation? Can the function *exceptionSignalHandler* be called directly when throwing an exception signal to itself?

2.13 Summary of the Chapter

The computational task is embodied in a program, which consists of two parts, code and data. The code being a sequence of instructions. When a program is executed by the CPU, the corresponding computational task is completed. The completion of a computational task usually involves interaction with peripherals, as well as human-computer interaction. The speed of response of the components of a computer varies greatly, and the CPU does not usually respond immediately to an instruction given during the execution of a program. The CPU is idle during the period from the time an instruction is given to the time the result is obtained. In order to fully utilize the CPU resources, the CPU can be allowed to jump to another computation task. Once

2.13 Summary of the Chapter

the response result is ready, then the CPU jumps back to process the response result. This is where concurrent multi-task execution comes from. Running instances of a program are called processes. When multiple processes execute concurrently, resources on the computer are shared by multiple processes.

The key concept in processes is the next instruction to be executed. Each process has its own next instruction to execute. When a process is in the start state, its next instruction to be executed is the first instruction of the program's main function. Concurrent execution of multiple tasks usually uses a time-division multiplexing strategy. Specifically, time is divided into time slices, the CPU executes one process in one time slice and another process in the next time slice, and all processes are executed by the CPU in turn. The process that is being executed by the CPU is called the current process. For the current process, when the conditions required for its next instruction to be executed are not yet satisfied, it actively gives up the CPU and performs a process switch to allow the CPU to jump to another process that is ready to be executed. This is the specific case of concurrent execution of multiple processes.

The operating system is the manager of the computer's resources and the application program is the client of the resources. The application program interacts with the operating system by calling API functions provided by the operating system. The data maintained in the operating system are shared data and are shared by all processes. The computer has an interrupt mechanism: every time a hard interrupt is triggered, the CPU goes to jump to execute the hard interrupt handling routine. After the hard interrupt handling routine returns, the CPU jumps again to continue the execution of the interrupted process. Access to shared data in the operating system involve not only processes, but also hard interrupt handling routines, so there is the problem of access conflicts. One strategy to guarantee data consistency and correctness is to block hard interrupts while the CPU executes a interrupt handling routine.

Executables and libraries are collectively referred to as modules. Modules contain both code and data parts. Module sharing refers to the sharing of code and constant data. Variable data in a module are the global and static variables in a program, which are not shared, but rather each process has its own copy. Module sharing suffers from the problem of inconsistency between the actual loaded address at runtime and the predefined loaded address at compile time. This inconsistency has two levels: (1) inconsistency in the read-only part of the module (i.e., the code part and the constant part of the data); and inconsistency in the read-write part of the module (i.e., the variable data part). To address the problems encountered in module sharing, relative addressing enables references within a module to be independent of the actual loaded address of the module in memory. Indirect addressing solves the problem of compilation-time indeterminacy of cross-module references. Dynamic allocation of data at runtime makes code reentrant: different processes execute the same code but manipulate different data and are out of bounds with each other.

There are signaling and messaging methods of interaction between processes. The signaling approach prioritizes startup signal handling, which can lead to multiple execution flows for a process, creating the problem of global variable access conflicts. In the messaging approach, messages are extracted and processed by the application program itself, which guarantees that a process has only one execution flow, thus eliminating the problem of global variable access conflicts. Just because you have a message approach does not mean you can eliminate the signal approach. Things that need to be handled urgently and with priority, such as exceptions, should still be handled by signaling. Since the hard interrupt handling routine is a separate execution flow, its interactions with processes can naturally be unified into process-to-process interactions. For a process to trigger a signal or send a message to another process, it needs to know the process id of the other process. There is a relationship between the processes. Process A creates process B, so the two are parent–child. The return value of the created process is the id of the child process, so the parent process knows the id of the child process.

Exercises

1. Creating instance objects of a class in the heap provides support for garbage collection. The application calls the API functions provided by the heap manager to request memory space for the objects. The heap manager records the starting address and size of each object. A program has no direct access to an object in the heap; it must access it through a pointer. Therefore, the only variable data that a program can access directly are local variables, global variables, static variables, and formal parameters. If the variable in these four categories is an object pointer variable, then the object it refers to can be accessed through that variable. If a member variable of an accessible object is a pointer variable, then the object to which it refers is also accessible. And so on, you can find out all the accessible objects.

   The implementation of automatic garbage collection is not really complicated. It is to check the above 4 types of variables to see which ones are object pointer variables, and if their value is not 0, it means that it points to an object, and the object it refers to is the one that can be accessed. Then we can find out all the accessible objects by following the trail. For all objects in the heap, after identifying the accessible objects, the remaining objects are inaccessible objects, i.e., garbage, and should be recycled to free up the memory they occupy.

   It is assumed that there are no global and static variables, and that the layout of each function's formal parameters and local variables in memory is known. That is, the id of each function, as well as the offset (i.e., the relative address) of each of its formal parameters and each of its local variables with respect to the function's base address, and whether or not the type is an object pointer, are constants recorded in the table *functionDefinitionList*.

   Runtime local variables and formal parameters are all allocated on the process stack. In order to identify the starting address of each local variable and formal parameter on the stack and its data type, it is necessary to keep track of the function call relationships at runtime. Assuming that the trace information is recorded in *functionCallList*, the table element is the function id, the current function id is at the end of the table, and its base address is stored in the base address register.

For each class, add a member variable to it, and make it the first member variable, which is named *classId*. For each class id, the relative address (i.e., offset) of each of its member variables, and whether or not the type is an object pointer, which are also constants, are recorded in the table *classDefinitionList*.

At garbage collection time, in addition to the local variables and formal parameters in the process stack, the signal objects in the *signalEventList* of the process and the message objects in the *messageList* are checked. The signal and message objects are data that the process has not yet processed, and naturally they are data that will be used later, and are accessible objects.

Write an algorithm for marking objects accessible in garbage collection based on the implementation of function calls and the dynamic allocation scheme for storing local variables described in Sect. 2.8.6. Note: For an object, its pointer may be stored in more than one place, so it is important to prevent duplicate marking when following the trail to avoid loopbacks.

2. Process object in the operating system is also called the process control block (abbreviated as PCB), the information recorded is divided into three parts: (1) code information, that is, the various modules making up an application, and their addresses in memory. Each module has two loading information: one is for a read-only part (i.e., the code and string constants), the other is for read-write part (i.e., global variables and static variables); (2) data information, including the stack to store local variables, the heap to store objects, the *signalHandlerList* to store signals, and *messageList* for storing messages; (3) run state information, i.e., context information, which is stored in registers. Consult the sources to see what each of these pieces of information is named in the PCB.

The Linux operating system provides a process cloning API function, *fork*, which is called to clone a new process that is a child of the calling process. For the child process, the return value of this function is 0; for the calling process, the return value of this function is the id of the child process. The two processes share the read-only part of the modules (i.e., code and string constants). The read-write portions each have their own share, as do the stack and heap. In the operating system kernel, the implementation of the fork function is not complicated. The global variable *currentProcess* refers to the current process object. The child process object is created by copying the current process object, and then added to the process table *processList*. After copying, first modify the value of the process id member variable of the child process object, because it plays a role in identifying the process. Can you write the code to implement the fork function?

In C language, the return value of *setjmp* and *longjmp* functions is assigned to the same variable. What is the connection and difference between this situation and fork? Linux operating system also provides API functions to create processes. Please check the information to find out the connection and difference with fork.

3. In the source program shown in Code 2.31, the meaning of line 2 is to call the API function *getProcessId* provided by the operating system to get its own process id. The meaning of lines 4–12 is to call the fork function by the main process to clone out three child processes. In this code, why don't any of the 3 child processes call the fork function? After the first child process is created, it knows the id of the parent process because it is stored in the processIdArray[0] variable. Is it right? After the second child process is created, it knows the id of the parent process and the first child process, why? After the third child process is created, it knows the ids of the parent, first and second child processes, why?
4. Bare metal virtual machine is a logical concept on which users can install an operating system. Assuming that the first operating system installed in a physical computer is Host, and Hypervisor is an application for creating bare metal virtual machines. After a bare metal virtual machine is created, an operating system called as Guest can be installed on it. In this situation, Host has APIs for creating a virtual machine and associating it with a process. Specifically, a new member variable *vm* is added to Process class. The specific implementation is as follows:

Hypervisor creates a VM, then a process and let its member variable *vm* pointing to the VM. The process execute Guest installation program. During the process of executing Guest installation program, when CPU encounters a privileged instruction, an exceptions occurs due to lack of privilege. So CPU jumps to execute the exception interrupt handling routine of Host, in which the attribute *vm* of the current process is checked. Thus, Host knows which virtual machine is associated with the exception, then takes corresponding measures such as sending a message to Hypervisor.

Intel Virtualization Technology for x86 (abbreviated as Intel VT-x) supports virtualization at the hardware level. Specifically, a bit is added to CPU for a new running mode, i.e., non-root mode. When a computer startups, CPU is in root mode. When creating a process, it can be set to run in non-root mode. When CPU executes a sensitive Instruction in non-root mode, an exception occurs. In terms of virtualization, compared to implementation in operating system level, what benefits can be achieved by Intel VT-x? Please refer to the literature on Intel VT-x to answer this question.

Code 2.31 Router Implementation
```
(1)    int processIdArray[4] = {0, 0, 0 , 0};
(2)    processArray[0] = getProcessId( );
(3)    int processIndex = 1;
(4)    int processId = fork( );
(5)    while( processId > 0 ) {,
(6)        processIdArray[processIndex] = processId;
(7)        processIndex++;
```

```
(8)     if (processIndex < 4)
(9)       processId = fork();
(10)    else {
(11)      processIndex = 0;
(12)      break;
(13)    }
(14)  }
```

After executing this code, the main process and the three child-processes cloned from it have *processIndex* values of 0, 1, 2 and 3 respectively. The *processIndex* value of each process indicates its own ranking among the four processes, so it also knows which part of the work it is responsible for doing. For example, suppose the computational task of the four processes is to do parallel processing of n-dimensional matrix multiplication, then each process is responsible for 1/4 of the work, based on the *processIndex* value to know which 1/4 of their own responsibility.

References

1. Abraham, S., Peter, B., Galvin, G. G., *Operating System Concepts (10th ed.)*. Wiley, 2018.
2. Andrew, S., Tanenbaum, H. B., *Modern Operating Systems (4th ed.)*. London: Pearson, 2020.
3. David, B., *Using and Administering Linux: Volume 1*. Springer Nature link, 2023.
4. David, B., *Using and Administering Linux: Volume 2*. Springer Nature link, 2023.
5. Wang, K. C., *Systems Programming in Unix/Linux*. Springer Nature link, 2018 [access date 10/27/2023]; Available from: https://link.springer.com/book/10.1007/978-3-319-92429-8.
6. Abhishek, B., Daniel, L., *Architectural and Operating System Support for Virtual Memory*. Springer Nature link, 2018.
7. SeungIl, L., Byung-Sun, Y., Soo-Mook, M., *Efficient Java Exception Handling in Just-in-Time Compilation*. Software: Practice and Experience, 2004, 34(15): p. 1463–1480.
8. Alan, H., Chi-Yu, H., *Embedded Operating Systems*. Springer Nature link, 2018 [access date 11/25/2023]; Available from: https://link.springer.com/book/10.1007/978-3-319-72977-0.
9. Kim, H., *Dynamic Binary Modification*. Springer Nature link, 2011.
10. Sri, M. P., *Practical System Programming with C*. Springer Nature link, 2021 [access date 10/22/2023]; Available from: https://link.springer.com/book/10.1007/978-1-4842-6321-1.

Chapter 3
Distributed Computing

The central problem in stand-alone computing is the concurrent execution of multiple tasks and the consequent sharing of resources. For this reason, the program code is structured into two parts, the operating system and the application, where the operating system plays the role of a resource manager, acting as a server, and the application plays the role of a client. The interaction between the application and the operating system is realized as a function call using the C/S model. Distributed computing [1] evolved from stand-alone computing, which is naturally a dialectical unity of inheritance and magnificence, and can also be described as a dialectical unity of change and invariance. The invariance is manifested in the sharing model, both using the C/S interaction model, and realized by function calls. The change lies in sharing boundary being extended. That is, the sharing scope is no longer limited to the local machine, but also extended to other computers. In distributed computing, resource sharing is represented as an interaction between two processes running on different computers, where one process acts as a server and the other as a client.

In distributed computing, services provided by service providers are still open to clients in the form of application programming interface (API) functions, and clients still access services by calling API functions. Since the service provider and the client are not in the memory space of a computer, it is necessary to add an intermediary at both ends. Specifically, a proxy is added to the client side and a stub is added to the server side [2]. Both proxy and stub are intermediary functions. A proxy acts as an intermediary for services on the client side and is called by the client. A Stub, on the other hand, acts as an intermediary for the client on the server side to call the service function. What the proxy does as an intermediary is as follows: (1) packages the client's request, including the function id and the real parameters to be passed, and then passes it to the service; (2) unpacks the result of the received response into a return value and returns it to the client. The stub acts as an intermediary as well, first unpacking the request into real parameters and then packaging the return value to pass to the client side. Function calls across computer boundaries are also called remote procedure calls [2], the implementation of which will be explained in detail in Sect. 3.1.

In distributed computing, the client has to pass the request to the service over the network and the service has to pass the response to the client over the network. Both the service side and the client side send and receive data through a network connection [3]. Network connection is a service concept provided by the operating system. A network connection has five identifying attributes: its own IP address, port number, communication protocol, the opposite party's IP address and port number. On a computer, a port number is attributed to only one process. Thus, a network connection identifies the two processes on both sides of the communication. Network transmission is equivalent to real-life courier logistics. The content to be transmitted is packaged as an IP packet, i.e., it is appended with the 5 identifying attributes of a network connection. How does an IP packet get from the sending process to the receiving process through layers of transit? What are the issues involved? The implementation of network transfers is explained in detail in Sect. 3.2.

In distributed computing, the resources owned by a server are shared by multiple clients. For shared data, there is an access conflict problem [4] when multiple clients access it at the same time, resulting in inconsistent and incorrect data. In addition, a client's request may involve updating multiple items of data, requiring the server to process them in an atomic manner, as is the case with bank transfers for example. Suppose the client's request is to transfer $300 from account number 1 to account number 2. The request involves subtracting 300 from the balance on account 1 and adding 300 to the balance on account 2. These two update operations must be handled by the server as a whole, and failures are not allowed to cause only one operation to be executed. For this reason, the concept of transaction is introduced. A client can define its request as a transaction and ask the server to handle it in an atomic way. For client requests, the server avoids access conflicts through concurrency control and guarantees atomicity of execution through transaction processing [5]. Concurrency control and transaction processing are explained in detail in Sects. 3.3 and 3.4, respectively.

Some servers are made up of multiple entity servers combined in a confederation. For example, the UnionPay server is a combination of servers from major commercial banks, where the commercial banks' servers are called entity servers, or member servers. For customer requests such as interbank transfers, the UnionPay server breaks down a transaction into two subtransactions, which are then submitted to its two member servers for processing respectively. The UnionPay server still requires atomicity to process the customer's transaction request. The two subtransactions are processed by the two member servers, and it is possible that one of them succeeds and the other one does not. Assume that member server A is successful and member server B is unsuccessful. If this happens, the UnionPay server will ask member server A to perform undo processing. Only in this way can the processing of the transaction of interbank transfer be atomic. Data consistency in distributed processing [6] is explained in detail in Sect. 3.5.

3.1 Function Calls Across Machine Boundaries

The most basic type of interaction in a program is function call. There are two concepts in function calls: the caller and the called function. The caller and the called function can be in the same module; this kind of function call is within a module. The caller and the called function can also be in different modules of the same process; this kind of function call is across the module boundary. The caller and the called function can also be in different computers; this kind of function call is across the machine boundary. Function calls are the most basic form of interaction, where the caller has to know the memory address of the called function, pass real parameters and return address to the called function. The called function, in turn, has to get the real parameters, pass the function return value to the caller, and return. When clear regulations are made for these things, they can be both independent and interactive. That is, they form a confederated system. Provisions about function calls are called function call specifications [7].

From a programming perspective, the implementer of a function is called the service provider and the callers of the function are called the clients. The function definition is a contract between the service provider and the clients. The implementation process is that the service provider first defines the function and provides an implementation of it, and then releases the function definition and function implementation to client sides. For the implementation of the function, the compiler can generate code based on the function definition at compile time, including the code for acquiring real parameters and return address, and the code for passing the return value. The function implementation that the service provider gives to the client sides can be a source program file, a compiled executable file, or an intermediate code file. Function definitions from the service provider to client sides are usually placed in a header file. For example, in C and C++, function definitions are placed in a header file with h as a suffix.

The developer of a client program introduces the header file into the source program file, and then can call the functions defined in the header file in the source program. When compiling the client source program, the compiler can generate the function call code based on the definitions of the functions, including the code for passing the real parameters and return address, and the code for extracting the return value. The compiler can also know the type of some function call based on its definition, and then do the corresponding processing. There are two types of function calls: function calls within a module and function calls across module boundaries. If it is a function call across the module boundary, when generating the executable file, the module file name and function name where the external function is located should be filled into the import address table, and indirect addressing should be used to jump to the called function [2]. If it is a function call within the module, then relative addressing is used to jump to the called function. The implementation of function calls is explained in Sect. 2.8.

3.1.1 Remote Procedure Calls

For function calls across machine boundaries, the concepts of proxy and stub need to be introduced in order to maintain the invariance of the original pattern of function calls (i.e., forward compatibility). On the client-side machine, the caller invokes the proxy function. On the server-side machine, the stub calls the called function. The proxy and the stub then interact over a network connection. The proxy function acts as an intermediary. From the client side, there is no difference between the proxy function and the called function, so function calls across machine boundaries are transparent to the client. What the proxy function does is to act as an intermediary, packaging the real parameters passed by the caller and relaying them to the stub on the service side, and then unpacking the response from the stub and returning it to the caller. The stub is on the service side, representing the caller to call the called function, then package the return value and relay it to the proxy. Specifically, the real parameter package sent by the proxy is unpacked, then the called function is called, then the return value is packaged and relayed to the proxy.

For function calls across machine boundaries, the interaction between the proxy and the stub is channeled through a network connection. If the caller and the callee are on different machines, the data are also translated in the packaging. The reason is that data such as integers and real numbers are expressed in binary in different ways on different computer models. For example, on a 32-bit machine, an integer is stored in 4 bytes, while on a 64-bit machine an integer is stored in 8 bytes. Therefore, data cannot be transferred between machines of different models using memory copies. When sending data, the memory object is first translated into a standard expression. For the received content, translation is also done to transform it into its own memory object. For data such as integers and real numbers, the WEB uses XML text as the standard expression.

Function calls across machine boundaries are also called remote procedure calls (Abbreviated as RPC) [2]. The core problem to be solved is to develop standards for the composition and format of packets passed between machines. With the standard, the service side can parse the client's request packet. Conversely, the client side will be able to parse the service's response packets. To address this problem, WEB has developed the WEB SERVICE standard [8], which contains three substandards, namely, the Simple Object Access Protocol (SOAP), the WEB Service Definition Language (WSDL), and the Service Delivery and Discovery Interface (UDDI). SOAP provides detailed guidelines on how to package and transmit objects in memory in function calls that cross machine boundaries. With SOAP, the compiler knows how to generate data packing code, and data unpacking code, based on the function definition.

For a given function definition, the functionalities of its proxy and stub are both explicit and specific. Therefore, for a given function, its proxy and stub do not need to be programmed by programmers, but can be automatically generated by the compiler. Since the scope of pointers is limited to a process, you cannot pass pointers when packing real parameters or return values; you must pass the object to which the pointer refers. When the member variables of an object are also of pointer type, the object to which the pointer refers must also be passed. As you can see, for pointer variables, the initial value is very important. When its value is 0, it is a null pointer. When the value is not 0, it indicates that it points to an object. When the stub parses the request packet, it creates the real parameter object and then initializes its member variables to construct the real parameter object of the service side, with which it calls the called function. Proxies do the same when parsing response packets, constructing the client-side return value object and returning it to the caller.

The following example illustrates the implementation of a remote procedure call. Assume that the service provider defines a function called *area*, which has one formal parameter, *polygon*, of type *Polygon*, and a return value of type double. The service provider creates an area.h file with one line:

double _declspec(dllexport) _cdecl area (Polygon *polygon);

Both _declspec(dllexport) and _cdecl are compilation indicators, where declspec is an abbreviation for declare specification. The meaning of _declspec(dllexport) is that when compiling the implementation of the function, the compiler will generate a target file of type dynamic link library, and will create an export address table in its header and then add the *area* function to it. In other words, the *area* function is a function that is open to the public for external calls. The meaning of _cdecl is to ask the compiler to follow the C function call specification to generate the code in order to get the real parameter and the function return address, and pass the return value.

The second thing the service provider has to do is to create an area.cpp file that provides the implementation of the *area* function. At the beginning of this file, there is a line: #include "area.h", which introduces the function definition into the source program file. After the implementation of the *area* function, it is compiled and linked to generate the area.dll file, which is a dynamic link library file.

A service program that is released by a service provider to a client should contain four subdirectories in its directory: head, origin, proxy, and stub, which hold header files, function implementation files, proxy files, and stub files, respectively. The name of the header file to be released to clients is still *area.h*. In its content, dllexport should be changed to dllimport. The modified function definition is:

double _declspec(dllimport) _cdecl area (Polygon *polygon);

The reason for the change from dllexport to dllimport is that the client side is programmed to call the *area* function. Therefore, the client side has to tell the compiler that the *area* function is a function from an external module and has to be imported. When generating the binary executable, an import address table is created in the header and the *area* function is added to it. When generating machine instructions to call the *area* function, the external function *area* is called with indirect addressing.

Code 3.1 Proxy Source Code Automatically Generated by the Compiler Based on the Function Definition

```
(1)   include <rpc.h>
(2)   double _declspec(dllexport) _cdecl area(Polygon *
      polygon) {
(3)     string connectInfo = getConnectInfoFromConfigure( );
(4)     Connect *connect = createNetworkConnection((con
        nectInfo);
(5)     RequestPackage *requestPackage = new RequestPackage
        (RPC_REQUEST );
(6)    requestPackage->setOperationIndicator
       (GET_MACHINE_MODEL);
(7)     ResponsetPackage *responsePackage = connect.
        Request(requestPackage);
(8)     bool homogeneous = FALSE;
(9)     if (isHomogeneous(responsePackage->getResult())
(10)       homogeneous = TRUE;
(11)    requestPackage->clear( );
(12)    requestPackage->setOperationIndicator(RPC_CALL);
(13)    requestPackage->setDllName("areaStub.dll");
(14)    requestPackage->setFunctionName("areaStub");
(15)    ParameterPackage * parameterPackage = new
        ParameterPackage(homogeneous);
(16)    Parameter *parameter = new Parameter();
(17)    if (homogeneous )
(18)      polygon->serializeInBinary(parameter)));
(19)    else
(20)      polygon->serializeInText(parameter)));
(21)    parameterPackage->addItem(parameter);
(22)    requestPackage->setParameterPackage(parameterPack
        age);
(23)    responsePackage = connect.Request(requestPackage);
(24)    ParameterPackage * returnPackage =
        responsePackage->getParameterPackage();
(25)    homogeneous =returnPackage->getHomogeneousFlag();
(26)    Parameter *returnParameter =
        returnPackage->getFirstItem();
(27)    if (homogeneous)
(28)      return Double.deserializeInBinary(returnP
          arameter);
(29)    else
(30)      return Double.deserializeInText(returnParameter);
(31)  }
```

3.1 Function Calls Across Machine Boundaries

The third thing the service provider has to do is to use the compiler to automatically generate the source code files for both the proxy and the stub at the *area* function. Let the source code files of proxy and stub be named as areaProxy.cpp and areaStub.cpp, respectively, and their contents are shown in Codes 3.1 and 3.2 respectively. As mentioned earlier, the functionalities of proxy and stub are clear and specific, thus their source code can be automatically generated by the compiler.

The proxy has to do 6 things. The first one is to read the network connection information from the system configuration file, i.e., the IP address of the server, the port number, and the account name and password for logging in, as shown in line 3 of Code 3.1. The second one is to establish a network connection with the server as shown in line 4. The third thing is to get the machine model information of the server, and then determine whether own machine model is isomorphic with the server, as shown in lines 6 through 10. If it is isomorphic, then a memory copy can be taken when packing the real parameters. If it is not isomorphic, then when packing the real parameters, they have to be translated and converted into text. The fourth thing to do is to construct the request packet, as shown in lines 11 through 22. The data items in the request packet include: the dynamic link library file name, the stub function name, and the real parameters to be passed. The fifth thing is to send an RPC request to the server and get the response result as shown in line 23. The last thing is to convert the response result into a return value, as shown in lines 24 through 27.

Code 3.2 Stub Source Code Automatically Generated by the Compiler from the Function Definition

```
(1)   include <rpc.h>
(2)   include "area.h"
(3)   ParameterPackage * _declspec(dllexport) _cdecl
      areaStub(ParameterPackage * parameterPackage) {
(4)     Polygon *polygon = new Polygon();
(5)     bool homogeneous =
        parameterPackage->getHomogeneousFlag();
(6)     Parameter* parameter = parameterPackage-
        >getFirstItem( );
(7)     if (homogeneous )
(8)        polygon->deserializeInBinary(parameter);
(9)     else
(10)       polygon->deserializeInText(parameter);
(11)    double result = area(polygon);
(12)    ParameterPackage *returnPackage = new
        ParameterPackage(homogeneous);
(13)    Parameter *returnParameter = new Parameter();
(14)    if (homogeneous)
```

```
(15)        Double.serializeInBinary( result,
            returnParameter ));
(16)      else
(17)        Double.serializeInText(result, returnParameter);
(18)      returnPackage->addItem(returnParameter);
(19)      return returnPackage;
(20)    }
```

Compile and link the proxy source program file areaProxy.cpp to generate the dynamic link library file areaProxy.dll, then copy it to the subdirectory proxy in the distribution directory, and then change its name to area.dll. The function name of the proxy is the same as that of the original function, and the name of its dynamic link library is the same as the name of the dynamic link library file of the source function, so that clients do not distinguish between the original function and the proxy when calling the area function in its source code. An example of a client application is shown in Code 3.3. Set the client source program file name as client. cpp, compile and link to it, specify the link to the area.dll library file, and generate the client.exe file.

Code 3.3 Client Program Example
```
(1)    include <stdio.h>
(2)    include "area.h"
(3)    int main( int argc, char **argv) {
(4)      Polygon *polygon= new polygon();
(5)      polygon->addPoint(new Point(1,2));
(6)      polygon->addPoint(new Point(20,36));
(7)      polygon->addPoint(new Point(30,9));
(8)      double a = area(polygon);
(9)      printf("area = %f6.2", a);
(10)     return 1;
(11)   }
```

When installing the client application client.exe on a user's machine, there are two ways to configure it: (1) invoke area locally; (2) invoke area remotely. If you choose the first way to configure it, you only need to copy the client.exe file and the area.dll file in the origin subdirectory of the area distribution directory to the client application installation directory c:\client, and the installation is complete. If you choose the second configuration method, you need to copy client.exe, as well as the area.dll file and area.fig file in the proxy subdirectory of the area distribution

3.1 Function Calls Across Machine Boundaries

directory to the client application installation directory, c:\client, and then configure the remote server's IP address, port, login username, login password in the area. fig file.

It can be seen that whether the client program runs locally or remotely is not a matter of program design and development, but a matter of installation and configuration. Since the original function and its proxy have the same function name, and dynamic link library files that both of them belong to have the same file name, the difference between them is transparent to the client applications. If *area.dll* with the proxy function is copied, then client.exe runs in a remote procedure call manner. If *area.dll* with the original function is copied, then client.exe runs in a local procedure call manner.

When a remote procedure is invoked, the proxy has to establish a network connection with the server, so the setup of the connection information is also part of the application installation and configuration. Under the proxy subdirectory of the distribution directory, there is also an area.fig file that records the configuration parameters for the network connection: IP address, port number, login account name, and login password. When installing the client program client.exe, if you use the remote procedure call manner, then in addition to copying the proxy file area.dll, you must also copy area.fig to the C:\client directory, and then set its configuration parameters. In the source code of the proxy, line 3 calls the *getConnectInfoFromConfigure* function, whose functionality is to read the connection parameters from the area. fig file.

The RPC server is implemented as shown in Code 3.4. Its workflow is to wait for the RPC request from the client side, then process the request and send the response to the client. There are only 2 types of requests, one is to get the model information of the server and the other is RPC request. For a RPC request, the request package contains 3 items: dynamic link library file name, function name, and real parameter package. The first task of processing RPC request is to check whether the dynamic link library file has been loaded into the memory space of the server process. If it has not been loaded, load it from disk into memory. Then get the memory address of the called function and then call it.

RPC servers cannot call called functions directly, only stubs of called functions. The reason is that, for the server, called functions are so diverse in terms of the number of formal parameters, their types, their order, and their return values that the server cannot call them. Unlike called functions, the stubs of all called functions are consistent, with only one formal parameter of type *ParameterPackage* * and a return value of type *ParameterPackage* *. The unity of diversity and consistency is achieved through stubs. Diversity is expressed in the called functions, and consistency is reflected in the stubs. What the stub does is to create the real parameter object, assign values to its member variables using the real parameter package, then call the original function, then package the return value and return it to the caller, as shown in Code 3.2.

For the area function, the contents of its stub source program file, *areaStub.cpp*, are shown in Code 3.2. Compile and link *areaStub.cpp* to generate the dynamic link library file *areaStub.dll*, and then copy it to the subdirectory stub of the distribution directory. Assuming that the installation directory of the RPC server *RpcServer.exe* is *c:\RpcServer*, then installing the called function, area, means that the stub file, *areaStub.dll*, as well as the original function file, *area.dll*, are copied to the *c:\ RpcServer* directory. The server program can then load the stub dynamic link library into memory based on its filename, and then get the memory address of the stub function and call the stub function *areaStub*.

When a file is loaded into memory and only the name of the file is given, but not the directory path, where does the operating system find the file? The operating system's solution is to look in the current directory of the application, and if it doesn't find it, to look in the directory path indicated by the environment variable PATH. If it doesn't find it, it reports a file not found error. When a process is created to run the *c:\RpcServer/RpcServer.exe* file, the current directory of the process is *c:\ RpcServer*. Therefore, when installing and configuring *areaStub.dll*, you should copy it and the original function file *area.dll* to the directory *c:\RpcServer*.

Reflection 3.1: In the stub source code shown in line 2 of Code 3.2, there appears *area.h*. In the *area.h*, first compilation indicator should be dllimport, not dllexport, why?

Reflection 3.2: The RPC server source code shown in Code 3.4, line 13, calls the function *getStub*, can you give its implementation?

In the stub function *areaStub*, you have to call the original function *area*, which is in the file *area.dll*. Since the stub function *areaStub* depends on the original function *area*, there is an entry in the import address table of *areaStub.dll* for the function *area*, which belongs to the dynamic link library file *area.dll*. Thus, after loading *areaStub.dll* into the memory of the server process, its import address table is checked, which leads to *area.dll* loaded into the memory. After *area.dll* is loaded, the memory address of the function *area* can be figured out by the loaded address plus offset (recorded in the *area* entry in the export address table), and then be filled in the area entry in the import address table of *areaStub.dll*. This solves the problem of locating functions in function calls across module boundaries.

Code 3.4 Implementation of RPC Server RpcServer.cpp
```
(1)    typedef ParameterPackage * (*pFunc)( ParameterPackage
       *) StubFunction;
(2)    int RpcServer(Connect *connect ) {
(3)      ResponsetPackage *responsetPackage = new
         ResponsetPackage (RPC_RESPONSE );
(4)      StubFunction stub;
(5)      while (1) {
(6)        RequestPackage *requestPackage =
           WaitforRpcRequest( );
```

3.1 Function Calls Across Machine Boundaries

```
(7)     if (requestPackage->getOperationIndicator()
             == GET_MACHINE_MODEL)
(8)         responsetPackage->setResult( getMachineInfo() );
(9)     else {
(10)        String dllName = requestPackage->getDllName( );
(11)        String functionName = requestPackage-
            >getFunctionName( );
(12)        ParameterPackage *parameterPackage =
            requestPackage->getParameterPackage( );
(13)        stub = getStub(dllName, functionName);
(14)        ParameterPackage *result =
            stub(parameterPackage);
(15)        responsetPackage->setParameterPackage(result);
(16)     }
(17)     connect->Reponse(responsetPackage);
(18)  } //while
(19) }
```

Note: When a proxy packs and passes a real parameter with type pointer, it is not the pointer that is packed, but the object to which it refers. For example, the area function above, which has only one formal parameter of type *Polygon* *. The definition of type *Polygon* is shown in Code 3.5. Assume that the real parameter to be passed contains 3 points: (1,2), (20,36), (30,9). When this real parameter is packaged in JSON format, the resulting JSON content is shown in Code 3.6, where the content in a pair of curly brackets is an object. For basic datatypes such as int, its instance object can omit the curly braces. For example, "int": 1,2, implies two instances of type int, one for 1, the other for 2.

Code 3.5 Definition of class Polygon and Its Dependent Classes

class Point	class PointItem	class PointList	class Polygon
{int x, y.}	{Point *point. PointItem *next.}	{PointItem * head.}	{PointList * pointList.}

Code 3.6 Example of a Real Parameter Packaged in JSON Format
```
"Polygon": {
 "PointList ": {
     "PointItem ": {
        "Point ": {
            "int": 1,2
         }
        "PointItem ": {
           "Point ": {
               "int": 20,36
            }
           "PointItem ": {
              "Point ": {
                  "int": 30,9
              }
              "PointItem ": null
           }
        }
     }
   }
}

 "China":{
    "province": [
         {
              "name": "Heilongjiang".
              "cities": {
                     "city": ["Harbin", "Daqing"]
                }
          }
          {
              "name": "Guangdong".
              "cities": {
                     "city": ["Guangzhou", "Shenzhen",
                     "Zhuhai"]
                 }
           }
      ]
}
```

3.1.2 WEB Interaction

WEB interaction is an implementation of RPC. In WEB interaction, the most common client application is the browser, the WEB server acts as the RPC server, and the called functions are identified by URLs. For example, "http://www.math.org/polygon/area?pointNum=3 &&points=1,2;20,36;30,9" is a WEB request, where www.math.org/polygon/area is the requested resource, which is equivalent to the called function, and "pointNum=3 && points=1,2;20,36;30,9" is a request parameter, which is equivalent to real parameters. Here, there are two real parameters whose names are *pointNum* and points, and whose values are 3 and "1,2;20,36;30,9", respectively. The resource is separated from the parameter by a question mark (?), and parameters are separated from each other by &&. The URL contains network connection information, and the port number of the WEB server is 80 by default. To obtain its IP address from the domain name www.math.org, it is done by sending a domain name resolution request to the domain name server (DNS).

In the above WEB interaction example, the data type of the real parameter is a list of key-value pairs. There are two items in the list, i.e., two key-value pairs. In the first key-value pair, the key is *pointNum*, and the value is 3. In the second key-value pair, the key is *points*, and the value is "1,2;20,36;30,9". In the WEB interaction, the return value is an XML document, with HTML and JSON as specific cases. Therefore, the return value can also be an HTML document or a JSON document. From a programming point of view, XML, HTML, JSON, and HTTP can be thought of as classes, i.e., data types. Thus, a JSON document is an instance of the JSON class, and an HTTP request or response is an instance of the HTTP class. Each class has member functions. The application parses the instance object by calling the member functions. Therefore, WEB interaction is actually a remote procedure call.

For the HTTP class, it has the member variables *contentType* and *content*. When an HTTP packet is received, the value of the member variable *contentType* is looked at first. If it is JSON, then you know that the value of the member variable *content* is a JSON instance object. If it is HTML, then we know that the value of the variable *content* is an HTML instance.

World wide web (WEB) is an interaction protocol for heterogeneous distributed systems. Therefore, translation is done for interaction. Clients and servers interact with each other in text data (i.e., strings). Text is a string and a character consists of multiple bits. The rules for defining characters are called encoding. There are encoding standards such as American standard code for information interchange (ASCII) and unicode transformation format-8 (UTF-8). In ASCII, a character is expressed in a byte, and the highest bit of the byte is 0. Therefore, ASCII can only express 127 characters, which is sufficient for English. For languages such as Chinese, the number of characters is much more than 127, so the UTF-8 encoding standard [9] has emerged. UTF-8 is compatible with ASCII.

In WEB interaction, the sender has to translate the binary instance object in memory into a text instance object, and the receiver has to translate the text instance object into its own binary instance object. In C, for example, an integer or real number is converted to a string by calling the function *sprintf*, a string is converted to an integer by calling the *atoi* function, and a string is converted to a real number by calling the *atof* function.

In the WEB, the called function does not have to be compiled into machine code in the form of a dynamic link library. The called function can be a source program, or intermediate code such as Java bytecode. For example, it could be a source program file with php as suffix, or a source program file with an aspx suffix. When the called function is not in the form of machine code, it is usually interpreted and executed by an interpreter, or compiled into machine code in real time and then is executed as a function call.

From the above, we can see that in WEB interaction, RPC request only takes one real parameter, its data type is string, and the data type of the returned result is also string. In the above example, the real parameter "pointNum=3&&points=1,2;20,36;30,9" is a string, and an XML/HTM/JSON document is also a string. To summarize, the data types of real parameters and return values are all strings. This interaction is equivalent to the interaction between a proxy and a stub, where the WEB server is responsible for parsing the real parameter string into a list of key-value pairs, which are then passed to the called function. The called function is responsible for packaging the return value into an XML/HTML/JSON document. In other words, the stub and the called function are now one.

In WEB interaction, the browser is the most common client-side application. Browsers have three functions: (1) sending WEB requests (i.e., RPC requests) to WEB servers; (2) visualizing the response results in a view window; and (3) human–computer interaction. The second and third functions are related to the HTML document, which consists of visual elements and nonvisual elements. Visual elements are divided into 2 categories: noninteractive elements and interactive elements. For example, the head element and paragraph element are noninteractive elements, and the input element is an interactive element. Interactive elements are used for human–computer interaction, including keyboard input, mouse clicks, and so on. The ultimate goal is to get the real parameters of a function call and send a WEB request.

In order to send a WEB request, HTML defines a form element, the action attribute of which specifies the URL resource to be requested, and the input elements placed in the form element are responsible for obtaining the real parameters, as well as triggering the WEB request. So the input elements can be divided into two categories: real parameter input elements and WEB request triggering elements. For example, text, checkbox, radio, etc., are parameter input elements, and submit is a WEB request triggering element. Input elements are identified by the value of the type attribute.

In a browser, an HTML document can be viewed as a program written in the HTML language. The browser translates the HTML document into a JavaScript program and then interprets and executes it, visualizing the document in a view window and providing human–computer interaction. From a programming point of view, HTML documents, and the visual elements within them, have classes defined for them. Therefore, an HTML document is actually an instance object of the document class *htmlDoc*. The WEB standard provides DOM, which stands for Document Object Model, an API programming interface defined for HTML documents and their visualization elements. Thus, DOM is equivalent to JavaScript library functions in browsers. It can be seen that the browser consists of three parts: (1) HTML language compiler; (2) JavaScript program interpretation executor; (3) DOM function library.

Search engines [10] are another type of common client-side applications in WEB interaction. A search engine sends a WEB request to a WEB server and gets a response result. The response result is naturally an HTML document. The search engine first transforms the HTML document into an *htmlDoc* object, and then parses the document through DOM function calls. The search engine then performs word segmentation and semantic processing on the parsed document elements to obtain the index words of the document. Finally, the document index is added to the database. The functionality of the search engine is to build an index database. HTML documents usually contain links, so the search engine can use the strategy of following the clues to constantly expand the scope of the search to build up a comprehensive index database.

3.1.3 Summary of Function Calls

Function calls began as a programming concept for code reuse. With the advent and popularization of networks, function calls evolved into a basic implementation of resource sharing. The introduction of proxies and stubs allowed function calls to cross machine boundaries and realize remote calls. Remote procedure calls are the cornerstone of distributed computing. WEB is an international standard for interaction between heterogeneous machines. With the WEB standard, clients and servers are ideally independent of each other while being able to interface and interact. Theoretically, WEB allows computers all over the world to be connected together to form a single computer, realizing world-class resource sharing.

The evolution of function calls is a unity of change and invariance. There are multiple scenarios for function calls: (1) the caller and the called function are in the same module; (2) the caller and the called function are in different modules of the same process; (3) the caller and the called function are in different processes. This diversity is transparent to clients. That is, despite the evolution of function calls, they have invariance for clients. To obtain this invariance, import and export address tables are introduced in modules and indirect addressing methods are introduced in CPUs. To make function calls across process boundaries transparent to clients, proxies and stubs were introduced.

3.2 Network Transmission

There are two levels of networks, namely, the local area network (LAN) and the Internet. For an organization, it builds its own LAN. The computers in the LAN are connected through switches, so that computers in a LAN can communicate directly with each other by establishing a network connection. Each LAN has a gateway.

The Internet is also called the public network or extranet. There are two network cards plugged into a gateway, one of which connects to the public network and the other to the LAN. Thus, the Gateway is a member of both the LAN and the Internet. In a public network, any two gateways can establish a network connection between them to communicate.

Communication between machines in different LANs is done with the help of gateways. This communication consists of three network connections in series. Let the gateways for LAN A and LAN B be gateway A and gateway B, respectively. Now, assume that machine α in LAN A wants to communicate with machine β in LAN B. The communication process is as follows: (1) machine α establishes network connection 1 with gateway A; (2) gateway A establishes network connection 2 with gateway B; and (3) gateway B establishes network connection 3 with machine β. Machine α sends the data to gateway A through network connection 1, and gateway A forwards the data to gateway B through network connection 2, and gateway B forwards the data to machine β through network connection 3. When machine β wants to send data to machine α, the data are sent from machine β to gateway B through network connection 3, then to gateway A, and then to machine α.

Either a gateway or a switch is actually a computer. There are 2 network interface controllers (NICs) plugged into a gateway machine and multiple NICs plugged into a switch. The gateway service program runs on the gateway machine and the switch service program runs on the switch. On the switch, the switching service program maintains a switching table that records the media access control (MAC) addresses of the machines to which NICs are connected. When a link packet is received from a NIC, the switching service program reads the destination MAC address, checks the switching table to determine which NIC should forward it, and then forwards the link packet. This is the switching functionality. Link packets have the dual concepts of class and instance objects. A link packet received from a network card is an instance object of the class link packet. The destination MAC address is a member variable of the class.

The gateway machine has one NIC connected to the external network and another NIC connected to the internal network. Therefore, it has an external IP address and an internal IP address. The gateway service program listens for connection requests from both the extranet and the intranet. When it receives a connection request from the intranet, it first establishes a network connection with the requester. The requester then tells the gateway service program the IP and port number of the extranet to which it wants to connect. The gateway service program then initiates a connection request in the extranet and establishes a network connection in the extranet. Let these two connections be called Network Connection 1 and Network Connection 2. When the gateway receives data from Network Connection 1, it forwards it from Network Connection 2. And vice versa, when it receives data from network connection 2, it forwards it from network connection 1. This is the gateway functionality.

The biggest benefit of a two-tier network is that it alleviates the problem of a shortage of IP addresses [11], which are 4 bytes long and are in short supply as the number of networked computers increases. With a two-tier network, only the gateway needs to be assigned a public IP address. The computers on the LAN use the intranet IP address. Thus, the problem of insufficient IP addresses was alleviated. However, the two-tier network also has its shortcomings. For a computer on the LAN, an external computer cannot actively establish a connection with it because it does not have a public IP address. If a computer on the LAN is acting as a server, then the problem of external computers being able to actively access it must be solved.

The above problem can be solved by a gateway. For a server on the LAN, from the outside, its public IP address is the IP address of the gateway on the LAN to which it belongs. The next problem is: when the gateway receives a network connection request from the outside network, how does it know which server on the inside network to connect to? The solution is to use port numbers to differentiate between machines on the intranet. For example, for a gateway on LAN A, it listens for connection requests on ports 80 and 25 on the extranet. When it receives a connection request from port 80 on the external network, it knows that the external computer is trying to access the WEB server, so it establishes another connection with the WEB server on the internal network. This way enables the external computer to access the WEB server on the intranet. Similarly, when it receives a connection request from port 25 on the external network, it knows that the external computer is trying to access the mail server. This solution is known as Tunneling Technology [3].

The essence of tunneling technology is that multiple servers on a LAN share a single public IP address, i.e., the public IP address of the gateway. The gateway assigns a unique port number to each server in the intranet, and uses the port number to distinguish the servers in the intranet. The port number assigned by the gateway to a server in the intranet is called the service port number. The gateway listens from the extranet, responds to connection requests from each service port number, and establishes a network connection with the corresponding server on the intranet to associate with it.

Network communication is in client/server (C/S) mode. Network communication is the communication between two processes on different machines, where one process acts as a client and the other acts as a server. For the client, the server is identified by an IP address, communication protocol, and port number. The IP address identifies the machine, and the communication protocol and port number identify the process (also called the application). A computer can have multiple applications running at the same time, which are distinguished from each other by communication protocols and port numbers. Therefore, packets transmitted over the network should contain the IP address, protocol and port number of the receiver. Only then can the receiver machine receive the packet and know which process to submit it to.

For a process running on a computer on a LAN, when it establishes a network connection with a server, it needs to know whether the server is running on a machine on the intranet or on a machine on the extranet. If the server is running on a machine on the intranet, it can directly establish a network connection with it and then communicate. If the server is running on a machine on an extranet, it must first establish a connection with the gateway, then send the server's IP address, protocol, and port number to the gateway, and tell the gateway to establish a connection with the server. Communication starts after the entire connection has been established.

For a server's IP address, how does a computer know whether it is an intranet IP address or an extranet IP address? This is where the subnet mask comes in handy. By Comparing the IP address with the subnet mask and its own IP address, it can know whether it is an intranet IP address or an extranet IP address.

Reflection 3.3: How is the comparison made? Write a detailed comparison process.

There are some basic data required for computers to communicate over a network. The first is that each computer on the LAN must have a unique IP address and know the subnet mask. When a computer wants to communicate with a server on an extranet, it must know the IP address, communication protocol, and port number of the gateway server. In addition, when a client process establishes a network connection, it is usually given not an IP address, but a domain name. A domain name server (DNS) is then required to resolve the domain name into an IP address. To access a DNS, you must know its IP address, communication protocol and port number.

These data are essential for network communication. The method of obtaining them is as follows: when a computer starts up, it broadcasts a dynamic host configuration protocol (DHCP) request packet across the LAN, where DHCP is abbreviation of Dynamic Host Configuration Protocol, the standard protocol for the Internet. The DHCP server responds to the request by assigning an IP address to the requester, and then telling the requester the IP address and subnet mask, as well as the IP address and port number of the gateway, and the IP address and port number of the DNS. The DHCP server usually runs on the gateway machine.

How does the DHCP response get from the DHCP server to the DHCP requester? It starts with link transmission. Computers on a LAN are connected together, and each computer is identified by its link MAC address. To differentiate, each NIC stores a globally unique NIC number at the factory. When a computer is turned on, it usually reads the NIC number and uses it as its link MAC address, so each computer on the LAN is distinguishable. The DHCP request packet contains the MAC address of the requester, so the DHCP server can pass the DHCP response to the requester.

In a LAN, a computer does not have a fixed IP address, which is assigned by a DHCP server in real time every time it is turned on. Therefore, at the application layer, you cannot use an IP address to identify a computer; you should only use a name to identify a computer. In the network layer, IP addresses are used to identify computers, while in the link layer, MAC addresses are used to identify computers. Thus, in network communication, there is a problem of obtaining an IP address from a name and a problem of obtaining a MAC address from an IP address. The former problem is called the domain name resolution problem and the latter problem is called the address resolution problem. To resolve a domain name, you send a domain name resolution request to the DNS. For address resolution, an ARP request is sent to the DHCP server, where ARP is abbreviation of Address Resolution Protocol. For DHCP request and response, domain name registration request and response, domain name resolution request and response, as well as address resolution request and response, these things have been stipulated, forming an international standard.

For the purpose of domain name resolution, after a computer obtains configuration parameters from a DHCP server, it registers its name and IP address to the DNS. For address resolution, after DHCP server responds to a DHCP request, it adds the MAC address of the requester, along with the IP address assigned to it, to the address resolution table for subsequent address resolution. A DHCP request can also be viewed as how to obtain an IP address by a MAC address, and is therefore also referred to as a RARP request. RARP is abbreviation of Reverse Address Resolution Protocol. Provisions are also called protocols in terms of interaction between two computers that are independent of each other. All of these protocols mentioned above are part of the standard protocols of the Internet.

As you can see from the above, the gateway plays a central role in a LAN. It runs the gateway server program, the DHCP server program, and in some cases the domain name resolution server program. When any computer is connected to a LAN, it broadcasts a DHCP request on the LAN as soon as it is powered on. When the DHCP server receives the request, it assigns an IP address to the requester and sends it, along with the subnet mask, the gateway IP address and port number, and the IP address and port number of the DNS, as a response to the requester. It also adds a row to the address resolution table it maintains, noting the IP address and MAC address of the requester. The DHCP protocol defines the data structure for DHCP request packet and DHCP response packet. Therefore, clients and servers are both independent of each other and can interact with each other.

In a LAN, each machine's IP address is assigned by a DHCP server with dynamic changeability. The benefit of this treatment is that the computers in the LAN do not need to be manually configured and can be plug-and-play. This feature is critical for data centers or cloud service providers. Some cloud service centers have 100,000 computers, with computers failing and new computers being added every day. When the number of computers is huge, the management of the LAN must be automated. Manual management is inefficient, prone to errors, and affects the overall situation. While automated IP address assignment brings benefits, it also brings new problems. On the client program side, a server cannot be identified by its IP address, but only by server name. However, the client program needs its IP address when it establishes a network connection with the server.

From the above analysis, it is clear that a DNS is necessary for a LAN as well. After a server program starts, it has to register its service to the DNS. The registration information includes service name, IP address, and port number. When a client program accesses the server, it has to look up the corresponding IP address and port number on the DNS based on the service name. In the gateway server program, the mapping table on server port number to service name is created. When the gateway receives a connection request from the external network, it first finds the service name in the mapping table based on the server port number. Then, based on the service name, the gateway goes to the DNS on the intranet to look up its corresponding IP address and port number. Once the IP address and port number are obtained, a network connection is established with the server. Services are usually named as domain names to avoid renaming problems. For example, Hunan University has its domain name "hnu.edu.cn." It should assign the domain name "cs.hnu.edu.cn" to its subordinate department of Computer Science. Similarly, Department of Computer Science should assign the domain name "www.cs.hnu.edu.cn" to its WEB server. Thus, in Hunan University, the services in its LAN will not have the problem of renaming.

Reflection 3.4: The gateway has two NICs connected to the external and internal networks, respectively. The IP address for the external network is to be applied to the Internet Management Center. The IP address for the intranet can be set by the organization itself. Why? What are the configuration parameters for the DHCP server program?

Enterprises usually use the LAN as the boundary to divide the security level for security reasons. For servers on the LAN, there are no restrictions if they are accessed from the intranet. If accessed from an external network, there are restrictions. For example, many universities have document repositories and faculty management systems that can be accessed from the intranet without any restriction, but when accessed from the extranet, the web pages cannot be opened. The implementation of this control is very simple. When accessing from an extranet, all requests are relayed by the gateway. Therefore, the security control can be done by the gateway server program. In this case, the gateway server program acts as a firewall. This security control can also be placed on the server side. On the server side, the network connection records the IP address, port number, and communication protocol of the communicating party. For a network connection on the server, if the IP address of the communicating party is the IP address of the gateway, it can be determined that it is an access from an external network.

Using the LAN as the boundary to divide the security level has both advantages and disadvantages. For enterprise employees, when they are traveling or working at home, they have to access through the extranet. As a result, the business systems cannot be opened, which affects the office. The solution is to install a VPN client software on their computers, so that there is no difference in accessing the business systems between by extranet and by intranet. VPN is the abbreviation of Virtual Private Network. Of course, only the VPN client software is not enough, the enterprise also needs to build a VPN server, which is accessible from the outside network to the server. The business servers are accessed via VPN from the extranet. In this situation, communication consists of 4 network connections in series. The first is the network connection between the client program and the client-side gateway, and the second is the network connection between the client-side gateway and the server-side gateway. The third is the network connection between the server-side gateway and the VPN server, and the fourth is the network connection between the VPN server and the business server.

The above four network connections are collectively referred to as a VPN connection. The process of establishing a VPN connection is a two-step process: (1) establish a connection with the VPN server; (2) send the IP address and port number of the business server you want to access, as well as the username and password for logging in, to the VPN server, which then establishes a connection with the business server. Since the VPN server is in the intranet, its access to the business servers belongs to intranet accesses. From the process of establishing a VPN connection, it can be seen that it is in fact exactly the same as the process of accessing an external computer through a gateway. If the process of accessing an external computer through a gateway is considered a pattern, then the establishment of a VPN connection is two iterations of that pattern: first, the gateway is used as a proxy to establish a connection with the VPN server, and then the VPN server is used as a proxy to establish a connection with the business server.

VPN is a way to access business servers. To make it transparent to applications, it needs to be supported by the operating system. This support can be placed in the support library level to achieve. Support library provides applications with the API function *registerVPN* for registration of VPN. Registration information includes three items: (1) domain name; (2) the IP address, the communication protocol and port number of the VPN server; (3) the username and password for logging into the VPN server. The VPN client software calls the function *registerVPN* to register the VPN information into the support library. Subsequently, when an application program wants to access the computer with domain name, it calls the function *createConnection*. In the implementation of the function *createConnection*, the domain name is first checked to see if it is under a VPN domain. If not, it is handled in the classic way. Otherwise, it uses the VPN registration information to establish a network connection with the VPN server, and then sends the IP address and port number of the domain name to the VPN server. After getting a response from the VPN server, the entire network connection is established.

An example of the above process is given. Assuming that the VPN client software is running on computer *A*, the VPN information registered in the support library is: the domain name is *hnu.edu.cn*, the IP address and port number of the VPN server are 127.6.92.79: 84, and the login username and password are 2004213 and 1122, respectively. Now, you can use a browser to access www.hnu.edu.cn. The browser naturally calls the API function *createConnection* with www.hnu.edu.cn as a real parameter to create a network connection. In the implementation of *createConnection*, the fact that www.hnu.edu.cn is a subdomain of the VPN domain hnu.edu.cn shows www.hnu.edu.cn should be accessed through VPN. Thus, a network connection is first established with the VPN server (noted as *conn1*), and then the IP address and port number of www.hnu.edu.cn are sent to the VPN server. Upon receiving the response result, it knows that the entire network connection has been established and returns *conn1* as a return value to the caller (i.e., the browser).

Reflection 3.5: Can you give an implementation of the function *registerVPN*? Can *createConnection* be improved to support VPN?

3.2.1 *Abstraction of Network Communications*

Network is a shared resource and therefore has a manager. On a computer, the network manager is an integral part of the operating system and manages the Network Interface Controller (abbreviated as NIC). For example, a gateway machine has two NICs plugged into it: one for the intranet and another for the extranet. Thus, on the gateway machine, the network manager manages two NICs. One NIC corresponds to one network, and each network has an IP address. From the object-oriented programming point of view, the operating system defines two classes: Network and Network Connection, whose class names are Network and Connection, respectively. The operating system provides the API function *getNetwork* to obtain the network object. The Network class has the member function *createConnection*. When a client wants to access a server using the network, it first calls the *createConnection* function to create a network connection object. Then, call the *send* member function of the network connection object to send the request and then the *recv* member function to receive the response.

The Network class has member variables *ipAddr* and *connectionList*, which store the IP address and the current connection objects, respectively. A network object can contain multiple connection objects, which is called multiplexing. Multiplexing is an external effect presented to clients, where multiple programs running on a single computer are communicating over the network at the same time. Internally, packets are still transmitted one by one in series through the network card. Network transmissions are duplexed, i.e., sending and receiving occur at the same time over different wires.

The connection class has member variables *port*, *protocol*, *oppositeIpAddr*, and *oppositePort*, which store the port number of own side, the communication protocol, the IP address and the port number of the other side, respectively. Connection objects of a network object are identified by port and protocol. The functionality of the member function *createConnection* is to create an instance object of the connection class, and then initialize its member variables, and add it to the connection table *connectionList*. The implementation of *createConnection* is shown in Code 3.7.

Line 2 of Code 3.7 is a call to Network's member function *getPort* to assign an identifying port number to the connection object to be created. Line 5 is a call to *requestConnection*, a member function of Network, to send a connection request IP packet to the server. The IP packet has the member variables *sourceIpAddr, sourcePort, protocol, destionationIpAddr*, and *destionationPort*. *requestConnection* uses the *ipAddr* member variable of the network object and its own 4 member variables to initialize the above five members of the connection request IP packet.

Code 3.7 Implementation of createConnection
```
(1)  Connection * Netwotk::createConnection( enum protocol,
     int serverIpAddr, int serverPort) {
(2)    int port = getPort(protocol);
(3)    Connection *connection = new Connection(port,
       protocol, int serverIpAddr);
(4)    connectionList->addItem(connection);
(5)    Response * response = requestConnection(port,
       protocol, serverIpAddr, serverPort);
(6)    connection ->setOppositeId(response->serverIpAddr,
       responset->serverPort);
(7)    return connect.
(8)  }
```

3.2 Network Transmission

When the server receives a connection request from a listening port, it also creates a network connection object to interface with it. The connection request contains the communication protocol, IP address and port number of the requester. For the connection object created by the server, they are the values of the member variables *protocol, oppositeIPAddr*, and *oppositePort*, respectively. The server's response to a connection request is to tell the requester the identifier (namely IP and port) of its connection object. To the requester, the identifier is used to initialize its own member variables *oppositeIpAddr* and *oppositePort*. This processing is shown in lines 5 through 6 of Code 3.7.

Globally, a connection object is identified by *ipAddr, port, protocol, oppositeIpAddr*, and *oppositePort*. To set up a communication channel between the client side and the service side, you actually create two connection objects, one on the client side and the other on the server side. Subsequently, when either the client or the service side sends data to the other side, it attaches connection information to the data. Thus, the data can reach destination side through the network. The correspondence between the two connection objects is shown in Fig. 3.1. For networking, a network cable is used to connect a computer to a switch.

Both the network object and the connection object are objects maintained by the network manager, i.e., kernel objects. The operating system detects the network cards on the computer at boot time and creates a network object for each card. For operating systems that support virtual networks, there are also API functions for creating network objects. Such network objects are virtual network objects. The virtual network object is essential if the operating system is to provide virtual machine functionality. The container functionality provided by the Linux operating system is, in fact, virtual machine functionality. Virtual networks are explained in detail in Chap. 5.

For network communication programming, the operating system provides the classic API functions: *socket, bind, listen, accept, connect, send, recv, close*, and *getsocketname*. In these functions, there are no obvious concepts of network object and connection object, but only the concept of socket. Socket function is actually to create a connection object above. For the sake of consistency, later in the discussion of the above nine API functions, the socket object is called connection object. The functionality of bind function is to bind a network object to a connection object. When calling the bind function, the real parameters include *ipAddr*, port, and

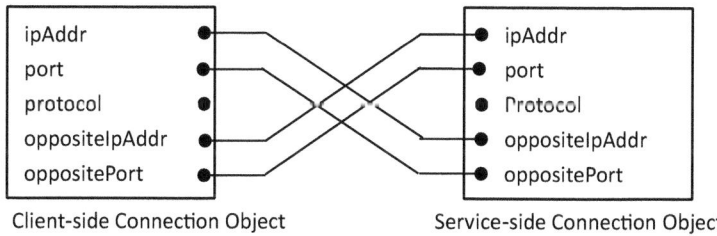

Fig. 3.1 Correspondence between two connection objects

protocol. *ipAddr* is an identifying attribute of the network object. Therefore, when *ipAddr* is given, a network object is bound to the connection object.

Much of the literature explains the use of network communication functions in a way that does not get to the heart of the matter. For example, for programming a client program, it is said that the socket function is called first, followed by the connect function. This creates a problem: neither the socket function nor the connect function binds a network object to the connection object. When multiple network cards are connected to different networks on a computer, which network object does the created connection object belong to? In this case, it is clearly incorrect to call the connect function after the socket function. The correct way is to call the bind function after calling socket, and then call the connect function.

For programming a client program that calls a bind function after calling a socket, there is a problem of not knowing how to set the port value. If a port value is given arbitrarily, there may be a conflict that will cause the bind to be unsuccessful. The correct way to handle this is to set the port parameter to 0. If you do this, the network object will automatically assign an available port number to the connection object. This means that the network class also has a member variable, *sortedUsedPortList*, that notes the currently used port numbers and sorts them. Every time a connection object is released, its port number is removed from *sortedUsedPortList*. When the bind function is called and the port value is 0, assign a port number to the connection object that does not appear in *sortedUsedPortList* and add it to the *sortedUsedPortList*. In other words, the network object is responsible for managing port numbers and ensuring that its connection objects have different port values when the protocol value is the same.

It follows that both server and client programs may not succeed when calling the bind function. For a server program, if the given port value is occupied by an existing connection object when calling the bind function, then the bind will not succeed. For a client program, calling the bind function with a port value of 0 to ask the network object to automatically assign it an available port number may also be unsuccessful. The reason is that there are at most 65536 available port numbers for a network object. When all of them have been assigned, there will be no free port number available. As you can see, when programming network communications, do not forget to call the close function. How did the integer 65536 come about? When the IP protocol was first developed, the storage allocated to a port was 2 bytes, 2^{16} is 65536.

For a better understanding of the bind function, its implementation is given as shown in Code 3.8. The data types are defined here for the IP address, the communication protocol and the port number (see line 1). The reason is that in the IP protocol definition, the IP address is stored in 4 bytes (i.e., a 32-bit integer), so it can be defined neither simply as an integer nor as a string. Different machines handle integers differently. For example, a 16-bit machine uses 2 bytes to store an integer, while a 64-bit machine uses 8 bytes to store an integer. The Network class has a member variable, *connectionList*, that holds the connection objects it owns, which facilitates the distribution of received network data to the connection objects. The connection class has a member variable *network*, which holds the network object it belongs to, to facilitate the sending of network data to the other end.

Connection objects belonging to a network object are identified by port and protocol. If the protocol value is the same, then the port is used to identify the connection object. Therefore, in the implementation of the bind function, it will check whether there is any conflict problem with the connection object, i.e., it will check whether the current connection object is distinguishable from other connection objects. If it is not distinguishable, the bind will not succeed.

In the above implementation of the bind function, the function of line 14 is to call the network object's member function *addUsedPort* to register the port number as a port number already used by the network object (recorded in the *sortedUsedPortList*). The function of line 17 is to call the member function *getAvailablePort* to assign an available port number to the connction object based on the port number already used by the network object.

Code 3.8 Implementation of the Bind Function
```
(1)   bool bind(Connection *conn, IpAddr ipaddr, Protocol
      protocol, Port port) {
(2)     conn->protocol = protocol;
(3)     Network *network = networkList->getFirstItem();
(4)     while (network) {
(5)       if (network->ipAddr == ipAddr) {
(6)         if (port > 0) {
(7)           Connection *connection =
              network->connectionList->getFirstItem();
(8)           while (connection) {
(9)             if (connection->port == port && conn-
                >protocol == protocol)
(10)              return false;
(11)            connection =
                network->connectionList->getNextItem();
(12)          }
(13)          conn->port = port;
(14)          network->addUsedPort(protocol, port);
(15)        }
(16)        else {
(17)          conn->port =
              network->getAvailablePort(protocol);
(18)          if (conn->port == 0)
(19)            return false;
(20)        }
(21)        network->connectionList->addItem(conn);
```

```
(22)          conn->network = network;
(23)          return true;
(24)      }
(25)      network = networkList->getNextItem();
(26)  }
(27)  return false;
(28) }
```

In the definition of *sortedUsedPortList*, in order to save storage space, each item in the table does not record only one port number, but a consecutive segment of port numbers. Each item has two member variables *from* and *to*, which write down the starting and ending serial numbers of a used port number, respectively. Every time a connection object is released, a port number is released, and it is removed from the *sortedUsedPortList*. There are three scenarios for deleting port number p: (a) if p is equal to *from* of an item in the *sortedUsedPortList*, then simply add 1 to *from* of that item; (b) if p is equal to *to* of an item in the *sortedUsedPortList*, then simply subtract 1 from *to* of that item; (c) if p lies between *from* and *to* of an item in the *sortedUsedPortList*, then the item should be split into two items: $(from, p - 1)$ and $(p + 1, to)$.

Reflection 3.6: When assigning an available port number to a connction object, it is common to assign the smallest available port number, which naturally does not appear in the *sortedUsedPortList*. This is why the items in the *sortedUsedPortList* are sorted. Can you write the implementation code for the above member functions *addUsedPort* and *getAvailablePort* of the Network class?

The accept function is dedicated to server programs. Its function is to wait for and process connection requests from clients. Once a connection request is received from a client, a new connection object is created for subsequent interaction with the client. This new connection object is the return value of the accept function. In contrast, the connect function is used exclusively by the client program to send a connection request to the server, get a response, and complete the initialization of the client's connection object. On the server side, the connection object obtained by calling the accept function has been initialized. Then, the client and the server can interact with each other. Business interaction using the C/S model. That is, the client calls the *send* function to send a business request, and then calls the *recv* function to get the response. On the server side, the *recv* function is called to obtain the client's business request, and then call the send function to send the response to the client.

The client and the server are independent of each other. Independence is reflected in the following three points: (1) the service side does not know when it will receive the client's request (including connection request and business request); (2) the client does not know when it will receive the response result (including that of the connection request and that of the business request); and (3) either the request or the response may be duplicated or lost. In the face of the above scenarios, there should be countermeasures. Countermeasures are divided into two levels: (1) operating system level; (2) application level.

At the operating system level, a request or response sent by one party to another in network communication is called a message for ease of presentation. When a network card receives a message, the network object first checks to see if there is a corresponding connection object associated with it. For unassociated messages, the network object simply discards them and responds with an error message to the sender. For related messages, the network object puts them into the *receiveList* of the corresponding connection object's receive buffer. When the application picks it up is up to the application, and the network object has no control over that. When the application wants to send a message, it first puts it into the connection object's send buffer *sendList*. As for when it can be sent out through the network card, it is the responsibility of the network object and the application cannot control it. In short, the asynchrony between the application and the network card is reconciled by the message cache.

The size of the send and receive buffers of a connection object cannot be unlimited, otherwise it may cause the memory on the computer to be exhausted, affecting the normal operation of the entire machine. Therefore, the connection object's send and receive buffer size is a configurable parameter, and there is an upper limit. The configuration can be done by calling the operating system API function *setsocketopt*. For the connection object used by the server to listen for connection requests, its receiving buffer size is not in bytes but in the number of connection requests. The size configuration is not done by the *setsocketopt* function, but by the listen function. Because the connection object has the concept of sending and receiving buffer size. Therefore, when calling the send and *recv* functions, it is important to check their return values to see the actual amount of sending or receiving to avoid errors.

Loss of messages is handled by a timeout mechanism. For the client program, after sending the request, it calls the *recv* function to wait for the response. If the wait timeout is exceeded, it is considered to be a lost message situation. Message loss can occur on the client side, or on the server side, or in the network transmission. A common way to deal with lost messages is to resend the request. Therefore, the timeout size is another configuration parameter for the *recv* and send functions. This parameter is also set by calling the *setsocketopt* function.

The client may retransmit the request, which can lead to message duplication problems on the server side. For connection requests, the accept function first checks the existing connection objects to see if the connection object to be created already exists when processing it. If it exists, the request is recognized as a duplicate request and is discarded directly. For business requests, it is not possible to identify duplicates in the *recv* function, which can only be handled by the server program. The most common method of identifying duplicates for business requests is that the client program attaches a sequence number to the business request. The service program keeps track of and records the valid sequence number as it processes the business request. When a server program receives a business request, if the serial number attached to it is not among the valid serial numbers, it considers it a duplicate business request and discards it.

Reflection 3.7: For duplicate messages for connection requests, they should not be handled by the network object, but by the accept function, why?

For messages received from the network card, the network object has to drop them into the *receiveList* of the corresponding connection object. For the message, it has member variables *destinationIpAddr, destinationPort, protocol, sourceIpAddr* and *sourcePort*, and all are definitely assigned values. For the connection object, there are three scenarios: (1) the connection object used by the server to listen for connection requests, whose member variables *oppositeIpAddr* and *oppositePort* both take the value of null; (2) the connection object used by the client to initiate the connection request, whose member variables *oppositePort* take the value of null; (3) the connection object after the two sides have established a connection, all of whose member variables are not null. Therefore, when the network object takes a message and matches it with its own connection object, it has to check whether or not the connection object's *oppositeIpAddr* and *oppositePort* are null. and *oppositePort* of the connection object are null, and if they are null, the match is omitted.

As you can see, for a message received from a network card, the network object first takes its d*estinationIpAddr* and matches it with its own *ipAddr*. If they are not equal, the message is discarded. Otherwise, match with its own connection objects one by one until the connection object to which the message belongs is found. Matching method is: Check if the destination Port and protocol of the message match the port and protocol of the connection object, respectively. If they are the same, the connection object to which the message should belong has been found; otherwise, further search is needed. After finding the connection object to which the message belongs, then check whether its *oppositeIpAddr* and *oppositePort* are null. If they are not null, perform further matching. If the match does not pass, the message is discarded; otherwise, the message is delivered to the *receiveList* of the corresponding connection object.

The accept function and the *recv* function take a message from the *receiveList* of the connection object and process it accordingly. If there is no message in the *receiveList* of the connection object, the process will enter the wait state until there is a message. The processing of the received message by accept is to create a new connection object and assign values to its member variables *oppositeIpAddr, oppositePort, protocol*, and *sourcePort*, so that it is connected to the connection object of the requester. Next, send a connection response message to the requester through the newly created connection object, and then return the newly created connection object as the return value. Accept function is implemented as shown in Code 3.9. The *pickOutFirstItem* called in line 2 is a synchronous function that will not return until there is a message. The processing done by *recv* is to copy the data part of the message to the storage space provided by the caller, and then return the length of the data part as the return value.

3.2 Network Transmission

Code 3.9 Implementation of the Accept Function

```
(1)  Connection * accept(Connection *conn) {
(2)      Message *msg =
         conn->receiveList->fetchOutFirstItem();
(3)      Connection * clientConn = new Connection ( );
(4)      clientConn->oppositeIpAddr = msg->sourceIpAddr;
(5)      clientConn->oppositePort = msg->sourcePort;
(6)      clientConn->protocol = msg->protocol ;
(7)      clientConn->sourcePort = conn->network-
         >getAvailablePort( msg->protocol );
(8)      clientConn->network = conn->network;
(9)      clientConn->network->connectionList->
         addItem(clientConn);
(10)     clientConn->send(CONNECTION_RESPONSE);
(11)     return clientConn;
(12) }
```

The client calls the connect function to establish a connection with the server. In the implementation of the connect function, first check whether the member variable *network* of the connection object is null. If it is null, it means that the client program did not call the bind function earlier. At this situation, bind it to the computer's current default network object, and complete the initialization of its member variable *port*. Next, complete the initialization of the member variables *protocol* and *oppositeIpAddr*. After that, send a connection request to the server, and then wait for the server's response. After receiving the response, initialize the connection object's member variable *oppositePort*.

In order to understand the connection process and its characteristics, an example is given. Suppose that before the client sends a connection request, it creates a connection object bound to a network object with the IP address 168.16.120.3, and the values of its member variables *port*, *protocol*, *oppositeIPAddr*, and *oppositePort* are 2356, INET_IPV4, 168.16.120.48, and null, respectively. *oppositePort* is null because it is unknown at this point of time. Assuming the listening port number of the server is 80, for the connection request message from the client, its five member variables *sourceIpAddr*, *sourcePort, protocol, destinationIpAddr,* and *destinationPort* have the values of 168.16.120.3, 2356, INET_IPV4, 168.16.120.48, and 80, respectively.

After the server receives the connection request, it creates a connection object whose member variables *port, protocol, oppositeIpAddr,* and *oppositePort* have the values 6848, INET_IPV4, 168.16.120.3, and 2356, respectively. The IP address of the attributed network object is naturally 168.16.120.48. The connection response message is sent through the newly created connection object, and the values of its five member variables are 168.16.120.48, 6848, INET_IPV4, 168.16.120.3, and

2356, respectively. After the client obtains the response, it sets its own connection object's member variable, *oppositePort*, to 6848. At this point, the network connection has been established. When the client sends a business request message, the values of its five member variables are 168.16.120.3, 2356, INET_IPV4, 168.16.120.48, and 6848, respectively.

When a program calls the send function to send a piece of data, the connection object encapsulates it into a message. The above five member variables of the message are initialized by the connection object. When the network object receives a message from the network card, it distributes it to the corresponding connection object based on the values of the above five member variables. If the corresponding connection object cannot be found, the message is discarded.

When the client program has completed its business interaction with the server, the close function should be called to release the network connection. In the implementation of close, first send a message to the other side to close the connection, and then release the connection object referred to. At this point, the server is usually in the *recv* wait state. When the network object on the server side receives a close message from the network card, it will set the state of the corresponding connection object to CLOSE. At this time, if the server program is in the *recv* wait state, it will be woken up and return. The return value is −1, which means that it returns with an error. Next, the server program should check the error code. If the connection is closed by the client, it should be closed accordingly. If the server program is not in the *recv* wait state, then when the *recv* function or *send* function is called later, it will immediately return, and the return value is −1. From this, it can be seen that checking the return values of *recv* and *send* function calls is crucial in programming.

After the server senses that the client has closed the connection, it calls the close function itself. At this point, the server does not need to send a close message to the client because the client's connection object has already been released. Both the server and the client call the close function, but the performance is different. The reason is: when the client calls the close function, the state of the connection object is NORMAL, but when the server calls the close function, the state of the connection object is CLOSE.

Reflection 3.8: Can you write the implementation code for the functions *connect*, *recv*, *send* and *close*?

3.2.2 Synchronous I/O and Asynchronous I/O

The classic functions, *accept, connect, send* and *recv*, are all synchronized functions that are called until a result is returned. For example, when the server calls the *accept* function, no connection request may have arrived yet; thus, there will be no result. From the other side, the connection request has arrived, but the server-side program has not been executed to the *accept* function call. In this situation, the connection request has to be cached to the *receiveList* of the listening connection object.

3.2 Network Transmission

The meaning of synchronization is: when the function is called, if the input data have not yet reached or output data have not been sent, the process will wait until the input reaches or the output is completed. Take *recv* as an example; its functionality is to receive data from the other side of the communication. If the network has not yet received the data from the other party, the caller process will wait until the data reaches, then the function returns. During the waiting period, the caller process is in a waiting state and will not proceed to the next execution.

For the function *send*, its functionality is to send data to the other party. Sending data is an I/O operation, which takes time by itself. In addition, for a multitasking operating system, there may be multiple processes that need to send data, but the network card can only send them one by one in a serial fashion. Thus, when one process is calling the send function, the card may be busy sending another data. The meaning of send synchronization is that the function will not return until the data have been sent by the card.

The implementation of synchronization functions is actually simple. For example, the implementation of the *recv* function is shown in Code 3.10. Here, for the sake of simplicity, the timeout and error handling are omitted. The implementation first checks whether there are data in the *receiveList* of the connection object. If there is, it is taken out as a return. If not, the process switch is actively carried out. Before switching, change the state of the current process to WAITING, and set the wakeup event to NETWORK_RECEIVE. Subsequently, when the network card receives a message, it will trigger an input hardware interrupt. In the interrupt handling routine, the corresponding connection object is found based on the *destinationPort* and *protocol* values of the received message, and then the data portion of the message is added to its *receiveList*. Connection object has a member variable *process* that records the process object associated with it. The state of the associated process object is changed to READY; thus, the process can resume running during the next round of process switching.

Code 3.10 Implementation of the Synchronization Function recv
```
(1)   Message *recv(Connection *conn) {
(2)      while (1) {
(3)         Message *msg =
            conn->receiveList->pickOutFirstItem();
(4)         if (msg == null) {
(5)            currentProcess->waitEvent = NETWORK_RECEIVE;
(6)            currentProcess->state = WAITING;
(7)            INT 90;    // process switching, see Sect. 3.2.2
(8)         }
(9)         else
(10)           return msg;
(11)     }
(12)  }
```

If synchronization mode is used, the server program has to create a process for each socket that is responsible for interacting with a client (including receiving requests and sending responses). When there are many clients accessing the server, there are many processes created in the system. Creating a process object consumes a certain amount of memory resources. In addition, when carrying out a process switch, the process table has to be scanned and traversed once, which consumes CPU resources. A more serious problem is that the context of the process has to be switched. Since the registers and cache are shared memory, they store the context of the current process. Therefore, when switching processes, the context of the abdicating process is moved from the registers and cache to memory, and then the context of the uploaded process is moved from memory to registers and cache. Therefore, process switching has CPU overhead. When there are many processes and frequent switching, the process switching overhead increases significantly, which seriously affects the system performance. So asynchronous I/O scheme [3] is proposed.

The intent of asynchronous I/O is to reduce the number of processes and eliminate process switching overhead. That is, one process is used to handle receiving and sending data on multiple network connections. The solution is to transform synchronous I/O mode into asynchronous I/O mode. When an application calls an asynchronous I/O function, it doesn't wait, but returns immediately, so it can get on with other things. Taking the asynchronous function *recv* as an example, when the application calls it to receive data, return immediately comes out, regardless of whether there are data in the *receiveList* of the connection object. If there are data, return is marked with a success indicator. Otherwise, return is marked with an error indicator. For the asynchronous function *send*, when it is called, it does not wait until the data are sent out by the network card before returning, but returns immediately.

This approach raises new questions. For receiving data, how to let the application know that there are already data in the *receiveList* of the connection object? For sending data, how does the application know that the data have been sent out by the NIC? This information is very important to the application. Only when the data have been sent by the card can the application call the send function again to send the next data. To do this, add two member variables to the connection class: *recvIndicator* and *sendIndicator*. For a connection object, when the value of its *recvIndicator* is 1, it indicates that there are data in its *receiveList*. When the value of its *sendIndicator* is 1, it indicates that it is now in an available state for sending.

The *recvIndicator* and *sendIndicator* values are changed as follows. When the connection object is created, its *recvIndicator* and *sendIndicator* are initialized to 0 and 1, respectively. When the NIC receives a message, a hard interrupt is triggered, and the *recvIndicator* of the corresponding connection object is set to 1 in the interrupt handler routine. When the NIC finishes sending a message, a hard interrupt will be triggered, and the *sendIndicator* of the corresponding connection object will be set to 1 in the interrupt handling routine. When there is only one piece of data in the *receiveList* of the connection object, and after the application calls the *recv* function

3.2 Network Transmission

to fetch it, the value of the *recvIndicator* will be modified to 0. After the application calls the send function, the *sendIndicator* value is changed to 0.

In addition, the operating system provides the API function *poll* for applications. Its functionality is to copy the recvIndicator and sendIndicator values of the referred connection object as a return value and pass it to the caller. Thus, the caller knows which connection objects have data for read, and which connection objects are ready for sending. Whenever an application wants to receive data or send data, it should call the poll function first. If the expected events do not occur, the application has to loop through calling the poll function.

If the expected event does not occur for a long time, polling repeatedly is obviously a waste of CPU resources. For this reason, it is necessary to implement the poll function as a synchronization function. In other words, the *recvIndicator* and *sendIndicator* of all connection objects are checked, and if they are all 0, the process is put into a wait state and a process switch is performed. In the NIC hard interrupt handling routine, check whether the process associated with the corresponding connection object is in the WAITING state. If it is, and the wait event is NETWORK, change its state to READY so that it can be subsequently dispatched as the uploaded process and resume operation.

The above asynchronous implementation is not fundamentally different from the asynchronous implementation scheme described in Sect. 2.11. The message queue-based scheme is a global scheme, i.e., it establishes a unified framework for asynchronous processing at the level of process-to-process interaction. The asynchronous I/O described here is limited to the network. In the message queue-based scheme, the data arrival event and the send completion event are processed as messages and directly put into the message queue of the process by the hard interrupt handling routine of the network card. In contrast, in this case, the data received from the network are placed in the *receiveList* of the connection object, and the send completion event is recorded in the *sendIndicator*. In the message queue-based solution, there is a synchronized function *pickOutMessage*, as opposed to the synchronized function *poll*. It can be seen that the asynchronous implementation in the message queue-based solution is more concise and clearer.

Reflection 3.9: For the *poll* function, different operating systems have different names, some are called *select* function. There is also the *epoll* function, which is optimized for the *poll* function, with e being the first character of enhanced. Consult the sources to see how these three functions are related and how they differ, and what exactly are the optimizations that *epoll* makes relative to poll? Then, compare the asynchronous implementations based on message queues and analyze which one has a higher computational overhead? Which is reflected in which point?

Reflection 3.10: There is really no difference between synchronous I/O functions and asynchronous I/O functions as far as function definitions are concerned. The difference is in the value of the socket's member variable *mode*. When the value of *mode* is BLOCKING, the I/O function behaves as synchronous I/O, which is another way of saying that the socket is working in blocking mode. When the value of *mode* is NONBLOCKING, the I/O function behaves as asynchronous I/O, which is another way of saying that the socket is working in non-blocking mode. The value of *mode* is set by a call to the *setsocketopt* API function. Please consult the literature to see what is the return value and error code of a call to *recv* when the socket is operating in non-blocking mode and the card has not yet received data?

Reflection 3.11: Considering both synchronous and asynchronous approaches, can you give an implementation of the six functions, *setsocketopt, accept, connect, send, recv,* and *poll*, as well as the hard interrupt handling routines for the NIC?

Reflection 3.12: *libevent* is an asynchronous network communication programming support library implemented in the application layer and open to the public with its own defined network programming interface. Consult the sources to see what *libevent* does? In addition to shielding against operating system differences, what other specific contributions does it make?

3.2.3 Gateway Servers

To better understand network transmission, an implementation of a gateway server is used to show how to write a network communication program. A gateway machine in an organization has two network cards plugged into it, connecting to the intranet and extranet, respectively. The gateway server listens for network connection requests from both the extranet and the intranet. Multiple servers on the intranet that are open to the public have the same IP address on the extranet for extranet customers, i.e., the gateway's extranet IP address, even though their domain names are different. In other words, to an extranet customer, an enterprise seems to have one machine that runs all its server programs. Similarly, to customers on the intranet, all servers on the extranet seem to be running on the gateway machine. In fact, for any network connection (denoted as α) from the extranet, the gateway server has to establish a network connection (denoted as β) to it in the intranet in order to reach the server (i.e., computer) in the intranet. The reverse is also true.

When a network connection request is listened to from the extranet, a connection object (noted as α) is created in the extranet. The gateway server then gets the domain name of its business server from the gateway configurations based on the listening port number (i.e., the server port number), and then gets its intranet IP address from the DNS based on the business server's domain name. Next, it creates a connection object (denoted as β) on the intranet in the client role and sends a connection request to the business server. After the connection is established, a row (β, α) is added to the internal and external connection mapping table. Finally, a connection response packet is sent to the requester in the extranet via the network connection α. Once the requester in the extranet receives the connection response packet, it knows that the entire connection has been established, and it can then send the business request packet.

When a gateway server receives a network connection request from the intranet, it indicates that a client in the intranet wants to access a server in the extranet. The gateway first creates a network connection object in the intranet corresponding to the request (denoted as α) and sends a response to the requester. Subsequently, when

3.2 Network Transmission

a relay connection request packet is received from the connection object α, it creates a connection object in the extranet in the role of a client (denoted as β) and sends a connection request to the target server. Then, a row of records (α, β) is added to the internal/external connection mapping table. Upon receiving a connection response from the target server, a relay connection response packet is sent to the requester in the intranet via the connection α. Once the requester in the intranet receives the relay connection response packet, it knows that the entire connection has been established, and then it can send the business request packet.

Subsequently, when the gateway server receives a business packet from an external connection (denoted as α), it looks up the corresponding row in the internal/external connection mapping table based on α to get its corresponding internal connection (denoted as β). Then the service packet is forwarded out from the intranet connection β. Similarly, when the gateway server receives a business packet from an internal connection (denoted as α), it looks up the corresponding row in the internal/external connection mapping table based on α to get its corresponding external connection (denoted as β). Then it forwards the business packet out from the extranet connection β.

When the gateway server receives a shutdown request from an external connection (denoted as α), it looks up the corresponding row in the internal/external connection mapping table based on α to get its corresponding internal connection (denoted as β). Then, a close connection request is sent through the intranet connection β. Finally, rows (α, β) are deleted from the internal/external connection mapping table and the network connection objects α and β are released from the external network and the internal network, respectively. The handling of shutdown requests from the internal network is exactly the same.

The message queue-based gateway server is shown in Code 3.11. The implementation uses an asynchronous mode where everything is done by a single process. When the NIC receives an IP packet, or finishes sending an IP packet, it sends a message to the process's message queue. Thus, the business processing framework of the gateway server is to extract the messages one by one from the message queue and then process them.

Lines 2 and 3 of Code 3.11 call the operating system API function *getNetwork* to obtain two network objects, the extranet and the intranet, and store them in the global variables *innerNetwork* and *outerNetwork*, respectively. Lines 4 through 6 are for clients on the intranet, as the server creates a connection object on the intranet that is used to listen for connection requests. Lines 7 through 13 are for clients in the extranet, representing each business server open to the public in the intranet, and creating a connection object in the extranet for listening to connection requests. The server table *serverList* stores the servers on the intranet that are open to the public, and is also a global variable that is used in message processing. Lines 14 through 38 are loops that extract network messages from the message queue and then process them. Network messages are divided into six categories identified by message id.

Network messages originate from the network card. A hard interrupt is triggered when the NIC receives an IP packet, or completes sending an IP packet. Each NIC has its own hard interrupt handling routine, which corresponds to a network object.

In the interrupt handling routine, for the received IP packet, it will find the corresponding connection object based on the values of *destinationPort* and *protocol*. A network card can only handle sending tasks from one connection object at any one time. For a network message, the application should know which connection object in which network object it comes from. Therefore, the content of a network message consists of three parts: (1) a pointer to a network object, (2) a pointer to a connection object, and (3) a pointer to network data. For gateways, there are only two network objects: the *outerNetwork* object and the *innerNetwork* object.

Question 3.13: When the network card finishes sending an IP packet, a hard interrupt will be triggered. In order to know which connection object that IP packet comes from in the hard interrupt handling routine of the network card, shouldn't there still be a member variable *currentConnection* in the Network class to write down which connection object the IP packet comes from?

There are six categories of network messages received by the gateway: connection request, connection response, relay connection request, connection closed, business data sent, and business data received. For the first five categories, the structure of the network data is defined by the network communication protocol. For the received business data, the structure is defined by the application and the gateway does not care. The gateway server handles the received business data by forwarding it.

Code 3.11 Implementation of the Gateway Server

```
(1)   int main (int argc, char **argv ) {
(2)      outerNetwork = getNetwork("outer");
(3)      innerNetwork = getNetwork("inner");
(4)      int port = getConfigureParam("GatewayPort");
(5)      Connection * conn = innerNetwork->createConnection(
              port, INET_IPV4);
(6)      conn->listen(5);
(7)      serverList = getConfigureParam("BusinessServer");
(8)      BusinessServer *server = servertList->getFirstItem();
(9)      while(server ! = null) {
(10)        conn = outerNetwork->createConnection( server-
              >port, INET_IPV4);
(11)        conn->listen(5);
(12)        server = servertList->getNextItem();
(13)     }
(14)     while (true) {
(15)        Message *msg = pickOutMessage( );
(16)        if (msg->id >= MIN_NETWORK_ID && msg->id <= MAX_
              NETWORK_ID) {
(17)           NetworkMessage * networkMsg = (NetworkMessage *)
                 msg->content;
```

3.2 Network Transmission

```
(18)        Network * network = (Network *)
            networkMsg->network;
(19)        Connection * connection = (Connection *)
            networkMsg->connection;
(20)        if (msg->id == CONNECTION_REQUSET) {
(21)           ConnectionRequestHandler(network, connection,
               networkMsg->data);
(22)        }
(23)        else if (msg->id == CONNECTION_RESPONSE) {
(24)           connectionResponseHandler(network, connect,
               networkMsg->data);
(25)        }
(26)        else if (msg->id == CONNECTION_RELAY) {
(27)           connectionRelayHandler(network, connect,
               networkMsg->data);
(28)        }
(29)        else if (msg->id == CONNECTION_CLOSE) {
(30)           closeConnectionHandler(network, connect,
               networkMsg->data);
(31)        }
(32)        else if (msg->id == BUSINESS_DATA_RECEIVE) {
(33)           DataReceiveHandler(network, connect,
               networkMsg->data);
(34)        }
(35)        else if (msg->id == BUSINESS_DATA_SEND) {
(36)           DataSendHandler(network, connect,
               networkMsg->data);
(37)        }
(38)      }
(39)    }
(40)  }
```

The gateway handles the incoming connection request message as shown in Code 3.12. If the connection request comes from an extranet client, a connection object is created in the outerNetwork object to interface with the client's connection, as shown in line 4. When calling the *createConnection* function, the first real parameter is the port number. If the value passed is 0, the implication is that the network object is told to automatically assign an available port number. For servers on the intranet that are open to the public, the port number is used to differentiate. The next step is to find the server on the intranet based on the port number, as shown in line 5. Based on the server's name, go to the DNS server to find its intranet IP address, as shown in line 6. Then create a network connection on the intranet, as shown in line 7. Then send a connection request to the server, as shown in lines 8 through 14. Finally, add a row to the internal/external connection mapping table to associate the two connections, as shown in line 15. Note: At this point, you cannot send a connection response to the requester on the external network; it is deferred until after the internal network connection is established.

Code 3.12 Gateway Handling of Network Connection Requests

```
(1)   void connectionRequestHandler(Network *network,
      Connection *conn, void* data) {
(2)     ConnectionRequest * request = (ConnectionRequest
        * ) data;
(3)     if ( network == outerNetwork) {
(4)       Connection *conn1 = outerNetwork->createConnection(
          0, request->protocol, request->sourceIpAddr,
          request->sourcePort);
(5)       Server * server = serverList->getItemByPort (
          conn->getPort( ) );
(6)       int serverIpAddr = getIpAddrByNameFromDNS(serv
          er->name);
(7)       Connection *conn2 = innerNetwork-
          >createConnection(0, request->protocol,
          serverIpAddr, server->port );
(8)       request = new ConnectionRequest(conn2);
(9)       if (innerNetworkSending == FALSE) {
(10)        conn2->send( request );
(11)        innerNetworkSending = TRUE;
(12)      }
(13)      else
(14)        innerUrgentSendbufferList->addItem(conn2,
            request);
(15)      connectionMapList->addItem(conn2, conn1);
(16)    }
(17)    else if ( network == innerNetwork) {
(18)      Connection *conn2 = innerNetwork-
          >createConnection(0, request->protocol, request-
          >sourceIpAddr, request->sourcePort );
(19)      ConnectionResponse *response = new
          ConnectionResponse(conn2->getPort());
(20)      if (innerNetworkSending == FALSE) {
(21)        conn2->send(response);
(22)        innerNetworkSending = TRUE;
(23)      }
(24)      else
(25)        innerUrgentSendbufferList->addItem(conn2,
            response);
(26)    }
(27)  }
```

3.2 Network Transmission

Both intranets and extranets may have multiple network connections established. Each network connection has data to send, but the network can only send them one by one in a serial fashion. Thus, when a network connection has data to send, it may not be able to send it immediately. If the network is busy sending, then it has to cache the data to be sent to the send queue. For this reason, the global variables *innerNetworkSending* and *outerNetworkSending* are set for *innerNetwork* and *outerNettwork* objects, respectively, to record whether they are currently in the sending state. In addition, data such as network connection requests and connection responses should be prioritized over business data. Thus, two send cache queues are set up for each network. For the intranet, *innerUrgentSendbufferList* and *innerSendbufferList* are set up to cache urgent data and normal business data, respectively. The same is true for the extranet.

If the connection request comes from an intranet client, a connection object is created in the *innerNetwork* object to interface with it, as shown on line 18. The connection response is then sent to the client through the created connection, as shown in lines 19 through 25.

Code 3.13 Gateway Handling of Connection Responses
```
(1)   void connectionResponseHandler(Network *network,
      Connection *conn, void *data) {
(2)     ConnectionResponse * response = ( ConnectionResponse
        * ) data;
(3)     conn->setOppositePort (response->port );
(4)     if ( network == outerNetwork) {
(5)       ConnectionMapItem *map =connectionMapList->getItemB
          yOuterConnection(conn);
(6)       RelayResponse *response = new RelayResponse( );
(7)       if (innerNetworkSending == FALSE) {
(8)         map->innerConnection->send(response);
(9)         innerNetworkSending = TRUE;
(10)      }
(11)      else
(12)        innerUrgentSendbufferList->addItem(map-
            >innerConnection, response);
(13)    }
(14)    else if ( network == innerNetwork) {
(15)      ConnectionMapItem *map =connectionMapList->getItem
          ByinnerConnection(conn);
(16)      response = new ConnectionResponse(map->
          outerConnection->getPort());
(17)      if (outerNetworkSending == FALSE ) {
(18)        map->outerConnection->send(response);
```

```
(19)            outerNetworkSending = TRUE;
(20)        }
(21)        else
(22)            outerUrgentSendbufferList->addItem(map-
                >outerConnection, response);
(23)    }
(24) }
```

The gateway's processing of the received connection response message is shown in Code 3.13. The connection response contains information about the other party's port number, so the initialization of the connection object's member variable *oppositePort* is completed first, as shown in lines 2 and 3. If the connection response comes from an external client, it means that it was an internal client that wanted to access the external server before that. More specifically, the gateway received a connection relay request from an intranet client, then initiated a connection request to the extranet server, and now gets a connection response from the extranet server. The work to be done at this point is to find the corresponding intranet connection, as shown in line 5. Then send a connection relay response message to the client on the intranet, as shown in lines 6 through 12. If the connection response comes from an intranet client, it means that it was an extranet client that wanted to access the server on the intranet before that. This is handled by finding the corresponding extranet connection and sending a connection response message to the client on the extranet, as shown in lines 15 through 22.

The gateway's handling of an incoming connection relay request is shown in Code 3.14. The connection relay request must have come from an intranet client. This means that the client has already sent a connection request to the gateway, and the gateway has already sent a connection response message to the connection requester. The connection requester then sends the gateway a connection relay request (which contains the IP address and port number of the external server) in accordance with the gateway access protocol. What the gateway does then is to create a network connection on the external network based on the connection relay request received and send a connection request message to the server on the external network, and then correlate the two connections and store them in the internal / external connection mapping table, as shown in lines 5 through 12.

Code 3.14 Gateway Handling of Connection Relay Messages
```
(1)  void ConnectionRelayHandler(Network *network,
     Connection *conn, void* data) {
(2)     ConnectionRelay * relay = (ConnectionRelay * ) data.
(3)     if ( network == innerNetwork) {
```

3.2 Network Transmission

```
(4)       Connection *conn2 = outerNetwork-
          >createConnection(0, relay->protocol, relay-
          >ipAddr, relay->port );
(5)       ConnectionRequest * request = new
          ConnectionRequest(conn2);
(6)       if (outerNetworkSending == FALSE) {
(7)          conn2->send( request);
(8)          outerNetworkSending = TRUE;
(9)       }
(10)        else
(11)           outerUrgentSendbufferList->addIem(conn2,
              request);
(12)       connectionMapList->addItem(conn, conn2);
(13)    }
(14)  }
```

The gateway's handling of incoming connection closure requests is shown in Code 3.15. In the C/S model, the request to close the connection must be initiated by the client. Therefore, if the connection closure request comes from the extranet, the corresponding intranet connection is found, and a connection closure request is sent to the server in the intranet, as shown in lines 3 through 11. Then you release the corresponding network connection object on the intranet and the corresponding network connection object on the extranet, and delete the corresponding rows in the internal/external connection mapping table, as shown in lines 12 through 14. If the request to close the connection comes from the intranet, the process is similar to the one described above, as shown in lines 17 through 26.

The gateway's processing of the received business data is naturally forwarded, as shown in Code 3.16. If the received business data come from an external network, the corresponding intranet connection is found, as shown in line 4. If the intranet is idle as far as sending data is concerned, then it is forwarded from the intranet, as shown in lines 5 through 6. If the intranet is busy as far as sending data is concerned, then the business data are stored in the intranet's send buffer queue *innerSendBufferList*, as shown in line 10. Note: When caching, you cannot just cache the data, but also the connection object pointer. The reason for this is that the subsequent forwarding is done through the connection object. If the received business data from the intranet, the process is similar to the above process, as shown in lines 13 to 19.

When the gateway receives a sending completion message, it naturally looks at the corresponding sending cache queue to see if there are any data to be sent. If so, it continues to send it; otherwise, it sets the sending state of the corresponding network object to idle. The implementation is shown in Code 3.17. If the message

Code 3.15 Gateway Handling of Close Connection Request Messages

```
(1)   void closeConnectionHandler(Network *network,
      Connection *conn, void *data) {
(2)     ConnectionMapItem *map.
(3)     CloseConnectionRequest *request = new
        CloseConnectionRequest( );
(4)     if ( network == outerNetwork) {
(5)       map = connectionMapList->getItemByOuterConnection(c
          onn);
(6)       if (innerNetworkSending == FALSE) {
(7)         map->innerConnection->send(request);
(8)         innerNetworkSending = TRUE;
(9)       }
(10)      else
(11)        innerUrgentSendbufferList->addItem(map-
            >innerConnection, request);
(12)      innerNetwork->closeConnection(map->
          innerConnection);
(13)      outerNetwork->closeConnection(conn);
(14)      connectionMapList->
          deleteItemByOuterConnection(conn);
(15)    }
(16)    else if ( network == innerNetwork) {
(17)      map = connectionMapList->getItemByInnerConnection(
          conn);
(18)      if (outerNetworkSending == FALSE) {
(19)        map->outerConnection->send(request);
(20)        outerNetworkSending = TRUE;
(21)      }
(22)      else
(23)        outerUrgentSendbufferList->addItem(map-
            >outerConnection, request);
(24)      outerNetwork->closeConnection(map->
          outerConnection);
(25)      innerNetwork->closeConnection(conn);
(26)      connectionMapList->
          deleteItemByInnerConnection(conn);
(27)    }
(28)  }
```

comes from an external network, then the data in the *outerUrgentSendbufferList* queue are prioritized when selecting the pending data, as shown in lines 4 through 13. If there is no pending data, the value of *outerNetworkSending* is changed from TRUE to FALSE, indicating that the network is idle as far as sending is concerned, as shown on line 12. If the message is from an intranet, the processing is similar to the above process, as shown in lines 16 through 25.

Code 3.16 Gateway Handling of Received Business Data
```
(1)   void DataReceiveHandler(Network *network, Connection
      *conn, void *data) {
(2)       ConnectionMapItem *map.
(3)       if ( network == outerNetwork) {
(4)           map = connectionMapList->getItemByOuterConnection(c
              onn);
(5)           if (innerNetworkSending == FALSE) {
(6)               map->innerConnection->send(data);
(7)               innerNetworkSending = TRUE;
(8)           }
(9)           else
(10)              innerSendbufferList->addIem(map-
                  >innerConnection, data);
(11)      }
(12)      else if ( network == innerNetwork)  {
(13)          map = connectionMapList->getItemByInnerConnection(
              conn);
(14)          if (outerNetworkSending == FALSE) {
(15)              map->outerConnection->send(data);
(16)              outerNetworkSending = TRUE;
(17)          }
(18)          else
(19)              outerSendbufferList->addIem(map-
                  >outerConnection, data);
(20)      }
(21)  }
```

The above implementation of the gateway server requires only one process to handle all client requests on both networks, including listening for connections, establishing connections to clients, and handling the receipt and sending of data on all network connections. In network transmissions, IP packets have a length limit. If the data to be sent by an application are large, the network manager splits it into multiple segments and then encapsulates each segment into an IP packet to be sent. The reason for limiting the length of IP packets is to prevent the network from being occupied by a single sending task for a long period of time, which may affect the timely delivery of instructional data such as connection requests and connection responses, and to allow the network bandwidth to be spread evenly across each network connection.

The interaction between hardware and process can be regarded as process-to-process interaction. The reason is that hard interrupt handling routines are independent of processes, and once a hard interrupt is triggered, the hard interrupt handling routines will be executed by the CPU for a trip. Take a network card as an example, a network card interrupt will be triggered when data are received or data have been sent. A message is sent to the message queue of the corresponding process in the card's hard interrupt handling routine, which is in essence an access to the shared data in the kernel space.

Code 3.17 Gateway Handling of Received IP Packet Delivery Completed Message

```
(1)  void DataSendHandler(Network *network, Connection
       *conn, void *data) {
(2)    ConnectionMap *map;
(3)    if ( network == outerNetwork) {
(4)      SendItem * sendItem =
         outerUrgentSendbufferList->pickOutItem();
(5)      if (sendItem ! = null)
(6)        sendItem->connection->send(sendItem->data);
(7)      else {
(8)        sendItem = outerSendbufferList->pickOutItem();
(9)        if (sendItem ! = null)
(10)         sendItem->connection->send(sendItem->data);
(11)       else
(12)         outerNetworkSending = FALSE;
(13)     }
(14)   }
(15)   else if ( network == innerNetwork) {
(16)     SendItem * sendItem =
         innerUrgentSendbufferList->pickOutItem();
(17)     if (sendItem ! = null)
(18)       sendItem->connection->send(sendItem->data);
(19)     else {
(20)       sendItem = innerSendbufferList->pickOutItem();
(21)       if (sendItem ! = null)
(22)         sendItem->connection->send(sendItem->data);
(23)       else
(24)         innerNetworkSending = FALSE;
(25)     }
(26)   }
(27) }
```

Concurrent multitasking can be achieved asynchronously through a single process when process-to-process interactions are unified using messages. This is the case with the gateway server described above. In contrast, in the asynchronous implementation of network communication described in the previous section, the application's call to the synchronous function *poll* waits only for network events (i.e., data received events or data sent completion events). This treatment takes into account the network only. If the application has to wait for events other than network events, then concurrent multitasking cannot be realized with only one process. The reason is that when a process calls the function *poll* to wait for a network event, other events (e.g., keyboard input events and mouse input events) cannot be processed in a timely manner.

The benefit of implementing process-network interactions through messages is that concurrent multitasking can be achieved with only one process, thus reducing the number of processes and optimizing performance. The trade-off is that much of the handling that was hidden in the operating system now has to be brought up to the application. For example, the sending and processing of data such as connection requests and connection responses, which were originally hidden in the implementation of the synchronization functions *accept* and *connect*, now need to be handled by the application. This scenario has been demonstrated in the implementation of the gateway server.

The implementation of the tunneling technology is also given in the gateway server. Servers in the intranet that are open to the public can be accessed by external clients even though they do not have an extranet IP address and are not connected to the extranet. It appears to the external client that the server in the intranet that is open to the public has an extranet IP address. This IP address is actually the IP address of the gateway on the external network. Even though servers in the intranet that are open to the outside world share an extranet IP address, they are distinguished in the gateway by the port number assigned to them. The gateway plays the role of a relay, sometimes referred to as a routing role. Of course, this routing is transport-level routing, not network-level routing. In transport-level routing, for an IP packet received from one NIC, the data portion of the packet is extracted and re-encapsulated into a new IP packet, which is then forwarded out from another NIC. In contrast, in network-level routing, IP packets received from one NIC are forwarded directly from another NIC.

There is also a situation where an organization has multiple servers that are open to the public and use the same port number. For example, a university has a WEB server, and each of its colleges has its own WEB server. These WEB servers all use port 80, open to the public. At this point, the tunneling technology cannot help. The solution is: if there are n WEB servers open to the public, you have to apply for n external IP addresses, including the external IP address of the gateway. However, all open servers are not connected to the external network, but on the intranet. Thus, interactions between external customers and intranet servers are limited to go through the gateway, in order to implement the total security control and traffic control at the gateway. How to implement network transmission at this situation? The answer to this question involves the concept of virtual networks and will be explained in detail in Chap. 5.

Reflection 3.14: A gateway can implement traffic control for an intranet client's access to an extranet server. The bandwidth for accessing the extranet is assumed to be 1000 M, and the control policy is to send IP packets for the current connection in turn. Assuming the current number of connections is 100, the bandwidth available to each connection is roughly 10 M. When an intranet customer installs a high-speed download component on his computer and uses it to upload or download large files, the speed can be increased several times. Of course, this kind of speed up is only possible with the support of the back-end server. How is the speed increase realized?

Reflection 3.15: ping and traceroute are two commonly used network inspection applications. Ping is used to test network reachability, and traceroute is used to show the path to a destination host. Instead of using the transmission control protocol (TCP) protocol to create a socket, these two applications use the Internet Control Message Protocol (ICMP), which is a connectionless protocol that means that when a network manager receives this type of IP packet, it gives a response to the requester, so there is no obvious server to handle this type of packet. Please consult the sources to write the implementation code for ping and traceroute.

3.2.4 Application Layer Protocols

The above functions, *accept*, *connect*, *recv*, and *send*, work at the transport layer. Above the transport layer, there is the application layer. The most common communication protocols in the transport layer are TCP/user datagram protocol (UDP), while the most common communication protocols in the application layer are HTTP, FTP, DHCP, DNS, and SMTP and POP3 [3]. Application layer protocols also provide API functions upwards for applications to call. Thus, what does an application layer protocol do? Data received or sent at the transport layer are of type ByteString. The data received or sent at the application layer are no longer of type ByteString, but of its own defined data type, e.g., in the HTTP protocol, the data type HttpPackage is defined. Therefore, the data received on the HTTP protocol are an HttpPackage object. One of the things that the HTTP protocol has to do, as far as data reception is concerned, is to convert one or more ByteString objects received into an HttpPackage object. As far as data sending is concerned, it is an HttpPackage object into a ByteString object.

Reflection 3.16: From the functionality of application layer protocols, it is clear that the application layer protocol code can be placed in the support libraries instead of in the operating system kernel, why? The network object and connection object are the objects to be accessed in the NIC interrupt handling routines, so they must be in the operating system kernel, is this statement correct?

3.3 Concurrency Control for Transaction Processing

Resource sharing and access conflicts are a symbiotic pair of concepts. Global variables in the operating system kernel space are shared by multiple processes. Since hard interrupts are process-independent, a trip to the execution of a hard interrupt

3.3 Concurrency Control for Transaction Processing

handling routine is also considered as a process. A simple implementation to avoid access conflicts is to mask hard interrupts during the execution of interrupt handling routines. This allows a process to have exclusive access to shared data in kernel space by calling the operating system API. Only after the access is complete (i.e., the interrupt returns) are other processes allowed to access the shared data in kernel space. This is an implementation of multi-process concurrency control.

In distributed computing, data in a server are shared by multiple clients. The server at runtime has a one-to-many relationship with clients, i.e., more than one client may be accessing the server at the same time. A single business request from a client is called a transaction. Every time the server receives a transaction request from a client, it processes it and returns the result to the client as a response. Concurrent processing of multiple transactions by the server can significantly improve its processing performance. This strategy stems from the following observations. In processing a transaction, it takes time for the CPU to access data from issuing a request to receiving a response result. During this period, the CPU is idle. The CPU can then be allowed to process another transaction, thus increasing the CPU utilization. When the response result arrives, then let the CPU jump back to process the previous transaction. Thus, from the outside, it appears as if the CPU is processing multiple transactions at the same time. This situation is called concurrent multi-transaction processing [4].

For multiple transactions, the comparison between concurrent processing and sequential processing is shown in Fig. 3.2. From this figure, it can be seen that to complete the processing of three transactions, the time to be spent in the sequential processing mode is $t_1 + t_2 + t_3$, while in the concurrent processing mode, the time to be spent is t_4. Concurrent processing can greatly improve the efficiency of data processing.

Concurrent processing strategies are often used in everyday work and life. For example, when a person is cooking at home, he or she cooks several dishes at the same time in order to increase efficiency. The approach is that when the first course takes some time to cook, the person moves on to the cleaning and chopping of the

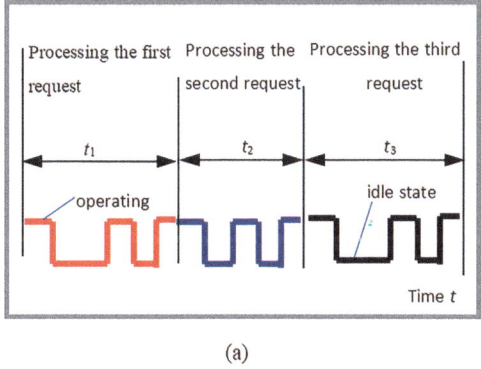
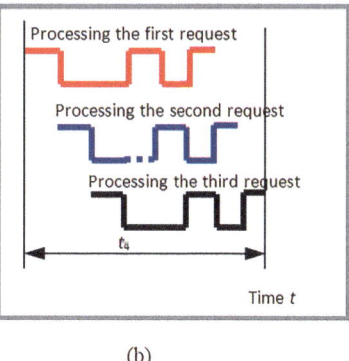

Fig. 3.2 Sequential processing vs. concurrent processing. (**a**) Sequential processing, (**b**) Concurrent processing

second course. When the first dish is done cooking, the person stops doing the second dish and turns back to do the first dish's bowl loading. As a result, the efficiency of the work is greatly increased and the time to cook a table is greatly reduced.

While concurrent processing gains efficiency gains, it also introduces access conflict problems that lead to inconsistent and incorrect data. For example, the first transaction wants to obtain the result of adding data A and data B, while the second transaction wants to do an addition of 50 to data A and then a subtraction of 50 to data B. The first transaction involves a 3-step operation and the second transaction involves a 6-step operation, as shown in Fig. 3.3a. In concurrent execution mode, the following processing is entirely possible: the CPU first executes step 1 of the first transaction, then goes to steps 1 through 6 of the second transaction, and then turns back to steps 2 and 3 of the first transaction, as shown in Fig. 3.3b. This processing is problematic, resulting in an inconsistency between A and B obtained in the first transaction and an incorrect response result that is 50 smaller than the true result.

The reason for the error is that the first transaction and the second transaction both access data A and B. Because of concurrent execution, the first transaction gets A as the value before the second transaction executes, but B as the value after the second transaction executes. It happens that the second transaction modifies both A and B. Therefore, A and B obtained by the first transaction are inconsistent, leading to wrong results.

By executing transactions in a sequential manner, there is no problem of inconsistent or incorrect data. Therefore, concurrent processing cannot be unconditional and should be predicated on ensuring that the data are correct and consistent. Concurrent execution of transactions should be controlled to ensure correct and consistent data. Concurrency control can be realized based on access conflict identification.

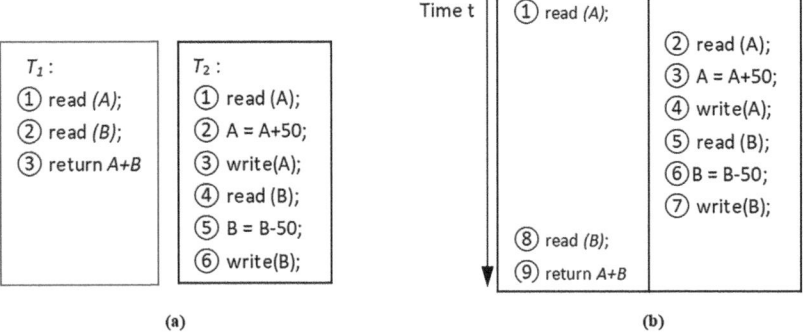

Fig. 3.3 Conflicts arising from the concurrent execution of two transactions. (**a**) Data operations contained in each of the two transactions, (**b**) Timing of CPU concurrent execution of the two transactions

3.3.1 Concurrency Control Based on Access Conflict Identification

In concurrency control based on access conflict identification, only transactions that do not have access conflicts are allowed to execute concurrently, and transactions that have access conflicts are constrained to execute sequentially. What is the meaning of access conflict? How is it identified? How to schedule the execution of transactions? These are the questions to be answered by concurrency control based on access conflict identification. The set of data items to be accessed by each transaction can be divided into two parts: read-only data items and write data items. For transaction T_α, its read-only data item set is denoted by α_r and its write data item set is denoted by α_w. For two transactions T_α and T_β, an access conflict exists between T_α and T_β if $\alpha_w \cap (\beta_r \cup \beta_w) \neq \emptyset$, or $\beta_w \cap (\alpha_r \cup \alpha_w) \neq \emptyset$. The meaning of this constraint is: (1) for two concurrently executing transactions, when one transaction is reading a data item, the other transaction can also read it, which is called shared read; (2) when a transaction wants to perform a write operation on a data item, no other transaction can perform a read operation or a write operation on it, which is called exclusive write.

In concurrency control, let the set of transactions currently waiting to be processed be $\{T_w\}$ and the set of transactions being processed be $\{T_x\}$. For any transaction T_w in $\{T_w\}$, if it does not conflict with all the transactions in $\{T_x\}$, then transaction T_w can be scheduled for execution. When the server accepts a transaction request submitted by a client, if it does not conflict with any of the transactions in $\{T_x\}$, then it schedules it for execution and adds it to $\{T_x\}$. Otherwise, it is added into $\{T_w\}$. After a transaction is executed, it is removed from $\{T_x\}$, and then the transactions in $\{T_w\}$ are checked one by one, and those that do not conflict with the updated $\{T_x\}$ are scheduled to be executed and moved from $\{T_w\}$ into $\{T_x\}$.

Reflection 3.17: Let any transaction T_w in $\{T_w\}$ conflict with $\{T_x\}$. After a transaction T_x in $\{T_x\}$ executes, it is to be excluded from $\{T_x\}$. For any transaction T_w in $\{T_w\}$, if T_x does not conflict with T_w, then T_w must still conflict with the updated $\{T_x\}$. Why? Please explain the reasoning.

For the concurrency control implementation, there are multiple threads executing in the server process. One of them, the main thread, is responsible for listening and accepting transaction requests from clients, as well as for concurrency control of transactions. The main thread creates multiple worker threads and hands over the accepted transactions to them for processing. The main thread and worker threads interact with each other through messages. When the main thread wants to give a transaction to the worker thread T_i for processing, it sends a message to T_i with the content of the transaction to be processed. The worker thread waits for messages from the main thread in a loop. Each time it waits for a message, it would receive a processing task from the main thread. After processing a transaction, the worker thread sends a message to the main thread to report the result and then waits for the next task. The code to be executed by the main thread and the worker thread is shown in Codes 3.18 and 3.19, respectively.

Code 3.18 Code to Be Executed by the Main Thread

```
(1)     Network *network = getNetwork( );
(2)     int port = getConfigureParam("ServerListenPort");
(3)     Connection *conn = network->createConnection( port,
        INET_IPV4);
(4)     conn->listen(5);
(5)     amount = getConfigureParam("workerThreadAmount");
(6)     for (int i = 0; i++; i < amount) {
(7)       int threadId = createThread( transactionHandler);
(8)       idleWorkerThreadIdList->addItem( threadId);
(9)     }
(10)    transactionCount = 0;
(11)    workingThreadCount = 0;
(12)    mainThreadId = getThreadId();
(13)    while (true) {
(14)      Message *msg = pickOutMessage( );
(15)      if (msg->id == TRANSACTION_COMPLETITION) {
(16)        transactionCompletionHandler(msg->content).
(17)      }
(18)      else if (msg->id == NETWORK_BUSINESS_RECEIVE) {
(19)        transactionAcceptanceHandler(msg->content).
(20)      }
(21)      else if (msg->id == NETWORK_BUSINESS_SEND) {
(22)        transactionResultSendHandler(msg->content);
(23)      }
(24)    }
```

In Code 3.18, lines 1 through 12 are initialization work: a network connection is created to listen for client requests, then multiple worker threads are created, and global variables are assigned initial values. The global variable *transactionCount* is used to assign a unique id to each transaction being processed, both to identify the transaction and to order it. The global variable *workingThreadCount* records how many worker threads are currently concurrently processing transactions. The total number of worker threads is recorded in the global variable *amount*, i.e., the maximum concurrency is *amount*. If each working thread is processing a transaction, even if the new transaction accepted by the main thread does not conflict with the ongoing transactions, its processing still needs to wait. Setting the maximum degree of concurrency is necessary, as too many worker threads can lead to congestion problems. Once congestion occurs, no one can operate normally. The global variable *mainThreadId* is used to record the id of the main thread so that worker threads can send messages to the main thread.

3.3 Concurrency Control for Transaction Processing

Code 3.19 Code to Be Executed by a Worker Thread
```
(1)  int transactionHandler( ) {
(2)    int threadId = getThreadId( );
(3)    while (true) {
(4)      Message *msg = pickOutMessage( );
(5)      Tranaction * transaction = (Tranaction *)
               msg->content;
(6)      transaction->responseResult =
               HandleTransaction(transaction);
(7)      postMessage(mainThreadId, TRANSACTION_COMPLETITION,
               (void *) transaction);
(8)    }
(9)  }
```

Code 3.20 Implementation of the TransactionAcceptanceHandler function
```
(1)  void transactionAcceptanceHandler(void *data) {
(2)    Transaction *transaction = new Transaction(data);
(3)    if (workingThreadCount < amount && conflict
             (activeTransactionList, transaction) == FALSE) {
(4)      transaction->id = transactionCount ++;
(5)      workingThreadCount++;
(6)      activeTransactionList->addItem(transaction);
(7)      transaction->threadId = idleWorkerThreadList-
             >pickOutItem( );
(8)      postMessage(transaction->threadId , ASSIGNMENT,
             (void *)transaction);
(9)    }
(10)   else
(11)     waitingTransactionList->addItem(transaction );
(12) }
```

In Code 3.18, lines 13 through 24 are a loop waiting for messages and then processing the received messages. There are 2 sources of messages: the network and the worker thread. When the network receives a transaction request, it sends a NETWORK_BUSINESS_RECEIVE message to the main thread. When the network finishes sending a transaction response result, it sends a NETWORK_BUSINESS_SEND message to the main thread. When a worker thread finishes processing a transaction, it sends a TRANSACTION_COMPLETITION message to the main thread. For the three kinds of messages, the main thread calls the functions *transactionAcceptanceHandler*, *transactionResultSendHandler*, and *transactionCompletionHandler* to process them, respectively. The implementation of these three functions is shown in Codes 3.20, 3.21, and 3.22, respectively.

Code 3.21 Implementation of the transactionResultSendHandler function

```
(1)  void transactionResultSendHandler(void *data) {
(2)     delete data;
(3)     SendItem *sendItem = SendbufferList->pickOutItem();
(4)     if (sendItem ! = null)
(5)        sendItem->connection->send(sendItem->data);
(6)     else
(7)        isSending = FALSE;
(8)  }
```

Code 3.22 Implementation of the transactionCompletionHandler function

```
(1)  void transactionCompletionHandler(void *data) {
(2)     Transaction *transaction = (Transaction *)data;
(3)     if (isSending == FALSE ) {
(4)        transaction->connection->send( transaction-
           >responseResult );
(5)        isSending = TRUE;
(6)     }
(7)     else
(8)        sendbufferList->addIem(transaction->connection,
           transaction->responseResult);
(9)     idleWorkerThreadIdList->addItem(transaction-
        >threadId );
(10)    workingThreadCount--;
(11)    activeTransactionList->deleteItem(transaction);
(12)    delete transaction;
(13)    transaction = waitingTransactionList-
        >getFirstItem( );
(14)    while (transaction ! = null && workingThreadCount <
        amount ) {
(15)       if ( conflict(activeTransactionList, transaction)
           == FALSE) {
(16)          transaction->id = transactionCount ++;
```

3.3 Concurrency Control for Transaction Processing

```
(17)            workingThreadCount++;
(18)            activeTransactionList->addItem(transaction);
(19)            transaction->threadId = idleWorkerThreadIdList-
                >pickOutItem( );
(20)            postMessage(transaction->threadId , ASSIGNMENT,
                (void *)transaction);
(21)            transaction = waitingTransactionList-
                >deleteItemAndGetNext( transaction);
(22)        }
(23)        else
(24)            transaction = waitingTransactionList-
                >getNextItem( );
(25)    }
(26) }
```

A new transaction request will be assigned to a worker thread only if two conditions are met. First, there must be a free worker thread, and there must be no conflict with the transaction being processed. Otherwise, it will be held in a waiting queue until both conditions are met before it is given to a worker thread to process. Transactions that are being processed are stored with the global variable *activeTransactionList*, while transactions waiting to be processed are stored with the global variable *waitingTransactionList*. This processing is shown in Code 3.20.

When a worker thread finishes processing a transaction, it sends a TRANSACTION_COMPLETITION message to the main thread. The main thread first looks to see if the network is currently in the sending state. If not, it sends the transaction result as the response to the client. Otherwise, the transaction result is placed in the pending queue *sendBufferList*. Next, the main thread removes the completed transaction from the *activeTransactionList* and groups the worker thread responsible for its processing into the *idleWorkerThreadIdList*. The pending transaction is then checked. If there are no conflicts, it is handed off to the idle worker thread t for processing. These processes are shown in Code 3.22.

Note: In the above implementation of transaction concurrency processing, global variables become shared variables due to multithreading. In order to avoid access conflicts, only the global variable *mainThreadId* is used in the worker thread, which is only assigned a value by the main thread during initialization and then only read by the worker thread, so there is no access conflict problem. The *transactionCompletionHandler* function can also be called in the worker thread, based on the timing of the business process alone. Due to the fact that there are multiple worker threads, and the fact that global variables are read and written in the function, the function cannot be called by the worker thread; otherwise, there would be access conflict issues. It is for this reason that the call to the function has to be transferred to the main thread by sending a message.

The above transaction concurrency control has a prerequisite that the data to be read and the data to be written by the transaction should be known from the transaction request. Only then can we determine whether there is an access conflict between the two transactions. Specifically, it is in line 3 of Code 3.20, as well as in line 15 of Code 3.22, where the conflict function is called to identify whether conflict exists or not. For the management of shared data, different servers have different management granularity. A file server has a minimum granularity of files, an object server has a minimum granularity of objects, and a database server has a minimum granularity of rows in a table.

For a database server, a client's transaction request is expressed as an SQL statement. If there are no SQL nested operations in the transaction request, then the SQL statement can be parsed to know which table and which rows are to be read or written by the transaction request. Thus, it is possible to know if there is an access conflict between two transactions before the transaction is executed. If the transaction request has nested SQL operations, then the outer SQL statement depends on the execution result of the inner SQL statement. In this case, it is conservative to assume that the outer SQL statement is targeting all rows in the table.

For the purpose of access conflict identification, a transaction should have a member variable *accessedObjectList*, which records the shared data to be accessed and the operations to be performed on it. *accessedObject* has two member variables: *objectId* and *accessMode*, where *objectId* is the data item identifier and *accessMode* is the operation type, whose values are read (R) and write (W). The transaction object is created based on the transaction request, as shown in line 2 of Code 3.20. Initialization of the member variable *accessedObjectList* is done in the constructor of the transaction object. If the transaction request is expressed as an SQL statement, then the initialization of *accessedObjectList* involves parsing the SQL statement. Once each transaction's member variable *accessedObjectList* has been initialized, determining whether two transactions have an access conflict is easy.

Reflection 3.18: Can you give an implementation of the conflict function called in line 3 of Code 3.20 and line 15 of Code 3.22?

The above concurrency control based on access conflict identification deals with a transaction as a whole and can be called coarse-grained concurrency control. Looking deeper inside a transaction, a transaction consists of operations. From the operation level, the waiting time of a transaction can be shortened in many cases. For example, transaction T_α contains three operations: read data item A, read data item B, and write data item C. Transaction T_β also contains three operations: read data item A, read data item B, and read data item C. At the transaction level, transaction T_α and transaction T_β have a conflict in accessing data item C. If transaction T_α is scheduled first, then transaction T_β will not be executed until transaction T_α has been processed. If we look at the operation level, the execution of transaction T_β can be advanced to increase the concurrency of transaction execution. The first two operations of transaction T_β, i.e., reading data items A and B, can be executed concurrently with transaction T_α because there is no conflict between them. Only the third operation, reading data item C, can be executed until transaction T_α is committed. Implementing concurrency control at the operation level is often referred to as fine-grained concurrency control.

3.3.2 Fine-Grained Concurrency Control

Implementing concurrency control at the operational level improves the concurrency of transaction processing compared to that at the transaction level. In operation-level concurrency control, whenever the server receives a transaction request from a client, it starts an idle worker thread to execute it. For the operations contained in the transaction, the worker thread executes them sequentially one by one. Typically, there are multiple worker threads executing concurrently in the server. To perform a read or write operation on shared data, a worker thread T_i must first send a message to the main thread asking whether there is an access conflict problem with performing the operation, and then wait for the main thread's response. This process is visualized in the operating system as locking. In this case, however, the lock manager is not the operating system, but the main thread. To lock is to send a lock message to the main thread. The synchronization of locking is reflected in waiting for the response message from the main thread.

In fine-grained concurrency control, the worker thread has three states: (1) idle state, (2) running state, and (3) blocking state. Initially, the worker thread is in idle state. When the main thread assigns a transaction task to an idle worker thread, the state of the worker thread changes from idle to running. The main thread assigns a task to a worker thread by sending an ASSIGNMENT message to it. For a running worker thread, when it wants to operate on shared data, it calls the function *postMessage* to send a lock request message to the main thread, and then calls the synchronization function *pickOutMesssage* to wait for the result of the main thread's response. At this point, the state of the worker thread changes from running to blocking. When *pickOutMesssage* returns, its state changes again from blocking to running. When the worker thread finishes processing a transaction, its state changes from running to idle.

The lock referred to here is actually an accessed object that records the id of the shared data to be accessed and the operations to be performed on it. Taking the database as an example, the id of the shared data includes the table name and the query condition, where the query condition identifies the rows to be accessed. There are two types of operations, read and write. Whenever the main thread receives a locking request, it first checks whether the requested accessed object has an access conflict with the accessed objects held by the currently active transaction. If there is no access conflict, the main thread performs the following two tasks: (1) adds the requested accessed object to the *accessedObjectList* of the transaction handled by the requesting thread; and (2) sends an uplock response message to the requester. If there is an access conflict, the lock request message is added to the *blockedTransactionList*, which is a global variable that records all blocked transactions and their requested locks (i.e., accessed objects).

For a worker thread in the running state, after it has finished accessing shared data, it sends an unlock request message to the main thread to increase the concurrency of transactions processed by the entire server. Once the main thread receives an unlock request message, it removes the lock it refers to (i.e., the accessed object) from the requester thread's *accessedObjectList*, indicating that it no longer holds the lock. All items in the *blockedTransactionList* are then checked one by one to see if the access conflict problem has been eliminated. If it has been eliminated, the accessed object of the current item is added to the *accessedObjectList* of the corresponding worker thread, and a lock response message is sent to the corresponding worker thread. Then, the worker thread will change from blocking state to running state.

The difference between fine-grained concurrency control compared to coarse-grained concurrency control is twofold. In fine-grained concurrency control, locks are not requested all at once in advance, but in real time, and only one lock is requested at a time, as many times as the transaction has locks. In coarse-grained concurrency control, on the other hand, all the locks needed are requested at once in advance. Requesting one lock is naturally easier to achieve success than requesting all locks, so fine-grained concurrency control increases the concurrency of transaction execution. As far as lock release is concerned, in coarse-grained concurrency control, locks are released all at once after the transaction has been processed. In fine-grained concurrency control, locks are released in real time, i.e., immediately after use. Because in fine-grained concurrency control, the application of locks is delayed, while the release of locks is advanced, so on the whole can increase the degree of concurrency of the server processing transactions, which is conducive to the enhancement of server processing performance.

In addition, when transactions have nested access to shared data, access conflicts are more accurately identified in fine-grained concurrency control, and thus concurrency can be improved. For example, suppose the transaction request to access the database is: "UPDATE employee SET salary= salary + 200 WHERE employId IN (SELECT employId FROM work WHERE sumHour > 500 AND year = 2023)". This transaction request contains two operations: (1) a read operation to the work table and (2) a write operation to the employee table. It is characterized by the fact that the data targeted by the latter operation depends on the result of the former operation. When the second operation is performed, the first operation has been completed, and the employee table is updated without locking the entire table, but only the rows to be updated. In contrast, in coarse-grained concurrency control, since the result of operation 1 is not known in advance, it is conservatively assumed that operation 2 will write all rows in the employee table.

In fine-grained concurrency control, when a transaction wants to have access to a piece of shared data, it first calls the lock function to lock it. The implementation of this function is shown in lines 1 through 5 of Code 3.23. The id of the data to be accessed and the type of operation to be performed (read or write) are stored in the formal parameter *accessedObject*, which is in essence a lock. The *pickOutMessage* call in line 4 is a synchronized function that does not return until the lock is successfully applied. After accessing the shared data, the unlock function is called to

3.3 Concurrency Control for Transaction Processing

perform the unlock operation. The implementation of the Unlock function is shown in lines 6 through 9 of Code 3.23.

Code 3.23 Implementation of Locking and Unlocking in Fine-Grained Concurrency Control

```
(1)  void * lock(Transaction *transaction, AcessedObject
     *acessedObject) {
(2)    transaction->lock = accessedObject;
(3)    postMessage(mainThreadId, LOCK, (void *)
       transaction);
(4)    pickOutMessage( );
(5)  }
(6)  void unlock(Transaction *transaction, AcessedObject
     *acessedObject) {
(7)    transaction->unlock = accessedObject;
(8)    postMessage(mainThreadId, UNLOCK, (void *)
       transaction );
(9)  }
```

After the main thread receives a lock request message from the worker thread, it calls the *lockHandler* function to process it. *lockHandler* is implemented as shown in Code 3.24. The processing is to check whether there is a conflict between the requested lock and the locks held by other executing transactions. If there is a conflict, the requested lock is added to the global variable *blockedTransactionList*; otherwise, the requested lock is changed to a held lock and a response message is sent to the requester thread indicating that the lock was successful. Changing the requested lock to a held lock means adding the requested accessed object to the transaction's member variable *accessedObjectList*, as shown on line 15.

When the main thread receives an unlock request message from the worker thread, it calls the *unlockHandler* function to process it. *unlockHandler* is implemented as shown in Code 3.25. The main thread first removes the lock to be released from the transaction's member variable *accessedObjectList* to indicate that it no longer holds the lock, as shown in line 3. The blocked transactions (recorded in *blockedTransactionList*) are then checked one by one to see if the locks they applied for can be locked successfully, as shown in lines 4 through 22. For the accesses they want to perform, after a lock is released, the conflict problem may have been eliminated, so the access conflict identification has to be redone for them. If the access conflict has been removed, then the requested lock is converted to a held lock and a response message is sent to the requester thread indicating that the locking was successful. At the same time, it is removed from the *blockedTransactionList*. The processing after the conflict is removed is shown in lines 16 through 18.

Code 3.24 Implementation of the lockHandler Function

```
(1)   void lockHandler(void *data) {
(2)     Transaction* transaction = ( Transaction *)data;
(3)     bool conflicting = FALSE;
(4)     Transaction* transaction2 = activeTransactionList-
        >getFirstItem( );
(5)     while ( transaction2 ! = null) {
(6)       if (transaction2->threadId ! = transaction-
          >threadId && conflict(transaction2-
          >accessedObjectList, transaction->lock) ) {
(7)         conflicting = TRUE;
(8)         break;
(9)       }
(10)      transaction2 = activeTransactionList-
          >getNextItem( );
(11)    }
(12)    if (conflicting)
(13)      blockedTransactionList->addItem(transaction);
(14)    else {
(15)      transaction->accessedObjectList->
          addItem(transaction->lock);
(16)      postMessage(transaction->threadId, LOCK_
          RESPONSE, null);
(17)    }
(18)  }
```

The difference between fine-grained concurrency control compared to coarse-grained concurrency control is mainly in the initialization of the transaction object. After a transaction object is created, initialization work is performed, which includes initialization of the member variable *accessedObjectList* and translation of the transaction request into a sequence of operation instructions. In fine-grained concurrency control, *accessedObjectList* is initialized to null, and the sequence of operation instructions contains lock and unlock instructions. In contrast, in coarse-grained concurrency control, all locks are added to the *accessedObjectList*, but there are no more locking and unlocking instructions in the sequence of operation instructions.

Reflection 3.19: In fine-grained concurrency control, see Code 3.23 through Code 3.25, how many items of accessed objects are in the member variable *accessedObjectList* for a transaction? The global variable *blockedTransactionList* records blocked transactions. Blocked transactions are also transactions that are being processed, so they must also be in the *activeTransactionList*. At what situation are the items in *blockedTransactionList* empty?

Reflection 3.20: In fine-grained concurrency control, when the main thread accepts a new transaction request, it is delegated to an idle worker thread to process as long as there are still free worker threads. Because of the real-time nature of lock

3.3 Concurrency Control for Transaction Processing

application as well as release, there is no accessed object in its member variable *accessedObjectList* at the time of initiating the processing of a transaction. In contrast, in coarse-grained concurrency control, all the locks to be requested are added to the *accessedObjectList* when the transaction object is created. It is then concluded that the number of accessed objects in coarse-grained concurrency control must be more compared to the number of accessed objects in fine-grained concurrency control. This conclusion is not necessarily correct, why? Please give an example.

Code 3.25 Implementation of the unlockHandler Function
```
(1)   void unlockHandler(void *data) {
(2)     Transaction * transaction = ( Transaction *) data;
(3)     transaction->accessedObjectList->deleteItem(
          transaction->unlock);
(4)     Transaction * transaction2 = blockedTransactionList-
          >getfirstItem( );
(5)     while (transaction2 ! = null) {
(6)       bool conflicting = FALSE;
(7)       Transaction *transaction3 = activeTransactionList-
            >getFirstItem( );
(8)       while (transaction3 ! = null) {
(9)         if ( transaction3->threadId ! = transaction2-
              >threadId && conflict(transaction3-
              >accessedObjectList, transaction2->lock) ) {
(10)          conflicting = TRUE;
(11)          break;
(12)        }
(13)        transaction3 = activeTransactionList-
              >getNextItem( );
(14)      }
(15)      if (conflicting == FALSE) {
(16)        transaction2->accessedObjectList->
              addItem(transaction2->lock);
(17)        postMessage(transaction2->threadId, LOCK_
              RESPONSE, null);
(18)        transaction2 = blockedTransactionList->deleteIte
              mAndGetNextItem(transaction2);
(19)      }
(20)      else
(21)        transaction2 =
              blockedTransactionList->getNextItem();
(22)    }
(23)  }
```

Reflection 3.21: When processing an unlock request, the main thread removes the released lock from the transaction's *accessedObjectList*. For the lock to be requested by the transaction in the *blockedTransactionList*, when identifying whether there is an access conflict between it and the locks held by other transactions, you can first identify whether there is an access conflict between it and the lock to be released. If there is no conflict, then do not check further, it can be directly concluded that it must still have an access conflict with locks hold by other transactions, why?

The above fine-grained concurrency control scheme does not guarantee that transactions are atomic, consistent, and isolated. Here is an example. Transaction T_α: reads shared data A and data B, and then finds the result of adding the two; transaction T_β: adds 50 to shared data A, and then subtracts 50 from data B. Transaction T_α involves 3 steps: read(A), read(B), A + B. Transaction T_β involves 6 steps: read(A), A = A + 50, write(A), read(B), B=B-50, write(B). When CPU executes transactions T_α and T_β concurrently, there are 9 steps. Assume that the sequence of these 9-step operations executed by CPU is: T_α: read(A), T_β: read(A), T_β: A = A + 50, T_β: write(A), T_β: read(B), T_β: B=B-50, T_β: write(B), T_α: read(B), and T_α: A + B. Then, naturally, the result of the execution of T_α is incorrect because the value of A read by T_α is the value before *the execution of T $_\beta$*, but the value of B read is the value after the execution of T_β. There is an inconsistency between the two situations. This scenario is labeled as Scenario 1.

The sequence in which these 9 operations are executed by the CPU can also be: T_β: read(A), T_β: A = A + 50, T_β: write(A), T_α: read(A), T_α: read(B), T_β: read(B), T_β: B=B-50, T_α: A + B, T_β: write(B). The scenario is now labeled as Scenario 2. Suppose the CPU encounters a problem executing T_β: write(B). It is then necessary to roll back T_β, i.e., undo the updates made to the shared data by transaction T_β. This causes the operation T_β: write(A) to be undone as well. As a result, T_α reads an undone shared data value, which is naturally incorrect. This problem is called the READ UNCOMMITTED problem.

In order to guarantee the atomicity, consistency, and isolation of transactions, i.e., to overcome the inconsistencies described in scenario 1 above, the isolation of transactions needs to be strengthened. One way to do this is to delay the unlocking operation until all the locks required by the transaction have been successfully acquired. That is, after the first unlock request message is sent, no more lock request messages are allowed to be sent. In this way, all the data to be accessed by a transaction logically becomes a whole. This ensures that there are no access conflicts between transactions. With this constraint, in the above scenario 1, transaction T_α holds the read lock of data *A*, and will not release the read lock of data *A* before requesting the read lock on data *B*. Therefore, transaction T_β will wait until T_α releases the read lock on data *A*. At this point, T_α reads both data items *A* and *B* before T_β modifies them. As a result, the delayed release of locks solves the consistency problem, but also has the side effect of reducing the concurrency of transactions.

In order to further overcome the problems in scenario 2 above, the isolation of transactions needs to be further strengthened. Specifically, the lock release for all write operations of a transaction should be further delayed until after the transaction commits. In the above scenario 2, transaction T_α has to wait until transaction T_β has finished processing before it can obtain the read lock of data item A. Therefore, there is no chance for T_α to read the data item A until the transaction T_β has finished processing. That is, T_α does not read a data value that has been revoked.

Delaying the release of a write lock can lead to the deadlock problem. For example, two concurrently executing transactions T_1 and T_2 both perform write operations on data items A and B. T_1 writes in the order of A followed by B, and T_2 writes in the order of B followed by A. If the CPU executes them in the order of T_1: write(A), T_2: write(B), T_1: write(B), T_2: write(A), the following phenomenon occurs. T_1 will fall into a permanent wait state when executing T_1: write(B) operation, and T_2 will also fall into a permanent wait state when executing T_2: write(A) operation. The reason is that T_1 does not release the write lock on data A after the write(A) operation, so T_2 cannot succeed in locking and keeps waiting when it executes write(A). T_2 does not release the write lock on data B after the write(B) operation, so T_1 cannot succeed in locking and keeps waiting when it executes write(B). In this way, T_1 and T_2 are consumed by each other and cannot move. This phenomenon is called deadlock.

Reflection 3.22: What is a necessary condition for a deadlock?

To avoid the deadlock problem, a simple and straightforward way is to request all the locks needed by a transaction as a whole (i.e., atomically). If it succeeds, it gets all the locks it needs. If it does not succeed, none of the locks are held. This scheme also degenerates into concurrency control at the transaction level. For the sake of comparison with the following scheme, this scheme is referred to as Scheme A.

Scheme A is to avoid deadlock by strengthening the lock application. In fact, deadlock avoidance can also be achieved by strengthening the conflict identification condition. The motivation is that the transaction is in the ordered case, and the main thread, when processing the lock request of transaction T_c, makes sure that it does not prevent transactions in front of T_c from acquiring the required lock when deciding to assign a lock to T_c. This strategy ensures that the transaction at the top of the queue will not encounter any obstacles in acquiring the required lock. Therefore, deadlocks will not occur.

3.3.3 Deadlock Avoidance by Enhancing Conflict Identification Conditions

In the enhanced conflict identification scheme, each transaction requests locks one by one, rather than requesting all the locks needed by the transaction as a whole. However, the transaction is still initialized with all of its locks in its member variable *accessedObjectList*. The scheme sorts the transactions. When the main thread assigns a transaction to an idle worker thread, it also assigns a sequence number to the transaction. Sequence number acts as the transaction id and expresses the order of transactions. For each lock in a transaction, it goes through three states during the life of the transaction. Each lock is first required, then held, and finally released. For the convenience of conflict identification rule description, let T_x be a transaction that is currently being processed, and all the locks it needs are expressed by $\{T_x\}$. The current $\{T_x\}$ can be divided into three parts: the released locks $\{T_{x,1}\}$, the currently owned locks $\{T_{x,2}\}$, and the subsequent locks needed $\{T_{x,3}\}$.

When a transaction T_c requests a lock from the main thread, the main thread allocates the lock based on the principle that T_c owning the lock will not prevent the transactions in front of T_c from acquiring the lock. In other words, for any transaction T_x in the *activeTransactionList* and in front of T_c, T_c can only apply for a lock that does not conflict with any of the locks in $\{T_{x,2}\} \cup \{T_{x,3}\}$. Only if this condition is met will the lock request of T_c succeed; otherwise, T_c will have to wait. The meaning of this condition is: the requested lock does not conflict with the lock currently held by T_x (i.e., $\{T_{x,2}\}$), and it is also required that it does not conflict with the subsequent locks required by T_x (i.e., $\{T_{x,3}\}$). For the convenience of comparison, this scheme is called scheme *B*.

In a fine-grained concurrency control scheme, when a transaction releases a lock, it removes the lock from its *accessedObjectList*, indicating that the lock is no longer held. In other words, the member variable *accessedObjectList* of transaction T_x stores only $\{T_{x,2}\} \cup \{T_{x,3}\}$. Thus, there are only three changes to the fine-grained concurrency control to avoid deadlocks. The first modification is to add all the locks of a transaction to the member variable *accessedObjectList* when the transaction object is created. The second modification is that the implementation of the function *lockHandler* shown in Code 3.24. Specifically, in line 6, "transaction2->threadId != transaction->threadId" is modified to "transaction2->id < transaction->id". The third modification is the deletion of line 15 of Code 3.24, because the requested lock is already in the transaction's member variable *accessedObjectList*. The assignment and ordering of transaction ids are given in the coarse-grained concurrency control implementation, see Code 3.20.

The handling of lock release should be modified in two places accordingly. The first is line 9 of the unlockHandler function shown in Code 3.25, which should be changed from "transaction3->threadId != transaction2->threadId" to "transaction3->id < transaction2->id". Line 16 of Code 3.25 should also be deleted. There is another place to optimize. When re-checking access conflicts for blocked transactions in *blockedTransactionList*, it is not necessary to check all of them, but only some of them. The reason is that when transaction T_c releases a lock, it does not have any effect on the transactions that are in front of T_c, but only on the transactions that are behind T_c. Therefore, blocked transactions in the *blockedTransactionList* and in front of T_c do not need to be checked.

Scheme *B* reinforces the conflict identification condition. It ensures that the transaction at the top of the *activeTransactionList* is not prevented from acquiring a lock by sorting the transactions. Therefore, it is able to complete its execution without deadlocks.

In order to compare the differences in the conflict identification conditions of the above schemes, let all the locks required by transaction T_x be $\{T_x\}$. In the time sequence, $\{T_x\}$ can be divided into three parts: the released locks $\{T_{x,1}\}$, the current locks $\{T_{x,2}\}$, and the locks needed in the future $\{T_{x,3}\}$. Let the transaction T_c request a lock. The scheduling thread performs a conflict check on the request. In scheme A, the conflict condition is whether $\{T_c\}$ conflicts with $\{T_x\}$, where $x \neq c$. In scheme B, the conflict condition is whether one of the locks in $\{T_c\}$ conflicts with $\{T_{x,2}\} \cup \{T_{x,3}\}$, where T_x refers to the transaction that is in front of T_c. In the coarse-grained (transaction-level) conflict identification, it depends on whether a lock in $\{T_c\}$ conflicts with $\{T_x\}$, where $x \neq c$. In the fine-grained conflict identification, it depends on whether a lock in $\{T_c\}$ conflicts with $\{T_{x,2}\}$, where $x \neq c$, and there is only one lock in $\{T_{x,2}\}$. It can be seen that in terms of conflict identification conditions, scheme A is the same as the coarse-grained (transaction-level) concurrency control scheme.

The essence of scheme B is that the lock request of transaction T_c is allocated by the scheduling thread on the condition that T_c owns the requested lock, which does not prevent the transaction ahead of T_c from acquiring the desired lock. Thus, the transaction at the top of the queue will not be prevented from acquiring a lock, i.e., its requests will always succeed. Another benefit of scheme B is that the transaction does not need to delay releasing the shared lock until it has all the required locks. In scheme B, a transaction releases the write lock it holds only when it commits. Thus, scheme B can achieve atomicity, isolation, and consistency of transactions in a very simple way.

Reflection 3.23: A transaction's release of a shared lock does not need to be delayed until it owns all the locks it needs, why? Also, scheme B increases the concurrency of the transaction compared to scheme A. Is this conclusion correct?

Reflection 3.24: Can the scheme B be improved further? Consider the following situation. Transaction T_x is in front of transaction T_c, and T_c requests a lock noted as $lock_c$. Assume that $lock_c$ conflicts with $lock_x$ in $\{T_{x,3}\}$, where $lock_c$ and $lock_x$ are both write locks, and refer to the same shared data. Thus, T_c's request will naturally not succeed due to the conflict. Actually, this conflict is not a conflict in a special case. This special case means that for any transaction T_y, which is scheduled between T_x and T_c, there is no read lock in $\{T_{y,3}\}$ to read the data that $lock_x$ refers to. The implication of this special case is that even though T_x is subsequently going to perform a write operation on the data that $lock_x$ refers to, this write is already meaningless because there are no transactions going to read it. Therefore, it is perfectly fine for T_c to go ahead and overwrite it. This override, however, requires that T_x subsequently abandons the write operation on the data that $lock_x$ refers to.

3.4 Transaction Processing and Fault Recovery

There is an issue of reliability of data managed by servers. Data reliability is rooted in system faults such as software faults, hardware faults, power outages, and even catastrophic events such as earthquakes and terrorist attacks. Faults can have a devastating effect on the data in the server, causing data loss and data inconsistency.

Faults are inevitable and for this reason the concept of transaction management is proposed and a fault recovery strategy is adopted to achieve data reliability. Fault recovery uses a redundancy strategy: in the absence of faults, the customer's data update operations (add, modify, delete) are not only applied to database, but also recorded in the logs. The logs are first stored in memory, then written to a log disk, and further transmitted to an off-site backup server over the network. With a redundant record of update operations, the logs can be used to recover data when it is damaged by a fault in the database, thus achieving data reliability.

The next Sect. 3.4.1 introduces the concept of Transaction and Sect. 3.4.2 categorizes faults and discusses fault recovery strategies. Log-based fault recovery techniques are shown in Sect. 3.4.3. Disk faults, disaster recovery are described in Sects. 3.4.4 and 3.4.5 respectively. Section 3.4.6 introduces the detection methods for the four types of faults.

3.4.1 Transaction Processing

For a single data operation request submitted by a customer, the server may encounter faults in performing it, resulting in lost, inconsistent, or incorrect data in the server's database. For example, a bank transaction server has an account table in its database, as shown in Table 3.1, whose primary key is the field *accountNo*. The balance of the customer's account is recorded in the field *balance*. When a customer withdraws money, the balance (the value of the field *balance*) decreases. When the customer deposits money, the balance increases. Customers send business requests to the server. For example, when customer Zhou Shan wants to pay back his friend Wang Bing $1000, he sends a transfer request to the server.

Assume that the business requests sent by clients to the server are expressed in SQL. Then, the SQL expression for the above transfer request would be:

UPDATE account SET balance = balance - 1000 WHERE accountNo = '2008043101';

UPDATE account SET balance = balance + 1000 WHERE accountNo ='2008043214';

This request contains two SQL statements. From the viewpoint of business logic, when this request is executed by the server, the two SQL statements it contains should be inseparable. However, because of the unavoidability of system faults, the nonsplit ability of the client request may not be satisfied. For example, after the server executes the first update statement, a power fault occurs. At this point, the

Table 3.1 Account table in the bank transaction databaseAccount

Name	accountNo	identityNo	balance
Zhou Shan	2008043101	430104198010101010	400
Wang Bing	2008043214	430104197611111111	4,500
Zhang Shan	2008043332	430104196912121212	137,000

3.4 Transaction Processing and Fault Recovery

second update statement has not yet had time to execute. When power is restored, the server reboots. After the restoration, the data in the account table reflects Zhang Shan's outgoing $1000, but not Wang Bing's incoming $1000. This situation is clearly unacceptable.

From the above example, it is clear that a system fault can devastate the indivisibility of a client request. In order to deal with this problem in a rational way, the concept of transaction is introduced. A customer can define its business request as a transaction. Business requires that a transaction must have four properties: atomicity, consistency, isolation, and persistence. These four attributes are also a consensus agreement between the server and the client. The meaning is: after the client submits a transaction request to the server; the response is either successful or unsuccessful. Successful means that the transaction was executed successfully, and whatever faults ensued, the transaction will be fully represented in the recovered database after the fault is recovered. Unsuccessful means that the server encountered a fault in processing the transaction, and the end result is as if the client did not submit the transaction request to the server at all.

When a client gets an unsuccessful response, he/she can accept it because the request has no negative consequences. The client can wait until the fault is recovered and submit that transaction request to the server again. Define the above transfer request as a transaction, expressed in SQL as follows:

```
TRANSACTION BEGIN
  UPDATE account SET balance = balance - 1000 WHERE accountNo = '2008043101';
  UPDATE account SET balance = balance + 1000 WHERE accountNo ='2008043214';
  END;
```

Where TRANSACTION BEGIN indicates the beginning of a transaction and END indicates the end of a transaction. The SQL statement contained therein is the business request submitted by the customer.

The transaction processing scheme described above is the result of a compromise between clients and the server. From the client's side, the ideal state is that the server will not encounter faults and all submitted transactions will be executed successfully. From the server side, because of the inevitability of faults, the non-splitability of transactions is challenged and the client's expectations cannot be met. Thus, both sides take a step back. On the client's side, no longer insisting that the submitted transaction requests must be successfully executed by the server, and then the server returns a successfully executed response result. The server can return a response result that the execution was unsuccessful. On the server's side, while committing to the indivisibility of the transaction, an additional manifestation of indivisibility is added.

Clients expect indivisibility to mean that the transaction request is executed as a whole and then persists without being affected by faults. Another type of indivisibility now added is that when the server returns an unsuccessful execution response to the client, it is equivalent to the server not executing the transaction at all. That is to say, there is no situation where a transaction contains multiple operations, some of which are executed while others are not.

This compromise is acceptable to clients. Faults will have an impact on the client, but they will not shake the nonsplittability of the transaction. Of the four attributes of a transaction, atomicity refers to the nonsplittability of a transaction, i.e., a client submits a transaction request and the server either executes it as a whole or acts as if it did not execute it at all. Consistency refers to the fact that when the atomicity of a transaction is not guaranteed, it can lead to inconsistent data in the database. For the transfer request above, the sum of the balances on the accounts of both Zhou Shan and Wang Bing before the transfer should be equal to the sum of the balances on their accounts after the transfer. Suppose the server fails after the first operation and before it has time to perform the second operation. After the fault is restored, the sum of their balances before and after the transfer will not be equal, which is a sign of inconsistency.

Transaction isolation is related to the concurrent execution of transactions. When a server executes a client's transaction request in a sequential manner, it can ensure that the execution result is correct. In order to improve the processing performance, the server processes the clients' transaction requests in a concurrent manner. Concurrent processing without any constraints will bring the problem of incorrect data. Transaction isolation means that multiple transactions are processed concurrently, and the effect and result must be as if they were executed sequentially, with no differences. The concurrent execution of transactions and the incorrectness they bring are explained in detail in the previous section.

Transaction persistence refers to the fact that once the server returns a successful response to a client's transaction request, the transaction will be fully reflected in the database after fault recovery regardless of subsequent faults, and will not be affected by the fault. In other words, the server returns a successful response to the client, which will not be undone because of a subsequent fault and become an unsuccessful response.

The four attributes of a transaction, also known as ACID attribute, are the initial letters of the four English words atomicity, consistency, isolation, and durability. The ACID attribute of a transaction is a consensus agreement between the server and clients. The next question is how the server honors the four attributes of the transaction.

3.4.2 System Faults and Their Recovery Strategies

In daily life and work, people encounter some unexpected situations. For example, for the door keys of the house, they are usually carried with them. Carrying around may encounter some unexpected situations, such as lost, stolen. Once the key is stolen or lost, the consequences of not being able to enter the house can be severe. In order to deal with such situations, it is common practice to take the key and get a

3.4 Transaction Processing and Fault Recovery

duplicate made before it is lost or stolen, and then keep the backup key in the office. This way, in the event that the key you have with you is lost, there are no serious consequences, and you can go to the office and pick up the backup key to open the door. An event that occurs infrequently but has serious consequences when it does occur is called a fault. Faults are unavoidable.

Fault recovery has two meanings. The first meaning refers to the precautionary measures taken before a fault occurs. The second level of meaning refers to the measures taken to recover from a fault after the fault has occurred. In the above case, the precautionary measure before a fault occurs is to make a copy of the key and put the backup key in the office. Fault recovery measures mean: go to the office to pick up the backup key. Precautionary measures are the prerequisite and foundation of fault recovery. Without precautionary measures, there is no way to talk about fault recovery.

Fault recovery has a cost. In the above case, the cost of fault recovery was paying someone to make a copy of the key and placing the backup key in the office. The impact of the fault was reduced from the serious consequence of not being able to enter the house to an extra trip to the office to pick up the backup key. Fault recovery is a game of cost versus benefit. It is often the case that the greater the cost of preparedness, the greater the benefit of remediation in the event of fault recovery. If the fault doesn't occur, then the cost of preparedness has been wasted. Insurance is a similar thing.

Faults in servers can be divided into four categories: transaction faults, system crash faults, disk faults, and disaster faults. These four categories of faults are in order of increasing in terms of the severity of the consequences brought about by the fault, and decreasing in terms of the probability of the fault occurring. A transaction fault is a fault of a server to continue down the line in processing a transaction request, i.e., it fails to complete. For example, for the transfer request described above, there is no problem executing the first operation, but problems may be encountered when executing the second operation. The reason is that the balance on Zhou Shan's account is not enough, only $400, which is not enough to pay the outgoing amount of $1000. Thus, the transaction cannot be completed properly. Another example is: to find the average monthly income of each employee, the method of finding is the sum of the actual monthly income divided by the number of months. It is possible that an employee will be suspended without salary, so there will be a 0 divided by 0 situation, which will cause an exception and the transaction will not be able to continue to the next level of execution.

Suppose a transaction performs an update operation (add, delete, modify) on data item *A* before the fault, and then a transaction fault occurs, then data item *A* is the data affected by the fault. Recovery from a transaction fault is relatively simple: return an unsuccessful execution response to the client, then undo the update operations that have been performed, and then abandon the transaction. To be able to undo an update operation that has already been done, you need to have precautions.

System crash faults are characterized by the loss of all memory data, such as power outage faults, blue screen of death faults due to software or hardware reasons.

Disk fault is characterized by the loss of disk data. Disaster faults are characterized by the destruction of the server room and the loss of the entire machine data, such as earthquakes, fires, floods, and terrorist attacks. Transaction faults are frequent faults, system crash faults occur only occasionally, disk faults may occur only once in a few years, and disaster faults are much rarer.

3.4.3 Log-Based Fault Recovery

Data in databases are usually stored using disks. Disks are characterized by high capacity and cost-effectiveness. What is more critical is that data are stored on disk, and even if there is a power outage, the data will not be lost. But disk also has its shortcomings: large access latency and slow speed. The reason is that the data are distributed in the disk space, and the magnetic head has to be moved to align the data when reading and writing. To reduce magnetic head movement and improve data processing performance, memory is usually used to cache data on disk, as shown in Fig. 3.4. When the server processes transactions, for data to be read, it reads it from the database buffer to the private buffer. To write data, it writes the data from the private buffer to the database buffer. The movement of data from disk to the database buffer is called a prefetch and can be done in batch manner. Updated data, which is also cached in the database buffer, is not usually written to the database disk immediately. Updates are not written to disk until the magnetic head is in the way or when necessary.

For fault recovery, a redundant backup of the data is performed when the update operation is performed. The redundant backup operation is also known as logging, as shown in Fig. 3.4. In addition to acting on the database buffer, the update also forms a log, which records the value of the data before the update and after the update, and is written to the log buffer. For example, suppose the value of data item A is 4500, and transaction T_α wants to add 1000 to the value of data item A, then transaction T_α first reads the value of A (4500) from the database buffer to its private

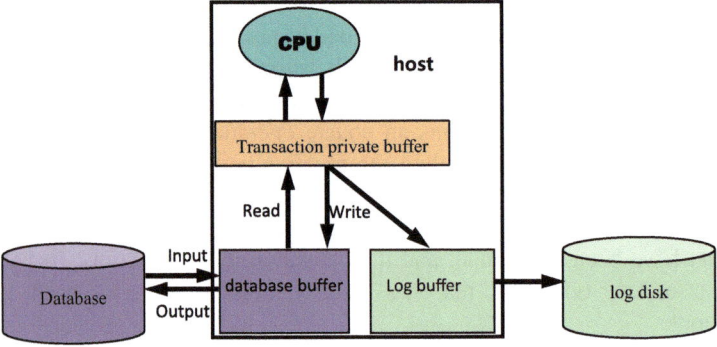

Fig. 3.4 Data processing model of the server

3.4 Transaction Processing and Fault Recovery

buffer, then adds 1000, and then writes the result (5500) to the database buffer. At the same time, a log record <α, A: 4500, 5500 > is formed and written to the log buffer for fault recovery. In this log record, α is the transaction id, A is the data item id, 4500 is the value before the update, and 5500 is the value after the update. In addition to being placed in the log buffer, log records can be output to a log disk or even to a remote backup machine.

Trivia: The word "log" comes from the ancient logbook. In ancient times, when sailing in the vast ocean, there were no clocks, no guides, only a compass, and if you were not careful, you would stray from your destination and get lost in the vastness of the ocean. Sailing all rely on the log, based on the naked eye observation of the speed, direction, wind, waves, meteorological, astronomical, time records, and then based on the entire voyage of the log records and past experience to estimate the position, decide how to maneuver the sails, so as to do not deviate from the course. It is because of the accumulation of a large number of logs, people continue to summarize the rules and characteristics, which led to the emergence of science and technology. It can be said that it was navigation that gave birth to the emergence and development of science and technology.

When a transaction fault occurs, it is only the failed transaction that cannot continue to execute. All other parts remain normal, and the data in the database buffer and log buffer remain intact. Assuming that a transaction fault occurs during the execution of transaction T_α, the recovery steps are as follows: (1) return an unsuccessful response to the requester of transaction T_α; (2) retrieve the log records of transaction T_α from the logs in the log buffer; (3) use the log records to perform a rollback operation: change the values of the data items in the database buffer back to the values before the update, which is also called the Undo operation; (4) abandon the T_α transaction. In this way, it is as if the transaction T_α was not processed at all.

Note: The log records have a sequential relationship, and their order is the order in which the transaction performs the update operation. Let transaction T_α do update operations on data items A, B, and C successively, and its log records are as follows:

```
α, <UPDATE, account, pk: '430125', balance: 4500, 5500>
α, <INSERT, account, pk: '430127', name: 'Yang Yi', balance: 0>
α, <DELETE, account, pk: '430129'>
```

In this example, the first log record reflects: data item A refers to the row with primary key '430125' in the account table, the operation is update, the update is the balance field, the old value is 4500 and the new value is 5500. The second log record reflects: data item B refers to the row with primary key '430127' in the account table, the operation is to insert a new row, with its field *name* set to 'Yang Yi' and the balance field assigned to 0. The third log record reflects: data item C refers to the row with primary key '430129' in the account table; the action is to delete the row. The rollback operation in transaction fault recovery is based on the order of log records, starting from the last line and executing the undo operation in reverse order to restore the original shape. Just like performing the undo operation when editing text in Word.

Note: In fault recovery of database, a data item refers to a row in a table, identified by the table name plus the value of the primary key.

When a system crash fault occurs, the entire memory is lost, naturally including the contents of the database buffer and the log buffer. If the logs are stored only in the log buffer, there is no way to recover from the fault. To guard against this type of fault, the log records in the log buffer are also output to the log disk, as shown in Fig. 3.4. When the transaction T_α has been successfully processed, a $< \alpha$, COMMIT> log record is to be written, and then all the logs of the transaction are to be output to the log disk. After the logs are written to the log disk, the state of the transaction at this point is called the commit state, which is the only time that the "successful execution" response can be returned to the client. Only in this way, when subsequent failures such as system crashes occur, can the persistent validity of "successfully executed" transactions be realized.

For a transaction, its logs must be output to the log disk before an "execution success" response is returned to the client. In addition, even if a transaction has not finished executing, the data items it has updated may have to be output from the database buffer to the database disk. In this case, the corresponding log records must be output to the log disk before the data items are allowed to be output to the database disk. This constraint is called the WAL constraint, which stands for Write After Log.

Data in the database buffer are output to the database disk when the following situations occur. When the amount of data in the database exceeds the size of the database buffer, some data cannot be cached. When a transaction wants to read a piece of data that is not in the buffer, it must first make room for it in the buffer. That is, to select some of the cached data and free up the buffer space it occupies. If the selected data item is an updated data item from a transaction that has not yet been committed, then its corresponding log must be output to the log disk first, and then its data must be output to the database disk before it can be freed. Thus, even if a transaction (T_α) does not complete successfully, there may be a log entry for it on the log disk, just without a $< \alpha$, COMMIT> entry.

When a system crash occurs, the recovery steps are as follows: (1) restart up the database server; (2) read the log records on the log disk; (3) start reverse scanning from the last log record, according to whether there is a $< x$, COMMIT> mark, to determine the transactions that have been successfully executed, as well as the unsuccessful transactions; (4) Starting from the first log record, scan in sequence and perform Redo operations on transactions that have been successfully executed to ensure their persistent validity. (5) Scan backwards from the last log record, and then execute Undo operation on the transactions that have not been successfully executed to ensure that they are as if they have not occurred. After the fault recovery, the system turns to normal operation and starts to accept customers' transaction requests.

For log-based fault recovery, an example is given. Assume that a bank transaction database server accepts two transactions, the first of which is a transfer

3.4 Transaction Processing and Fault Recovery

transaction and the second is a withdrawal transaction. The server assigns an identification serial number to each transaction, let the two transactions be T_0 and T_1. The operations to be performed are shown in Code 3.26. Assume that a system crash fault has occurred. Upon recovery, the log records read from the log disk are shown in Table 3.2. From the commit flag in the log, it can be seen that transaction T_0 has been successfully executed, while transaction T_1 has not been successfully executed. Therefore, first, perform Redo operation on T_0, set the value of data item A in the database to 3500, and set the value of data item B to 3000, so as to ensure the persistent validity of transaction T_0 after the fault recovery. Then, perform an Undo operation on T_1 and set the value of data item C to 700, so that T_1 can be seen as if nothing happened.

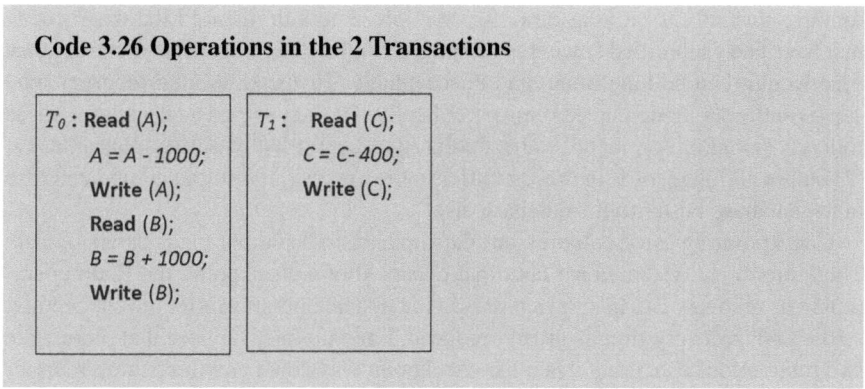

Code 3.26 Operations in the 2 Transactions

```
T₀ : Read (A);            T₁ :   Read (C);
    A = A - 1000;                C = C - 400;
    Write (A);                   Write (C);
    Read (B);
    B = B + 1000;
    Write (B);
```

In the above example of fault recovery, after restarting the system, the value of data item A on the database disk at this point is either 4500, or 3500, and both are possible. Even though the T_0 transaction has completed successfully, its updates may have been applied only to the database buffer and not output to the database disk. At the time of the crash fault, the value of data item A on the database disk was the value before the update (namely 3500). Of course, it is also possible that in the time between the update of the A value and the crash fault, the buffer occupied by data item A was vacated and its value was output to disk. If this is the case, then the value of A after the fault restarts is 4500. Doing a Redo operation when the fault recovers ensures that the transaction T_0 is persistent. The same is true for the value of C, which may be 700 or 300. Although the T_1 transaction has not yet completed

Table 3.2 Logs for fault recovery

$<T_0$ start$>$
$<T_0, A, 4500, 3500>$
$<T_0, B, 2000, 3000>$
$<T_0,$ commit$>$
$<T_1$ start$>$
$<T_1, C, 700, 300>$

successfully, the buffer occupied by data item C may have been emptied and its value exported to disk during the period between the update of the value of C and the crash fault.

From the above analysis, it can be seen that although a transaction has not been successfully executed yet, its updated data items may have to be output from the database buffer to the database disk. In this case, its log records must be output to the log disk first. This constraint is necessary. If this is not done, then in the event of a system crash, there is no way to roll back a transaction that has not successfully completed execution, and the atomicity of the transaction is not guaranteed.

From the above recovery process of a system crash fault, it can be seen that for the transactions that have been successfully executed, a Redo operation should be done to ensure that their updates are persistent and valid. If the system has been running normally for a long time, for example, 1 month, then all the transactions that have been submitted since this month have to be Redo once. The fault recovery time would then be long, long, and unacceptable. To speed up fault recovery, you can have the server do checkpoints periodically. The steps to do a checkpoint are as follows: (1) add a log record <checkpoint, the current list of active transactions>; (2) output all log records in the log buffer to the log disk; (3) output all updated data in the database buffer to the database disk.

Checkpointing causes all previous data updates to be output to the database disk. Therefore, for a system crash fault that occurs after a checkpoint, the Redo operation in its recovery can be targeted only at the update operation after the checkpoint, so the fault recovery time is greatly reduced. For example, suppose that there were two transactions executing when the checkpoint was done, and three more transactions were executed after the checkpoint was done, and then a crash fault occurred, as shown in Fig. 3.5. For fault recovery, the reverse scanning of log records can be done as long as <checkpoint, (T_3, T_4)> is reached, and for the transactions that have been successfully executed, it is enough to do Redo operation on T_3, T_4, T_5, T_6. For T_1, T_2 transactions before the checkpoint moment, there is no need to do Redo operation for them. After Redo is completed, then do Undo operation on T_7.

The moment of execution of checkpoints and the length of the interval is a configuration parameter of the server. Checkpoint intervals that are too short have an impact on performance. Too long an interval has an impact on fault recovery time. Therefore, the checkpoint interval should be chosen appropriately. Usually, the

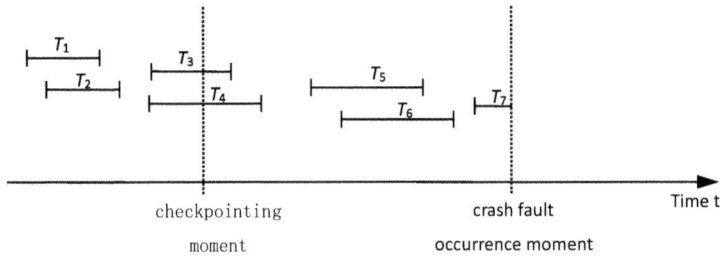

Fig. 3.5 Recovery from a system crash fault using checkpoint

3.4 Transaction Processing and Fault Recovery

checkpoints are executed at night when the load on the database server is small, and are executed once a day.

From the logging methods described above, log data and database data are associated with each other, but have completely different characteristics. Log data are semantic records of data updates, noting not only the values before the update, but also the values after the update. The database contains a large number of data items that are scattered throughout the disk space of the database disk. For every read/write of a data item, it is necessary to move the magnetic head to locate it before the read/write operation can be performed. Therefore, reading and writing data items from disk has high latency and low performance, and disk reads and writes should be minimized. The characteristics of log data are completely different. During fault-free operation, log data are constantly generated and is write-only. There are two synchronization constraints on log output to disk: (1) before a transaction commits to a client, its log must first be output to disk; (2) before updated data are written from buffer to disk, its corresponding log must first be output to disk. These two synchronization constraints result in log data being output to disk very frequently.

Log data and database data should not be stored on the same disk. If they are stored on the same disk, the performance of the database server becomes very low. Assuming that the magnetic head stops at the log data storage area to write logs, when reading and writing database data, the magnetic head needs to move to the database data storage area. When outputting logs, the magnetic head has to move back to the log data storage area. Since the frequency of outputting logs is very high, the magnetic head will keep moving back and forth between the database data storage area and the log storage area, resulting in inefficient disk access, high latency, and low performance.

During fault-free operation, log data output to disk is of write-only and non-read, as well as of high-frequency. From this characteristic, it is clear that a dedicated log disk must be configured. Only in this way can we realize that in the continuous disk storage space, let the magnetic head to write log data exclusively, to avoid moving back and forth, to obtain the high efficiency and rapidity of the log data output to the disk.

The disk storage location for log data is another configuration parameter of the database server. It is usually something that the customer is asked to set when the server is installed. The system has a default setting. When installing the server, the installer is prompted and asked to specify the installation directory for the database management system. The default setting for logs is a log subdirectory of the installation directory. So why is that default setting not another dedicated disk? The reason is that the vendor follows the principle of minimizing installation usage. If the default setting is a dedicated disk, then computers with only one disk cannot install and run its product. This is a situation that the vendor does not want.

If log data and database data are stored on the same disk, it can seriously affect system performance. However, this impact will not be obvious in the initial period when the database is up and running. The reason for this is that the amount of data at the beginning of the operation is not large, and the database buffer is able to hold all the data in the database. In this case, the data required for query operations are available in the database buffer, and the new data brought by update operations can be accommodated in the database buffer. As a result, there are essentially no disk operations occurring for the database, and there is only one thing to do, i.e., write logs. In this case and in this situation, there will be no need to read and write database data at once and then switch to writing logs at another time. That is, the magnetic head doesn't constantly switch back and forth between these two things.

Over time, the amount of data in the database increases. When the database buffer does not hold the entire database, if the required data are not in the buffer, it is necessary to write the data back to disk in order to free up a storage space and then read the required data. Thus, the frequency of disk accesses to the database data keeps increasing. This causes the magnetic head to move back and forth between the log storage area and the database storage area so frequently that performance begins to degrade. The larger the amount of data in the database, the more pronounced the performance degradation becomes.

There is another problem with storing log data and database data on the same disk. That is, it can only accommodate system crash faults, not disk faults. Once a disk fault occurs, log data and database data are lost at the same time, and fault recovery is impossible to talk about.

Reflection 3.25: For a transaction, delete its logs from memory once it has been output from memory to disk. Is this OK to do? Please justify. The life cycle of logs in memory does not end until after the corresponding transaction has been successfully committed or aborted, why?

3.4.4 Recovery from Disk Fault

Disk faults are classified into database disk faults and log disk faults. Database disk fault results in the loss of all data stored on it. Once a database server detects a database disk fault, it aborts the execution of the currently executing transactions, gives the corresponding clients a response result of unsuccessful execution, and then recovers from the fault. Theoretically, a database disk fault can be recovered from the logs made during the period from the moment of database creation to the moment of fault. However, the recovery time is too long and unacceptable. The way to speed up database disk fault recovery is to make a database backup (Dump).

The steps of a database backup are as follows: (1) pause the acceptance of client requests and finish processing the currently executing transactions; (2) output all logs in the log buffer to the log disk; (3) output all updated data in the database buffer to the database disk; (4) make a copy of the database disk and archive it for backup purposes; (5) write a <dump> log entry to the log disk, marking the disk backup; (6) resume acceptance of client requests and turn to normal operation; .

The moment of execution of database backups and the length of the interval is also a configuration parameter of the database server. A backup interval that is too long has a significant impact on the fault recovery time. Therefore, the choice of database backup time as well as the interval length should be set appropriately.

3.4 Transaction Processing and Fault Recovery

Database backups, which usually result in system unavailability or significant performance degradation, are generally set to be performed at 1:00 p.m. on Sundays, when the load on the database server is minimal. There are also many database products that support hot backups. Hot backups are covered in the recovering from disaster faults section.

The steps to recover from a database disk fault are as follows: (1) for the currently executing transactions, abort their execution and return an unsuccessful execution response result to the corresponding clients; (2) shut down the server system; (3) take out the most recent database backup disk and replace the failed database disk; (4) reboot the server system, and then perform a reverse scan of the logs starting from the last entry up to the <dump >record; (5) Starting from this record, scan forward and perform Redo operations on successfully completed transactions; (6) switch to normal operation.

For recovery from a database disk fault, data prior to the most recent backup moment is on the backup disk. Updates made during the period from the backup moment to the fault moment are recorded in the logs after <dump>. Therefore, any transaction that successfully completes during this time, i.e., a transaction marked with <x, COMMIT> in the logs, should be Redo to bring the database back to its prefault state.

Reflection 3.26: In database disk fault recovery, an Undo operation is not required for transactions that do not have an <x, COMMIT> tag in the logs, why?

When the log disk fails, the recovery steps are as follows: (1) suspend accepting client requests; (2) abandon the execution of currently active transactions and return unsuccessful response results to the corresponding clients; (3) output all updated data in the database buffer to the database disk; (4) do a database backup; (5) take a new log disk to replace the failed log disk; (6) write a <dump> log entry; (7) switch to normal operation.

The purpose of logs is for fault recovery, and they are only useful when data in the database is lost due to a fault. Thus, in the event that only the log disk fails and everything else is normal, the recovery method is to ensure the database data at the current moment is not subsequently lost due to a fault. This makes the logs that have been done no longer needed. Making a database backup makes the logs that have been made no longer useful.

If both the database disk and the log disk fail at the same time, then there is no way to recover. Therefore, keeping logs in the log buffer as well as on the log disk does not guarantee absolute system reliability, but only improves it. To what extent has reliability been improved? This can be quantified from theoretical calculations. Assuming that the probability of a disk fault is p, the probability of two disks failing at the same time is p^2. The normal operating time of a disk is about 5 years, i.e., the probability of a fault p is about 0.001. *The probability of p^2 is about* 10^{-6}, which translates back to time, which is about 200 years. That is, reliability has increased from 5 to 200 years. For a single disk, you see a fault in about 5 years on average; for two disks failing at the same time, you see one in about 200 years on average. So that is a significant improvement in reliability. The fault of two disks at the same time is a small probability event. Usually, there appear the news that a levee has been strengthened and expanded, and its flood resistance has been increased from one in 20 years to one in 100 years. Two events say the same truth.

Reflection 3.27: When you make a database backup, you have to suspend the external service. During the backup period, no operation requests from clients are accepted. Is it possible to do a database backup while the service is being provided to the public?

Reflection 3.28: Database backups take a certain amount of time to complete due to the large amount of data. Clients' business requests are usually not entertained during the backup period. Is it possible to realize incremental backup of the database to shorten the database backup time? Incremental backup means that only those disk blocks where update operations have occurred since the last backup need to be backed up. Those disk blocks for which no update operation has occurred are subject to the last backup and there is no need to rewrite them again. Incremental backups speed up backup and reduce the length of time the database is unavailable. Can you design a database disk incremental backup implementation?

Tip: The database server accesses the disk in blocks; a block size is usually 64 KB. Disk storage space consists of blocks; each block is identified by a serial number. In other words, when the server reads the disk data, given the block id, and the memory start address, it reads the specified disk block into the specified memory. The same is true when writing disk, i.e., writing data from the specified memory to the specified disk block.

3.4.5 Recovery from Disaster Fault

Disaster faults, such as floods, fires, earthquakes, and terrorist attacks, although rare, have the most serious consequences when they do occur. It leaves the entire server room devastated, and both the database disk and the log disk are unavailable. For disaster recovery, it is not enough for logs to be stored in the log buffer and local log disks, but they must be exported to a remote backup machine. The remote backup is shown in Fig. 3.6, where the logs are sent over the network to the remote backup machine in addition to being output to the log disk.

The remote backup machine accepts logs sent from the host, outputs them to a log disk, and uses them to update its own database to synchronize it with the host database. In the event of a disaster fault, the backup machine takes over from the host and provides service to its clients. This type of backup is called a hot backup. The remote host can also just keep logs and not do database updates in real time; this backup is called a cold backup. The fault recovery time for a hot backup is very short, while the fault recovery time for a cold backup is much longer. However, cold backups are much cheaper to run.

The logs of a transaction can only be guaranteed to be persistently valid if they reach the remote backup machine for subsequent disaster fault recovery. Therefore, for a transaction, only after receiving sign-off responses from both the log disk and the remote backup machine, can the client be given a response result that the

3.4 Transaction Processing and Fault Recovery

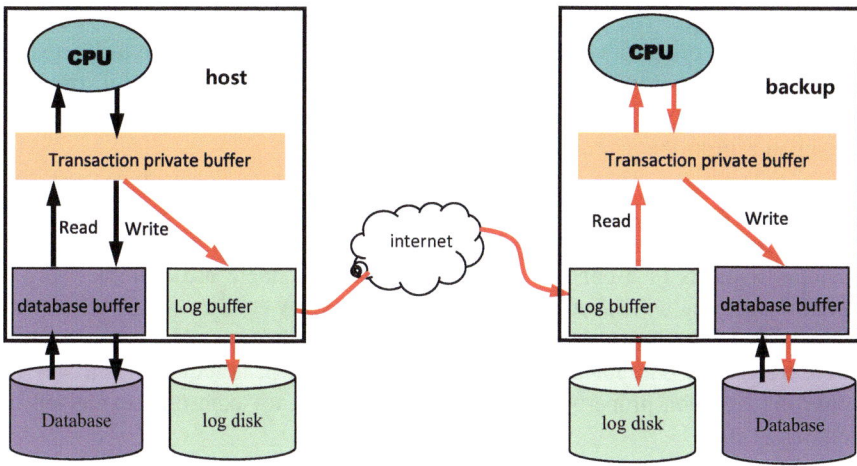

Fig. 3.6 Remote backup

execution has been completed successfully. This is the two-safe commit protocol. This practice results in a significant performance degradation of the database server. The reason is that the latency of network transfers over long distances is much greater than the latency of local disk transfers. This means that the point in time at which a response is given to the client is significantly delayed, and the processing time for a transaction is significantly extended.

For performance reasons, the one-safe commit protocol can also be used. In this protocol, it only waits for a sign-off response from the log disk before giving the client the response result that the execution was completed successfully, and does not wait for a sign-off response from the remote backup machine. This protocol weakens the reliability. In the event of a catastrophic fault, it may happen that the remote backup machine does not receive the logs, and the recovery is inconsistent: the client is told that the transaction was successfully completed, but this is not reflected in the data after the fault is recovered. Nevertheless, the one-safe protocol has its viability. The reason is that disaster faults are uncommon, and it is rare that a remote backup machine happens to receive no logs. Furthermore, even if logs of one or two transactions are lost, the impact is much smaller compared to the impact of the disaster itself, and the customer will understand and can negotiate a solution.

3.4.6 Implementation of Fault Detection and Recovery

A client uses an application program to access a database server. The process of accessing is to first log in to the database server with the account information, establish a connection, then send a business request to the database server and wait for the response result. The client's business request is expressed in the form of a SQL statement, and a request contains one or more SQL statements. When a client submits a transaction request, the database server commits the transaction if it is processed successfully, otherwise it rolls back the transaction. Regardless of success, the server returns the processing results to the client.

A single request from a client is usually a transaction. For each request, the server usually schedules a worker thread to process it. A database server has many clients. All clients have to access the database, so the server processes the clients' business requests in a concurrent manner. Therefore, there are multiple worker threads executing concurrently in the server process. A conflict occurs when two concurrently executing worker threads want to access the same data item. In order to ensure correct data manipulation, concurrency control is required as a way to honor the isolation property of transactions. Concurrency control is explained in detail in Sect. 3.3.

For transaction faults, detection and recovery can be done based on an exception handling mechanism. The framework for transaction processing in the worker thread is shown in Code 3.27, where the processing of the transaction request from the client is placed in the try statement block. When a transaction fault occurs, it is expressed by throwing an exception. After catching the exception in the catch statement, the log is used to undo the executed operation, thus honoring the atomicity of the transaction.

For detection of system crash faults, a server crash flag parameter can be set and written to disk. Every time the server is started, the main thread reads this parameter from disk and checks its value. If its value is CRASH, it indicates that a system crash fault has occurred before and recovery from the system crash fault needs to be performed. If its value is NORMAL, no system crash has occurred before. In this case, the default is CRASH. When performing a normal shutdown of the server, after the server writes updates from the database buffer to disk, change the value of this parameter to NORMAL and write to disk. This treatment allows the server to know at startup whether a system crash has occurred beforehand.

For disk fault, it is sensed when the server accesses the disk. As soon as the server senses that a disk fault has occurred, it starts the disk fault recovery process and automatically recovers. For disaster faults, the remote backup machine detects and senses them, and notifies the gateway to switch routes and forward clients' requests to the backup machine.

Reflection 3.29: When a client goes to a bank to apply for an account, he or she is required to provide a phone number and email. What purpose can a phone number and email serve? Suppose a client withdraws money from an ATM machine and may not see the result of the response to his or her service request because of a sudden power outage at the ATM. What can the bank server do to help the client in this situation so that he/she is aware of the response result?

Reflection 3.30: What are some of the causes of transaction faults?

Code 3.27 Transaction fault Detection and Recovery Based on Exception Handling

```
(1)  try {
(2)     log->startTransaction(transaction->id ); //generate a
            <t_id, start> log entry
(3)     handleTransactionRequest( transaction );
(4)  log->commit( transaction->id ); //generate a <t_id,
     commit> log entry and wait until all its logs have been
     written to the log disk.
(5)  } catch exception(e)   { // Perform a rollback:
(6)     LogRow *curLogRow = log->lastRow(transaction->id);
(7)     while (curLogRow != null)  {
(8)         undo(curLogRow);
(9)         curLogRow = log->prevRow(transaction->id);
(10)    }
(11)    log->abort( transaction->id); //generate a <t_id,
            abort> log entry
(12)    response->status =failure;
(13)    response->detail = e.description;
(14)    return response;
(15) }
(16) response->status = success;
(17) response->detail = 'OK';
(18) return response;
```

3.4.7 Summary of Transaction Processing and Fault Recovery

Data in a database server is stored on disk. Due to the huge amount of data, the data in the database is scattered throughout the disk space and is both read and written. If clients need to output data updates to the disk every time, the magnetic head will move all over the entire disk space, resulting in poor efficiency, high latency, and low performance. Log data have completely different characteristics compared to data in a database. When the system is running without faults, the log data output to the disk has a write-only and non-read nature, as well as a high frequency. From this characteristic, it can be seen that the database data and log data cannot be stored on the same disk, and a dedicated log disk must be configured. Only in this way can the efficiency and speed of transferring log data to disk be achieved.

Faults faced by databases can be classified into four categories: transaction faults, system crash faults, disk faults, and disaster faults. From the point of view of the severity of the consequences, the four types of faults are enhanced in order. In terms of probability of occurrence, they become smaller in that order. A transaction fault leads to unsuccessful completion of transaction execution, a system crash fault leads to total loss of data in memory, a disk fault leads to total loss of data on disk, and a disaster fault leads to loss of data on the entire machine. Fault recovery uses a redundancy strategy. Logging enables fault recovery, i.e., fault tolerance. Logs are stored in memory and can tolerate transaction faults. Logs are stored in disk, which can tolerate system crash faults. If the log data are stored on separate disks from the database data, then a single disk fault is tolerated. Logs stored on a remote backup machine can tolerate disaster faults. In terms of performance, storing logs in memory has the lowest overhead, storing to disk has the second highest overhead, and storing to a remote backup machine has the highest overhead.

Doing checkpoints speeds up recovery from system crash faults, and doing database backups speeds up recovery from database disk faults. The log storage location, checkpoint execution time and interval length, and database backup execution time and interval length are all configuration parameters for the database server.

3.5 Distributed Transaction Processing

3.5.1 *Distributed Servers*

Distributed server [6] means: combining several servers of the same kind in the form of confederation into one server, forming an external service window to provide services to clients. For example, each university has its own academic affairs management database server, and now we want to set up a university academic affairs management database server whose data covers all universities in the country. Thus, this university academic affairs management database server is a distributed server. It combines the academic affairs management database servers of all universities in the country to form one database server. Assuming that each university's academic affairs management database is a relational database, then in the view of a client, the university academic affairs management database is also a relational database. There is no change in the data model in it, there is still only one student table which contains student data of all universities.

The following is an example of a distributed database server to illustrate the compositional characteristics of a distributed server. The composition of a distributed database server is shown in Fig. 3.7. It consists of a distributed database management system (abbreviated as DDBMS), and multiple DBMS servers, which are connected to each other through a network. DDBMS is a server program whose external service interface is identical to that of a DBMS. Thus, when a client accesses a DDBMS server, it does not know whether it is a DDBMS or a DBMS. Internally, a DDBMS is an intermediary that does not manage business data itself. The business data are managed by the DBMS servers under it. In a distributed database server, the DBMS servers under its umbrella are called entity database servers, also called member database servers.

3.5 Distributed Transaction Processing

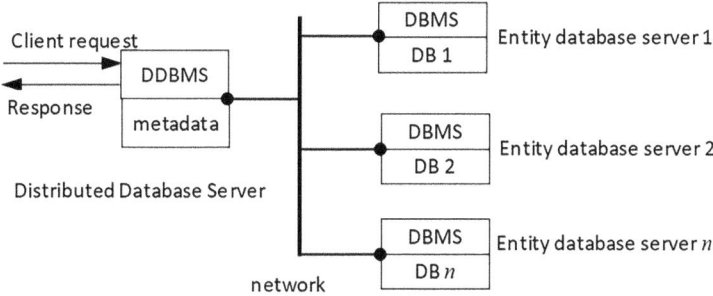

Fig. 3.7 Distributed server

When a DDBMS accepts a business request (i.e., SQL request) from a client, it first parses the request, checks in which entity database servers the data it involves is distributed, and then breaks the request into multiple subrequests, which are, respectively, handed over to the corresponding member database servers for processing. For a member database server, the DDBMS is one of its clients. When the DDBMS dispatches a subrequest to a member database server, it is actually sending it a business request (i.e., an SQL request). When the DDBMS receives all the response results from the corresponding member servers, it then summarizes them and returns the summarized results to the client as the response result.

The establishment of distributed database servers can bring three benefits as follows. First, the concept of physical storage of data is shielded for clients, realizing the simplicity of data operation. Clients can just focus on their business in accordance with the relational model, without caring about which server the data come from and where it should be stored. The second benefit is to improve processing performance. When the amount of data in a database server increases and cannot meet the performance requirements, it can be split into multiple database servers, through parallel processing of multiple computers to increase throughput and shorten response time. The third benefit is that it can improve the reliability and availability of the system. This is achieved by replication, i.e., replicating a database server into multiple database servers to form multiple replicas. When a replica server is unavailable due to maintenance, upgrade, or fault, other replica servers that are running normally can take over the work and maintain uninterrupted service.

Another way of saying the above three benefits is called network transparency, segmentation transparency, and replication transparency. This is all for the clients. With a DDBMS, clients do not have to care or know about the physical storage of data. Clients only need to focus on business processing in accordance with the relational model, use SQL to express the operation of semantic data. Which server should the data be stored on? It is entirely the responsibility of DDBMS. Network transparency refers to the physical storage structure of data that clients do not need to care about or be aware of. Segmentation transparency means that the data table seen by clients is actually cut into multiple data sub-tables, which are scattered and stored on different entity database servers.

There are two forms of segmentation: horizontal and vertical. Horizontal segmentation is to cut a data table horizontally into several subtables, with each subtable storing only part of the rows. All subtables do the merge operation, you get the full table. For example, the student table in the above university academic management database is a combination of student subtables from each university. Vertical segmentation is to vertically slice a data table into multiple subtables, each of which holds only a portion of the columns. All the subtables do a natural join operation to get the full table. For example, the student's tuition payment data are stored in the financial database server, while the academic performance data are stored in the academic administration database server. To get the complete information of students, we need to use the student table in the financial database server to do a natural join operation with the student table in the academic administration database server.

Replication transparency means that replication is not visible to clients. In order to increase throughput and improve reliability and availability, an entity database is often replicated to form multiple replicas. When an update is made to a piece of data, it is made to all replicas. When reading a piece of data, it is read from only one replica. With DDBMS, clients do not have to care about replication. In the client's view, there is only one copy of the data in the DDBMS, which can be manipulated at any time, is always available, and is responsive.

Network transparency, segmentation transparency, and replication transparency to clients is what DDBMS is trying to do and where it functions. In a DDBMS, business data are not stored, but only meta data. Meta data are the data needed to achieve network transparency, segmentation transparency, and replication transparency. For example, the IP address of each entity database server, port number, database name, and the account (client name and password) to log in to these entity database servers are part of the meta data. This meta data are indispensable for the DDBMS to establish network connections with its member database servers.

In addition, what data tables are in each member database server and the extent of the data covered by the tables are also metadata. These metadata are essential for the DDBMS to decompose a client request into multiple subrequests, and also provide support for summarizing the response results of member database servers. For example, if it is horizontally segmented, the DDBMS has to do a concatenation operation when doing the summarization; if it is vertically segmented, it has to do a natural join operation. When there is replication, metadata records how many copies of the data are available and in which member database servers they are stored. This metadata provide support for replication transparency in order to parse client requests and generate multiple subrequests that are dispatched to the appropriate member database servers for processing.

A distinctive feature of a distributed server is that it is a confederated system. The meaning of confederation is that each individual has independent autonomy, and the individual has a docking combination, can work together. Individual independent autonomy refers to the internal realization of the functionality. That is to say, how to do a specific thing, you can make your own decision, in order to fully mobilize the individual initiative. If it is done well internally, it will be competitive in the same category. Dockable combinability refers to the interaction with the outside. That is

3.5 Distributed Transaction Processing

to say, access to external services should follow the standard, their own services open to clients should also follow the standard. As far as access to database servers is concerned, standards have been established: the SQL language to express data operations, and the ODBC/JDBC programming interface to express the access process. Existing DBMSs and DDBMSs follow this standard.

As you can see, when building a distributed database server, there will not be any additional special requirements for member database servers. Any database server can naturally become a member of a distributed database server. Thus, building a distributed database server is as simple as installing a DDBMS server software and then providing network-transparent, segmentation-transparent, and replication-transparent configuration information, i.e., metadata. A DDBMS is also a DBMS in the eyes of external clients, and a DDBMS can be a member of another DDBMS. Thus, the confederated system is very scalable.

Distributed servers exert a group effect and have completely different qualities compared to individual physical servers. In the eyes of clients, distributed servers have large storage space, extreme computing power, and are never down, always available, and responsive. These qualities are exactly what clients expect from a system. These qualities are not possible for a single physical server.

The group effect has a wide range of uses. For example, bus companies use the group effect to provide uninterrupted bus service. For a bus driver of a bus company, he may not be able to go to work due to illness, or accident. For a bus of a bus company, it may also not be able to be put into operation normally due to breakdown, or accident. Thus, for an individual, it cannot guarantee uninterrupted service. But for a company, it is possible to realize that the service is never interrupted. When a bus driver cannot go to work normally, the company will arrange another employee who is on vacation to take his place, and when a bus cannot be put into service normally, the company will dispatch another spare bus to take its place.

This collaborability is only available to groups, and the larger the group, the more fault-tolerant it is. For example, suppose there are 10 bus routes that provide 24-h-a-day service. Also, an employee works 8 h a day, 5 days a week. For a one-week period, the company has to hire 40 bus drivers and schedule 30 to work each day and another 10 on vacation. It would not be a problem at all to find one of the 10 vacationing employees to fill in for the breakdown driver. Assuming that there is only 1 route, then it would only be necessary to hire 4 car drivers, scheduling 3 to work each day and 1 on vacation. When one driver breaks down, the one on vacation may not be available to cover the shift. This does not allow for uninterrupted service.

For distributed servers, to be able to play the group effect, its premise is that the DDBMS knows what happen in its members and can guide its members to do what it expects. The DDBMS should promptly monitor the operational status of each member server. Once a member server is found to be unable to perform its duties due to a fault, it is necessary to hand over its share of the work to other entity database servers to undertake, in order to realize the external provision of uninterrupted service. After the fault is eliminated, fault recovery should also be carried out. The DDBMS typically uses the heartbeat method to monitor the operational status of each member server. That is, the DDBMS inquires with member servers at regular intervals to see if they are functioning properly. This method is also often called watchdog method. Once a fault is detected, the DDBMS has to make adjustments to the metadata to isolate the failed member server for fault tolerance. After the faulty member server recovers, it notifies the DDBMS. Once the DDBMS receives a recovery notification, it initiates fault recovery, allowing the faulty member server to restore its data to a state consistent with the system.

3.5.2 Transaction Processing and Fault Recovery in a Distributed Server

In a distributed database server, a client submits a transaction request to the DDBMS for execution, which parses the client's submitted transaction and decomposes it into multiple subtransactions based on metadata, and then submits them to the corresponding member servers for processing. The member servers return the results of the subtransactions to the DDBMS. When each subtransaction has been successfully processed, the DDBMS notifies each subtransaction bearer to commit the subtransaction for which it is responsible. Once the DDBMS receives feedback from all bearers on successful commits, it returns the summarized results to the client, informing it that the transaction was successfully committed. The above process consists of two phases: the first phase is the execution phase and the second phase is the commit phase. If the execution of a subtransaction is unsuccessful in the first phase, the DDBMS receives this response and immediately notifies each subtransaction bearer to abort the subtransaction. At the same time, the client is also notified that the transaction commit was unsuccessful.

Transaction commit in distributed database servers is called two-phase transaction commit protocol. It is a solution to implement the ACID properties of transactions in distributed servers. Before discussing fault recovery in distributed servers, the automatic and nonautomatic commit modes of database servers are introduced. After a client establishes a connection with a database server, he or she can call the *setAutoCommit* function provided by the connection interface to set the commit mode to nonautocommit mode. In nonautocommit mode, when a client submits a transaction request, the database server returns the execution result, but does not commit the transaction. When the client receives a successful result, he or she has to send another commit request to the database server for committing the transaction. Of course, the client can also send a rollback request to the database server to tell the database server to abort the transaction.

The default mode of a DBMS is autocommit mode. In autocommit mode, when a client submits a transaction request, the database server processes the request and returns the execution result to the client. If it is successfully processed, then the transaction is committed; otherwise, the transaction is aborted. The client does not need to send a commit request or a rollback request to the database server.

3.5 Distributed Transaction Processing

In nonautocommit mode, when the DBMS is executing a transaction T_i, the state of the transaction is called active. When the DBMS has successfully completed executing a transaction, another <T_i, READY> record is added to the log to identify that the transaction has been successfully executed. The log buffer is flushed to the log disk immediately afterward. The response can be sent to the requester only after flushing. The state of the transaction at this point is referred to as semicommitted. For an active transaction T_i, when a transaction fault is encountered, the DBMS adds a < T_i, ABORT> record to the log, identifying the transaction as being in the aborted state. For a transaction in a semicommitted state, when the DBMS receives a commit request from the client, it will add another <T_i, COMMIT> record to the log, identifying the transaction is committed. The state of the transaction at this time is called the commit state. If the DBMS receives a rollback request from the client, then a < T_i, ABORT> record is added to the log, identifying the transaction as aborted, and a rollback is performed to undo the changes made to the database by the transaction T_i.

In a distributed database server, the DDBMS establishes connections to member servers that are set to nonautocommit mode. When a subtransaction is successfully processed, it is in a semicommitted state. When the DDBMS learns that all subtransactions are in a semicommitted state, it sends a commit request to all subtransaction bearers to notify them to commit. When the DDBMS learns that the execution of a subtransaction was unsuccessful, it sends a rollback request to all subtransaction bearers to notify them to abort.

Each member server, at any time, may fail. At the moment of fault, for a transaction, it may be active, aborted, semicommitted, or committed. Of the four types of faults, only transaction faults can be detected and handled immediately. Transaction faults can occur only when a transaction is active. Assuming that a subtransaction T_i fails during processing, its bearer sends an unsuccessful response to the DDBMS. Once he DDBMS receives a unsuccessful response, it sends a rollback request to all subtransaction bearers to notify them to abort the execution of the subtransaction they bear. Once a member server receives a rollback request, it aborts the execution of the subtransaction, adds a < T_i, Abort> record to the log, and then uses the log of T_i to perform a rollback operation to cancel the changes that have been made to the database by T_i. The DDBMS also sends a response to the client informing that the execution of the transaction was unsuccessful. Thus, the transaction fault is handled. After the client receives the response result, according to the reason of unsuccessful execution, he or she either modifies the content of the transaction request and then make a transaction request again, or just gives up.

When a system crash fault occurs in a member server, the DDBMS senses that one of its member servers has failed due to a wait timeout or through heartbeat detection. At this time, for the DDBMS, it may be in the following two possible states. The first state is that the DDBMS has issued a subtransaction T_i to the failed member server but has not yet received the result of its execution. In this case, the transaction is in phase 1. The DDBMS can then conservatively assume that the failed member server's execution was unsuccessful, send a rollback request to all subtransaction bearers, abort the transaction, and return an unsuccessful result to the client. The transaction is thus processed. The reason there is no problem with this processing is that the transaction has not yet entered the commit phase and the DDBMS has the right to make a decision. The second state is that the DDBMS has issued a subtransaction T_i to the failed member server and has received its execution result. In this case, the DDBMS still follows the two-phase commit protocol. DDBMS outputs the instructions to be sent to the failed member server to its own fault recovery log for later recovery of the failed member server.

In distributed servers, if replication is not configured for member servers, when a member server experiences a system crash, its service is interrupted. Subsequently, if a client's request is not related to the failed member server, the DDBMS can process it as usual. Otherwise, the DDBMS sends the client a direct response result that cannot be executed and gives the reason as server fault. The client has to wait until the fault is restored before requesting again.

The faulty server is restarted up and plugged into the system after the fault has been cleared. For example, if it was a power outage, the fault is lifted when the power comes back on, if it was a device fault, the fault is lifted when the device is replaced, or if it was a software fault, the fault is lifted when it is upgraded. The DDBMS re-establishes a connection to the restored member server and checks the fault recovery logs to see if there are any commit or rollback requests associated with it. If there are, they are extracted and sent to the failed member server for processing to bring it back to a state consistent with the system.

After restarting the DBMS, the recovered member server will first check the logs in its own log disk and use its logs for fault recovery, the process of which is explained in Sect. 3.4. It is just that in nonautocommit mode, there will be one more $<T_i$, READY$>$ record in the log of transaction T_i. If it is found that there is a $< T_i$, READY$>$ record in the log of a transaction T_i, but there is neither a $< T_i$, COMMIT$>$ record nor a $< T_i$, ABORT$>$ record thereafter, then it is necessary to wait for a recovery command from the DDBMS, which will be added to the log. You can then decide whether to perform a REDO or an UNDO on it.

In a distributed server, if a member server is configured with replication, its service will not be interrupted after it fails in a system crash. Let the member server D_i have two replicas $D_{i,1}$ and $D_{i,2}$. When the DDBMS wants to send a subtransaction T_i to the member server D_i for execution, it should send T_i to both $D_{i,1}$ and $D_{i,2}$ for both to execute. When sending T_i to $D_{i,1}$, check its status first. If $D_{i,1}$ is in normal state, send T_i to $D_{i,1}$ for execution. If $D_{i,1}$ is faulty, DDBMS stores $<D_{i,1}, T_i>$ records in the fault recovery log for future use. When the fault of $D_{i,1}$ is lifted and the system is reconnected, the DDBMS extracts the subtransactions from the fault recovery log that were to be sent to $D_{i,1}$ for execution, and sends them to $D_{i,1}$ for execution in order to bring $D_{i,1}$ back to a state consistent with the system. During the fault of $D_{i,1}$, its service was not interrupted because $D_{i,2}$ was providing the service. The same is true for $D_{i,2}$.

Note: During the above process, the $<D_{i,1}, T_i>$ records stored in the fault recovery log may also be deleted by the DDBMS later. The reason is that the subtransaction T_i may be aborted by DDBMS. If T_i is aborted, then $<D_{i,1}, T_i>$ records should be deleted from the fault recovery log.

Reflection 3.31: For applications, when connecting to a database server, it should be strictly managed and usually not allowed to be set to nonautomatic commit mode, why? Please analyze the reasons from security point of view, and processing performance point of view. Nonautomatic commit mode is usually used only when the DDBMS establishes a connection to the DBMS, why?

A DDBMS server may also meet faults. When it fails, the service becomes unavailable. However, DDBMS servers have completely different qualities than member servers and are much less likely to fail. First of all, DDBMS servers have relatively simple things to deal with and therefore have a small amount of program code. Simple things are highly reliable, so the probability of a DDBMS server fault is low. In addition, DDBMS servers maintain less state data, and fault recovery is relatively easy and the recovery time is short. To increase the availability of the DDBMS server, replicas can also be set up for it.

Who is responsible for fault sensing and fault recovery of the DDBMS server? Clients send requests to the DDBMS server and get responses. Therefore, clients can sense the fault of the DDBMS server, but cannot do anything to recover from the fault. The DDBMS server is started up and operated by the cluster/cloud manager of the service provider. Therefore, it is the cluster/cloud manager that is responsible for DDBMS server fault sensing and fault recovery. Fault sensing can be done by heartbeat detection. The cluster/cloud manager is the top manager and must be available at all times. The implementation is still replication. The difference is that there is no more manager on top of the cluster/cloud manager, so the replicas of the cluster/cloud manager have to sense faults among themselves.

3.6 Summary of the Chapter

Distributed computing has evolved from stand-alone computing and has elevated resource sharing to new heights. With the support of network communication, the concept of the boundary of resource sharing has been broken and borderless sharing has been realized. The evolution of computing is a dialectical unity of change and invariance. The invariance is manifested in the sharing mode, and the change is manifested in the sharing boundary being expanded and extended, as well as the improvement of service quality. The sharing model remains unchanged, indicating that the threshold for realizing sharing has not increased. As a service provider, the concern is still the definition of service interfaces and the realization of service functions. As a service client, the concern remains the invocation of service functions. Distributed computing enables the service to be uninterrupted and to respond to client requests in a timely manner.

The access conflict problem is always the most fundamental problem in resource sharing. Resources in a server are shared by multiple clients and must be managed effectively to ensure orderly sharing. Among them, data sharing is the most representative and common way of sharing. In distributed computing, data consistency is the most critical issue. In a server, concurrency control is used to solve the access conflict problem, and transaction processing and fault recovery are used to ensure data consistency and persistence. Therefore, in distributed computing, data consistency, concurrency control, transaction processing, and fault recovery are the most core concepts.

Interaction across a computer boundary is an interaction between two processes running on different computers, where one acts as a client and the other as a server. Function calls across computer boundaries are also known as remote procedure calls. In the implementation of remote procedure call, the concept of proxy is introduced at the client side and the concept of stub is introduced at the server side. The client calls the proxy function and the service function is called by the stub. This structured processing has the advantage of making function calls across computer boundaries transparent to the programmer. Since the functions of proxies and stubs are clear and fixed, their source code can be automatically generated by development tools based on the function definitions.

Two processes running on different computers interact over a network connection. A network connection is a logical communication channel that connects a client to a server. For data to be transmitted, adding network connection information to it is the same as labeling it with the sender's address and the receiver's address. There are 4 types of transmission devices in network communication: routers, gateways, switches, and bridges. These four types of transmission devices are actually computers, but they run different applications, such as routing programs, gateway programs, switching programs, and bridge programs. If a LAN is configured with a DHCP server, a DNS server, and a gateway server, then the computers on the LAN can connect to the network without having to be manually configured, and can be plug-and-play. This feature is critical for data centers or cloud service providers.

A server has a one-to-many relationship with its clients, so the load on servers is usually heavy. To improve processing performance and efficiency, servers adopt concurrent execution strategies to handle multiple requests simultaneously. This gives rise to the access conflict problem. Concurrency control is to ensure that the effect of concurrent execution is exactly the same as that of executing in a sequential manner, so as to ensure the correctness and consistency of the data. For this purpose, the concept of transaction processing has been introduced. Transactions are atomic, consistent, isolated, and persistent. Concurrency control only ensures the isolation of transactions. It is the transaction processing and fault recovery that ensures the atomicity, consistency and persistence of transactions. There are four types of faults: transaction faults, system crash faults, disk faults, and disaster faults. A system is usually considered reliable when the probability of its unreliability occurring is very small.

In distributed computing, multiple closely related servers can be combined into a larger server, which is called a distributed server. Distributed servers have the property of confederation, in which each member server has independent autonomy. Distributed servers have good scalability and can realize network transparency, segmentation transparency, and replication transparency to clients. In the view of clients, a distributed server has large storage capacity, strong computing power, uninterrupted service, and timely response. These qualities are very popular among clients. Inside a distributed server, these qualities are obtained by parallel computing and replication. Distributed servers use a two-phase commit protocol to ensure the four attributes of a transaction.

Exercises
1. Serverless/FaaS (Function as a Service) is also a hot topic in cloud computing. Its idea is to let the server be transparent to developers of server programs. The concept opposite to serverless is serverful. Serverless means that developers do not need to consider such matters as fault-tolerance/fault recovery and scalability. These matters are left to platforms that support serverless. In Sect. 3.1, the implementation of RPC is transparent to developers. Specifically, such concepts as proxy, stub, RPC server, and deployment of RPC are transparent to developers who implement functions. The platform supporting RPC include 3 components: RPC server, RPC support library, and development tool. The development tool is responsible for generating the source code of proxy and stub. Please consult the serverless literature and think about the following question: Is deploying a website directly on an operating system a serverless example or a serverful example? Should development tool be a component of a platform supporting serverless?
2. For the function creating a network connection, it is assumed to be defined as "Connection *createConnection(char * domainName, int port)". In the implementation of this function, the VPN registry is first checked to see if the domain to be connected to belongs to one of the registered VPNs. If so, it is treated as a VPN. If not, look at the local hosts file to see if there is a record line. If there is, you get its IP address. If not, access the DNS server and find out the IP address of the domain. Next, add a line to the hosts file, noting the mapping relationship. Then, determine whether the resulting IP address is a local IP address or an external IP address. If it is an extranet IP address, then first establish a connection with the gateway, and according to the gateway protocol, after the connection is established, send the IP address and port number to be connected to the gateway, and after getting a response from the gateway, the network connection is established. In case of an intranet IP address, the network connection to the server is established directly. Based on the above description, write an implementation of the createConnection function in the operating system support library.
3. In the transaction execution framework shown in Code 3.27, is it possible that from the beginning of its execution until the execution of logCommit( ), the data update logs preceding it have been written to the log disk? During this period, can those log records that have been written to the log disk be deleted from the log buffer? Please justify. logCommit( ) does not just add a <t_id, COMMIT> log record to the log buffer, but also waits until all its log records have been written to the log disk. Why? For logAbort( ), it just adds a <t_id, ABORT> log entry to the log buffer, but does not wait. Why? When a transaction is aborted, all its log records, still need to be written to the log disk? Please explain the reasoning.
4. For a distributed database server DDBMS, the metadata it maintains include which member servers are present, how connections are established with mem-

ber servers, which member servers have replicas, and the segmentation of the data table (including horizontal and vertical segments). Please write a data structure definition for these metadata. Then, based on the defined data structure, write a decomposition algorithm for the DDBMS to generate subrequests for the client's SQL request, and then delegate the subrequests to the member servers for processing. Then, derive the processing method that performs the aggregation of the response results from the member servers.
5. For transaction processing and fault recovery in a distributed database server, can you write the implementation code for a two-phase commit protocol? Can you draw a flowchart for fault recovery in a distributed database server.

References

1. Andrew, S. T., Maarten, V. S., *Distributed Systems: Principles and Paradigms (Third Edition)*. Prentice Hall, 2017.
2. Don, B., *Essential COM*. Addison-Wesley Professional, 1998.
3. James, F. K., Keith, W. R., *Computer Networking: A Top-Down Approach (8th ed.)*. London: Pearson, 2020.
4. Huawei Technologies Co., Ltd., *Database Principles and Technologies – Based on Huawei GaussDB*. Springerlink, 2023 [access date 05/21/2024]; Available from: https://link.springer.com/book/10.1007/978-981-19-3032-4.
5. Louis, D., *Pro SQL Server Relational Database Design and Implementation*. Springer Nature link, 2021 [access date 12/25/2023]; Available from: https://link.springer.com/book/10.1007/978-1-4842-6497-3.
6. Tamer Özsu M., Patrick, V., *Principles of Distributed Database Systems*. Springer Nature link, 2021 [access date 01/25/2024]; Available from: https://link.springer.com/book/10.1007/978-3-030-26253-2.
7. Zhang, Y., Guo, K., Ren, J., et al, *Transparent Computing: A Promising Network Computing Paradigm*. Computing in Science & Engineering, 2017, 19(1): p.7-20.
8. Milanovic, N., Malek, M., *Current Solutions for Web Service Composition*. IEEE Internet Computing, 2004, 8(6): p. 51 - 59.
9. Bartlett, J., *ASCII, Unicode, and UTF-8. In: Learn to Program with Assembly*. Apress, 2021.
10. Dirk, L., *Understanding Search Engines*. Springer Nature link, 2023.
11. Agnaldo de, S., B., Aldri, L. D. S., *A Survey on Resilience in Information Sharing on Networks: Taxonomy and Applied Techniques*. ACM Computing Surveys, 2024, 56(12): p. 1 - 36.

Chapter 4
Decentralized Computing

Traditionally, an internet service is usually provided to customers by a single company. For example, each bank, as a service provider, has its own banking service system. This system is a centralized system, which is characterized by the fact that there is only one service provider, and customers use its service system based on their trust in the service provider. In the case of banking service, for example, customers deposit their money into the bank's service system based on their trust in the bank and conduct transactions through the service system. The banking service system is actually a database system. The money deposited by a customer in the bank is represented as data in the database. The maintenance of the data is the responsibility of the service provider. The correctness of the data, as well as the fairness of transactions, presupposes that customers trust the service provider. Fairness of transactions exists in service systems such as stock trading. In the customer's view, it is only fair that trade requests should be filled on a first-come, first-served basis, under the same conditions.

A centralized service system is controlled by a single service provider. The service provider has the ability to tamper with the transaction data in the system, as well as the ability to move a transaction request from the back of the queue to the front. In addition, the service is provided by a single point, and in the event of a single point of fault, the service becomes unavailable to customers. In the face of these problems with centralized service systems, decentralized solutions [1] have emerged. The idea is that a service is no longer provided by a single service provider, but by multiple service providers. In terms of system composition, the system is no longer composed of a single node, but of multiple nodes. Different nodes belong to different service providers. Each node runs the same program, stores the same data, and has the same nature, so the nodes in a decentralized system are also called replicas.

A decentralized systems has two distinct new qualities compared to a centralized system: (1) anything is no longer up to a single service provider, but is decided by multiple service providers in a deliberative manner, and (2) any replica (or any service provider) is no longer essential to the service, but optional. As long as more than half of the replicas are working, the system remains available to customers [2].

Decentralized systems are very popular among customers. Bitcoin and Ethereum [3] are two transaction service systems built with decentralization in mind. In both systems, any company can become a service provider at any time. Becoming a service provider is as simple as providing a computer (including computing and storage resources), downloading the service software, and running the service program. Once the service program starts up, it performs a synchronization operation to read existing data from existing nodes. Once the synchronization operation is complete, it becomes a new replica in the system. The service software is open-sourced to prove its trustworthiness and feasibility to customers. The system is also designed with a set of incentives to attract companies to join as service providers. Transaction revenues are automatically distributed to the service providers in accordance with their contributions as a result of providing the service.

Decentralization is an effective way to improve service availability [4]. In the case of a single-node service, the service becomes unavailable to customers in the event of a fault. In contrast, a service system consisting of three replicas, where any one of the replicas fails, is still available to customers. As a result, the availability of the service is significantly improved. In other words, the fault tolerance of the system is significantly improved. From another perspective, the service is unavailable only if two replicas fail at the same time. Assuming that the probability of one replica failing is p, the probability of two replicas failing at the same time is p^2. For a service system consisting of five replicas, the service will be unavailable to customers only if three replicas fail at the same time. The probability that three replicas fail at the same time is p^3. It follows that the higher the number of replicas, the lower the probability that the system will be unavailable. On the positive side, the higher the number of replicas, the higher the availability of the system.

In a decentralized system, jointly negotiated decisions are called Consensus [5]. Consensus is a prerequisite for replicas to remain identical. The sameness of the replicas is also called consistency. The process of reaching a consensus is called a consensus protocol, or sometimes a consensus algorithm. Paxos is a well-known consensus protocol [6], proposed by Leslie Lamport in 1990, which is widely used in various service products, such as Zookeeper [7], etc. Lamport is also known for this contribution. Lamport also won the Turing Award in 2013 for this contribution. Figuring out the Paxos protocol is not easy. The reason is that the concepts involved are too abstract and difficult to understand. Due to the difficult nature of the Paxos protocol, it did not attract much attention in the 16 years after it was proposed. It was not until 2006, when Google used the Paxos concept to implement a decentralized distributed system, that its value became apparent.

There is a lot of literature explaining the Paxos protocol. However, most of them are still abstract and difficult to understand, and the explanation is not thorough and convincing. Looking at the source code of the Paxos protocol is another way to learn. However, it is still difficult because of the many details considered, the large amount of code, and the complexity of the logic, which is poor in readability. The author of this book, after long research, has finally found a practical example that defuses the abstraction, and understands the real meaning of those abstract concepts. Subsequently, driven by the problem, a solution was gradually derived, finally showing the true face of the Paxos protocol. Once this fortress of the Paxos protocol is conquered, there will be no more roadblocks in learning other consensus protocols in decentralization. For example, after understanding the Paxos protocol, learning the Practical Byzantine Fault Tolerance (PBFT) consensus protocol [8] feels like a natural progression. The next Sects. 4.1 and 4.2 explain the Paxos consensus protocol, Sect. 4.3 explains the PBFT consensus protocol, and Sect. 4.4 provides a summary of the chapter.

4.1 Paxos Consensus Protocol

What problems are encountered in decentralization? What are the ideas for solving them? An example is given. Suppose a decentralized database server consists of $2f + 1$ replicas, where f is a positive integer. Each replica is an external service window, i.e., each replica can entertain transaction requests from clients. Whichever replica accepts a transaction request, it is broadcast to every replica in the system to process it. Initially, the state of each replica is the same, and naturally consistent, and is denoted as s_0. After all replicas have processed the transaction trx_1, their state changes from s_0 to s_1. After transaction trx_1 is processed, all replicas are in the same state and are also consistent. It follows that for the transaction requests that each replica in the system receives individually, it is important to have an order in the system, and then each replica processes the transactions one by one in that order. If this can be done, the replicas in the system are said to be consistent [9]. If the replicas in a decentralized system can be consistent, then it is equivalent to having only one replica, and there is no difference in efficacy logic with the centralized system.

The problem is what can be done to sort the transaction requests received by each replica in the system? When a replica receives a transaction request from a client, it broadcasts it to the other replicas. Although this allows each replica to receive all transaction requests from clients, it does not guarantee that each replica will receive them in the same order. For example, replica $R1$ broadcasts transaction $T1$, and replica $R2$ broadcasts transaction $T2$. For replica $R1$, it receives $T1$ first, then $T2$. In contrast, for replica $R2$, it receives $T2$ first, then $T1$. Replicas $R1$ and $R2$ do not receive transactions in the same order. If replica $R1$ processes transaction $T1$ before transaction $T2$, and the replica processes transaction $T2$ before transaction $T1$, then $R1$ and $R2$ may become inconsistent. The fact that all replicas process transactions in the same order is necessary to ensure that they are consistent. If they are processed in a different order, they may become inconsistent.

Inconsistency problems can be triggered by replicas processing transactions in a different order. An example is given. Enterprise α is a customer in a bank database with account number a. Two financial officers of enterprise α are each handling their own business. One of them is handling an incoming transaction: depositing $100 into account number a. The other one is handling an outgoing transaction:

transferring $200 from account number *a*. Thus, the bank database receives two transaction requests: an incoming request and an outgoing request. Assume that replica *R*1 processes the incoming request first and the outgoing request second, while replica *R*2 processes the outgoing request first and the incoming request second. Now, assume that the original balance on account number *a* is $180. At this point, replica *R*1 processes both transaction requests successfully, and the balance on account number *a* is $80 after execution. Replica *R*2, on the other hand, will not succeed in processing the outgoing request because the balance is not enough for $200. The incoming request is processed again after the rollback, and the balance on account number *a* is $280 after execution. There is a clear inconsistency between replica *R*1 and replica *R*2.

In a decentralized system, it is necessary to ensure that each replica processes transactions in the same order to ensure that all replicas are consistent. The idea is that when a replica receives a transaction request from a client, it assigns it a globally unique id, and once the transaction requests have ids, their order of precedence is determined. Although each replica receives transactions in a different order, according to the size of the id after sorting, the order will be the same. The way this is handled is that each replica has a receive queue *receiveQueue* that holds transaction requests received from clients. In addition, each replica has a global queue, *globalQueue*, which is used to store transactions that are in the same order. For each transaction in the *receiveQueue*, the replica requests a globally unique id for it. Transaction has an id attribute that records the globally unique id assigned to it. Once the replica assigns an id to a transaction, it moves it from the *receiveQueue* into the *globalQueue* and broadcasts it to the other replicas.

Once a replica receives a transaction with an id from another replica, it puts it into the *globalQueue*, where the transactions are sorted by their ids. Note: the order in which a replica receives transactions from other replicas is not necessarily the same as the order of transactions. For example, replica *R*1 receives transaction request α with a globally unique id of 8; replica *R*2 receives transaction request β with a globally unique id of 9. For replica *R*3, it is possible that it receives transaction request β first, and then transaction request α. The reason is that the transmission delays are different. The above scenario occurs when the transmission delay of transaction request β is small and that of transaction request α is large. Therefore, when putting a transaction with id into *globalQueue*, it is not simply adding it to the end of the queue, but putting it in the right place so that the transactions are sorted by id size.

For the above id assignment and placing transactions with ids into *globalQueue*, an example is given. Suppose that there are three replicas in the system, and each of them receives two transaction requests from clients into their own *receiveQueue*, respectively. Thus, the system accepts a total of six transaction requests. Suppose replica *R*1 requests twos globally unique ids 1 and 6, replica *R*2 requests two globally unique ids 2 and 3, and replica *R*3 requests two globally unique ids 4 and 5. These six transactions with ids go into the *globalQueue* of the three replicas, and they are all queued up in the *globalQueue* in the order of 1, 2, 3, 4, 5, and 6. Each

4.1 Paxos Consensus Protocol

replica processes the transactions in the *globalQueue* in order of id size, so the three replicas are consistent.

The question has now been transformed into how a replica can obtain a globally unique id for a transaction from a client. The Paxos protocol is used to answer that question. The Paxos protocol itself is somewhat abstract and difficult to understand. With the above case, it is possible to bring the Paxos protocol down to earth. The id in the above case is the proposal number in the Paxos protocol, and the transaction is the value in Paxos that corresponds to the proposal number. A replica has to apply a globally unique id for a transaction it receives from a client, corresponding to a single initiation of a proposal in Paxos. For an id application, the applicant corresponds to the proposer role in Paxos, and the other replicas act as acceptors of Paxos. A successful application corresponds to a proposal in Paxos that is approved by more than half of the members, i.e., consensus is reached. With this case, the abstract concepts in Paxos are easy to understand.

4.1.1 Id Application in the Absence of Faults

Each replica performs the same procedure. Let the replica use the variable *idCount* to keep track of the last assigned id. Thus, when a replica wants to apply for a globally unique id, the value of this id is *idCount* + 1. When applying, it broadcasts a proposal message in the system with the id it wants to apply for, i.e., its own value of *idCount* + 1. When an acceptor receives the proposal message, it checks to see if the attached id is equal to its own *idCount* + 1. If it is, the application is reasonable, and it gives the applicant a favorable vote. As long as the applicant receives more than half of the total favorable votes, the application is considered successful. Once the application is successful, the applicant broadcasts the transaction with the id to the other replicas. The other replicas put the transaction with id into the *globalQueue* and update their *idCount*, i.e., do the increment by one. From this, it can be seen that the function of consensus is twofold: (1) to ensure that the applied id has global uniqueness; (2) to make each replica know which id is available for the next id application.

To make the applied id globally unique, the measure is that each replica has only one favorable vote for any id application. This ensures that when more than one replica applies for the same id at the same time, there will be no case where two applicants both get more than half of the total favorable votes. Thus, there is no situation where two applicants are both successful. When multiple replicas receive transaction requests from clients at the same time, they all apply for the same id at the same time. For a replica acting as an acceptor, the received proposal messages are processed sequentially. For the first received proposal message, the acceptor votes in favor of it. For proposal messages that arrive later, there are no more favorable votes in hand, and therefore no favorable votes to cast. For any applicant, it is required to get more than half of the total votes in favor of its proposal to indicate that its application is successful. This is a much lower threshold compared to getting favorable votes from all replicas. The implication is that a simultaneous fault of f replicas can be tolerated in a system consisting of $2f + 1$ replicas.

When a globally unique id is successfully applied, the requester assigns that id to a transaction it receives from a client. This transaction becomes the value of that id in the Paxos protocol. The applicant then broadcasts a decision message to all replicas. The decision message contains the transaction with the id. Once a replica receives a decision message, it knows that it has a transaction with an id attached to it and that it should be placed in the *globalQueue*. It also knows that the transaction's id is an assigned id, so it should update its *idCount* value, i.e., increment it by 1, so that it knows the next available global id to assign. One id corresponds to one decision message. Each decision message drives each replica's *idCount* to increment by 1. This scenario implies that a replica is not allowed to initiate a new id application between the time it receives a proposal message and the time it receives a decision message. Otherwise, the following scenario is possible: a replica receives a decision message with id 9 first, and then receives a decision message with id 8.

For simplicity and clarity of the protocol description, a state machine is used to describe the replica. A replica starts in FREE state, and if a replica is in FREE state and its *receiveQueue* queue is not empty, it initiates an id application and broadcasts a proposal message, at which point its state changes from FREE to PROPOSING. If a replica in the FREE state receives a proposal message, its state changes from FREE to VOTING. An id application is allowed only when a replica is in the FREE state. It is entirely possible for more than one replica to apply the same id at the same time. This situation is called competition, where multiple applicants compete for the same id. In order for one applicant to receive more than half of the total votes in favor of an id, the notion of priority is introduced. Suppose that the replicas in the system are identified by serial numbers. For simplicity, assume that the higher the serial number, the higher the priority.

From the above state change, it is clear that only the applicants will be in the PROPOSING state. Each replica uses the variable *agreeNum* to store the number of favorable votes it has currently received. Each applicant initializes its *agreeNum* value to 1 after broadcasting a PROPOSAL message in the system, indicating that this favorable vote comes from itself. Subsequently, all the favorable votes received are added to the *agreeNum*. Once the value of *agreeNum* reaches $f + 1$, it means that more than half of the total votes received are in favor of the proposal, and the application is successful. At this point, the applicant's state changes from PROPOSING to DECIDING.

For a replica in the PROPOSING state, the receipt of a proposal message from another replica indicates an id competition situation. Each proposal message has the *senderId* attribute, which records the serial number of the applicant. If an applicant finds a competitor having a higher priority than itself, it has to transfer all the favorable votes held by itself to the competitor, so that the competitor can get more than half of the total favorable votes as soon as possible. Then, it changes its role from PROPOSER to ACCEPTOR, i.e., its state changes from PROPOSING to VOTING.

4.1 Paxos Consensus Protocol

After a replica's state changes from PROPOSING to VOTING, it is possible that it will also receive favorable votes. For example, in the messaging scenario shown in Fig. 4.1, replica $R3$ is first an id applicant that broadcasts a PROPOSAL message in the system. The delivery of the proposal message is indicated by solid arrows in the figure. The response to the proposal message is called a vote message and its delivery is indicated by a dashed arrow. After $R3$ receives a PROPOSAL message from replica $R4$, its state changes from PROPOSING to VOTING. Subsequently, $R3$ also receives a VOTE from replicas $R5$ and $R1$. The reason is that $R5$ and $R1$ receive $R3$'s PROPOSAL message first, and therefore will vote in favor of $R3$. In this case, $R3$ has to forward the favorable votes from $R5$ and $R1$ to $R4$ so that $R4$ gets more than half of the total favorable votes as soon as possible.

It is possible that a replica in VOTING state will also receive PROPOSAL messages. For example, in Fig. 4.2, replica $R3$ is first an applicant. Because it receives a PROPOSAL message from replica $R4$, $R3$'s role is changed from PROPOSER to ACCEPTOR, its state changes to VOTING, and it transfers the two favorable votes it holds to $R4$. One of these two favorable votes is from $R3$ itself and the other is from $R2$. $R3$ then receives a PROPOSAL message from $R5$. Since $R5$ has a higher priority than $R4$, when $R3$ subsequently receives a favorable vote from $R1$, it should not forward it to $R4$, but to $R5$. Therefore, the replica should have a variable, *votee*, to keep track of the applicant with the highest priority that it currently knows. For $R3$, when it receives a proposal message from $R4$, its *votee* value should be changed to $R4$. When $R3$ then receives a proposal message from $R5$, its *votee* value should be changed again to $R5$.

Even though id applications are competitive and prioritized, the possibility of a successful application exists for low-priority applicants. If a low-priority applicant has received more than half of the total votes in favor of its application before it receives a PROPOSAL message from other applicants, then its application is successful. This scenario is shown in Fig. 4.3. Replica $R3$ in the figure, despite its lower priority than $R4$, has received more than half of the total favorable votes from $R1$ and $R2$, plus its own favorable vote, before it receives $R4$'s proposal message. So $R3$'s application is successful.

Fig. 4.1 Receiving favorable votes after losing competition

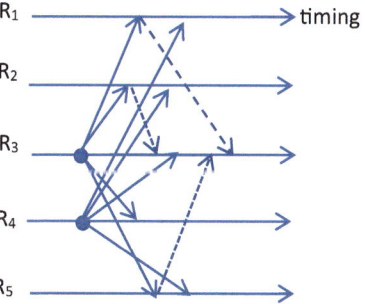

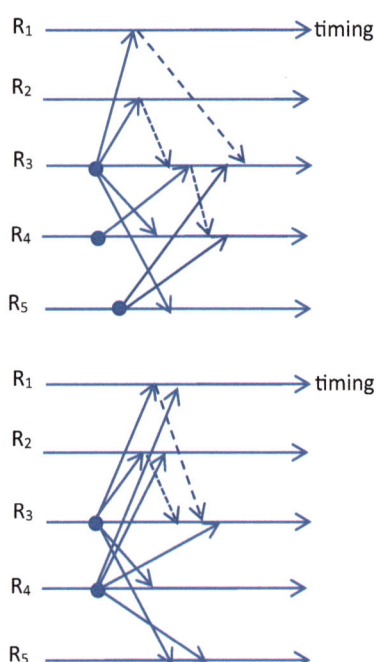

Fig. 4.2 Receiving a PROPOSAL message after losing competition

Fig. 4.3 Scenario in which applicants with low priority can also apply successfully

4.1.2 Impact of Faults on Id Applications

Faults can occur in two ways: (1) replicas fail; (2) replicas cannot communicate with each other due to network faults. Network faults may cause the replicas in the system to be split into two or more partitions. The system is available to clients only when the number of normal replicas in the largest partition exceeds half of the number of replicas in the system. Therefore, whether a replica can continue to work depends on whether it is in the largest partition. Those replicas that are not in the largest partition cannot continue to work. The reason is that they fail to communicate with replicas in the largest partition. They all need to wait for troubleshooting before performing fault recovery and then integrating into the system.

The impact of faults on id applications is on the replicas in the largest partition. The impact is twofold: (1) the applicant in the PROPOSING state stays in the PROPOSING state for a long time because it does not get more than half of the total votes in favor of its application, resulting in a blocking situation; (2) the replica in the VOTING state stays in the VOTING state for a long time because it does not receive an applicant's decision message, resulting in a blocking situation as well. The applicant in the PROPOSING state does not get more than half of the total votes in favor of its application because the favorable votes are swallowed up by faults. A replica in the VOTING state stays in the VOTING state due to not receiving an applicant's DECISION message. There are two reasons: (1) the applicant fails

4.1 Paxos Consensus Protocol

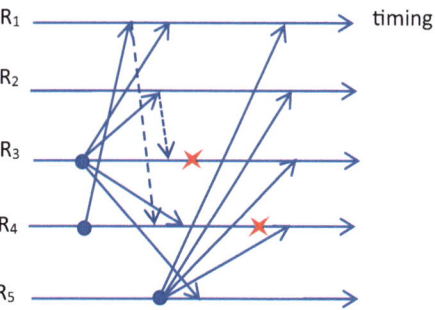

Fig. 4.4 Scenario in which faults swallow favorable votes

before broadcasting the DECISION message, and (2) the applicant is in the largest partition but does not get more than half of the total favorable votes.

Let us first look at the situation where the applicant is fault-free and is in the largest partition. When a low-priority applicant has received a favorable vote, but fails to transfer the favorable vote to the higher-priority applicant due to a fault, which may lead to the higher-priority applicant not receiving more than half of the total favorable votes. This situation can also be described as: the favorable votes are swallowed up by a fault. An example is given. In Fig. 4.4, replicas $R3$, $R4$, and $R5$ apply for the same id at the same time. Replica $R1$ receives $R4$'s proposal message first, and therefore votes in favor of $R4$. Replica $R2$ receives $R3$'s proposal message first, and therefore votes in favor of $R3$. Replica $R3$ fails after receiving $R2$'s vote, Replica $R4$ fails after receiving $R1$'s vote. Both $R3$ and $R4$ swallow two favorable votes, respectively. In this scenario, the normal replicas in the largest partition are $R1$, $R2$, and $R5$, numbering more than half of the total number of the system. Fault-free replica $R5$, despite having the highest priority, never receives more than half of the total favorable votes.

4.1.3 Impact of Faults on System Consistency

A replica accepts a transaction request from a client and responds to the client with a processing result. Because of faults, for a transaction, the replica must ensure that it has entered the *globalQueue* of at least $f + 1$ replicas before it can process it and respond to the client with a result. This is the only way to ensure that the system is consistent in front of the client. Otherwise, inconsistencies may occur. Here is an example. Suppose replica $R1$ assigns an id to transaction T, then broadcasts it to f replicas (including itself), then processes the transaction T, and returns the successful result to the client. If it happens that all f of these replicas fail at this point, then the system behaves inconsistently with respect to that client. The fact that f replicas have failed does not mean that the client cannot access the system. The client can continue to access the system through other normal replicas. The problem is that since the other $f + 1$ normal replicas have not received transaction T from replica $R1$, the client will not see the result of transaction T being successfully processed.

From the above analysis, it is clear that simply obtaining a globally unique id is not enough. The replica broadcasting the decision message must ensure that at least $f + 1$ replicas (including itself) have placed the transaction with the id in the *globalQueue* before it is allowed to process the transaction and send the result to the client. If no response result is given to the client, then the end result of the client's request is acceptable to the client whether it was successfully processed or not. If it is not processed, it is equivalent to not submitting the transaction request earlier. The client can submit the request again. As long as there is at least one normal replica in the largest partition that has put transaction T in its *globalQueue*, the situation is different. When the client queries the result through another normal replica, the id assigned to the query request is greater than the id of transaction T. That is, the system processes transaction T first, and then the query request is processed. Thus, the consistency of the results is ensured.

In order to achieve system consistency, each replica that receives a decision message has to give a response, i.e., reply with an acknowledge message. The sender of the decision message is allowed to process the transaction only after it has received at least $f + 1$ acknowledge messages. Of course, it is possible that the previous transaction has not yet been processed and the transaction cannot be processed immediately. For this reason, a validation attribute is added to each transaction. Only transactions with a validation attribute value of TRUE are allowed to be processed. Once the number of received acknowledge messages reaches $f + 1$, the value of the validation attribute of the corresponding transaction in the *globalQueue* is changed to TRUE, and a validation message is broadcast in the system to notify the other normal replicas that the value of the validation attribute of the transaction is also changed to TRUE. Thus, a transaction from receiving to being processable has to go through three phases: (1) applying for a globally unique id; (2) putting it into each replica's *globalQueue*; and (3) being processable (i.e., the validation attribute is TRUE).

The timing of the 3-phase processing is shown in Fig. 4.5. First, the applicant (i.e., proposer) broadcasts a proposal message with the globally unique id to be applied for. Each acceptor receives the proposal message and responds with a vote message with the id and the number of votes in favor. The number of favorable votes can be 0, 1, or greater than 1. When the proposer receives at least $f + 1$ favorable

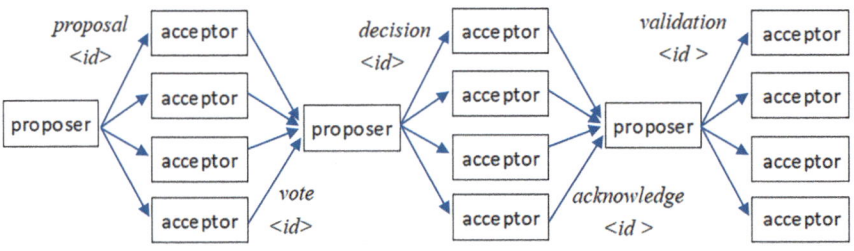

Fig. 4.5 Transaction from receipt to being processable

4.1 Paxos Consensus Protocol

votes, it broadcasts a decision message with the transaction (i.e., value) attached to the id. When an acceptor receives the decision message, it puts the attached transaction into its *globalQueue* and responds with an acknowledge message with the id. When the number of acknowledge messages received by the proposer reaches $f + 1$, it broadcasts a validation message with the id attached. Once an acceptor receives the validation message, it sets the validation attribute of the corresponding transaction in its *globalQueue* to TRUE.

The state change scenario for replicas is as follows. When a replica needs to apply for a unique id for a received transaction and is in the FREE state, it broadcasts a PROPOSAL message and migrates its state from FREE to PROPOSING. When the applicant has received at least $f + 1$ votes in the PROPOSING state, it broadcasts a DECISION message and migrates its state from PROPOSING to the DECIDING state. When the number of ACKNOWLEDGE messages received by the applicant in the DECIDING state reaches $f + 1$, a VALIDATION message is broadcast and it returns to the FREE state from the DECIDING state. In contrast, when a replica in FREE state receives a PROPOSAL message, it responds with a VOTE message and migrates its state from FREE to VOTING. When a replica in VOTING state receives a DECISION message, it responds with an ACKNOWLEDGE message and migrates its state from VOTING to VALIDATING. When a replica in VALIDATING state receives a VALIDATION message, it sets the validation attribute of the corresponding transaction in the *globalQueue* to TRUE and returns to FREE state from the VALIDATION state.

Due to the situation of application competition, when an applicant loses the competition, its role will change from PROPOSER to ACCEPTOR. The specific situation is: when a replica in PROPOSING state receives a higher priority PROPOSAL message, it will transfer its own favorable votes to the competition winner and change to VOTING state. Subsequently, when a favorable vote is received, it should also be immediately forwarded to the competition winner. Thus, replicas have the state machine shown in Fig. 4.6.

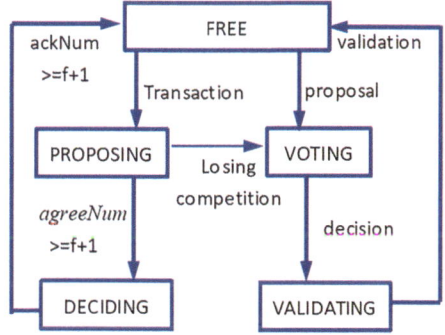

Fig. 4.6 State machine for replicas

4.1.4 Implementation of Replica Consistency in the Presence of Faults

From the above analysis, it can be seen that because of faults, the transaction from receiving to having processability needs to go through 3-phase message interactions to reach. The hazards brought by faults are: (1) faults may swallow the favorable votes, so that fault-free proposer may fail to at least $f + 1$ favorable votes and fall into a waiting state; (2) if the proposer fails to receive at least $f + 1$ favorable votes, it will make fault-free acceptors fail to receive the DECISION message and fall into a waiting state; (3) if the proposer fails, or network faults lead to the proposer not in the largest partition, the fault-free acceptors may fail to receive the VALIDATION message and fall into a waiting state. The system cannot be blocked due to faults. The way to deal with this is to set up a timeout mechanism. When something should have happened but does not happen within the specified time, it is considered to be due to faults. Once the timeout period is exceeded, state information is collected and measures are taken to terminate the application of the current id so that the fault-free replicas return to the FREE state and can continue to work.

Terminating the current id application is also a system-wide matter and requires consensus in the system. Therefore, terminating the current id application can succeed only in the largest partition. The idea is to check if there is a fault-free replica in the largest partition that has received a validation message for the current id application. If there is, a validation message is broadcast directly to compensate for the validation messages swallowed by faults, in order to complete the current id application. If not, further check whether there is a fault-free replica in the largest partition that has received a decision message. If so, that replica knows the value of the current id and broadcasts a decision message to finish the rest of the application in place of the failed proposer. If none of them has received a decision message, the value corresponding to the current id should be set to null because it is unknown, and the rest of the follow-up is also done.

For an id application, the replica timeout can be categorized into two scenarios: proposer timeout and acceptor timeout. Proposer timeout occurs in following two cases: (1) the proposer fails to receive enough favorable votes in the PROPOSING state; (2) the proposer fails to receive enough acknowledge messages in the DECIDING state. In contrast, acceptor timeout also has two scenarios: (1) an acceptor fails to receive a decision message in the VOTING state; (2) an acceptor fails to receive a validation message in the VALIDATING state. Therefore, there are four situations on replica timeout in total. For ease of description, that four situations are noted as timeout 1 through 4, respectively.

When timeout 1 occurs in a proposer, or timeout 3 occurs in an acceptor and all acceptors in the largest partition have not received a decision message, it implies that a decision does not appear in the largest partition. At this point, a new consensus should start up. Of course, this consensus is not for an id application but for aborting the current application. Abort consensus is initiated by the timeout replica: either the proposer or an acceptor. This timeout replica broadcasts a termination

4.1 Paxos Consensus Protocol

message, which is also a kind of proposal message. It is possible that multiple replicas broadcast the same termination message at the same time. The reason is that these replicas time out at the same time. There is no problem in this situation, because their motivation is the same. The decision in abort consensus is to set the value of the current id to null.

When timeout 2 occurs, the proposer fails to receive enough acknowledge messages in the DECIDING state; it shows that the proposer has been off the largest partition due to network faults. At this point, the proposer has to wait for fault recovery.

When timeout 3 occurs in an acceptor, there are two possible scenarios: (1) the timeout acceptor is in the largest partition; (2) not in the largest partition. In the first scenario, there are two subscenarios: (1) there is no acceptor in the largest partition having received a decision message; (2) there is at least one acceptor in the largest partition having received a decision message. The first subscenario is easy to understand. The reason is that the proposer has failed or has not received enough favorable votes. The second subscenario shows that the proposer failed in the process of broadcasting the decision message, resulting in some acceptors receiving the decision message but others not. The second scenario is caused by network faults, the timeout acceptors have to wait for fault recovery.

Under the first subscenario, an abort consensus should start up. In contrast, under the second subscenario, the acceptor having received the decision message should broadcast the decision message in place of the failed proposer to continue to complete the current id application. In this situation, the broadcasting acceptor becomes a new proposer. After it receives at least $f+1$ acknowledge messages, it broadcasts a validation message.

When timeout 4 occurs in an acceptor, there are also two possible scenarios: (1) the timeout acceptor is in the largest partition; (2) not in the largest partition. In the first scenario, there are two subscenarios: (1) there is no acceptor in the largest partition having received a validation message; (2) there is at least one acceptor in the largest partition having received a validation message. The first subscenario is easy to understand. The reason is that the proposer has failed before broadcasting the validation message. The second subscenario shows that the proposer failed in the process of broadcasting the validation message, resulting in some acceptors receiving the validation message but others not. Similarly, the second scenario is caused by network faults, the timeout acceptors have to wait for fault recovery.

Under the first subscenario, the timeout acceptor should broadcast a decision message in place of the failed proposer to continue to complete the current id application. In this situation, the timeout acceptor becomes a new proposer. After it receives at least $f+1$ acknowledge messages, it broadcasts a validation message. In contrast, under the second subscenario, the acceptor of the validation message should broadcast a validation message in place of the failed proposer to complete the current id application.

In summary, once a replica times out, it broadcasts a message in the system to promote the consensus. Specifically, when the proposer times out in the PROPOSING state, it broadcasts a termination message in the system and changes the state from

PROPOSING to EXPIRING. Its purpose is to start up an abort consensus. If an acceptor times out in the VOTING state, it also broadcasts a termination message and changes the state from VOTING to EXPIRING. Its purpose is to find out if there is a replica that has received the decision message or the validation message. If there is, application consensus continues. Otherwise, an abort consensus is started up. If an acceptor times out in the VALIDATING state, it knows the proposer has failed, thus broadcasts a decision message in the system and changes the state from VALIDATING to DECIDING. Its purpose is to promote consensus on behalf of the proposer.

When a replica receives a termination message, it checks its own state. If the state shows that it has received a decision message or a validation message, it will know from the termination message that the original proposer has failed, and it should replace the original proposer to broadcast a decision message to complete the subsequent processing. If it does not receive a decision message, it responds with an approval message to the sender of the termination message.

If a replica remains in the EXPIRING state and has received at least $f+1$ approval messages, it shows that an abort consensus is feasible. Thus, it broadcasts a decision message with null as the value of the current id and changes its own state from EXPIRING to DECIDING. Apparently, it is acting as a proposer in abort consensus. When it has received $f+1$ acknowledge messages in the DECIDING state, it broadcasts a validation message and returns to FREE state. It is also possible for a replica in the EXPIRING state to receive a decision message. If so, it changes the state from EXPIRING to VALIDATING and responds with an acknowledge message to the sender of the decision message.

Reflection 4-1: When a replica receives a termination message on some id application, its state may be FREE, PROPOSING, VOTING, DECIDING, or VALIDATING on this id application. Why? Please give an example for each case. Furthermore, it is possible that it has received the validation message on this id application and now goes on another consensus larger than this id. Why?

Reflection 4-2: For a replica in the EXPIRING state, it is also possible to receive a validation message. Why?

The above scheme ensures the consistency of the system. In the largest partition, for the current id application, if none of the replicas receives a DECISION message, it is impossible for the proposer to have received $f+1$ acknowledge messages before a fault occurs. This is because if $f+1$ acknowledge messages were received, then at least one of them was from the largest partition. That is, at least one replica in the largest partition received a DECISION message. Now that none of the replicas in the largest partition has received a decision message, it can be inferred that the proposer has not received $f+1$ acknowledge messages, which is a prerequisite for the proposer to process the corresponding transaction. It can be further deduced that the proposer has not yet processed the transaction corresponding to the current id, and has not sent the result to the client.

In contrast, if at least one replica has received a decision message in the largest partition, it is possible that the proposer has received $f+1$ acknowledge messages before the fault. In this scenario, the final result is that the transaction T with the assigned id is placed in the *globalQueue* of each replica in the largest partition and has processability. Of course, it is possible that the proposer fails before processing the transaction T and thus does not send a response result to the client. The client would definitely inquire the result through another fault-free replica, the id assigned to the inquiry request is naturally greater than the id of transaction T. That is, the system processes transaction T first, and then the inquiry request. This result does not violate the principle of consistency.

If a network fault makes a replica off the largest partition, the replica cannot succeed in assigning a globally unique id to a transaction received from a client. In this case, the replica cannot hold the transaction until the network fault is lifted, and then reapply for it. The reason is that the client does not get a response in time, and then timeout occurs. After the timeout, the client may go through other replicas in the system to inquire about the final result of the transaction. In the largest partition, no replica may have received a DECISION message about the transaction, and the response result to the client is that no such transaction was processed. Therefore, as soon as a replica senses that it is not in the largest partition, after fault recovery, it should discard all transactions in its *receiveQueue*, as well as all transactions in the *globalQueue* whose validation attribute does not have a value of TRUE, in order to maintain the consistency of the system.

Reflection 4-3: For a replica in the EXPIRING state, it is possible that it has neither received a decision message nor a validation message nor $f + 1$ approval messages. Why? Thus, it will time out in the EXPIRING state. That is, it is stuck in a timeout loop until the network fault is lifted.

In the abort consensus, the system assigns null to the value of the current id, which does not lead to inconsistency. It means the proposer should have assigned an id to a transaction, but it has failed. Thus, the proposer has to abort this transaction, which is equivalent to the client's transaction request being rejected by the system. Abort consensus is necessary, because it can make IDs in the *globalQueue* of each replica successive.

In the maximum partition, once the current id application has completed, it means that consensus is reached, so the fault-free replicas return to FREE state and the next id application can be initiated. For example, suppose the current application is for id 8, and a fault occurs during the consensus, causing the proposer to fail to get enough favorable votes. Once the proposer times out, an abort consensus is initiated. Finally, the value of the id 8 is set to null, all fault-free replicas return to the FREE state, and then the application with id 9 can be initiated.

4.1.5 *Characterization of the Protocol*

The consensus-reaching scheme described above does not require that the delivery of a message be necessarily reliable. That is, a message is broadcast or sent without concern for whether it is received by the receiver. This assumption is more realistic. When a network fault occurs, the receiver does not receive the message. When the receiver fails, it naturally does not receive the message. For message delivery latency, it is assumed that when there is no system fault, a message will not take longer than a certain value for a round trip. If it is greater than this value, a fault is considered to have occurred. This is the basis for setting up a timeout mechanism so that consensus is reached without getting stuck due to the presence of faults. This consensus is characterized by the fact that out of the $2f + 1$ replicas, the system can provide services normally as long as $f + 1$ replicas are fault-free and can communicate with each other. Under this premise, any replica is dispensable and any fault will not block the normal service of the system. This is the essential property of decentralization.

Knowing the above system characteristics, the following scenarios are all possible. When a replica receives a proposal message, it finds that the id attached to it is smaller than its own $idCount + 1$. This situation indicates that the applicant missed one or more consensuses due to a fault, resulting in an outdated id application. Therefore, the applicant should be informed of this situation via a vote message, so that the applicant can abort the application and perform fault recovery until it is in agreement with the system, and then reapply. It is also possible for a received proposal message to be accompanied by an id that is greater than one's own $idCount + 1$. This situation indicates that you have missed one or more consensuses due to a fault, causing you to fall behind the global state of the system. At this point, you can ignore the proposal message and recover from the fault yourself.

For an id application, it is possible to receive a decision message or even a validation message instead of a proposal message. This situation is caused by a temporary network fault. Temporary network faults cause messages to be lost. Instead of receiving favorable votes from all replicas, the applicant only needs to receive $f + 1$ favorable votes to broadcast a decision message. Instead of receiving acknowledge messages from all replicas, the applicant only needs to receive acknowledge messages from $f + 1$ replicas to broadcast the VALIDATION message. This is a concrete manifestation of the fact that a replica is optional, and that faults do not prevent the system from providing normal service. What is more, the id of the received decision message or validation message may be larger or smaller than its own $idCount + 1$. This is all due to faults.

Consensus in Paxos protocol is divided into two phases, pre-prepare phase and prepare phase. The presence or absence of validation phase is related to the reliability assumptions of message delivery. When communicating based on transmission control protocol (TCP), there is the concept of network connection. In communication based on network connection, when a message is sent, the other party's network transport layer gives a response. Thus, the reliable transmission of the message is taken care of by the network communication subsystem. When communicating based on user datagram protocol (UDP), there is no concept of network connection and the reliable transmission of messages is the responsibility of the application program. That is, when a message is sent, the response is given by the other application program. In this paper, it is assumed that message delivery is not required to be reliable, corresponding to UDP communication, where the application responds to the received message. In this case, the validation phase is essential. If TCP communication is used, then the proposer broadcasts the DECISION message with the knowledge of how many replicas received the message. This is equivalent to getting the acknowledge message in the broadcast, so there is no need for a separate validation phase.

Broadcasting a VALIDATION message is necessary for the protocol to be non-blocking in situations where message delivery is not necessarily reliable. The fact that a replica receives a DECISION message does not mean that at least $f + 1$ replicas have received that DECISION message. For example, suppose replica $R1$ receives $f + 1$ favorable votes and then there is a network fault, replica $R2$ can receive $R1$'s DECISION message, but the largest partition cannot receive $R1$'s DECISION message. $R2$ cannot process the transaction attached to the decision message; otherwise, it will be inconsistent with the largest partition. Only when $R2$ receives the validation message can it conclude that the largest partition will definitely make a decision for the id application, and the corresponding transaction will be processable.

For a replica that is not in the largest partition due to a network fault, when it initiates a consensus, it will not be able to reach a finalization because it will not get a response from $f + 1$ replicas. In addition, it does not receive a finalized consensus from the largest partition. Therefore, it stays in a blocking state, i.e., it is stuck in a timeout loop until the network fault is lifted.

The maximal partition is not blocked by a fault because there are at least $f + 1$ fault-free replicas in it. When the id applicant fails, if no replica in the largest partition receives a decision message, then it can be inferred that the applicant must not have gotten $f + 1$ acknowledge messages. Therefore, the largest partition can set the value corresponding to the id to null. This decision does not cause an inconsistency because if the applicant does not get $f + 1$ acknowledge messages, it must not have processed the corresponding transaction, and it must not have given the client a response. As long as the client is not given a response, the system can discard the client's transaction request. The client will then continue to access the system through other replicas to inquire about the final outcome of the previous transaction. In the largest partition, the id value is set to null, which is equivalent to rejecting the customer's transaction request. The prerequisite for rejection is that no replica in the largest partition receives the corresponding decision message.

4.1.6 Fault Recovery of Replicas

For a replica, whether it fails itself or encounters a network failure, it will miss the receipt of the consensus message, causing it to fall behind the global state. The sign of network failure being lifted is the ability to receive messages from the largest partition. If the replica itself has failed, the replica will reboot after the fault has been cleared. After restarting, it checks its *globalQueue* for the last consensus id, then broadcasts a recovery message to get the latest system consensus id from fault-free replicas, and when it receives a response message that reaches $f + 1$, it indicates that it is in the largest partition and knows which ids it is missing from the finalized id. After that, find a fault-free replica and send it a fetch message requesting the case. Once all the missing files have been filled, the replica becomes a normal replica again. This is signaled by the fact that its own proposal message has not been rejected by other replicas, or that it has received a message with an id equal to its own *idCount* + 1.

When a replica fails, not only are all the transactions in its *globalQueue* lost, but also the transactions being processed are not in a committed state. Therefore, when the replica is restarted after the fault is removed, its *receiveQueue* and *globalQueue* are empty. At this point, you need to check the processed transaction logs to see which transaction was the last one you committed. For the finalizations that you missed due to the fault, you have to fill them in. This is what fault recovery is going to do. Only after you have aligned yourself with the system will you become a normal replica again.

When a replica receives a message id greater than its own *idCount* + 1, it knows that it has missed the reception of a finalized message due to a network fault. At this point, if the received message id is equal to one's *idCount* + 2 and one is in the VALIDATING state, then one can infer that one is only just missing the reception of a VALIDATING message. It can be assumed that a validation message was received before the above message was received. If this is not the case, then the received message is ignored and a request is made to the sender of the message to obtain a finalization and perform a fault recovery. The sign of a full recovery is the same as the recovery from replica fault described above, i.e., one's own proposal message has not been rejected by other replicas, or the received message id is equal to one's own *idCount* + 1.

In the process of performing fault recovery, after replica $R1$ sends a fetch message to another replica $R2$, there is a possibility that $R1$ cannot wait for the response result because of a fault of $R2$ or a network fault. At this point, a timeout occurs for $R1$. Once the timeout occurs, $R1$ broadcasts a recovery message in the system. If it receives a response message that reaches $f + 1$, it indicates that it is in the largest partition and knows which ids it is missing from the finalization. After that, it looks for another fault-free replica and sends a fetch message to it, requesting a fix. If it does not wait for an $f + 1$ response message, it is stuck in a wait timeout loop until the fault is lifted or it receives a message from another replica.

4.2 Specific Implementation of the Paxos Protocol

Each replica in the decentralized system is a server that accepts transaction requests from clients. For an accepted transaction, the processing flow is: (1) request a globally unique id for it and broadcast it to the other replicas; (2) the transaction becomes processable (i.e., the validation attribute has a value of TRUE) only after it has been placed into the *globalQueue* of at least $f + 1$ replicas; (3) each replica processes transactions with a value of TRUE in the *globalQueue* in order of their id size to maintain consistency. In the above processing, for the replica applying for the id, it also acts as a client (i.e., proposer role) to broadcast proposal/decision/validation messages to other replicas. Any other replica acts as a server (i.e., acceptor role) and responds to the received proposal and decision messages with vote messages and acknowledge messages, respectively.

For the proposer, after broadcasting the PROPOSAL message, it waits for the VOTING message in the PROPOSING state. For the acceptor, after processing the PROPOSAL message, it waits for the DECISION message in the VOTING state. Once either the proposer or the acceptor times out either in the PROPOSING or in the VOTING state, it enters the EXPIRING state and broadcasts a termination message in an attempt to start an abort consensus. When a replica receives a termination message, it responds with an OUTCOMING message. In addition, when the replica is restarted due to a fault, or when it realizes that it has fallen behind, it broadcasts a recovery message in an attempt to be informed of the latest progress of the system and to perform fault recovery. During the fault recovery process, the replica sends a fetch message to ask the fault-free replica for its own missing finalization. When a replica receives a recovery message, it responds with a progress message to the requester. When a replica receives a fetch message, it responds to the requester with an item message.

In Paxos protocol, a state machine is used to portray the state of the replica. A replica has seven states: (1) FREE; (2) PROPOSING; (3) DECIDING; (4) VOTING; (5) VALIDATING; (6) EXPIRING; and (7) RECOVERING. The first five states are the operating states when there are no faults, and the last two states are introduced due to faults. The initial state of a replica is FREE. A replica is allowed to initiate a globally unique id application only when it is in the FREE state. Initializing an id application is to broadcast a PROPOSAL message to the other replicas in the system and then change state from FREE to PROPOSING. The state change scenario for a replica is shown in Fig. 4.7. This figure extends the state machine shown in Fig. 4.6 by adding the processing when there is a fault. The red portion of the diagram expresses how a fault-free replica responds to a fault in the system, while the black portion expresses fault recovery.

The implementation of the Paxos protocol is the processing of the 12 types of messages described above. Assuming that the client's transaction request is also sent as a message to a replica, the implementation of the Paxos protocol is shown in Code 4.1. Each replica executes this code and processes each message as it is received. The replica's start state is FREE, and the start message must be a transaction request from a client. When a replica receives a transaction request, it calls the *processTransactionArrival* function to process it. The implementation of this function is shown in Code 4.2. The replica first puts the received transaction into the *receiveQueue*, then checks its state, and if it is in the FREE state, it acts as a

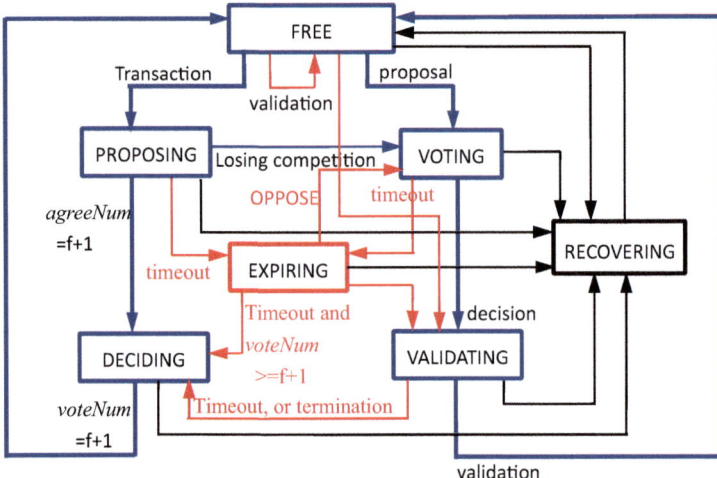

Fig. 4.7 State machine for replicas in the Paxos protocol

proposer to apply for a globally unique id for the received transaction. The specific implementation is to call the *startupConsensus* function.

Code 4.1 Implementation of Paxos Protocol
```
(1)     while(1) {
(2)       Messsage *msg = waitForMessage( );
(3)       if (msg->type == TRANSACTION)
(4)         processTransactionArrival( (Transaction *)
            msg->content);
(5)       else if (msg->type == PROPOSAL)
(6)         processProposal((Proposal *)msg->content);
(7)       else if (msg->type == VOTE)
(8)         processVote((Vote *)msg->content);
(9)       else if (msg->type == DECISION)
(10)        processDecision((Decision *)msg->content);
(11)      else if (msg->type == ACK)
(12)        processAck((Ack *)msg->content);
(13)      else if (msg->type == VALIDATION)
(14)        processValidation((Validation *)msg->content);
(15)      else if (msg->type ==TIMEOUT)
(16)        processTimeout( );
(17)      else if (msg->type ==TERMINATION)
(18)        processTermination((Termination *)msg->content);
(19)      else if (msg->type ==POSTURE)
(20)        processOutcome((Outcome *)msg->content);
```

```
(21)        else if (msg->type ==RECOVERY)
(22)           processRecovery((Recovery *)msg->content);
(23)        else if (msg->type == PROGRESS)
(24)           processProgress((Progress *)msg->content);
(25)        else if (msg->type ==FETCH)
(26)           processFetch((Fetch *)msg->content);
(27)        else if (msg->type ==ITEM)
(28)           processItem((Item *)msg->content);
(29)     }
```

The implementation of the *startupConsensus* function is shown in Code 4.3, where the global variable *myselfId* is used to store the replica's own identification number. Each replica in the system has a unique identification number. The global variable *idCount* is used to store the id of the latest finalized case. So when a replica wants to request a globally unique id for a transaction, the value of that id is *idCount* + 1. The global variables also include *state*, *voteNum*, *agreeNum*, and *timer*, which store the replica's current state, the number of votes it has received, the number of favorable votes it has received, and the value of the timer. Because there is a competitive situation for the application of id, the global variable *votee* is used to store who one is currently voting for. To initiate an application, first broadcast a PROPOSAL message to the other replicas in the system with the applicant's identification number and the value of the id to be applied for. The state value is then changed to PROPOSING to indicate that the replica is currently in the PROPOSING state.

Code 4.2 Implementation of the processTransactionArrival function
```
(1)     void processTransactionArrival( (Transaction *
        transaction) {
(2)        receiveQueue->addItem(transaction);
(3)        if (state == FREE) {
(4)           startupConsensus();
(5)        }
(6)        return;
(7)     }
```

Code 4.3 Implementation of the startupConsensus function

```
(1)     void startupConsensus( ) {
(2)         broadcast(PROPOSAL, myselfId, idCount + 1);
(3)         state = PROPOSING;
(4)         votee = -1;
(5)         voteNum = 1;
(6)         agreeNum = 1;
(7)         timer->restart( );
(8)         return;
(9)     }
```

When starting the id application, set both *voteNum* and *agreeNum* to 1 to indicate your own vote as well as a favorable vote from yourself. Setting *votee* to −1 indicates that no votes are currently cast for another replica, i.e., there are no vote recipient. Once the id application is initiated, *restart*, a member function of timer, is called to start the timer. If not enough votes and enough favorable votes are received within the specified time, then a fault must have occurred and the id application is closed.

4.2.1 Handling of Proposal Messages

When a replica receives a proposal message, the *processProposal* function is called to process it. The implementation of this function is shown in Code 4.4. Under normal circumstances, the id attached to the proposal message (i.e., the requested id) should be equal to its own *idCount* + 1. Since the maximum id assigned is *idCount*, the next id to be requested is naturally *idCount* + 1. In the case of a randomized delay in message delivery, a scenario such as the one shown in Fig. 4.8 is possible: replica $R2$ broadcasts a validation message, and replica $R3$ broadcasts a validation message. After $R2$ broadcasts the validation message, replica $R3$ receives the validation message first compared to $R1$, and $R3$ returns to the FREE state after processing the validation message, and then initiates the id application and broadcasts the proposal message. For replica $R1$, it is possible that it receives the proposal message from $R3$ first and the validation message from $R2$ later.

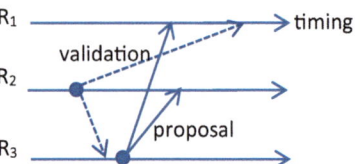

Fig. 4.8 Reversal of reception order triggered by random message delivery delay

4.2 Specific Implementation of the Paxos Protocol 265

When the above situation occurs, $R1$ will find that its id is equal to *idcount* + 2 and it is in VALIDATING state when it processes $R3$'s proposal message. At this point, $R1$ can deduce from the proposal message that it should first complete the *idCount* + 1 application and return to the FREE state before processing the proposal message. This is the origin of lines 2 through 9 in Code 4.4.

Code 4.4 Implementation of the function processProposal
```
(1)     void processProposal(Proposal *proposal) {
(2)        if(state == VALIDATING && proposal->id ==
           idCount + 2) {
(3)           transaction *trx = globalQueue-
              >getItemById(idCount + 1);
(4)           if (trx ! = null) {
(5)              trx->validation = TRUE;
(6)              idCount++;
(7)              state = FREE;
(8)           }
(9)        }
(10)       if (proposal->id == idCount + 1) { // reasonable
(11)          if (state == PROPOSING) { //indicates the
              presence of a competitor
(12)             if (proposal->senderId > myselfId) { // meet
                 stronger competitor
(13)                response(proposal->senderId, VOTE, proposal-
                    >id, AGREE, agreeNum);
(14)                state = VOTING;
(15)                agreeNum = 0;
(16)                votee = proposal->senderId;
(17)                timer.restart( );
(18)             }
(19)          else if (proposal->senderId < myselfId)
(20)             response(proposal->senderId, VOTE, proposal-
                 >id, DISAGREE, 0);
(21)          }
(22)          else if (state == FREE) {
(23)             response(proposal->senderId, VOTE, proposal-
                 >id, AGREE, 1);
(24)             state = VOTING;
(25)             agreeNum = 0;
(26)             votee = proposal->senderId;
(27)             timer.restart( );
(28)          }
```

```
(29)            else if (state == VOTING) { //indicates that
                there is competition
(30)              if (proposal->senderId > votee) { //this
                  applicant has a higher priority than the
                  previous one
(31)                response(proposal->senderId, VOTE, proposal-
                    >id, AGREE, 0);
(32)                votee = proposal->senderId;
(33)                timer.restart( );
(34)              }
(35)              else if (proposal->senderId < votee)
(36)                response(proposal->senderId, VOTE, proposal-
                    >id, DISAGREE, 0);
(37)            }
(38)          }
(39)          else if (proposal->id > idCount + 1) // own
              lagging behind
(40)            processOutdating(proposal->senderIdId,
                proposal->id);
(41)          else if (proposal->id < idCount + 1) //applicant
              is outdated
(42)            response(proposal->senderId, VOTE, proposal->id,
                OPPOSE, idCount);
(43)          return;
(44)        }
```

fetching is used to record whether you are currently requesting a missing item. The global variable *provider* is used to record from which replica one should claim one's missing items in fault recovery. The meaning of line 10 is to ask the provider for the desired item.

When the id attached to the proposal message is equal to *idCount* + 1, the replica only needs to process the proposal message if it is in the FREE state, or the PROPOSING state, or the VOTING state. If the replica is in the PROPSING state, it means that there is a contention situation. It is important to determine who has priority. If the sender of the PROPOSAL message has an identification number greater than its own, then it has failed the competition and should change from the PROPOSER role to the ACCEPTOR role, while casting all the favorable votes it holds for the other party. This processing is shown in lines 12 through 18. If the competition wins, the opposing party is given a negative vote, as shown in lines 19 through 20. If the replica is in the FREE state, it casts this one favorable vote of its own for the applicant, and the role naturally becomes acceptor, which is handled as shown in lines 22 through 28.

4.2 Specific Implementation of the Paxos Protocol

If the replica receives a PROPOSAL message in the VOTING state, this indicates a contention situation. At this point, it is also important to determine who has priority. If the sender of the proposal message has an identification number greater than *votee*, a higher priority applicant has been encountered. The value of *votee* is updated at this point. A replica in the VOTING state does not hold a favorable vote in its hand and therefore casts a favorable vote of 0. This processing is shown in lines 29 through 37.

When the id attached to the proposal message is greater than *idCount* + 1, it means that one missed the reception of the validation message due to a fault and fell behind the system state. At this point, the *processOutdating* function should be called to recover from the fault, as shown in lines 39 through 40. When the id attached to the proposal message is less than *idCount* + 1, it means that the sender of the proposal message missed the receipt of the validation message and fell behind in the system state. At this point, it should tell the sender of the proposal message its *idCount* to recover from the fault. This processing is shown in lines 41 through 42.

The *processOutdating* function is implemented as shown in Code 4.5. It first determines whether it is in the RECOVERING state. If it is not, then it moves to the RECOVERING state. In the RECOVERING state, three global variables are used: *lastRecoveryLine*, *fetching*, and *provider*. *lastRecoveryLine* is used to store the id of the last fix that was received, so the id of the next fix that is to be fetched from the other replicas in the fault recovery. *lastRecoveryLine* is updated for each request in the recovery. When *lastRecoveryLine* is equal to *idCount*, the recovery is complete.

Code 4.5 Implementation of the function processOutdating

```
(1)     void processOutdating(int senderId, int newestId) {
(2)         if (state ! = RECOVERING) {
(3)             state = RECOVERING;
(4)             fetching = FALSE;
(5)             lastRecoveryLine = idCount;
(6)         }
(7)         idCount = newestId - 1;
(8)         provider = senderId;
(9)         if (fetching == FALSE) {
(10)            request(provider, FETCH, lastRecoveryLine +
                1, null );
(11)            fetching = TRUE;
(12)            timer->restart( );
(13)        }
(14)        return;
(15)    }
```

4.2.2 Handling of Vote Messages

Vote message is the acceptor's response to a proposal message. After the proposer receives a vote message, it calls the *processVote* function to process it, the implementation of which is shown in Code 4.6. For the vote message received by the proposer, its category is recorded in its member variable *option*, and there are four categories: (1) OPPOSE; (2) AGREE; (3) DISAGREE; and (4) TRANSFER. When the category of the vote message is OPPOSE, it means that the id application is lagging behind in the system state, and the applicant should perform fault recovery. The handling of the OPPOSE category is shown in lines 2 through 3. Processing is only required if the *idCount* attached to the vote message is greater than its own *idCount*. The reason for this is that it is possible to receive multiple OPPOSE category vote messages. When the first OPPOSE category vote message is received, the above condition is satisfied and the replica calls the *processOutdating* function to transfer to the fault recovery state. For subsequent OPPOSE category vote messages received, the above condition is not satisfied and no further processing is required.

A vote message is a response to a proposal message. This correspondence is expressed by the accompanying id. Therefore, for the other three categories of vote messages, processing is performed only if their accompanying id is equal to their own *idCount* + 1 and they are in the PROPOSING or VOTING state; otherwise, they are ignored. This processing is shown in lines 4 through 23. The replica may be in the VOTING state when the VOTE message is received. The reason for this is that the replica was originally a proposer, then became an acceptor due to a failed contention, and was then in the VOTING state. If this is the case, and the VOTE message has a favorable vote attached to it (i.e., its member variable *agreeNum* is greater than 0), then the favorable vote should be forwarded to the winner of the competition. This processing is shown in lines 21 through 22.

Code 4.6 Implementation of the function processVote

```
(1)     void processVote((Vote *vote) {
(2)        if (vote->option == OPPOSE && idCount < vote->idCount)) //handle laggards
(3)           processOutdating(vote->senderId, vote->idCount);
(4)        else if(vote->id == idCount+1 && (state == PROPOSING || state == VOTING)) {
(5)           if (state == PROPOSING) {
(6)              if (vote->option ! = TRANSFER)
(7)                 voteNum++;
(8)              agreeNum += vote->agreeNum;
(9)              if (voteNum >= f+1 && agreeNum >= f +1 ) {
(10)                Transaction trx* = receiveQueue->pickOutItem( );
```

4.2 Specific Implementation of the Paxos Protocol

```
(11)            trx->id = vote->id;
(12)            trx->senderId = myselfId;
(13)            trx->validation =FALSE;
(14)            globalQueue->addItem(trx);
(15)            broadcast(DECISION, myselfId, vote-
                >id, trx);
(16)            state = DECIDING;
(17)            voteNum = 1;
(18)            timer.restart( );
(19)          }
(20)        }
(21)        else if(state == VOTING && vote->agreeNum> 0)
(22)            response(votee, VOTE, vote->id, TRANSFER,
                vote->agreeNum );
(23)      }
(24)      return;
(25)    }
```

If the replica state is PROPOSING, the number of votes and the number of favorable votes are accumulated. Vote messages in the TRANSFER category are not votes, they are transitory favorable votes, so do not credit them to the votes, only to the favorable votes. This is where lines 6 through 8 come from. Note: For votes in the DISAGREE category, the *agreeNum* must be 0. For votes in the AGREE category, the *agreeNum* may be 0 or 1. So the count of favorable votes can be written in the way shown in line 8. If the number of votes received and the number of favorable votes obtained both reach $f + 1$, it means that the id application was successful. A DECISION message is then broadcast and the state changes to DECIDING. This processing is shown in lines 9 through 19. Line 24 assigns *voteNum* to 1. The intent is that this variable is subsequently used to count the acknowledge messages received.

4.2.3   Handling of Decision and Acknowledge and Validation Messages

After the proposer succeeds in applying for an id, it broadcasts a decision message to the other replicas in the system. The other replicas receive the decision message and call the *processDecision* function to process it. The implementation of this function is shown in Code 4.7. The normal scenario is to put the transaction attached to the message into its own *globalQueue*, change its state to VALIDATING, and then respond with an acknowledge message. This processing is shown in lines 2 through 10. In a faulty situation, the normal replica may receive multiple DECISION messages. For example, the proposer fails during the broadcast of a DECISION message, resulting in only a portion of the replicas receiving the DECISION message. The result is that the replicas that received the decision message time out in the VALIDATING state and then broadcast the decision message. Thus, it is possible for a replica to receive more than one decision message. Each time it receives a DECISION message, it replies with an acknowledge message as long as it is not in the RECOVERING state, as shown in line 9.

Code 4.7 Implementation of the processDecision function
```
(1)    void processDecision(Decision*decision) {
(2)      if ( decision->id == idCount + 1 && decision-
         >senderId ! = myselfId) {
(3)        if (state == FREE||state==PROPOSING||state==VOTING||s
           tate==EXPIRING)) {
(4)          globalQueue->addItem(decision->transaction);
(5)          state = VALIDATING;
(6)          timer->restart( );
(7)        }
(8)        if (state ! = RECOVERING)
(9)          response(decision->senderId, ACK,
             decision->id);
(10)     }
(11)     else if (decision->id > idCount + 1)    // own
         falls behind
(12)       processOutdating(decision->senderId,
           decision->id);
(13)     return;
(14)   }
```

For a received decision message, if its attached id is greater than its own *idCount* + 1, it means that it missed the reception of the consensus message due to a fault. At this point, it should be transferred to the fault recovery state, which is handled as shown in lines 11 and 12. Unlike a proposal message, the id attached to a decision message cannot be less than its own *idCount* + 1. The reason for this is that the id attached to a proposal message is the applicant's own *idCount* + 1 value, whereas a decision message is a message that is sent after a consensus has been achieved by the system, and the id attached to it is global information.

The Proposer waits for the acknowledge message in the DECIDING state after broadcasting the DECISION message and counts it. The processing of acknowledge messages is shown in Code 4.8. When the number of acknowledge messages received reaches $f + 1$, it broadcasts a VALIDATION message and returns to the FREE state. Once in the FREE state, the *receiveQueue* is checked to see if it is empty. If it is not empty, the next global unique id application is initiated. After returning to the FREE state, the timer is turned off, as shown in line 8. The reason is that there is no concept of timeout in the FREE state.

Code 4.8 Implementation of the processAck function
```
(1)    void processAck(Ack* ack) {
(2)        if (state == DECIDING && ack->id == idCount + 1) {
(3)            voteNum ++;
(4)            if (voteNum == f+1) {
(5)                Transaction *trx =
                     globalQueue->getItemById(ack->id);
(6)                trx->validation = TRUE;
(7)                broadcast(VALIDATION, myselfId, ack->id, trx);
(8)                timer->stop();
(9)                idCount ++;
(10)               state = FREE;
(11)               if ( not receiveQueue->isEmpty())
(12)                   startupConsensus();
(13)           }
(14)       }
(15)       return;
(16)   }
```

Once an acceptor receives the DECISION message, it waits for the VALIDATING message in the VALIDATING state. The processing of the VALIDATING message is shown in Code 4.9. Note: The proposer brings the transaction on again when broadcasting the VALIDATING message for the convenience of those replicas that did not receive the DECISION message. For example, when there is a temporary fault in the network, this may result in one or some replicas not receiving a DECISION message, but receiving a VALIDATION message. Also, the DECISION message received earlier may be inconsistent with the VALIDATION message received later. For example, suppose a network fault occurs while the proposer is broadcasting a decision message, resulting in none of the replicas in the largest partition receiving the decision message. Subsequently, a wait timeout occurs in the largest partition and the current id application is aborted. For the validation message in the abort consensus, its transaction is null. This is where the inconsistency between validation and decision occurs. This is the origin of lines 5 and 6.

For validation messages, the attached finalization is placed in the *globalQueue* only if the replica is not in the RECOVERING state. If it is in the RECOVERING state, only the *idCount* is updated, as shown in line 3. In fault recovery, the missing finalized items are claimed in turn. The advantage of this processing is that the finalizations in the *globalQueue* are sequential and there are no gaps in between. In addition, when a validation message is received, it is possible that the id attached to it is greater than its own *idCount* + 1. This is due to a fault. The replica should be transferred to the fault recovery state, as shown in lines 13 and 14.

Code 4.9 Implementation of the processValidation function
```
(1)     void processValidation( Validation *validation) {
(2)        if (validation->id == idCount + 1 && validation-
           >senderId ! = myselfId) {
(3)          idCount ++;
(4)          if (state ! = RECOVERING) {
(5)             globalQueue->deleteItemById(validation->id);
(6)             globalQueue->addItem(validation->trx);
(7)             timer->stop( );
(8)             state = FREE;
(9)             if (not receiveQueue->isEmpty())
(10)               startupConsensus();
(11)         }
(12)       }
(13)       else if (validation->id > idCount + 1) // own
           lagging behind
(14)         processOutdating(validation->senderId,
                validation->id + 1);
(15)       return;
(16)    }
```

4.2.4 Handling of Termination and Outcome Messages

If a replica times out in the PROPOSING state, it means that either it is not in the largest partition itself, or the favorable votes were swallowed up by a fault. If a replica times out in the VOTING state, there are three possibilities: (1) it is not in the largest partition and cannot receive a DECISION message; (2) the proposer has a fault and did not send a DECISION message; and (3) the proposer cannot send a DECISION message because it did not receive enough favorable votes. In short, in the PROPOSING state or VOTING state timeout, the DECISION message is missing. So it broadcasts a termination message, which is motivated by ending the current id application. When a replica receives a termination message, it calls the *processTermination* function to process it, which is implemented as shown in Code 4.10. The states in which no decision message is received are FREE, PROPOSING, VOTING, and EXPIRING, so in these states, a posture message is replied to the termination message with the option AGREE, as shown in lines 3 through 6.

If you receive a termination message in VALIDATING status, it means that you have already received a decision message before, but the sender of the termination message has not received it. This indicates that the proposer has failed in broadcasting the decision message. Therefore, the decision message should be broadcast on behalf of the proposer, which is where lines 7 through 14 come from. Multiple replicas may time out at the same time, so one replica may receive multiple termination messages. When the first termination message is received, the state changes from VALIDATING to DECIDING, so if the termination message is received in the DECIDING state, simply reply with a posture message with the option OPPOSE as shown in lines 15 through 16.

For the sender of a termination message, after broadcasting the termination message, it possibly receives a posture message. The processing of the posture message is shown in Code 4.11. There are only two option values attached to the posture message: (1) AGREE and (2) OPPOSE. If it is OPPOSE, then it is sufficient to change its state to VOTING, since the ensuing message will be a DECISION. If it is AGREE, it is counted with the variable *voteNum*. When it times out again, if it is still in the EXPIRING state and the value of *voteNum* is greater than or equal to $f + 1$, it indicates that it is in the largest partition and that no replica has received a DECISION message. So the abort consensus is reached: set the transaction associated with the id to null.

Code 4.10 Implementation of the processTermination Function

```
(1)      void processTermination(Termination *termination ) {
(2)        if( termination->id == idCount +1) {
(3)          if (state==FREE||state == PROPOSING || state == VOTING||state == EXPIRING) {
(4)            response(termination->senderId, POSTURE, termination->id, AGREE);
(5)            timer->restart();
(6)          }
(7)          else if (state == VALIDATING) {
(8)            response(termination->senderId, POSTURE, termination->id, OPPOSE);
(9)            Transaction * trx = globalqueue->getItemById(termination->id);
(10)           broadcast(DECISION, myselfId, termination->id, trx);
(11)           voteNum = 1;
(12)           state = DECIDING;
(13)           timer->restart();
(14)         }
(15)         else if (state == DECIDING)
(16)           response(termination->senderId, POSTURE, termination->id, OPPOSE);
(17)       }
(18)       return;
(19)     }
```

Code 4.11 Implementation of the processOutcome function
```
(1)     void processOutcome(Posture *posture) {
(2)         if (posture->id == idCount +1 && state ==
            EXPIRING) {
(3)             if (posture->option == AGREE)
(4)                 voteNum ++;
(5)             else {
(6)                 state = VOTING;
(7)                 timer->restart();
(8)             }
(9)         }
(10)        return;
(11)    }
```

4.2.5 Handling of Timeout Messages

Timeout messages do not come from a replica, but from a timer. The replica has seven states: FREE, PROPOSING, VOTING, DECIDING, VALIDATING, and EXPIRING and RECOVERING. All states except FREE have a time limit concept. The time limit is timed with a timer. Once it has expired, the timer delivers a timeout message. The processing of the timeout message is shown in Code 4.12. If the replica is timed out in the PROPOSING or VOTING state, the processing is to change the state to EXPIRING and then broadcast the termination message to the other replicas in the system, as shown in lines 2 through 7. If the timeout is in the EXPIRING state, it depends on whether the favorable votes received are greater than or equal to $f + 1$. If so, abort consensus is reached, and a DECISION message is broadcast, as shown in lines 8 through 15. Line 9 is constructing a transaction with empty content, whose id value is *idCount* + 1 and whose validation value is FALSE.

If a replica times out in the VALIDATING state, the proposer has failed or is not in the largest partition, preventing itself from receiving validation messages. Therefore, It should take over for the proposer to do the rest of the work, as shown in lines 16 through 22. First, the decision message is broadcast, with the intention that any replicas that did not receive the decision message will receive it. Subsequently, when $f + 1$ acknowledge messages have been received, a validation message is broadcast, thus completing the application for the current id.

During the EXPIRING state, the replica will change to the VOTING state as soon as it receives a posture message with an OPPOSE option value. Therefore, the timeout in the EXPIRING state indicates that all the received posture messages have an option value of AGREE, and if the number of posture messages in the AGREE category is less than $f + 1$, the replica is not in the largest partition due to a network fault. A replica that is not in the largest partition is behind the system state because it does not receive a validation message, and therefore should be transferred to the

4.2 Specific Implementation of the Paxos Protocol

fault recovery state. This processing is shown in lines 23 through 28. When a replica times out in the DECIDING state, it is because it cannot receive enough acknowledge messages. It can then infer that it is not in the largest partition and should also execute the code shown in lines 23 through 28. Both scenarios cause the replica to migrate to the RECOVERING state, as shown in line 24.

There are two scenarios where the replica changes to the RECOVERING state. The first scenario, as described above, is that the replica is acting as a proposer and has inferred that it is not in the largest partition due to a network fault because it has not received enough response messages. In this case, once the timeout in the RECOVERING state has expired, an attempt should be made to broadcast a recovery message to proactively try to see if the network fault has been lifted. This processing is shown in lines 29 through 34. Another scenario is that the replica, acting as an acceptor, receives a PROPOSAL message, or DECISION message, or VALIDATION message, and realizes that the attached id is greater than its own *idCount* + 1. This scenario indicates that it is missing the validation message due to a fault. If you are not in the RECOVERING state, you should migrate to the RECOVERING state and request the missing validation message from the sender of the above message. This processing is placed in the implementation of the *processOutdating* function, as shown in Code 4.5.

Code 4.12 Implementation of the processTimeout function
```
(1)    void processTimeout( ) {
(2)        if (state == PROPOSING || state == VOTING) {
(3)        broadcast(TERMINATION, myselfId, idCount + 1);
(4)        state = EXPIRING;
(5)        voteNum = 1;
(6)        timer->restart( );
(7)        }
(8)        else if (state == EXPIRING && voteNum >= f+1) {
(9)        Transaction trx* = new Transaction( null, idCount+1, FALSE);
(10)       globalQueue->addItem(trx);
(11)       broadcast(DECISION, myselfId, idCount + 1, trx);
(12)       voteNum = 1;
(13)       state = DECIDING;
(14)       timer->restart( );
(15)       }
(16)       else if (state == VALIDATING) {
(17)               Transaction * trx = globalqueue->getItemById(idCount +1 );
(18)       broadcast(DECISION, myselfId, idCount + 1, trx);
(19)       voteNum = 1;
```

```
(20)      state = DECIDING;
(21)      timer->restart( );
(22)    }
(23)    else if ((state == EXPIRING && voteNum < f+1) ||
          state == DECIDING) {
(24)      state = RECOVERING;
(25)      lastRecoveryLine = idCount;
(26)      fetching = FALSE;
(27)      timer->restart( );
(28)    }
(29)    else if (state == RECOVERING) {
(30)      broadcast(RECOVERY, myselfId, lastRecoveryLine);
(31)      voteNum = 1;
(32)      fetching = FALSE;
(33)      timer->restart( );
(34)    }
(35)    return;
(36) }
```

4.2.6 Handling of Recovery and Progress Messages

When a replica times out in the RECOVERING state, it broadcasts a recovery message to the other replicas in the system. For the other replicas, once the recovery message is received, the *processRecovery* function is called to process it. The implementation of this function is shown in Code 4.13. Processing is very simple, that is, in response to a progress message, and accompanied by their *idCount* value.

Code 4.13 Implementation of the function processRecovery

```
(1)  void processRecovery(Recovery *recovery) {
(2)    if (recovery->senderId ! = myselfId)
(3)      response(recovery->senderId, PROGRESS,
              idCount);
(4)    return;
(5)  }
```

4.2 Specific Implementation of the Paxos Protocol

Code 4.14 Implementation of the processProgress function

```
(1)     void processProgress(Progress *progress) {
(2)         if (state == RECOVERING) {
(3)             voteNum ++;
(4)             if ( progress->idCount > lastRecoveryLine )
(5)                 provider = progress->senderId;
(6)             if ( progress->idCount > idCount ) {
(7)                 idCount = progress->idCount;
(8)                 provider = progress->senderId;
(9)             }
(10)            if ( voteNum == f+1) {
(11)                if (lastRecoveryLine == idCount) {
(12)                    timer->stop();
(13)                    state = FREE;
(14)                    receiveQueue->clear( );
(15)                }
(16)                else if (lastRecoveryLine < idCount &&
                        fetching == FALSE) {
(17)                    request(provider, FETCH,
                            lastRecoveryLine + 1);
(18)                    fetching = TRUE;
(19)                    timer->restart();
(20)                }
(21)            }
(22)        }
(23)        return;
(24)    }
```

After the replica in RECOVERING state broadcasts the recovery message, it receives the response message *progress*. The processing of the progress message is shown in Code 4.14. First, the progress message is counted and stored in the global variable *voteNum*. The purpose of counting is to determine whether or not one is in the largest partition. Only if one is in the largest partition can it complete fault recovery and become a normal replica again. It is also important to check whether the *idCount* value attached to the progress message received is greater than own *idCount* value. If it is, it means that one is missing the receipt of the validation message, and should update own *idCount*, as well as the provider value. This processing is shown in lines 6 through 9.

For the received progress messages, if the number reaches $f + 1$, it means that one is in the largest partition. At this point, if the *lastRecoveryLine* value is equal to the *idCount* value, it means that the reception of validation message is not missing. Thus, the fault recovery is complete and the changeover to the FREE state is done, as shown in lines 11 through 15. After the fault is recovered, all the transactions in the *receiveQueue* should be cleared, as shown in line 14. The reason is that these transactions lost their timeliness due to the fault. The client should also have experienced a wait timeout at this point. If the *lastRecoveryLine* value is less than the *idCount* value, it means that it is missing the receipt of validation message and should ask the provider for it. This processing is shown in lines 16 through 20.

4.2.7 Handling of Fetch and Item Messages

When a replica in the RECOVERING state finds itself missing the receipt of a validation message, it sends a fetch message to the provider for the specified item. When the replica receives a fetch message, it calls the *processFetch* function to process it, which is implemented as shown in Code 4.15. Processing is as simple as responding to an item message with the requester's desired customization. Specifically, it looks up the corresponding transaction from the *globalQueue* based on the id attached to the fetch message, as shown in line 2.

Code 4.15 Implementation of the processFetch function
```
(1)     void processFetch(Fetch *fetch) {
(2)         Transaction * trx =
            globalQueue->getItemById(fetch->id);
(3)         response(fetch->senderId, ITEM, fetch->id, trx);
(4)         return;
(5)     }
```

Once the replica in the RECOVERING state receives the item message, it calls the *processItem* function to process it, the implementation of which is shown in Code 4.16. All that is done is to place the finalized item attached to the message into the *globalQueue*, and then check to see if the recovery is complete. If recovery is complete, it changes to the FREE state, as shown in lines 5 through 9. Otherwise, it continues to ask for the next missing item.

After the replica issues a fetch request, it is possible that the response message item is not received because the provider of the fixation fails. A timeout occurs in the RECOVERING state. Once the timeout is reached, the replica broadcasts a

4.2 Specific Implementation of the Paxos Protocol   279

RECOVER message in order to find a new fixation provider and ask it for its missing items. This processing is shown in lines 28 through 33 of Code 4.12, and lines 4 through 9 of Code 4.14.

Code 4.16 Implementation of the function processItem

```
(1)     void processItem(Item *item) {
(2)         if (state == RECOVERING && item->id ==
            lastRecoveryLine + 1 ) {
(3)             globalQueue->deleteItemById(item->id);
(4)             globalQueue->addItem(item->trx);
(5)             if (lastRecoveryLine +1 == idCount) {
(6)                 timer->stop();
(7)                 state = FREE;
(8)                 receiveQueue->clear( );
(9)             }
(10)            else {
(11)                lastRecoveryLine++;
(12)                request(provider, FETCH,
                    lastRecoveryLine + 1);
(13)                timer->restart();
(14)            }
(15)        }
(16)        return;
(17)    }
```

4.2.8 Characterization of Implementations

A replica is always in one of the seven states and has no timeout only when it is in the FREE state. When a replica is not in the largest partition due to a network fault, it always receives a timeout message as long as it is not in the FREE state, and does not return to the FREE state. If the timeout is in the PROPOSING state or VOTING state, the replica moves to the EXPIRING state. If the timeout is in the EXPIRING state, it will not receive $f + 1$ posture messages and will migrate to the RECOVERING state. If the timeout occurs in the VALIDATING state, it is migrated to the DECIDING state. In the DECIDING state, a timeout occurs because $f + 1$ acknowledge messages are not received, and the state is migrated to the RECOVERING state. In the RECOVERING state, a timeout loop occurs because $f + 1$ progress messages are not received.

The largest partition does not block due to system faults. If a decision message is not received in the largest partition due to a fault, the replica in the largest partition times out in the PROPOSING state or the VOTING state and migrates to the

EXPIRING state. If the EXPIRING state times out, the replica in the largest partition will either migrate to the DECIDING state because it receives $f + 1$ posture messages, or it will migrate to the VALIDATING state because it receives a decision message; in the DECIDING state, it will migrate to the FREE state because it receives $f + 1$ acknowledge messages. In the VALIDATING state, the state is changed to FREE because a validation message is received.

A replica is definitely able to complete fault recovery after troubleshooting and becomes a normal replica in the largest partition again. If a replica fails, it reboots after troubleshooting. The first thing it does after rebooting is to broadcast a recovery message in the RECOVERING state. If it is a network fault, then the replica will keep timing out in the RECOVERING state and keep broadcasting recovery messages. After broadcasting a recovery message, at least one of the first $f + 1$ progress messages received must be from the largest partition. Therefore, after receiving $f + 1$ progress messages, it will be able to restore its *idCount* to the latest state of the system. During the subsequent request for those missing items, the requester may time out due to a fault of the provider of the expected item. Once the timeout occurs, the replica broadcasts the recovery message again to find a new provider. Thus, the request for the missing items is always completed. Fault recovery is signaled by the replica state changing from RECOVERING to FREE.

4.3 Practical Byzantine Fault Tolerance Protocols

Practical Byzantine Fault Tolerance protocol is abbreviated as PBFT protocol. In the Paxos protocol described above, when a replica has applied for a globally unique id, it broadcasts it, along with its value (i.e., the transaction), to other replicas in the form of a DECISION message to achieve system consistency. In a system such as Bitcoin, any organization can join and add replicas to the system. The Paxos protocol makes each replica dispensable for the purpose of providing services to the public, provided that more than half of the replicas are able to communicate with each other and function properly. The system consistency achieved by the Paxos protocol has a prerequisite, which is that the replica does not commit any wrongdoing. If the replicas are evil, system consistency is a dead letter. For example, when replica R broadcasts a decision message, if the ID value sent to replica $R1$ is transaction $T1$ and the ID value sent to replica $R2$ is transaction $T2$, then system consistency will be completely lost.

In the framework of the Paxos protocol, it is impossible to break the consistency of the system even if there are one or more evil-doing replicas in the system. Can this be done? How can it be done? This is the question that the PBFT protocol [8] is trying to answer. It is feasible for a replica to do evil. For example, in a decentralized system like Bitcoin, any business can join and add replicas to the system. The program that the replicas run is open source, so a business can modify the program, add malicious code, and then launch one or more replicas in the system. For example, the Paxos protocol originally stated that each replica had one and only one

4.3 Practical Byzantine Fault Tolerance Protocols

favorable vote for an id. A business can modify the program to vote in favor of every proposal it receives, maliciously messing with the system's rules. In the original protocol, the proposer passed the same id value (i.e., transaction) to each replica via a DECISION message. An enterprise can modify the program to send different transactions to different replicas to intentionally disrupt the consistency of replicas in the system.

In the case where a replica may do evil, replicas in decentralized systems are divided into two categories: (1) normal replicas and (2) faulty replicas. Normal replicas do not do evil and perform the work specified in the protocol properly. Faulty replicas, also called Byzantine replicas, include both replicas that do not work due to faults and replicas that work, but do evil. Evil-doing faults are also called Byzantine faults [10]. In the PBFT protocol, the maximum number of faulty replicas that can be tolerated is f when the number of replicas in the system is $3f + 1$. In other words, even if there are evil replicas, as long as their number does not exceed f, the system will not be inconsistent due to the faulty replicas, and will still be able to provide services normally. Consistency here refers to the consistency of normal replicas.

In the PBFT protocol, the replica does evil with the intention of messing up the consistency of the system. A replica cannot achieve the purpose of messing up the system by not accepting a client's transaction request. Suppose a client accesses the system through replica R. If R does not accept its transaction request, then the client cannot get the response result from it. The client will then assume that R has failed and will choose another replica to access the system again. The replica also cannot mess up the system by tampering with the client's transaction request. This is because the client uses a private key to encrypt the transaction request before sending it. Asymmetric encryption [11] makes the transaction request tamper-proof. A replica can violate the rule on assigning ids to transactions based on their arrival order. This operation only disrupts the fairness of the system's service, not its consistency. A replica can process a transaction incorrectly. This also does not break system consistency. Because the result of its processing is inconsistent with the results processed by other normal replicas. Clients and normal replicas can recognize inconsistent results and then discard them.

In the Paxos protocol, each replica has one and only one favorable vote for an id. For this rule, there are two ways for a replica to be evil: (1) not vote in favor of its own id, and (2) vote in favor of ids all over the place. For this reason, in the PBFT protocol, when a replica applies for an id, the number of favorable votes required is no longer more than 1/2, but more than 2/3. Because of the addition of the Evil Fault, the threshold has been raised. The failure of an evil replica to vote in favor is equivalent to the occurrence of a nonworking fault. The Paxos protocol has taken this scenario into account. In the case of violating the rule that each replica has one and only one favorable vote for an id, given the two competing proposers, the total votes are at most $4f + 1$, of which $3f + 1$ come from one-person-one-vote, and the other f come from duplicate votes by the f faulty replicas. With a maximum of $4f + 1$ favorable votes, it is not possible for two competing proposers to both receive $2f + 1$

favorable votes. This is the origin of the requirement to get up to $2f + 1$ favorable votes.

In the PBFT protocol, each acceptor verifies the legitimacy of the received DECISION message to prevent the proposer from being evil. This requires the proposer to broadcast the DECISION message with the $2f + 1$ favorable votes it has received. In order to validate one-person-one-vote, each replica has to use its private key encrypt its favorable vote to prevent it from being tampered with by other replicas. A favorable vote encrypted with a private key is also called a signed favorable vote. Once an acceptor receives a decision message from a proposer, it checks each of the attached $2f + 1$ favorable votes to ensure that they are valid and that there are no duplicates. This is done by decrypting each signed favorable vote using the issuer's public key to get the voter's identification number and the id value voted for. The decision message is only recognized as legitimate if it is confirmed that each favorable vote is legitimate and there are no duplicates.

Another way for the Proposer to do evil is to assign different values to the globally unique ids, i.e., different transactions. Assuming that the evil replica R applies a globally unique id of 9, it broadcasts a decision message to the other three normal replicas of the system, $R1$, $R2$, and $R3$, transmitting the value of the id, transactions $T1$, $T2$, and $T3$, respectively, which causes the normal replicas, $R1$, $R2$, and $R3$, to be inconsistent with each other. In order to enable the normal replicas to distinguish such inconsistencies, the PBFT protocol requires that the proposer encrypts its content (i.e., id and its value) with a private key to form a signed decision message, and then broadcasts it to the other replicas in the system together with the signed favorable votes obtained. After receiving the decision message, each acceptor signs the decision using its own private key, and then attaches it to the acknowledge message as the response to the proposer. When the proposer receives $2f + 1$ acknowledge messages, it broadcasts a validation message, which is accompanied by the $2f + 1$ acknowledges it received.

The proposer signs the decision message with the intention that any acceptor cannot tamper with it. Similarly, the acceptor signs the received signed decision with the intention that the proposer cannot tamper with it. Thus, when each acceptor receives the validation message, it knows the content of the decision that the proposer sent to $2f + 1$ acceptors. This forces the proposer not to arbitrarily set different id values for different acceptors when broadcasting the decision message. Otherwise, after broadcasting the validation message, this malicious behavior will be known by acceptors. For the $2f + 1$ acknowledges attached to the validation message, each acceptor first decrypts the acknowledges with the public key of the acknowledge sender to get the signed decision, and then decrypts the decision with the public key of the proposer to get the content of the decision. If all $2f + 1$ decisions are the same, accept the validation message. Otherwise, reject it.

For a system with $3f + 1$ replicas, the number of acknowledges attached to the validation message by the proposer is required by the PBFT protocol to be more than 2/3 (i.e., $2f + 1$ acknowledges) rather than more than 1/2. An example is given to illustrate the necessity of this condition. For ease of presentation, the $2f + 1$ normal replicas are divided into two groups, A and B, where group A has $f + 1$ normal replicas and group B has f normal replicas. The proposer is a faulty replica, and when broadcasting the decision message, the id value passed to group A is transaction $T1$, and the id value passed to group B and the other f-1 faulty replicas is transaction $T2$. Since the number of group B plus f faulty replicas exceeds half, the proposer can intentionally select only the acknowledge messages from group B and the f-1 faulty replicas when broadcasting the validation message, and intentionally broadcast the validation message only to group B and the f-1 faulty replicas. Thus, group B and the f-faulty replicas accept the proposer's validation message with id value $T2$.

Subsequently, the normal replicas in group A experience a timeout waiting for a VALIDATION message. It is then concluded that the proposer has failed, and a decision message is broadcast instead of the proposer. The id value at this point is $T1$. The combination of group A and the f faulty replicas also exceeds half through the process. At this point it is assumed that all f faulty replicas are evil and also respond to acknowledge the decision messages. Assuming that those acknowledge messages from group A and the f faulty replicas happen to be received first, before that from group B, thus a new VALIDATION message with an id value of $T1$ is formed and accepted by group A. The reason is the number of acknowledge messages from group A and the f faulty replicas reaches $2f+1$. This leads to an inconsistency between group A and group B. If the number of acknowledges is required to be $2f+1$, then group B plus the f faulty replicas is not enough to form a validation message.

For the above scenario, an example is given. Suppose f is equal to 1 and the proposer is the faulty replica R. When broadcasting a decision message, the id values passed to the normal replicas $R1$, $R2$, and $R3$ are transactions $T1$, $T1$, and $T2$, respectively. When broadcasting a validation message, it is sent only to $R1$ and $R2$, with $2f+1$ (i.e., 3) acknowledges from R, $R1$, and $R2$, respectively. Thus, validation is legal and accepted by $R1$ and $R2$. Subsequently, $R3$ times out in waiting for the validation message, and then broadcast the decision message instead of the proposer, with the ID value being transaction $T2$. Replica R, despite having accepted validation, does evil and responds with an acknowledge message to $R3$. At this point, $R3$ can only get two acknowledges, from R and $R3$ itself, less than $2f+1$. Thus, $R3$ fails to form a new validation. In response to $R3$'s decision, both $R1$ and $R2$ respond with a validation message. Because the validation messages from $R1$ and $R2$ are legitimate, $R3$ will accept them. In this case, the normal replicas $R1$, $R2$, and $R3$ remain consistent despite the fact that R is evil three times.

Reflection 4-4: In the above example, replica R did evil 3 times, specifically which 3 evils?

It follows that in the PBFT protocol, each client in the system, as well as each replica, has its own private key for signing. Each replica holds the public keys of all client as well as all other replicas. Clients sign their own transaction requests with their private keys, and replicas sign their own favorable votes and acknowledge messages with their private keys to prevent tampering by faulty replicas. In addition, the proposer broadcasts a decision message with $2f+1$ signed favorable votes, and a validation message with $2f+1$ signed acknowledges, so that the acceptors can verify the legitimacy of the message.

After consistency is achieved, the transaction is executed by each replica. The last problem is how to return the execution result to the client. Each replica takes the execution result of the transaction and signs it with a private key to get a signed reply in case the proposer tampers with it. The signed reply is then sent to the proposer as a response to the validation message, and the proposer receives the signed reply, decrypts it with the issuer's public key, and obtains the execution result. Once it receives $f + 1$ identical replies, the proposer sends them to the client along with $f + 1$ signed replies. At this point, the entire transaction is processed. In this process, the proposer cannot do evil. Because if it does, it will be known by the client. Assuming that the proposer does not send a reply to the client, it causes the client to timeout. Once the client times out, it inquires the other replicas for the final end of the transaction request. $f + 1$ signed replies indicate that at least one of them is from a normal replica. $f + 1$ replies that are all the same indicate that the reply is correct.

From the above analysis, it can be seen that the PBFT protocol is based on the Paxos protocol, with the addition of the verification function, in order to prevent the evil replica from not adhering to the protocol and disrupting the system. The PBFT protocol makes it impossible for evil replicas to disrupt the consistency of the system, i.e., to tolerate the Byzantine fault. In the PBFT protocol, processing a client's transaction request involves three rounds of message interactions, as shown in Fig. 4.9. The enhancements of the PBFT protocol to the Paxos protocol are embodied in the following seven points: (1) each acceptor has to sign the favorable vote when it votes in favor of the proposal; (2) each acceptor has to sign its acknowledge

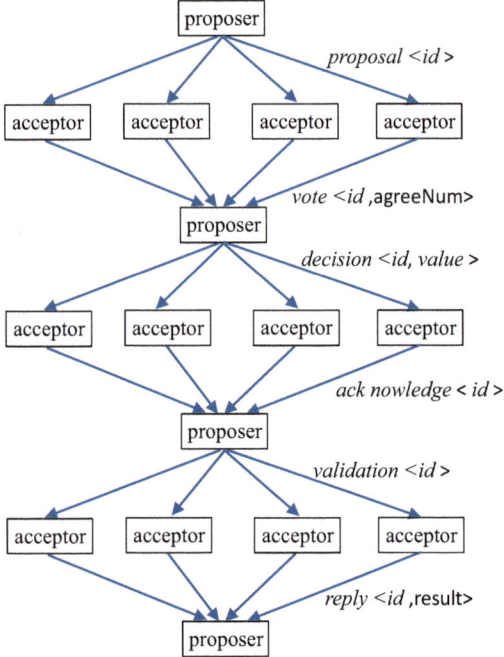

Fig. 4.9 Replica interactions in the PBFT protocol

when it replies to the decision message; (3) each acceptor has to sign the received decision; (4) when the proposer broadcasts a decision message, it is accompanied by a $2f + 1$ signed favorable votes; (5) when the proposer broadcasts a validation message, it is accompanied by a $2f + 1$ signed acknowledges; (6) when each acceptor replies to the proposer with a processing result, it signed the processing result; (7) the proposer, when replying to the client with the response result, needs to receives $f + 1$ identical replies from acceptors, and then replies to the client with the $f + 1$ signed replies.

4.4 Implementation of the PBFT Protocol

The PBFT protocol described in the previous section uses a private key signing method that has two purposes: (1) to make it impossible for a malicious replica to tamper with it, and (2) to force the malicious replica to have to comply with the protocol. The benefit of this approach is that the PBFT protocol is implemented by simply augmenting the Paxos protocol. However, the computational overhead of encrypting with a private key and decrypting with a public key is very high, especially when the amount of data to be encrypted is large. The problem that signatures are meant to solve can actually be solved by broadcasting. For example, instead of just sending a vote message to the proposer when voting in favor of a proposal, the vote message is broadcast to every replica in the system. Each replica then knows where each favorable vote is going. Again, this can force a malicious replica to have to follow the protocol, making it impossible to tamper with. Similarly, when replying to a decision with an acknowledge, instead of just sending an acknowledge message to the proposer, the content of the acknowledge is broadcast to every replica in the system. Thus, every replica knows the content of the decision that the proposer sends to each replica.

To prevent the client's transaction request from being tampered with by the proposer, the client may send the transaction request to $f + 1$ replicas. In order to ensure that normal replicas in the system can receive transaction requests that have not been tampered with, each of the $f + 1$ replicas that receive client's transaction request can be required to attach the transaction to the vote message when it broadcasts it to other replicas in the system. Thus, each replica can receive $f + 1$ id values. At least one of these $f + 1$ id values comes from the normal replica and has not been tampered with. Each replica checks to see if all of the $f + 1$ id values it receives are the same. It accepts the id value only if they are all the same. Otherwise, the id value is rejected. This ensures that transaction requests reach every normal replica without being tampered with. It also forces a malicious replica not to tamper with a client's transaction request. Once tampered with, it is discovered by the other replicas.

The above method has a prerequisite: when a replica receives a proposal message, it has to know that it has received the id value from the client. To do this, an index attribute is added to the transaction; the value of the index attribute consists of the client id and access timestamp, being able to globally identify the transaction request. It is the client's responsibility to assign a value to the transaction's index attribute. In addition, the proposer broadcasts a proposal message with the transaction's index value. When a replica receives a proposal message, if it can vote in favor of it, it has to look up in its *receiveQueue* based on the index value attached to the proposal to see if there is a transaction with that index value. If there is, the transaction is attached to the favorable vote and the vote message is broadcast.

The value of the transaction's index attribute can be used to solve another problem in addition to the above uses. After a client submits a transaction request, if it does not get a response, or if it finds an inconsistency in the response, it will come back to the system through another replica to inquire about the final outcome of the transaction. At this point, the client needs to be able to present transaction identification information. The value of the transaction's Index attribute is specified by the client and is naturally known to the client. Therefore, the value of the transaction's Index attribute can also be used as the transaction's identification information, which can be used by the client to access the system and inquire the final end of the transaction.

To prevent the execution result of a transaction from being tampered with by a malicious replica, each of these $f + 1$ replicas receiving the client's transaction request can be required to return its own execution result to the client so that the client can verify that the execution result has not been tampered with. At least one of these $f + 1$ returned execution results is from a normal replica whose execution result is correct. The client checks these $f + 1$ returned results, and if they are not all identical, it knows that there is a Byzantine fault. This treatment ensures that the execution results are not tampered with, and also forces the malicious replica not to do evil. Because if it does, it will be detected by the client.

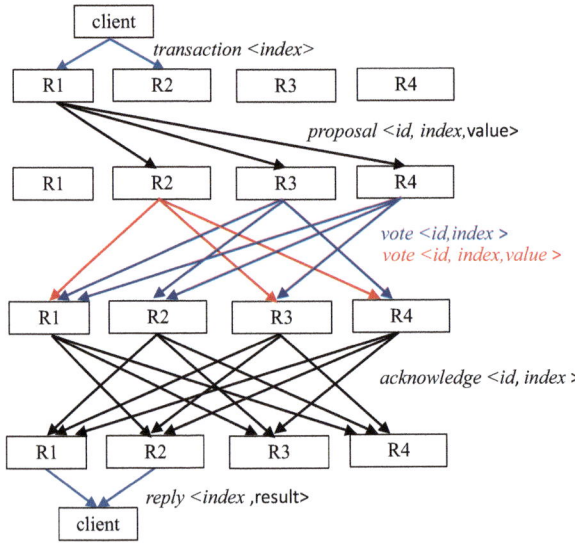

Fig. 4.10 Message broadcast-based tamper-proof implementation of the PBFT protocol

An example of a broadcast-based implementation of PBFT to protect against tampering and replica mischief is shown in Fig. 4.10. The system in this example consists of four replicas $R1$, $R2$, $R3$, and $R4$, hence the value of f is 1. The client sends the transaction request to two replicas. When $R2$ in the Figure votes in favor of the proposal, the broadcast vote contains the id value, which is the content of the transaction request. Due to the id value attached to the proposal message and the fact that the vote message is broadcast to other replicas in the system, each replica can come up with its own DECISION as long as it receives $2f + 1$ favorable votes on its own and $f + 1$ identical ID values, and then broadcasts the acknowledge message. Since the acknowledge message is broadcast, each replica can derive the validation by itself as long as it receives $2f + 1$ acknowledge messages by itself. It can be seen that when the vote and acknowledge are broadcast, the broadcasting and receiving of the decision message and validation message are eliminated.

4.5 Summary of the Chapter

A centralized system is controlled by a single service provider. Clients use the service system based on trust in the service provider. Maintenance of data is the responsibility of the service provider. The correctness of the data, as well as the fairness of the service, is predicated on the clients' trust in the service provider. In addition, the service is provided by a single point, and in the event of a single point of fault, the service is unavailable to clients. In contrast, a decentralized system no longer consists of a single node, but of multiple replicas. Different replicas are attributed to different service providers. Decentralized systems have three distinct new qualities compared to centralized systems: (1) anything is no longer up to a single service provider, but is decided by multiple service providers by mutual deliberation; (2) under the premise that more than half of the normal replicas are available, any replica (or any service provider) is no longer essential for service provision, but is optional; and (3) even if there is a malicious replica in the system, it is no longer necessary to provide the service. There is a malicious replica that wants to disrupt the system's consistency by messing up, it will not succeed.

In the Paxos protocol, as long as the number of normal replicas exceeds half, any fault will not block the normal service of the system. In the PBFT protocol, the consistency of the system is guaranteed even if the number of Byzantine faulty replicas reaches f in a system consisting of $3f + 1$ replicas. That means the system can tolerate f Byzantine faults. Fault tolerance is realized by consensus. In Paxos protocol, any decision only requires more than half of the replicas to agree, and does not require all of them to agree. In the PBFT protocol, the threshold for consensus is raised from more than half to more than two-thirds due to the addition of Byzantine faults. The decentralized transaction commit protocol consists of three elements: (1) a protocol for committing transactions when there are no faults; (2) a protocol for how normal replicas continue to work when there are faults (i.e., a termination protocol); and (3) a fault recovery protocol.

Exercises

1. In the PBFT protocol, how does a normal replica respond in the presence of a fault scenario? And how does a faulty replica recover from the fault? Write the implementation code of the PBFT protocol with reference to the specific implementation of the Paxos protocol in Sect. 4.2.
2. What are the costs of the gains made by decentralization?
3. In the Paxos protocol implementation given in Sect. 4.2, when there is competition, it is simply the size of the replica's identification number that determines who takes priority. Consult the sources to see what is used to determine who takes priority in the three decentralized implementations of the blockchain: Bitcoin, Ethereum, and Conflux.
4. Blockchain is a decentralized distributed database that is divided into three categories: (1) public chain; (2) federated chain; and (3) private chain. Typical public chains are Bitcoin, Ethereum, and Conflux, which are characterized by the fact that any enterprise is free to add replicas to the system with a large number of replicas. For public chains, should we consider Byzantine faults? Why? Private chains are usually managed and maintained by a single enterprise, with replicas provided by its various departments. For private chains, should we consider Byzantine faults? Why? What is the difference between a federated chain as opposed to a public chain and a private chain?
5. What are the differences between a private chain and the distributed database explained in Sect. 3.4?
6. Look up information to see how long it takes for bitcoin to get out of a block? Why is Bitcoin's transaction throughput so small? Please analyze the reasons.

References

1. Gengrui, Z., Fei, P., Yunhao, M., et al, *Reaching Consensus in the Byzantine Empire: A Comprehensive Review of BFT Consensus Algorithms*. ACM Computing Surveys, 2024, 56 (5): p. 1–41.
2. Leslie, L., Dahlia, M., Lidong, Z., *Vertical Paxos and Primary-Backup Replication*. In Proceedings of the 28th ACM symposium on Principles of distributed computing, 2009, p. 312–313.
3. Gencer, A. E., Basu, S., Eyal, I., et al, *Decentralization in Bitcoin and Ethereum Networks*. 22nd International Conference on Financial Cryptography and Data Security, 2018, p. 439–460.
4. Jinglin, Z., Debiao, H., Sherali, Z., et al, *Integrated Blockchain and Cloud Computing Systems: A Systematic Survey, Solutions, and Challenges*. ACM Computing Surveys, 2021, 54(8): p. 1–36.
5. Jim, G., Leslie, L., *Consensus on Transaction Commit*. ACM Transactions on Database Systems, 2006, 31(1): p. 133–160.
6. Leslie, L., *The part-time parliament*. ACM Transactions on Computer Systems, 1998, 16(2): p. 133–169.
7. Jie, X., Cong, W., Xiaohua, J., *A Survey of Blockchain Consensus Protocols*. ACM Computing Surveys, 2023, 55(13s): p. 1–35.

References

8. Miguel, C., Barbara, L., *Practical byzantine fault tolerance and proactive recovery.* ACM Transactions on Computer Systems, 2002, 11(1): p. 62–97.
9. Leslie, L., *The part-time parliament.* Concurrency: The Works of Leslie Lamport, 2019, p. 277–317.
10. Leslie, L., Robert, S., Marshall, P., *The Byzantine Generals Problem.* the Works of Leslie Lamport, 2019, p. 203–226.
11. Eiichiro, F., Tatsuaki, O., *Secure Integration of Asymmetric and Symmetric Encryption Schemes.* In Proceedings of the 19th Annual International Cryptology Conference on Advances in Cryptology, 1999, p. 537–554.

Chapter 5
Virtualization and Cloud Computing

The meaning of cloud computing [1] is that cloud service providers provide platform services to enterprise customers, so that enterprise customers do not need to consider their own infrastructure such as server rooms, networks, servers, and so on, and do not need to hire business information systems operation and maintenance personnel, thus reducing information systems construction, operation, and maintenance expenses. By migrating their business information systems to the cloud and leaving them to the cloud service provider, enterprise customers can not only significantly reduce costs, but also achieve better service quality. For cloud service providers, deepening resource sharing improves resource utilization and reduces costs through large-scale sharing effect, making cloud services inexpensive.

A business information system is an umbrella term for applications and their data. A common business information system has two applications. One is a WEB application, also called a WEB server. The other is a data management application, also called a database server. Each application consists of two parts: (1) the application itself; (2) the runtime environment. An application depends on its runtime environment to run. For example, for a Windows 32 application, its most basic runtime environment is an X86 model computer and the Windows 32 operating system. Specifically, to the WEB application, it can only run normally when the network is normal and can access the database server. Therefore, its runtime environment further includes the network as well as the database server.

In the traditional approach, the runtime environment comes first, and then an application is built. For example, you build a Windows 32 application after you have an X86 computer and a Windows 32 operating system. Web applications are built after the network and database servers are in place. In other words, applications are designed, developed, and deployed based on the runtime environment. In many cases, the runtime environment is even assumed to be statically invariant. For example, the IP address of the database server to be accessed is treated as a constant. For applications that have already been built, they are now migrated to run on the cloud.

This requires the cloud platform to provide the environment for it to run. The next Sect. 5.1 details the coupling between an application and its runtime environment.

When you want to run an application, you need to build the environment for it. Traditionally, this is done by selecting a computer, installing support software such as an operating system on it, and then installing and configuring it. Cloud computing imposes a new requirement: to build the runtime environment under the premise of resource sharing. Specifically, an application should be able to run everywhere on the cloud; multiple applications running on a single computer should be isolated from each other and not interfere with each other. This goal cannot be achieved by asking applications to adapt to the cloud platform, but only by the cloud platform adapting to applications. The reason is that the customer's applications are usually so well established that it is not possible to modify them to fit the cloud platform. The solution is virtualization [1].

There appear many problems in making an application work everywhere on the cloud. The first one is the diversity of programming languages. An application is associated with a language, and a computer is also associated with a language. When the language associated with computer A is not the same as the language associated with application α, application α can not run directly on computer A. One solution to make computer A capable of running application α is to install a virtual machine (VM) [2] on computer A. A typical example would be to install a Java virtual machine (JVM) on Computer A to enable Computer A to run Java applications. The next Sect. 5.2, explains how applications run, showing how virtual machines are implemented to make a computer support multiple languages.

It is not enough to make a computer capable of running an application program. There is a deeper problem of whether it can run successfully or not. When an application migrates to the cloud, the resources in its runtime environment are shared by multiple applications from various customers. Services are also no longer in a static, unchanging state. This poses problems: resources may not always be available to an application; service ids may change dynamically. Both of these scenarios can prevent an application from running successfully. The solution to this problem is still virtualization. This virtualization is that of the runtime environment [3]. Specifically, a virtual machine is embedded between the application and the operating system. Instead of running directly on top of the operating system, the application runs on top of the virtual machine. The virtual machine provides an unchanging virtual runtime environment for the application. The next Sects. 5.3–5.14 explain what causes applications to run unsuccessfully, as well as strategies and methods for solving the problem.

Treating one physical resource as multiple virtual resources is a direction of virtualization. In contrast, treating multiple physical resources as one virtual resource is another direction of virtualization [4]. The first type of virtualization is disaggregated sharing, while the latter is combined sharing. Both cluster computing and cloud computing combine multiple computers to be used as a single computer. This combination is a dialectical unity of invariance and variability. Invariance is reflected in the fact that the way customers use the system remains the same. The variability is reflected in the quality of service of the system. In the eyes of customers, clusters and clouds have new qualities: infinite storage capacity, infinite throughput, responsive, always available, and cost-effective. Section 5.15 explains cloud service management systems.

5.1 The Application and Its Runtime Environment

An application is code written in a programming language. Programming languages are categorized into low-level programming languages and high-level programming languages. Machine language is a low-level programming language. Each model of computer has its own machine language. High-level programming languages are independent of the computer model and are universal. High-level programming languages can be divided into two categories: (1) compiled runtime languages, such as C/C++; (2) interpreted runtime languages, also called scripting languages, such as Shell scripting language and JavaScript language. To run an application program written in a compiled runtime language, it is necessary to select the runtime environment, i.e., to determine which model of computer will be used to run it. The selected computer is called the target computer. The application is then compiled into target code using the appropriate compiler [5]. If you want the application to run on more than one model of computer, you have to compile it once for each model of computer to generate the corresponding target code. Only the target code will run on the target computer.

When it comes to applications, you cannot get away from programming languages. When it comes to programming languages, you cannot get away from the computers that run applications. Computer here does not necessarily mean hardware. For example, an application written in a scripting language is run using an interpreter [6]. The interpreter is not hardware, but software. Java bytecode is run using the Java Virtual Machine, which is not hardware, but software. When the computer running an application is not hardware but software, it is often referred to as a virtual machine. Thus, the interpreter for application programs written in the Shell scripting language can be called a Shell virtual machine. The virtual machine itself is an application program. The virtual machine is used to run applications. This suggests that applications can be used to run applications. This iterative nature is one of the distinguishing qualities of software.

An application program cannot run without a runtime environment [6]. To illustrate the meaning of runtime environment, basic input & output system in ROM (BIOS) is an application program run by the CPU as soon as the computer is powered on. Its function is to detect computer hardware, and then load the operating system from disk to memory, and then let the CPU jump to execute the first instruction of the operating system. BIOS runs only on the bare metal computer and does not depend on any other software. In addition to BIOS, many embedded applications also run on bare metal. They, like BIOS, are burned into ROM memory and are run by the CPU as soon as the computer is powered on. The operating system is software, which can also be referred to as an application program. The operating system depends on BIOS to load it from disk into memory and for the CPU to jump to execute its first instruction. Therefore, the operating system's runtime environment refers to BIOS.

The runtime environment is the prerequisite on which an application program runs. Commonly, an application program's runtime environment is the operating system. The application relies on the operating system to load it from disk into memory and then to make the CPU jump to execute its first instruction. In addition, the application has to call the operating system's application programming interfaces (APIs). From this point of view, the application is also dependent on the operating system. An application written in a scripting language is run by an interpreter, so it runs in an interpreter environment. An interpreter is also an application, and its runtime environment is usually the operating system.

The runtime environment can also be regarded as the resources required for the normal operation of a program and the conditions that should be met. Resources include both hardware and software resources, and sometimes include data. For example, for a database management system, the amount of memory allocated to it cannot be lower than a certain threshold. When a WEB application wants to access a database server, the database server becomes its runtime environment. When the WEB application specifies that it wants to access a MySQL database, the database server must also be a MySQL server in its runtime environment. If the WEB application writes the IP address of the MySQL database as a constant in the source code, then its requirements for the runtime environment are even more strict: the IP address of the MySQL server must be the value it specifies.

The more constraints and limitations an application has on its runtime environment, the less adaptable it will be. Take the above WEB application as an example, if it solidifies the IP address of the MySQL server, then it will not be able to run properly when the IP address of the MySQL server cannot be set to the value it specifies. Applications are designed, developed, and deployed based on the runtime environment. Therefore, when determining the runtime environment, it is important to consider the constructability and ease of construction of the runtime environment. Still take the above WEB application as an example, if the IP address of MySQL server is set as a configurable parameter during the design and development, then the constructability of its runtime environment is significantly enhanced. If you further use the ODBC/JDBC driver to connect to the database server and use SQL to interact with the database server, the restriction of requiring the database server to be a MySQL server is lifted. If the WEB application is developed using the Java language, then its runtime environment is independent of the operating system.

In cloud computing [1], it is required that the customers' applications can run everywhere on the cloud. To achieve this goal, efforts can be made in two dimensions: (1) applications should be designed and developed in such a way that constraints and limitations should be minimized as far as their runtime environments are concerned, and (2) the cloud service providers' ability to build runtime environments to satisfy applications' runtime requirements can be improved. The problem-solving idea for both aspects is virtualization. In the design and development of applications, logical concepts should be summarized and abstracted from physical concepts, and then code should be written based on logical concepts to avoid physical concepts in the code. Leave the mapping of logical concepts to physical concepts to runtime. For example, the IP address of a database server should be expressed as a variable in the program, not as a constant. Leave the value of the variable to be read from the configuration file at runtime. In the construction of the runtime environment, physical resources are abstracted into virtual resources to meet the resource requirements of applications.

In cloud computing, applications are required to run everywhere. Given an application α, and a computer β, running involves two dimensions: (1) can the computer β run the application α? and (2) can the application α run successfully on the computer β? The question of whether it can run starts with the programming language. If application α is written in programming language A, and computer β supports programming language A, then computer β can run application α. If computer β does not support programming language A but supports programming language B, then computer β cannot directly run application α. There are two ways to make computer β run application α: (1) compile application α so that it is adaptable to computer β; (2) install an interpreter on computer β to make computer β support program language A. The next Sect. 5.2 explains the concrete implementation of these two strategies.

5.2 Compilation Versus Interpretation of Application Programs

Programming languages are divided into high-level programming languages and low-level programming languages. Both high-level and low-level programming languages are diverse. High-level programming languages are used to write applications due to their flexibility, simplicity, popularity, and versatility. Applications are characterized by the fact that developers and users are independent of each other. An application has only one developer but many users. Users differ in the ability of their computers to support the language. A bare metal computer supports only its own machine language. If a Java virtual machine is also installed, then that computer also supports the Java language. If a C/C++ compiler is also installed, then it further supports the C/C++ language. A computer pays a cost when it provides support for languages other than its own machine language. The cost comes from two sources: (1) the support software itself consumes computer resources, and (2) performing translations between languages also consumes computer resources.

The problem of linguistic diversity also exists in everyday life and work. A lot of important literature is in foreign languages. Suppose that employee α has to handle the literature written in language A. If employee α does not know language A but only language S, then it is necessary to find a person who knows both language A and language S to translate the literatrue into the document written in language S, and then give the translated document to employee α. This kind of processing is called compilation run on the computer. To be precise, it is called a postcompilation run. Another way is to give employee α a translator A, so that he can figure out the literature with the help of translator A and then process it. This processing is called interpreted run on the computer. This is similar to installing a Java virtual machine software on a computer so that it can run Java programs. If employee α is also told to process the literature in another language, then he or she will have to be equipped with another translator. The more translators an employee α carries, the heavier the burden becomes. It is inefficient to have to do the translation for every task that is processed.

The traditional meaning of compilation is: to translate a program expressed in a high-level programming language (also called a source program) into a program expressed in some machine language (also called a target program). The target program can be run directly on the corresponding model of computer. The program is compiled and then run, which is called the compiled execution method. Interpreted execution means that an application program written in a certain language is run by an interpreter for that language. The interpreter is an application program. There are advantages and disadvantages to both compiled and interpreted execution. In the next section, we will start from the analysis of the characteristics of high-level programming languages, explain the implementation methods of compilation and interpretation, and then analyze and summarize their respective features, exploring how to complement each other's strengths and weaknesses.

5.2.1 Features of the High-Level Programming Language

Applications written in high-level programming languages have good readability, maintainability, generalization, and reusability. The high readability of high-level programming languages is reflected in the use of names to identify variables. As opposed to it, low-level programming languages use addresses to identify variables. In addition to this, high-level programming languages offer a rich variety of feature expressions. For example, branching statements are expressed not only in terms of if, but also in terms of switch, while, for, and so on. When a variable has multiple values that are discrete, it can be expressed by switch. When the number of loop iterations to be determined at runtime, then use while to express. Thus, programs written in a high-level language have good readability, so that people can see at a glance.

Programming in a high-level programming language also allows you to use the laws of union, commutativity, precedence, and so on, to make the expression of the code as consistent as possible with custom and with the actual situation of things. For example, the statement "y = a*x^2 + b*x + c;" in a high-level programming language makes it clear at first glance that it is a computational expression to find the value of *the y-coordinate* on a parabola. If this expression were expressed in a low-level language, there would be five lines of code, in this order: (1) t1 = x * x; (2) t2 = a * t1; (3) t1 = b * x; (4) t2 = t2 + t1; (5) y = t2 + c. The readability of these five lines of code is obviously very poor. It can be seen that lines of code written in a high-level programming language literally express a complete concept and have good readability. In contrast, lines of code written in a low-level programming language are characterized by each line being short, but the number of lines is large and readability is poor.

Programming in a high-level programming language can be handled by abstraction in order to make the program well-generalized and widely applicable. A typical example is to abstract all input and output devices into files [7]. Thus, when inputting, the read function is uniformly called on the file, and when outputting, the write function is uniformly called on the file. The application behaves differently when called with different file descriptor parameters. For example, when the write function is called to output data, if the given file descriptor parameter is the id of the display file, then the data will be output to the display; if the given file descriptor parameter is the id of the ordinary file, then the data will be output to the file; if the given file descriptor parameter is the id of the printer file, then the data will be printed out. An application written in a high-level programming language is universal and has to be programmed only once. If you want it to run on a certain model of computer, you only have to use a compiler to compile it into the target code supported by that model.

5.2.2 Compositional Characteristics of the Source Program

Compilation is the translation from a source program language to a target program language. Specifically, it is the translation of a program written in the source language into a program written in the target language. For a compiler, its input is a text file containing the source code and its output is an executable file containing the target code. The source file is a string of characters, also called a sequence of characters. A word sequence is obtained by slicing the sequence of characters in the input. For example, line 3 of the source code shown in Code 5.1, "area = 0;", can be sliced into "area", "=", "0" and ";". The first of these words, area, is made up of the four characters 'a', 'r', 'e' and 'a' concatenated. The line of code is an assignment statement, consisting of four words concatenated. A sequence of statements is obtained by slicing the sequence of words in the input. The entirety of Code 5.1 is a function implementation statement that contains a sequence of five statements. The fifth statement in the sequence is a for statement that contains a sequence of two statements.

It follows that, in terms of compositional relations, a program is composed of one or more statements, a statement is composed of one or more words, and a word is composed of one or more characters. For the purpose of translation, some intermediate structure concepts are also usually introduced between statements and words. For example, an arithmetic expression is an intermediate structure concept between statements and words. The expression "(xEnd - xStart)/100" that appears in line 4 of Code 5.1 is an arithmetic expression. The notion of intermediate structure is usually defined for the purpose of translation, taking into account the characteristics of the high-level programming language and the target language. Thus, in addition to words, the compositional elements of statements include intermediate structure, statement, and the sequences of statements. An example of a statement containing an intermediate structure is the assignment statement in line 7 of Code 5.1, where "area + fun(x) * stepLen" to the right of the equal sign is an arithmetic expression. An example of a statement containing a sequence of statements is the for statement in line 8 of Code 5.1, which contains a sequence of two statements. It can be seen that statements are no longer linear in their composition, but are tree-like. Programs are composed of statements, which are naturally also tree-structured.

Code 5.1 C Source Code Example
```
(1)     float area (float xStart, float xEnd) {
(2)         float area, stepLen, x;
(3)         area= 0;
(4)         stepLen = (xEnd - xStart) / 100;
(5)         x = xStart;
(6)         for (int i = 0; i < 100; i++) {
(7)             area = area + fun(x) * stepLen;
(8)             x = x + stepLen;
(9)         }
(10)        return area.
(11)    }
```

5.2.3 Compilation Process and Methods

In high-level programming languages, words are the smallest constituent elements of a program. For words, each high-level programming language defines its own composition rules. For example, in C, a variable can only be composed of three types of characters: underscore, letter, and number, and the first character cannot be a number, which is the composition rule about variables. The law of word formation is also called lexicon. The compiler analyzes the input character sequence based on the lexicon and cuts it into word sequences, which is called lexical analysis. Lexical analysis is the first thing that the compiler has to do.

The second job the compiler has to do is to build a syntax analysis tree of the source program by slicing and dicing the word sequence based on the grammar. For example, line 7 in Code 5.1 is an assignment statement. Its syntax analysis tree is shown in Fig. 5.1. The root of this syntax analysis tree is the symbol S, which stands for Statement. From the child nodes of S, it is clear that this is an assignment statement. An assignment statement consists of four elements: the assigned variable V, the equal sign (=), the arithmetic expression E, and the semicolon (;). Looking again at the assigned variable V, it is clear from its child nodes that it consists of a variable

5.2 Compilation Versus Interpretation of Application Programs

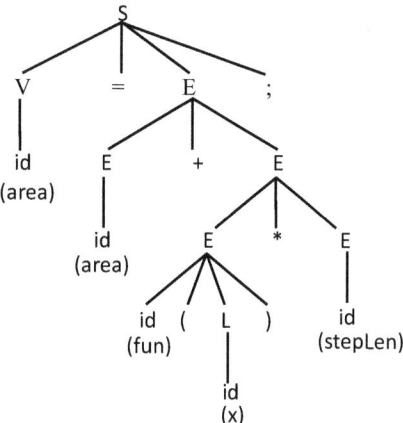

Fig. 5.1 Syntax analysis tree for the assignment statement "area = area + fun(x) * stepLen"

(denoted by *id*), which is *area*, and the expression *E*, which is the result of an addition expression, as shown by its subnodes. An addition expression consists of two operands that are added together. These two operands are also the result of other arithmetic expressions, hence *E*.

A variable counts as an arithmetic expression, and its value is the value of the arithmetic expression. Thus, the first operand *E* has a subnode of a variable called *area*, and the second operand is the result of a multiplication expression, as shown by its subnodes. A multiplication expression consists of two operands doing multiplication. The first operand is of course also an expression *E*, which is the result of a function call, as shown by its subnodes. A function call consists of four elements: the function name *id*, the left parenthesis, the argument list *L*, and the right parenthesis. Here, the function name is *fun*. From the subnode of the argument list *L*, it consists of one variable, which is *x*. The second operand of the multiplication operation is also an arithmetic expression *E*. From its subnodes, it consists of one variable. This variable is *stepLen*.

Looking at the syntactic analysis tree, it is clear that (1) the non-leaf nodes are structural concepts such as statements (*S*), arithmetic expressions (*E*), etc., which have their own constituent grammars, and (2) the leaf nodes are all words. Stringing all leaf nodes of the tree from left to right is the input word sequence, i.e., "area = area + fun(x) * stepLen;". In addition, from the syntax analysis tree, it can be seen that although the addition operation is written before the multiplication operation in the input word sequence, the multiplication operation is executed before the addition operation, realizing the reversal of the computation order. The reason is that one of the two operands that do the addition operation is the result of the multiplication operation. The priority of operations is expressed by the syntax.

As can be seen from this example, the basic strategy of syntactic analysis is to first define structural concepts, such as program (*P*), statement (*S*), arithmetic expression (*E*), and list of variables (*V*). Then, look at how many different scenarios, i.e., how many categories, exist for each of these concepts. The syntax for each category is then summarized. For example, statements have categories such as variable definition statements, assignment statements, and for statements. Expressions have categories such as additive expressions, multiplicative expressions, and so on. For a variable definition statement, it consists of three elements: data type, variable list, and semicolon. The strategy of syntactic analysis is to derive the rules of syntactic composition of a program by induction and abstraction, and then use them to match the word sequences of a program to construct a syntactic analysis tree of the program.

In addition to the lexical and syntactic rules mentioned above, there are also semantic rules for the composition of programs. The meaning of semantic rules is illustrated by an example. In C, pointer variables cannot perform multiplication or division, nor can they add or subtract data other than integers, which is a semantic rule. Break statements can only be used in loops or switch statements, which is another semantic rule. The use of functions should be consistent with their definition, which is also a semantic rule.

Semantic rule and syntactic rule are two completely different concepts. Syntax expresses composition, while semantics expresses constraints. Syntax describes the composition of a structure, including the constituent elements and the order of the elements. For example, an assignment statement is a structure consisting of a list of variables V, an equal sign (=), an expression E, and a semicolon (;). The equal sign (=) and the semicolon (;) are words, i.e., basic elements. Variable list V and arithmetic expression E are intermediate structures, each with its own syntax. In contrast, the use of a function is consistent with its definition, which is a semantic rule. The meaning is: in the syntax analysis process, once you see the structure of the function call appears, you have to go to check the previous function definition record, first of all to see whether the function has been defined. If defined, then further check whether the number, order, and type of parameters in the function call are consistent with the function definition. If undefined or inconsistent, it is considered that the program does not comply with the semantic rules.

The third job the compiler has to do is to ensure that the input source program does not violate all the semantic rules defined in the language. When the compiler does a semantic check, as soon as it finds that the input source program violates the semantic rules, it reports an error, stops compilation, and asks the programmer to correct the source program. Of course, when a lexical error is found in the first task, or a syntax error is found in the second task, an error will also be reported and the programmer will be asked to correct the source program. In concrete implementations, semantic analysis is usually not a stand-alone session, but is done incidentally to the process of syntactic analysis.

After the compiler has constructed the syntax tree for the input source program, the next task 4 is to generate the intermediate code. It is logical that with the syntax tree of the program, the target machine code can be generated directly. However, this is not usually done, but rather the intermediate code is generated and then translated into the target machine code. In other words, going from the syntax tree to the target machine code is a big step, not a very good step to climb. Setting another intermediate code step in the middle of this big step turns a big step into two small steps. This has better maneuverability.

5.2 Compilation Versus Interpretation of Application Programs

To illustrate the benefits of having an intermediate code link, here is a similar example. There are many languages in the world, such as Chinese, Russian, German, Japanese, and so on. In the computer world as well, there are many high-level programming languages and many machine languages. Translation between human languages is usually not a direct translation from the source language to the target language, but rather a translation from the source language to English and then from English to the target language. The advantage of using this model is that for translators in any country, they only need to master the translation between their own language and English. Choose any two languages, assuming A and B, to do its translation just need to find a translator in country A, find a translator in country B, through the two-step translation to complete. This is far better in terms of maneuverability, reliability, quality, efficiency, and cost than finding an interpreter who understands both A and B languages. The same is true for translations of programming languages.

Setting up an intermediate language can make the compilation and running of programs more flexible. Program code expressed in an intermediate language can be interpreted and run by an interpreter or further compiled into target code. Another advantage is: any program written in a high-level language, only after two steps of compilation, you can get the target code of any kind of computer model, so that the high-level programming language and machine language are both independent of each other, but also a combination of docking.

The translation from source code to intermediate code is done in the process of syntactic analysis. Syntactic analysis scans the sequence of words obtained from lexical analysis one by one, from beginning to end, and matches them with the grammar rules as a way of discovering the complete occurrences of structural instances. Structures are concepts defined in grammars, such as addition expressions, function calls, variable definition statements, assignment statements, if statements, function definition statements, etc. They are all structures. In syntactic analysis, once a complete instance of a certain structure appears, its intermediate code is derived based on the meaning of that structure.

Taking the syntax analysis tree shown in Fig. 5.1 as an example, the first complete instance of a structure to appear is the function call "fun(x)", and so its intermediate code is derived from the meaning of the function call, as seen in lines 1 and 2 of Code 5.2. The meaning of line 1 is to create a temporary variable of type float (whose type id is 1) to temporarily store the return value of the function call. The return value of this creation operation is the id of the temporary variable being created. The second occurrence of a complete instance of a structure is a multiplication expression, so its intermediate code is derived from the meaning of the multiplication expression, see line 3 in Code 5.2. The third occurrence of a complete instance of a structure is an addition expression, so the intermediate code is derived from the meaning of the addition expression, see line 4 in Code 5.2. The fourth occurrence of a complete instance of a structure is an assignment statement, so its intermediate code is derived from the meaning of the assignment statement, see lines 5 and 6 in Code 5.2. The meaning of line 6 is to release the temporary variable with id equal to 0.

Code 5.2 Intermediate Code for the Assignment Statement "area = area + fun(x) * stepLen;"

```
(1)   NewTempVariable 1.
(2)   tmp:0 = call function:2 local:2
(3)   tmp:0 = floatMultipleWithVarToVar tmp:0 local:1
(4)   tmp:0 = floatAddWithVarToVar local:0 tmp:0
(5)   local:0 = floatVarAssign tmp:0
(6)   freeTempVariable 0
```

In Code 5.2, "NewTempVariable", "tmp:", "=", "function:", "local:", "floatMultipleWithVarToVar", "floatAddWithVarToVar", "floatVarAssign", and "freeTempVariable" are all keywords in the intermediate language. The meaning of floatMultipleWithVarToVar is to perform multiplication of two variables of float type, while floatVarAssign is to assign the value of one variable of float type to another variable of float type. In the intermediate language, variables are no longer identified by name, but by logical address. In line 2, "function:2" is the logical address of the function *fun*, which means: this function is that with serial number 2 among all the functions of the program. "local:2" is the logical address of the local variable *x*, which means: in the local variables of the function, the variable is that with serial number 2. "tmp:0" indicates the temporary variable with serial number 0.

Translating the source code into intermediate code will separate the code from the data. Thus, the intermediate code consists of two parts: (1) code table; (2) symbol table. The code table records the intermediate code, and each line of intermediate code is identified by a line number. The symbol table records the data types, variables, functions, and string constants defined in the program. Symbol table is a general term that contains four kinds of tables: (1) data type table; (2) function table; (3) variable table; (4) constant table. Since variables are further divided into five types: (1) global variables; (2) local variables; (3) member variables; (4) formal parameters; and (5) temporary variables. Therefore, there are five types of variable tables: (1) global variable tables; (2) local variable tables; (3) member variable tables; (4) formal parameter tables; and (5) temporary variable tables. In the process of syntactic analysis, every new data type definition encountered is added to the data type table; every new function definition encountered is added to the function table. Other analogies. For data types, variables, functions, etc., every time you encounter its use, you have to look up its definition in the symbol table, check whether it meets the semantic rules, and get its logical address for intermediate code generation.

Examples of the contents of the type table, function table, and local variable table are shown in Tables 5.1, 5.2, and 5.3, respectively. Types, functions, and variables are identified by serial numbers (also called line numbers). In the intermediate code, data and functions are identified by logical addresses. For example, the logical address "function:2" identifies a function, the details of which are recorded in the function table in the row with the serial number 2. The logical address "local:1"

5.2 Compilation Versus Interpretation of Application Programs

Table 5.1 Table of types

Serial number (index)	Type name	The id of the reference type (referenceTypeId)	Type width
0	int		
1	float		
2	char		
3	char *	2	
4	Student		
5	Student *	4	

Table 5.2 Table of functions

Serial number (index)	Function name (name)	Type id of the return value (typeIndex)	Serial number of the first line of code (startIndex)	Total width of the formal parameter (formalTotalWidth)	Total width of the local variable (localTotalWidth)
0	main	0	0		
1	area	1	67		
2	fun	1	198		

Table 5.3 Table of local variables

Function id (functionIndex)	Serial number (index)	Variable name (name)	Type id (typeIndex)	Size (width)	Offset (offset)
1	0	area	1		
1	1	stepLen	1		
1	2	x	1		
1	3	i	0		

identifies a local variable, and its details are recorded in the local variable table of the function in the row numbered 1. There are basic data types and custom data types. The basic data types are int, float, and char, which are assumed to have type numbers 0, 1, and 2, respectively, as shown in Table 5.1. Each custom type (e.g., struct in C and class in C++) has its member variables, which are recorded in the member variable table. The other type is the pointer type. For pointer types, there is the concept of reference types. For example, in the type example shown in Table 5.1, there are two pointer types, char * and Student *, whose reference type ids are 2 and 4, respectively.

For both types and variables, there is the concept of width (i.e., the number of bytes in memory). The width of a custom type is the sum of the widths of its member variables. The width of a variable is that of its type. Knowing the width of a variable, you know how much memory to request for it at runtime. Types and variables have only the concept of width in intermediate languages, but not a specific value. The width value is not filled in until the target computer is determined. The reason is that the widths of basic data types such as int, float, and so on, vary from one computer model to another. For example, the width of a float is 4 on a 16-bit computer, but 8 on a 32-bit computer, and 16 on a 64-bit computer.

Once the target computer is determined, then the width of the base data type is known, and so the width of the custom data type can be calculated. The width of a variable is that of its data type, so it is also a known constant. Assuming that the target computer is a 32-bit computer, the widths of the int, float, and pointer types are 4, 8, and 4, respectively, and the widths of the four local variables shown in Table 5.3 are 8, 8, 8, and 4, respectively. Variables or functions in a program are identified at runtime by memory addresses. A memory address consists of a base address and an offset. For local variables of a function, the first one has 0 as its offset value. The first variable's offset plus the width of the first variable is the second variable's offset value, and so on. Thus, for the four local variables shown in Table 5.3, their offset values are 0, 8, 16, and 24, respectively, and the same is true for other types of variables.

When translating intermediate code into target code, all logical addresses are converted into memory addresses. Each program and each function can be considered as a data type. Thus, global variables are members of the program type, and local variables are members of the function type. When you run a program, you create an instance of the program type; when you call a function, you create an instance of the called function type. The memory address of the instance object is the base address of its member variables. The base address, plus the offset value of a member variable, is the memory address of the member variable. Offset values are also called relative addresses. When the target computer supports relative addressing, using a register to store the base address of a variable makes all memory addresses appearing in the target code constants.

From the above examples and analysis, it is clear that the intermediate code is close to machine code. Each line of intermediate code represents an operation. Each line of intermediate code is short, but there are many lines. In intermediate code, however, there is only one type of memory. Whereas in a physical computer, there are registers and memory. In addition, intermediate code is poorly readable due to the fact that functions, variables, and string constants are no longer expressed by name, but by logical address.

5.2.4 Intermediate Code Optimization

From the compilation process and methodology in the previous section, it can be seen that the translation from source code to intermediate code is a mechanical translation based on the meaning of structures (i.e., syntax) and does not take into account the association between contexts. The intermediate code resulting from this translation is optimizable. The following example demonstrates this translation property. Code 5.3 is a fragment of source code with the function of matrix transpose transformation, where the local variable a is a two-dimensional array, assumed to be defined as: int $a[10][20]$. In the intermediate code, data are to be expressed in terms of its logical address. The address space is linear. Array elements are data and therefore are to be expressed with their logical addresses in intermediate code as well. Suppose the logical address of an array element $a[i, j]$ is expressed as $a[x]$,

5.2 Compilation Versus Interpretation of Application Programs

where a denotes the logical address of the array variable a, and x is the logical address of another variable, whose value is the offset of the array element $a[i, j]$ with respect to the start address of the array a, in bytes. Thus, we have $x = (20 * i + j) *$ WIDTH (int). Where WIDTH (int) denotes the width of the integer.

Code 5.3 Source Program Fragment
```
(1)    k = a [i, j].
(2)    a [i, j] = a [j, i];
(3)    a [j, i] = k;
```

The program in Code 5.3 consists of three assignment statements. So they are translated one by one. When translating the first assignment statement, the intermediate code for calculating the offset of array element $a[i, j]$ is generated. When translating the second assignment statement, it also generates intermediate code that calculates the offset of array element $a[i, j]$. The reason is that the translation is done independently statement by statement and the translation of the previous statement does not affect the translation of the subsequent statement. From the optimization point of view, the intermediate code for calculating the offset of array element $a[i, j]$ can be omitted in the translation of the second assignment statement. The reason is that it has already been calculated in the translation of the first assignment statement and there is no need to repeat it. The code for calculating the offset of array element $a[j, i]$ in the third assignment statement can also be omitted because it has already been calculated in the translation of the second statement. Performing the translation of the three lines of source code shown in Code 5.3 results in the intermediate code shown in Code 5.4, which assumes that the local variables a, i, j, k are numbered 0, 1, 2, and 3, respectively, in the function's table of local variables. Optimization can be performed to remove 10 lines of this code, and the optimized result is shown in Code 5.5.

Code 5.4 Intermediate Code from Translation
```
(1)     newTempVariable 0
(2)     tmp:0 = intMultipleWithConstToVar 20 local:1
(3)     tmp:0 = intAddWithVarToVar tmp:0 local:2
(4)     tmp:0 = intMultipleWithVarToConst tmp:0 WIDTH(int)
(5)     local:3 = intVarAssign local:0[tmp:0]
(6)     freeTempVariable 0
(7)     newTempVariable 0
(8)     tmp:0 = intMultipleWithConstToVar 20 local:1
(9)     tmp:0 = intAddWithVarToVar tmp:0 local:2
(10)    tmp:0 = intMultipleWithVarToConst tmp:0 WIDTH(int)
(11)    newTempVariable 0
(12)    tmp:1 = intMultipleWithConstToVar 20 local:2
```

```
(13)    tmp:1 = intAddWithVarToVar tmp:1 local:1
(14)    tmp:1 = intMultipleWithVarToConst tmp:1 WIDTH(int)
(15)    local:0[tmp:0] = intVarAssign local:0[tmp:1]
(16)    freeTempVariable 0
(17)    freeTempVariable 1
(18)    newTempVariable 0
(19)    tmp:0 = intMultipleWithConstToVar 20 local:2
(20)    tmp:0 = intAddWithVarToVar tmp:0 local:1
(21)    tmp:0 = intMultipleWithVarToConst tmp:0 WIDTH(int)
(22)    local:0[tmp:0] = intVarAssign local:3
(23)    freeTempVariable 0
```

It is clear that intermediate code optimization is an important part of compilation. Intermediate code optimization is all about shrinking the amount of intermediate code. When the code to perform a particular computation is repeated, the repeated portion can be eliminated. The amount of code is reduced, so the amount of computation at runtime is reduced, thus the computation time is reduced, which helps to get the result of the computation as soon as possible. In addition, code that performs a calculation in a loop can be moved out of the loop and forwarded to the front of the loop if the result of the calculation is the same each time the loop is performed. This reduces repeated calculations. For a computational task, there may be multiple equivalents, such as finding x^2, which is equivalent to $x*x$. In terms of computational overhead, multiplication is preferable to power operations. Thus, equivalence transformations are also an important aspect of intermediate code optimization. There are other ways and methods of intermediate code optimization. For example, for a variable in an operator, when it can be reasoned that its value is some known constant, replacing the variable with a constant eliminates the overhead of reading the variable.

Code 5.5 Optimized Intermediate Code
```
(1)     NewTempVariable 0
(2)     tmp:0 = intMultipleWithConstToVar 20 local:1
(3)     tmp:0 = intAddWithVarToVar tmp:0 local:2
(4)     tmp:0 = intMultipleWithVarToConst tmp:0 WIDTH(int)
(5)     local:3 = intVarAssign local:0[tmp:0]
(6)     NewTempVariable 0
(7)     tmp:1 = intMultipleWithConstToVar 20 local:2
(8)     tmp:1 = intAddWithVarToVar tmp:1 local:1
(9)     tmp:1 = intMultipleWithVarToConst tmp:1 WIDTH(int)
(10)    local:0[tmp:0] = intVarAssign local:0[tmp:1]
(11)    freeTempVariable 0
(12)    local:0[tmp:1] = intVarAssign local:3
(13)    freeTempVariable 1
```

5.2 Compilation Versus Interpretation of Application Programs 307

Reflection 5.1: In intermediate code optimization, how do you identify repeated calculations? How do you determine that the value of a variable is a known constant? Answer these two questions by doing a sandboxing exercise, i.e., rehearsing the running of the program and performing a data flow analysis. Consult the information to answer these two questions.

5.2.5 Interpreted Execution on Applications

Compilation takes as input a program written in the source language and as output a program written in the target language. Each model of computer has its own machine language. Assuming that the machine language supported by the computer of model A is language A, then the compiled output program can run directly on the computer of model A when the target language is language A. This is the meaning of compiled run. A program written in a machine language is a sequence of instructions that are taken and executed by the computer one by one. The computer jumps when it encounters a branching instruction during the execution instead of proceeding to the next instruction.

When running a program in the interpreted mode, the program is the input to the interpreter. The interpreter takes out the sequence of instructions contained in the program and processes them one by one. When the interpreter encounters a branch instruction during the process of execution, it performs a jump to the instruction indicated by the branch, instead of moving on to the next instruction. When the interpreter reaches the return instruction of the main function, the interpreted run is complete.

An interpreter is a program that has inputs and outputs. The program being interpreted and executed can be viewed as a data file. The data in the file serve as input to the interpreter. The output of the interpreter is the result of processing the input. If viewed from the perspective of the program being interpreted and executed, the output of the interpreter is equivalent to the result of its execution. It follows that the program being interpreted and executed as input to the interpreter indicates the execution path of the interpreter, resulting in the output of the interpreter being exactly the same as the result obtained by running the program being interpreted and executed. The intermediate code described in the previous section is actually a program written in an intermediate language. An interpreter that supports the intermediate language can take the intermediate code as input, and its output is the result of executing the intermediate code. In the following, the intermediate code obtained by compiling the C source code shown in Code 5.1 is given first, and then the implementation of the interpreter is explained.

For the C source code shown in Code 5.1, it is compiled and the intermediate code is obtained as shown in Code 5.6. The meaning of the first line is to add a temporary variable of data type id 1 (i.e., float type) to the temporary variable table to store the intermediate computation result. This instruction returns the serial number of the temporary variable, which in this case is 0. The logical address of the temporary variable is therefore "tmp:0". The meaning of line 4 is to release the temporary variable with serial number 0. Line 7 adds a temporary variable of data type id 0 (i.e., int type) to the temporary variables table. Because the temporary variable requested in line 1 has already been released earlier, the serial number of the returned temporary variable is still 0. Line 8 performs a comparison operation and stores the result in the temporary variable "tmp:0". Line 9 is a conditional branch jump instruction, which means: if the value of the temporary variable "tmp:0" is 1, then jump to the execution of the 18th line; if it is 0, then continue to execute the next line (i.e., line 10).

Code 5.6 Compiled Intermediate Code

```
(1)   newTempVariable 1
(2)   tmp:0 = floatSubtractWithVarToVar formal:1 formal:0
(3)   local:1 = floatDivideWithVarToConst tmp:0 100
(4)   freeTempVariable 0
(5)   local:2 = floatVarAssign formal:0
(6)   local:3 = intConstAssign 0
(7)   newTempVariable 0
(8)   tmp:0 = intEqualOrLargerWithVariableToConst
      local:3 100
(9)   branch tmp:0 18
(10)  newTempVariable 1
(11)  tmp:1 = call function:2 local:2
(12)  tmp:1 = floatMultipleWithVarToVar tmp:0 local:1
(13)  local:1 = floatAddWithVarToVar local:0 tmp:0
(14)  freeTempVariable 1
(15)  local:2 = floatAddWithVarToVar local:2 local:1
(16)  intIncrement local:3
(17)  goto 7
(18)  freeTempVariable 0
(19)  return local:2
```

As can be seen from the intermediate code shown in Code 5.6, each line of intermediate code represents only one operation, and so each line is short. In addition, each line of intermediate code contains an operation indicator. For example, the operation indicator *floatVarAssign* in line 5 means to assign the value of a variable of type float to another variable of type float. The operation indicator *intConstAssign* in line 6 assigns a constant value of type int to another variable of type int. The meaning of the operation indicator is very clear and specific, operable, and conducive to interpretation and execution.

Intermediate code is a program written in an intermediate language and stored in a file. The file contains a table of intermediate code, a table of data types, a table of functions, a table of global variables, a table of temporary variables, and a table of string constants. For each function in the function table, there is a table of local variables and a table of formal parameters. For each custom data type (i.e., class) in the data types table, there is a table of member variables. In an intermediate language, there are seven types of data that can be accessed: (1) global variables; (2) local variables; (3) formal parameter variables; (4) member variables of instance objects; (5) temporary variables; (6) numeric constants; and (7) string constants. The interpreter encapsulates the above contents of the application file into an *Application* object, and then obtains the information therein through the member variables and member functions of the object. This information is used by the interpreter for allocating memory for the variables, deriving the memory address of each variable, and interpreting and executing the intermediate code.

5.2.6 Interpreter Implementation

When the interpreter interprets and executes a program, it first allocates memory space for its global variables. Think of a program as a class, so allocating memory space for global variables is equivalent to creating a program object. In terms of functional logic, the interpreter next calls the application's main function. When calling a function, the interpreter first allocates memory for the formal parameters of the called function. Formal parameters of a function can also be treated as a class, so by allocating memory space for the formal parameters of the called function, the interpreter creates a formal parameter object. Next, you assign values to each member variable of the formal parameter object using real parameters, completing the parameter passing. Then allocate memory space for the local variables of the called function. Each function's local variables can be treated as a class, so allocating memory space for the local variables of the called function creates a local variable object. The interpreter then executes the first line of the main function.

When the interpreter executes a line of code in a program, it derives the corresponding memory address for the logical address that appears in it. When a variable is treated as a member of an object, its memory address is the base address plus its offset. The base address is the memory address of the object, and the offset can be found in the symbol table. The memory address of each logical address can then be derived.

When a computer executes machine code, there is the concept of the memory address of the next instruction to be executed, which is stored in the instruction register. After executing the current instruction, the CPU automatically calculates the memory address of the next instruction to be executed based on the functional semantics of the current instruction. Similarly, when the interpreter executes a program, it has the notion of the serial number of the next line of code to be processed. This number is stored in the variable *application->nextCodeRowIndex*. After the interpreter has processed the current line of code, it derives the serial number of the next line of code to be processed based on its functional semantics. If the functional semantics of the current line of code is not a branch jump, then the serial number of the next line of code to be processed is the serial number of the current line of code plus 1. Otherwise, the serial number of the next code line to be processed will be obtained during the processing of the current code line. For example, in the intermediate code shown in Code 5.6, the functional semantics of line 9, "branch tmp: 0 18", is a conditional branch jump. Its meaning is: if the value of the variable with logical address tmp:0 is 1, then the next line of code to be processed is numbered 18, otherwise it is 10.

As far as the running of a program is concerned, there is the concept of the current function. When the interpreter starts executing the program, the current function is the main function. When another function is called in the main function, the current function changes to the called function. When the called function returns, it changes to the main function again. For each line of code, the formal parameters and local variables that appear are those of the current function. For function calls, in addition to allocating memory space for the formal parameters and local variables of the called function, the interpreter also has to deal with the passing of real parameters, as well as the passing of the return address and the return assignment of the return value. This can be solved by adding two more variables to the formal parameter. The first variable is added to store the return address and the second is added to store the memory address of the variable that receives the return value. When the interpreter executes the return instruction of the called function, it first assigns the return address to the *application->nextCodeRowIndex* variable, then writes the return value to the memory of the variable that receives the return value, then releases the memory space occupied by the local variables and the formal parameter, and changes the current function to the caller function.

An example of the implementation of a function call is given. It is assumed that the interpreter is running on a 32-bit computer. Take the function call "tmp:0 = call function:2 local:2" in line 11 of Code 5.6 as an example, where the logical address of the called function is function:2, and there is only one real parameter, whose logical address is local:2. The value of the return address is the serial number of the next line of code, i.e., integer 12, whose width is 4. The logical address of the variable that receives the return value is tmp:0, whose width is 4. The logical address of the current function is function:1. Checking its local variable table, we can see that the width of the variable with the logical address of local:2 is 8. Thus, the interpreter would request a 16-byte (8 + 4 + 4) memory space to the parameter pass of the function call. The interpreter uses the variable *application->currentFormalBaseAddr* to store the address of the requested memory, so the offsets of the three items of data in the parameter pass are 0, 8, and 12, respectively.

In order to realize the current function switching back and forth between the caller function and the callee function, the interpreter has to have a function call stack *callStack*. When the interpreter executes to a line of function call code, it has to push the feature information of the current function into the function call stack *callStack* to save it, and create a callee function object to make it the new current function. When the interpreter executes to a function return instruction, it has to release the current function object and then pop the top element from the function call stack *callStack* to make it the new current function.

5.2 Compilation Versus Interpretation of Application Programs

In the intermediate code, when calling a function implemented by the program itself, the logical address of the function is used to express the called function. Take the function call "tmp:0 = call function:2 local:2" in line 11 of Code 5.6 as an example, it is to call the function *fun* realized by the program itself, and the logical address of the function is function:2. In the line with serial number 2 in the function table, the details of the function are recorded, such as the serial number of its first line of code in the intermediate code table, the total width of the formal parameters, and the total width of the local variables, shown in Table 5.2. When the interpreter executes this line of intermediate code, it first calculates the size of the memory space for parameter passing, then applies for memory space for parameter passing, and completes parameter passing. Next, the total width of the local variables is obtained and memory space is requested for the local variables. After this, the current function is switched to the callee function: the current function is pushed into the function call stack, *callStack*, to be restored when the function returns, and then the callee function is set to the current function.

From the above analysis, it is clear that in the interpreter's implementation, the program file is first loaded from disk into memory, and then the data in it are used to create an instance object of the Application class. After creation, the width of each basic data type in the type table is filled in, then the width of each custom data type is calculated and filled in, then the width and offset of each variable in the variable table is calculated and filled in, as well as the total width of the formal parameters and the total width of the local variables of each function in the function table. After this, the interpreter calculates the total width of the global variables, and then allocates memory space for the global variables to get the base address *globalBaseAddr*. This is the initialization work that the interpreter does before executing a program.

After initialization, the interpreter next calls the application's main function. To do this, it first calculates the size of the memory space for parameter passing, then requests the memory space and completes the parameter passing. Here is an example. Assuming that the file name of the interpreter application is *interpreter.exe* and the file name of the program to be interpreted is *application.dat*, the command line for interpreting and executing this program is "interpreter.exe application.dat 10 20". The meaning of this command line is: when calling the main function of the program *application.dat*, three real parameters are passed: "application.dat", "10" and "20". According to the definition of the main function, the real parameters to be passed are *argc* and *argv*, where *argc* has a value of 3. *argv* has a value of a memory address where an array of three elements is stored, and the values of these three array elements are the memory addresses of those three strings.

The first real parameter to be passed is an integer, the second real parameter is a pointer (i.e., address), both of which have widths of sizeof(int) and sizeof(char **), respectively, and the other two parameters to be passed are the return address and the memory address of the variable to be assigned, where the first one is of the type int, and the second one is of the type pointer, both of which have widths of sizeof (int) and sizeof(void *). When the interpreter is running on a 32-bit computer, the width of each of these types is 4, so the interpreter should request 16 bytes of memory for parameter passing. For the requested memory, the interpreter stores its address in the member variable *application->formalBaseAddr*. Thus, the offsets of these four items of data are 0, 4, 8, and 12, respectively.

The meaning of the above command line "interpreter.exe application.dat 10 20" has two layers: (1) specify the application to be run, that is, *interpreter.exe*; (2) specify the values of the real parameters of the main function of *interpreter.exe*, where *argc* is 4, *argv* is a memory address value of an array containing 4 elements. The values of these four array elements are the memory addresses of the four strings "interpreter.exe","application.dat", "10", and "20", respectively. Therefore, when the interpreter calls the main function in the *application.dat*, the first real parameter value to be passed is its own *argc* value minus 1, and the second real parameter value to be passed is its own *argv* value plus sizeof (char *). When the interpreter executes to the return instruction in the main function of *application.dat*, there is no next line of code to be executed. Therefore, when passing the return address for the call to the main function, −1 is used to indicate that the interpreted execution has finished.

After the interpreter completes parameter passing for the call to the main function, it next allocates memory space for its local variables. The interpreter first needs to find the details of the main function in the function table through the Application object, including its id, the serial number of the first line of code in the code table, and the total width of the local variables, etc. After getting the total width of the local variables, it requests memory space for them. Once the total width of the local variables is obtained, memory space is requested for them. The address of the requested memory is stored in the variable *application->currentLocalBaseAddr*. After getting the serial number of the first line of code, it is assigned to the variable *application->nextIRowCodeIndex*. Then the interpreter starts executing the main function of *application.dat*.

Each time the interpreter executes a line of code in *application.dat*, it first takes the line of code out of the code table based on the value of *application->nextIRowCodeIndex*, then parses it to get all elements contained in it, placing it in the array *element*. The array element *element*[0] holds the operation indicator. The interpreter does processing based on the operation indicator and performs the operation shown in the line of code.

The implementation of the interpreter is shown in Code 5.7. The function of the third line of code is to load the program file to be interpreted from disk into memory and create an object of the Application class. The value of the formal parameter *argv*[1] is the name of the program file being interpreted. The function of the code in line 4 is to initialize the application object: fill in the width of each type in the type table, the width and offset values of each variable in the variable table, and the total width of the formal parameters and the total width of the local variables of each function in the function table. The function of the code in lines 5 and 6 is to get the total width of the global variables and then allocate memory space for the global variables. The meaning of line 7 is to get the main function from the function table and set it as the current function. The function of lines 8 through 17 is to call the main function of the program, including calculation of the total width of the formal parameters, memory allocation for the formal parameters, and assignment of each formal parameter to complete the parameter passing. From *argv*[1] to *argv*[*argc*-1], these *argc*-1 parameters are the real parameters to be passed to the main function. Therefore, the number of real parameters is *argc*-1.

Lines 18 and 19 are to get the total width of the local variables of the current function (i.e., the main function), and then allocate memory space for them by assigning the resulting memory address to the variable *application->currentLocalBaseAddr*. The function of line 20 is to get the serial number of the first line of code of the current function (i.e., the main function) in the code table and assign it to *application->nextCodeRowIndex*, which is the first line of code to be executed by the interpreter. The function of lines 21 through 26 is to interpret and execute the program line by line. The value of *application->nextCodeRowIndex* is updated after each line of code is executed. When the interpreter executes to the return instruction of the main function, the value of *application->nextCodeRowIndex* is −1, indicating that the interpreted execution is complete.

Code 5.7 Implementation of the Interpreter

```
(1)    int main(int argc, char ** argv) {
(2)        int result;
(3)        application = createApplicationFromFile(argv[1]);
(4)        application->initialize();
(5)        int globalVariableTotalWidth = application->getGlobalVariableTotalWidth( );
(6)        application->globalBaseAddr = malloc(globalVariableTotalWidth);
(7)        application->currentFunction = application->functionTable->getItemByName("main");
(8)        int fomalTotalwidth = application->currentFunction->getFormalTotalwidth();
(9)        fomalTotalwidth += sizeof(int) + sizeof(unsigned int *);
(10)       application->currentFormalBaseAddr = malloc(fomalTotalwidth);
(11)       *(int *)application->currentFormalBaseAddr = argc - 1;
(12)       xxxchar *itemAddr = (char *)application->currentFormalBaseAddr + sizeof(int);
(13)       *(char **)itemAddr = argv + 1;
(14)       itemAddr += sizeof(char **);
(15)       *(int *)item = -1;
(16)       itemAddr += sizeof(int);
(17)       *(unsigned int *)itemAddr = &result;
```

```
(18)    int localTotalWidth =
        application->currentFunction-
        >getLocalVariableTotalWidth();
(19)    application->currentLocalBaseAddr =
        malloc(localTotalWidth);
(20)    application->nextCodeRowIndex = application-
        >currentFunction->getCodeRowStartIndex( );
(21)    while (application->nextCodeRowIndex >= 0 ) {
(22)       char * codeRow =
           application->codeTable->getRowByIndex(application-
           >nextCodeRowIndex);
(23)       char * element[16].
(24)       int elementNum = resolve( codeRow, element);
(25)       executeCodeRow(elementNum, element);
(26)    }
(27)    return result;
(28) }
```

5.2.7 Interpreted Execution on Instructions

Interpreter executes a line of code by first parsing it into a sequence of elements, which are stored in the array *element*, as shown in line 24 of Code 5.7. The number of elements is stored in the variable *elementNum*. In a code line, elements are separated from each other by spaces. This parsing is similar to command-line parsing. In command-line parsing, the elements are stored in the array *argv* and the number of elements is stored in *argc*. The difference is that the order of the elements may have to be adjusted by bringing the operation indicator to the front and storing it in *element*[0]. Here is an example. For the code line "tmp:0 = floatSubtractWithVarToVar formal:1 formal:0", it is parsed and adjusted to "floatSubtractWithVarToVar formal:1 formal:0 tmp:0". The parsing result is similar to an instruction written in assembly language. Once the line of code is parsed, the function *executeCodeRow* is called to execute it, as shown in line 25.

The implementation of the *executeCodeRow* function is shown in Code 5.8. *element*[0] stores the operation indicator, which specifies how many elements follow and what each element means. For example, the operation indicator *floatSubtractWithVarToVar* means that two variables of type float are subtracted and the result is stored in a variable of type float. The processing of this operation is shown in lines 3 through 9. In contrast, the operation indicator *floatSubtractWithVarToConst* means that a variable of type float is subtracted from a constant of type float and the result is stored in a variable of type float. This operation is handled as shown in lines 10 through 16. Since all the elements are strings, the atof function in C language is called on the second operand to convert it to a constant of type float, as shown in line 12.

When a line of code functions as a conditional branch, the interpreted execution is shown in lines 17 through 23 of Code 5.8. The operation indicator "branch"

5.2 Compilation Versus Interpretation of Application Programs

indicates that it is to be followed by two arguments, the first of which is a variable of type int and the second an integer constant. When the value of the first parameter is 1, a jump is performed and the target line is numbered with the value of the second parameter. Since *element*[2] is a string, the atoi function in C language is called to convert it to a constant of type int, as shown in line 20.

Every high-level language has system functions defined. For example, in C language, malloc and atoi are system functions. When compiling the source code into intermediate code, the system function calls remain unchanged. The implementation of the system functions is provided by the program executor. Here, the program executor is the interpreter, so the interpreter should provide the implementation of the system functions. In Code 5.8, lines 24 through 31, the call to the system function *readFile* is interpreted and executed. The operation indicator *readFile* is followed by four parameters, the meaning of which are: file descriptor id, the starting address of the memory where the data are stored, the number of bytes that should be read, and the return value (the number of bytes actually read). The definition of the function requires that all four parameters be variables. The interpreter does what *readFile* should do by calling its own implementation of the function *read*, as shown in line 29.

When the function of a line of code is a function call, the processing done by the interpreter is shown in lines 32 through 34 of Code 5.8. A function call is a call to a function that is implemented by the program itself. The functions implemented by the program itself are identified by logical addresses, for example, "function: 2" is the logical address of a function, indicating that the corresponding information of the function is recorded in the row numbered 2 in the function table. Function information includes: the type id of the return value, the serial number of the first line of code in the code table, the total width of formal parameters, the total width of local variables and so on. Since the processing of function calls is relatively more complex, for the sake of simplicity and clarity, it is encapsulated separately in the function *processFunctionCall*, the implementation of which is shown in Code 5.9. A special case of function calls is the main function call, which is the first function to be called, as explained earlier. Subsequent function calls involve a switch to the current function: the current function information is pushed into the function call stack, *callStack*, to be restored when the call returns, as shown in lines 2 through 4. The called function is then established as the new current function.

Code 5.8 Implementation of the executeCodeRow Function

```
(1)     void executeCodeRow(int elementNum, char
        *element[ ]) {
(2)         switch( element[0]) {
(3)             case "floatSubtractWithVarToVar":
(4)                 float *operand1 = getMemAddrByLogicAddr(el
                    ement[1]);
(5)                 float *operand2 = getMemAddrByLogicAddr(el
                    ement[2]);
```

```
(6)         float * result = getMemAddrByLogicAddr(el
            ement[3]);
(7)         *result = *operand1 - *operand2;
(8)         application->nextCodeRowIndex += 1;
(9)       break;
(10)      case "floatSubtractWithVarToConst":
(11)        float *operand1 = getMemAddrByLogicAddr(el
            ement[1]);
(12)        float operand2 = atof(element[2]);
(13)        float * result = getMemAddrByLogicAddr(el
            ement[3]);
(14)        *result = *operand1 - operand2;
(15)        application->nextCodeRowIndex += 1;
(16)      break;
(17)      case "branch":
(18)       int *param1 = getMemAddrByLogicAddr(element[1]);
(19)       if (*param1 == 1)
(20)         application->nextCodeRowIndex =
             atoi(element[2]);
(21)       else
(22)         application->nextCodeRowIndex += 1;
(23)      break;
(24)      case "readFile":
(25)        int *param1 = getMemAddrByLogicAddr(el
            ement[1]);
(26)        char *param2 = getMemAddrByLogicAddr(el
            ement[2]);
(27)        int *param3 = getMemAddrByLogicAddr(el
            ement[3]);
(28)        int *result = getMemAddrByLogicAddr(el
            ement[4]);
(29)        *result = read(*param1, *param2, *param3);
(30)        application->nextCodeRowIndex += 1;
(31)      break;
(32)      case "call":
(33)        processFunctionCall(elementNum, char *element);
(34)      break;
(35)      ......
(36)    }
(37) }
```

5.2 Compilation Versus Interpretation of Application Programs

Code 5.9 Implementation of the processFunctionCall Function

```
(1)   void processFunctionCall(int elementNum, char
      *element[ ]) {
(2)      callStack->push( (void *)
         application->currentFunction);
(3)      callStack->push(
         application->currentFormalBaseAddr);
(4)      callStack->push( application->currentLocalBaseAddr);
(5)      application->currentFunction =
         application->functionTable-
         >getItemByIndex(element[1]);
(6)      int fomalTotalWidth =
         application->currentFunction->getFormalTotalWidth();
(7)      fomalTotalWidth += sizeof(int) +
         sizeof(unsigned int *);
(8)      application->currentFormalBaseAddr =
         malloc(fomalTotalWidth);
(9)      char *itemAddr = application->currentFormalBaseAddr;
(10)     int i = 2;
(11)     while (i < elementNum && *element[i] ! = '=' ) {
(12)        Variable *Variable = application-
            >currentFunction->formalTable->getItemByIndex(
            i - 2 );
(13)        if ( isLogicAddr(element[i] ) {
(14)           void *realParamAddr = getMemAddrByLogicAddr(el
               ement[i]);
(15)           memcpy( itemAddr, realParamAddr
               ,Variable->width);
(16)        }
(17)        else {
(18)           if (Variable->typeIndex == 0)  //int type
               constant
(19)              *(int *) itemAddr = atoi(element[i]);
(20)           else if (Variable->typeIndex == 1)  //float type
               constant
(21)              *(float *) itemAddr = atof(element[i]);
(22)           else if (Variable->typeIndex == 2) //char type
               constant
(23)              *(char *) itemAddr = *element[i];
(24)        }
(25)        itemAddr += Variable->width;
(26)        i++;
(27)     }
```

```
(28)    *(int *)itemAddr = application-
        >nextCodeRowIndex + 1;
(29)    itemAddr += sizeof(int);
(30)    if (elementNum > 3 && *element[elementNum - 2]
        == '=') {
(31)       void *assignedVarAddr = getMemAddrByLogicAddr(ele
           ment[elementNum - 1]);
(32)       *(unsigned int *) itemAddr = assignedVarAddr;
(33)    }
(34)    else
(35)       *(unsigned int *)itemAddr = 0;
(36)    int localTotalWidth
        =application->currentFunction->getLocalTotalWidth();
(37)    application->currentLocalBaseAddr =
        malloc(localTotalWidth);
(38)    application->nextCodeRowIndex = application-
        >currentFunction->getCodeRowStartIndex( );
(39)    return;
(40) }
```

In a function call, the logical address of the called function is stored in *element*[1], and the interpreter first goes to the function table to find its definition based on it, as shown in line 5 of Code 5.9. The next step is to calculate the size of the memory space for the parameter passing, and then request the memory space to complete the parameter passing, as shown in lines 6 through 35. There are two scenarios for function calls: (1) to assign the function return value to a variable, e.g., "tmp:0 = call function:2 local:2"; and (2) not to return the value, e.g., "call function:3 local:1 100". When parsing the function call code line, if it is the first case, the order will be adjusted, and the assigned variable will be adjusted from the first element to the last element, and then the equals sign (=) will be adjusted to the penultimate element. The real parameters passed start at *element*[2], although cases without real parameters are possible. The passing of real parameters is shown in lines 9 through 27. For a real parameter, it may be either the value of a variable or a constant. The distinction is made by seeing if it is a logical address, as shown on line 13.

For a real parameter to be passed, if it is the value of a variable, a direct memory copy is made when passing, as shown in lines 14 through 15. When copying, the width of the variable needs to be known. The width can be obtained from the function's formal parameter definition, as shown in line 12. The reason is that real and formal parameters have one-to-one correspondence. If the real parameter to be passed is a constant, its data type should be obtained from its corresponding formal parameter definition, and then it should be handled in different categories, as shown

5.2 Compilation Versus Interpretation of Application Programs

in lines 18 through 23. After passing the real parameter, the return address is passed, as shown in line 28. The last thing passed is the memory address of the assigned variable. To do this, first determine if there is an assigned variable, as shown in line 30. If there is, then the logical address of the assigned variable is stored in the *element[elementNum - 1]*. First, its memory address is obtained, and then passed, as shown in lines 31 through 32. Otherwise, the value to be passed is set to 0, as shown in line 35.

After processing the parameter passing, the next step is to get the total width of the local variables of the called function, allocate memory space for the local variables, and assign the memory address of the local variables to the variable *application->currentLocalBaseAddr* as shown in lines 36 through 38. Finally, the serial number of the first line of code of the called function is obtained in the code table, which is assigned to the variable *application->nextCodeRowIndex* so that the first line of code of the called function can be executed next, as shown in line 39.

The return instruction *return* corresponds to the function call instruction *call*. The interpreter calls the *processCallReturn* function to process the return instruction line, the implementation of which is shown in Code 5.10. The meaning of return is fourfold. First, the return address is assigned to *application->nextCodeRowIndex* for return, as shown in lines 2 through 4. Next, the caller is checked to see if the return value is needed and then the corresponding processing is done, as shown in lines 7 through 22. The last parameter passed by the caller is the memory address of the variable being assigned. If the value of this parameter is 0, it indicates that the caller does not need a return value. Otherwise, a return value is required, which should be passed to the assigned variable. When the caller needs a return value, there are two cases: (1) the value of a variable; (2) a constant. When it is the value of a variable, it is handled as shown in lines 11 through 12. When it is a constant, it is handled as shown in lines 15 through 20.

Code 5.10 Implementation of the processCallReturn Function

```
(1)   void processCallReturn(int elementNum, char
      *element[ ]) {
(2)       int fomalTotalwidth =
          application->currentFunction->getFormalTotalwidth();
(3)       char *itemAddr = (char *)application-
          >currentFormalBaseAddr + fomalTotalwidth;
(4)       nextCodeRowIndex = *(int *)itemAddr;
(5)       itemAddr += sizeof(int);
(6)       unsigned int assignedVarAddr = *(unsigned int *)
          itemAddr;
(7)       if (assignedVarAddr != 0) {
(8)           int typeId = application->currentFunction-
              >getReturnTypeId( );
```

```
(9)        Type *type
           =application->typeTable->getItemByIndex(typeId);
(10)       if ( isLogicAddr(element[1] ) {
(11)           void *returnValueAddr = getMemAddrByLogicAddr(
               element[1]);
(12)           memcpy(assignedVarAddr, returnValueAddr ,
               type->width);
(13)       }
(14)       else {
(15)         if (typeId == 0) //int type constant
(16)           *(int *) assignedVarAddr = atoi(element[1]);
(17)         else if (typeId == 1) //float type constant
(18)           *(float *) assignedVarAddr = atof(element[1]);
(19)         else if (typeId == 2) //char type constant
(20)         *(char *) assignedVarAddr = *element[1];
(21)       }
(22)     }
(23)     free(application->currentLocalBaseAddr);
(24)     free(application->currentFormalBaseAddr);
(25)     application->currentLocalBaseAddr =
         callStack->pop( );
(26)     application->currentFormalBaseAddr =
         callStack->pop( );
(27)     application->currentFunction = (Function *)
         callStack->pop( );
(28)     return;
(29)   }
```

After processing the return value, the memory space occupied by local variables and formal parameters should be freed, as shown in lines 23 through 24. Finally, the current function should be switched to the caller function, i.e., three elements should be popped out of the function call stack *callStack*, and new values should be assigned to the variables *application->currentLocalBaseAddr*, *application->currentFormalBaseAddr*, and *application->currentFunction*, respectively, as shown in lines 25 through 27.

Reflection 5.2: How does the interpreter handle the unconditional jump instruction *goto*, and the instruction *intAddwithVarToConst* for an integer variable plus an integer constant? Can you write the implementation code?

5.2.8 Mapping Logical Addresses to Memory Addresses

The interpreter calls the *getMemAddrByLogicAddr* function to map a logical address into a memory address when it encounters a variable use in processing a line of code. The implementation of this function is shown in Code 5.11. The logical address consists of two parts: the variable category and the variable id. The variable categories include global variable, local variable, formal parameter, member variable, and temporary variable. They are recorded in the global variable table, the local variable table, the formal parameter table, the member variable table, and the temporary variable table, respectively. In the Application object, there is a global variable table and a temporary variable table. Each custom data type has its own member variable table, and each function has its own formal parameter table and local variable table. The memory address of a variable is derived from the base address plus its offset. Once you have the memory address of a variable, you can read its value or assign a value to it. Finding the memory address of a variable by category is shown in lines 4 through 34.

In intermediate languages, there is the concept of temporary variables. When translating source code into intermediate code, temporary variables are introduced to store the results of intermediate calculations. For example, when translating the expression "area + fun(x) * stepLen", a temporary variable of type float is introduced to store the result of the function call fun(x), which is then used to further store the result of the multiplication operation and the result of the addition operation. When the temporary variable is used up, it loses its significance and therefore the memory space it occupies should be freed. In intermediate languages, the instruction *newTempVariable* is used to create a temporary variable, while the instruction *freeTempVariable* means to free a temporary variable. Creating a temporary variable involves defining a new variable by adding a row of data to the temporary variable table. The row number is the serial number of the temporary variable. Releasing a temporary variable is to delete an existing row in the temporary variable table. When the compiler compiles the source code, it notes the maximum number of temporary variables to be used at the same time as part of the program.

When running a program, the interpreter reads the maximum number of temporary variables in the program file during the initialization phase of the Application object, estimates the maximum amount of memory space required for the temporary variables, and then allocates memory space for them. The interpreter stores the starting address of the temporary variable memory space in the *tempBaseAddr* member variable of the Application object, which also has the *tempTable* member variable for storing the temporary variables currently in use. When the interpreter executes the *newTempVariable* instruction, it adds a row of data to the *tempTable* table, creating a new temporary variable. The line number is the index of the temporary variable. When the interpreter executes the *freeTempVariable* instruction, it removes the specified row from the *tempTable* table, releasing an existing temporary variable. The creation and release of a temporary variable is confined to a single statement in the source code. Thus, a temporary variable that is created at compile time and one that is created at interpreted execution will have exactly the same serial number. This is the origin of lines 17 through 20 in Code 5.11.

Code 5.11 Implementation of the getMemAddrByLogicAddr Function

```
(1)   void *getMemAddrByLogicAddr( char *logicAddr) {
(2)      int id = resolveId(logicAddr);
(3)      Variable *Variable = null;
(4)      switch (*logicAddr) {
(5)        case: 'f': //formal parameter
(6)           Variable = application->currentFunction-
              >formalTable->getItemByIndex( id);
(7)           return (char *)application-
              >currentFormalBaseAddr + Variable->offset;
(8)        break;
(9)        case: 'l': //local variable
(10)          Variable = application->currentFunction-
              >localTable->getItemByIndex( id);
(11)          return (char *)application-
              >currentLocalBaseAddr + Variable->offset;
(12)       break;
(13)       case: 'g': //global variable
(14)          Variable = application->globalTable-
              >getItemByIndex( id);
(15)          return (char *)application->globalBaseAddr +
              Variable->offset;
(16)       break;
(17)       case: 't': //temporary variable
(18)          Variable = application->tempTable-
              >getItemByIndex( id);
(19)          return (char *)application->tempBaseAddr +
              Variable->offset;
(20)       break;
(21)       case: 'c': //string constant
(22)          Variable = application->constantTable-
              >getItemByIndex( id);
(23)          return (char *)application->constantBaseAddr +
              Variable->offset;
(24)       break;
(25)       case: 'm': //member variable
(26)          char * objectLogicAddr = resolveObjectLogicAddr
              (logicAddr);
(27)          void *baseAddr = getMemAddrByLogicAddr(
              objectLogicAddr );
```

5.2 Compilation Versus Interpretation of Application Programs 323

```
(28)         Variable = getVariableByLogicAddr(
             objectLogicAddr );
(29)         Type *type =
             application->typeTable-
             >getItemByIndex(Variable->typeId);
(30)         Type *referenceType = application->typeTable-
             >getItemByIndex(type-> referenceTypeId);
(31)         Variable = referenceType->memberTable-
             >getItemByIndex( id );
(32)         return *(unsigned int *)baseAddr +
             Variable->offset;
(33)      break;
(34)    }
(35)  }
```

String constants are expressed as logical addresses in intermediate code. For example, the logical address "const:2" expresses a string constant whose definition is recorded in the line numbered 2 in the string constant table. When the compiler translates the source code into intermediate code, every time it encounters a string constant, it adds it to the string constant memory and adds a row to the string constant table, noting its offset in the string constant memory. The string constant table is shown in Table 5.4. The string constants are then represented by their logical addresses in the intermediate code. The string constant table, as well as the data in the string constant memory, are all part of the intermediate code.

After the interpreter loads the program file into memory, the memory address of the loaded location plus the offset of the string constant data in the file is the base address of the string constant. The interpreter stores it in the member variable *constBaseAddr* of the Application object. Thus, when you get the memory address from the logical address of the string constant, you go to the string constant table and look up the offset value of the corresponding row. The base address plus the offset value is the memory address of the string constant. This is the origin of lines 21 through 24 in Code 5.11.

The other type of variable is the member variable, whose logical address is slightly different from the other categories and whose memory address is a bit more complicated to find, as shown in lines 25 through 33. The logical address of a member variable takes the base address (i.e., the object's memory address) with it. For

Table 5.4 String constant table

Serial number (index)	Offset
0	0
1	18
2	35

example, "member:3[local:5]" is the logical address of a member variable, which means that the memory address of the object is stored in a local variable with logical address "local:5". Thus, the base address is the value of this variable with a logical address of "local:5". The next thing to do is to find the member variable in order to get its offset value. In order to find the definition of the member variable, we first need to find the definition of the variable with the logical address "local:5".

In an intermediate language, when you want to access a member variable, the memory address of the object must already be stored in one of the four categories: local variable, formal parameter, global variable, and temporary variable. In the above example, after finding the definition of the variable "local:5", we know the id of its data type, and then we go to the type table to find its type definition. The type must be a pointer type, which contains the id of the reference type, and from the id of the reference type, go to the type table to find its definition. The type must be a custom datatype with a table of member variables. From the id of the member variable (three in this case), you can get its offset value from the table. This is where lines 25 through 33 of Code 5.11 come from.

Getting the definition of a variable based on its logical address is accomplished by calling the function *getVariableByLogicAddr*, as shown in line 28 of Code 5.11. The implementation of the function *getVariableByLogicAddr* is shown in Code 5.12. Note: The use of this function is limited to obtaining the type definition of a member variable. For pointer chains that appear in the source code, such as "*application->typeTable->rowNum*", the compiler creates a temporary variable of type *TypeTable* pointer when generating intermediate code to store the value of *application->typeTable*, and then uses the value of that temporary variable as the base address of the member variable *rowNum*. Therefore, in Code 5.12, there will only be four types: formal parameter, local variable, global variable, and temporary variable.

Code 5.12 Implementation of the getVariableByLogicAddr Function

```
(1)    Variable*getVariableByLogicAddr( char *logicAddr) {
(2)       int id = resolveId(logicAddr);
(3)       Variable *Variable = null;
(4)       switch (*logicAddr) {
(5)          case: 'f': //formal parameter
(6)             Variable = application->currentFunction-
                    >formalTable->getItemByIndex( id);
(7)          break;
(8)          case: 'l': //local variable
(9)             Variable = application->currentFunction-
                    >localTable->getItemByIndex( id);
(10)         break;
(11)         case: 'g': //global variable
```

5.2 Compilation Versus Interpretation of Application Programs

```
(12)            Variable = application->globalTable-
                  >getItemByIndex( id);
(13)       break;
(14)       case: 't': //temporary variable
(15)            Variable = application->tempTable-
                  >getItemByIndex( id);
(16)       break;
(17)     }
(18)     return Variable.
(19) }
```

Reflection 5.3: When the interpreter processes the *call* instruction, it pushes *application->currentLocalBaseAddr* and *application->currentFormalBaseAddr* into the function call stack *callStack*, which is well understood. Why should *application->currentFunction* also be pushed into the function call stack *callStack*? Please explain. The interpreter is stateless in its interpretation of intermediate code. That is, each line of intermediate code processed does not depend on the previous processing. That is why, when processing a function call, the memory address of the assigned variable is also passed to the called function, which completes the assignment operation by using the return value when it RETURNS. Is this the only way to achieve statelessness in interpreted execution? Please explain the rationale.

Reflection 5.4: When the interpreter processes the temporary variable creation instruction *newTempVariable*, it adds a row of data to the temporary variable table, i.e., defining a variable. The instruction is followed by a parameter with the id of its data type, and the values of the width and offset fields are filled in when it is added. How are the values of these two fields determined? Can you write the implementation code to handle this instruction? For the instruction *freeTempVariable*, which is followed by the id of the temporary variable, can you write the implementation code to handle this instruction?

Reflection 5.5: The implementation of the *getMemAddrByLogicAddr* function shown in Code 5.11 does not consider how to translate the logical addresses of array elements into memory addresses. The logical address of the array element "local:0[tmp:0]" appears in Code 5.6, where "local:0" represents the logical address of the array variable, and the variable with logical address "tmp:0" stores the offset of the array element relative to the array variable in bytes. Therefore, the memory address of the logical address "local:0[tmp:0]" is the memory address of the variable "local:0" plus the value of the int type variable "tmp:0 ". What does the interpreter do with the logical addresses of the array elements? Can you write the implementation code?

Reflection 5.6: The member variables of the Application object include the function table *functionTable*, the type table *typeTable*, the global variable table *globalTable*, the temporary variable table *tempTable*, and the string constant table *constTable*. The data type of *functionTable* is an array, where the data type of its elements is Function. The member variables of the function object include: function id, type id of return value, the id of first line of code in the code table, total width of formal parameters, total width of local variables, and *formalTable* and *localTable*. Other tables are similar. The member variables of the type object include: type id, width, the id of the referenced type, and *memberTable*. The member variables of the variable object include: variable id, type id, width, and offset. The intermediate code file is a text file consisting of two parts: (1) metadata, and (2) an intermediate code table and symbol tables. The metadata records the line width of each type of table, the number of lines, and the starting position of its data in the file. Can you write the initialization implementation code for the Application object?

Reflection 5.7: When talking about binary executables, a certain model of computer is usually anchored. The reason is that the binary representation of a piece of data may not be the same for different models of computers. Therefore, binary executables are not universal, only text files are. However, text files cannot be processed directly by the computer, but through an application program. For example, intermediate code files cannot be executed directly by the computer, but by an application program called interpreter. Thus, it can be seen that there is a cost to be paid for genericity. The interpreter is a binary executable. Why not just compile the intermediate code file into a binary executable, thus eliminating the need for an interpreter? Please give reasons.

Reflection 5.8: Programs, also called software, are classified as operating system software, system software, and application software. Are compilers part of system software, or application software? What about interpreters? What are the characteristics of each of the three types of software and how are they related to each other?

Reflection 5.9: Programs written in high-level languages are clearly less structured than programs written in intermediate languages. In high-level programming languages, there is only the notion of source code, and code and data are mixed together. In an intermediate language, the program is structured into a code table and multiple symbol tables. Symbol tables are further divided into four categories: type table, function table, global variable table, and constant table. For each function in the function table, there is a formal parameter table and a local variable table. For each custom data type in the type table, there is a member variable table. What are the advantages of high-level languages? Why is it important to program in a high-level programming language?

5.2.9 Characteristics of Interpreted Execution

As can be seen from the implementation of the interpreter in the previous section, the greatest advantage for a program generated in an intermediate language is its generality. Regardless of the model of computer, a program can run on it as long as the interpreter is installed. The gain of the interpreted implementation is generality, and the cost paid is performance overhead. Performance overheads include

5.2 Compilation Versus Interpretation of Application Programs

computational overheads and storage overheads. Computational overhead is manifested in the fact that for each variable accessed, the interpreter has to look up a table, get the variable's offset, compute its memory address, and then use a variable to store its memory address. In contrast, when generating a binary executable, the compiler first replaces the logical address with the relative address at once. The relative address is also known as the offset. This eliminates the need for a table lookup at runtime, thus saving the overhead of table lookup. When the computer supports relative addressing, the compiled mode of operation eliminates the need to explicitly calculate the memory address of a variable, which is done incidentally by the CPU during the execution of operation. At the same time, the overhead of storing the memory address and transferring the memory address value back and forth between the CPU and memory is eliminated. As a result, the interpreted mode of operation is clearly inferior to the compiled mode of operation in terms of performance.

The performance overhead of interpreted execution is even more pronounced when a piece of code is executed in a loop. Every time it loops, it repeats the address translation. When running in compiled mode, the conversion is done once and for all at compile time; thus, the problem of repeated address translation does not exist. In addition, when running in compiled mode, the symbol table in the program has lost its meaning and can be removed, thus saving memory space. The interpreter is also no longer needed, further saving memory overhead.

Another problem with interpreted execution is that it does not utilize the hardware characteristics of the computer to improve execution efficiency. When the interpreted mode of operation is used, all of the contents of the program being interpreted for execution (both program and data) are in memory, and high-speed memory such as registers is not utilized at all. When the compiled mode of operation is used, the translation of intermediate code into machine code is usually done by a compiler provided by the computer vendor. The compiler therefore knows the hardware characteristics, such as the number of registers, whether relative and indirect addressing is supported, whether pipelining is supported, whether parallel processing is supported, and so on. The full utilization of hardware features can significantly improve the computational performance [9]. Comparative performance tests show that the efficiency of the interpreted mode of operation is usually less than 15% of that of the compiled mode of operation. Therefore, only when the program is short, or the function of the program is human–computer interaction, it is appropriate to use the interpreted mode of operation.

Scripting languages can be categorized into two types: (1) directly interpreted execution classes, such as the Shell scripting language, and (2) indirectly interpreted execution classes, such as the JavaScript language. Programs written in indirectly interpreted execution class scripting languages are first compiled into code written in an intermediate language and then run in an interpreted manner by an interpreter. In this case, a script engine, which is an application that runs script programs, naturally consists of two components: the compiler and the interpreter. The compilation and interpreted execution can be strictly divided into two sessions, or they can be alternated. When split into two sessions, a script program is compiled first and then interpreted for execution. When alternating, it means that after compiling a statement or function, the generated code is interpreted and executed, and the two alternate.

Reflection 5.10: What are the characteristics of shell scripts and web front-end JavaScript scripts, both of which use the interpreted mode of operation? Why is the interpreted mode of operation appropriate, rather than the compiled mode of operation? For data processing and scientific computing programs, loops are usually included, so why is the interpreted mode of operation not suitable?

5.2.10 Intermediate to Machine Code Translation

Once the interpreter implementation is known, translating the intermediate code into machine code is a natural step. The first task of translation is to fill in the width of each type in the type table, the offset of each variable in the variable tables, and the total width of the formal parameter and the total width of the local variables in the function table. Then, for the base address of each variable, a register is allocated to store it exclusively. The logical address in the intermediate code can then be replaced by the register id plus the offset, i.e., it is converted to a memory address. The next step is to translate the intermediate code into machine code line by line according to the machine language specification. The function call instruction means: allocate memory for parameter passing, pass real parameters and return address and memory address of the assigned variable, and then jump. For the called function, the added start code performs the switching of the current function and the allocation of memory for local variables. Return instruction means: pass back the return value to the assigned variable, restore the return address, free the memory occupied by local variables and formal parameters, switch the current function, and then jump.

In the translation of the return instruction, when restoring the return address, it cannot be restored directly to the instruction register, otherwise it would be an instant jump. Instead, it should be restored to another register. Finally, it is restored to the instruction register, and the restoration and jump are completed by one instruction. In addition, the switching of the current function not only refers to the base addresses of formal parameters and local variables, but also includes registers. Registers are a kind of shared memory, available in every function. Therefore, in the starting code of the function, the value of the registers to be used should be saved to memory for restoration when the function returns.

Translating intermediate code into machine code is not complicated in terms of translation alone. An important task for the compiler is to take full advantage of the physical characteristics of the target computer to generate high-quality machine code. High-quality machine code generation is also called object code optimization [5]. The meaning of object code optimization is to make the target code require as little storage space as possible at runtime, the computational overhead is as small as possible, as well as the transportation of code and data between different classes of memories is as small as possible, and the result of the computation is obtained as soon as possible. The optimization strategy is based on the execution timing of the intermediate code to identify the dependencies among the data, and the life cycle of the data, and then make use of the physical characteristics of the target computer to make the running time of a program as short as possible, so as to get the computational results as soon as possible.

Typical physical characteristics of a computer include: addressing mode, number of registers, cache, instruction pipelining, multicore processing [5], etc. Registers are the most responsive memory, so storing frequently accessed data in registers can increase computing speed. Deciding what data to store in registers and how to pair data with registers is known as the register management issue. Register management is implemented at two levels: first register assignment and then register allocation. Register assignment is the specialized storage of specific registers for those data that are used frequently while the program is running. For example, the memory address of the next machine instruction to be executed, and the base address of the local variables for the current function, are the data to be frequently accessed in a program. The remaining registers after register assignment are used to store the program's data.

The problems to be solved by register allocation are: which variables should be stored in registers and how to assign registers to variables. Since the number of registers is very limited, it is not enough to store all the data commonly used by the program. At this point, it is necessary to perform register vacating. The thing to do in register allocation is to identify the most commonly used data to be stored in registers. Data has life cycle characteristics and variables with non-intersecting life cycles can share the same register. Register allocation consists of three components: live variable identification algorithm, graph coloring-based register allocation method, and register vacating selection method. The utilization of addressing modes has been explained earlier in Sect. 2.8.

5.2.11 Code Optimization Based on Instruction Pipelining Processing

Pipeline processing is an efficient organizational model for factory production. This mode is also adopted by CPUs to increase the efficiency of program operation. In this model, the CPU consists of multiple processing subunits, which are connected in an assembly line fashion. Each subunit does only specific processing, and when it is done, it flows to the next subunit for other processing. The CPU has the ability to start the execution of an instruction in each clock cycle. In other words, at a single moment in time, multiple instructions can be executed in a ladder. Thus, in the case of n subunits, the CPU can execute n instructions at the same time. The processing scenario is as follows: in the first clock cycle, the first subunit processes the first instruction; in the second clock cycle, the first instruction flows to the second subunit for processing, and the first subunit processes the second instruction. And so on. Thus, the CPU runs the program, and in an ideal situation, multiple instructions can be processed in parallel, with one clock cycle completing one instruction.

A prerequisite for an instruction to be submitted to the CPU for execution (i.e., to come online) is that its input data are ready. To ensure that each subunit of the CPU is not idle in every clock cycle, it is required that each instruction does not depend on the operation results of the $n - 1$ instructions that precede it. If this is not possible, the instruction submission can only be delayed until its input data are ready. A clock cycle is said to be in the NOP (no operation) state if no instruction is online. In the extreme cases, where each instruction is dependent on the result of its predecessor, the entire pipeline processing becomes meaningless and takes n clock cycles to complete the processing of an instruction. CPUs with instruction pipeline processing are sometimes called VLIW (Very Long Instruction Word) processors, or superscalar processors.

Therefore, an important part of object code optimization is to analyze the dependencies between instructions, adjust the order between them, or do some simple equivalent transformations to maximize the CPU's pipeline processing power. For example, to find the sum of the elements of an array, the most common source program is shown in Code 5.13. This code cannot utilize the CPU's pipeline processing capabilities. If it is rewritten as the source program shown in Code 5.14, it can take advantage of the CPU's pipelining feature and increase the computation speed by nearly four times.

Code 5.13 Codes That Do Not Adapt to Pipeline Processing
```
for (i = 0; i ++; i < 4*n)  {
  t1 += a[i];
}
```

Code 5.14 Codes That Take Full Advantage of Pipeline Processing
```
for (i = 0; i += 4; i < 4*n) {
  t1 += a[i]; t2 += a[i+1]; t3 += a[i+2]; t4 += a[i+3];
}
t1 += t2; t3 += t4;
t1 += t3.
```

5.2.12 Cache-Based Code Optimization

Cache has much faster read and write responses compared to regular memory. The memory data to be accessed while the program is running have to be in the cache. The transfer of data between the cache and memory is managed by the hardware and is therefore transparent to the compiler. Thus, to the compiler and the programmer, there is only the concept of memory, not the concept of cache. The transfer of data between cache and memory is not done with word as a unit, but with cache line as a unit, typically ranging from 32 to 256 bytes in size. In contrast, when accessing memory, the smallest unit is the byte. When program data are localized, the cache can provide significant performance gains. If the program data are not localized, the cache does not provide a performance boost, but even impacts the performance. Therefore, it is very important to increase the locality of program data.

Increasing the localization of program data usually involves simple equivalent transformations based on the semantics of the code segment. For example, the source program segment shown in Code 5.15 has poor data localization. If it is equivalently transformed into the source program shown in Code 5.16, then the data localization is significantly enhanced. For the sake of comparison, it is assumed that the size of the cache line is 32 bytes (i.e., 8 integers), and the integer two-dimensional array $z[8][8]$ in the program shown in Code 5.15 is stored line by line in memory. Let the space size of the cache be 32 bytes, i.e., it can only hold one line of data. For the program shown in Code 5.15, each access to an array element involves a round-trip transfer of data from memory to the cache. The reason is that a transfer of 32 bytes is exactly one row of data, of which only one element is used, i.e., the availability is only one-eighth.

Code 5.15 Source Program Example with Poor Data Localization
```
for (i = 0; i <= 5; i ++)
   for (j = i; j <= 7; j ++)
       z[j][i] = z[j][i] - average;
```

Code 5.16 Code Optimization That Enhances Data Localization
```
for (j = 0; j <= 7; j ++ )
   for (i = 0; i <= min(j, 5); i ++ )
       z[j][ i] = z[j][i] - average;
```

Since the space in the cache can only hold one row of data, the desired next array element is not always in the cache. Thus, each loop involves one transfer from memory to the cache and one transfer from the cache to memory. The entire loop has to assign values to 33 elements of the two-dimensional array z containing 64 elements. The total number of transfers back and forth is therefore up to 66. If the program shown in Code 5.15 is equivalently transformed into a program such as the one shown in Code 5.16, then data localization is significantly enhanced. From row 1 to row 6 of the two-dimensional array z, the usefulness of each row of data increases by one-eighth of a step. From row 6 to row 8, the availability of each row of data is six-eighths. Thus, the data are transferred from memory to the cache only eight times, and returned eight times, for a total of 16 times. This is a 4× performance improvement compared to 66 times. From this example, it is clear that increasing the locality of program data is an important aspect of code optimization.

Reflection 5.11: Indexes are created in a database with the goal of improving query performance. Please analyze why indexes can contribute to performance improvement in terms of reducing inefficient transportation of data?

5.2.13 Multicore Processor-Based Code Optimization

A multicore processor consists of multiple CPUs and thus has parallel processing capabilities. Most of the multicore processors are symmetrical multiple processes (SMP) type processors, where each core has its own cache and all cores share memory. For multicore processors, it is critical to tap into the parallelizability of the computation. Codes for parallel computation usually have the single program multiple data (SPMD) feature. The function of the program shown in Code 5.17 is to find the variance matrix of a matrix. The program has parallelism. The result of transforming it into a parallel processing program is shown in Code 5.18. Each core in the parallel computation executes the same program, i.e., the program shown in Code 5.18. M in line 1 is the number of cores and is a constant. The variable p in line 2 refers to the serial number of the core. Each core has its own unique serial number. The serial numbers of the cores are from 0 to $M - 1$.

From the program shown in Code 5.18, it can be seen that the matrix z is divided into M blocks, with each b rows of data constituting a block, and the blocks being numbered from 0 to $M - 1$. Each core is responsible for processing one block, and the ith core is responsible for processing the ith block. Thus, the entire computational task is divided into M independent subtasks, with each core responsible for one subtask. This is a typical scenario of parallel computing. From the above analysis, it is clear that the program shown in Code 5.18 has SPMD characteristics.

Code 5.17 Examples of Parallelizable Programs
```
for (i = 0; i < n; i ++)
   for (j = 0; j < n; j ++)
       z[i][j] = (z[i][j] - average)^2;
```

Code 5.18 Parallel Computing Programs with SPMD Features
```
b = n / M;
for (i = b*p; i < b*p + b; i ++ )
   for (j = 0; j < n; j ++ )
       z[i][j] = (z[i][j] - average)^2;
```

Parallel computing involves a number of things such as job partitioning, job scheduling, result aggregation, collaboration, and synchronization between processing units. Thus, the parallel computing architecture, which models and abstracts parallel computing as a way to shield the underlying differences and details. Parallel Computing architecture consists of three components: data types, API interfaces, and application frameworks. Parallel Computing platform providers implement the architecture, while parallel computing application developers develop applications based on the architecture. The well-known parallel computing architectures are MPI, compute unified device architecture (CUDA), OpenMP, OpenCL, OpenACC, and Map/Reduce [8].

High-performance computing has shifted from CPUs alone to a collaborative processing approach that combines CPUs and GPUs. The CUDA architecture is launched by NVIDIA, which utilizes the advantages of both CPUs and GPUs to enhance the parallel processing power of computers. CUDA provides the math libraries CUFFT (discrete fast Fourier transform) and CUBLAS (discrete elementary linear computation) math libraries, which encapsulate the specific implementation details of parallel processing. Once a CUDA-based program is compiled, the target code consists of a Host Code running on the CPU and a Device Code running on the GPU, which share memory and interact with each other to achieve parallel processing.

5.2.14 Interpretation-Compilation-Based Hybrid Run Mode

For an application program, when it is not known what model of computer it is going to run on, interpreted execution is thought of. The diversity of computer and operating system models is shielded by the interpreter, making the application program universal, or portable. Interpreters are language-oriented by nature. That is, for an interpreter of language A, it can interpret and run any application program written in language A. This is where the advantage of interpreted execution comes in. For cloud computing, it is required that applications run everywhere. Interpreted execution adapts to this requirement. But the inefficiency of interpreted execution constrains its application.

Under the traditional way of compiled execution, the developer of the application compiles the source code into a binary executable file. This type of compilation is characterized by being computer model and operating system model oriented, and is therefore not universal or portable. When the application is required to run everywhere, the application developer has to generate binary executables for each model of computer and operating system. This approach creates a dilemma for both application developers and users. There are many models of computers and operating systems, and they are constantly growing. When distributing an application, the developer has to generate binary executables for each model of computer and operating system, which is a large amount of work, inefficient, costly, and difficult to maintain. For users, they have to select a binary executable that matches their computer and operating system model before the application can run on their computer. With a long list of options, it is difficult to know which one is the right one to choose. It is because of this dilemma that an interpreted execution solution is proposed.

The traditional way of compiling has another drawback, which is the problem of version mismatch leading to unutilized machine potential. Here is an example. Suppose a developer generates a binary executable for an X86 32-bit computer and a Windows 32 operating system. There are many versions of X86 32-bit computers, such as 80386, 80486, Pentium, Core, Ryzen, etc. These versions have forward compatibility. The developer had to compile the binary executable conservatively based on 80386 in order to make it run on any X86 32-bit computer. When the user's computer running the application was a newer version such as core, the machine potential was wasted because the additional resources relative to 80386 were not used by the compiler. For example, the core version has many more registers than the 80386, which are wasted if not used by the compiler.

Java is an improvement program for the problems of traditional compilation and operation. Java divides the compiler into two: one is called the front-end compiler and the other is called the back-end compiler. The front-end compiler compiles the Java source code into byte code, i.e., intermediate code generated with an intermediate language. The back-end compiler then compiles the bytecode into target machine code. In the Java scenario, the front-end compiler remains at the developer's end of the application. The back-end compiler, on the other hand, is pushed forward to the user's machine and built into the Java virtual machine. The back-end compiler is installed on the user's machine and naturally knows the model and version of the computer. Thus, the back-end compiler can take full advantage of machine features to do optimizations when translating intermediate code into machine code. This is a major reason why Java has become popular.

Each operating system now provides its own Java virtual machine, which is distributed and installed with the operating system. This means that the Java virtual machine has become an integral part of the operating system. With Java programming, the developer of an application only has to maintain a distribution and keep the source code to himself. This trait is naturally very popular. Microsoft .NET technology is similar to Java technology in that it features a front-end compiler that compiles various high-level language programs into MSIL intermediate code [9].

Scripting languages [10] are very popular these days, such as Node.js, Python, etc. From a compilation point of view, scripting languages have taken a step forward from Java by bringing the front-end compiler forward to the user's machine as well. The developer of an application distributes the source program directly to users. The popularity of scripting languages is closely related to the boom in Internet applications and the generalization of open-source software. Software open source reflects changing times. It no longer makes sense to recognize the source program as a programming secret. In this context, scripting languages became popular. Scripting languages are attractive to users. Since scripting languages appeared later than traditional high-level programming languages, it is natural to introduce many new features in response to the shortcomings of the original languages exposed in practice. For example, programming in Python can reduce the amount of code to a teeny tiny fraction of programming in C++ or Java. The smaller code size not only improves programming efficiency and makes the code concise, but also ensures the quality of the code and enhances the reliability of the software. In addition, when the code size is very small, it becomes feasible to use the interpreted execution mode.

The Java program, in order to achieve the generality and portability of applications, started not with the program of moving the back-end compiler forward to users' computers, but with the interpreted execution. Later, it was found that the efficiency of the interpreted execution is too low to be acceptable. Thus, JIT compilation program (abbreviation of Just in Time Compile) was proposed. That is, during the interpreted execution, when a looping code segment or a function that is frequently called is encountered, it is translated into machine code and then executed. This program mixes interpretation and compilation together, alternately, to improve the execution efficiency of Java applications. In order to further improve the operational efficiency, many JVMs have introduced the AOT compilation program (abbreviation of Ahead of Time) [11]. The essence of the AOT compilation program is to move the back-end compiler forward to users' computers. AOT means, before running an application, the entire byte code is translated into machine code, and then the machine code is executed.

From the optimization based on the physical properties of computers described in Sects. 5.2.10 through 5.2.12, it is clear that the realization of a computer's potential is closely related to both programming and compilation. A computer's potential is wasted if its physical properties are not exploited by applications. An effective solution to exploit the full potential of computers is to organize software hierarchically. For example, for basic and common problem solving such as matrix operations, Fourier transforms, partial differential equation solving, neural network gradient optimization, as well as querying data in a set, it is up to the professionals to explore the data processing characteristics and the physical characteristics of computers, define the data structure, write efficient parallel computation code, and then encapsulate it into a service function as the underlying support software. Thus, computers execute these codes with their potential fully utilized. When an application program is developed, it is based on a ready-made architecture to choreograph the calls to these service functions. This explains why writing an application in a modern scripting language can reduce the amount of code to a tenth, or even a few tenths, of programming in C++ or Java.

Interpreted execution becomes fully viable when the application code is small and does not process the data directly, but indirectly through system function calls. At this point, the interpreted execution plays the role of a baton in a large recital, and itself consumes only a very small percentage of computer resources. Computers spend most of their time executing code in system functions. This is the fundamental reason why scripting languages have become so popular. In essence, they are a mixture and alternation of interpretation and compilation.

5.3 Virtualization of the Runtime Environment

In cloud computing, it is very important for customers' applications to be able to run everywhere to deepen resource sharing and improve service quality. The previous section discusses how to enable a program to run everywhere in response to the question of whether it can run or not. A program can be made to run everywhere by interpreted execution. An interpreter is essentially a virtual machine. However, the interpreted execution is very inefficient. To overcome this problem, one strategy is to layer the software. The solution of fundamental and common problems is encapsulated into system functions, which are treated as public infrastructure services and become part of the system software. When developing an application, the calls to the system functions are orchestrated using a ready-made architecture, so the amount of code to be interpreted and executed is very small. When an application program is interpreted and executed, the computer spends most of its time executing the code in the system functions. Interpreted execution takes up very little time. This is the fundamental reason why scripting languages have become popular.

After an application can run, there is the question of whether it will run successfully. For example, if an application uses port 80 to listen for network connection requests, it will not run successfully if port 80 has already been occupied by another application. The second example is: when an application connects to the database server with the IP address "192.10.168.12", if the database server has been migrated to another computer with an IP address other than "192.10.168.12", then the run will also be unsuccessful. The failure is due to the change. If a computer only runs one application, there is no port conflict issue. Now running multiple applications on one computer at the same time raises the issue of port conflicts. If the database server is not migrated, the operation of old clients will be successful. Now that the database server has been migrated, it has led to the problem of old clients not being able to find the server.

Runtime environment refers to the resources and services that an application will access. In the above example, ports are shared resources managed by the operating system. The database server is an external service that the application relies on. In the case of cloud computing, a customer's application originally ran successfully on its own computer. Since the runtime environment remains the same, the run is always successful. Now it is migrated to run on the cloud, which is a change. When an application runs on the cloud, it is not fixed to run on a particular computer. That is, change is the norm. Migration makes an application's runtime environment change, which triggers the problem of the application running unsuccessfully. How to solve the problem? Next, let us first analyze what is meant by the runtime environment, and then analyze the specific manifestations of unsuccessful execution, lastly explain the solution to the problem.

An application has to call the APIs provided by the operating system to access the services provided by the operating system. Thus, there is a client/service relationship between applications and the operating system. An application as a client makes a request for a resource and the operating system gives the result in response.

5.3 Virtualization of the Runtime Environment

This client–service interaction occurs in the form of API function calls. If the operating system cannot fulfill the resource request made by a client, then the application's call to the operating system's API is unsuccessful. The application runs unsuccessfully because of the unsuccessful calls to the OS APIs. Thus, the runtime environment in which the application runs is the operating system. From an object-oriented perspective, the operating system also has two layers of concepts: classes and instance objects. Here, the operating system is the instance object. The same application may have different API call results when facing different operating system instance objects. Some calls are successful, while others are unsuccessful.

The problem of unsuccessful application execution due to changes is to be solved using virtualization strategies. Virtualization is a common strategy used in software engineering. Virtualization sounds very familiar, but it is not easy to put it into practice in solving real-world problems. Diversity problems caused by changes are basically solved by virtualization strategies. For example, in the early days of networking, it seemed natural to identify a computer on a network by its IP address. Since a server program ran on a single computer, it was natural to use the IP address plus the port number to access the server in client programs. Later, due to a change in the company, the server program was moved to run on another computer. This change caused a problem with clients not being able to find the server. In order to solve this problem, the client program no longer uses the IP address, but uses the domain name to identify the computer where the server is located. The domain name is then resolved (or mapped) to an IP address in real time at runtime.

In the above scheme, the domain name is the logical id of the computer and the IP address is the physical id of the computer. In the terminology of virtualization, the domain name is the virtual id of the computer and the IP address is the real id of the computer. The virtual id has invariance while the real id has variability. This is the virtualization of computer identity in the network. Clients access the server using its virtual id. In the original implementation, clients accessed the server with its real id. In order for a client to access a server with a virtual id, a domain name resolution module has to be added between the client and the server to map the virtual id to the real id. This intermediate module is often called an intermediary or proxy. In this scenario, the server has invariance on the client side. That is, the virtual id remains constant. The server has variability on the provider side, which is reflected in the variability of the real id. The handling of this invariance-variance interface is often referred to as a virtualization solution.

The virtualization of the above IP addresses is static in nature, as evidenced by the fact that the virtualization solution is first available and then the client program is developed. This scenario is clearly not adapted to cloud computing scenarios. In cloud computing, the concept of cloud computing does not come first and then the application is designed and developed. The meaning of cloud computing is to migrate an enterprise customer's existing business information system from its own local area network to run on the cloud without changing the original configuration of the application. At this time the physical resources id changed. For example, Customer A's database server had an IP address of "192.10.168.12" before migration. After migration, it is running on a computer in the cloud with IP address

Fig. 5.2 Realization scenarios where changes due to migration are transparent to applications

"129.95.37.45". Customer A's another application, β, wants to connect to the database server, and the IP address given is still "192.10.168.12". If left alone, the connection will obviously not succeed. To make the connection successful, you must treat the IP address "192.10.168.12" given by application β as a virtual IP address, and map it to the real IP address "129.95.37.45" before you perform the connection. After mapping it to the real IP address "129.95.37.45", you can connect to it successfully.

From the above example, it can be seen that before the migration, the resource id given by an application when it requests a resource is the real id. After the migration, the real resource id has changed. For the application to run successfully, the resource id given by the application must be treated as a virtual resource id. At runtime, an intermediary is added between the operating system and the application to map the virtual resource id to the real id. This addition is called a virtual machine. The original 2-tier structure is now a 3-tier structure, as shown in Fig. 5.2. Since the application is on top of the virtual machine, it is also said that the application runs on the virtual machine.

The virtual machine is responsible for mapping virtual ids to real ids. How does the virtual machine know the mapping between virtual ids and real ids? When a server migrates, its real id changes. The virtual machine on which a client resides must be aware of this change in order to perform the correct mapping. How should virtualization be implemented in the cloud? To answer these questions, it is important to understand the evolution of virtualization technology. The first virtualization that occurred was the virtualization of files and then of functions. Once the intent and implementation of virtualization of these two resources are understood, it is not difficult to understand and master virtualization technology in cloud computing.

5.4 Virtualization of Files

The problem that virtualization addresses is the interaction between a client and a server. The variability of the server id requires that it be transparent to the client. That is, the client holds a virtual id of a resource, which is mapped to a real id in real time as the client accesses the server. A virtual ID could be mapped to a different real ID, which results in different service outcomes. This interface between invariance and variability can sometimes be described as a generalization of the client

5.4 Virtualization of Files

program. Here is an example. A Shell interpreter is used to execute Shell commands. When a single Shell command is executed, the keyboard is used as input, and the results of the run are displayed on the screen. When two Shell commands are executed together using a pipe character, the results of the first command are no longer displayed on the screen, but become the input for the second command. Going to check the source code of the Shell commands (written in C++), it can be seen that it does not take into account whether or not there is such a difference as a pipe character. It uses cin for input and cout for output, which means it uses the keyboard as input and the screen as output.

Why do the behavioral characteristics of Shell commands change when two Shell commands are connected by a pipe character? The implementation of this generalization is considered in the operating system. The operating system treats all peripheral resources as files. Thus, keyboard input is to open the keyboard file and then read that file. Screen output is to open the screen file and write to that file. cin and cout in C++ are actually file ids. The shell interpreter is a client program that accesses the file service, and the operating system is the provider of the file service. The client program reads data from a file by calling the API function *fread* provided by the operating system and writes data to a file by calling the *fwrite* function. The first parameter in these two functions is the file descriptor, i.e., the file id. The operating system virtualizes files, so the file id given by a client is a virtual id. The execution of the above Shell commands, with or without the pipe character, affects the behavior of the service because the operating system maps the virtual id to a different real id.

The operating system provides virtualization support for three files [12]. In C++ terminology, these three files are cin, cout, and cerr, respectively. The operating system opens these three files for a process when it is created. Therefore, the application program only needs to use these three files without opening them. The virtual ids of these three files are 0, 1 and 2, respectively. When an application calls the operating system API function *fopen* to open a file, the return value will not be the memory address of the file object, but the file descriptor. In other words, the return value is not the real id of the opened file, but the virtual id. The process object in the operating system kernel has a member variable *fileTable*, which stores the mapping relationship between the virtual ids and the real ids of the opened files. Every time an application program opens a new file, the operating system will add a row to its process's *fileTable*, recording the file's virtual id and real id. At the point, the virtual id is called the file descriptor, returned to the application program.

cin, cout, and cerr are the first three files to be opened by a process, and their file descriptors are naturally 0, 1, and 2, respectively. The operating system also provides an API for applications to modify the real ids of the cin, cout, and cerr files. An application can open a file and then call the operating system's API to set it to cin, or cout, or cerr. When the real id of cin is changed, the application will no longer read the cin file as keyboard input. When the real id of cout is changed, the application will no longer write to the cout file as screen output.

The Shell interpreter takes advantage of the file virtualization capabilities provided by the operating system to implement pipelined stream processing. The interpreter checks to see if there is a pipe character between two Shell commands in a line of commands. If it does, it creates a temporary file before executing the first Shell command and modifies cout to change it to the temporary file that was created. Thus, the output of the first command is deposited into the temporary file. Before executing the second Shell command, the interpreter resets cout, so the output of the second Shell command is still the screen. In the meantime, it also modifies cin to change it to the temporary file that was created. Thus, the input of the second command is no longer the keyboard, but the temporary file that was created.

The virtualization provided by the operating system for the three files cin, cout and cerr provides a powerful support for the generalization of applications. Taking Shell commands as an example, when executed remotely, no modifications are required. A user can use a telnet terminal to log in to a telnet server on a remote computer, and then keyboard in the Shell command line on the telnet terminal to have it executed on the remote computer. The result of the execution is displayed on the telnet terminal. With the virtualization of the above three files, the implementation of this function is very simple. Telnet terminal and telnet server have to establish a network connection to interact. In the operating system, the network connection is also abstracted as a file. Therefore, the telnet server only needs to change cout to this network connection. When the shell commands are subsequently executed, the output is sent to the telnet terminal over the network connection.

The virtualization of the file cerr also has a wide range of applications. Applications output logs to cerr. By default, cerr refers to the screen file. Thus, logs are output to the screen. If the cerr is changed to a local file, then the logs are written to the local file. If you change cerr to a remote file, then the logs are written to the remote file. If you establish a network connection to a remote database server and modify cerr to that network connection, then the logs are written to the remote database server. In cloud computing, it is common to collect logs from all customer applications into a log database for unified analysis and management. With the virtualization of the file cerr, it is very simple to implement this function. Just create a process, then let the process establish a network connection with the log database server, then modify cerr to that network connection, and then call the main function of the application.

The operating system encapsulates all resources into files, allowing applications to access any resource and service simply by knowing how to access a file. This treatment greatly improves the generalizability of applications. For example, the operating system provides applications with API functions that allow a network file system (NFS) to be mounted in a directory of the local file system [12]. Applications can then access the remote files no differently than the local files. In other words, the network is transparent to applications in terms of file usage.

From the virtualization of the above files, it is clear that services are on the provider's side, with variability, in the form of real ids. Services, on the client side, have invariance and appear as virtual ids. The interface between invariance and variability at runtime is realized through mapping. Resource ids are used to identify resource objects on the service provider side. Resource virtualization only enables client programs to have universality from the aspect of resource object identification. For client programs, at runtime, they also need to call the member functions of the resource objects provided by the service provider. The service provider may provide different implementations for the same function in different classes. Therefore, there is a diversity of function implementations. Can this diversity of function implementations appear in a single form on the client side? That is, can it appear in the form of virtual function? This is where virtual functions come from. The virtualization of functions is crucial for the generalizability of client programs, which is explained next.

5.5 Virtualization of Functions

In many scenarios, when the number increases to a certain level, there is a need for hierarchical management. For example, when the number of students is small, it can be managed at one level. When the number of students increases to 60 or more, it will be found that one level of management will encounter a series of problems, such as students' renaming. The way to deal with this is to carry out split-class management. Thus, one level of management becomes multiple levels of management, and the linear structure becomes a tree hierarchy. The same is true for programming. In procedure-oriented languages, programs are composed of functions in a one-level structure. Functions are identified by function names. As more functions are added, problems like renaming come out. For this reason, the concept of classes was introduced for hierarchical management. Procedure-oriented programming evolved into object-oriented programming. Functions became members of classes and thus are called member functions. A function may be repeated in more than one class. For this reason, the concept of inheritance was introduced by extracting commonalities, making the program structure and lineage both clear and concise, and easy to maintain.

Polymorphism [13] is the most central concept in object-oriented programming languages. Polymorphism is a high-level abstraction that enhances the generality of program code. The essence of polymorphism is function virtualization. The following program example shows the ins and outs of function virtualization. In a drawing program, a graph document consists of various classes of graphical objects. Graphics classes are added through inheritance. For example, the five-ringed flag graph is inherited from the circle graph. To add an object of a graphics class to a graph document, you create an instance object of that graphics class and add it to the graph document. The drawing program uses a linked list *pShapeList* (an instance object of List class) to store the graphics objects in the graph document. When the drawing program creates an object of the List class, the type of element must be given in advance. Although the type of element is pointer, the referenced type by the pointer must also be given in advance. Now the problem is: when adding an element to *pShapeList*, it may be a pointer to various graphic classes. Thus, there is a contradiction.

To solve the above problem, a forced type conversion strategy can be adopted to solve the problem of elements into the list. Element type of *pShapeList* is set to "void *" at the time of definition. Before adding a pointer value of a graphics class object to *pShapeList*, first convert it to "void *" type. Thus, you have made diversity into singularity and solved the problem of getting elements into the list. But then a second problem popped up. When displaying a graph document on the screen, the *draw* member function of each element in *pShapeList* is called one by one. But the type of all elements in the *pShapeList* is "void *". At this point, each element in *pShapeList* has to be forced to type conversion again, back to its original type. However, its original type is not known at this time. Therefore, it is not possible to convert the pointer of type "void *" back to the original type.

In order to solve the problem of converting pointers of type "void *" back to pointers of the original type, the type of each element in the list had to be tracked. One way to do this is to define an ancestor class, *Shape*, which has a member variable, *classId*, that records the class id. Then, each time a graphics class is defined, the *Shape* class is used as the root class through inheritance. The member variable *classId* is assigned to the class id in the constructor of the *Shape* class. Element type of *pShapeList* is no longer defined as "void *", but "Shape *". When a pointer to a graphics object comes into the list, it is forced to be converted to a "Shape *" type. When reading an element from *pShapeList*, forced type conversion is performed once again, back to a pointer of the original type. The implementation scheme example is shown in Code 5.19.

There are obvious flaws in the program's ability to sense the type of pointer by checking the value of the member variable *classId*. There are many places in the drawing program where elements in *pShapeList* are read. Every time a graphics class is added, the source code has to be modified to add a case statement at these reading places. There are many modifications, involving multiple source code files, and it is inevitable that something will be missed, resulting in an incorrect program. In addition, the developer of the drawing program may not be independent on the vendor who defines and implements the graphics classes. The vendor that defines and implements the graphics classes is called the library provider. The developer of the drawing program is called the client of the library. The above scheme requires that the client and the provider are linked at the source code level. That is, when the provider defines a new graphics class, the client has to modify its source code.

Code 5.19 Example of Conversion of Type Pointers from Singularity to Diversity

```
void Document::onDraw(Canvas* p) {
    Shape *pShape ;
    pShape = pShapeList->GetFirstElement( );
    while (pShape) {
```

5.5 Virtualization of Functions

```
        switch (pShape->classId) {
          case TEXT:
              (Text *)pShape->draw(p);
          break;
          case CIRCLE:
              (Circle *)pShape->draw( p);
          break;
          case FIVE_CIRCLE_FLAG:
              (FiveCircleFlag *)pShape->draw(p);
          break;
          ........
        }
        pShape = pShapeList->getNextElement( );
    }
}
```

Another problem with the above scheme is that the provider of the library must release the header file of the graphics class definition to clients. Only then can clients create an instance of the graphics class in their source code and then call its member functions. In this case, the object-oriented encapsulation feature becomes a dead letter. Clients can see the definitions of all the graphics classes and the entire inheritance history from the root class. This is not encapsulation. Encapsulation should only allow clients to see member functions that are open to the public by the provider.

The bigger problem with the above scenario is version coupling. It is common for providers to revise and upgrade function libraries. Revisions include adding new classes and making changes to existing classes (e.g., adding new member variables, modifying the implementation of member functions). As a result, there are multiple versions of a library. In addition, libraries are often used by multiple applications. For example, on a single machine, there are program A and program B installed, both of which use version v1 of library α. For the purpose of saving disk space and memory, the operating system usually stores only one copy of library α in a public location. At runtime, program A and program B also share library α in memory. When program C is newly installed, it happens to use the library α as well, but a newer v2 version. The new version is copied to a public location, overwriting the v1 version. At this point, the originally installed program A may appear to run unsuccessfully. The reason is that it has a version coupling problem with library α.

An example is given to explain why program A appears to run unsuccessfully. Let us say that there is a graphics class *Text* in library α. The two versions of the class are defined in Codes 5.20 and 5.21, respectively. The modification in version v2 is the addition of a member variable *length*. Program A is developed with version v1, which creates an instance object of the graphics class *Text*, and then calls its member function with the object pointer as the first real parameter. The implementation code for the member function is in library α, which accesses the instance object via the first formal parameter. In the v2 version of library α, the *length* member variable is accessed in the implementation of the member function. However, the instance object provided by Program *A* is a v1 instance object, which has no memory space for *length*. Thus, program *A* appears to run unsuccessfully.

Code 5.20 Definition of class Text in v1
```
class Text {
  char *pText;
  int x, y, width, height;
  Text (char *pString);
  ~Text ( );
  void draw(Canvas *p);
};
```

Code 5.21 Definition of class Text in v2
```
class Text {
  char *pText;
  int x, y, width, height;
  int length;
  Text (char *pString);
  ~Text ( );
  void draw(Canvas *p);
};
```

From the above analysis, it is clear that class definitions released by the provider to clients cannot be modified permanently. In particular, member variables cannot be deleted or added, nor can the types of member variables be changed. Otherwise, programs developed by clients will not run successfully due to the version update problem. However, things are always evolving, and class definition revisions and upgrades are inevitable. The following four subsections discuss in detail the solutions to these three problems.

5.5.1 Proxy-Based Decoupling and Encapsulation Scheme

The above case reveals three problems encountered in object-oriented programming. One of the most intuitive solutions to the latter two problems (i.e., encapsulation and coupling problems) is for the provider to add a proxy (or intermediary) class for each class. The original class is now called the entity class, so each entity class has a corresponding proxy class. All member function definitions of the entity class that are open to the public are copied into the proxy class. Thus, to clients, there is no difference between the proxy class and the entity class. The proxy class always has only one member variable, *pEntity*, of type entity class pointer. In version upgrades, the existing member functions of the proxy class remain unchanged forever, and new member functions can only be added later. The provider now only distributes the definition of the proxy class to clients and no longer publishes the definition of the entity class to clients.

An example of the entity classes is shown in Code 5.22. Its proxy class is shown in Code 5.22, in which a class name *Text* is declared first, and then a pointer variable *pEntity* pointing to that class is defined. In the header file released to clients, even though there is only a definition of *TextProxy* and no definition of the class *Text*, no semantic error is considered when compiling clients' source code. The reason is that, regardless of the type of pointer, the memory address stored in the pointer variable is the same width. When defining a pointer type, the referenced type must be given, which means that when assigning a value to a pointer variable, the memory address of an instance object of class *A* cannot be used to assign to a pointer variable of class *B*. There is no statement in the clients' source code that assigns a value to the member variable *pEntity*. The assignment to *pEntity* is made in the constructor of the proxy class. The implementation of the proxy class constructor is part of the library and is located in the provider's source code.

Code 5.22 Example of an Entity Class Definition
```
class Text {
  char *pText;
  int x, y, width, height;
  void draw(Canvas *p);
  bool focus(bool option);
};
```

Code 5.23 Example of a Proxy Class Definition for an Entity Class
```
class TextProxy {
  class Text;
  Text *pEntity;
  void draw(Canvas *p);
  bool focus(bool option);
};
```

The provider must open all member functions of the proxy class to the public in the library, including constructor and destructor. The reason is that in clients' source code, the instance of the proxy class will be created, and then released. When created, the constructor of the proxy class is called. When released, the destructor of the proxy class is called.

The above scheme solves the version coupling problem. In clients' source code, the instance object of the proxy class is first created and then the member functions of the proxy class are called. The proxy class acts as an intermediary. The implementation of its member function has only one line of code, which is to call the corresponding member function of the entity class object *pEntity*. The initialization of the member variable *pEntity* is done in the constructor of the proxy class, i.e., an instance object of the entity class is created and then its pointer is assigned to *pEntity*.

The definition of a proxy class has the unique feature of having only one member variable and not inheriting from any other class. Thus, it is also very simple and popular among clients. The proxy class achieves decoupling between the provider and its clients. This decoupling is achieved through the invariance of the proxy class. The solution also solves the encapsulation problem together. In the header file that the provider publishes to its clients, there is only the definitions of the proxy classes, no longer the definitions of the entity classes.

5.5.2 Solutions Based on Function Virtualization

The introduction of proxy classes, while solving the coupling and encapsulation problems, came at a cost. Member function calls are relayed through the proxy, which has both time and storage overheads. Is there a better solution that solves the problem without introducing overhead, while also solving the first problem (i.e., modification linkage problem) as well? This question leads to the virtualization of functions.

For the first problem, it is summarized as follows. A program creates a lot of instance objects of many classes, and stores their pointers in a linked list. Because the pointer types of these objects do not match that of element in the list, when a pointer value is put into the list, a forced type conversion has to be performed to convert it to the pointer type of element in the list. When you want to call the member function of an object referred to by an element in the list, you have to perform the forced type conversion again to convert it back to the original pointer type. However, the original pointer type is not known at this time. The tracking scheme shown in Code 5.19 is then used. When a new type appears, this scheme requires clients of the new type to link with the provider at the source code level, making clients' source code less generalizable and generic.

If the source code shown in Code 5.19 is changed to that shown in Code 5.24, and if the desired effect is obtained at runtime, then this code is generalizable and generic, and the first problem is solved. The desired effect is that the member

5.5 Virtualization of Functions

function *draw* called in line 5 of Code 5.24, although expressed through the variable *pShape*, is not bound to the class *Shape* of the variable *pShape*, but rather to the class of the object pointed to by the value of *pShape*. This effect is called polymorphism. For example, if the class of the object to which the pointer value refers is *Circle* for an element in the list, then the member function d*raw* of class *Circle* should be called at runtime instead of the member function *draw* of class *Shape*.

Code 5.24 Broadly Applicable and Generic User Source Code
```
(1)   void Document::onDraw(Canvas* p) {
(2)      Shape *pShape ;
(3)      pShape = pShapeList->GetFirstElement( );
(4)      while (pShape) {
(5)         pShape->draw(p);
(6)         pShape = pShapeList->GetnextElement( );
(7)      }
(8)   }
```

For the call to the member function *draw* in line 5 of Code 5.24, to bind it to the class of the object to which the pointer value *pShape* refers, it means that the starting memory address of the called function *draw* cannot be determined at compile time, but only at run time. This type of member function call is called a dynamic call. In other words, there should be additional member variables in the object pointed to by the pointer value *pShape* that records the starting addresses of the class member functions in memory. The most straightforward way to accomplish this goal is to think of the class's member functions as member variables. Thus, there are two kinds of class member variables: data member variables and function member variables. When an instance of the class is created, memory space is allocated for both types of member variables. Then both types of member variables are assigned initial values in the constructor. For function member variables, the initial value is the starting address of the member function in memory.

An example is given below. For the class *Text* shown in Code 5.25, in the original semantics, there is only memory space for the data member variables *pText*, *x*, *y*, *width*, and *height* in its instance object, and there is no memory space for the member function variables *draw* and *focus*. In order to achieve polymorphic effects, the memory space for the function member variables *draw* and *focus* is added to the instance object. Both variables are naturally of type function pointer. In the constructor of a class, initial values are assigned not only to data member variables but also to function member variables. In this example, the initial values of the function member variables *draw* and *focus* are the starting addresses of the member functions *draw* and *focus* in memory, respectively.

Code 5.25 Ordinary Member Function Definition in the Text Class
```
class Text {
  char *pText;
  int x, y, width, height;
  void draw(Canvas *p);
  bool focus(bool option);
};
```

Code 5.26 Virtual Function Definition in the Text Class
```
class Text {
  char *pText;
  int x, y, width, height;
  virtual void draw(Canvas *p);
  virtual bool focus(bool option);
};
```

However, the above memory layout for instance objects of a class is not the original scheme. In the original scheme, when an instance object of a class is created, memory space is allocated only for its data member variables and not for its function member variables. The reason is that for a member function variable of a class, it takes the same value in all instance objects, so there is no need to store it repeatedly in each instance object. Because in the original scheme, no memory space is allocated to the member functions in the instance objects, the call to the member function *draw* in line 5 of Code 5.24 refers to the call to the member function *draw* of class *Shape*.

In order to achieve polymorphic effects based on the original scheme, a new category must be added to the member function. The original category is called ordinary member function, and the new category is called dynamic member function. Dynamic member function is also called virtual function. In C++, a member function is called a virtual function when the virtual modifier is added in front of its definition. For a virtual function, memory space is allocated for it when an instance of the class is created, and the compiler adds code to the constructor to assign initial values to the virtual function member variables.

To make the code shown in Code 5.24 exhibit polymorphic effects, the *draw* function should be defined as a virtual function. For example, for the definition of the class *Text* shown in Code 5.25, its member functions are defined as virtual functions accordingly, as shown in Code 5.26. For a class containing virtual functions, the virtual function variable takes the same value in all of its instance objects, so the virtual function variable portion can be stripped out of the instance objects, with only one copy in memory, and shared among all instance objects. The shared portion of the virtual function variable is called the virtual table and is named *vtab* (short for virtual table). Each instance object simply adds a pointer variable whose

5.5 Virtualization of Functions

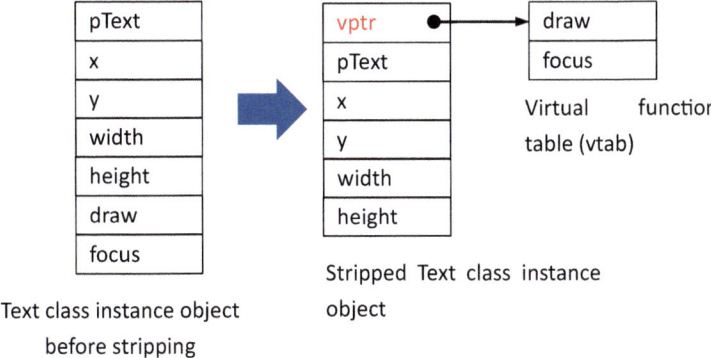

Fig. 5.3 Example of stripping function member variables from an instance object

value points to the virtual table. This pointer variable is called a virtual pointer and is named *vptr* (short for virtual pointer). The initialization of the virtual pointer is done in the class constructor. An example of this stripping is shown in Fig. 5.3. This example is an instance object of the class *Text* defined in Code 5.26.

From the above analysis, it is clear that defining member functions as virtual functions solves the first problem encountered in object-oriented programming, allowing the program shown in Code 5.24 to exhibit polymorphic effects. However, the encapsulation and coupling problems have not been solved. In order to solve these two problems, the concept of pure virtual functions [13] has to be further introduced, and the proxy class has to be transformed into an interface. In the definition of a virtual function, the virtual function variable is further assigned a value of 0, then it becomes a pure virtual function. If the definition of a class contains only pure virtual functions, then the class is called interface. A pure virtual function in an interface is called an interface function. An example of an interface definition in C++ is shown in Code 5.27. In Java, the keyword interface was introduced, and an example of an interface definition is shown in Code 5.28.

Code 5.27 Shape Interface Definition in C++
```
class Shape {
    virtual void draw(Canvas * p) = 0;
    virtual bool focus(bool option) = 0;
};
```

Code 5.28 Shape Interface Definition in Java
```
interface Shape {
    void draw(Canvas * p) ;
    bool focus(bool option) ;
};
```

With the concept of interface, an entity class inherits an interface and implement its interface functions, achieving the unity of virtual and real, so that the instance objects of the interface class and the entity class are integrated into one. As a result, the relay overhead of member function calls no longer exists. On the other hand, the provider only needs to publish the interface definition to clients, not the entity class definition. The source program written by clients (as shown in Code 5.24) not only has no syntax problems, but also exhibits polymorphism at runtime. Thus, all three of the above problems in object-oriented programming have been solved perfectly.

The last thing left to do is that the service provider must provide a global function open to the public for clients to call to get an instance object of the interface class. A client can only call the member functions of the interface class if he or she has obtained an instance object of the interface class from the service provider. For the service party, it is the creation of an instance object of an entity class. Since the instance object of the entity class contains the instance object of the interface class, it is only necessary to perform a forced type conversion to convert a pointer to the instance object of the entity class to a pointer to the instance object of the interface class. Code 5.29 gives a sample implementation of this global function for clients to call to get a pointer to an instance object of the interface class. In this implementation, an instance object of the entity class *Text* is created first. This object contains an instance object of the interface class *Shape*. Therefore, after performing a forced type conversion, a pointer to the interface *Shape* instance object is obtained.

Code 5.29 Method for Obtaining Interface Pointers by Users
```
Shape * CreateText(const char *psz, int x, int y, int width,
int height) {
    return (Shape *) new Text(psz, x, y, width, height);
};
```

Now return to the drawing program described earlier. With the definition of the interface *Shape*, the elements in the *pShapeList* table are of type "*Shape* *". For the different graphics classes, they all inherit the *Shape* interface and implement the interface functions therein. Regardless of which instance of the graphics class is created, what is returned to clients is a pointer to the *Shape* interface, so it can be deposited directly into the *pShapeList* list without the need for forced type conversion. In addition, when the program shown in Code 5.24 is run, the member function *draw* called at line 5 is polymorphic, and its memory address is obtained from the interface object pointed to by the value of the pointer *pShape*. The member variable *vptr* of the interface object points to the virtual function table, the first entry of which is the memory address of the member function *draw*.

The instance object of an interface has two parts: (1) the member variable *vptr*; and (2) the table of virtual functions *vtab*. Since the entity class inherits the interface class, the instance object of the entity class contains an instance object of the interface class. When entity class *E* inherits interface *A*, it must implement every pure virtual function from the interface class. Implementing a pure virtual function is the same as creating an instance object of that pure virtual function. Therefore, when entity class *E* inherits interface *A*, it creates an instance object of interface *A*'s virtual function table *vtab*, named *vtabByE*. Each instance object of entity class *E* contains an interface object. The member variable *vptr* of all interface objects has the same value, pointing to *vtabByE*. The assignment of the member variable *vptr* is handled by the constructor of entity class *E*. *vtabByE* is similar to the function export table, belonging to the content of the executable. Once the executable is loaded into memory, the memory address of *vtabByE* is a known constant.

5.5.3 Interface Characterization

Interfaces are the baseline for interaction between the library provider and clients, and must be immutable. That is to say, once the provider defines an interface and publishes it, it can never be modified. If you want to add a new interface function, you can only define a new interface, let it inherit the original interface, and then add the interface function in the new interface. In addition, interface inheritance can only be single inheritance, not multiple inheritances, to ensure that the child interface is compatible with the parent interface. That is to say, interface *C* can inherit interface *A* or interface *B*, but cannot inherit both interface *A* and interface *B*. For an entity class, it can inherit multiple interfaces and implement the functions in each interface, not leaving the interface function unimplemented. Clients cannot create an instance of an interface by themselves, but can only call a function in the library to get a pointer to an instance of the interface.

An interface changes from abstract to concrete only when it is inherited by some entity class that implements it. An interface may be inherited by many entity classes, each of which has its own implementation of the interface functions. Therefore, the behavior of an interface varies from one entity class to another. For example, for the above *Shape* interface, each graphics class inherits it and gives its own implementation of the *draw* function in the interface. For example, the implementation of the *draw* function by the graphics class *Text* is clearly different from that by the graphics class *Circle*. When the compiler generates the object code for the entity class *E*, it generates a virtual function table *vtab* for its inherited interface *A*. For each implementation of a function in *A*, the compiler records its start address (an offset from the start of the library file) in the virtual function table *vtab*. The compiler also adds code that assigns an initial value to the virtual function pointer *vptr* in the constructor of the entity class *E*.

A virtual function table is like a function export table in an executable file, it is the content of a function library file. When a client's application runs, the function library file is loaded into memory. Let the loaded address be *loadedAddr*. At this point, the data in the virtual function table *vtab* have to be changed, from an offset relative to the start position of the library file, to a memory address. Only then can the interface function calls be realized. This change is very simple, i.e., the original value (i.e., the offset) plus *loadedAddr*.

In addition, the compiler reserves a storage location for *loadedAddr* when generating the function library file, for the purpose of assigning an initial value to *vptr*. At runtime, the memory address of the virtual function table *vtab* is assigned to the member variable *vptr* every time an instance of the entity class E is created, which involves the calculation of the memory address of *vtab*. *vtab*'s offset in the library file is known at compile time, and is therefore a constant. This constant, plus *loadedAddr*, is its memory address. Therefore, assigning an initial value to *vptr* in the constructor of the entity class E is not a problem.

5.5.4 Getting Another Interface by One Interface

An entity class may inherit from multiple interfaces and give implementations for all of them. For example, suppose class E is defined as "class E: public A, B {......}", whose implication is that the entity class E inherits and implements interfaces A and B. When a user calls the global function *createA* in the library, the return value is a pointer to an instance of interface A. When the user wants to get a pointer to an instance of interface B, how to get it? At this point, it is natural to think of forced type conversion. For example, the user first obtains a pointer to interface A through the statement "A* pA = CreateA();". The member function in interface A is then called. Subsequently, a pointer to interface B can also be obtained via the forced type conversion statement "B* pB = (B *)pA;" in order to call the member function in interface B.

The forced type conversion here differs from the common forced type conversion. When the user knows the definition of class E and knows that the pointer *pA* originates from an instance object of class E, the above forced type conversion is perfectly feasible. The compiler can determine the reasonableness of this forced type conversion based on the definition of class E and knows how to convert it. The problem now is that the value of *pA* comes from the service provider. On the user side, the compiler can only see the definitions of interface A and interface B, and there is no notion of class E. Interface A and Interface B are independent on each other and are not necessarily related to each other. Therefore, the compiler does not know how to convert them. Therefore, the forced type conversion statement "B* pB = (B *)pA;", which appears in the user's source program, does not work from the conventional point of view. But then again, the Java language allows such a statement. How can this be explained?

The above forced type conversion has its own peculiarities. The compiler knows that the meaning of the statement is: from an interface pointer value, get another interface pointer value. For this particular conversion, the compiler translates it as follows: a member function *transform* of interface A is called, where the real parameter passed is the name of interface B. If the return value of this function is not 0, then it is a pointer to interface B. Conversely, if it is 0, it indicates that a pointer to interface B cannot be obtained from *pA*, i.e., the two are not linked.

In the above example, on the service provider side, the instance object of interface A referred to by *pA* is derived from the instance object of class E. Class E inherits and implements interfaces A and B, and naturally implements the purely

5.5 Virtualization of Functions

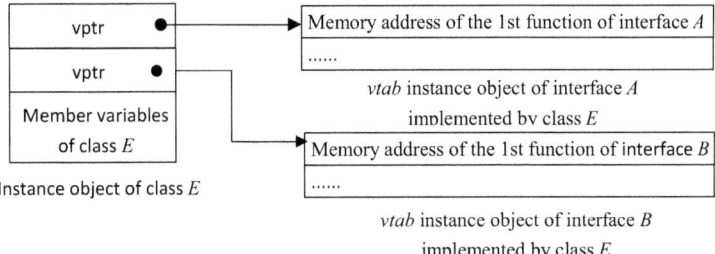

Fig. 5.4 Memory layout of an instance object of class *E* that inherits and implements interfaces *A* and *B*

virtual function *transform* of interface *A*. Here, the member function *transform* of interface *A* is implemented by class *E*, and therefore the definition of class *E* is known. Knowing the definition of class *E* and its memory layout, we also know the relationship between the memory addresses of the three instance objects. These three instance objects are: the instance object of class *E*, the instance object of interface *A*, and the instance object of interface *B*. The memory layout of the instance object of class *E* is shown in Fig. 5.4. From this, we know that the instance object of class *E* has the same memory address as the instance object of interface *A*. The memory address of the instance object of interface *A* plus the width of the pointer variable *vptr* is the memory address of the instance object of interface *B*. The implementation of the member function *transform* for interface *A* and interface *B* in this example is shown in Codes 5.30 and 5.31, respectively.

Code 5.30 Class *E*'s Implementation of the Member Function transform in Interface A

```
(1)   void * E::A::transform( char *inferfaceName) {
(2)     if (strcmp(inferfaceName, "B") == 0) {
(3)       return (void *)this + WIDTH( POINTER);
(4)     else
(5)       return 0;
(6)   }
```

Code 5.31 Class *E*'s Implementation of the Member Function transform in Interface B

```
(1)   void * E::B::transform( char *inferfaceName) {
(2)     this = (void *)this - WIDTH( POINTER );
(3)     if (strcmp(inferfaceName, "A") == 0) {
(4)       return this;
(5)     else
(6)       return 0;
(7)   }
```

For the member functions of interface *B*, the first statement in any implementation given by class *E* will be "this = (void *)this - WIDTH(POINTER);". This scenario is shown in line 2 of Code 5.31. The implication is that from the value of the pointer to the instance object of interface *B* (i.e., the value of the formal parameter *this*), the value of the pointer to the instance object of class *E* is obtained (here it is still stored in the parameter *this*). In contrast, for the member functions of interface *A* implemented by class *E*, the formal parameter *this* is the value of the pointer to the instance object of interface *A* as well as the value of the pointer to the instance object of class *E*.

5.5.5 The Essence of Function Virtualization

The essence of function virtualization is that a function has multiple implementations on the service provider's side, while it is called in a single form on the client's side. As a result, the client program is adaptive and will not be modified by the increase in the number of implementations on the service provider side. This also achieves complete decoupling of the client module from the service module. It can be seen that the virtualization of functions is still about the interaction between the client and the service, and still deals with the problem of connecting singularity to diversity, i.e., the problem of mapping at runtime. The mapping is placed at the beginning stage where the client obtains the interface pointer from the service provider. Subsequently, the client uses the interface pointer only to care about its functionality (i.e., the meaning of its member functions), not its implementation. This is because the implementation is a service-side matter.

A function may have many implementations on the service provider side. For example, for the graphics mentioned in the previous section, regardless of the type of graphics, there is a display output issue, as well as an issue of saving them from memory to disk and reading them from disk to memory. Therefore, the three functions *draw*, *save*, and *load* have to be implemented. So these three functions can be composed of an interface. In a graphics library file, several implementations of graphics classes are provided. For each graphics class, it inherits and implements the interface. In other words, each interface has multiple implementations. When there are many functions, they are organized in an object-oriented form, which is not only clear and concise, but also easy to understand. For an interface, in addition to having multiple implementations in one library file, it is also possible to have implementations in many library files. For example, the file interface is implemented in many library files.

Function virtualization enables programs to have good traits. For example, a cell phone networking communication program has generalization. When Wi-Fi is available, the cell phone communicates using Wi-Fi networking. When Wi-Fi is not available but Bluetooth is available, the cell phone automatically switches to Bluetooth networking communication. If Bluetooth is also unavailable but mobile data network is available, the phone automatically switches to mobile data network

5.5 Virtualization of Functions

communication. When Wi-Fi becomes available again, the phone automatically switches again to Wi-Fi communication. This automatic switching is transparent to clients, giving clients the impression that the network is available at all times. When communication is viewed as a service, this auto-switching keeps the service available to its clients at all times. This is a desired trait.

Wi-Fi, Bluetooth, and mobile data network in this example refer to different communication links. Assuming that the libraries that provide services for these three links are named *wifi*, *bluetooth*, and *mobile*, respectively, and that they all implement the interface *LinkComm*. In the network hierarchy model, the network layer calls the LinkComm interface open to it by the link layer, where the member function *send* is used to send data to the outside world (i.e., passes data down). For data received from the outside, the link layer calls the *Network* interface open to it by the network layer, in which the member function *receive* is used to receive data (i.e., passes data up). Here, the network object and the link objects are in a one-to-three relationship, so it is necessary to add an intermediary between the two of them to take care of the mapping. This intermediary is called the link manager, which also implements the *LinkComm* interface. Suppose the link manager is implemented in the library file *linkManager*.

During the operating system startup process, when the link manager is initialized, it stores all the link objects in its own link object table, *linkTable*, and orders them so that the link objects that have priority for use are listed first. The link object here is the *LinkComm* interface pointer. The implementation of the above auto-switching is placed in the link manager, as shown in Code 5.32.

Code 5.32 Realization of Automatic Switching of Communication Links
```
(1)   int LinkManager::LinkComm::send( char *data,
int size) {
(2)       for (int i= 0; i < linkNum; i++) {
(3)           LinkComm *link = linkTable->getItemById(i);
(4)           if (link->available())
(5)               return link->send(data, size);
(6)       }
(7)       return -1;
(8)   }
```

In the file virtualization described in Sect. 5.4, the process object has a member variable, *fileTable*, which is used to store the mapping of virtual and real ids for opened files. In the concrete implementation, the real id is actually the file interface pointer. When a process, as a client, requests the operating system to open a file, the operating system returns a file interface pointer. Next the operating system adds a row in the process's *fileTable*, recording the return value, and then returns the row number to the application as the virtual id. Subsequently, when the application accesses the file, it calls a member function of the interface. As you can see, the implementation of file virtualization is simple. The operating system provides applications with the API function *fopen*, the implementation of which is shown in Code 5.33. *File* in line 2 is the name of the file interface, and *os_fopen* is an internal service function of the operating system. Application programs call the API function *fread* provided by the operating system to read the data in the file, and its implementation is shown in Code 5.34.

Code 5.33 Implementation of the fopen Function in File Virtualization
```
(1)   int fopen(const char * fileName, const char * mode) {
(2)       File *file = os_fopen( fileName, mode);
(3)       int rowId = currentProcess->fileTable->addRow(file);
(4)       return rowId;
(5)   }
```

Code 5.34 Implementation of the fread Function in File Virtualization
```
(1)   int fread(int fileId, char * buffer, int size) {
(2)       File *file =
              currentProcess->fileTable->getFileByRowId(fileId);
(3)       return file->read( buffer, size);
(4)   }
```

5.6 Migration of Applications

Migration [14] is the process by which application program A, which originally ran on computer α, is moved to computer β to run. When running on computer β, program A may encounter problems where its required resources cannot be met. For example, if server program A wants to use port 80 to listen for connection requests from clients, when it is migrated from computer α to computer β, the resource port 80 on computer β may not be available to it. This will cause server program A to run unsuccessfully on computer β. Even if server program A is successfully migrated, since the IP address of Computer β is not the same as the IP address of Computer α, there will be a problem for clients of server program A to find it. In other words, the migration of server program A will result in unsuccessful operation for its clients. Cloud computing is about migrating the applications of enterprise customers to run on the cloud. These two problems in migration are to be solved by virtual machine [15].

5.6 Migration of Applications

Before explaining the implementation of virtual machines, let's look at the traditional way that enterprise customers run and maintain their server programs. An enterprise customer has its own local area network (LAN), which is interconnected to the public network through a gateway. Each server program is fixed to run on a particular computer on the LAN. To bring a new server program online, the computer is first selected, then the server program is installed and configured until it can run successfully. The startup scripts for the server programs are placed in a boot Shell script program that is automatically executed by the operating system when the computer is booted. So as soon as the computer is turned on, the server program is started up and running. In this approach, the service id (i.e., IP address and port number) of each server program is a known constant. For any server program (denoted as program A), when it wants to access another server program (denoted as program B), it establishes a network connection with program B based on its service id and then interacts with it. In Program A, the service id of Program B appears as a configuration parameter, sometimes even is written directly into the source code of Program A. In the traditional way, the configuration parameters are stored in the local configuration file.

It can be seen that in the traditional operation and maintenance model, An application and the computer running it are bound. This binding is manifested by the fact that the service id of the application is represented by the IP address and port number. To migrate an enterprise customer's application from its own LAN to run on the cloud, it has to build an identical LAN on the cloud. This LAN is, of course, a virtual LAN. The computers running the server programs on the enterprise customer's own original LAN are also built together and are called virtual machines. Once the virtual machines are built, they can communicate with each other to indicate that they are on the same LAN. After the migration, the customer's business information system remains logically the same, with the same concept of computers and applications. The fact that the computers can communicate with each other indicates that they are on a LAN.

Next, look at a specific scenario of migrating an enterprise customer's business information system to the cloud. After the enterprise customer completes registration and login on the cloud service provider's website, the cloud service system builds a virtual LAN for him. The customer fills in the number of computers on the LAN. Once filled in, the virtual machines in the virtual LAN are created. The customer then packages the file system of each computer on his LAN into an image file and uploads it to the corresponding virtual machine. After all the uploads, press the start button and then the entire business information system is running on the cloud. It is that simple. Each virtual machine will use the image file uploaded to it as its own file system. For the boot Shell script program in the file system that should be run at boot time, the virtual machine executes it. Thus, the server programs is then up and running. For each virtual machine, its IP address, with Linux for example, is stored in the file /etc/sysconfig/network-scripts/ifcfg-eth0. The virtual machine reads this file and knows its own IP address.

After migrating their business information systems to the cloud, enterprise customers can install new applications on existing virtual machines, or add virtual machines to the virtual LAN and install new applications on them. In other words, the way customers run and maintain their business information systems remains the same. Only everything becomes done in the virtual world. The benefits of moving their business information systems to the cloud are that they do not have to worry about failures, lack of physical resources, or the quality of service of the system. In addition, they can get statistical information about the load characteristics of their business information systems from the cloud service.

For a cloud service provider, it starts by creating virtual LANs and virtual machines for its business customers. After a customer uploads an image file for a VM, the VM's file system is ready. The cloud service provider then schedules the virtual machines to run on physical computers. Physical computers are later called hosts on the cloud. For a host computer, when it receives a task to run a virtual machine, it first calls the API function *createVM* provided by the operating system to create a virtual machine. Then, it completes the initialization of the virtual machine, i.e., prepares its file system and connects it to the virtual LAN. Finally, *startupVM*, an API function provided by the operating system, is called to start the virtual machine. Starting a virtual machine is actually executing the boot Shell script program in the VM's file system. The startup scripts for all applications that will be run at boot time are in the boot Shell script program. Therefore, starting the virtual machine is actually starting the running of application programs.

Virtual machine is simply a concept added to the operating system that is transparent to applications. The function of virtual machine is to map the virtual ids of resources to real ids. When an application runs on top of a virtual machine, its original interaction with the operating system becomes an interaction with the virtual machine. In the interaction, the resource ids given by the application become virtual ids, and the virtual machine maps the virtual ids to real ids and then interacts with the operating system. The virtual machine forwards the response from the operating system to the application. The next section explains the implementation of virtual machine.

5.7 Implementation of Virtual Machine

The cloud service provider's clients are enterprise customers whose business information systems were originally running on their own LANs, interconnected to the public network through gateways. Now they want to migrate their business information systems to run on the cloud. If the configuration of a business information system is not changed, then the cloud service provider has to build an identical running environment for it. Assuming that Customer A has two computers on its original LAN with IP addresses 192.168.76.100 and 192.168.76.101, running a web server program and a database server program, respectively. The ports used by the two servers are 80 and 3306, respectively. When the cloud service provider builds the runtime environment for Customer A, it has to create a virtual LAN and two virtual machines for Customer A. The two virtual machines can communicate with

5.7 Implementation of Virtual Machine

each other with the migrated IP addresses of 192.168.76.100 and 192.168.76.101 respectively.

Assume that there are also two computers on the original LAN of Customer *B* with IP addresses 192.168.76.100 and 192.168.76.101, respectively. This scenario is entirely possible because Customer *A* and Customer *B* are independent of each other. When the cloud service provider builds the runtime environment for Customer *B*, it also creates a virtual LAN and two virtual machines with IP addresses 192.168.76.100 and 192.168.76.101 respectively. For presentation purposes, the virtual LAN created for Customer *A* is named *VN_A*, and the two virtual machines on it are named *VM_A1* and *VM_A2*, respectively. The virtual LAN created for customer *B* is named *VN_B*, and the two virtual machines on it are named *VM_B1* and *VM_B2*. For resource sharing purposes, the runtime VMs *VM_A1* and *VM_B1* may be scheduled on the same physical computer on the cloud (denoted as host PC_x). At this point the two virtual machines *VM_A1* and *VM_B1* on PC_x have the same IP address (192.168.76.100).

In the above scenario, how to make the applications running on both *VM_A1* and *VM_B1* run successfully? In other words, how can virtualization be implemented? Applications access the services provided by the operating system kernel through soft interrupt instructions, so virtualization can be implemented in the operating system kernel. That is, add a virtual machine module to the operating system kernel. Once added, any application can call the OS API function *createVM* to create a virtual machine object. In order to associate a process with a virtual machine, a new member variable, *vm* (short for virtual machine), is added to the process object to record the virtual machine object to which the process belongs. When a process is created, the operating system assigns the *vm* value of the parent process to the child process, i.e., the child process is also included in the virtual machine to which the parent process belongs. The parent process can also create a virtual machine, and then assign it to the child process's member variable *vm* to make the child process belong to another virtual machine. The runtime virtual-real mapping is then done by the virtual machine.

The following is an example of establishing a network connection to illustrate the specific implementation process of virtual-real mapping. Assume that the virtual machines *VM_A1* and *VM_A2* created for customer *A* in the above example are scheduled to run on hosts PC_x and PC_y with IP addresses 129.95.37.23 and 129.95.37.45, respectively. *VM_A1* is running a Web server program and wants to connect to the database server running on *VM_A2*. The Web server program knows that the database server's IP address is 192.168.76.101 (i.e., the IP address of *VM_A2*), and the port number is 3306. Since the database server is part of the runtime environment of the Web server program, it should start up first. Once the database server is started up, a socket is created to listen for network connection requests. Due to the database server running on a virtual machine, there is a dual layer concept of virtual and real servers. The virtual server is the concept in *VM_A2* with the id (IP: 192.168.76.101, port: 3306). The real server is a concept in PC_y with id (IP: 129.95.37.45, port: 3306).

Let's look again at the virtual-real mapping involved in establishing a network connection to the database server for the Web server program. The Web server program knows the database server with the id (IP: 192.168.76.101, port: 3306). Since the Web server program runs on *VM_A1*, this is a virtual server id. When establishing a network connection, the real server id to connect to is (IP: 129.95.37.45, port: 3306). *VM_A1* is responsible for performing the mapping, i.e., getting the real server id (IP: 129.95.37.45, port: 3306) from the virtual server id (IP: 192.168.76.101, port: 3306). After getting the real server id, *VM_A1* calls the network connection function provided by host PC_x to establish a network connection with the database server. As the concept of virtual machine is added to the operating system, the original operating system has to be said to be the host. Now the question is: How does *VM_A1* know that the virtual server id (IP: 192.168.76.101, port: 3306) corresponds to the real server id (IP: 129.95.37.45, port: 3306)?

Since the virtual LAN *VN_A* and the virtual machines *VM_A1* and *VM_A2* in it are built by the cloud manager. The scheduling of these two VMs to run on hosts PC_x and PC_y is also determined by the cloud manager. In addition, the cloud manager can get the IP addresses of a virtual machine from the image file uploaded by the enterprise customer for it. The image file is the file system of the virtual machine. In the case of Linux, for example, the file /etc/sysconfig/network-scripts/ifcfg-eth0 contained in it stores the IP address of the local machine. This IP address is the IP address of the virtual machine. For the hosts PC_x and PC_y, their IP addresses are naturally known to the cloud manager. Therefore, cloud manager knows the IP address of every virtual machine and the IP address of the host on which it resides, and thus the mapping between the virtual IP address and the real IP address. Taking virtual LAN *VN_A* as an example, which contains only two VMs, *VM_A1* and *VM_A2*, the cloud manager can derive the mapping table of their virtual and real IP addresses, as shown in Table 5.5. Name the table as *ipAddrMapTable*.

The cloud manager passes this *ipAddrMapTable*, the mapping table for the virtual LAN *VN_A*, to all of its virtual machines, *VM_A1* and *VM_A2*. Once *VM_A1* gets this table, it simply looks up the table and comes up with the real IP corresponding to the virtual IP (192.168.76.101) as 129.95.37.45.

After the concept of virtual machine is added to the operating system kernel, the virtual machine module is embedded between application programs and the operating system kernel. An application program's original calls to the OS kernel APIs should be changed to calls to the corresponding APIs in the virtual machine module. After the virtual machine completes the mapping, it then calls the OS kernel API to complete the actual operation. The virtual machine returns the response results from the OS kernel API to the application program. Since the virtual machine is implemented in the operating system kernel, the operating system kernel module is divided into two modules: the virtual machine module and the host module. The

Table 5.5 IP address virtual-real mapping table for all virtual machines in *VN_A*	Virtual machine name	Virtual IP address	Real IP address
	VM_A1	192.168.76.100	129.95.37.23
	VM_A2	192.168.76.101	129.95.37.45

host module is the original OS kernel module. This embedding is therefore transparent to applications.

This embedding is demonstrated below with an API example. The original *connect* function in the operating system kernel functioned to establish a network connection with a server. Now, because of the addition of the virtual machine as an intermediate module, the function is renamed as *host_connect*, indicating that it is a host implementation. The implementation of the new *connect* function is placed in the virtual machine module, as shown in Code 5.35. The implication is that if the process belongs to a virtual machine, then it is given to the virtual machine to handle. Otherwise, it is still handled by the host.

Line 3 of Code 5.35 is going to call the member function *connect* of the virtual machine object, the implementation of which is shown in Code 5.36. The first job

Code 5.35 Implementation of the System Function Connect
```
(1)  int connect(int socketId, char *ipAddr, int port, int
     protocol) {
(2)    if (currentProcess->vm ! = null )
(3)      return currentProcess->vm->connect(socketId,
         ipAddr, port, protocol);
(4)    else
(5)      return host_connect( socketId, ipAddr, port,
         protocol);
(6)  }
```

the function has to do is to complete the mapping of virtual IP addresses to real IP addresses, as shown in line 2. Next, the mapping of virtual port number to real port number is completed, as shown in line 3. The virtual machine has member variables *ipAddrMapTable* and *portMapTable*. The former stores the mapping between the virtual IP addresses of all virtual machines and the real IP addresses of the hosts they reside on, and the latter stores the mapping between the virtual port numbers and the real port numbers of all servers on the virtual LAN. Note: The virtual LAN here is not the VLAN in network technology, but the virtual LAN to which the virtual machines belong. In this function, the formal parameter *ipAddr* is the IP address of the virtual machine where the server is located, and the formal parameter *port* is the virtual port number of the server. The meaning of line 4 is that if there is no mapping entry between the virtual port number and the real port number, then the real port number is equal to the virtual port number.

In the above example, the web server wants to create a network connection socket to the database server. The virtual machine *VM_A1*, to which the web server belongs, performs the mapping for it, mapping the virtual IP (192.168.76.101) to the real IP (129.95.37.45). This shows that when a process is a concept under the operating system, the network resources it has to access are real resources and there

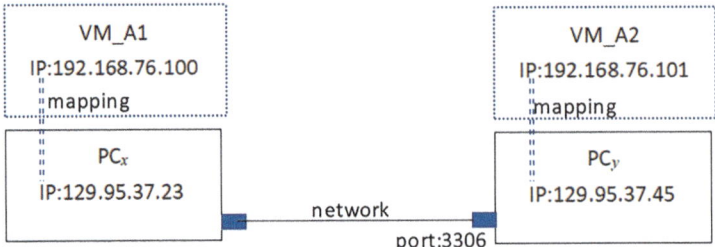

Fig. 5.5 Example of network connection mapping in virtualization

is no mapping issue. When the process becomes a concept under the virtual machine, the network resources it wants to access are also virtual resources, and the mapping is performed by the virtual machine it belongs to. The mapping is performed at runtime. The mapping relationship is shown in Fig. 5.5. In this example, the real and virtual port numbers of the database server are the same, both are 3306. The cases where they are not the same will be explained later.

Code 5.36 Implementation of the Virtual Machine's Member Function Connect

```
(1)   int VM::connect(int socketId, char *ipAddr, int port,
      int protocol) {
(2)     char *RealIpAddr =
        ipAddrMapTable->getRealByVirtual(ipAddr);
(3)     int realPort = portMapTable-
        >getRealByVirtual(ipAddr, port);
(4)     if (realPort == -1)
(5)        realPort = port;
(6)     return host_connect( socketId, realIpAddr, realPort,
        protocol);
(7)   }
```

The above networking method for virtual machines is called Host-Only method. There are three advantages to it. When this approach is used in cloud computing, each customer's own original computers and its networking is virtualized transparently. Thus, there is no need to change any configuration when migrating a customer's application to run on the cloud. The second benefit is that there are no constraints on the IP address settings of the virtual machines; multiple virtual machines on a single host computer can have the same IP address. This is exactly the kind of program migration trait one would expect. The third benefit is that the mapping only needs to be performed when the socket is created, and then there is no more mapping to do when sending or receiving data through the socket. Thus, there is no additional overhead for sending and receiving data. Creating a socket and establishing a network connection is an occasional event, while sending and receiving data are a frequent event. Therefore, the mapping overhead is so small that it is almost negligible.

For operating systems that support virtual machines, there are usually three configuration methods available for networking virtual machines. In addition to the Host-Only method mentioned above, the other two methods are called Bridged and NAT (short for network address translation) [16]. In the Bridged method, each virtual machine is assigned a real IP address, which means that the IP address of a virtual machine and the IP address of a host are equivalent. Multiple VMs can be created on a single host, so a host has multiple IP addresses. According to the network model described in Sect. 2.2, i.e., there are multiple Network objects in the operating system kernel. Therefore, a routing layer has to be added between the network layer and the link layer. For a IP packet passed up by the link layer, the routing layer checks its IP address and then passes it up to the Network object that matches it. For an IP packet passed down by a Network object, the routing layer either passes it down to the link layer or transfers it to another Network object based on its destination IP address.

In the NAT approach, virtual machines on a host and the host itself form a LAN. The host also acts as a gateway to that LAN. So the IP address of the host is also the IP address of the gateway in the extranet. Here the extranet is only relative to the LAN. The implementation of the router in the bridged approach and the gateway in the NAT approach is explained in the Network Model section in Chap. 2. The advantages of these two networking methods are that VMs are able to communicate with each other, and VMs do not need to maintain IP mappings between each VM in the virtual LAN and the hosts they reside on. Between them, the bridged approach has more connectivity. The disadvantage is that the IP address of a virtual machine cannot be set arbitrarily. If NAT is used, two VMs on the same host cannot have the same IP address and must meet the LAN configuration requirements. If bridged approach is used, there are more restrictions: any two virtual machines on the entire physical LAN cannot have the same IP address, and any IP address of virtual machine must meet the configuration requirements of the physical LAN.

There are no restrictions on the IP address settings of virtual machines only when using Host-Only method for networking. However, for the establishment of a network connection between two VMs, an IP address mapping table is required and the mapping also needs to be performed. This approach has the advantage of application migration without the need to change the configuration of applications. It is because of the unique advantages of the Host-Only method that it is widely utilized in application migration.

From the above implementation of virtual machines, it is clear that a virtual LAN is only a logical concept. It means that the virtual machines in a virtual LAN can establish a network connection with each other directly. The implementation is reflected in the mapping table *ipAddrMapTable*. When virtual machine *VM_A1* wants to establish a network connection with virtual machine *VM_A2*, the IP address of *VM_A2* and its host IP address mapping relationship must appear in the *ipAddrMapTable* table of *VM_A1*. If it does not appear, then *VM_A1* assumes that it is an extranet IP address and establishes a network connection with the gateway in the virtual LAN, which is handled in the same way as establishing a network connection with an extranet server. The gateway is a server in the virtual LAN, and its virtual IP address must appear in the *ipAddrMapTable* of *VM_A1*. The process of establishing a network connection with an extranet server is explained in Sect. 2.2 of Chap. 2.

Virtual LANs as described here are not the same thing as VLANs in networking technology. VLANs, also known as Virtual Local Area Networks (VLANs), are a network communication technology. It can be associated with VLANs only if the virtual machines are networked in a bridged way. VLANs consider the problem that if a message is broadcast in a LAN with n computers, then the message is to be delivered to $n-1$ computers. Each of these $n-1$ computers has to receive the message and check whether the message should be handled by itself. Out of these $n-1$ computers, only one computer will actually process the message, and all the receiving and checking done by the remaining $n-2$ computers is useless. The number of broadcast messages is proportional to n. Therefore, reducing n reduces the amount of useless work. What VLANs are trying to do is to divide a large LAN into multiple smaller LANs in order to reduce the amount of useless work.

5.8 The Virtual Machine's Own File System

Another important element of the runtime environment is the file system. For an application program, from the point of view of the composition of its code, it includes private and public shared parts. The public shared part refers to the support libraries in the user space, such as the system function libraries of the C language. The public shared code accesses public shared files. For example, when an application accesses a computer based on its domain name, it first resolves the domain name to an IP address. This work is done by public shared code. In Linux, the mapping of domain names to IP addresses is stored in the public shared file /etc/hosts. Thus, domain name resolution is a matter of opening the /etc/hosts file and finding out the IP address that corresponds to the domain name.

The concept of accessing a computer based on its domain name changes when an application runs on a virtual machine. The domain name here refers to the domain name of the virtual machine, and the IP address found out also refers to the IP address of the virtual machine. Take the above customer *A* as an example, its web server program and database server program run on virtual machines *VM_A1* and *VM_A2*, respectively. On Customer *A*'s own original LAN, the domain name of the computer running the database server program is *dbServer*. Suppose the web server program accesses the database server with the domain name *dbServer*. Now that the web server program is running on virtual machine *VM_A1*, the IP address obtained when resolving the domain name *dbServer* should be the IP address of virtual machine *VM_A2*. The domain name resolution at this point should not be to open the /etc/hosts file on the host PC_x, but should be to open the /etc/hosts file on the virtual machine *VM_A1*.

From the above analysis, it is clear that when an application is running on a virtual machine, the files that are opened refer to the files on the virtual machine and not to the files on the host. The files of the virtual machine refer to the files contained in the image file uploaded by the enterprise customer for the virtual machine. This is accomplished by mounting the root directory of the virtual machine in a directory on the host file system. Thus, the virtual machine object has to have a member variable *mountedDir* that records the host directory that is mounted. The implementation of *fopen*, the file open function provided by the operating system kernel, should be modified. The modified implementation is shown in Code 5.37. For example, suppose the root directory of virtual machine *VM_A1* is mounted under the directory /vm/VM_A1 on host PC_x, and the domain name resolution opens the file /etc/hosts. Here, the actual file that is opened is /vm/VM_A1/etc/hosts. In line 4, *strcat* is a C library function whose function is to concatenate two strings to form a string.

Code 5.37 Implementation of the System Function fopen
```
(1)   int fopen(const char * fileName, const char * mode) {
(2)      char *realFileName;
(3)      if (currentProcess->vm ! = null )
(4)         realFileName = strcat(currentProcess->vm-
                >mountedDir, fileName);
(5)      else
(6)         realFileName = fileName;
(7)      return host_fopen( realFileName, mode);
(8)   }
```

From the above analysis, we can see that when the cloud manager assigns the host PC_x to run *VM_A1*, it needs to transfer the image file and *ipAddrMapTable* file of *VM_A1* to the host PC_x. The host PC_x first creates a mount directory /vm/VM_A1 for *VM_A1*, and then unpacks the image file to the mounted directory /vm/VM_A1, so that the file system of the virtual machine *VM_A1* is ready. Subsequently, the host PC_x creates a virtual machine, assign its member variable *mountedDir* to "/vm/VM_A1", and then uses the data in the *ipAddrMapTable* file to initialize the virtual machine's member variable *ipAddrMapTable*. Next create a process to run the boot Shell script program of *VM_A1*. Before starting up the process, set its member variable *vm* to the virtual machine created earlier. After the process is started up, the boot Shell script program in the file system of the virtual machine *VM_A1* is executed. The startup scripts for applications to be run at boot time are written in this boot Shell script program. Therefore, by executing this script program, applications are started up.

5.9 Virtual-Real Mapping of Server Port Numbers

An organization usually has multiple servers with dependencies between them. In the example described in the previous section, enterprise customer A has two servers: a web server and a database server. Of these two servers, the web server depends on the database server, i.e., the database server is part of runtime environment of the web server. Before starting the web server, the database server should be started, otherwise the web server will fail to establish a network connection with the database server and runtime errors will occur. The listening port of a server is usually determined at design time and is a constant. After a server has been migrated to the cloud and is running in a virtual machine, the required port number may have been taken up by another program on the host where it resides. In order for the server to run successfully, the virtual machine has to ask the host it resides on to assign an available port number. At this point the server's listening port changes. This change must be made known to the other virtual machines on the virtual LAN, otherwise client programs will not be able to establish a network connection with the server.

Taking the above example, the database server publishes on listen port number 3306 and runs on *VM_A2* virtual machine. Suppose *VM_A2* is scheduled to run on host PC_y. However, port number 3306 on host PC_y is already occupied by another program. *VM_A2* has to ask host PC_y to assign an available port number. Assuming the assigned port number is 2564, thus host PC_y listens for connection requests on port number 2564. The web server is running on the *VM_A1* virtual machine, and is assumed to be scheduled to run on host PC_x. For the web server to be able to connect to the database server, *VM_A1* needs to be aware of the fact that the listening port of the database server has changed. How can *VM_A1* be made aware of this change? This involves the architecture of cloud computing.

In cloud computing, enterprise customers and their virtual LANs, as well as virtual machines on the virtual LANs, are managed by a cloud manager, *CloudManager*. An Agent program runs on each host of the cloud provider, and *CloudManager* gives instructions to the Agent such as creating a VM, starting a VM, etc. The Agent also reports the VM's runtime information to *CloudManager*. For a VM created by the Agent, it should report the runtime virtual-real mapping information to the Agent. The Agent forwards this to the *CloudManager*, which in turn disseminates it to other VMs on the VLAN. In the above example, *VM_A2* reports the virtual-real mapping information of the listening port number (virtual id: 3306, real id: 2564) to the Agent on the host PC_y. This information is passed through the *CloudManager* to the Agent on the PC_x, and finally passed to *VM_A1*. Thus, when the web server connects to the database server, *VM_A1* will map 3306 to 2564.

The next question is: how does a VM know that an application is going to request a port number for listening to network connection requests? One of the functionalities of the *bind* function in the socket API functions provided by the operating system is to set a port number for the network connection object. The virtual machine provides an implementation of this function, as shown in Code 5.38. The

5.9 Virtual-Real Mapping of Server Port Numbers

formal parameter *ipaddr* of this function is the IP address of the virtual machine, and *port* is the port number to be requested. If the value of *port* passed in is equal to 0, the implication is that the operating system is requested to assign an available port number. When a client program creates a network connection to a server, the port value is usually set to 0. In contrast, a port value greater than 0 means that the operating system is being asked to assign a given port number. When a server requests the operating system to create a network connection object for listening to connection requests, it sets the port value to greater than 0.

The first task in the virtual machine's implementation of the *bind* function is the virtual-real mapping, where the IP address of the virtual machine is used to get the IP address of the host on which it resides, as shown in line 2. When the formal parameter *port* is greater than 0, it means it is a listening port. Thus, the port number is first checked to see if it is available. If it is not available, the operating system is requested to assign an available port number. This creates a virtual-real mapping entry for the server port number. This mapping is both added to the virtual machine's own port mapping table, *portMapTable*, and reported, in a message, to the virtual machine's creator process. This processing is shown in lines 4 through 9. When the creator of the VM is an Agent, the Agent receives the message and uploads it to *CloudManager*. The final step is to call the host's *host_bind* function to complete the binding, as shown in line 10.

Code 5.38 Virtual Machine Implementation of the bind Function
```
(1)   bool VM::bind(Connection *conn, char *ipAddr, Protocol
      protocol, Port port) {
(2)     char * realIpAddr =
        ipAddrMapTable->getRealByVirtual(ipAddr);
(3)     Network *network =
        networkList->getItemByIpAddr(realIpAddr);
(4)     if ( port > 0 && not network-
        >portAvailable(protocol, port)) {
(5)       conn->port = network->getAvailablePort(protocol);
(6)       portMapTable->addItem(ipAddr, port, conn->port));
(7)       postMessage(creatorProcess, PORT_MAP, ipAddr,
          port, conn->port);
(8)       port = conn->port;
(9)     }
(10)    return host_bind(conn, realIpAddr, protocol, port);
(11)  }
```

It can be seen that when an enterprise customer migrates its business information system to the cloud, it has to specify the dependencies among the virtual machines. The cloud manager starts the virtual machines in sequence according to the dependencies specified by the customer to ensure that applications on the virtual machines can run successfully.

5.10 Persistent Storage of Data in VMs

An application may generate data at runtime and then put it into a file for persistent storage. This is the case, for example, with a database server, which adds rows to a data table and does persistent storage when it receives a request from a client to add data. Persistent storage means that no matter when the application is restarted, the data originally deposited are still there and can continue to be read. Persistent storage runs into problems when an application is running in a virtual machine. In the example described in the previous section, virtual machine *VM_A1* was scheduled by Cloud Manager to run on host PC_x. The Agent running on PC_x then creates a VM object, then creates a mount directory "/vm/VM_A1" for the VM, and then unpacks the image file of *VM_A1* to that mount directory. The next step is to set the value of the member variable *mountedDir* of the VM object to "/vm/VM_A1". The last thing is to start the virtual machine running.

Subsequently, when the Agent shuts down *VM_A1*, it is freeing the virtual machine objects in the operating system kernel and then deleting the mount directory "/vm/VM_A1". The host PC_x then returns to the state it was in before running *VM_A1*. Here's the problem. Deleting the mount directory "/vm/VM_A1" means deleting the file system of the virtual machine running on the host PC_x. The files opened or created by the VM while it is running are all part of the VM file system. Deleting the mount directory "/vm/VM_A1" also deletes all the data generated by the virtual machine while it is running. Therefore, the data generated by the virtual machine running on PC_x are not persistently stored.

The most straightforward way to solve the persistent storage problem is to write new and modified files back to the virtual machine's image file before deleting the mounted directory. That is, the image file is updated. The problem with this approach is that there is no separation of program and data. Over time, the image file of the virtual machine will become larger and larger. If the image file is large, it takes a long time to download the image file when starting a virtual machine. In other words, the startup of the virtual machine is slow. Also, the shutdown of the virtual machine is long because the updated files have to be uploaded to the image file. When an application on the virtual machine needs to be updated for a new version, the virtual machine needs to be shut down and restarted. The services provided by the virtual machine during the shutdown phase and startup phase are not available to clients. Therefore, a long shutdown time and a long startup time of the VM equals a long unavailability of the VM to clients. This scenario is naturally undesirable.

5.10 Persistent Storage of Data in VMs

Volume is an abstraction that arises in response to the above problem [3]. Volumes are used to separate programs from data, so that the image file of a virtual machine contains only the program and not the data generated by applications. With a small image file, the virtual machine starts faster. When shutting down a virtual machine, there is no problem of updating the image file, so the shutdown of the virtual machine is also fast. A volume is a directory of files on a host. A volume can be mounted to one of the file directories of a virtual machine. For example, create a volume named *vol_a1* and associate it with the host's file directory "/usr/data/vm/a1". Then associate the volume *vol_a1* with the virtual machine object's file directory "/usr/data". Thus, the virtual machine object's file directory "/usr/data" becomes a virtual directory, corresponding to the real directory "/usr/data/vm/a1" on the host machine. In other words, when an application on the virtual machine opens the file "/usr/data/www/index.html", it actually opens the "/usr/data/vm/a1/www/index.html "file on the host machine.

When shutting down a virtual machine, Agent deletes the virtual machine's mount directory on the host, i.e., it deletes the file system on which the virtual machine is running. This deletion does not affect the volume. The reason is that a volume is actually a pointer (also called a reference). Deleting a pointer does not delete the object it refers to. In the Windows operating system, a file pointer is also called a file shortcut. The implementation of a volume is very simple, just add a member variable *volumeMapTable* to the virtual machine. The creator of the virtual machine is responsible for the initialization of the member variable. To support volumes, the *fopen* function implementation shown in Code 5.37 is modified. The modified implementation is shown in Code 5.39. The file to be opened is first checked to see if it is the contents of a volume, as shown in lines 4 through 12. The meaning of line 7 is: check if the virtual directory of the volume is the beginning of the file name. If it is, the file to be opened is in the volume, and should be processed in the volume mode. Otherwise, it will be processed in the normal way.

The meaning of lines 14 and 15 in Code 5.39 is that the virtual directory in the preceding part of the filename is replaced with a real directory. *strstr* in line 7 and *strcat* in line 15 are C library functions for string processing.

Code 5.39 Implementation of the System Function fopen
```
(1)    int fopen(const char * fileName, const char * mode) {
(2)        char *realFileName;
(3)        if (currentProcess->vm ! = null ) {
(4)            MapItem *mapItem = volumeMapTable->getFirstItem();
(5)            bool match = FALSE;
(6)            while( mapItem ) {
(7)                if (strstr(fileName, mapItem->virtualDir) == fileName) {
(8)                    match = TRUE;
```

```
(9)              break;
(10)           }
(11)           mapItem = volumeMapTable->getNextItem();
(12)       }
(13)       if(match) {
(14)           int len = strlen(mapItem->virtualDir);
(15)           realFileName = strcat(mapItem->realDir,
                   fileName + len);
(16)       }
(17)       else
(18)           realFileName = strcat(currentProcess->vm-
                   >mountedDir, fileName);
(19)   }
(20)   else
(21)       realFileName = fileName;
(22)   return host_fopen( realFileName, mode);
(23) }
```

For a host, a network file system can be mounted to a directory within its own file system, making the network transparent to applications. If the volume is associated with a host directory that is the contents of a network filesystem, then the data files that applications in the virtual machine wants to access are still remote files. As a result, the virtual machine can access its data files regardless of which host the cloud manager schedules the virtual machine to run on. This is achieved by the following implementation approach. When the cloud manager wants to schedule the virtual machine VM_A1 to run on the host PC_x, it notifies the Agent on the host PC_x to first mount the disk storage resources assigned to VM_A1 to a directory on the host PC_x in the form of a network file system. The Agent then creates a volume and associates it with that directory, and then initializes the VM_A1's member variable *volumeMapTable* to associate the volume with the specified directory of the VM. The virtual machine VM_A1 can then access the disk storage resources allocated to it by the cloud manager.

An example is given. Assume that the cloud service provider assigns disk storage resources to enterprise customer A on host PC_s, and the corresponding file directory is "/usr/data/A". The virtual machine VM_A2 of enterprise customer A is running MySQL database server, and its database storage directory is /usr/mySQL/database. To do so, the cloud service provider first tells the host PC_s to set its directory "/usr/data/A" to network share directory A. When the cloud manager schedules the virtual machine VM_A2 to run on the host PC_x, it tells the Agent on the host PC_x to mount the network file system "//PC_s/A" to a directory on the host PC_x. Suppose the Agent on PC_x gives the mount directory as "/usr/NFS/PC_s/A".

Cloud Manager then tells the Agent on PC_x to create a volume associated with the virtual machine VM_A2's directory "/usr/mySQL/database". Next, when the Agent on PC_x performs the initialization of the created VM object, it adds a volume to its *volumeMapTTable*, setting its virtual directory to "/usr/mySQL/database" and its real directory to "/usr/NFS/PC_s/A". After the virtual machine VM_A2 is started up on PC_x, when the MySQL database server performs an open operation on the database files in the directory "/usr/mySQL/database", the actual files opened are those in the directory "/usr/data/A" on the host PC_s.

5.11 Volume of Resources Owned by the Virtual Machine

Threats to the successful operation of applications come not only from changes in the runtime environment, but also from interfering with each other. In cloud computing, multiple virtual machines from different customers may be running on a single host in order to fully utilize the resources. Applications on these virtual machines may interfere with and disrupt each other. For example, when a program has vulnerabilities such as dead loops and memory leaks, it can cause shared resources such as CPU, memory, service port numbers, etc., on the host to be consumed and exhausted, thereby affecting the normal operation of other programs. Some programs even intentionally exhaust resources to disrupt the system. This kind of interference and destruction is related to the characteristics of the operating system. The operating system uses a preemptive mechanism for resource allocation. That is, when an application requests a resource, the operating system handles it in such a way that if it can fulfill it, it does. This model creates a fatal problem of programs interfering and disrupting each other in cloud computing.

For an application to run successfully and properly, VMs have to have the concept of resource quantity and the concept of isolation from each other. When a virtual machine is to be scheduled to run on a host, the volume of resources is allocated to the virtual machine before it is started up. The resources that an application on a VM can use are limited to the resources allocated to the VM, not to any resources on the host. Thus, virtual machines do not have the problem of interfering and destroying each other. For example, if you allocate 8 GB of memory to virtual machine *A*, applications running on virtual machine *A* can use up to 8 GB of memory, and if virtual machine *A* runs out of memory, the impact is limited to virtual machine *A* and does not affect applications on other virtual machines.

Allocating resources to virtual machines and isolating them from each other can be accomplished with the Linux operating system's existing CGroup and Namespace technologies [17]. The Linux operating system provides applications with API functions to create CGroup and Namespace kernel objects, which are then bound to the created child processes. Once the operating system starts up, a CGroup object and a Namespace object are created and bound to the starting process. The initial CGroup object has the hardware resources of the entire computer, including CPU, memory, disk bandwidth, network bandwidth, and so on. For process *A* bound to the

CGroup1 object, when it creates the CGroup2 object, only the hardware resources owned by CGroup1 can be allocated to CGroup2. Process *A* creates child process *B* and binds it to CGroup2. So subsequently the hardware resources that child process *B* can use are limited to those owned by CGroup2.

The scenario of CGroup technology in cloud computing is as follows. The Agent process on a host is created by the starting process and thus inherits the CGroup object of the starting process. Thus, the CGroup object bound to the Agent process is the original CGroup object that owns the hardware resources of the entire host. The Agent process then creates a child process to run the boot *S*hell script program of *VM_A1* once it receives the command to run *VM_A1* from the cloud manager. The Agent process also creates a CGroup object (named *CGroup_A1*) and allocates hardware resources to *CGroup_A1* as instructed by the cloud manager. The Agent process next binds *CGroup_A1* to child process *A1*, so child process *A1* can only use the hardware resources in *CGroup_A1*.

Subsequently, child process *A1* creates another child process to run each application on virtual machine *VM_A1*, respectively, when it executes the boot Shell script program. When the parent process creates a child process, the child process inherits the CGroup object from the parent process. The CGroup object bound to the child process changes only when the parent process binds a new CGroup object to the child process. From this, it can be seen that the hardware resources that can be used by an application on virtual machine *VM_A1* are limited to those in *CGroup_A1*. Therefore, it will not affect the normal operation of applications on other virtual machines.

Cloud Manager knows the amount of hardware resources each host has and the amount of hardware resources each virtual machine requires. When enterprise customers migrate their information systems to the cloud, they specify the amount of hardware resources required for each virtual machine. Subsequently, the cloud service provider and the enterprise customer also make adjustments to the amount of hardware resources required for the virtual machines based on changes in the amount of data and business load. In short, the cloud manager can go about scheduling virtual machines based on the current system state. In other words, for virtual machine *VM_A1*, the cloud manager can determine which host should run it, which can satisfy the virtual machine's demand for hardware resources and also optimize the use of the entire system resources.

Namespace is a namespace isolation technique. As far as a computer is concerned, it has the concepts of host name, IP address, subnet mask, gateway IP address, IP address of domain name resolution server, as well as currently running processes, etc. These contents constitute the namespace of a computer. For two processes in the same namespace, the communication between them belongs to the communication between processes on the same machine, using inter-process communication (IPC) method [12]. In contrast, communication between two processes on different machines is networked. The operating system usually stores its configuration information and operation status information in files. From Sect. 5.9, it is clear that each virtual machine has its own file system, and therefore each virtual

5.11 Volume of Resources Owned by the Virtual Machine

machine has its own namespace. However, the namespace embodied through the VM's filesystem is limited to the namespace in the user space. For the contents of the namespace in kernel space, it is managed by the host and is not reflected in the file system of the virtual machine. For example, process ids are part of the namespace in kernel space.

For namespace content that belongs to the kernel space, the isolation between virtual machines is also realized with the help of Namespace technology. When parent process *A* creates child process *B*, child process *B* inherits the Namespace of parent process *A*. Parent process *A* can also create a new Namespace object (named *Namespace2*) and bind it to child process *B*. At this point, the Namespace of child *B* changes to *Namespace2*. In cloud computing, when the Agent process creates a child process to run the boot Shell script program for virtual machine *VM_A1*, it creates a new Namespace object and binds it to the child process. Each virtual machine thus has its own Namespace, achieving isolation in the namespace. Any process that looks at the contents of the namespace can only see the contents of its own Namespace.

CGroup and Namespace technologies also bring flexibility to the configuration of virtual machines. The Pod concept was introduced in Kubernetes [18], a cloud manager product from Google, with the aim of making VM configuration more flexible. For multiple VMs of an enterprise customer, they can be very closely connected and interact very frequently. For example, in the example mentioned earlier, the interaction between Enterprise Customer *A*'s web server and database server is very frequent. The web server runs on virtual machine *VM_A1* and the database server on virtual machine *VM_A2*. The cloud manager can schedule *VM_A1* and *VM_A2* to run on the same host when scheduling the virtual machines. If the Agent on that host binds the same Namespace object to both *VM_A1* and *VM_A2*, then they are both in the same Namespace.

VM_A1 and *VM_A2* share the same Namespace, so the web server and the database server are in the same Namespace. The advantage of this is that the communication between the two will use the IPC method instead of the network method. In terms of performance, the IPC method is much better than the network method. In other words, two VMs sharing the same Namespace can significantly improve the performance. Pod is an abstraction concept introduced for structural clarity. With the concept of Pod, the virtual machine is divided into two levels: the upper level is called Pod, and the lower level is called virtual machine. Multiple VMs can be run in a Pod. For multiple VMs of an enterprise customer, when scheduling them to run on the same host, a Pod is created and then they are all run in that Pod.

There are also benefits to having multiple VMs in a Pod share the same CGroup. This allows multiple VMs to share hardware resources. It is for this reason that the Kubernetes user guide says that a Pod is the smallest resource allocation unit. Essentially, a Pod corresponds to a CGroup object and a Namespace object. Multiple VMs in the same Pod have the dual meaning of sharing and independence, while pods are completely isolated from each other. As you can see, naming this concept Pod is very vivid and imaginative.

5.12 Virtual LAN Implementation

In cloud computing, enterprise customers are a first level concept, which includes the concept of virtual local area networks. According to the network model, virtual machines on a virtual LAN are able to communicate directly with each other. Each virtual LAN has a virtual gateway that is responsible for the communication between virtual machines within the virtual LAN network and servers outside the network. The previously described VM-to-VM communication uses the Host-only method. The network connections between VMs in this implementation are called virtual network connections. Each virtual network connection corresponds to a real network connection.

For the one-to-one correspondence between virtual and real network connections, an example is given. In the preceding example, the web server on virtual machine *VM_A1* of enterprise customer *A* wants to establish a network connection with the database server on virtual machine *VM_A2*. The virtual network connection is: (192.168.76.100, 4328) vs (192.168.76.101, 3306), where 192.168.76.100 is the IP address of *VM_A1*, and 4328 is the port number on the client side, while 192.168.76.101 is the IP address of *VM_A2*, and 3306 is the virtual listening port number on the server side. The corresponding real network connection is: (129.95.37.23, 4328) versus (129.95.37.45, 2564), where 129.95.37.23 is the IP address of the host PC_x where *VM_A1* resides, 4328 is the real port number on the client side, while 129.95.37.45 is the IP address of the host PC_y where *VM_A2* resides, 2564 is the real listening port number of the server.

The Host-only method to VM-to-VM communication has the potential for multiple VMs on the same host to interfere with and affect each other. As an example, assume that VM1 and VM2 are running on the same host. An application on VM1 has a vulnerability where it forgets to release the network connection after using it. This vulnerability causes the application on VM1 to request the creation of a network connection without releasing it, eventually exhausting all port number resources on the host. In this scenario, if the application on VM2 wants to create a network connection, it will not succeed and thus will not be able to run normally.

To overcome the above problems, overlay approach can be used for VM-to-VM communication. In the overlay approach, the virtual machine no longer uses the host's network services directly, but has its own network object. The virtual machine's network object treats the host's UDP communication interface as a link communication interface for sending and receiving IP packets. In other words, the host's UDP communication interface becomes the link communication interface of the virtual machine. Overlay means that the virtual machine network is layered on top of the host network [19]. Specifically, the IP packets sent by the VM will appear to the host as application data. That is, the host will encapsulate the IP packets of the VM into IP packets of the host, and then send them out through the link layer of the host. The data received by the host's UDP component are then passed up to the virtual machine's network object. The data passed up here are naturally the IP packets of the virtual machine. The virtual machine's network object dispatches the data portion of the received IP packet to the corresponding network connection object.

5.12 Virtual LAN Implementation

A virtual LAN realized using the above overlay approach is called an overlay network [19]. A comparison of the original network communication model with the overlay network model is shown in Fig. 5.6. This implementation is characterized by the fact that each virtual machine occupies only one UDP port number of the host, i.e., each virtual machine only needs to apply for the creation of one network connection object in the host. Thus, the aforementioned problem of host port numbers being exhausted by a particular VM is solved. But this gain comes at a cost. The cost is that data are transferred from one VM to another VM with one more encapsulation and unpacking of IP packets and one more IP header for the transferred data.

The stack architecture of network protocols facilitates the implementation of overlay networks. The Connection, Network, and Link classes of network communication are implemented in the Transport, Network, and Link layer modules, respectively. All three classes implement the interface *Transfer*. The definition of the interface *Transfer* and the three classes are shown in Code 5.40. To recognize a socket in network communication programming from an object-oriented perspective, it is the connection object in the network model. Connection has the process object above it and the network object below it. It therefore has member variables *process* and *network*. The connection object calls the *send* function in network to transfer the data down to the lower level. When data are received from the lower level, the connection object calls the *postMessage* function in process to transfer the data up to the upper level.

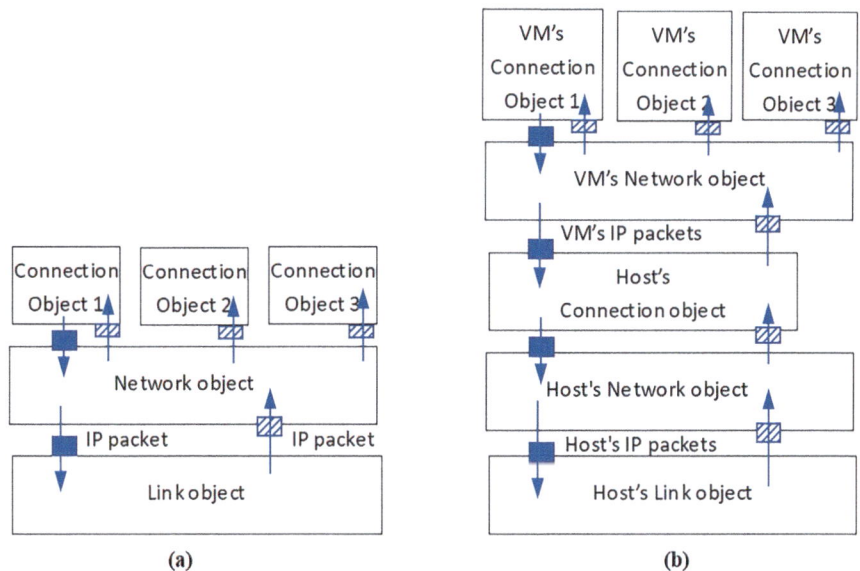

Fig. 5.6 Comparison of communication model between original network and overlay network. (**a**) Communication model of the original network. (**b**) Communication model of the overlay network

Similarly, the network object has connection objects above it and a link object below it. Therefore, it has the member variables *connectionList* and *link*. Network object has a one-to-many relationship with connection objects, so the member variable is *connectionList* instead of *connection*. When there is an IP packet to be sent, network object calls the *send* function in link to transfer the data down. Note: The data type of the member variable *link* is a *Transfer* pointer. Whether it is the transport layer, the network layer, or the link layer, from an external client's point of view, their function is to send data and receive data. Therefore, they are all abstracted to the *Transfer* pointer type. The benefit is that the protocol stack can be built flexibly. Overlay networks are realized with the help of this abstraction. When an IP packet is received from a lower layer, the network object determines which connection object to pass the data based on the *destinationIP* and *destinationPort* values in the IP header, and then calls its *recv* function to pass the data up.

Code 5.40 Abstraction and Data Structure Definition for Communication Module
```
(1)     class Transfer {
(2)         virtual int send(void *pData, int size) = 0;
(3)         virtual int recv(void *pData, int size) = 0;
(4)     }
(5)     class Connection: public Transfer {
(6)         Transfer *network;
(7)         Process * process;
(8)         int port, destinationPort;
(9)         IpAddr destinationIp;
(10)        int protocol;
(11)    }
(12)    class Network: public Transfer {
(13)        Transfer *link;
(14)        List<Connection *> *connectionList;
(15)        IpAddr ipAddr;
(16)    }
(17)    class Link: public Transfer {
(18)        Transfer *device;
(19)        Transfer *network;
(20)    }
```

The transport layer module has the *createConnection* function open to clients for creating a connection object and initializing it. Similarly, the network layer module has the *createNetwork* function open to clients for creating a network object and initializing it. When the operating system starts up, it detects how many network cards are on the computer and then creates a network object and a link object for

5.13 Updates to Applications on Virtual Machines 377

each of them. *createConnection* function and *createNetwork* function are defined as shown in Code 5.41. The data type of the return value of both functions is a *Transfer* pointer. Therefore, the *createConnection* function can be called first, and its return value can be used as the second real parameter in the call to the *createNetwork* function. This results in the creation of a network object with a Connection object underneath. This is how overlay networks are implemented.

Code 5.41 Definition of the Functions createConnection and createNetwork

```
(1)     Transfer * CreateConnection(IpAddr ip, int port,
        IpAddr oppositeIp, int oppositePort );
(2)     Transfer * CreateNetwork(IpAddr ipAddr,
        Transfer *link);
```

When the Agent on the host wants to create a virtual machine, it first calls the *createConnection* function to create a connection object and then calls the *createNetwork* function to create a network object. For the member variable *ipAddr* of this network object, initialize it to the IP address of the virtual machine. This network object becomes the network object of the virtual machine. Initialize its member variable *link* to the connection object created earlier. The network object then uses the connection object as its link layer. Subsequently, when the application on the virtual machine calls the *createConnection* function, the given IP address is that of the virtual machine, so it is bound to the virtual machine's network object. For this connection object acting as link layer of the virtual machine, its UDP port number becomes the identification information of the virtual machine on the host. This UDP port number should be advertised to other virtual machines on the virtual LAN. Virtual machines communicate with each other by UDP.

Reflection 5.12: When the network object of a VM is identified by its IP address, then multiple VMs on a single host are not allowed to have the same IP address. So when two enterprise customers' VMs have the same IP address, they cannot be scheduled to run on the same host. How to remove this restriction?

5.13 Updates to Applications on Virtual Machines

In an organization, it is common for applications to be revised and updated for reasons such as business expansion. The traditional way to get a new version of an application online is to shut down the old version of the application, install the new version of the application to replace the old one, and then start up the new version of the application. The problem with this traditional approach is that during the replacement process, services provided by the application are not available to clients. For many applications, availability is a critical metric, especially for Internet applications such as e-commerce. In cloud computing, instead of using the traditional replacement method, application upgrades use a switching method. The switching method has little or no impact on the availability of the services.

In cloud computing, when an enterprise customer wants to upgrade an application on virtual machine *VM_A1*, it finds another host and starts up virtual machine *VM_A1*. This startup is not called an online state startup, but a maintenance state startup. The difference in a maintenance state startup is that instead of executing the boot Shell script program on the VM file system, the Telnet server program is executed. After the Telnet server program is started up, the operation staff logs on using a telnet terminal program. Next, the operator can install the new version of the application, replacing the old one. After the upgrade is complete, the file system of the virtual machine is changed. Using a tool such as Docker [17], the operator can repackage the virtual machine's file system into a new image file and upload it to the cloud repository. During the above upgrade process, the original virtual machine *VM_A1* on the production line runs as usual on the cloud.

After the new version of the image file is uploaded to the cloud repository, the cloud manager is notified to perform the switchover. When the cloud manager performs the switchover, it schedules a host to run *VM_A1* first, and then performs the switchover job after *VM_A1* has started up. The so-called switchover job is to notify other running VMs in the virtual LAN to update the entry in their *ipAddrMapTable* and *portMapTable* about *VM_A1*. For example, assume that the original *VM_A1* is running on the PC_x host (whose IP address is 129.95.37.45). The upgraded virtual machine *VM_A1* runs on the PC_y host (whose IP address is 129.95.37.69). Then all other VMs running on the virtual LAN should have their *ipAddrMapTable* and *portMapTable* changed. Specifically, the entry 129.95.37.45 is changed to 129.95.37.69. The switchover is achieved after the change. The last task is to shut down the *VM_A1* on host PC_x after it has no load.

After changing the original host IP address 129.95.37.45 to the new host IP address 129.95.37.69 in *ipAddrMapTable* and *portMapTable* of the other virtual machines on the virtual LAN, when an application wants to establish a network connection with the server on virtual machine *VM_A1*, the connection request will be initiated to the listening port on the host PC_y instead of to the listening port on the host PC_x. This is an indication that the switchover is complete.

5.14 Containerization of Applications

The life cycle of an application usually goes through a process of development, testing, deployment and operation, as well as revision and upgrade. This involves a transfer issue. Specifically, the development department designs and codes an application and then transfers it to the testing department. The testing department installs the application in its own runtime environment and then tests it. After the testing department completes the testing, the application transfers to the operation

5.14 Containerization of Applications

department. The operation department also installs and deploys the application in its own runtime environment and makes it run successfully. There may be differences in the runtime environments provided by the three departments for the application. Therefore, there is an installation and deployment problem in both the testing and operation departments [20]. Once the application does not run successfully, the testing department usually suspects that the root cause of the problem lies in the development department and believes that the development department has not done a good job with the application. The development department, on the other hand, thinks that it is due to the poor skill level of testing department. The same is true between operation and testing.

The above issue leads to a synergy problem with very serious consequences. Shirking of responsibilities and pulling the strings between departments can result in applications not going live as scheduled. To solve this problem, the DevOps software development management model [20] is proposed. DevOps is a combination of two words development and operations, which means inter-departmental collaboration and integration. The idea to solve the problem is containerization of applications. A container is a lightweight implementation of a virtual machine. The implementation of virtual machine described earlier is a lightweight one. The so-called lightweight implementation is relative to implementation schemes such as VMware [21]. In the VMware solution, the Hypervisor is installed on the computer before the operating system is installed. In this scenario, the Hypervisor acts as the operating system and the operating system becomes an application. This scenario has the problem of high overhead of performance. The reason is that Hypervisor is not an intermediary role but a manager role. Thus, there are two managers, and the real manager of the hardware resources is the Hypervisor, which leads to frequent interactions between the two managers.

Containerization of an application means that the development of an application takes place right in the virtual machine. Thus, the process of program development is: (1) the development department selects a base image file as the file system of the virtual machine; (2) the virtual machine is started up on a computer where the development environment is installed and configured; and (3) the application is developed. The base image file referred to here is usually the file system after the operating system is installed. The development department may also continue to install and configure the runtime environment during the development of the application. Whenever the file system of a virtual machine is changed, the image file of the virtual machine is regenerated and uploaded to the image file repository. Whenever application development is performed, the latest version of the image file is downloaded, the virtual machine is started up, and development is performed in the virtual machine. When it is time to submit it to the testing department for testing, it is time to notify the testing department to download the image file, start up the virtual machine, and test it in the virtual machine. The same is true for the operations department.

Once an application is containerized, there is no longer a problem of installing, deploying and configuring the application. Thus, there is no more shirking of responsibilities between departments. Note: Application containerization here does not mean the containerization of a single application, but the containerization of all server programs. For example, suppose an enterprise wants to develop a new web server program, and the database server is its part of runtime environment. Although each of the three departments has its own physical LAN, all three departments will have the same virtual LAN with two VMs: (1) VM1 to run the web server program; (2) VM2 to run the database server program. In both the testing and operation departments, the image files for these two VMs come from the development department, so they are exactly the same. The difference is the application data. All three departments have their own database files. For all three departments, it is simply a matter of mounting the directory where the database files are located (as NFS) in a specified directory on the host running VM2. This scenario was explained in Sect. 5.10.

Containerization of applications requires tools to support it. The first step is to provide the base image, then comes the creation and initialization of the virtual machine, the download of the image file, and the startup of the virtual machine. There is also a key task of packaging the updated VM filesystem into an image file, and updating and replacing the original image file. Docker is the best-known software tool for supporting the containerization of applications [22]. Docker consists of three components: the Docker Daemon, the Docker Client, and the Docker Repository. The Docker Daemon is the core component, equivalent to the Agent in the cloud computing described earlier, and runs on each host. The Docker Client is the equivalent of a cloud manager in cloud computing and gives operational instructions to the Docker Daemon. The most common commands are to run the virtual machine, configure the virtual machine, and package the updated virtual machine filesystem into an image file to be uploaded to the Docker Repository. The Docker Repository is a database server used to store the image file.

5.15 Cloud Service Management Systems

Cloud service providers use cloud service management systems to manage their cloud services. The management consists of two parts: resources management and customers management. Resources include hardware resources and information service resources. Hardware resources mainly refer to hosts and networks. Each host contains hardware resources such as CPU and GPU, memory, and disk. Customers are the business customers. Customers migrate their business information systems to the cloud and run them on the cloud. The management system opens to customers the following functions: registration, login, create virtual LAN, add virtual machines to the virtual LAN, and delete the existing virtual machines. Functions that customers can perform on virtual machines include: setting the volume of resources for a virtual machine, uploading an image file, starting a virtual machine, shutting down a virtual machine, uninstalling an application on a virtual machine, and installing an application on a virtual machine. It can be seen that after enterprise customers migrate their business information systems to the cloud, the

5.15 Cloud Service Management Systems

original system structure concept and operation and maintenance methods remain unchanged. The change is that the operations and maintenance are no longer performed in the physical world, but in the virtual world.

It can be seen that the cloud service management system has to have two data tables to support host management and customer management. One of them is the host resource table and the other is the customer table. Sample data in these two tables are shown in Tables 5.6 and 5.7, respectively. The host resource table gives the data of four hosts and the customer table gives the data of two customers. The hosts of the cloud service provider are organized according to regions. There are a number of hosts in each region. Therefore, the identification of a host consists of two parts: region id and host id. Customers can create their own virtual LAN and add VMs to the virtual LAN. Therefore, the identifier of a virtual machine consists of three parts: the customer id, the virtual LAN id, and the virtual machine id. The last three columns of the host resource table and the last two columns of the customer table record runtime information. The other columns record static information.

The cloud service management system consists of three applications: the cloud manager, the executor, and the data manager. The cloud manager is the service center that is responsible for interacting with customers, collecting host information, and scheduling virtual machines. The executor runs on each host and receives commands from the cloud manager to perform operations such as creating virtual machines, configuring virtual machines with virtual-real mapping, starting up virtual machines, and shutting down virtual machines. The executor also collects information about the operation of the virtual machine and reports it to the cloud manager. The virtual machine also reports the listening port number virtual-real mapping information of the server programs on it to the executor. The executor transfers it to the cloud manager. The cloud manager, in turn, passes it down to the other VMs in the virtual LAN. Once the other virtual machines get the server port number virtual-real mapping information, they can successfully establish network connections with

Table 5.6 Table of host resources

Region id	Host id	Model	IP address	Resource	Utilized resources	Free resources	VM load
R1	H1	64-bit ARM	129.95.37.45	32 cores 32G mem	24 cores 24G mem	8 cores 8G mem	C1:VN1:VM1 C1:VN1:VM1 C1:VN1:VM1
R1	H2	64-bit ARM	129.95.37.69	32 cores 64G mem 8T disk	16 cores 48G mem 6T disk	16 cores 16G mem 2T disk	C1:VN1:VM1 C4:VN1:VM2 C5:VN1:VM1
R2	H1	32-bit X86	129.95.37.33	16 cores 32G mem	16 cores 32G mem	0 cores 0G mem	C1:VN1:VM1 C1:VN1:VM1
R2	H2	32-bit X86	129.95.37.74	16 cores 32G mem	2 cores 8G mem	14 cores 24G mem	C1:VN1:VM1

Table 5.7 Table of customers

Customer id	Virtual LAN id	VM id	Model	Name	Image file	Startup index	IP address	Resource requirement	State	Assigned host
C1	VN1	VM1	64-bit ARM	WEB server	Image 1	3	192.168.76.100	24 cores 24G mem	Running	R1:H1
		VM2	64-bit ARM	Database server	Image 2	1	192.168.76.101	16 cores 48G mem 4T disk	Running	R1:H2
		VM3	32-bit X86	Email server	Image 3	2	192.168.76.102	16 cores 32G mem	Shutdown	
C2	VN1	VM1	32-bit X86	WEB server	Image 4	1	192.168.76.100	4 cores 4G mem	Running	R2:H1
		VM2	32-bit X86	Database server	Image 5	2	192.168.76.101	8 cores 16G mem	Running	R2:H2

the servers in the virtual LAN. The data manager is responsible for data management. For example, the host and client tables described above, as well as image files are stored in the data manager.

There are many cloud service management system products such as Kubernetes [23], Openstack [24], Mesos [25] and Docker Swarm [26]. Among them, Kubernetes is the most well-known and widely used cloud service management system product. Kubernetes is an open-source product from Google. Its cloud manager is called Kubernetes Master and its executor is called Kubernetes Node. Kubernetes uses etcd, a database product, as its data manager. Once you understand the essence of cloud computing and virtual machines, it is easy to understand the components in Kubernetes. The Kube-proxy component in Kubernetes Node performs virtual-real mapping, including virtual-real mapping of IP addresses and virtual-real mapping of service port numbers. The Kubelet component in Kubernetes Node uses the Docker Daemon to perform specific operations such as creation, configuration, startup, and shutdown of virtual machines.

After an enterprise customer migrates its business information system to the cloud, the operation and maintenance work is all handed over to the cloud service provider. The cloud service management system monitors the operation status and service quality of virtual machines to keep track of the operation in real time. Once irregularities are detected, measures are taken to safeguard service quality. The measures include adding resources to the virtual machine, migrating the virtual machine to a more suitable host, replicating the virtual machine, and so on. As a result, enterprise customers who migrate their business information systems to the cloud will no longer encounter problems such as insufficient resources or dropped connections due to failures. For common applications, such as database management systems [27], enterprise customers can also use products provided by cloud service providers. In this case, they do not need to think about upgrading their applications. Cloud service providers can make their services more affordable through scale and aggregation.

From another perspective, the function of cloud service management system is to organize many hosts into a mega host for users. The users here are the enterprise customers and the system operation and maintenance personnel of the cloud service provider. In the user's view, this host has oversized computing power, storage space, and communication capability to carry the operation of all the business information systems of the enterprise customers. And this oversized host has the good characteristics of never failing and always available.

5.16 Summary of the Chapter

Cloud computing evolved from cluster computing, motivated by the idea of combining many hosts into a single oversized host for use by enterprise customers. Externally, this host has some desired characteristics such as supporting many program languages, huge capacity, never failing, always available, and so on. Internally, it enables enterprise customers to migrate their business information systems to the cloud without any change and run them successfully on the cloud. Compared to cluster computing, cloud computing takes resource sharing to a whole new level. On top of cluster computing, cloud computing enables enterprise customers to run their applications everywhere on the cloud. Cloud computing enables applications to run successfully even when the runtime environment in which they are running changes. For cloud service providers, it enables them to make their services affordable through large scale sharing effect.

The evolution of computing is a dialectical unity of change and constancy. An application consists of two parts: (1) the application itself and (2) the runtime environment. The application accesses resources and services in the runtime environment in a client role. The resources and services in the runtime environment are shared and independent, so they are variable in terms of identification and availability to the application. This variability can prevent the application from running successfully. Migrating an application to the cloud, or migrating an application from one host to another in the cloud, introduces the issue of variability in the runtime environment. The strategy adopted to make applications run and be able to run successfully is virtualization. Specifically, virtual machines are used to run applications. Virtual machines are categorized into two tiers.

The first level of virtual machines, also called interpreters, can interpret and execute instructions in an application line by line. Interpreted execution is very inefficient. An effective solution is to organize the software in layers. The code for solving those fundamental and common problems is compiled and deposited as underlying service functions, which are distributed with the operating system. The application is then written to orchestrate the calls to these service functions based on an off-the-shelf architecture. Applications written in this way are characterized by a small amount of code. When the application is interpreted, the interpreted portion is only a small percentage. The computer spends most of its time executing the code in the system functions. This is the fundamental reason why scripting languages have become popular. In essence, it is a mixture of interpretation and compilation.

A second tier of virtual machines can provide an unchanging virtual runtime environment for an application. Alternatively, a second-tier virtual machine makes the changing runtime environment transparent to the application. The second tier of virtual machines is between the application and the operating system. When it is implemented in the operating system kernel, the operating system kernel changes from a single layer to a two-tier structure. The top layer is called the virtual machine layer and the bottom layer is called the host layer. The host layer is the original operating system kernel. As a result, applications that were running on top of the OS kernel became running on top of a virtual machine. Thus, the application program has to access the resources and services in the runtime environment through the intermediary of the virtual machine.

There are two scenarios for virtualization. The first scenario is where the concept of virtualization and the implementation of virtual-real mapping comes first and then the application is developed. For example, applications are developed with domain names to identify computers. There are existing implementations for

5.16 Summary of the Chapter

mapping domain names to IP addresses. The second scenario is that the application comes first and then the virtualization concepts and the implementation of virtual-real mapping. Cloud computing falls into this scenario. In this scenario, the original identification concepts of resources and services are given two meanings: real ids and virtual ids, e.g., IP addresses, which are divided into virtual and real IP addresses. By transforming the operating system so that the application runs on top of a virtual machine, all the real ids in the application become virtual ids, and the mapping of the virtual ids to real ids is done by the virtual machine.

With virtual machines, it is possible for enterprise customers to migrate their business information systems to the cloud without modification. In the view of enterprise customers, after migrating their business information systems to the cloud, the original system structure concept and operation and maintenance methods remain unchanged. What has changed is that their original physical LAN has become a virtual LAN on the cloud, and physical computers have become virtual computers on the cloud. Enterprise customers originally performed operation and maintenance operations in the physical world, but now perform them in the virtual world on the cloud. There is no difference between performing O&M operations on a virtual machine and performing O&M operations on a physical computer. The physical world on the cloud is completely transparent to enterprise customers, i.e., enterprise customers neither knows nor needs to know on which host the virtual machine is actually running. The computer communication considered by enterprise customers is the communication between the virtual machines. When connecting to a server, the IP address given is the IP address of the virtual machine on which the server resides, and the port number given is also the server's port number on the virtual machine.

A cloud service management system consists of three applications: the Cloud Manager, the Executor, and the Data Manager. The cloud manager is the service center. Enterprise customers perform operation and maintenance operations through the cloud manager, such as creating virtual LANs, adding virtual machines to virtual LANs, configuring hardware resources for virtual machines, and starting up virtual machines. The cloud manager is also responsible for collecting host information as well as scheduling VM operations. The executor runs on each host and receive commands from the cloud manager to perform actions such as creating VMs, configuring VMs, starting up VMs, and shutting down VMs. The VMs also report server port mapping information to the executor. The executor transfers it to the cloud manager. The cloud manager in turn passes it down to the other VMs in the virtual LAN. Once the other virtual machines get the service port number virtual-real mapping information, they can successfully establish network connections with the servers in the virtual LAN. The data manager is responsible for managing host information, customer information, and virtual machine operation information.

For multiple virtual machines running on the same host, they should be isolated from each other in terms of hardware resources and namespaces. Only in this way can they not interfere with each other. These two kinds of isolation can be realized with the help of CGroup technology and Namespace technology on Linux.

Exercises
1. The implementation of overlay networking described in Sect. 5.12 uses a network connection object on the host as the link layer for a virtual machine. The transport protocol for this network connection object is udser datagram protocol (UDP), not transmission control protocol (TCP). Please analyze and explain why UDP is used rather than TCP. Is it feasible to use TCP? Please analyze and explain from the following scenario. Suppose two virtual machine α and β. A client program on VM β wants to establish a network connection to a server on VM α. VM α and β can reside either on one host or on two different hosts.
2. The default networking mode that Docker provides for containers (another name for virtual machines) is Bridged. In this mode, each virtual machine has its own physical IP address. In other words, when n VMs reside on a host, the host has n additional IP addresses, each of which is assigned to one VM. Alternatively, a virtual machine is also a computer on the physical LAN. The advantage of this mode is that any two virtual machines in the physical LAN can communicate directly without IP address mapping and service port number mapping issues. Can this mode enable enterprise customers to migrate their business information systems to the cloud without modification? How to implement the Bridged networking mode? What are its characteristics?
3. Docker also supports an overlay network. An example of a Docker command to create an overlay network is "docker network create --driver overlay my_overlay", which gives the name *my_overlay* to the overlay network that is created. When you subsequently create a container, you can specify the network for the container. For example, the Docker command "docker run --it --name my_container --network my_overlay my_image" creates a container using the image file *my_image*, names the container *my_container*, and connects the container to network *my_overlay*. Many people think that an overlay network means layer 2 of a network is stacked on top of layer 4 of another network. But the overlay network described in Sect. 5.12 means layer 3 of a network is stacked on top of layer 4 of another network. Layer 2, layer 3, and layer 4 here refer to the link layer, network layer, and transport layer, respectively. Please analyze the advantages of the overlay network implementation described in Sect. 5.12 over that described in the sources.
4. In cloud computing, a virtual gateway is essential for a virtual LAN of an enterprise customer. Logically, the virtual gateway has two virtual NICs, which connect to the public network and intranet, respectively. Suppose there are n enterprise customers on the cloud and each enterprise customer has only one virtual LAN. Then there will be n virtual gateways on the cloud. These n virtual gateways are all connected to the public network and therefore can communicate with each other. Logically, these n virtual gateways should form a higher-level virtual LAN, named virtual LAN g. Virtual LAN g should also have a gateway to the public network. It follows that the virtual gateway for an enterprise customer should be provided by the cloud service provider. Is this reasoning correct? Please justify it. If it is correct, what information should the enterprise

5.16 Summary of the Chapter

customer tell the cloud service provider in the construction of the virtual gateway? And what should the cloud service provider do?

5. In cloud computing, enterprise customers want to view the logs of their applications running on the cloud. To satisfy this requirement, the cloud service provider takes the step of redirecting the logs of applications running on virtual machines to a network connection through a redirection technique (i.e., the file virtualization technique in Sect. 5.4). The other end of this network connection is a log server. Thus, the application's running logs are deposited into the log server of the cloud service provider. When an enterprise customer wants to view historical logs, it queries the log records from the log server. How can the above functionality be realized? Please give the implementation scheme. What are the things that Agent has to do in the implementation of this feature?

6. In cloud computing, can an enterprise customer use a telnet terminal program to log in to a virtual machine running on the cloud? If there is a need for this functionality, how should it be implemented? Assuming that logging in is possible, can an enterprise customer perform actions such as installing a new application? Can they shut down a running application? Please answer the above questions based on your knowledge of Sects. 5.13 and 5.14. Please also consult the information to see what functions Docker provides for manipulating image files? Can these functions of Docker be utilized to perform the above operations?

7. In addition to scheduling and running VMs, a cloud service management system needs to monitor the operational state of VMs, and keep track of the operational state of VMs and the applications on them. How to sense the operation state of virtual machines? Tip: Processes have a creator/created relationship, i.e., a parent–child relationship. The Agent process is the root process of all processes on the virtual machine, so it can control and manage the processes on the virtual machine.

8. Virtual machines, CGroups, and Namespaces are all kernel objects in the operating system. There is no direct association between the three, but they are connected through processes. Because processes have attributes *vm*, *cgroup*, and *namespace*, which record the virtual machine, CGroup, and Namespace to which the process belongs, respectively. There is a one-to-many relationship between the virtual machine and the process, between the CGroup and the process, and between the Namespace and the process. When a parent process creates a child process, the child process inherits these three attribute values from the parent process. However, the parent process can change the values of the three attributes of the child process. Is it correct to say that suspending VM *A* actually suspends those processes whose *vm* attribute value is VM *A*? Please give reasons. The operating system provides the application with creation API functions, and release API functions for these three objects. Suppose the operating system provides the application with the *pauseVM* function, whose function is to suspend the virtual machine. Can you write an implementation of this function?

References

1. Thomas, E., Zaigham, M., Ricado, P., *Cloud Computing: Concepts, Technology & Architecture*. London: Pearson Education, 2016.
2. Violeta, M., Juan, M, G., *A survey of migration mechanisms of virtual machines*. ACM Computing Surveys, 2014, 46(3): p. 1–33.
3. Tianzhang, H., Rajkumar, B., *A Taxonomy of Live Migration Management in Cloud Computing*. ACM Computing Surveys, 2023, 56(3): p. 1–33.
4. Rajkumar, B., *Mastering Cloud Computing: Foundations and Applications programming*. Morgan Kaufmann Publishers Inc., 2013.
5. Alfred, V. A., Monica, S. L., Ravi, S., Jeffrey, D. U., *Compilers: Principles, Techniques, and Tools*. Addison Wesley, 2006.
6. Mads, S. A., Dariusz, B., Olivier, D., Jan, M., *From Interpreter to Compiler and Virtual Machine: A Functional Derivation*. Basic Research in Computer Science, 2003.
7. Wang, K. C., *Systems Programming in Unix/Linux*. Springer Nature link, 2018 [access date 10/27/2023]; Available from: https://link.springer.com/book/10.1007/978-3-319-92429-8.
8. Chuntao, H., Dehao, C., Wenguang, C., *MapCG: Writing Parallel Program Portable between CPU and GPU*. In 19th International Conference on Parallel Architectures and Compilation Techniques, 2010, p. 217–226.
9. Thuan, L. T., Hoang, L., *.Net Framework Essentials (3rd edition)*. O'Reilly Media Inc., 2003.
10. Lutz, P., *Are Scripting Languages Any Good? A Validation of Perl, Python, Rexx, and Tcl against C, C++, and Java*. Advances in Computers, 2003, 57: p. 205–270.
11. April, W. W., Prasad, A. K., Michael, R. J., *AOT vs. JIT: Impact of Profile Data on Code Quality*. ACM SIGPLAN Notices, 2017, 52(5): p. 1–10.
12. Andrew, S., Tanenbaum, H. B., *Modern Operating Systems (4th ed.)*. London: Pearson, 2020.
13. Don, B., *Essential COM*. Addison-Wesley Professional, 1998.
14. *Container migration with Podman on RHEL*. 2019 [access date 3/12/2023]; Available from: https://www.redhat.com/en/blog/container-migration-podman-rhel.
15. Fei, Z., Guangming, L., Xiaoming, F., et al., *Survey on Virtual Machine Migration: Challenges, Techniques, and Open Issues*. IEEE Communications Surveys & Tutorials, 2018, 20(2): p. 1206–1243.
16. Dan, K., *Virtualization: A Manager's Guide*. O'Reilly, 2011.
17. Merkel, D., *Docker: Lightweight Linux Containers for Consistent Development and Deployment*. Linux Journal, 2014, 239(3): p. 76–90.
18. *Why you need Kubernetes and what it can do*. 2020 [access date 12/11/2023]; Available from: https://kubernetes.io/docs/concepts/overview/#why-you-need-kubernetes-and-what-can-it-do.
19. Mallik, M., Dinesh, D., Kenneth, D., *Virtual Extensible Local Area Network (VXLAN): A Framework for Overlaying Virtualized Layer 2 Networks Over Layer 3 Networks*. 2020 [access date 3/11/2024]; Available from: https://datatracker.ietf.org/doc/rfc7348/.
20. Armin, B., Abbas, H., *Microservices Architecture Enables DevOps: Migration to a Cloud-Native Architecture*. IEEE Software Magazine, 2016, 33(3): p. 42–52.
21. Orran, K., Phil, M., Arkady, K., *Enabling a Marketplace of Clouds: VMware's VCloud Director*. ACM SIGOPS Operating Systems Review, 2010, 44(4): p. 103–114.
22. Rodriguez, M. A., Buyya, R. *Container-Based Cluster Orchestration Systems: A Taxonomy and Future Directions*. Software: Practice and Experience, 2019, 49(5): p. 698–719.
23. Zeineb, R., Javad, C., *Custom Scheduling in Kubernetes: A Survey on Common Problems and Solution Approaches*. ACM Computing Surveys, 2022, 55(7): p. 1–37.
24. Antonio, C., Mario, F., Luca, F., *VM Consolidation: A Real Case Based on OpenStack Cloud*. Future Generation Computer Systems, 2014, 32(3): p. 118–127.
25. Pankaj, S., Madhusudhan, G., Suresh, M., Marlon, P., *Integrating Apache Airavata with Docker, Marathon, and Mesos*. Concurrency and Computation: Practice and Experience, 2015, 28(7): p. 1952–1959.

26. Adrian, M., *Container Orchestration with Kubernetes, Docker Swarm, Mesos/Marathon and Nomad*. O'Reilly Media, Inc., 2016.
27. Nane, K., Peter-Christian, Q., *Understanding Cloud-Native Applications After 10 Years of Cloud Computing - A Systematic Mapping Study*. Journal of System Software, 2017, 126(4): p. 1–16.

Chapter 6
Microservices

When it comes to services, there is the concept of client/server (C/S), which involves both clients and service providers, or in other words, clients and servers. A server consists of two parts: the server program and the data. There is a large amount of data in a server because both the service data and the client data are stored on the server. Servers are also load centers because clients are coming to access them. Servers can be built in a one-stop manner or a combined one [1]. In a one-stop manner, all problems to be considered in a service are solved in a single application. Whereas in the combined manner, a large server is made up of multiple subservers. Each subserver focuses on the solution of a particular problem. For example, a database server can be composed of three subservers: a resolution server, a security server, and a data processing server [2]. These three subservers are responsible for request resolution, security checking, and data processing, respectively.

There is no clear definition of microservices [3]. In many literature, microservices are understood as a traditional one-stop server that is split into multiple subservers based on the business. The subservers are also called microservices. Each microservice provides for a single business function, i.e., one service does one thing. Thus, a big server is made up of multiple microservers combined in a confederate fashion. The micro in microservices does not really just mean small. Micro comes from the word microcosmic, which means that the whole thing is reliable and trustworthy if the small things are carefully and thoughtfully considered. Therefore, microservices technology [4] should refer to the strategies and methods to realize the efficient operation, elastic operation, secure operation, fast update, and fast startup of server programs.

For a big server, how many subservers should it be divided into? How should it be divided? The guideline for division should not only be the functionality, but also the frequency of interaction between modules. If two modules are in the same application, then their interactions are of direct function calls. If they are in two applications running on the same computer, then their interactions are of process-to-process communication, i.e., inter-process communication (IPC) communication. If they are in two applications running on different computers, then their interactions depend on network communication. When the two computers are heterogeneous, the two ends of the communication also need to translate. It can be seen that when interactions between two functional modules are frequent, it is better to put them both into the same server application. This division principle is also often used in daily life. For example, when arranging dormitories for students, those in one class should be accommodated in close proximity to each other. For students of a department, dormitories should be prioritized close to the department building, because the most common place for students to go is the building.

A distinctive feature of modern server programs is the high frequency of revising and upgrading. When a program has bugs, it needs to be updated. When the program structure becomes unreasonable, it also needs to be updated. The function expansion leads to the program being updated. When the function implementation needs to be improved, it also needs to be updated. Program update involves program design and development, program test and verification, as well as program online deployment. Update to be fast, not only refers to each link being fast, the transfer from one link to the next should be fast. For fast source code update, the prerequisites are: (1) popular frameworks are used for developing applications; (2) coding follows the standard in the naming and formatting; (3) the document structure is clear and easy to understand. Only in this way will it be easy for developers to understand the original programs and quickly locate the places to be modified. In other words, when there is already a standard for a job, it should be followed. In addition, in the process of the development, testing, as well as online deployment, when there are automation tools that can assist, you should try to use them.

The transfer from one link to the next should also be fast. That is, applications should be installed, configured, and debugged quickly. After the development department completes the development, the application should be transferred to the test department for testing and verification. After the test department completes testing, the application flows to the operation department for online deployment. An application contains two parts: (1) the application itself; (2) the runtime environment. For an application, the development, test, and operation departments all have their own runtime environments, which are different from each other. Because of this, there is a problem of installing, configuring, and debugging the application in both the test and operation departments. In the interface between the application and the runtime environment, some exceptions and difficulties often emerge, leading to the departments to pull each other's punches and shirk their responsibilities. The ultimate consequence is that the application does not go live as scheduled.

The above problems can be solved by application containerization [5]. Containerization technology has been explained in Sect. 5.14. It means that an application runs in a container. Containers are virtual machines and have invariance. Thus, the runtime environment of an application is virtualized and has invariance. The mapping of the virtual runtime environment to the real one is done by the container. The mapping relationship is determined by an application manager, such as Cloud Manager, or Cluster Manager. The entire mapping is done automatically by software tools without human involvement. Thus, with containerization, there is no more installation, configuration, or debugging of applications. The application is packaged into an image file by the development department and then released to the test and operation departments. The image file has the good characteristic of being ready to use out of the box [6].

On the cloud or on the cluster, updates to online server programs are no longer done by the original replacement method, but by switching [7]. Replacement means shutting down and uninstalling the old version of an application, and then installing and starting its new version. When the replacement method is used, the service is unavailable during the replacement period. The service is unavailable for a long period of time, which is not acceptable in many application scenarios, such as the passenger identification service at a train station. The switchover method involves starting the new version of an application on another computer and then notifying the service gateway to switch the client requests from the old version to the new version. After the switchover is complete, the old version is shut down and uninstalled. As you can see, with the switchover approach, the service remains available to clients without interruption. This is a desired feature.

To make a server process data efficiently, it is necessary to analyze the process of data processing and its characteristics, and then take effective measures to improve the processing efficiency [8]. The next section (Sect. 6.1) will explain the ways and measures to improve the efficiency of data processing. All assets and activities of enterprises and clients are digitized and represented by data. Data are stored in servers. Therefore, Servers need to be safe and secure [9]. What exactly are the security threats to servers? Section 6.2 explains the security technology to deal with these security threats. When the amount of data in a database server increases to a certain level, it will be split into two database servers. Splitting affects the service availability [10]. What are the measures and methods to minimize the impact of splitting on service availability? Section 6.3 will explore server scalability. Servers need to be dynamically adaptive [11]. Sections 6.4 through 6.6 explain service clustering [12], abstraction and dynamic adaptation [13], as well as serverless [14], respectively.

6.1 Efficient Data Processing

In a server, there is a large amount of similar data. For example, in an e-commerce server, the registration information of a client is one item of client data. Because there are many clients, there are many items of client data on the server. These similar data are usually stored in one table. Assume that the client data are stored in the *client* table, where one row of data corresponds to one client. A client has only one row of data in the *client* table. When a client logs in, it gives its username and password. The server then has to query the *client* table based on the username and password to get that row of registration data for the client. Queries are one of the most common and frequent operations in servers. The most intuitive way to query is to take the table data row by row from memory and see if it is the data that match the condition. If so, it means that it has been found. If it does not match, then take the next row. The process continues in a loop until it is found.

In the above query method, the judgment of whether or not it matches the condition is done by the CPU. The data are stored in memory. The four most common types of memory are cache, RAM, local disk, and remote computer. Fetching a row of data from memory means transporting a row of data from memory to the CPU. If it does not match, then the transport is a futile one, and the judgment made by the CPU for that trip is futile processing. The query time is proportional to the number of futile transports and also proportional to the data volume of futile transports. In terms of a transport, the data volume of futile transportation is the amount of a row of data. When querying a row from a table with n rows, in accordance with the above method to perform, the average number of futile transportations is about $n/2$. Querying efficiency of the method is very low, especially when n is large.

One effective way to improve query efficiency is to create indexes for data tables and then query the data based on the indexes [15]. Indexing is a common and effective way to reduce ineffective transportation and ineffective processing, thus improving query efficiency. The catalog of a book seen in daily life is a kind of index. For a book with hundreds of pages, if you know that it contains a certain content, how to find this content? If there is no catalog, then you have to start from the first page, page by page, until you find the content you want. For a 500-page book, it takes an average of 250 pages to find it. This kind of search is so inefficient that it is unbearable. If there is a catalog of contents, we will first look it up, find the page number where the target content is located, and then directly jump to the target page. The catalog of contents is usually only 2 or 3 pages long, so it is quick and easy to find it. For a book, the establishment of the catalog, although it costs a few more pages, can play a big role in improving the efficiency of the search. The larger the dataset, the greater the efficacy of the index for finding.

6.1.1 Tree Indexing

In a server, creating an index for a table is to copy the selected one or more columns from the table and build them into an index table that is stored in memory. The selected columns are called the search key. The index table contains two columns: the search key column and the address column. Compared to the amount of data in the original table, the amount of data in the index table is drastically reduced, as shown in Fig. 6.1. The area is used in the figure to indicate the size of the data volume, and it is clear from the figure that the data table has a large amount of data. The amount of data in the index table constituted by the search key extracted from the data table is reduced a lot. When querying, if there is no index, then the entire data table has to be transported from the memory to the CPU for row-by-row checking to see if the query condition is satisfied. The amount of data to be transported is large. If there is an index, then the index table is first transported from memory to

6.1 Efficient Data Processing 395

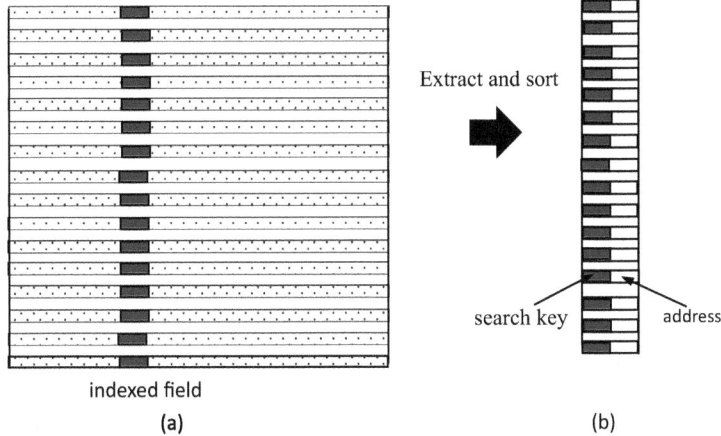

Fig. 6.1 Comparison of the data table and its index table in terms of data volume. (a) Data table; (b) Index table

the CPU for checking to find out the data rows that satisfy the query condition. Then, the desired data rows are read from the memory based on their address.

From the above analyses, it can be seen that the use of indexes can significantly reduce the amount of data to be transported and the query efficiency is improved. The index-based query consists of two steps: (1) first query the index table to get the storage addresses of the target rows; (2) based on the addresses to extract the desired data rows directly from the memory. The measure of reducing data transport by index-based querying does not end there. Rows of an index table are sorted based on the search key values. After sorting, the query no longer uses a sequential lookup method, but a binary lookup method. In binary lookup, when the number of rows in an index table is 2^n, on average only n rows need to be transported to find the target rows. For example, when the number of rows in an index table is 4 billion (i.e., 2^{32}), the average number of rows to be transported in a query is reduced from 2 billion to 32. It can be seen that sorting is very helpful in improving the efficiency of the query, especially when the amount of data are large.

Futile transportation and futile processing are drastically reduced by index-based queries. The reduction comes from two sources: (1) the amount of data in an index table is much less than that in the corresponding data table, and (2) the number of rows to be read is reduced by sorting the rows in an index table. The essence of indexing is to reduce the data, additionally forming a reduced version, which is then sorted to reduce the number of memory accesses. The catalog of contents of a book can be considered as a reduced version of it. The larger the reduction ratio, the more significant increase in query efficacy. For a 500-page book, if the catalog of contents is only two or three pages long, the increase in efficacy is naturally very significant. If the catalog of contents is 60 pages long, then the effect will not be obvious.

For a table, multiple indexes can be created. For example, for the Book table in the Library Management Server, the book name field can be extracted to create an index, and the author field can be extracted to create another index. Other extraction perspectives include publisher, year of publication, keywords, and so on. The more indexes you create, the easier it is to query. Of course, creating an index also brings additional overhead. The overhead consists of two main aspects: (1) the index table itself; (2) update to the indexed field. When the data update in the data table involves indexed fields, the index table should also be updated accordingly. The more indexes you create, the more additional overhead you incur. Every time a row is added to the data table, all the index tables have to be updated. Therefore, indexes should be created carefully and not randomly.

Indexes not only help improve query performance, but can also be used for statistics and data integrity control [16]. For example, an index created for an account id field in the *client* table can be used to count the number of clients. The reason is: (1) a client in the client table has only one row of data; (2) the number of rows in the index table is the same as the number of rows in the data table. When a new client registers, it will have to add a row of data to the *client* table. Additionally, an old client may also want to modify its account id. For adding a row to the client table or modifying a row already in the client table, it is required that the account id values of any two rows of data must not be the same in the table. Processing method is to first query the account id index to see whether it violates the uniqueness principle. If violated, then refuse to accept client's row addition operation or account id modification operation.

Indexes should not be used blindly. For a table with a small amount of data, do not create an index for it. Just as you would not create a catalog for an article if it is only a few or a dozen pages long. This is especially true when the data are stored on disk. The reason is that access to disk data is not performed in bytes, but in blocks. A block of data is typically 8 kB in size, and an indexed table, regardless of its size, takes up at least one disk block. When a query is performed based on an index, the disk is accessed at least once to read the index table, and then again to read the target data row. This results in at least two disk accesses to read two disk blocks. When the data table occupies only one disk block due to a small amount of data, without the index, only one disk block would have to be read. At this point, instead of bringing about a performance improvement, the index is bringing about a performance degradation.

The search key refers to one or more columns in a data table, being used to create an index. Only when the ratio of its data volume to the total data volume is small, the creation of the index makes sense. An intuitive analogy is: for a 500-page book, if the catalog is only one to three pages, the query efficiency is naturally very significant. If the catalog is 80 pages long, then it makes little sense to create a catalog. Therefore, do not create index for one search key with large amount of data. Such an index leads to a large amount of data in the index table. Additionally, do not create indexes for a column with a small value range. For example, for the *client* table, do not create an index for the column *gender*. The reason is that possible values for the column *gender* are only male and female. In any disk block that stores the data table, there are at least dozens of rows of data, which certainly contain both male and female clients. Thus, whether you are looking for male or female clients, all disk blocks need to be read. In this situation, the index loses its meaning.

In the above example, creating an index with the gender column as the search key does not bring benefits for query performance improvement. However, it can bring benefits for statistics. When it comes to counting the number of male and female clients, reading the index can solve the problem without having to read the client table. This leads to statistics-oriented indexes, also called aggregation indexes [15]. It is not the same as a query-oriented index. For the column *gender*, its aggregation index contains only two rows of data, one for the number of male clients and the other for the number of female clients. It has very little data. In contrast, a query-oriented index needs to record every row in the data table, resulting in a large amount of data.

When creating an index, the search key can be more than one column. For example, for a transaction table in an e-commerce server, a combined index can be created based on two columns: client id and product id. In this case, the rows in the index table are first sorted by the client id column and then by the product id column. In this case, the sorting feature of the index cannot be utilized when executing a query based on the product id. That is, all disk blocks of the index table are read and then their rows are scanned sequentially to check whether the query condition is satisfied. Nonetheless, the index's reduction feature can be utilized. For example, if you want to query the transaction rows for the purchases of product id "A2306", only a few of the disk blocks in the transaction table will contain rows that meet the condition. In other words, using an index significantly reduces the number of disk blocks to be read on the data table. At this point, the index provides a query performance improvement, even though the sorting feature of the index is not utilized.

In e-commerce servers, buyers and sellers, as the largest group of customers, often have to check their own transaction records. Each seller has a unique id for its each product. Sellers check their own transaction records to understand their product sales. Buyers check transaction records to understand their own shopping situation. It is better to create two indexes on the transaction table: one with the buyer id as the search key, and the other with the seller id as the search key. The former serves buyers, the latter serves sellers. In addition, when buyers shop, they have to query the products. Thus, for the product table, it is better to create an index with product id as the search key. In the design of the product id, the front part is preferably the category id of the product, and the back part is the serial number. The reason is that the most common way for buyers to query products is based on the category from coarse to fine to query.

6.1.2 Hash Indexes

The index described above is known as a tree index. It is a mapping table that records the mapping relationship between the search key values and the storage addresses of the rows in the data table. When querying, the index table is looked up first to derive the addresses of the desired rows, and then the desired rows are read. The mapping is from the value of variable X to derive the value of variable Y. Here, variable X is the search key and Y is the address of the data row. Mathematically, this can be expressed as a function $Y = f(X)$. Creating an index table means that for different values of X, the function f is different and f does not have to be known. The benefit is that there is little constraint on where a row of data should be stored. If for every value of the variable X, the function f is the same and known, then the index table can be eliminated. Eliminating the index table not only saves storage space, but also eliminates the overhead of accessing the index table. Such indexes are called hash indexes [15].

For a hash index, you need to design a hash function f. When adding a row to a data table, use its search key value as the X value, calculate the storage address (i.e., the Y value) of the row, and then store it at the location with the address Y. When the search key value of a row in the data table is modified, the new location where the row of data should be stored should be calculated, and if it is not the same as the old location, the row should be moved to the new location. Compared with tree indexes, Hash indexes have the advantage that there is no need to build index tables, so the query will not have the overhead of reading index tables. In a tree index, pinpointing the target record is accomplished by looking up the index table. In a hash index, pinpointing the target record is achieved by computing the hash value. Specifically, Using the hash function f, taking the search key value given in the query condition as input, calculate the corresponding hash value, which is the storage address of the target record.

Hash indexing reaches the ultimate in terms of reducing futile transportation and futile processing. But it also has many drawbacks. At the time of adding a row of data, the hash value is computed and then the row is stored in the storage location determined by the hash value. The value range of the search key can be derived from its meaning, and its space size is set to M. When constructing the hash index, the number of rows in the data table is specified (set to N) in order to determine the hash function f, and the storage space is reserved. As a result, there is the problem of low utilization of disk blocks when there are still very few rows in the data table. When there are more rows in the data table, there is the problem of conflict of row storage location. In other words, it is poorly scalable and is only suitable for those tables that the number of rows does not change much, such as the course table in the university academic management database. In addition, the hash index is only suitable for equal-value queries, not for range or fuzzy queries.

Reflection 6-1: Hash indexes are only suitable for equal-value queries, not for range or fuzzy queries, why?

Both tree indexes and hash indexes are polarized in nature. In tree indexes, there are no constraints or limitations on where the rows in a data table can be stored. In hash indexes, the rows in the data table must be stored in the specified location. In tree indexes, the mapping relationship between the search key value and the storage location is recorded. In hash indexes, the mapping relationship does not need to be recorded at all, and the storage address can be obtained by calculating the search key value. Hash indexes have address conflict problems, and their scalability is poor. Tree indexes and hash indexes can be used in conjunction with each other to maximize their strengths and avoid their weaknesses. For example, for the student table in the university student management server, its characteristic is that there are new students enrolled every year, and the number of rows is incremental. Therefore, for the student table, a tree index can be established based on the year and major, and then a hash index can be established based on the serial number. When querying, the tree index is used first, followed by a hash index. This combination of indexes is characterized by: the number of rows in the tree index is very small, and the problem of poor scalability of hash index is overcome by the use of tree index.

When querying the data in a table, the expression of query conditions should consider whether indexes can be utilized. For the above student table, suppose you want to check the students of a certain major. In the student table, there is a column for major. If the query condition is expressed in terms of the major column, then the student number index will not be utilized. In fact, the student number contains the major information. Therefore, it is better to use the major information in the student number to express the query condition. This kind of query condition expression can utilize the student number index. Use the student number index to query students of a certain major, although the sorting characteristics of the index cannot be utilized, but the reduction characteristics of the index can be used. Therefore, the query performance can still be significantly improved.

6.1.3 Organizing Data Storage Based on Access Characteristics

Traditionally, data storage is organized using a relational data model [16]. The relational data model is very concerned about update anomalies and data inconsistencies caused by data redundancy. The core idea of relational data model is: data are strictly stored in tables according to categories, where each table stores one category of data, and the same category of data are stored in one table. Take the e-commerce server as an example, client data are stored in the *client t*able, product data are stored in the *product* table, and transaction data are stored in the *transaction* table. When the amount of transaction records in a server reaches the upper limit, a new server is added to store the new transaction records. Thus, the single server becomes a distributed server. In this way, data are organized by distributing the transaction data on different member nodes in the order in which they are generated.

The above organization is not adapted to the data access characteristics and can lead to very poor system performance. One of the significant access characteristics of e-commerce systems is that for both buyers and sellers, they only care about their own transaction records, and they have to access their own transaction records frequently. Adopting the above data storage organization will result in each customer's transaction records being sparsely distributed across the member nodes in the e-commerce distributed database, where customer refers to either buyer or seller. Whether a customer is a buyer or a seller, when her/she wants to query his/her own transaction records, the manager has to send subquery tasks to all member nodes. Each member node has to retrieve the transaction records based on the customer id and then return the query results to the manager. The manager can respond to the customer only after it receives the response results from all member nodes and does the summarization. The performance of this query is very poor because it involves all member nodes. Furthermore, this query is the most frequent query, so the overall performance of the system will also be very poor.

If the organization of transaction data are changed to a per-customer layout, the situation will be completely different. Organizing transaction data by customer means that all customers are evenly dispersed to the member nodes of the distributed system in advance, and then whenever a transaction record is generated, it is stored under the name of the buyer, and then a copy is stored under the name of the seller. Organizing the transaction data in this way makes each customer's transaction records aggregated and stored on one member node. When a customer wants to query his transaction record, the manager then needs to access only one member node. The entire query result is provided by one member node instead of calling all member nodes. Thus, the performance is significantly improved.

Another benefit that comes from organizing transaction data by customer is load balancing [17]. All customers are spread evenly across the member nodes of the distributed system in advance. Thus, the load of adding transaction records is also evenly distributed across the member nodes, and the load of querying transaction records is also evenly distributed across the member nodes. When the amount of data on a member node reaches the upper limit, it is split into two by customer and one of them is transferred to a new member node. Splitting in this manner still maintains the aggregated storage of transaction records of each customer on a member node. After the split, the metadata maintained by the manager should be modified accordingly in the mapping relationship between the customer id and the member node id to reflect the situation after the split.

From the above analyses, it can be seen that for big data systems, the storage organization of data is very critical, which has a direct impact on system performance and load balancing. As the amount of data increases, the performance problem becomes more and more prominent. For system performance and load balancing, sometimes the relational data model is broken. In the above example, for the sake of system performance, the transaction records are replicated and stored under the names of both the buyers and sellers respectively. This clearly introduces data redundancy and violates the principles of relational databases. The reason for this approach is that transaction data has a characteristic of rarely being modified. Even if it is modified, there are only two changes to be made. As a result, few data inconsistencies are triggered.

Key–value pair data model [18] is a widely used data model today. In this model, a table is regarded as a collection of key–value pairs. For any two rows of data in the table, their VALUE data type can be the same or different. The key–value pair data model is not opposed to the relational data model. In the relational data model, the columns of a table can be divided into two parts: primary key column and non-primary key column, where the primary key column corresponds to the KEY, and the non-primary key column corresponds to the VALUE in the key–value pairs data model. From this point of view, the two data models are unified. However, the key–value pair data model is more flexible than the relational data model. For the key–value pair data model, when all rows of data in a table are limited to have the same data type for their VALUE and not a set type, it degenerates into a relational data model. Thus, it can be said that the relational data model is a special case of the key–value pair data model.

The key–value pair data model, also called the NoSQL model, provides good support for the proper organization of data. Take the above e-commerce server as an example, in which there is a customer table, whose KEY is the customer id and VALUE is the transaction records, where the data type of VALUE is a collection. Thus, for a row of data in the customer table, the value of its VALUE is a table of transaction records. This makes a customer's transaction records aggregated and stored in a row in the customer table.

In a clustered environment, in the early days of the server, when the number of customers is small and the transaction records are few, it is sufficient for the customer table to be stored in only one member node. This member node is denoted by A. In the manager, its metadata has a row of record <A, customer, range of values for KEY>. Over time, the number of customers grows, and so does the number of transaction records for each customer. When the amount of data in A reaches the upper limit, a new member node B is added, and half of the data rows from the customer table in A are migrated to member node B. At the same time, a row of record <B, customer, range of values for KEY> is added to the manager's metadata, and the value of the third column in the original record <A, customer, range of values for KEY> is modified accordingly. This process can be continued recursively.

From the above example, it can be seen that the key–value pair data model has good scalability, can achieve good load balancing as well as good query performance. For any member node in the system, when its data volume reaches the upper limit, it is split into two. That is, the customers it carries are split in two parts. Thus, all the customers are evenly spread over the member nodes of the system, and load balancing is well achieved. When a customer wants to query its transaction records, the manager first checks, from its metadata records, on which member node the customer's id falls, and then dispatches that query to that member node. Since a customer's transaction records are aggregated in one row in the customer table, the query performance will be very good.

The key–value pair data model has relaxed restrictions on non-primary key columns in the relational data model, which has both advantages and disadvantages. In terms of querying functionality, the key–value pair data model is far less powerful than the relational data model. In the relational data model, a class corresponds to a table, all instances of a class are placed in a table, and the table is global. In addition, there is no subordinate relationship between tables, and they are peer-to-peer. Therefore, its query function is very powerful, and the query conditions can be flexible, such as range query, fuzzy query, join query, and so on. While in the key–value pair data model, queries can usually only be performed based on the KEY equal to a certain value.

Particularly significant difference is: in the relational data model, all rows in a table have the same data type, while in the key–value pair data model, rows in a table can have different data types for their VALUE. Therefore, in the relational data model, a table has array properties. When extracting a certain column from it, there is no need to scan row by row and then column by column, and it can be jumped at a fixed step size. In the key–value pair data model, a table does not have the characteristics of an array; rows are stored in a sequential mode. When you want to look up the content based on VALUE, you have to scan the whole table row by row and then column by column, which is of very poor performance. Because of this, many products developed based on the key–value pair data model usually do not provide a lookup function based on the content of the VALUE. When you need to look up based on VALUE content, it is necessary to create an index for the searched VALUE to improve search performance.

In some applications, for a single table, different columns have different access frequencies by customers. An example is the email database, which is characterized by the fact that customers all access only their own emails, and often have to open the email list to see if there are any new ones. When looking at the email list, the decision to open an email in detail is usually based on the sender of the email, and the title of the email. Some emails come with attachments, but most emails usually do not. Customers only access attachments when they are interested and then download them locally. From these characteristics of emails, it can be seen that customers visit the basic information of emails (sender, title, time of receipt, accessed mark) very frequently, and visit the detailed content of emails much less frequently than the basic information. In addition, only a small portion of emails have attachments, and the frequency of access to attachments is very low.

For the above access characteristics of email, a customer table is constructed in the email server based on the key–value pair data model, with customer id as KEY and an email table as VALUE. The email table is also a collection of KEY–VALUE pairs. The VALUE in the email table consists of three Column Family: Basic Information Column Family, Details Column Family, and Attachments Column Family. Each Column Family of the email table constitutes a separate table. Thus, there are three tables: <KEY—Basic Information> table, <KEY—Details> table, <KEY—Attachments> table.

The data organization method of storing columns in groups not only brings good access performance, but also makes the storage space efficiently used. For each customer, its basic information of emails is aggregated and stored on a member node. When a customer wants to access the basic information of his emails, the manager only needs to notify one member node to process it, instead of calling all members to participate. Thus, the processing performance will be very good. The same is true when a user wants to access the details of an email, or wants to access the attachments of an email. The advantage of having each Column Family as a separate table is that there is no wasted storage space when an email has no attachments.

The above organization based on Column Family is actually supported by the relational data model. In the relational data model, it is called the vertical segmentation of a table. The difference is that in the key–value pair data model, when adding a row of data to a table, the number of columns in a Column Family, the column name and the column value of each column can be specified at the time of adding. In other words, the columns in a family are not defined in the schema in advance as in the relational data model. In the key–value pair data model, only the Column Families need to be defined in the schema, not the columns contained in a family. In addition, multi-version has been introduced for a column value in a row of data to meet the needs of some applications.

Documents in a document server have another characteristic. Document data includes content and attributes. It is characterized by a large amount of data for the content and a small amount of data for the attributes. Document attributes include file name, category name, creation time, last modification time, creator, size, etc., mainly used for document query. For this characteristic, the document table is divided into two tables in storage: content table and attribute table. The storage of the content table adopts a key–value pair data model, where the KEY is automatically generated by the server and the VALUE is the document content. KEY is not specified by customers, but automatically generated by the server. Its advantage is that the server can set the storage address of the document content as its KEY. Thus, when customers use KEY to query, they can directly locate and quickly obtain data, achieving efficient search. The KEY of the document content is also a column of the attribute table. Because of the small amount of data, the attribute table plays the role of an index table, which is convenient for customers to query documents from different perspectives.

Having the server generate the KEY is good for locating the VALUE, but it also has a drawback. That is, the server cannot determine if the data are redundant. Specifically, when a customer wants to add a row of data, the server cannot make a judgment as to whether that row of data already exists in the server. Therefore, for a certain type of data, when the business requirement is that its instances are not allowed to be duplicated, it should not be added to the server alone, but should be added to the server together with its attribute values. At that point, the server can determine whether it already exists in the server based on its attribute values.

To improve the efficiency of data processing, many servers place restrictions on data types. For example, only one data type, string, is used. This has the advantage of avoiding differences in the expression of types such as integers and real numbers across computer models and operating systems, eliminating the need for translation when exchanging data between heterogeneous computers. For text data, as long as the same standard is used for character encoding, all computer models and operating systems will express it in the same way. UTF-8 is a widely used international standard for character encoding. Therefore, many servers use the UTF-8 encoding standard and provide only one data type, string, so as to eliminate data conversion, improve data processing performance, and increase the throughput of the server.

In short, the storage organization of data must be comprehensively considered based on application characteristics, especially user access characteristics. In the data storage organization, the access types should be sorted according to their operation frequency, and then the access types with high frequency should be given priority. For the access types with high frequency, the data should be aggregated and stored together as much as possible, so as to avoid the situation of extensive search in the whole system. For example, an e-commerce server has buyers as its largest customer group, followed by sellers. One of the most frequent operations of buyers and sellers is to query their transaction records. Therefore, the transaction records should be stored in separate tables according to customers, and then clustered with the customer registration data. For the product table, the access characteristics are: customers check the basic information first. Only when they are interested in a product, will they click on its details. It can be seen that, in terms of access frequency, the basic information is very different from and detailed information in the product data, and it should be stored in a separate table. Let the basic information table play the role of index table.

6.1.4 Thread Pool and Connection Pool

For each client request, the server usually creates a thread to process it, thus enabling concurrent or parallel processing. Once the request is processed, the thread's life cycle ends. The time it takes to process a request is usually very short, so the life cycle of a thread is also very short. So, in a server, threads are constantly being created and then quickly destroyed. Threads are managed by the operating system, and creating a thread, or destroying a thread, consumes some resources. If threads are created and destroyed very frequently, it will impact system performance. The solution is to use thread pooling technology [19]. In other words, some threads are created in advance to act as worker threads and placed in the thread pool. These threads are in an idle waiting state. When a request is received from a client, the server takes an idle thread from the thread pool to process it. After processing, the thread does not terminate, but returns to the idle waiting state. This avoids the overhead of creating and destroying threads, which improves system performance.

With thread pooling technology, it is natural for the server's scheduling thread to manage the worker threads. The scheduling thread and any worker thread work together via messages. When a client request is accepted, the scheduling thread takes a thread from the pool of idle threads to handle it. Specifically, a new task message is sent to the selected thread. The idle threads are all in a state of waiting for a message. When a message comes in, it ends the wait state and processes the incoming message. The new task message naturally comes with information about the task to be performed. Thus, the thread comes and executes the assigned task. When the thread has finished processing the assigned task, it sends a completion message to the scheduling thread to notify it that the task has been processed. When the scheduling thread receives this message, it adds the message sender thread to the free thread pool.

In addition, servers may have close relationships with each other and interact very frequently. For example, an organization's WEB server interacts frequently with its database server, always accessing the database server when processing client requests. When the WEB server wants to access the database server, it must first establish a network connection with the database server and then send business requests to it. Establishing a network connection is like making a phone call to someone in daily life. The process is to dial first, connect and then wait for the other party to pick up. After the other party answers, the caller reports own name. After verified by the other party, both parties get down to business topic. After the discussion is over, hang up.

The process of communication is like having a messenger run from the client's end to the server's end with a letter and handing it to the server. After the server has processed the letter and written a reply, it runs back to the client end with the reply and gives it to the client. Such a process is called a round trip. In terms of time composition, it consists of two parts: road time and server processing time. Road time cannot be ignored. The round-trip transport goes through layers of check points, where data are checked and processed by each layer of the protocol stack. It takes three round trips to establish a network connection. If the time spent negotiating business is short, the time spent establishing a network connection is a large percentage of the whole time. One way to deal with this characteristic is to not close the network connection after it is established, but to leave it open for use in processing the next client requests. This eliminates the overhead of establishing and closing a network connection again and again.

When multiple clients access a WEB server at the same time, there are multiple concurrent requests. Each request requires a network connection to the database server. This requires the creation of a connection pool, where the WEB server creates some network connections to the database server at startup and places them in the connection pool. Like the worker threads in the thread pool, all network connections are managed by the scheduling thread. When the WEB server receives a client request, it selects an idle thread from the thread pool and an idle connection from the connection pool to take care of the request. When there is no free thread, or no free network connection can be assigned, the scheduling thread will put the client request into the waiting queue until the conditions are met, and then processed.

The WEB server uses a connection pooling scheme, which eliminates network connection overhead and significantly improves processing performance. However, it also brings new security issues. When a network connection to access a database server is shared by multiple clients, the access privileges held by the person who logged in when the network connection was established are given to all clients using that network connection. This creates a security problem. The way to deal with this is to categorize the clients and then create some network connections for each category of clients. For example, for a university academic administration WEB server, its clients are categorized into student, faculty, and administrator. Assuming that when the WEB server initializes the connection pool, it creates 30 network connections for the student class, eight network connections for the faculty class, and two network connections for the administrator class. When the request comes from a student, the scheduling thread assigns only the student class network connection. When the request comes from a faculty, only the faculty class network connection is assigned.

In the case of a thread pool and a connection pool, the processing logic for the scheduling thread and the worker thread is shown in Code 6.1 and Code 6.2, respectively. When a client's request reaches the server, a message of type CLIENT_REQUEST is sent to the scheduling thread. The scheduling thread then takes a free worker thread and a free network connection from the thread pool and the connection pool respectively to process the client's request. This processing is shown in lines 4 through 7 of Code 6.1. If there is no free thread or network connection, the client's request is placed in the wait queue *waitQueue* and waited for conditions to be met before processing. This processing is shown in lines 8 through 14 of Code 6.1. Once the worker thread receives a NEW_TASK class message from the scheduling thread, it knows that a processing task has come and calls the *executeTask* function to process it. After processing, it sends a message of type TASK_COMPLETE to the scheduling thread, which is processed as shown in lines 3 through 6 of Code 6.2.

Once the scheduling thread receives a TASK_COMPLETE message from a worker thread, it knows that the worker thread has finished processing and is idle. It then goes to *waitQueue* and checks to see if there are any more client requests queued up. If there is, transfer it to the idle worker thread to process. If not, the idle worker thread and the network connection are put into the thread pool and the connection pool, respectively. This processing is shown on lines 16 through 26 in Code 6.1. Note: When scheduling a network connection, it should match the category of the client, this processing is shown in lines 5 and 17 of Code 6.1.

Code 6.1 Processing logic for the scheduling thread

```
(1)   while (TRUE) {
(2)     waitForMessage( msg );
(3)     if (msg->type == CLIENT_REQUEST) {
(4)       msg->thread = threadPool->fetchItem( );
(5)       msg->connection = connectionPool->fetchItemByType
              (msg->clientType);
(6)       if (msg->thread ! = null && msg->connection
              ! = null)
(7)         postMessage(msg->thread, NEW_TASK, msg);
(8)       else {
(9)         if (msg->thread ! = null)
```

```
(10)              threadPool->addItem(msg->thread);
(11)           if (msg->connection ! = null)
(12)              connectionPool->addItem(msg->connection);
(13)           waitQueue->addItem(msg);
(14)         }
(15)       }
(16)       else if (msg->type == TASK_COMPLETE) {
(17)         Request *request = waitQueue->fetchItemByType
                 (msg->clientType);
(18)         if (request ! = null) {
(19)            request->thread = msg->thread;
(20)            request->connection = msg->connection.
(21)            postMessage(request->thread, NEW_TASK,
                   request );
(22)         }
(23)         else {
(24)            threadPool->addItem (msg->thread);
(25)            connectionPool->addItem ( msg->connection );
(26)         }
(27)       }
(28)    }
```

Code 6.2 Processing logic for a work thread
```
(1)    while (TRUE) {
(2)       WaitForMessage( msg );
(3)       if (msg->Type = NEW_TASK) {
(4)          executeTask(msg);
(5)          postMessage(dispatcherThread, TASK_
                COMPLETE, msg);
(6)       }
(7)    }
```

6.1.5 Batch Processing

Another effective way to achieve efficient processing is batch processing. Here is an example. In version 4 of the HTML protocol, when a browser sends a request for a web page to a WEB server, the WEB server first responds to the client with an HTML document. In the HTML document, there are usually references to many other files, such as image files, CSS files, and so on. The browser in the process of parsing the HTML document, each encounters a reference; it will again send a request to the WEB server to obtain the referenced file. Thus, the browser has to interact with the WEB server many times to display a complete web page. This processing is inefficient. In version 5 of the HTML protocol, batch processing is used: the WEB server transmits the HTML document and referenced files to the browser all at once. The browser then only has to request it once to get all the files it needs. The performance improvement brought by this batch processing is very significant, up to tens or even hundreds of times.

Application development should make full use of batch processing to improve system performance. For example, in the university academic management, a teacher has to input the grades for students. In the grade entry interface, the teacher can enter grades for all students at once, and then click the Save button. In terms of the SQL language used to access the database, a single SQL update statement can only modify the grade of one student. Assuming that there are n students, then it is necessary to interact with the database server n times. This processing is inefficient. In fact, these n updates are independent of each other and can be packaged into a batch and sent to the database server for execution. In this way, n round of interactions become one round interaction, thus the efficiency will naturally be greatly improved. Programming interfaces for applications to access the database server, such as java database connectivity (JDBC) and open database connectivity (ODBC), as well as activex data objects (ADO), all support batch processing. Therefore, programmers need to explore the batch processing characteristics of business operations and make good use of them.

Batch processing is often used in people's daily lives. For example, a trip to the bank usually takes a lot of time. Therefore, instead of making a trip to the bank to deposit a small amount of income, people keep it in their wallets. When they have accumulated to a certain amount, they go to the bank and deposit it again. This greatly reduces the number of trips to the bank. Going to the bank once a month will not have a significant impact on oneself. If you go to the bank every day, you will feel that you cannot do much in a day and your efficiency is low. The same applies to computer processing.

6.2 Security Technology

Clients using front-end tools to access servers over the public Internet face security threats. The reason is that the data that a client interacts with a server must be transmitted through the public Internet. Hackers can intercept or peek at the interactive data between the client and the server on the public Internet, and then fake the client to cheat the server, or fake the server to cheat the client. Hackers can also exploit vulnerabilities or defects in the system to carry out attacks through abnormal operations, illegally stealing information for profit, or disrupting the normal work of the system. Therefore, security is a very prominent issue [20] that needs to be given

6.2 Security Technology

high priority. When developing server programs, in addition to realizing business functions, it is also necessary to apply security techniques to make the server safe and reliable.

Security threats come from four sources, as shown in Fig. 6.2. The first type of security threat comes from vulnerabilities in application programs. Hackers can take advantage of the vulnerabilities of a program to distort its normal semantics and make it deviate from the preset logic by entering special characters when accessing the server, so as to achieve the purpose of the attack. Typical examples of this type of attack are SQL injection attacks and HTML injection attacks [21]. The second type of security threats is rooted in the Internet. The data of client-server interactions are transmitted over the public Internet. Thus, hackers can peek, tamper, and replay the interaction data between clients and servers on the public Internet. Clients can also deny the transaction operations they have performed. The third type of security threat comes from impersonation. On the client party, there is doubt about the response data coming from the server: is it coming from the server, or a hacker? On the server party, there is also doubt about the request data from clients: from a client, or from a hacker? The last type of threat arises when a client misbehaves and performs an illegal operation.

6.2.1 Defense Against Injection Attacks

Common attacks that utilize system vulnerabilities to perform attacks are SQL injection attacks and HTML injection attacks. Specific examples of such attacks are explained in Sect. 1.11 of Chap. 1. In order to have a more in-depth understanding

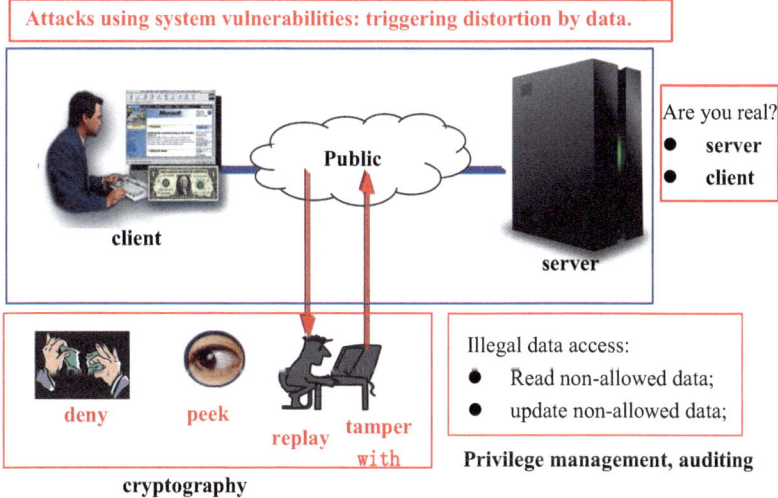

Fig. 6.2 Four categories of security threats

of the harm caused by such attacks, the following is another example of a SQL injection attack. Suppose a hacker successfully logs in to a server and opens the interface to modify the client's mailbox. The interface is shown in Fig. 6.3. The content entered by the hacker in this interface is also shown in the figure. Assume that the application handles this interface as well by concatenating a SQL statement first:

```
string sqlState = "UPDATE user SET mail='"+ mailbox + "' WHERE user_id ='" + user_account + "';"
```

where "mailbox" and "user account" are the email and client id entered by the client in the interface for modifying the client's email, respectively. Then, the SQL request is sent to the database to complete the modification of the client's mailbox.

When the hacker enters the user account as 'OR '1' = '1, shown in Fig. 6.3, the concatenated SQL statement will be "UPDATE user SET mail=' HYPERLINK "mailto:909485030@qq.com"909485030@qq.com' WHERE user_id ='' OR '1' ='1';". This SQL statement also breaks through the designer's preconceived logic. Its selection condition is TRUE for every row of data in the user table, so e-mail addresses of all clients in the database are changed to "909485030@qq.com", which is the hacker's mailbox. Subsequently, when a client changes his/her password, the system informs the client of the change by email. As a result, the email is sent to the hacker. Thus, the hacker obtains the client's account information in the database, which is a very serious consequence.

From the above example, we can understand the meaning of SQL injection attack. Hackers first guess the processing logic of an application, and then take advantage of the concatenation of a SQL statement in the program to make it deviate from the original intention by inputting SQL reserved words, achieving the purpose of the attack. In order to defend against SQL injection attacks, it is necessary to make sure that the content entered by clients in the operation interface does not contain SQL reserved words, such as single quotes, semicolons, commas, comment characters, and logic operators OR and AND, etc. If the content entered by a client in the operation interface contains SQL reserved words, they need to be escaped in the concatenation of a SQL statement to make them regular words. Therefore, it should be prohibited to concatenate a SQL statement when programming applications. The correct programming approach is to call the *prepareStatement* function in the access interface to parameterize the client input, as shown in Code 6.3. This

Fig. 6.3 Example of SQL injection attack

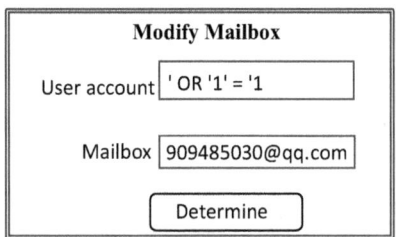

function checks the parameters and escapes the SQL reserved words contained in them to ensure that the SQL statement is not misshapen or malformed.

HTML injection attacks are similar to SQL injection attacks in that they utilize reserved words in the syntax to make semantic distortions. In SQL injection attacks, hackers utilize SQL reserved words. In HTML injection attacks, hackers utilize HTML reserved words. In Sect. 1.11, an example is given of a hacker attacking a web page containing a client comment feature. Under normal circumstances, when Client A opens a comment page and posts a comment, his comment can be seen by clients who also open the page later. If client A is a hacker and enters content in the comment box that contains HTML reserved words and JavaScript attack code, then the WEB server will deviate from the designer's intended logic when it generates the web page, so that JavaScript attack code injected by the hacker will be executed in the browser of the subsequent clients. Attacks can be stealing data on the clients' computers, or installing a virus or Trojan horse on the clients' computers.

Code 6.3 Examples defending against SQL injection attacks
```
(1)   String sqlState="UPDATE user SET mail=? WHERE user_
      id =?;";
(2)   PreparedStatement ps = connection.
      prepareStatement(sqlState);
(3)   ps.setString(1, mailbox);
(4)   ps.setString(2, user_account);
(5)   ps.ExecuteQuery( );
```

The defense against HTML injection attacks is to make the content entered by clients in the comment interface not contain HTML reserved words. If the content entered by a client in the operation interface contains HTML reserved words, it should be escaped and turned into ordinary words. Therefore, when programming applications, it is necessary to check and disinfect the content input by clients. Many front-end development toolkits, such as JQuery, provide disinfection function to defend against HTML injection attacks. When writing front-end code, the disinfection function should be called to purify the client input content.

6.2.2 Authentication of Client and Server to Each Other

One security threat faced by clients using front-end tools to access servers over the public Internet is impersonation. For example, when a client is about to open www.boc.com to access the transaction server, a hacker can intercept the request on the public Internet, and then impersonate www.boc.com to respond with a transaction login page to the client. The appearance of this fake web page is no different from the real one, and the client cannot perceive the authenticity from its appearance. When the client enters a username and password and presses the login button, this login information is sent to the hacker. The hacker then learns the client's account information. This is an example of impersonation. Therefore, when a client accesses a web page, it is important to have the ability to recognize authenticity and ensure that the web page that is opened is from a real server. This security requirement is known as client-to-server authentication. The opposite of this is server-to-client authentication, which ensures that the client is a legitimate one.

To solve the above authentication problem, encrypted transmission technology [22] is used. Encrypted transmission means that when a client wants to transmit data to a server through the public Internet, for security reasons, the client first encrypts the data to be transmitted with a cipher to obtain the ciphertext, and then transmits the ciphertext to the other party. The Server receives the ciphertext and then decrypts it with a cipher to get the data. These data are also known as plaintext. In turn, the server transmits data to the client with encryption. In this scenario, hackers cannot know what is being transmitted between the client and the server because they does not know the cipher.

There are two types of encryptions: symmetric encryption and asymmetric encryption. Symmetric encryption means that a server and its clients use the same cipher for encryption and decryption. The advantage of symmetric encryption is that the encryption and decryption overhead is small, while the disadvantage is that it does not have the authentication function. Asymmetric encryption means that a server and its clients do not hold the same cipher. The cipher held by one party is called the private key, while the cipher held by the other party is called the public key. The ciphertext obtained after encrypting the plaintext with the private key must be decrypted with the public key. The reverse is also true; the ciphertext obtained by encrypting the plaintext with the public key must be decrypted with the private key. The advantage of asymmetric encryption is that it provides authentication, but the disadvantage is that the computational overhead for both encryption and decryption is very large.

The private key *SK* (abbreviation for secret key) consists of a pair of integers (n,d), while the public key *PK* (abbreviation for public key) consists of another pair of integers (n,e). They pair up. The private key *SK* is kept by oneself and cannot be known to anyone. The public key *PK* can be distributed to others for asymmetric encrypted communication with it. Let client *A* use an asymmetric cryptography tool to set a private key *SK* for himself, denoted as (n,d), and then generate a public key *PK*, denoted as (n,e). Client *A* tells Server *B* about the public key *PK*. When Client *A* is going to communicate with Server *B*, it first encrypts the plaintext α with the private key *SK* to get the ciphertext β, and then sends the ciphertext β to Server *B* through the Internet. Server *B* can decrypt the ciphertext β to get the plaintext α by the public key *PK*, which means that the ciphertext β must be sent by Client *A*. This realizes the authentication of Server *B* to Client *A*. Thus, encryption with private key becomes a signature mechanism.

The security of asymmetric cryptography lies in the fact that for a large number n, even though the public key PK(n,e) is known, it is not possible to guess the private key SK(n,d) by computation. The proof of this security belongs to a mathematical problem, which has been given by mathematicians. Therefore, the authentication process is as follows: if Client A wants Server B to authenticate itself, it uses a cipher generator tool to set a private key SK for itself, and generates a public key PK for Server B. It then tells the public key PK to Server B. After Server B receives a ciphertext, if it can be decrypted into plaintext by the public key PK, the ciphertext must come from Client A.

Asymmetric encryption seems esoteric and mysterious, but it is not. The method of setting the private key SK(n,d) and the algorithm of generating the public key PK(n,e) are actually very simple, as shown in Fig. 6.4. According to this algorithm, it can be seen that (33,3) is a public key PK when the private key SK is set to (33,7). The encryption and decryption algorithm is shown in Fig. 6.5. For example, suppose the plaintext is an integer 7, then the ciphertext obtained after encryption with the private key is an integer 28, and the plaintext obtained after decrypting the ciphertext 28 with the public key is an integer 7. This encryption and decryption can be done manually in <10 s. But when n is a very large number, the computational overhead becomes very large.

To achieve certification on the public Internet, a certification center is also required. The certification center is similar to the national notary office, which is a specially established and recognized Internet certification service organization. The certification center has its own private key. Its public key is public. For companies or individuals who need others to certify themselves, they have to go to the certification center to apply for a certification. The applicant has his own private key and public key. When applying for a certificate, the applicant provides its public key and server domain name to the certification center. After verifying the uniqueness of an applicant's server domain name and public key, the certification center encrypts the public key and domain name provided by the applicant with its own private key to form an authentication certificate, which is issued to the applicant. Certificates are immutable. The reason is that certificates are ciphertext, and the encrypted key is the private key of the certification center, which no one else knows. Certificates have

---

(1) Find two prime numbers p and q. Let $n = p * q$ and then let $t = (p - 1) * (q - 1)$;
(2) Take any number e, but require that $e < t$ and that e and t are mutually prime;
(3) Then produce a number d such that $d * e \% t == 1$;

Fig. 6.4 Setting of private key SK(n,d) and generation of public key PK(n,e)

---

(1) Encryption: ciphertext = (plaintext **d) % n;
(2) Decryption: plaintext = (ciphertext **e) % n;
(3) To simplify the encryption and decryption calculations, there is the formula: $b*c \% n = (b \% n)*(c \% n) \% n$

Fig. 6.5 Asymmetric encryption and decryption algorithms

credibility. Any certificate that can be decrypted with the public key of the certification center must be issued by the certification center. The public key of the certification center is usually built into front-end tools such as browsers.

When a client accesses a server, the front-end tool completes the authentication to the server. For example, a client accesses a transaction server by entering https://www.boc.com/ in the address bar of the front-end tool. Note: Here, instead of http://www.boc.com/, the client enters https://www.boc.com/. If http://www.boc.com/ is entered, it means to access the server using normal HTTP protocol. If https://www.boc.com/ is entered, it indicates that the server is accessed using the secure HTTP protocol. When a client accesses the server using the secure HTTP protocol, the front-end tool first establishes a connection with the server before encrypted communication takes place. The connection is a two-step process that first authenticates the server and then generates a symmetric encrypted cipher that is passed confidentially to the server.

When a front-end tool accesses a server using the secure HTTP protocol, it first sends a secure connection request to the server. The server's response to the front-end tool is the server's authentication certificate. When the front-end tool receives the server's certificate, it decrypts the certificate using the public key of the certification center to obtain the plaintext of the certificate, which contains the server's public key and domain name. The front-end tool then compares the domain name it wants to access with the domain name on the certificate. If they are exactly the same, the certificate is that of the server you want to access, not that of the fake server. At this point, the front-end tool completes the authentication to the server.

This authentication process is reliable. If a client's secure connection request is intercepted by a hacker on the public Internet, then the response that the client gets will be from the hacker. The hacker's response can also only be a certificate, either the certificate of the real server or the hacker's own certificate. Since all certificates are public, the hacker can get the certificate of the real server and use it as the response. However, as the hacker does not have the private key of the certification center, so it cannot forge the certificate, or tamper with someone else's certificate. If the hacker's response is the hacker's own certificate, then the front-end tool will find that the domain name it wants to access is inconsistent with the domain name on the certificate when it performs the domain name comparison mentioned above. Thus, the front-end tool fails to authenticate to the server. Therefore, the authentication scheme based on asymmetric encryption is not only reliable but also feasible.

After the front-end tool completes the authentication to the server, the next problem to be solved is to realize the two-way security of data transmission between the client and the server. After authenticating the server, when the front-end tool sends data to the server, it can encrypt it using the public key on the server certificate, and then transmit the ciphertext to the server through the public Internet. Although a hacker can intercept the ciphertext sent by the client to the server over the public Internet, it cannot decrypt it. The reason is that the hacker does not have the server's private key. That is, the hacker cannot obtain the plaintext sent by the client to the server. Therefore, the data sent by the client to the server is secured. However, this security is unilateral. The data sent by the server to the client is not secure. The reason is that the server's public key is public. For the ciphertext sent by the server to the front-end tool, the hacker can decrypt it with the public key of the server and get the plaintext.

To realize the two-way security of data transmission between the client and the server, the strategy is to utilize the fact that the data sent by the front-end tool to the server is secure. Such a basis can enable the data sent to the client by the server to be secure. Specifically, after the front-end tool authenticates to the server, it calls the advanced encryption standard (AES) function [22] to generate a symmetric encryption cipher, and then encrypts it with the server's public key to form a ciphertext, which is sent to the server. Subsequently, when the server wants to send data to the front-end tool, it encrypts the plaintext with the symmetric encryption cipher, rather than with its private key. After obtaining the ciphertext, the server sends it to the front-end tool. The front-end tool decrypts the ciphertext using the symmetric encryption cipher to get the plaintext.

It is secure for the front-end tool to send the symmetric encryption cipher to the server. Although hackers can peek at the public Internet and intercept the ciphertext sent by the front-end tool to the server, they do not have the private key of the server and therefore cannot decrypt it to get the symmetric encryption cipher. After the server gets the symmetric encryption cipher sent by the front-end tool, when the front-end tool sends data to the server again, it no longer uses the server's public key for asymmetric encryption, but uses its own symmetric encryption cipher for encryption. As we can see, asymmetric encryption is only used for two things: the front-end tool authenticates to the server, and the front-end tool sends a symmetric encryption cipher to the server. Subsequent data transfers use symmetric encryption to achieve security. Thus, the secure HTTP protocol achieves two-way security for data transfer between the front-end tool and the server.

The authentication of the front-end tool to the server and the encrypted transmission between the front-end tool and the server described above are implemented in the secure HTTP protocol, which is transparent to clients. Specifically, the implementation is in SSL/TLS, which stands for Secure Socket Layer. TLS stands for Transportation Layer Security. Symmetric encryption uses the AES algorithm. The international standard for the secure transmission of data is X.509. This standard specifies the data structure of certificates, the process of authentication, and the interfaces for encryption and decryption.

The above symmetric encryption cipher is randomly generated by the front-end tool for confidential communication between the front-end tool and the server. The symmetric encryption cipher is encrypted by the front-end tool using the public key of the server and transmitted to the server. The server can decrypt it using the private key to get the plaintext, but hackers cannot. The reason is that hackers do not have the server's private key. Therefore, the symmetric encryption cipher will only be held by both the front-end tool and the server, and no one else can get it. Subsequently, both the front-end tool and the server use the symmetric encryption cipher to encrypt the data to be transmitted to each other. As a result, hackers cannot peek at the data transmitted over the public Internet. Symmetric encryption has the advantage of low overhead for both encryption and decryption compared to asymmetric encryption.

In addition to the client authenticating the server, the server also needs to authenticate the client. The server authenticates clients in the form of account. When a client accesses a server, the first page that opens is the login page, by which a client enters user name and password. Only after successful login can the business operation pages be opened.

Reflection 6-2: When a client wants to access a server, if he goes to the wrong door (i.e., entering the domain name wrong in a front-end tool) and mistakenly enters a hacker's site, then there is no way to talk about security. For example, someone wants to access some transaction server, but cannot remember its domain name. Thus, he goes to open a search engine. If there is a mistake in the search results, e.g., the hacker server is mistaken for the transaction server, then the prerequisite of security is no longer met, why? Because of this, when clients use a search engine, it is necessary to authenticate it to ensure that the search results are genuine, not a fake version. Assuming no authentication, try to analyze what security risks will be brought?

Reflection 6-3: After the front-end tool authenticates to the server, it calls the advanced encryption standard (AES) function to get a symmetric encryption cipher, encrypts it with the server's public key, and sends it to the server. Subsequent communications between the server and the client are encrypted and decrypted using that symmetric encryption cipher. Imagine that the symmetric encryption cipher obtained by the AES algorithm must be irregular and randomized; otherwise, the hacker will be able to guess it. So, how can we make the symmetric encryption cipher generated by the AES algorithm on every machine different, irregular, and random? Can you give a scheme?

6.2.3 Defense Against Other Internet Attacks

The fact that the authentication problem has been solved and the encrypted transmission of data has been realized does not mean that the security problem has been completely solved. For example, a client accesses a transaction server to transfer money. For each transfer operation, the client sends encrypted data to the server once. Assume that client A transfers $100 to client C. Client C can ask a hacker to intercept the encrypted packet of this transfer from the public Internet and then keep copying and sending it to the server. The server will then keep repeating the operation of transferring $100 from client A to client C, resulting in client A's money being swindled. In this operation, the hacker does not need to make any changes to the encrypted packet, but only needs to keep copying and sending it to achieve the purpose of fraud. This attack is called a replay attack.

This problem is solved by adding a CAPTCHA. Each time a client opens the transfer interface, the server generates a CAPTCHA for the client, stores it in the local queue of valid CAPTCHAs, and sends it to the client along with the transfer interface. When the client performs a transfer operation, it carries this CAPTCHA in the transfer packet it sends to the server. When the server receives a transfer

6.2 Security Technology

packet, it parses the CAPTCHA attached to the packet, and then searches the local queue of valid CAPTCHAs to see if it is valid. If it is valid, the request is recognized as legitimate, accepted, and the CAPTCHA is removed from the queue of valid CAPTCHAs. Subsequently, if the server receives the transfer packet for the second time, the CAPTCHA attached to it no longer exists in the queue of valid CAPTCHAs. Thus, the second received transfer packet will be discarded as garbage.

For critical business operations such as money transfers, there is also a problem of deniability in terms of security. For example, a client performs a transfer over the public Internet, but refuses to admit it, accusing the bank of stealing his money or of leaking his account information to someone else. At this point, the bank will also counterclaim that the client is denying. In this case, the problem of not being able to determine who is right and who is wrong arises. In order to solve this problem, the client's signature is required for the transfer operation. In other words, the client must have his own private key, encrypt the transfer operation packet with the private key, and then transmit it to the bank. The bank then takes the client's public key to decrypt it. The packet that can be decrypted with the client's public key must come from the client. Thus, the problem of deniability is solved. In order to prevent client's repudiation, the bank has to archive the ciphertext of the transfer packets sent by clients. In the event of a client denial, the archived transfer packet ciphertext is used as evidence that the client is denying the transaction.

In order to provide a client with a private key, the U-shield was created, which is manufactured by a specialized security agency and contains a private key, while the public key is distributed to banks. Because the U-shield contains the client's private key, when the bank gives the client a U-shield, it emphasizes that the client should carefully inspect it to make sure that the seal is intact and that it has not been tampered with. The client uses the U-Shield to access the banking system, and key operations such as money transfers are encrypted using the private key in the U-Shield, so the problem of repudiation is overcome. With U-Shield, in the event of a legal dispute, there will be evidence.

When using an Internet banking system, it is common to require the use of a U-shield for large transfers and a cell phone authentication code for small transfers. The authentication code is a means of verifying that the person making the transfer is actually the account holder. In addition, the banking system will notify the account holder by SMS and email whenever a transfer occurs. Therefore, even if a client account is stolen, there is no chance that the funds will be transferred and lost. From a technical point of view, the Internet banking system is reliable. However, it is still common to hear about cases of financial fraud. The reason is that the customers themselves are defrauded. Therefore, it is important for everyone to be aware of security and to be on guard against fraud and deception.

Reflection 6-4: Many servers ask for a CAPTCHA when you open the login page. By definition, the CAPTCHA should be invisible to clients, meaning that there is no need for a client to enter it again. When the client clicks on the login button, the CAPTCHA should be taken as a parameter of the login. Is not it redundant to ask a client to enter the CAPTCHA shown in the login page? Please give the reasons.

6.2.4 Management of Client Access Privileges

The server is a centralized place for business data, and all kinds of clients have to access the server to complete their business operations. For example, the university academic management server is the centralized place of academic affairs data. Students, teachers, and administrators have to access the server to complete their business operations, respectively. Administrators have to enter courses and schedule classes; students have to enroll courses and check their records; teachers have to enter student grades. For security reasons, the server should have clearly defined access privileges for clients. Once a client logs in to the server with an account, a session to the server is established. The client submits an operation request to the server through the session. When the server receives an operation request from a client, it checks whether the client has the appropriate operation privileges. If it does, it accepts the request, executes the process, and then returns the result to the client. If the client is not authorized, the server refuses to accept the client's request and returns a message of no operating privilege to the client.

The concepts and rules of privileges management need to be clear and concise in order to be effective. There are only five concepts in privilege management: Authorizer, Object, Privilege, Authorized person, and Authorization Flag. The privilege of a client is granted by another client. Taking the university academic management server as an example, Client A grants Client B the privilege to perform adding and updating data on the course table, which is one case of privilege management. If the authorization flag is RELAY, it indicates that Client A allows Client B to grant this privilege to other clients.

Privilege management includes three components: (1) supporting clients to grant privileges; (2) supporting clients to revoke privileges; (3) determining whether a client has a certain privilege. Granting privileges includes creating a client and then authorizing privileges to the client, while revoking privileges means revoking the originally granted privileges from a client, even deleting the client. There are only three criteria for privilege management: (1) the creator of an object owns all privileges to access it; (2) a client can grant the privileges it owns to other clients; and (3) an authorizer can revoke the privileges it has granted, and the revoking of privileges is cascading. For the meaning of cascading revocation, an example is given. For a privilege, client A grants it to client B, and client B grants it to client C. When client A revokes the privilege from client B, the privilege owned by client C can also be revoked. As you can see, privilege management is simple and can effectively ensure the security of data access in the server.

In order to make privilege management simple and clear, in addition to the concept of clients, there is the concept of roles. Role is a general term for a category of clients. For example, in the university academic management server, its clients can be divided into three categories: student, teacher, and administrator. Therefore, there should be student role, teacher role, and administrator role in the university academic management Server. With the concept of roles, privilege management changes from directly granting privileges to clients to granting privileges to roles and then assigning roles to clients. This change brings simplicity to privilege management.

Only two data tables are required to support privilege management in the server. These two tables are the *user* table and the *privilege* table, as shown in Table 6.1 and Table 6.2, respectively. The *user* table records client account information and role information, whose fields include *userTtype*, *userId*, *password*, and *creatorId*. Each client or role has a row in the *user* table. When the *userType* field of a row takes the value 'USER', it identifies the row as a client. When the value is 'ROLE', it identifies the row as a role. Privilege table records the privilege grant information, whose fields include *granterId*, o*bjectId*, *privilegeType*, *granteeId*, and *grantTag*. The meaning of the first row of data in Table 6.2 is that the root user grants to the role *administrator* the privilege to add rows to the *course* table, and the role *administrator* can continue to grant this privilege to others.

A row is added to the *user* table for each successfully created client or role. A row is added to the *privilege* table for each successful privilege grant performed. From the data in the *user* table shown in Table 6.1, you can see that there are three roles and three clients in the server. From the data in the *privilege* table shown in Table 6.2, four privilege grants are recorded.

When the server is installed, it prompts for the creation of a root user and asks the installer to enter the account name and password for that user. This root user has all privileges and is the root of the privilege management hierarchy tree. Thus, after the system is installed, there is a row for this user in the User table, as shown in the first row in Table 6.1. After the server is initially up and running, you log on to the server with the root account, then you create the business data tables, roles and users, and then grant the roles privileges to access the business data tables. Each user created is a login account that can be used to log on to the server.

Table 6.1 User table

userType	userId	password	creatorId
USER	root	123,456	SYSTEM
ROLE	administrator		root
ROLE	teacher		root
ROLE	student		root
USER	A	1	root
USER	B	2	A
USER	C	333	B

Table 6.2 Privilege table

granterId	ObjectId	privilegeType	granteeId	grantTag
root	course	INSERT	administrator	RELAY
root	enroll	SELECT	student	RELAY
root	administrator	ROLE	A	
A	student	ROLE	B	

When a client logs on to the server, the account is given, i.e., username and password. The server looks up the account information in the *user* table based on the username submitted by the client. If there is a row of data where the value of the u*serId* field is equal to the login username and the value of the *userType* field is "USER" and the value of the password field is equal to the login password, then the login user is recognized as legitimate and the login is successful. When the client sends a request for a business operation to the server, the server first performs a privilege check. Only after the permission check is passed will the request be executed by the server.

If a request sent by a client is to grant privilege, the server first checks whether the client has the privilege on the privilege grant. For simplicity, it is assumed that the client's privileges are derived from the roles it plays. For example, in a university academic management server, client A submits a request to grant the privilege of querying the *enroll* table to the *student* role. The server first checks whether the roles of client A have the privilege to perform queries on the *enroll* table. If it does, it further checks whether it has the privilege to grant it. Only when both conditions are met will the server accept the client's privilege grant request and perform it.

For a privilege revocation operation, a client can only revoke the privileges he/she has previously granted. Therefore, when a client submits a privilege revocation request, the server has to check in *privilege* table to see whether there is a corresponding grant record for the roles played by the client. Only granted privileges can be revoked, otherwise the revocation operation becomes meaningless. When a revocation operation is performed, cascading revocations are also performed.

Reflection 6-5: Can you write a detail processing flowchart for a privilege revocation operation based on the data in the *user* and *privilege* tables?

6.2.5 Audit on Client Access Operations

In server security, there are four layers of defense: (1) mutual authentication of clients and server to each other; (2) encrypted transmission of data; (3) privilege management within the server; and (4) audit within the server. Audit is a technical means and tool used to detect data security problems and find out the truth. Audit is like installing a camera in a public place to record every operation of clients who log in the server. Once a security problem occurs, the audit records can be accessed to find out the truth and provide clues and evidence for case investigation.

Auditing is the process of recording what clients have done in the server so that they can be tracked later. The audit log includes login information and operation information. Login information includes login accounts, IP addresses of clients' computers, and login time. Operation information includes the operation command and operation time. If an operation is of update or deletion, the data value before the change is further recorded. If an operation is of addition or update, the data value after the change is also recorded.

Auditing is configurable. Auditing can be performed only on selected tables, selected clients, and selected types of operations. For example, in a university academic management server, only the course grade field in the *enroll* table can be audited, specifically for update operations. Because grades are critical data, their security is important. After a teacher enters a grade, no modification is allowed. Therefore, auditing the modification of grades can be used to find out where the security problem lies.

Auditing is a feature provided by the server and only needs to be configured and turned on. The server also provides an audit trail tool, which makes it easy to access the audit history and query/count the audit records from various perspectives. The applications of auditing include: (1) discovering account leaks, illegal operations, management loopholes and other security problems; (2) finding out the truth of cases and providing evidence for the investigation of cases; (3) correcting illegal operations. For example, if a student's grade is found to be problematic, the audit history can be accessed to locate who, when, and from where the modification operation of the student's grade was performed. The trace is then extended to check what other illegal operations were performed by that client and then to correct the illegal operations.

When a user discovers that a data operation is not performed by himself, it means that his account has been compromised by an intruder. At this point, the anomaly is reported to the system administrator. The system administrator can then access the audit logs to find out when and where the fake user logged in the system and what illegal operations were performed. That is, audit logs can provide evidence and clues for the detection of cases, and provide support for the elimination of hidden problems as soon as possible.

Auditing can bring many benefits, but it also comes at a cost. Auditing takes up system resources, including CPU resources and storage resources, and therefore has an impact on system performance. Server administrators should be careful about the configuration of auditing, and plan carefully so that it is not abused arbitrarily. Usually, only key data and key operations are audited. Auditing should not be placed on less important data and operations.

Reflection 6-6: Should an audit be performed on privilege grant and revocation operations? Please provide a justification.

Reflection 6-7: The transaction server is very important, and clients' money and transactions are recorded on the server. How can a security defense be constructed against the illegal operations from administrators of the transaction server? How can they be deterred from performing illegal operations?

6.3 Server Scalability

When a server has the amount of data reach its capacity limit, it is split into two servers. For example, an e-commerce server, as its data volume increases, is split into two servers when its upper limit is reached. When splitting, half of the clients' data are migrated to the added server. To make this split transparent to clients, turn a single server into a distributed server. A distributed server consists of a management server and multiple member servers. The management server, also called the service broker, is the client-facing service window. After receiving a request from a client, the management server breaks it down into multiple subrequests and then submits them to the corresponding member servers for processing. The management server is also responsible for summarizing the returned results from the member servers and then submitting it to the client. Thus, the distributed nature of the server is transparent to clients. In the view of clients, there is only one server.

In the case of an e-commerce server, for example, the data that grows rapidly is mainly transaction data and client data. For every item purchased by a client, a new transaction record is added. For every new client, a new account record is added. When the amount of data in a server reaches the upper limit, one way to deal with it is: add a new server to store the data added newly. After a new server is added to the system, the management server forwards client requests for adding new data to the new server. For a data query request or a data modification request from a client, the management server tells every member server to process it and then summarizes their return results to get the return value for the client. This method is characterized by poor scalability. The reason is that every query from a client calls all member servers to participate. The response time is limited by the slowest member server.

The second way to handle this is to split the clients into two parts account in half in a member server, and then migrate the data of half of the clients to the added server. Thus, after the split, the management server only needs to hand over requests from each client to one member server for processing. The reason is that all the data of a client is in one member server. The scalability of the system is significantly improved compared to the previous solution. However, the drawback of this solution is that during the data migration process, which involves splitting one server into two, the service is not available to clients. The reason is that client data are stored in multiple tables. For example, client account data are in the *account* table and transaction data are in the *transaction* table. Only after both account data and transaction data have been migrated, the service becomes available to clients.

The third processing scheme is to cluster the account data and transaction data for storage based on the key–value pair data model. In this scheme, the transaction record becomes a part of the account table and its data type is table. That is, the account data and transaction data are stored in one table. Specifically, each row of data in the account table has another transaction table embedded in it. The advantage of this kind of data storage organization is that when a server is split into two, a half of clients is migrated in the form of one by one. When a row of client account data is migrated, its transaction data are also migrated in the meantime. Therefore, after a row of data in the account table id migrated, it becomes available on the added server immediately. This scenario provides a significant improvement in service availability compared to the second scenario. The essence of this enhancement is to change the migration granularity from the entire database to one client at a time.

6.4 Service Cluster

As the amount of data in a single server increases, the server needs to be split into two. At this point, the single server evolves into a distributed server. A distributed server consists of a management server and multiple member servers. Each member server is responsible for storing and managing only a portion of the whole data. This is a kind of form of distributed servers. For a server, in the case of a large number of concurrent client requests, its load is so heavy that it is too busy to provide a timely response. When the response time cannot meet the requirements, it is necessary to add a new server replica to increase the system throughput and shorten the response time. Adding a new server copy is called replication. Replication not only improves system throughput, but also improves system availability. When a server consists of multiple replicas, even if one replica is unavailable due to a failure, other replicas can provide service, so there is no interruption in service.

The management server in a distributed server manages not only the member servers but also the replicas. The management server holds information about all its members and all its replicas. This information is called Metadata. In the case of multiple member servers, the management server relies on the metadata to decompose a client request into multiple subrequests, and then passes them to the corresponding members for processing, which is also called MAP. The management server is also responsible for summarizing the response results from the member servers, and then returns the summarized result to the client as the response result, which is also called REDUCE. In the case of a replica, if a client's request is for query data, the management server simply submits it to one of the replicas for processing. This process is sometimes called load balancing [23].

A distributed server is sometimes called a service cluster. Many enterprises have a very large amount of business data, up to the P-level, often called Big Data [24]. Big data are scattered across the member servers in the cluster and is managed by a distributed file server or a distributed database server. These data support not only the daily business operation of the enterprise, but also data analyses and mining such as drawing customer profiles, discovering abnormal customer behaviors, and AI model training. Data analysis and mining can support enterprises to better conduct business and expand business.

Big data contains both a large amount of useful data and a huge amount of useless data, even junk data. It is characterized by a large total amount of value but a low density of value. This characteristic means that in data analyses, the ratio of the amount of output data to the amount of input data is small. Data analysis software is like a factory. In the case of a factory, there is an issue of siting. Does the company build the factory close to the source of raw materials or close to the company's location? The traditional approach is to build the factory near the company's location. This is a good solution when the production scale is small, because it can bring convenience to the production without any bottleneck problems. However, when large-scale and efficient production is desired, the transportation of raw materials is a constraint even a bottleneck. Thus, it is difficult to achieve the goal. The reason is that the throughput of the transportation network is much less than the throughput of the factory to raw materials.

Therefore, the smart approach is to change the strategy and build the factory near the origin of raw materials. This allows for a large-scale supply of raw materials and efficient production. After raw materials are processed into products, their transportation will not be constrained by the transportation network because the ratio of the volume of products to the volume of raw materials is very small. The same is true for data analyses. Traditionally, data analysis software is deployed separately on dedicated computers, and data are fetched from storage over the network and analyzed. In the case of a large amount of data, this traditional approach is no longer feasible and cannot meet the needs of big data processing. The reason is: it is difficult to achieve high traffic transportation of data over long distances. The solution to the problem is to deploy the data analysis software on or near the computer where the data are stored, and process it nearby. Thus, data analysis changes from a centralized model to a distributed model. The problem faced by clusters in this scenario is no longer about splitting and replication, but about adaptation. The focus of attention is that on which computer an application should be scheduled to run.

A cluster means a distributed system. One form of clustering is the use of cluster management software to organize multiple computers networked together into a single computer. This type of cluster consists of three applications: the cluster manager, the executor, and the metadata server. The cluster manager is the service window. Clients use the cluster through the cluster manager, including installing applications, launching applications, and so on. The cluster manager is also responsible for managing the computers in the cluster and scheduling applications to run on them. Executors run on each computer in the cluster and receive commands from the cluster manager to perform actions such as starting and stopping applications. The metadata server is responsible for storing and managing installed applications, as well as information about their operation. After a server is started up, its runtime service information should be registered in the metadata server. To access a service, you go to the metadata server to get the service information.

Another form of clustering is a distributed server. This type of cluster consists of two applications: (1) a management server and (2) one or more member servers. The cluster manager is responsible for starting the management server. The management server is the service window and is responsible for receiving requests from clients. The management server is also responsible for managing members and replicas. When a member server needs to be started, the management server sends a request to the cluster manager, which arranges and specifies a computer to run the member server. The same is true when a new replica needs to be added. The management server is also responsible for decomposing a client request and then dispatching subtasks to the corresponding member servers, as well as summarizing their response results.

YARN [25] is a well-known cluster management software product. YARN stands for Yet Another Resource Negotiator. The cluster manager is named ResourceManager and the executor is named NodeManager. YARN provides support for distributed servers running on a cluster. Each computer in the cluster runs the NodeManager software, which is responsible for managing processes on the local computer, including creating processes to run applications, allocating resources to processes, and so on. When a customer wants to start a distributed server on a cluster, he/she submits the request to ResourceManager. In YARN, the management server of a distributed server is called Application Master, and the member servers are called Application Workers. The ResourceManager first arranges for a NodeManager to run the Application Master, and after the Application Master starts, it sends a request to the ResourceManager to run the Application Workers.

Despite the evolution of computing, how applications are programmatically implemented remains the same. Computing has gone through two evolutions: from monolithic computing to cluster computing and then from cluster computing to cloud computing. Servers have also evolved from monolithic servers to distributed servers. In terms of programming to implement an application, the application is still composed of two parts: the application itself and the runtime environment. To access the resources and services in the runtime environment, the application still obtains the resource and service information from the configuration file. Accessing resources and services is still done by calling API functions. Parallel processing is still realized by creating child processes. What has changed is the implementation of API functions in the support libraries. The meaning of configuration file is no longer limited to local file, but also remote file and configuration server. The meaning of child process is no longer limited to the local computer, but can also be a process on a remote computer. In other words, both configuration file and child process have become abstract concepts, with a virtual-real mapping in implementation. Abstraction enables applications to be adaptive.

6.5 Abstraction and Dynamic Adaptation

Abstraction is a strategy and method, while dynamic adaptation is a system characteristic resulting from abstraction. Apache Spark (SPARK) [25] is a well-known distributed big data processing platform that abstracts data into a data type called RDD, which stands for Resilient Distributed Datasets. SPARK also defines attributes for RDDs, and a rich set of data processing functions for clients to invoke, thus making a wide variety of data processing simple and easy for clients. The internal implementation of distributed processing is completely transparent to clients. The following is an example to demonstrate this feature. Given an English text document with the file name HDFS:/data/document.txt. The data processing task is to determine which English words appear in this document and the number of times each word appears in the document.

On the SPARK platform, the processing code to be written by a client to accomplish this data processing task is:

```
sc.textFile("hdfs:/data/document.txt").flatMap(_.split(" ")).
map((_,1)).reduceByKey(_+_).collect()
```

This code expresses the five-step operations to reach the goal. The first operation is *sc.textFile*("hdfs:/data/document.txt"), where *sc* is a Spark Context object that can be directly used by clients, whose interface function *textFile* is called with the file "hdfs:/data/document.txt" as the input parameter. This function returns an object of type RDD. For the convenience of expression, here we name the returned RDD object *paragraphs*, which is a list of objects. Each paragraph of data in the file that ends with a CRLF becomes an element in the list.

The second operation is *paragraphs.flatMap(_.split(" "))*, where '_' is a special character that represents any element in the *paragraphs* object. The meaning of _.split(" ") is: given an element in *paragraphs*, i.e., a paragraph of text data, it is scanned from beginning to end, and every time a space is encountered, it is cut. Thus, the sequence of English words in that paragraph is obtained. The sequence of words is then constructed into a list, whose elements are English words. Thus, each element in *paragraphs* becomes a list of words. That is, one-level list *paragraphs* is turned into a two-level nested list. *flatMap* means that the two-level nested lists is flattened into a one-level list, whose elements are words. In summary, the second operation returns an object of type RDD, named *words*, which is a list of objects that contain all the words that appear sequentially in the document.

The third operation is *words.map((_ ,1))*, whose functionality is to transform each element in *words* from one item to two items, i.e., it adds an item for every element. Here, the added item is an integer with the value 1. This operation also returns an object of type RDD, which is given the name *words_2* here. The fourth operation is *words_2. reduceByKey (_ + _)*. Here, each element of *words_2* has two items, the first item is called KEY, and the second term is called VALUE. *reduceByKey(_ + _)* means: any two elements in *words_2*, as long as their KEYs are the same, merge them into one element, with the KEY remaining unchanged and the VALUE becoming the sum of the two. This process continues recursively until there are no more elements in the list with the same KEY value. This operation also returns an object of type RDD, named *result_words*.

result_words is also a list of objects that contains all the words that appear in the document and counts the number of times each word appears in the document. This is the desired result. The fifth operation is *result_words.collect()*, which returns the contents of *result_words* to the client as the response result.

The concept of distributed processing does not appear at all in the above code, so it is said that distributed data processing is completely transparent to clients. Inside SPARK, when receiving the above processing code submitted by a client, first go to the HDFS file server to query the file hdfs:/data/document.txt to understand how many parts it is composed of in terms of storage, and on which member node each part is stored. Then, based on the available resources in the system as well as the storage distribution of the file, a parallel processing scheme is developed. The scheme consists of four operations: (1) allocating a machine for the Application Master, (2) deciding how many Application Workers to be created, (3) allocating machines for each Worker, and (4) assigning processing task to each Worker.

The principle of assigning machines to Workers is to process data nearby. Suppose the *document.txt* file is inside the HDFS server and consists of three parts:

H1://d1.txt, *H2://d2.txt*, and *H3://d3.txt*, which are stored on the member nodes *H1*, *H2*, and *H3* in the cluster, respectively. Then, it is best to create three Workers for this processing task and let them run on the three-member machines H1, H2, H3, respectively, processing d1.txt, d2.txt, d3.txt, respectively.

As far as the above processing task is concerned, for the first three operations, all Workers do parallel processing, each processing its own data, and there is no interaction and collaboration among Workers. The fourth step is different and requires all Workers to collaborate. The reason is that a word may appear in all three files: d1.txt, d2.txt, and d3.txt. One way is to have all Workers send the results of the third step to the Master, who summarizes them and performs the fourth step. The fifth step is also performed by the Master. This solution is simple and straightforward, but there is a problem that all three Workers send their data to the Master, resulting in a huge amount of data for the Master to receive. The Master may not be able to accommodate those data.

The second option is to have the three Workers process the words with initial character ranging from a to h, j to r, and s to z, respectively. That is, each Worker sends the elements with initial character ranging from a to h to Worker1 for processing, the elements from j to r to Worker2 for processing, and the elements from s to z to Worker3 for processing. The process of exchanging data among the Workers is called the process of data shuffle. After shuffling, each Worker performs the fourth step. In the fifth step, all Workers send the results of the fourth step to the Master, which summarizes the results and then returns the final result to the client as a response.

In order to reduce the amount of data to be transferred during data shuffling, each Worker can also perform the fourth step operation on the output of its own third step operation before performing data shuffling. After shuffling, each Worker performs the fourth step once more. The fourth step is a global operation, but with local compatibility. That is, each Worker performs it once for the portion of data for which it is responsible, without affecting the correctness of the global result. This global operation, which is performed locally first, is called data merging. The merge operation helps to reduce the amount of data transfer during data shuffling.

From the above case, it is clear that a client writes data processing code that expresses the logical process of data processing based on abstract concepts. The places where a client has to be concerned is the data structure and its transformations. In the above example, the client has to know that the *sc.textFile* function turns a file into a list of objects, and the paragraphs in the file into the elements of the list. When performing the second operation, it is clear to the client that the words in a paragraph are separated by spaces, that the split operation is slicing an element into a list of objects, and that the *flatMap* operation flattens a two-level nested list into a one-level list. In the execution of the third operation, it is clear to the client that the elements in the input object are words, each element contains only one item, and each element is changed from one item to two items by the *map* function. In the fourth operation, the client knows that the elements in the input object are a key–value pair, and the *reduceByKey* function can merge the elements with the same key, and in the merge the values of the elements are summed.

It is the responsibility of the platform to translate abstract concepts and logical solutions into implementation solutions, i.e., physical solutions. The platform must first understand the size of the input data and its storage distribution, and then develop an implementation scheme in real time based on the available resources in the system. The implementation scheme includes: (1) assigning machines to Application Master; (2) deciding how many Application Workers to be created; (3) assigning machines to each Worker; (4) assigning input data and processing task to each Worker; and (5) establishing protocols for collaboration between Master and Workers, as well as for collaboration among Workers.

Clients express abstract concepts and logical solutions in a scripting language, enabling SPARK to analyze tasks and implement comprehensive optimization, as well as real-time optimization. SPARK has universal data processing capabilities, rooted in the introduction of abstract concepts. The traditional approach is to compile the client's code into a binary executable file using development tools beforehand, and then install it on the target machine to run. As a result, runtime optimization cannot be implemented. The SPARK approach is equivalent to moving the compiler to the target machine where the program is to run, and then executing the client's code in an interpreted manner. Therefore, the platform can formulate implementation schemes in real time based on the size of the data to be processed, its storage distribution characteristics, as well as the available resources in the system, to achieve the overall optimization, as well as real-time optimization.

As can be seen from the above example, the client's scripting code is very short, despite the huge amount of data processing work. Therefore, the time spent on executing the script can be considered to be negligible compared to the time spent on executing the system functions. This example also further explains why scripting languages have become popular. The interpreted execution strategy of scripting languages has been analyzed in Chap. 5.

6.6 Serverless

Serverless is a hot technology in cloud development [26]. The motivation is to program based solely on logical servers without considering physical servers in server-related application development. Since virtualization is the most core concept in cloud computing, logical servers are also called virtual servers. The programs related to servers include client programs and server programs. The ideal way to implement a client program is to let the server transparent to developers. Specifically, Accesses to the server are done through function calls. This goal is easy to achieve. The remote procedure call implementation described in Sect. 3.1 achieves transparency to developers of client programs. When calling a function, clients do not need to consider whether it is a local call or a remote call.

The ideal way to implement a server program is to let developers only consider the implementation of service functions, without worrying about matters related to physical servers. In traditional server programming, developers need to consider

6.6 Serverless

physical servers. For example, physical servers have limited storage capacity and computing power, so developers need to consider server's throughput and response latency. Physical servers may experience failures, so developers need to consider fault recovery. Virtual servers are completely different from physical servers, with infinite storage capacity and computing power, as well as being fault-free. For large servers, a significant proportion of the development workload is related to physical servers. Manual development usually lacks comprehensive consideration. That is why the serverless programming pattern was proposed. Its goal is to use automation technology to accomplish tasks related to physical servers.

The benefits of the Serverless programming pattern are that it not only simplifies the development of server programs, but also makes servers robust, secure, dependable, and resilient. For a virtual server, its runtime physical server may be a stand-alone server or a distributed server. Its form changes in real-time due to data volume and load. When the amount of data managed by the server increases, it will transform from a stand-alone server to a distributed server. When the load on a server increases or its availability needs to be improved, it is necessary to add replicas to it. In this case, the stand-alone server will also become a distributed server.

A server has two aspects: class and instance object. The Spark example mentioned in the previous section is a good case. This server has three levels. The top-level server is the SPARK server, responsible for interacting with clients. The second and third level servers are respectively Master and Worker. When the SPARK server receives a client request, it creates a Master instance to process the client request. After the Master instance is created, it checks the amount of data in the specified data file, and then decides how many Worker instances should be created. If the amount of data is small, only one Worker instances is created. If the amount of data is large, multiple Worker instances are created for parallel processing. On which host does SPARK server schedule a Master instance or a Worker instance to run? When multiple Worker instances need to be created, how many instances should be created? The above things are all considerations in physical servers. The ideal scenario is that these things are transparent to developers. Serverless aims to achieve this goal.

In the Serverless programming pattern, the development scenario for the aforementioned server is as follows. First, there is a SPARK development platform that developers use to create server-class projects. Once a project is created, the platform will automatically generate framework code based on the SPARK architecture, which includes the definitions of the Master class and the Worker class. Then, the developer defines service functions open to clients for calling. Next, the developer completes the initialization of the server based on the SPARK framework, and then provides the implementation of service functions. Finally, the developer builds the project to generate an executable file. This is all that developers need to do. In this example, all things related to physical servers are completely transparent to developers. The executable file is submitted to SPARK operation platform to complete the deployment of the server.

Reflection 6-8: In the above server development example, in order to enable the server to run everywhere, it is better to use Java or a scripting language as the programming language. Why? The SPARK operation platform provides powerful support libraries for the development of various applications such as database applications, stream data applications, and AI applications. Developers can utilize these support libraries to simplify the implementation of server programs. What other benefits can these libraries bring besides simplifying application development?

6.7 Summary of the Chapter

Services are very important to clients. It is because of the variety of services that life has become better. The reverse is also true; clients are also very important to service providers. Clients are the cornerstone on which service providers' survival and development depend. The competitiveness of a service provider is reflected in the quality of its services. Service quality is directly perceived by clients in terms of responsiveness, security, and availability. The improvement of service quality cannot be separated from the support of technologies and tools. The strategies and methods to make servers run efficiently, safely and elastically, as well as to realize the rapid development and deployment of service programs, rapid revision and upgrade, and rapid startup are collectively known as microservice technologies.

Ways and means to achieve efficient processing of data include: (1) indexing; (2) rational organization of data storage based on access characteristics; (3) thread pool and connection pool; (4) batch processing. In terms of security, the first step is to defend against SQL injection attacks and HTML injection attacks. In addition, the secure HHTP protocol should be used to do client-to-server authentication and encryption transmission. In the client-server interaction, asymmetric encryption is only used for two things: decrypting certificates, and transmitting symmetric encryption cipher to the server. There are three layers of server-to-client authentication: (1) account number; (2) cell phone verification code; and (3) U-shield. In transaction processing, servers use the verification code to defend against replay attacks.

Servers running on a cluster or a cloud are dynamic in nature. This dynamism is manifested in three aspects. First, the computer on which a server program runs cannot be determined in advance, but in real time. The second aspect is that the number of replicas of a server is dynamically variable for the sake of service availability and throughput. When the business volume increases or availability needs to be improved, the number of replicas will have to be increased in real time. When the business volume decreases, the number of replicas should be reduced in real time to save resources. The third aspect is that when the amount of data in a server grows to the upper limit, the server is split into two. This feature requires that a server program not only runs everywhere but also starts up quickly. The availability of the service during the splitting process is related to the way the data storage is organized. Properly organizing the storage of data improves not only system performance but also service availability.

Exercises

1. Assume that data are stored on disk and the computer accesses the disk in blocks. The rows of data in the index table have been sorted by the search key. When the amount of data in the index table is also large, many disk blocks are required to accommodate it. When looking for a search key value from the index table, due to the fact that the entire index table is not fully read into memory from the disk and stored continuously, binary search may encounter the problem: which disk block is the middle data in? To address this issue, it is necessary to establish a statistical index table for the index table. In the statistical index table, a row of data records a disk block. Recorded disk block is, of course, the disk block to store the index table. The recorded content includes the disk block ID (i.e., the address of the disk block), the starting search key value, and the ending search key value. When the statistical index table still needs a lot of disk blocks to accommodate it, the statistical index table should be built further. And so on, until the amount of data in the last statistical index table does not exceed the capacity of one disk block. Is this the essential meaning of the B^+ tree?

2. Given an English document, count the words that appear in it and the number of times each word appears. To do this, set up a table called *words*, which has two columns: the word column and the number of occurrences column. Scan the English document, every time a word appears, we will look for the existence of the word in the *words* table. If not, add a row, the column value of number of occurrences is set to 1. If there is, the number of occurrences of the word to do plus 1 processing. Is it necessary to sort the *words* table based on the word column? Justify. Assuming sorting, is it necessary to create a statistical index for the *words* table? Assuming no sorting, is it necessary to create a tree index for the *words* table? Would building a hash index for the *Words* table achieve better processing efficiency? Explain the reasons.

3. The processing logic for the scheduling thread shown in Code 6.1 assumes that there are many requests from clients and the server is busy. It is characterized by the fact that there are no more free worker threads or network connections. Thus, the scheduling thread puts the client's request into the *waitQueue*. If the client waits for a long time without a response, it will time out and treat the request as unsuccessful. Therefore, is it necessary to set a length limit for *waitQueue*? Suppose the length of *waitQueue* is set to 10, i.e., only 10 client requests can be held. If the *waitQueue* is full, it will give a response of "I'm too busy to accept" to the subsequent client requests. This treatment is not reasonable, why? The correct treatment is to fetch out the earliest request from *waitQueue,* and give it a response of "I'm too busy to accept". Justify. What is the risk to the server if there is no length limit on *waitQueue*? Can the server increase its throughput by increasing the number of worker threads and network connections when it is too busy? Justify.

4. For accessing the database programming interface JDBC, review the information to understand how it supports batch processing? For a teacher entering grades for the students he teaches, write the implementation code for batch submission based on JDBC.

5. For a MySQL database server, given the *user* table shown in Table 6.1 and the *privilege* table shown in Table 6.2, assume that the four functions for creating a user, creating a role, granting privilege, and revoking privilege are implemented as stored procedures. Write the code that implements these four stored functions.
6. For a MySQL database server, assume that student grades are stored in the *enroll* table. The table has fields: *studentId*, *courseId*, and *score*, which record the student id, course id, and grade, respectively. Please create a trigger that implements the following audit function: If a client makes changes to the grades in the *enroll* table after the instructor submits the grades, an audit will be performed. The details of the audit are: the client login id, the IP address of the computer used to access the database server, the time of the operation, and the values of the *studentId*, *courseId*, and *score* fields in the row that was modified, as well as the grades after the modification. The seven items are recorded in the *scoreUpdateAudit* table.
7. Edge computing is a hot topic in the field of Internet of Things, similar to big data processing. In Internet of Things, there are three roles: data producing, data processing, and data consuming. Additionally, geographic distribution is an important factor, which is reflected in latency, bandwidth, and stability of communication between data producers and data processor, or between data processor and data consumers. When data processor is far from data producers, or data consumers, service quality such as response time is difficult to meet. The idea of edge computing is to migrate data processor closer to the data producers or consumers. Please consult the literature and think about the following question: What is the difference between edge computing and big data processing?

References

1. Gos, K., Zabierowski, W., *The Comparison of Microservice and Monolithic Architecture*. In Proc. In IEEE 16th Int. Conf. Perspective Technology Methods MEMS Design (MEMSTECH), 2020, p. 150–153.
2. Surajit, C., Gerhard, W., *Rethinking Database System Architecture: Towards a Self-Tuning RISC-Style Database System*. In Proceedings of the 26th International Conference on Very Large Data Bases (VLDB '00), 2000, p. 1–10.
3. Alshuqayran, N., Ali, N., Evans, R., *A Systematic Mapping Study in Microservice Architecture*. In Proc. of IEEE 9th Int. Conf. Service-Oriented Computing and Application, 2016, p. 44–51.
4. Jawaddi, N. A., Johari, M. H., Ismail, A., *A Review of Microservices Autoscaling with Formal Verification Perspective*. Software Practice Experience, 2022, 52(11): p. 2476–2495.
5. Zhou, H., Hoppe, D., *Containerization for High Performance Computing Systems: Survey and Prospects*. IEEE Transaction on Software Engineering, 2023, 49(4): p. 2722–2740.
6. Rajdeep, D., Reddy, R., Dharmesh, K., *Virtualization vs Containerization to Support PaaS*. In 2014 IEEE International Conference on Cloud Engineering, 2014, p. 610–614.
7. Kavis, M. J., *Architecting the Cloud: Design Decisions for Cloud Computing Service Models*. New York: Wiley, 2018.
8. *Best Practices Design Patterns: Optimizing Amazon S3 Performance: AWS Whitepaper*. 2024 [access date 7/12/2024]; Available from: https://d1.awsstatic.com/whitepapers/AmazonS3BestPractices.pdf.

9. Barlev, S., Basi, Z., Kohanim, et al, *Secure yet Usable: Protecting Servers and Linux Containers*. IBM Journal of Research Development, 2016, 60(4): p. 1–10.
10. Eric, J., Johann, S., Vikram, S., et al, *Cloud Programming Simplified: A Berkeley View on Serverless Computing*. 2019 [access date 8/12/2024]; Available from: https://www2.eecs.berkeley.edu/Pubs/TechRpts/2019/EECS-2019-3.pdf.
11. Anna, B., Brad, C., *Deployment Archetypes for Cloud Applications*. ACM Computing Surveys, 2022, 55(3):p. 1–48.
12. Verma, V., Pedrosa, L., Korupolu, M., *Large-Scale Cluster Management at Google with Borg*. In 10th European Conference on Computer Systems, 2015.
13. Thomas, E., Ricardo, P., Zaigham, M., *Cloud Computing: Concepts, Technology & Architecture*. Prentice Hall, 2013.
14. Hossein, S., Ahmad, K., Payam, M., *Serverless Computing: A Survey of Opportunities, Challenges, and Applications*. ACM Computing Surveys, 2022, 54(11): p.1–32.
15. Kaisong, H., Tianzheng, W., *Indexing on Non-Volatile Memory*. Springer Nature link, 2024.
16. Huawei Technologies Co., Ltd., *Database Principles and Technologies – Based on Huawei GaussDB*. Springerlink, 2023 [access date 05/21/2024]; Available from: https://link.springer.com/book/10.1007/978-981-19-3032-4.
17. Grosu, D., Chronopoulos, A. T., Leung M. Y., *Cooperative Load Balancing in Distributed Systems*. Concurrency & Computation: Practice & Experience, 2008, 20(16): p. 1953–1976.
18. Yishan, L., Sathiamoorthy, M., *A Performance Comparison of SQL and NoSQL Databases*. In IEEE Pacific Rim Conference on Communications, Computers and Signal Processing (PACRIM), 2013, p. 15–19.
19. Subhasri, D., Rupinder, V., Manoj, N., *Predicting Performance in the Presence of Software and Hardware Resource Bottlenecks*. In International Symposium on Performance Evaluation of Computer and Telecommunication Systems, 2014, p. 542–549.
20. Arpan, R., Santonu, S., Rajeshwar, G., et al, *Secure the Cloud: From the Perspective of a Service-Oriented Organization*. ACM Computing Surveys, 2015, 47(3): p. 1–30.
21. Donald, R., Jay, L., *Defining Code-Injection Attacks*. In Proceedings of the 39th annual ACM SIGPLAN-SIGACT symposium on Principles of programming languages, 2012, p. 179–190.
22. William, S., *Cryptography and Network Security (2nd edition.): Principles and Practice*. Prentice-Hall, Inc., 1998.
23. Amir, N., Ariel, O., Danny, R., *Replication-Based Load Balancing*. IEEE Transactions on Parallel and Distributed Systems, 2016, 27(2): p. 494–507.
24. Fay, C., Jeffrey, D., Sanjay, G., et al, *Bigtable: A Distributed Storage System for Structured Data*. ACM Transactions on Computer Systems, 2008, 26(2): p. 1–26.
25. Dazhao, C., Xiaobo, Z., Palden, L., et al, *Cross-Platform Resource Scheduling for Spark and MapReduce on YARN*. IEEE Transactions on Computers, 2017, 66(8): p. 1341–1353.
26. Zijun, L., Linsong, G., Jiagan, C., et al, *The Serverless Computing Survey: A Technical Primer for Design Architecture*. ACM Computing Surveys, 2022, 54(10): p.1–34.

GPSR Compliance

The European Union's (EU) General Product Safety Regulation (GPSR) is a set of rules that requires consumer products to be safe and our obligations to ensure this.

If you have any concerns about our products, you can contact us on ProductSafety@springernature.com

In case Publisher is established outside the EU, the EU authorized representative is:

Springer Nature Customer Service Center GmbH
Europaplatz 3
69115 Heidelberg, Germany

Batch number: 08673141

Printed by Printforce, the Netherlands